Faces of the Feminine in Ancient, Medieval, and Modern India

Faces of the Feminine in Ancient, Medieval, and Modern India

EDITED BY

Mandakranta Bose

New York Oxford
Oxford University Press
2000

65.00

Oxford University Press

Oxford New York
Athens Auckland Bangkok Bogotá Buenos Aires Calcutta
Cape Town Chennai Dar es Salaam Delhi Florence Hong Kong Istanbul
Karachi Kuala Lumpur Madrid Melbourne Mexico City Mumbai
Nairobi Paris São Paulo Singapore Taipei Tokyo Toronto Warsaw

and associated companies in
Berlin Ibadan

Published by Oxford University Press, Inc.
198 Madison Avenue, New York, New York 110016

Oxford is a registered trademark of Oxford University Press

Library of Congress Cataloging-in-Publication Data

Faces of the feminine in ancient,
medieval, and modern India/edited by Mandakranta Bose.
p. cm.
Includes bibliographical references.
ISBN 0-19-512229-1
1. Women—India—History. 2. Women—India—Social conditions.
3. Women—Religious aspects—India. I. Bose, Mandakranta
1938–HQ1741. C36 1999
305.4'0954—dc21 98-8137

9 8 7 6 5 4 3 2 1

Printed in the United States of America
on acid-free paper

To my husband,
Tirthankar Bose

Preface

This study of women in India explores some of the less frequented areas in the field. In recent years, studying women's issues or reevaluating literature by and about women has been a major activity in the academic enterprise and the world, and lives of Indian women have been fertile ground for both fieldwork and theorizing. Indeed, so many of these studies are coming out of India, as well as the Western world, that one might think we have exhausted the field. Why, then, do we need another collection of essays? The reason for undertaking it is to provide a path to many untapped primary sources of information about women's lives. To examine India's three-thousand-year-old culture, including vast bodies of literature spanning every area of public and personal life, is, indeed, a daunting task. Not surprisingly, although valuable contributions have been made in some areas, a scholarly sense of the entire domain awaits development. Our incomplete knowledge of sources affects both research and pedagogy. As teachers of Indian studies, some of us constantly lack the reading material to offer our students who want to explore primary texts and documents in order to prepare themselves for historical research on women's issues. We hope that the present study, while by no means a final map, will be a critical guide to this vast field.

The purpose here is twofold: to point researchers toward primary material and to analyze specific issues critically on the basis of such material. The writers of this collection are women who have made special studies in the history, literature, and culture of India. Most of them have lived in India for a number of years or for their entire lives. What they have written comes from their own experience and understanding of the culture and is firmly grounded in their research. Not all of them share the same viewpoint or proceed along the same tracks. Some of the essays attempt feminist critical analyses, some concentrate on textual and historical evidence, and some are historical surveys. This mix, I hope, will enable readers to recognize some of the central issues of women's lives and their cultural roots, to become aware of the resources for studying them, and to find ways to approach them.

The essays in this collection are organized in a broadly chronological scheme, going from early Indian history through its medieval period to the nineteenth and twentieth centuries. We begin with studies in the lives of women of ancient times, their roles in society, their access to education, and their power and control over their own lives. This was the period when the society gradually established itself as patriarchal, controlling every aspect of women's existence. As society became stratified, women's roles were defined as subservient to men in the name of social, legal, and moral stability. Early literature on codes of conduct and law makes this quite clear. Treatises on law founded on the sacred books of the Hindus had a far-reaching and defining influence on social life. As foundational documents of the Hindu way of life that codified both social relations and personal belief as religious imperatives, these texts have exerted a deep impact on women's lives and conduct through history, and their teachings have not yet entirely lost their force. They are thus some of the most useful sources for understanding women's lives in India. Of particular interest is the fact that the conditions governing the lives of women in India that appear in the earliest texts of the tradition seem more egalitarian than those in texts from later times, as we may gather from references to learned women going back to 1500 B.C.E.[1] Later texts reflect the increasing rigidity of Hindu society and its elaborate structuring of power relations and ethical principles. Confined within that structure, women's lives from about 500 B.C.E. became more patrifocal and thus constricted and homebound. From law books to literature, the emerging picture of a woman's life in India is total subjugation and submission. One can see why judgments such as the following are broadcast: "women, rooted in their families, remain graceful subordinates of men."[2] One of the aims of this book is to look closely at the provisions in Hindu sacred law that prescribed and idealized that subordination. The texts examined are those in which Manu and other ancient Hindu lawgivers laid the bases of women's status, roles, rights, and duties. On this basis, we may attempt to understand the intimate connection between the religious framework and the social, as expressed in the lives of women. Other kinds of literature that we propose to examine are the ancient Hindu epics and literary and philosophical works. This is the task of the first part of the book, which covers the ancient period, reaching back before the beginning of the common era and continuing to its early years.

A vital part of the history of women in India is that, denied the authority of public presence, they nonetheless left their mark, sometimes faint but often strong, in the form of poetry. Although the earliest recorded poetry by women in India—by Buddhist nuns of the sixth century B.C.E.—are very early, there are not many of them, and very few writings by women are extant from the first few centuries of the common era. However, the poems by these nuns stand as testaments to these women's joy at finding freedom from the drudgery of everyday life and at achieving not merely social but spiritual liberation. Because they are as much philosophical speculations as simple avowals of love for the ascetic life, these poems help us understand the power that religious life gave to the writers. The excerpts below give us a taste of their sense of life:

Muttā:

So free am I, so gloriously free,
Free from three petty things—
From mortar, from pestle and from my twisted lord,
Freed from rebirth and death I am,
And all that has held me down
Is hurled away.

tr. Uma Chakravarty and Kumkum Roy, *Women Writing in India*, vol. 1, p. 68

Paṭācārā:

The way by which men come we cannot know;
Nor can we see the path by which they go.
Why mournest then for him who came to thee,
Lamenting through thy tears: "My son! My son!"

Poems of Early Buddhist Nuns (*Therīgāthā*), p. 63.

Quite different from these spiritual perceptions are Tamil poems by women of the Sangam period (150 B.C.E–250 C.E.). The hundred and fifty or so short poems from the early years of the common era, mostly founded on a warrior ethic, instruct a mother how to bring up her child as a warrior or a wife to prepare her husband to march out to the battlefield.[3] These poems are written in the heroic mode and tell us little about women except that their ideals of self-worth conformed wholly to the demands warfare made on their menfolk. Other women poets are mentioned in ancient texts, but their works are now lost. The only exception is Vidyā or Vijjakā, who probably lived around the sixth century C.E. and wrote poems about love and life.[4] Never voluminous, women's writing became scarcer as society became more rigid, pushing women into the margin of a male-dominated society and making education less accessible to them. The first part of this volume traces this erosion of women's options and ends with an analysis of rituals dealing with goddesses and women in Hinduism.

The second part of the collection is concerned with the medieval period—that is, from about the ninth to the early eighteenth century. It begins with an essay on the goddess-woman equation in Tantra. The articles that follow deal with aspects of the Buddhist and Jain faiths and the new wave of devotional Hinduism that revolutionized women's perception of the world and the self, expressed in some of the most enduring poetry and music of India. Songs and poems by the best known women poets of devotional Hinduism, such as Āṇṭāl from Tamilnadu (ninth century), Ākka Mahādevi (twelfth century), Jānā Bāi, Bahinā Bāi, Ātukuri Mollā, and others (fifteenth to eighteenth centuries), appear throughout this long period.[5] Devotional Hinduism swept through India, taking root as an ideology that offered an irresistible alternative to the mystique of Brahmanical religion and gave legitimacy to the common individual, at least in the spiritual context. It gave space to people on the margin, such as women, lower castes, and outcastes. Women, powerless and silent in many domains of community life, found strength in their sense of the divine and their own voice in poetry and songs. One of the most original minds of the twelfth century belonged to the poet Ākkā Mahādevī of the *Vīraśaiva* sect, who left a set of powerful poems expressing her love for the divine.

R. K. Ramanujan's fine translation and critique of Ākkā's poems make an extended commentary on her superfluous for the present volume, but a few excerpts will give an idea of her vision and philosophy,[6] expressed specifically as a woman's spiritual quest and rejection of the material world:

Mahādevīyākkā:
Till you've earned
knowledge of good and evil
it is
lust's body,
site of rage,
ambush of greed,
house of passion,
fence of pride,
mask of envy.

tr. Ramanujan, *Speaking of Śiva*, p. 126, verse 104

with peace, patience, forgiving and self-command,
who needs the Ultimate posture?
The whole world become oneself
who needs solitude.

tr. Ramanujan, *Speaking of Śiva*, p. 128, verse 120

Among the subjects chosen for this part are a Rāma tale by a medieval woman devotee-poet, Candrāvati, and the perception of the feminine in the genre of medieval Bengali literature known as *maṅgala kāvya* (the poetry of divine beneficence) as it appears in one of the genre's most popular exemplars, the *Manasā Maṅgala*. Our inquiry then takes us to examine the relationship between women's wealth and worship in medieval Tamilnadu. Also included is a study of women saint poets of Maharashtra and an extended study of the sixteenth-century princess Mīrābai, one of India's most celebrated devotional poets, whose songs are still sung in Hindu households and regarded as the paradigm of joyous spiritual surrender.[7] Expanding our inquiry from this base, we examine in this part how the songs have affected the people of India and have continued as a living tradition of women's spiritual quest. Finally, the lives and political agency of women of the Mughal court are examined to trace a gendered map of power negotiations in late medieval India.

The subject of the third part is the perception of women, their nature, and their place in the nineteenth and twentieth centuries, including women's self-perception and British and Anglo-Indian women's perceptions of Indian women of the time. This was an era of radical change in India, political as much as social, in which the "woman question" became part of the discourse of nationhood, foregrounding the issue of women's education. The meliorist impetus behind the movement for women's advancement is subject to debate, but there is no question that it energized women's cultural and political aspirations. In earlier periods, women's writings conformed to idealized images of the female in Indian society as mediated by religion, law, and social practice. Within these boundaries arose a literature of beauty and sensitivity but not one that articulated the writers' identities beyond gender stereotypes. But the growth in women's education through the nineteenth century made the few but increasingly vocal women writers of the time actively aware of women's roles, work, and status. That awareness became critical as economic and political crises overwhelmed India in the twentieth century, chiefly the two world wars, the man-made famine of World War II, independence from British rule, and the traumatic partition of India. The political imperatives of the struggle for freedom in particular forced a redefinition of identities of subaltern groups, including such obvious minorities as women and low-caste and tribal people. That redefinition and the recognitions it implies have been the primary preoccupation of much of early-twentieth-century Indian fiction and drama. Two of the commonest subjects are freedom for the masses and freedom in particular for women. For many writers, this twin emphasis has converged into a paradigmatic representation of a woman's personal struggle, leading to explorations of the meaning of the political freedom of the Indian people and perhaps even of human freedom in the widest sense. The emerging validation of women's perceptions is the most exciting single social phenomenon in present-day India; necessarily, Indian women writers' consciousness of gender has become the central site of their representation of the world, of women, and of men. The aim of this part is to explore the themes, strategies, and assumptions of women writers within the historical framework of colonialism, modernization, and global linkages. Writings by and about women from four regions of India—namely, Maharashtra, Bengal, Tamilnadu, and Punjab—are included to give an idea of women's perceptions and self-evaluations in the India of today. The last two essays focus on women's movements in Bengal in the 1940s and in the last three decades.

Views on the women of India, both popular and academic, are usually beset with stereotypes, which, like other generalities, tend to attribute the condition of South Asian women to race or gender characteristics rather than social conditions. Labels such as docile, gentle, or nurturing undoubtedly connote some social realities but through uncritical usage have become such universal verities that they invite little or no attention to the conditions that gave rise to them, obscure facts, and demand conformity. They also disregard women's own initiatives, often futile but never abandoned. This collection of essays attempts to see clearly these conditions of being a woman in India by tracing them historically. What were the conditions of women's lives in early India? What was their position in society? Through what ideologies and pressures have women evolved into stereotypes? By examining the roots of India's culture, the present studies seek answers to these questions and lay the foundation for understanding women's predicaments today and their responses.

Because the contributors reach back into time for the roots of women's history, this collection of studies begins by drawing a historical and cultural profile of India with special reference to ideas of power, status, and gender roles in early sources. We then go on to see how social prescriptions began on the one hand to idealize women and on the other to define women's lives in increasingly rigid and repressive terms through the medieval and modern periods till the beginning of the twentieth century. Given the force of religion in India, it is particularly necessary to examine the structures of duty and concepts of worth within which the different religious communities set the lives of women. To these frames are related women's self-expression, achievements, and initiatives as known in legends, literature, and historical records. The research presented here will, we hope, help us reassess the received image of the women of South Asia and show not only how women were (and are) thought of but also how they have thought of themselves.

In a fundamental way, these essays typify a women's project: to assert an independent judgment. The value of that judgment is for readers to assess, but the authors take the view that these considerations are essential for a disciplined approach to women's studies; it is also their belief that attempts such as these are perhaps equally important to the history of ideas because in their explorations of women's lives they illustrate how ideas are transformed into action and ethics into politics.

Rounding off this introduction is a quote from one of the principal writers on *smṛti*, who questions the inconsistency in the inheritance rights of a daughter and a son:

> *aṅgādaṅgāt saṁbhavati putravat duhitā nṛṇāṁ/*
> *tasmāt pitṛdhanaṁ tvanyaḥ kathaṁ gṛhṇīta mānavaḥ//*
>
> *Bṛhaspatismṛti*, pp. 217–18.
>
> A daughter is born from [the same] human bodies as does a son.
> Why then should the father's wealth be taken by another person?

Notes

1. The *ṚgVeda* on Lopāmudrā (i.179), Apāla (viii.91), Yami (x.10), Indrāṇī (x.86), Ūrvaśi (x.95), Saramā, (x.108); and the *Bṛhadāraṇyaka Upaniṣad* on Maitreyī (ii.4).
2. *India* (1961), p. 25.
3. Tharu and Lalitha (1991), pp. 72–77.
4. Ingalls (1979), pp. 86, 156, 187–8, 221–2, 265.
5. The works of most of these poets appear in Tharu and Lalitha (1991), pp. 77–98, except for Āṇṭāl. Vidya Dehejia (1990) has drawn attention to the high literary value of Āṇṭāl's work.
6. Ramanujan (1977).
7. Since Mīrābai is only briefly touched upon in the Tharu anthology, the sustained critique offered in this volume will, it is hoped, encourage further work on this important medieval figure.

References

Bṛhadāraṇyaka Upaniṣad. Hindu Scriptures [ser.]. Tr. R. C. Zaehner. London: Everyman's Library, 1984.

Bṛhaspatismṛti. Ed., K. V. R. Aiyanagar (reconstructed text). Barode: Gaekwad Oriental Series lxxxv, 1941.

Dehejia, Vidya. *Āṇṭāl and Her Path of Love*. New York: State University of New York Press, 1990.

India. Life World Library [ser.]. New York: Time, 1961.

Ingalls, Daniel H. H. *Sanskrit Poetry*. Cambridge, Mass.: Harvard University Press, 1979.

Poems of Early Buddhist Nuns (Therīgatha). Transl. C. A. F. Rhys Davids and K. R. Norman. Oxford: Pali Text Society, 1989.

Ramanujan, R. K. *Speaking of Śiva*. Harmondsworth: Penguin, 1977.
The ṚgVeda with Sāyanabhāṣya. Ed. Ramgovinda Trivedi. Varanasi: Chowkhamba Vidyabhavan, 1990.
Tharu, Susie, and K. Lalitha, eds. *Women Writing in India*. New York: Feminist Press, 1991.
The Upaniṣads. Ed. Juan Mascaro. London: Penguin, 1965.

Acknowledgments

It is a pleasure to acknowledge the many forms of support I have received from many quarters. This venture began when I organized a one-day conference entitled, "Engendering Voices: A South Asian Perspective," at the University of British Columbia in March 1994 with support from the Centre for India and South Asia Research and the Centre for Research in Women's Studies and Gender Relations at the University of British Columbia. I am particularly indebted to Veronica Strong-Boag and Jo Hinchliffe of the latter Centre for their sustained support. When I decided to put together a volume of essays on the women of India, many friends and colleagues not only from my own institution but from many parts of the world encouraged me and lent their active help to my ambitious project by contributing articles. To all of them my grateful thanks. One friend from whom I received support throughout my effort was John Straton Hawley, to whom I am grateful not only for his valuable scholarly suggestions but also practical advice. Another friend and colleague, Kenneth Bryant, has remained a constant source of help in more than one way over the past two decades. It is within the nurturing climate of this scholarly community that the present volume, the result of three years of effort, has come to fruition.

My children, Sarika and Pablo, have helped me consistently by typing, editing, and proofreading the manuscripts. I must also acknowledge my great and continuing debt to my husband, Tirthankar Bose, whose help in making this volume possible has been immense.

Finally, I would like to extend my thanks to Cynthia Read for undertaking the publication of this volume and her colleagues at the Oxford University Press, MaryBeth Branigan in particular, for seeing it through the press with meticulous care.

Vancouver
January 1998

M. B.

Contents

Contributors

VIDYUT AKLUJAKAR is a research associate at the Centre for India and South Asia Research at the University of British Columbia, where she has also taught in the Departments of Philosophy and Asian Studies. She studied in the University of Poona, Tufts University, and the University of British Columbia. Her research interests range from poetry and fiction to critical studies in classical Sanskrit literature, Marathi, and contemporary South Asian literature. She has published in both North America and India as a poet, journalist and fiction writer.

MANDAKRANTA BOSE is the director of the Program in Intercultural Studies in Asia in the University of British Columbia. She also teaches in the Department of Religious Studies at the same university. She studied Sanskrit and comparative literature in the universities of Calcutta, British Columbia, and Oxford. She has published books and articles on dance and drama in the Sanskrit tradition and on South Asian women's issues. One of her recent books is *Movement and Mimesis* on the idea of dance in India.

SARIKA PRIYADARSHINI BOSE studied English in the Universities of British Columbia and Birmingham, England. Her doctoral work at the latter university was on gender roles in Oscar Wilde's plays. She has been teaching English at Simon Fraser University for the past three years.

MAITREYI CHATTERJEE, formerly a professor of English, has been a freelance journalist in Calcutta for many years and a grassroots activist in raising the social and legal awareness of women as a member of *Nārī Niryātan Pratirodh Mañcha* (Forum against the Oppression of Women). Her works on women's movements in contemporary India are regularly published both in India and North America.

TRIPTI CHAUDHURI teaches history at Rabindra Bharati University in Calcutta. She studied modern history in Calcutta and Oxford, specializing in missionary studies, and has published several studies of nineteenth-century India. A member of the Historical Records Commission and the University Grants Commission of India, she is a long-time social activist for many volunteer women's organizations.

SUMA CHITNIS recently retired as vice-chancellor of S.N.D.T. Women's University in Bombay and is now the director of a national organization for women there. Trained as a sociologist, she is the author of many books and articles about India before and after independence.

MADHUSRABA DASGUPTA has devoted many years to studying the *Mahābhārata* in the original. The result of her meticulous effort is her recent book, *A Descriptive Concordance of the Characters in the* Mahābhārata.

MANASI DASGUPTA, who studied psychology in Calcutta and at Cornell, recently retired as principal of a women's college in Calcutta. Her publications include many books and articles in Bengali and English in scholarly journals.

KRISHNA DATTA taught Sanskrit at Vidyasagar College for Women in Calcutta for many years till her recent retirement. She studied Sanskrit, as well as law, in the University of Calcutta and did her graduate work on *smṛti* and *mimāṁsā* (codes of conduct), on which she has published many articles and presented papers at scholarly conferences.

NABANEETA DEV SEN is a professor of comparative literature at Jadavpur University, a poet, and a novelist with thirty books to her credit. An alumnus of the universities of Calcutta, Harvard, and Indiana, she has published critical studies in comparative literature and gender studies. A visiting professor at many European and North American universities, she delivered the 1997 Radhakrishnan lectures at All Souls at Oxford, an acclaimed series on a late medieval Bengali feminine rendering of the epic *Rāmāyaṇa*.

MATILDA GABRIELPILLAI studied English in Singapore, England, and Vancouver and has taught in the universities of British Columbia and Singapore. A former journalist, she is interested in hegemonic politics, especially nationalism.

JAYATRI GHOSH studied Sanskrit in Calcutta. Her research interests span Indian philosophical systems and their impress on classical Sanskrit literature. She is currently working on a study of *Sāṅkhya* philosophy.

SAMJUKTA GOMBRICH GUPTA, formerly of Utrecht University, now teaches in the Faculty of Oriental Studies at Oxford. Author of numerous books and articles, including the well-known definitive study, *Lakṣmī Tantra: A Pañcarātra Text*, she commands a wide range of scholarship, from classical Sanskrit literature and Indian philosophy to contemporary women's studies.

KARYN HUENEMANN studied English at the Universities of British Columbia and London and has recently completed her graduate degree on Anglo-Indian women's perception of Indian women at the School of Oriental and African Studies in London. She has published articles on Anglo-Indian women's perceptions.

DORIS R. JAKOBSH, whose degree was in Religious Studies at Harvard, is now working on Sikh women for her doctorate in Asian Studies at the University of British Columbia. She has presented many papers at scholarly conferences and published articles in North American journals.

MADHU KHANNA is an associate professor in the Indira Gandhi National Centre for the Arts, New Delhi. She studied at Oxford University for her doctorate and has published several books and articles on tantra and women. She co-authored *The Tantric Way* with A. K. Mookerjee.

NANCY MARTIN-KERSHAW received her graduate degrees from the University of Chicago and Graduate Theological Union. She has taught at the University of California at Berkeley and is at present teaching at Chapman University. Author of many articles, she is currently completing a book on the sixteenth-century woman saint Mīrābai and is also engaged in extensive fieldwork on devotional Hinduism among low-caste people in western Rajasthan.

LESLIE ORR studied at McGill University and teaches religious studies at Concordia University. Author of numerous articles and the forthcoming *Donors, Devotees and Daughters of God*, she specializes in Buddhism and Jainism in ancient and medieval India.

MRIDUCCHANDA PALIT studied history in the universities of Calcutta and Visvabharati and has recently retired from teaching history at Vivekananda College for Women in Calcutta. Her publications are mainly on Brahmo women of Bengal in the nineteenth and twentieth centuries. Her most recent book is *Itihasacintāy Rabindranath* (Rabindranath Tagore's idea of history).

CHAPLA VERMA studied Buddhism in Allahabad, Bodhgaya, and Magadh and has taught Zen Buddhism in the Religious Studies Department in the University of British Columbia.

ELEANOR ZELLIOT recently retired as Laird Bell Professor of History at Carlton College. Author of numerous books and articles, editor of many scholarly books and journals, and member of several international academic bodies, she has contributed widely to studies in Maharashtrian religious movements; "Stri Dalit Sahitya: The New Voice of Women Poets" appeared in 1996 in *Images of Women in Maharashtrian Religion and Society*, edited by Anne Feldhaus.

Faces of the Feminine in Ancient, Medieval, and Modern India

PART ONE

VISIONS OF VIRTUE

This part explores some of the traditional ideas that used to govern the lives of Hindu women in South Asia and to a certain extent still do. These chapters are by scholars working in this field who address a wide variety of issues. The aim of this part is twofold: first, to review the rules and ideals that have been generally understood in India to be the historical bases for defining women's lives; second, to examine how scriptural injunctions and their exegesis have been used as levers in the political machinery of sexual domination.

Because one of the concerns of this book is with primary sources, this first part focuses on women's lives as represented in the Hindu tradition of *smṛti* literature, particularly the *dharmaśāstras* (texts on codes of conduct), tales from the epics, religious rituals, and early Buddhist tradition. Of this part's seven chapters, some are relatively short explorations and some are fuller examinations of social, ethical, and moral issues.

The most ancient sacred texts of the Hindus, the Vedas or records of revealed truth, which go back to 1500 B.C.E., show us a society that had room for women to take part in religious and intellectual activities. From the texts we consider in these essays, which describe and prescribe women's status, privileges, and duties, such as *satī* (wife-burning), *punarvivāha* (remarriage), or participation in intellectual activities, it appears that in the period of *śruti* or Vedic literature, women led less subjugated lives. This is also attested by the epic *Mahābhārata* and by the early *smṛti* literature, which prescribe detailed codes of conduct governing every facet of social and personal life for men as well as women at every social level. Later, as society began to settle into the ruts of tradition, stricter rules were advocated under the umbrella of *dharma* (from root *dhṛ*, to sustain) to sustain order and maintain a strong social structure. The burden of maintaining order within the family, and thus within society as a whole, fell on women, as the *Bhagavad Gīta* points out.[1] This becomes apparent when we examine the less-known tales of women in the *Mahābhārata*, the *Rāmāyaṇa*, and the later *smṛti* literature. Buddhist sources equally confirm this view. But this was a responsibility within which women quickly became imprisoned by the needs of conserving tradition. Instead of embodying positions of decision-making power and defining order, women became vehicles of orthodoxy. Thereby, whatever power or equality women might have had in ancient times was lost at a relatively early period. It is true that against the distressingly frequent examples of women lauded for their submissiveness one might cite women who took active roles in intellectual discourses in very early Hindu society. Because women in such roles were not numerous and their authority as scholars was often shown to be subsumed under patriarchal requirements, however, their reputation cannot be extrapolated to public life at large to presume women's access to scholarship and elevated discourse as anything but a rarity.[2]

It seems that by about the fifth or sixth century B.C.E. women's position began to slide into one of subservience, as evident from a thorough examination of *smṛti* texts with their commentaries. They record the shrinking social space of women and offer proof of their eroded social and intellectual activity from about the eighth century C.E. The lawgivers of the time begin to redefine women's position in increasingly subordinating terms. Given the penchant of the Hindu scholarly establishment for textual interpretation and commentary, the ethical discourse of the time gives rise to conflicting directives as to details but the general discourse adds up to the imposition of severe restrictions of women's lives. Note, however, that even though the original writers of the *smṛtis* are often blamed for tightening the noose around Hindu women's lives, often it is the commentators who are to be blamed for their interpretations. The chief case in point is, of course, the modern indictment of Manu, who is blamed for many such regulations. Manu was not liberal in his prescriptions, but his zealous disciples and critics alike have rushed to emphasize only his interdictions against women and ignored the rights he recognized. This is precisely the kind of inadequacy in studying the Hindu tradition that this book is designed to correct.

With this reappraisal in view, this part takes a close look at two of the most controversial issues that have shaped women's lives in India and at an ambivalent representation of an epic heroine. One major issue studied here, by Krishna Datta, is *punarvivāha* or the remarriage of women, and the other is *satī* or the burning of a widow, a custom explored by Mandakranta Bose. Each essay goes back to the earliest evidence and, while tracing the development of the ideas, attempts to uncover the forces that shaped the ideas into social sanctions. The essay by Jayatri Ghosh on the epic heroine Satyavatī of the *Mahābhārata* attempts to throw new light on an inexplicably neglected character in the *Mahābhārata*, whose life and actions seem to contradict the basic pattern of approved conduct in the epic, a work that has exerted on Hindu life an influence of inestimable depth. An essay by Madhusraba Dasgupta on two other neglected characters of the *Mahābhārata*, Ambā and Mādhavī, examines an instance of the subordination of women that amounts to the dispossession not only of social capital but also of the female body itself. Looking at yet another woman from the epics, Vidyut Aklujkar analyzes the legend of Anasūyā, a figure of virtue drawn in the *Rāmāyaṇa*, which shows us how the strength and power of a woman lies in her *pātivrātya*—that is, her unqualified loyalty to her husband. This study demonstrates how legend equates Anasūyā's virtue with her miraculous power, both of which are defined by her identity as a wife.

Two of the chapters in this part examine the roles of women in religious life. The chapter by Chapla Verma on women's position in Buddhist religious life weighs the evidence for the authorizing of women's subordination in light of the transmission of Buddhist scriptures and the Buddha's own well-known espousal of liberation for all. The other chapter, by Samjukta Gombrich Gupta, explores the roles accorded to women in rituals and the implications of their frequent deification, reaching into the paradox of the customary elevation of the goddess figure set against the disempowerment of women in actual social life.

The chapters in this part, then, attempt to follow the general aim of the book—that is, to encourage a critical reappraisal of some of the central principles, belief systems, and social practices that have historically underpinned women's lives and identities in India. The particular aim of this part is to explore some of the earliest formulations and expressions of these ideological and actual terms under which women have lived. Whether these explorations uncover enduring patterns is a question that the succeeding parts may answer.

Notes

1. . . . when duty is lost,
chaos overwhelms the family.

In overwhelming chaos, Kṛṣṇa,
women of the family are corrupted;
and when women are corrupted,
disorder is born in society.

Bhagavad Gītā.1.40–41

The *Bhagavad Gītā* is believed to have been written about the first century C. E. (Barbara Stoller-Miller, tr. *The Bhagavad-Gita*, New York: Bantam Books, 1986, Introduction, p. 3).

2. This is not to ignore the achievements or reputation of the female sages of ancient India. Women like Maitreyī and Gārgī Vācaknavī rejected material wealth and pleasures in favor of a contemplative life and pursued profound questions about the nature of existence, the cosmos, and Brahman. Women's participation in esoteric discourse was evidently acceptable in ancient times. But these privileges proved to be short-lived.

KRISHNA DATTA

A Controversy over a Verse on the Remarriage of Hindu Women

In *dharmaśāstra* literature, the verse *naṣṭe mṛte* . . . *(Parāśarasmṛti* iv.28),[1] ordaining the remarriage of women, occupies a unique position from the sociological point of view. This verse has given rise to serious controversies that have continued for centuries. Even its authorship has not been beyond question. The verse appears in the *Parāśarasmṛti:*

> *naṣṭe mṛte pravrajite klīve ca patite patau /*
> *pañcasu āpatsu nārīṇāṁ patiranyo vidhīyate.//*
>
> *Parāśarasmṛti* iv. 28
>
> In [case of] the disappearance or death or renunciation or impotence or lost caste-status of her husband: in these five predicaments, a woman is allowed to take another husband.

Garuḍa Purāṇa (107.8) reproduces this verse, attributing it to Parāśara.[2]

If the context of the *smṛti* texts in which the verse appears is considered, then one is forced to admit the superior claim of the *Nāradasmṛti* on this verse because it includes the verse most appropriately under *strīpuṁsaṁyoga* (*Nāradasmṛti*, chapter xii) and offers a systematic study of the verse, along with related issues. In the *Parāśarasmṛti*, by contrast, the verse occurs in chapter 4, which is part of the *prāyaścitta* (expiation) section, and the verse has no relevance either to the aims of the section or to the topics in the chapter. Surprisingly enough, in most of the many digests of the *śāstras* in which the verse has been quoted, it has been ascribed to Parāśara and in none to Nārada. Some digest writers refer to the verse as by Manu and others as by Bṛhaspati. On this issue, we comment later.

The verse *naṣṭe mṛte* . . . is simple in language and does not necessarily provide any reason for controversy on grounds of ambiguity. Yet it has become the most controversial verse on the topic of marriage because it provides for the remarriage of a woman, even though only under specific conditions of distress. We must conclude that the controversy arose because at some historical point in the evolution of Hindu society, female remarriage began to be seen as a threat. Whether the threat was to the dominant power structure or to its ethical superstructure is, of course, a matter for a more modern controversy.

The controversy over the legitimacy of a woman's remarriage is relatively recent in the scale of Indian history and certainly does not reach back to the roots of Hindu culture. If we look back to the Vedic texts, we find that women's remarriage was not unknown in the Vedic age. The term *punarbhū*, meaning a remarried woman (literally, a woman married again) appears in the *Atharvaveda* for the first time.[3] Even in the *dharmaśāstra* texts, we find that Baudhāyana uses the term *punarbhū* (a remarried woman) in connection with his definition of *paunarbhava* (the son of a remarried woman). He states,

> *klīvam tvaktvā patitaṁ vā yā'nyam patiṁ vindeta tasyāṁ punarbhavāṁ yo jātas sa paunarbhava.*
>
> *Baudhāyana Dharmasūtra* ii.3.27
>
> A *paunarbhava* is he who is born of a *punarbhū*, who having left the impotent or outcast husband takes another husband.

Baudhāyana further states,

> *niḥsṛṣṭāyāṁ hute vā'pi yasyai bhartā mriyeta saḥ sā ced akṣatayoniḥ syād gatapratyāgatā satī paunarbhavena vidhinā punaḥ saṁskāram arhati/*
>
> *Baudhāyana Dharmasūtra* iv.1.18
>
> If a woman whose husband dies after offering ceremony and *homa*, remains a virgin, as also a woman who comes back to her husband after going away with another—such a woman deserves the performance of fresh marriage rites behooving a *punarbhū*.

Thus Baudhāyana recognizes remarriage of a woman under three conditions: when her husband is impotent, outcast, or dead. The *Vaśiṣṭha Dharmasūtra* adds to these three conditions one more for allowing a woman to remarry: when the husband is insane:

> *yā ca klīvam patitam unmattaṁ vā bhartāraṁ utsṛjyānyaṁ patiṁ vindate mṛte vā sā punarbhūr bhavati//*
>
> *Vaśiṣṭha Dharmasūtra* xvii.20
>
> She is *punarbhū* who takes another husband having left an impotent or outcast or lunatic husband or on the death of her husband.

Vaśiṣṭha prescribes fresh marriage rites for a widow who had been given away at her wedding with mantras but whose marriage was never consummated:

> *pāṇigrahe mṛte vālā kevalaṁ mantrasaṁskṛtā/*
> *sā ced akṣatayoniḥ syāt punaḥ saṁskāram arhati//*
>
> *Vaśiṣṭha Dharmasūtra* xvii.74
>
> The acceptor of the hands [= husband] being dead, a woman ritually [offered] only with mantras deserves fresh rites of marriage if she remains a virgin.

In the *Manusaṁhitā*, the term *punarbhū* has been defined indirectly by the author's definition of the term *paunarbhava*. Manu says:

> *yā patyā vā parityaktā vidhavā vā svayecchayā/*
> *utpādayet punarbhūtvā saḥ paunarbhava ucyate//*
>
> *Manusmṛti ix. 175.*

She, on being deserted by [her] husband marries again by her will or on being a widow and gives birth to a son who is called *paunarbhava*.

This nomenclature would become meaningless without Manu's acceptance of the provision for women's remarriage. However, we must draw a careful distinction between acceptance, which is forthcoming, and approval, which is lacking. That this attitude was indeed general is indicated by the fact that, like Baudhāyana and Vaśiṣṭha, Manu prescribes the performance of fresh marriage rites for a widow whose marriage remained unconsummated:

sā ced akṣatayoniḥ syād gatapratyāgatā'pi vā/
paunarbhavena bhartrā sā punaḥ saṁskāram arhati//

Manusmṛti ix. 176.

Should she be a virgin or one who having gone away (with another) comes back (to her husband), such a woman deserves fresh marriage rites with a *paunarbhava* husband (= one who marries a married woman).

These verses show that Baudhāyana, Vaśiṣṭha, and Manu distinguish between two categories of *punarbhūs*, depending on whether a woman's marriage has been consummated. There is no instance, however, of any difference in society's treatment of the two categories because the sons of such *punarbhūs* are called *paunarbhavas* in the texts, irrespective of whether their mothers were virgins at the time of their second marriages. In the text of *Yājñavalkyasmṛti*, this distinction is done away with. Yājñavalkya says:

akṣatā ca kṣatā caiva punarbhūḥ saṁskṛtā punaḥ/

Yājñavalkyasmṛti i. 67.

Both nonvirgin and virgin are *punarbhūs* if they have gone through the marriage rites again.

The *Viṣṇusmṛti* defines *punarbhū* in two ways, first:

akṣatā bhūyaḥ saṁskṛtā punarbhūḥ

Viṣṇusmṛti xv. 8.

A virgin [who has] gone through the rites [of marriage] again is called *punarbh* .

Second:

bhūyas tv asaṁskṛtāpi parapurvā

Viṣṇusmṛti xv. 9.

[A woman] previously enjoyed by another [man] [is called *punarbhū*] even though she has not gone through the rites again [= more than once].

The *Nāradasmṛti* (xii.46–48) defines three different types of *punarbhūs*, but for our purposes such intricacies are of less moment than the fact that Nārada does approve of the remarriage of women, for he makes categorical statements on the five enabling conditions.

Thus, different *dharmaśāstras* and *smṛti* texts directly or indirectly approve the remarriage of married women. Against this, it must be admitted that Manu, the foremost *smṛti* writer, declares his strong disapproval of the remarriage of women in real life, even while he accepts the provision for it in law, eulogizing a woman's chastity during her husband's lifetime as well as during widowhood.[4] The principle

Manu lays down is that for those women who value chastity most, taking a second husband can be prescribed under no circumstances:

> *na dvitīyaśca sāddhvīnāṁ kvacid bhartopadiśyate/*
>
> Manusmṛti v. 160.
>
> No second husband for chaste women is ever advised.

In another context, he states:

> *pāṇigrahaṇikā mantrāḥ kanyāsveva pratiṣṭhitāḥ/*
>
> Manusmṛti. viii. 226.
>
> Mantras relating to *pāṇigrahaṇa* [accepting the hand—a formality of marriage] is applicable only in the case of a maiden.

In this verse, he indicates that those who have lost maidenhood cannot go through the proper marriage rites. The aversion to the whole idea of women's remarriage is also apparent from the proscription in some *smṛti* texts against accepting *paunarbhava* sons as bridegrooms.[5] It seems that the only reason that the provision for women's remarriage was at all mentioned in these texts was a conventional reverence for tradition.

Thus, the rules of Manu (*Manu.* ix.176–77), Yājñavalkya (*Yāj.* i.67), Viṣṇu (*Viṣ.* xv), and Nārada (*Nār.* 12.97) that define *punarbhū* or *paunarbhava* (meaning remarried women and sons born of such women, respectively) directly or indirectly attest to the remarriage of married women as a social reality that they had to record as a rule because the practice was embedded in tradition. At the same time, the lawmakers seem to find such a social reality unpalatable and attempt to alter it by eulogizing constancy to one husband and one alone as the ideal for married women. The remarriage of women is certainly looked upon with contempt in Manu (*Manu.* vv. 155–56). Indeed, the *Manusmṛti* sets down some rules that appear to prohibit the remarriage of women. (*Manu.* v.160, viii.226, ix.47).

Against this background, it is useful to bring out the implications of the verse *naṣṭe mṛte* . . . after critically examining the different commentators' and digest writers' interpretations of the verse. In general, it is among these writers of a later age that the resistance to women's remarriage begins to gather force to the point of reinterpreting the old texts, notably the verse *naṣṭe mṛte* . . . . The first among these exigesists to quote this verse is Asahāya (700–750 C.E.), the celebrated commentator on the *Nāradasmṛti*, from whom we might expect an exposition of the verse because it appears in *Nāradasmṛti* (xii. 97) in a form identical to that in *Parāśarasmṛti* (iv.28). Unfortunately, Asahāya's commentary is not available to us in its entire form, and we do not know what, if any, was his interpretation of the verse. However, there does exist a reference to the verse in Asahāya's commentary on Nārada's rule (i.40) relating to the superiority of custom (*vyavahāra*) over dharma. Here Asahāya cites the instances of remarriage and *niyoga* (a system akin to levirate). He holds that though both remarriage and *niyoga* had been sanctioned by the *dharmaśāstras*, both had been abandoned in actual practice.[6] Asahāya's comments perhaps reflect the actual practice not only of his own time but also of an earlier period, when the customs of *niyoga* and remarriage of women were gradually losing acceptability.

By Asahāya's time, social opinion, at least the preferences of the lawgivers, had turned irrevocably against women's remarriage, but no reason is forthcoming as to why and how the *śāstric* provision for remarriage was overridden by custom. On the contrary, Asahāya's age marks a distinct trend toward questioning the *śāstric* authority of remarriage. Although Asahāya himself does not deny that remarriage of women was sanctioned by the *śāstras*, Medhātithi (825–900 C.E.), the celebrated author of a gloss on the *Manusmṛti*, does not consider the verse *naṣṭe mṛte* . . . to be proof of *śāstric* validation of remarriage.

Medhātithi quotes the verse *naṣṭe mṛte* twice without, however, mentioning its author. One reference occurs in the course of explaining the following verse:

> *kāmaṁ tu kṣapayed dehaṁ puṣpamūlaphalaiḥ subhaiḥ/*
> *na tu nāmāpi gṛhṇīyat patyau prete parasya tu//*
>
> *Manusmṛti v. 155.*
>
> One should rather waste away her body [subsisting] on auspicious flowers, roots and fruits, but should not even take the name of another man when the husband is dead.

To defend this injunction, he gives his own interpretation of the controversial verse:

> *yattu naṣṭe mṛte. . . vidhīyate iti—tatra pālanāt patim anyam āśrayeta.*
>
> *Medhātithi on Manusmṛti v. 155, p. 492*
>
> [As regards] The rule "another husband [*pati*] is ordained etc. etc." . . . there it is meant that one should seek the protection of a *pati*.

Medhātithi is claiming here that the term *pati* in the verse *naṣṭe mṛte* . . . yields the sense of *pālaka* or protector. In the context of *Manusmṛti* ix. 75–76, he elaborates this contention. Drawing analogies to *grāmapati* and *senāpati* (where the term *pati* is used to convey the idea of the lord of the village or the commander of the army, respectively), he interprets the term *pati* as protector or guardian.[7] Commenting on *Manusmṛti* ix.75–76, again dealing with the question of the required period of waiting and the means of livelihood to be adopted by a woman in the absence of her husband, Medhātithi refers to the different views of different schools of opinion and in that context again cites the verse *naṣṭe mṛte* . . . as the view of one group of thinkers prescribing the remarriage of women but he himself condemns it as amounting to adultery.[8] This shows that Medhātithi is decidedly averse to the marriage of women, notwithstanding the fact that Manu's rules indirectly justify remarriage by sanctioning fresh rites of marriage for women who marry a second time.[9] On the contrary, Medhātithi tries hard to invalidate the idea of women's second marriage. In his first reference to the verse in question (gloss on *Manusmṛti* v. 155 and ix. 75–76), Medhātithi tries to do this by simply twisting the meaning of the word *pati* to suit his own preference, while in the later place (on *Manusmṛti* ix.75–76) he can hardly hide his extreme aversion to the system of women's remarriage. In support of his position, he quotes a verse from *Manusmṛti* ix.46, which states "a wife cannot be divorced by sale or by desertion."[10] He resorts to sheer casuistry to advance his position, knowing full well that the term *pati* has been used in the verse in the sense of husband and that nothing else is evident from the two different meanings he attaches to the two occurrences of the term in the verse. Although he takes the term *pati* in the first line as declined in the seventh case ending (*patau*) and yielding the sense of husband, he takes *pati* in the second line in the sense of protector. By this subterfuge, Medhātithi attempts to disprove that the verse *naṣṭe mṛte* . . . is the *śāstric* sanction for women's remarriage, which he equates with nothing less than adultery. In this way, a *śāstric* prescription ensuring choices for women could be distorted by the neo-*śāstrakāras*—that is, the commentators and digest writers who interpreted the meaning of the *śāstras* to fit their own views and thereby set the ethical and legal boundaries for future ages.

Maskari (900–1100 C.E.), commenting on the *Gautama Dharmasūtra* xviii.4 refers to the verse *naṣṭe mṛte* . . ., assuming it to be a text from Bṛhaspati, explains it in the light of *niyoga*. He takes the term *apati* in the *sūtra* (*apatir apatyalipsur devarāt/Gautama Dharma Sūtra* xviii. 4) in two different ways. *Apati* is a woman without a husband (evidently meaning that the husband is either dead or untraceable or is unfit to perform the duties of a husband). In that context, Maskari refers to the verse *naṣṭe mṛte* . . . and goes on to explain that if such a woman is childless and wishes to have a child, she can seek to do so by the agency of her brother-in-law.[11] Although Maskari does not speak of remarriage, his recommendation for solving the problem of a woman's childlessness implicitly precludes remarriage. The text of Bṛhaspati is not available to us in its original form but only in a reconstruction by K. V. R. Aiyanger (G.O.S. lxxxv, Baroda 1941), which, however, does not contain the verse *naṣṭe mṛte* . . . . Even if the rule were part of Bṛhaspati's text, it cannot be held as prescribing *niyoga* because the reconstructed text contains a verse in which Bṛhaspati states that *niyoga* has been acknowledged by Manu but has been prohibited by him. According to Manu, *niyoga* should not be practiced in the present age on account of the progressive deterioration of the ages.[12] In raising the issue of *niyoga*, therefore, Maskari is perhaps not speaking of the actual practice of his time. Long before Maskari, Asahāyācarya had stated that both remarriage and *niyoga* had ceased to exist in actual practice, and the *Manusmṛti* itself condemns *niyoga* as a bestial practice. The reason that Maskari glosses the verse *naṣṭe mṛte* . . . in the light of *niyoga* is that, as a commentator on the *Gautama Dharmasūtra*, he has to give precedence to the topic of *niyoga* to follow the line of Gautama, who aphorizes on the rule of *niyoga*. This emphasis on *niyoga* effectively prohibits remarriage.

A different argument is invented by Devaṇabhaṭṭa (1150 C.E.–1225 C.E.) in his *Smṛti Candrikā* to deny women the right of remarriage. Quoting the verse *naṣṭe mṛte* and ascribing it to Manu (on what grounds we do not know, because the verse appears in no edition of the *Manusmṛti*), he agrees that it recommends the remarriage of a woman whose marriage has not been consummated. At the same time, he states that such marriages are prohibited in the *kali* age and supports his view by citing the *Ādipurāṇa*.[13] Thus he allows a *purāṇic* text greater authority than the *smṛti* text despite the standard scholarly practice that the *smṛti* text overrides the *purāṇic* text when there is a conflict between the two.

Devaṇabhaṭṭa's attempt to nullify the provision for remarriage by citing the needs and conditions of the *kali* era gains force with time. Mādhavācārya (1300 C.E.–1386 C.E.), the first and the most important commentator on the *Parāśarasmṛti*, whose scholarly reputation encourages us to look for a rational and critical exposition, falls back on the same feeble argument. While commenting on this verse, which he ascribes to Parāśara, he simply says, "Such a marriage is intended for ages other than the *kali* age" and supports this view with the same text of *Ādipurāṇa* cited by Devaṇabhaṭṭa.[14] In a different context of marriage, Mādhava refers to the verse *naṣṭe mṛte* . . . as by Manu, recycling the same argument (*Parāśara Mādhavīya*, aratrc one vol. 1, p. 491). It becomes quite apparent here that Mādhava is slavishly imitating Debaṇabhaṭṭa and following his interpretation almost word for word. What is surprising is that Mādhava has singled out the verse *naṣṭe mṛte* . . . from the whole text of Parāśara, which sets itself up as the central code of conduct for the age of *kali*. His emphasis on this verse makes sense only as an attempt to explain away the one verse that might be seen as an inconvenient contradiction of the patriarchal program of the *Parāśarasmṛti*.[15]

This is by no means the end of the scholarly inventiveness called forth by the verse *naṣṭe mṛte* . . . . Nandapaṇḍita (1550–1630 C.E.) in his *Vidvānmanoharā*, a commentary on the *Parāśarasmṛti*, explains the verse in a novel way. Though at the beginning of his commentary he declares that he has followed in the footsteps of Mādhavācārya,[16] in his exposition of the verse he offers a completely different explanation without criticizing Mādhavācārya. Nandapaṇḍita interprets the term *pati* in the verse as the groom in whom the formal status of husbandhood will be generated in a future time (*sambhāvitotpattikapati*). Nandapaṇḍita states that "subsequent to the act of betrothal (*vāgdāna*) and before the actual performance of the rite of *pāṇigrahaṇa* (which according to *Manusmṛti* VIII. 227 generates wifehood in the maiden and consequently husbandhood in the groom) if the person in whom the status of husbandhood is likely to arise in future be involved in any one of the aforesaid calamities, the maiden as such is allowed to take a second husband."[17] Whereas Mādhava takes the verse to recommend remarriage but narrows its scope by restricting its application to ages other than *kali*, Nandapaṇḍita justifies the applicability of the verse to the *kali* age by changing the connotation of the term *pati*. In his reading of the term, the husband mentioned in the verse is not actually a husband but only potentially one. Therefore, the woman betrothed to such a person is really not married, and in case of his incapacitation she remains free as an unmarried woman to remarry. In effect, then, by seeming to accept the provision of the verse, Nandapaṇḍita actually denies the remarriage of a married woman.

Bhaṭṭojī Dīkṣita (1057–1150 C.E.) in his *Caturviṁśatimatasaṁgraha* ascribes the verse to the *Parāśarasmṛti* and explains it by virtually copying the words of Nandapaṇḍita.[18] Nor is he alone in doing so. Bālambhaṭṭa (1740–1830 C.E.) also copies Nandapaṇḍita word for word (see Bālambhaṭṭa on *Mitākṣarā* (*Yāj*. II. 1127). Mitramiśra (1610–1840 C.E.) quotes the verse *naṣṭe mṛte* . . . three times in his *Vīramitrodaya*. In the context of the rites of remarriage of women, he refers to the verse as a text of Parāśara and states, "This rule applies to verbally offered maiden."[19] Again in the context of *adhivedana* (plurality of marriage), he quotes this verse but inexplicably attributes it to Manu and takes it as referring to the remarriage of women. Earlier (see *Vīramitrodaya Saṁskāra*, p. 681), however, he had argued that the remarriage of women as ordained by the verse *naṣṭe mṛte* . . . must be prohibited in the age of *kali* on the basis of a text of *Brahmapurāṇa*, which is identical with the text of *Ādipurāṇa* as quoted by Devaṇabhaṭṭa and Mādhavācārya (see n.13).[20] Mitramiśra appears simply to combine two different sets of views, those of Devaṇabhaṭṭa and Mādhavācārya on the one hand and those of Nandapaṇḍita and Bhaṭṭojī on the other.

A distinctly contrary note is struck by a later writer, Kāmeśvara (eighteenth century), who in his commentary on the *Parāśarasmṛti*[21] entitled the *Hitadharma* or *Laghuhitadharma*, agrees that the verse *naṣṭe mṛte* . . . does ordain the remarriage of married women. He introduces his discussion on the verse by stating that, like *parivedana* and *paryādhāna*, the remarriage of women also has been prescribed on certain conditions specified in the verse. In that case, there can be no demerit arising out of such marriages.[22] He criticizes Mādhava's view that the remarriage of women as prescribed by the rule *naṣṭe mṛte* of Parāśara applies to ages other than the *kali*.[23] Thus Kāmeśvara interprets the rule of Parāśara in its literal sense but it is not clear whether in his time and place the provision for women's remarriage was actually followed in practice. However, his words suggest that unlike others he was in favor of the remarriage of women as prescribed by the verse *naṣṭe mṛte* . . .

The last in the list of commentators on the *Parāśarasmṛti* is Vaidya Gaṅgādhara (1798–1885 C.E.), who in his commentary *Upaskara* interprets the verse in the light of *niyoga*.[24] Surprisingly for a nineteenth century commentator, Gaṅgādhara tries to justify *niyoga* in preference to the remarriage of women, given that the practice of *niyoga* had been condemned by Manu himself and it could not even be dreamed of as a *śāstric* prescription in his time.

To sum up the historical expositions of the different commentators and digest writers, we may note that Asahāya, Devaṇabhaṭṭa, Mādhavācārya, and Kāmeśvara accept that the verse *naṣṭe mṛte* . . . ordains the remarriage of married women but while Asahāya informs us that the practice had been overruled by custom, others except Kāmeśvara hold that this right to remarriage is not allowed to the women of the *kali* age. Devaṇabhaṭṭa, who ascribes the verse to Manu, can explain the verse in this way to keep it consistent with other texts of Manu, but it is beyond one's imagination how Mādhavācārya, as an exponent of the text of Parāśara who declares his text to be applicable to the *kali* age, can explain the rule relating to women's remarriage as applicable for ages other then *kali* and that, too, on the basis of a *purāṇic* text when he knows quite well that no *purāṇic* verse can overrule the *smṛti* text. Only Kāmeśvara thinks that the remarriage of women is permissible according to the rule *naṣṭe mṛte* . . . of Parāśara and that there is no demerit in such a remarriage. Medhātithi, on the contrary, thinks that those who attach the meaning of remarriage to the verse *naṣṭe mṛte* . . . encourage adulterous conduct because he equates remarriage with adultery and twists the term *pati* to mean protector. Unlike Medhātithi but impelled by the same aversion to remarriage, Nandapaṇḍita and Bhaṭṭojī Dīkṣita direct their ingenuity to the term *patau* (the seventh case ending of *pati*) in the first line of the verse *naṣṭe mṛte* . . ., taking the term *patau* to mean the bridegroom in whom husbandhood is as yet latent. Attacking the idea of remarriage from yet another angle, Maskari and Gaṅgādhara argue that the provision in the verse *naṣṭe mṛte* . . . is not for remarriage but for *niyoga*.

In this context, we must also consider a controversy over the grammatical irregularity in the use of the term *patau*. The form of the term *pati* in the seventh case ending should have been *patyau* instead of *patau*. This has given an opportunity to a section of orthodox pundits to read it as *apatau* and explain it as a husband not formally wedded but betrothed. These interpreters ignore the fact that this irregular use of the term *patau* is found elsewhere in *smṛti* texts, where it invariably means a formally wedded husband. For instance, the term appears in both Parāśara (*Parāśarasmṛti* x. 28–29) and Nārada (*Nāradīyasmṛti* xiii.12), and in both it unambiguously denotes a formally wedded husband. Nandapaṅḍita and Bhaṭṭojī follow this line of interpretation without, however, referring to the irregular use of *patau*.

Another problem relating to the verse *naṣṭe mṛte* . . . arises from a different reading of the text. The alternative reading is *patir anyo na vidyate* rather than *patir anyo vidhīyate*. This reading is a precise negation of the other and prohibits the remarriage of women under the same five conditions that ordain remarriage. But the reading *patir anyo na vidyate* is palpably incorrect because it construes the verse into sanctions of unlimited latitude to women. If the prohibition of the acceptance of another husband is legislated under a rigorously specified set of five conditions, then logic demands that women may remarry under all other conditions, some perhaps socially calamitous. Not only would such license go against the general spirit of the *śāstras* but also, ironically, reverse precisely the strict code to which the proponents of the alternative reading would subject women.

This survey demonstrates that Parāśara's prescribing bold, fivefold provision of women's remarriage failed to elicit support from orthodox commentators and digest writers. Allowing even the limited freedom of a second marriage to a woman appears to have been so unpalatable that these writers stretched scholarly ingenuity to the limit to deny that freedom without directly contradicting or challenging ancient authority, which would have been unthinkable within the tradition-bound ethos of patriarchy. The conflicting tasks of following authority while contradicting it could be performed only by leaps of reinterpretation. In this quest, the later commentators on *smṛti* reconstruct both language and context.

The history of responses to the verse *naṣṭe mṛte* . . . that we have charted here testifies to the growing constriction of women's lives in Hindu society through time. The ethicolegal proscription against women's remarriage is rooted in the general attitude of a society that placed no great value on women's autonomy and systematically annulled their rights and privileges. The invocation of *śāstra* to validate, fortify, and perpetuate that annulment underlines, not for the first time or for the Hindu tradition alone, how powerfully knowledge can be manipulated to serve social interests. It is, of course, a double-edged weapon. As we have seen previously, the effort to deny women the right of remarriage proceeded in full force from the time of Asahāya if not from an earlier time, and the weight of *śāstric* authority behind that effort seemed crushing. By an appropriate irony, a great Hindu scholar founded the resistance to women's subjection on his own reading of the *śāstras* in the nineteenth century. This was Pandit Ishwar Chandra Vidyasagar, a man of "oceanic compassion," who by his lonely efforts placed a petition before the Legislative Council of India, along with a draft bill that passed on July 26, 1856, legalizing the remarriage of Hindu widows. As the title of the act suggests, only widows were allowed to remarry. It is satisfying to record that it was Vidyasagar's scholarship that gave legitimacy to this particular right of women to equality, but it is a melancholy fact that the social will to extend these rights to marriage in general took another hundred years in India. In the Hindu Marriage Act of 1956, Hindu women finally received what the oldest sources of the Hindu tradition tell us they once at least partially had—namely, equal rights with men in marriage, divorce, and remarriage.

Notes

1. A similar verse also appear in *Nāradasmṛti* xii.97, *Agni Purāṇa* 154.6, and *Viṣṇudharmottara Purāṇa* ii.87.11, iii.329.14.

2. In the *Nāradīya Manusaṁhitā*, which does not give that ascription, it appears with a slight variation:

> *patyau pravrajite naṣṭe klive'tha patite mṛte/*
> *pañcasu āpatsu nārīṇāṁ patiranyo vidhīyate//*
>
> (*Nāradīya Manusaṁhitā* xii.99)
>
> In case of the husband's renunciation or disappearance or impotence or loss of caste or death: in these five predicaments a woman is allowed to remarry.

3. *yā pūrvam patim vittvāthānyaṁ vindate'paraṁ /.*
pañcaudanaṁ ca tāv ajaṁ dadāto na viyoyataḥ/
samānaloko bhavati punarbhuvāparaḥ patiḥ/
yo'jam pañcaudānam dakṣiṇājyotiṣam dadāti/

Atharva Veda ix.5.27–28

One who at first marrying a husband afterwards marries another may not be separated if five dishes of rice and a goat are offered by them. If five dishes of rice, goat and fees are offered, the second husband attains same world with the remarried wife.

4. *Manusmṛti* v.144–147

5. *Gautama Dharma sūtra* ii.6.18. *Manusmṛti* iii. 145–56; *Yājñavalkyasmṛti* i.222, 224.

6. The custom of *niyoga* stands for the practice of appointing a substitute male to procreate progeny for a deceased man in his wife's body. As the following judgments show, custom came to override the scriptural provision for *niyoga.*

> *dharmaśāstravirodhe tu yuktiyukto vidhiḥ smṛtaḥ/*
> *vyāvahāra hi valavān dharmas tenāvahīyate//*
>
> *Nāradasmṛti. 1.40*
>
> When *dharmaśāstra* (religious law) is controversial, a rule based on logic is to be followed. Custom is powerful, and religious law is overruled by it.
>
> *tathā ca dharmaśāstroktam aputrām gurvanujñāto devaraḥ putrakāmyaya sapiṇḍo vā sagotro vā ghṛtābhyakta ṛtāv iyāt* (*Yājñavalkyasmṛti.* i. 60) *tathā ca naṣṭe mṛte . . . . vidhīyate* (*Nāradasmṛti* xii. 97) *ityādi dharmaśāstroktam api lokavyavahāre parityaktaṁ/*
>
> *Asahāya* on *Nāradasmṛti*. 1.40

The injunction of the *dharmaśāstra* (that) "the brother-in-law or a *sapiṇḍa* or a *sagotra* intending to procreate a son, with the permission of the preceptor, will approach a sonless woman in the monthly period, being annointed with clarified butter," and also the rule that "a woman is ordained [to take another husband in five calamitious conditions, such as] the disappearance or death of her husband," though prescribed by the *dharmaśāstra*, have been abandoned in actual practice.

Asahāya's interpretation of the verse *naṣṭe mṛte* . . . is not available, as Asahāya's commentary has not yet been obtained in its entire form.

7. *patiśabdo hi pālanakriyatmakaḥ —grāmapatiḥ senāyāḥ patir iti*

Medhātithi on *Manusmṛti* ix.76, p. 264

The word *pati* refers to the act of protection (as in the case of) protector of village (*grāmapati*) and protector of army (*senāpati*).

8. *anye tu vyabhicāram icchanti*
   tathā ca smṛtyantare 'naṣṭe mṛte . . . Vidhīyate.'

Medhātithi on *Manusmṛti* ix. 76. p. 263

Others prescribe adultery. Thus in another *smṛti* (it is stated that) another husband is ordained, and so on.

9. *yā patyā vā parityaktā vidhavā vā svayecchayā/*
   utpādayet punarbhūtvā sa paunarbhava ucyate//
   sā ced akṣatanyoniḥ syād gatapratyāgatāpi vā/
   paunarbhavena bhartrā sā punaḥ saṁskāram arhati//

Manusmṛti ix. 175–76

10. *na niṣkrayavisargābhyāṁ bhartur bhāryā vimucyate/*

Manusmṛti ix.46

11. *apatir apatyalipsur devarāt/*

Gautama Dharmasūtra. xviii.4

Lacking a husband, [a wife] intending to have progeny [should have it] from the brother-in-law.

apatir avidyamānabhartṛkā ayogyapatir vā/
tathā ca Bṛhaspati-'naste mrte . . . vidhīyate iti/
apatyalipsuḥ yady anapatyā saty apatyam icchanti punar devarād utpādayed ity arthaḥ/
devaro bhrātur jyeṣṭho yavīyān vā/

Maskari on *Gautama Dharmasūtra.* xviii.4

Apati means one whose husband does not exist or one whose husband is unfit. Bṛhaspati says, "another husband is ordained in five calamitous conditions etc. etc." (It means) if a childless woman is desirous of having a child she can procreate from brother-in-law (*devara*). [Brother-in-law is husband's elder or younger brother.]

12. *ukto niyogo manunā niṣiddhaḥsvayam eva tu/*
    yuga-hrāsād aśakyo'yam kartum anyair vidhānataḥ//

Bṛhaspatismṛti. 25.16

The *niyoga* having been prescribed by Manu has been prohibited by Manu himself. It cannot be practiced by others because of the deterioration of the ages.

13. *manurapi naṣṭe mṛte . . . vidhīyate/ evaṁ ca yāni saṁskārād ūrdhvam akṣata yonyāḥ punar udvāhaparāni tāni yugāntarābhiprāyāṇi iti mantavyaṁ/ ata eva Ādipurāṇe uḍhāyāḥ punar udvāhaḥ jyeṣṭhāṁsaṁ gobadhas tathā kalau pañca na kurvīta bhrātṛjāyām kamaṇḍaluṁ//*

Smṛti Candrikā—Saṁskāra, p. 221

Manu also [states another husband is] ordained in case of [the husband's] disappearance, death etc. etc. Thus [the rule relating to] remarriage of a virgin woman after [previous] marital rites is intended for other [than the *kali*] ages. That is why it is stated in the *Ādipurāṇa*, remarriage of a married woman, share of the eldest, killing of cows, [procreation on] brother's wife and accepting the *kamaṇḍalu* [*saṁnyāsa* or asceticism]—these five should not be practiced in the age of *kali*.

14. *ayam ca punar udvāho yugāntaraviṣayaḥ/*
    tathā ca Ādipurāṇam -uḍhāyāḥ punar udvāho etc./

Parāśara Mādhavīya, vol. 2, p. 44

Bhaṭṭojī Dīkṣita rightly criticizes this view of Mādhava by stating:

na ca kaliniṣiddhasyāpi yugāntarīyadharmasyaiva naṣṭe mṛte ityādi Parāśaravākyam aṣṭv iti vācyaṁ/ kalāv anuṣṭheyān dharmān eva vakṣyāmīti pratijñāya tad granthapraṇayanād iti dik./

Caturviṁśatimatasaṁgraha, p. 39

The text *naṣṭe mṛte* . . . cannot be contended to be prohibited in the *kali* and applicable to *yugas* other than *kali* since the text [Parāśara] has been compiled with the avowed object of declaring the *dharmas* to be observed in the *kaliyuga*.

15. See in this connection *Marriage of Hindu Widows* by Eswar Chandra Vidyasagar (rejoinder, pp. 22–25) for the author's criticism of Mādhavācārya's views.

16. *mādhavācāryanirdiṣṭa rathamārgānusāriṇaḥ/*
skhalane'pi na me doṣaḥ parapratyayagāminaḥ//

Vidvānmanoharā, Introductory verse 5

17. *vāgdānāntaram pāṇigrahaṇāt prāk patāv utpatsyamanapatitve purvasmin vare naṣṭe dunadesa-jamanenāparijñātavṛttānte nārīṇāṁ kanyānāṁ anyaḥ patir vidhīyate/*

Vidvānmanoharā on *Parāśarasmṛti* IV. 29

18. *duṣṭe tu pūrvavare vāgdattāpi varāntarāya deyā/*
tathā ca Parāśarāḥ -naśṭe.mṛte . . .vidhīyate/
asyārthaḥ vāgdānāntaraṁ pāṇigrahaṇāt prāk patau
sambhāvitotpattikapatitve pūrvasmin vare naṣṭe sati . . . etc.

Caturviṁśatimatasaṁgraha, p. 87

19. *vīvāhavicāre punarbhvādīnāṁ saṁskārav cāraḥ/*
parāśaraḥ —naṣṭe mṛte . . . vidhīyate/
. . . .
etacca vāgdattāviṣayaṁ/

Vīramitrodaya Saṁskāra, p. 738

20. *vivāhavicāre adhivedanaṁ/ Tad uktam Aitareyabrāhmaṇe*—(iii.3; xii.11)
tasmād ekasya vahavo jāyā bhavanti naikasyai vahavas sahapatayaḥ/ sahaśabdasāmarthayāt krameṇa patyantaraṁ bhavatīti gamyate/ ata eva naṣṭe mṛte . . . vidhīyate iti manunā strīṇām api patyantaraṁ smaryate.

Vīramitrodaya Saṁskāra, p. 871

Concerning plurality of marriage: Thus it is stated in the *Aitareya Brāhmaṇa*, a man can have many wives but a woman cannot have many husbands at a time. On the basis of the word *saha* (= at a time) acceptance of another husband is possible in succession (but not more than one husband at a time). Taking another husband had been prescribed by Manu (also in the verse) *naṣṭe mṛte* . . . .

21. The commentary of Kāmeśvara is still in manuscript form and is yet to be published.

22. *parivedanaparyadhānayor iva nimittaviśeṣe sati punarvivāham anujānāti/*
bhartary evamvidhe sati patyanantaram parigrāhyam/
vidhīyate ity uktya punarbhūtvadoṣo nāstīti nigamyate/

Hitadharma, folio 81

As in the case of [the dispensation for] the younger brother marrying or laying the sacred fire before the elder brother, remarriage is [also] allowed under special circumstances.

Similarly, in case of the husband's [death, impotence, etc.] another husband can be taken.

By the statement *vidhīyate* [= ordained] it is to be understood that there is no demerit arising out of one's being married again.

23. *naṣṭe mṛte iti vacanasya Mādhavācāryair akaliviṣayatvenokter iti cen na/*

Hitadharma, folio 81

The applicability of the rule *naṣṭe mṛte* . . . for the ages other than *kali* as stated by Mādhavācārya is not correct.

24. *pañcasu naṣṭādiṣu patiṣu santānābhāvātmakāpadi satyām āpad rūpeṣu nārīṇām santānābhāvātmakāpad upaśamanāya pūrvokta kṣetrajasantānotpadanārtham anyaḥ svapater anyaḥ pati niyogavidhinā vidhīyate/ kṣetrajaputrasya kalāv uktatvāt/*

Upaskara, folio 28b

Under five calamitous conditions when the husband is untraced and so on (naṣṭe mṛte . . .) when there is a calamity in the form of sonlessness, to remove such calamity of sonlessness of women, another husband other than one's own is ordained according to the rule of *niyoga* because in the *kali* the *kṣetraja* son has been prescribed.

The commentary of Gaṅgādhara on Parāśarasmṛti, like Kāmeśvara's, is still in manuscript form and is yet to be published.

Approximate dates of the texts and/or their authors as they appear in P. V. Kane's *History of Dharmaśāstra*:

Aparārka: 1200 C.E. (p. xxxiii)
Asahāya: 600–750 C.E. (p. xxvii)
Bālaṁbhaṭṭa: 1730–1820 C.E. (p. xliii)
Baudhāyana: 500–200 B.C.E. (p. iv)
Bṛhaspati: 300–500 C.E. (p. xxii)
Caturviṁśati Matasaṁgraha: 800–900 C.E (p. xviii)
Devaṇabhaṭṭa: 1150–1225 C.E. (p. xxxiv)
Gautama: 600–400 B.C.E. (p. iii)
Jīmūtavāhana: 1100–1200 C.E. (p. xxxiii)
Mādhavācārya: 1400 C.E. (p. xxxvii)
Manu: 200 B.C.E.–200 C.E. (p. xvi)
Medhātithi: 900 C.E. (p. xxix)
Nandapaṇḍita: 1600–1700 C.E. (p. xlii)
Nārada: 100–300 C.E. (p. xxi)
Parāśara: 100–500 C.E. (p. xx)
Raghunandana: 1600 C.E. (p. xli)
Vaśiṣṭha: 300–100 B.C.E. (p. vi)
Vijñāneśvara: 1100–1120 C.E. (p. xxxii)
Vīramītrodaya Saṁskāraprakāśa: 1800–1900 C.E. (p. xlii)
Viṣṇusmṛti: 300–100 B.C.E.; additions: 300–600 C.E. (p. vii)
Yājñavalkya: 100 B.C.E.–300 C.E. (p. xix)

References

Manuscripts

Parāśara Dharmaśāstra with commentary *Hitadharma* or *Laghuhitadharma* of Kāmeśvara (ms 5519, Government Oriental Library, Madras).

Parāśarasmṛti with commentary *Upaskara* of Vaidya Gaṅgādhara (ms *Smṛti* 984, Government Sanskrit College, Calcutta).

Texts

Agnipurāṇa. Ed. H. N. Apte. Poona: Anandasrama Sanskrit Series 41, 1900.

Atharvaveda, vols. 1–4. Ed. S. P. Pandit. Bombay: 1895–98.

Atharvaveda with Sāyanabhāṣya, vols. 1–8. Ed. Pandit Ramswarup Sharma Gaud. Varanasi: Chowkhamba Vidyabhavan, 1990.

Baudhāyana Dharmasūtra. Ed. A. Chinnaswami Sastri. With the commentary *Vivarana* by Govindaswami. Benares: Kashi Sanskrit Series 104, 1934.

Bṛhaspatismṛti. Ed. K. V. R. Aiyanger (reconstructed text). Baroda: Gaekwad Oriental Series lxxxv, 1941.

Caturviṁśatimata. Bhaṭṭojī Dīkṣita. A commentary on *saṁskāra* and *śrāddha*. Benaras: Benares Sanskrit Series, n.d.

Garuḍapurāṇa. Ed. P. Tarkaratna. Calcutta: Bangabasi Press, 1812 (*śaka*). Repr. Calcutta: Nababharata Publishers, 1985.

Gautama Dharma Sūtra. With *Māskarī Bhāṣya*. Ed. L. Srinivasacharya. Mysore: Trivandrum Sanskrit Series 1917.

Parāśarasmṛti. Nagesvara Panta Dharmadhikari, with the commentary *Vidvānmanoharā* of Nandapaṇḍita. Benaras, 1913.

Parāśarasmṛti with *Mādhavabhāṣya*, vols. 1–2. Ed. C. R. Tarkālankāra. Calcutta: Bibliotheca Indica Series, 1890–92. Bibliotheca Indica Series, repr. 1973–74.

Manusmṛti or *Manusaṁhitā* with *Medhātithibhāṣya*, vols. 1–2. Ed. G. N. Jha. Calcutta: Bibliotheca Indica Series, 1932.

Nāradasmṛti. Ed. J. Jolly. With extracts from *Asahāyabhāṣya*. Calcutta: Bibliotheca Indica Series, 1885.

Nāradīya Manusaṁhitā. Ed. Sambasiva Sastri. With the commentary of Bhavasvāmī. Mysore: Trivandrum Sanskrit Series xvii. 1929.

ṚgVeda. Ed. F. Max Müller. London: 1849–74.

Ṛgveda with Sāyanabhāṣya. Ed. Ramgovinda Trivedi. Varanasi: Chowkhamba Vidyabhavan, 1990.

Smṛti Candrikā of *Devanabhaṭṭa*. Ed. L. Srinivasacharya. Mysore: 1914–16.

Vaśiṣṭha Dharmasūtra, vols. 1–3. Ed. A. A. Fuhrer. Bombay: 1939.

Vīramitrodaya of *MitramiŚa*, *Saṁskāraprakāśa*. Ed. Nityānanda Pārvatīya. Benaras: Chowkhamba Oriental Series, 1939.

Viṣṇudharmottara. Ed. Srikrishnadas Ksemaraja. Bombay: Venkateswar Press, 1921.

Viṣṇusmṛti. Ed. J. Jolly. With extracts from *Vaijayantī*. Benaras: Chowkhamba Oriental Series, 1881. Repr. Calcutta, 1962.

Yājñavalkyasmṛti. With commentary *Mitākṣarā* of Vijñāneśvara and *Bālambhaṭṭi* on *Mitākṣarā* by Bālambhaṭṭa. Ed. Narayana Rama Acharya. Delhi: Nag Publishers, 1985.

General Works

Vidyasagar, Eswar Chandra. *Marriage of Hindu Widows*. Calcutta: 1856. Repr. Calcutta: K. P. Bagchi, 1976.

2

MANDAKRANTA BOSE

Satī

The Event and the Ideology

In September 1987, in a village in India's northwestern province of Rajasthan, an eighteen-year-old woman, Roop Kanwar, died in the funeral pyre of her 24-year-old husband, apparently in an act of exemplary devotion to her husband and to a Hindu practice supposedly hallowed by creed and custom. The couple had been married for less than a year. A photograph of the funeral shows a smiling Roop, bedecked in her wedding outfit and holding on to her husband's body as the flames rise around her. The picture was widely distributed all over Rajasthan to prove the triumphant survival of an ancient tradition—namely, the voluntary choice of self-immolation as the highest wifely duty, one that ensured for the wife the ultimate accolade of a *satī*, a wife wholly dedicated to her husband. The word *satī* means a woman who is virtuous and truthful and, as an extension of the term, a woman who is chaste and totally devoted to her husband. After Roop Kanwar's death, which was witnessed by thousands of worshipful supporters, including large numbers of women chanting Roop's praise, she was virtually deified by those who organized the event. It was, they claimed, an entirely voluntary act and one that reiterated the ancient values of Hindu society and rediscovered the power of spiritual and physical self-sacrifice that, in their view, is at the core of the Hindu religion and elevates it above all others. Soon, however, this view of noble self-sacrifice was questioned. Roop Kanwar was said to have been in a drugged state and the famous photograph a fake. The ecstatic smile the crowd saw on her dying face was suspected to be the rictus of death. Her death took place without the knowledge of her parents, who learned of it from newspaper reports. Her in-laws were found to be earning enormous sums from worshipers at a shrine erected to Roop on their property, where they had held the funeral instead of at the public cremation site. Most telling of all, local custom would have allowed the widowed Roop to return to her parents' home with the very substantial dowry that she had brought as a bride.

Roop Kanwar's death triggered the age-old controversy over the issue of *satī* (spelled *suttee* in older British writings) or wife-burning (until the cremation of her dead husband, a Hindu woman cannot be called a widow). Her fate came to be known all over India and much of the rest of the world, and it gave new force to many of the well-known notions about Hindu women's lives, centering on the institution of *satī* as a symbol of the systemic repression of women said to be entrenched in the Hindu tradition. At the same time, many voices spoke up in defense of *satī* as the most persuasive example of the power and glory that attaches to womanhood in Hinduism.

Following the incident, many articles and books appeared, and many conferences addressed the controversial issue of *satī*.[1] Anti-*satī* groups have focused not merely on the cruelty of *satī* as a physical act but even more on the institutionalized subjugation of women implicit in it. Feminist writers in particular have reminded us that revulsion is an obvious human response to *satī*, along with anger and grief, but it must not blind us to other critical questions about India. The sheer inhumanity of *satī* is of such magnitude that we begin to wonder what forces within the Indian polity, armed with what kinds of validating pressures, drive human beings, apparently including the subjects of the custom themselves, to accept and even extol *satī*. Who does accept *satī*? What in the Hindu belief system and social theory can validate *satī*? Equally to the point, how widely has Hindu society accepted that validation and when? Because the ancient sacred texts of Hinduism have been used both to promote *satī* and oppose it, I shall try here to bring together the textual evidence and to show how the ideology of *satī* has evolved through time and how it has served personal and social agendas. This is a fairly large undertaking, so in dealing with the present-day issue of *satī*, I shall be able to comment only briefly on the use of that ideology today. By doing so, I hope to work toward answering the question that became insistent after Roop Kanwar's death: Why is this resurgence of *satī* happening now?

First, let me explain the term *satī* and its history. The word is derived as a feminine noun from *sat*, which means "goodness, virtue, truth." Satī is one of the names of the goddess of energy, often known as a form of Durgā, who is the consort of the god Śiva. As the story goes, in one of her incarnations Satī was the daughter of the demigod Dakṣa, who spoke insultingly of Satī's husband publicly at a sacrificial ceremony in his palace. She could not bear her husband's humiliation and died of grief at the sacrificial ground. Her death infuriated Śiva, who came and took up the body of Satī and began a dance of destruction. As he danced in a fury, the body of Satī broke into 51 parts, which Śiva then deposited at 51 sites. Later, these 51 sites became some of the holiest places of pilgrimage for all Hindus. In this legend, Satī does not join her husband after his death and although the story shows her devotion toward her husband, it shows equally her husband's devotion to her.

A second explanatory note is necessary. From the earliest times, Hindus have regarded fire as the great purifier, and a ritual flame is an integral part of most religious ceremonies. This context makes the correlation between purity and faithfulness an obvious one and explains why fire became the ultimate proving ground for female virtue. Both great epics of India affirm this. *Satī* appears in the *Mahābhārata*, where we find that the mother of two of the five *Pāṇḍava* brothers voluntarily chose to die with her husband when she was unable to prevent her husband's death and realized that, in fact, she had been instrumental in bringing about his death. She ascended the funeral pyre of her husband and purified herself. Sītā, the heroine of *Rāmāyaṇa*, the other epic, had no need to die as a *satī* but had to prove her purity by going through fire more than once. These mythical examples have worked as powerful models of female virtue that retained their potency irrespective of the numbers of women who died as *satīs*, which in actual practice was never large.

If we turn from myth to the earliest recorded history of India, from about 1500 B.C.E., we find from the sacred Vedic texts, which are the only available records from that age, that *satī* was neither advocated nor in practice.[2] Yet, the proponents of *satī* insist that it has the sanction of the Vedas. In support of this claim, they cite a hymn from the *ṚgVeda*, which, they say, requires the widow to sit within the fire that burns her dead husband's body. But Vedic scholars have proved that this reading of the hymn is based on an orthographic mistake: the significant word is *agre* (in front), not *agne* (O Agni). Even if we were to accept the reading *agne*, it would not mean "into the fire," for the word would still be in the vocative case and signify that *agni* was being addressed. The sense of "into the fire" would be yielded only if the word were in the dative case, which would be *agnaye*. The fact is that the hymn actually directs the widow to sit facing her dead husband after moistening her eyes with ghee, or clarified butter, evidently to bring tears to her eyes.[3] Vedic funerary rituals described elsewhere similarly direct all female relatives of the dead man to put ghee in their eyes while throwing *kuśa* grass in the funeral pyre (*Āśvalāyana Gṛhyasūtra*, iv.6.12). That the disputed *ṚgVedic* verse could not possibly require the widow to die with her husband becomes clear beyond doubt in the verse that immediately follows. Directing the wife to accept her loving husband's death, it instructs her to arise from his side to resume her place in the world (*ṚgVeda*. x.18.8).[4] This has been taken by early writers and commentators such as Āśvalāyana and Sāyana to imply a directive to the wife to continue her dead husband's line by means of *niyoga*.[5] The *Atharvaveda* uses the same command to the wife to arise (*Atharvaveda* xviii.3.1); it also prescribes the continuation of the line through the same wife. A ritual prayer for blessings to continue the line would be ludicrous if the widow were to burn herself to death with her husband. Baudhāyana, another early writer on *smṛti* or codes of conduct, prescribes both these verses to be recited, one while sitting beside the corpse, the other when rising from the place (*Baudhāyana Pitṛmedhasūtra* 1.8.7). *Bṛhaddevatā* says that the first verse is to be recited when the wife ascends the funeral pyre and the second verse is to be recited by the brother of the deceased husband who prevents her from dying.[6] Equally important, the manuals of conduct known as the *gṛhyasūtras*, which lay down the daily regimen for family life to the last detail, contain no directions for *satī*. These examples from a body of sacred law that is considered to be the fountainhead of the entire Hindu tradition persuasively suggest that the custom was neither approved nor practiced in the Vedic age.

At the same time, *satī* is mentioned in quite early times. As early as the fourth century B.C.E., examples of *satī* can be found in the northwestern corner of India, particularly in Taxila and near the banks of the Irāvatī, now in Pakistan, where the custom seems to have been introduced by Scythian invaders.[7] But the long tradition of validating *satī* in religious law did not begin till early medieval times—that is, about the eighth century C.E. The *Brahmapurāṇa* and Aparārka, commentator on the *Yājñavalkyasmṛti*, cite the *ṚgVedic* verse in the corrupted form mentioned previously as proof of ancient authority (Aparārka, p. 111), and the influential sixteenth century scholar Raghunandana follows them in the error in his *Śudhhitattva*.[8]. By Raghunandana's time, the practice of *satī* had become common, at least partly because his scholarly prestige perpetuated the misreading of the *ṚgVedic* verse. Amazingly, the error proved most enduring and influenced some of the greatest of nineteenth century scholars, such as Max Müller and H. H. Wilson, who concluded that *satī* was known during the Vedic period, evidently on the basis of the misreading of the word *agre* for *agne*. Interestingly, Max Müller blames the Brahmins for validating *satī*, which he considers to be part of their general strategy to keep society under their control. There might be something to this argument because Brahmin women were discouraged from following their husbands to death.

But *satī* was not simply a Brahmin conspiracy, for it was also assimilated in the Buddhist tradition. Aśvaghoṣa, an early Buddhist author, writes:

viṣayād viṣayāntaram gatā pracaretyeva hṛtāpi gauḥ/
anavekṣitapurvasauhṛdā ramate'nyatra gatā tathānganā//
praviśantyapi hi strīyaścitāmanubdhnantyapi muktajīvitāḥ/
api bibhrati caiva yantraṇā na tu bhāvena vahanti sauhṛdam//
ramayanti patīn kathañcana pramadā yāḥ patidevatāḥ kvacit/
calacittatyā sahasraśo ramayante hṛdayaṁ svameva tāḥ//

Saundarānanda by Aśvaghoṣa, viii.41–43

Just as a cow if restrained from grazing on one plot goes straight to another, so a woman regardless of a former love, goes elsewhere to take her pleasure.
For women may mount their husband's funeral pyre, they may follow them closely at risk of their lives, they may be subjected to no restraint, but they never bear love wholeheartedly.
Even those women who treat their husbands as gods and sometimes in one way or the other give them pleasure, please themselves a thousand times from fickleness of mind.

As this passage shows, *satī* had become part of the systematic demeaning of women that was the social reality in post-Vedic ages, although we do not know how common *satī* by itself was. We do know, however, that the custom received no support from the Hindu lawgivers till much later. The authoritative *Manusmṛti*, a second century C.E. text known for its restrictive injunctions on women, does not prescribe the act of wife burning. Manu, the author of this work and perhaps the chief architect of the subordination of women, says:

asvatantrāḥ striyaḥ kāryāḥ puruṣaiḥ svairdivāniśaṁ/
viṣayeṣu ca sajjantyaḥ saṁsthāpyā ātmano vaśe//
pitā rakṣati kaumāre bhartā rakṣati yauvane/
rakṣanti sthavire putrā na strī svātantryamarhati//

Manusmṛti, 9. 2–3

Men must make their women dependent day and night, and keep under their own control those who are attached to sensory objects. Her father protects her in her childhood, her husband protects her in youth, and her son protects her in old age. A woman never gains independence.

Manu also disapproves of widows' marriages and, generally speaking, has the reputation of having authorized the systematic subordination of women, as, indeed, the verse just quoted proves. Yet even Manu does not prescribe *satī*, possibly because he considers a woman to be *pujārhā gṛhadīptayaḥ*—"worthy to be worshiped and the lamp that lights up the household." Nor is any support forthcoming from Medhātithi, the ninth century commentator on Manu. Other early writers on *smṛti*—that is, texts on codes of conduct, such as Vaśiṣtha or Yājñavalkya (roughly third century C.E.)—are also silent on the issue of *satī*. Vaśiṣṭḥa allows the remarriage of women in certain unusual circumstances, such as a husband who is insane, lost, or impotent.[9] Rather than allowing remarriage, Yājñavalkya prescribes the duties of a widow.[10] Strict as these are, Yajñavalkya remains one of the most liberal-minded *smṛti* writers, who thought of wives as gifts of the gods who must be respected and valued. He also laid down rules of inheritance for wives, which, of course, created more problems for women in later times. Obviously, if codes of conduct and inheritance for widows were to make any sense, the burning of wives and widows was not being sanctioned at that time. However, one verse from another fifth century writer, Parāśara, famous for advocating the remarriage of women, has often been interpreted as support for *satī*. The same verse appears in a work by Nārada, another writer on *smṛti*, who again supported the remarriage of women. It therefore needs to be looked at closely and in context:

naṣṭe mṛte pravrajite klīve ca patite patau/
pañcasu āpatsu nārīṇāṃ patiranyo vidhīyate//
mṛte bhartari yā narī brahmacaryavrate sthitā/
sā mṛtā labhate svargaṃ yathā te brahmacāriṇaḥ//
tisraḥ koṭyo ardhakoṭī ca yāni lomāni mānave/
tāvatkāla baset svarge bhartāraṃ yā anugacchati// [11]

Parāśara Smṛti 4.30–32

In case of the following five impediments affecting the husband, namely, disappearance, death, renunciation, impotence, or loss of caste, a woman may take another husband.
In case of the death of her husband if the woman pursues celibacy she gains heaven just as a celibate man does.
One [= a woman] who follows the path of her husband resides in heaven for three and a half million years, that is, the number of hairs on a human body.

Note first that Parāśara approves of the remarriage of women who suffer under five impediments: the disappearance or death of the husband, the husband's being declared an outcast, the husband's renunciation of worldly life, or his impotence. In the two verses that follow, Parāśara prescribes for a widow either *brahmacarya* or *anugamana* as virtuous choices. *Brahmacarya* means celibacy, but in light of the provisions laid down in the preceding verses the widow is not denied the right to remarry. It is the term *anugamana*, which literally means "to follow in the path [of the husband]," that raises the problem here because it has been taken to mean an injunction to follow the husband to death. But this interpretation of the term creates a serious inconsistency: if Parāśara allows a woman to remarry after the death of her husband, can he, in the very next verse, also require her to die when her husband dies? Moreover, the widow cannot practice celibacy if she dies. The term *anugamana* has been taken to mean *anumaraṇa* (following [the husband] in death), even though the terms are not synonymous. If we accept this equation of the terms, then the verses on remarriage and celibacy become meaningless. If Parāśara identified the conditions for women's remarriage, how can we justify translating *anugamana* as *anumaraṇa*? There is no authority in Sanskrit usage to substitute *maraṇa* (death) for *gamana* (going or following). *Gamana* definitely refers to following the path, which would mean that ideally a virtuous wife should follow the path traveled by her husband. To interpret that path as the path of self-immolation and the term *anugamana* as *anumaraṇa* strains common sense and suggests a deliberate rewriting of the social code, a twisted interpretation to enforce *satī*. Some apologists for *satī* have suggested that Parāśara was perhaps offering both *anugamana* and *anumaraṇa* as valid alternatives for a widow, but this alternative still seems to be a piece of wishful thinking because the term *anumaraṇa* does not actually appear in the text. Rather, what we have here is the same kind of linguistic manipulation to force a particular meaning that we have seen in the case of the *ṚgVedic* verse.

The increasing restriction of and control over women's lives become evident around the fifth century B.C.E., when *satī* gradually became much more common. In addition to the incidence of *satī* in the *Mahābhārata*,as previously mentioned, we find *satī*hood claimed also by the wives of Vasudeva, the Yādava king and the mortal father of Kṛṣṇa.[12] With time, Hindu society became more and more elaborately structured, and women's lives became more repressively constrained in more than one way. By the late medieval period, *satī* was accepted and often encouraged. That is when Raghunandana's *smṛti* appeared.

Yet, even then, as in later times, opposition to *satī* continued. Indeed, as the practice grew, so did opposition to it. In the seventh century, King Harṣavardhana tried to dissuade his mother from committing *satī*, though without success.[13] The poet Bāṇabhaṭṭa (seventh century C.E.) condemned it as inhuman. In his *Kādambarī* he explicitly says that it is a form of escape that is upheld only by fools.[14] Unfortunately, the practice surged again and again and reached epidemic proportions in the 18TH and 19TH centuries. In Rajasthan, the troubled 14TH and 15TH centuries saw the growth of the custom of *jauhar* (from *jīvahara*,[15]—that is, the taking of life), in which Rajput women either took poison or burned themselves to death when their sons, husbands, or brothers faced certain death in battle. Note that the custom reflected the occupational predicament of the warrior class. If the king and his followers were defeated, their womenfolk faced slavery, rape, or slaughter. Suicide in the form of *jauhar* was a desperate act to avoid that fate but an act that was glorified as the supreme example of both faith and courage. Significantly, Roop Kanwar has been held up as an example of the essential Rajput virtues of faith and courage.

Whether *jauhar* can be called *satī* is debatable because it was not limited to wives. But the Rajasthani practice does open a different window to the custom of *satī* because it can be invoked to legitimize *satī* as a social instrument for permanently removing women whose lives might become an inconvenience. In such calculations, pragmatism rather than idealism is the driving force, and I believe we need to ask whether in the heyday of *satī* it was the idealization of female virtue that motivated *satī* or the self-interest of people around its subject. When we look at the pattern of growth in its practice, we begin to glimpse motives other than a noble if tragic pursuit of virtue.

The largest number of *satīs* from the eighteenth century onward occurred in Bengal and Maharashtra. Why there? The explanation for Bengal is that the law of inheritance that was followed there, in contrast with the rest of India, was the law prescribed in Jīmūtavāhana's *Dāyabhāga*, a commentary on *Yājñavalkyasmṛti*, by which widows could inherit their husbands' property in full or in part. Because this provision meant disinheritance for other family members or the fragmentation of property, as well as power for women, it clashed directly with the conditions of a patriarchal, predominantly agrarian society in which the splitting of land parcels could mean financial disaster for a family. In European history, the solution for this predicament was the reservation of property to the male line by entailment.

But the calculations were not only financial. Especially in the case of a young widow, there was always the risk of unwanted sexual entanglements. Thus, as a way of getting an inconvenient female out of the way, *satī* was supremely efficient. The property would go to other relatives with no legal complications. If, in addition, we take into account the unrelieved harsh regimen of a widow's life and her inauspiciousness, it is not altogether surprising that some widows should have chosen *satī* as a way out. A diary kept by a Maharashtrian woman describes in detail her life after her husband's death.[16] One solution in India to all this was *satī*. Whereas in England women could be simply pushed outdoors (Jane Austen's readers will recognize this), Hindu society invented a strategy to drive widows out of active social roles and into the status of passive family appendages or, in extreme cases, out of life altogether by the custom of *satī*.

But attributing pressures to commit *satī* exclusively to motives of material gain or desperation does not tell the whole story. On the contrary, it ignores the weight of ideology, no less powerful because it is intangible. Often ideological indoctrination led well-meaning men and women to believe in the moral and spiritual transformative power of *satī*. Wrapped up in the glamor of virtue and spirituality, *satī* was said to ensure salvation not only for the *satī* herself but also for the families of her husband and her father going back seven generations. As Julia Leslie points out in her comments on *Strīdharmapaddhati*, an eighteenth century guide to right conduct for women, the author Tryambaka encourages women to commit *satī*, by asserting that it is the only way to reach salvation for a woman.[17] This is the voice of idealistic zeal. If at the same time it benefited dominant interests, no wonder that it was echoed loudly and often. Ironically, at about the same time, we hear a contrary voice, that of the author of the *Mahānirvāṇatantra*, who condemns the act as a form of suicide, which, he says, was sure to consign the perpetrator's soul to hell:

> *tava svarūpā ramaṇī jagati ācchannavigrahā/*
> *mohād bhartuścitārohād bhavennarkagāminī//*
>
> *Mahānirvāṇatantra* 10.80
>
> Every woman, O Goddess, is your very form, your body concealed within the universe; and so, if in her delusion a woman should mount her husband's pyre, she would go to hell.[18]

The fact that this condemnation was silently passed over by the Hindu establishment of the time shows how active the promoters of *satī* were in constructing a supporting ideology from a selective reading of the sources of the Hindu belief system.

We must not make the mistake of thinking that *satī* was the universal lot of Hindu women. Very few women actually ascended their husbands' funeral pyres. What mattered more was the potency of *satī* as an ideal energetically marketed by the arbitrators of conduct. At the same time, as the opposition of Harṣa, Bāṇabhaṭṭa, and the author of *Mahānirvāṇatantra* shows, both the ideology and the practice were persistently challenged. With the rise of liberalism in nineteenth century India, opposition to *satī* began to gather effective force. In an ethos that favored the establishment of women's rights, even if in a limited way, and emphasized the need for women's formal education, legislation for widow remarriage, and the abolition of child marriages and polygamy, *satī* began to be seen as a barbaric practice. Finally, a movement led by Raja Rammohan Roy in Bengal and supported by Lord Bentinck, the governor-general of India, succeeded in 1829 in having *satī* banned and declared a criminal act. The law was vigorously applied, and by the end of the century *satī* seemed to be a nightmare of the past. When the abolition of *satī* was reiterated after the independence of India in 1947, it seemed that the issue had been laid to rest once and for all.

That is why the burning of Roop Kanwar and several other women in the past few years has shocked the Indian nation into a reexamination of its present and past. Why this resurgence of *satī*? And why particularly now? Why and how has Roop Kanwar taken on an iconic status?

In answering these questions, we encounter problems of both interpretation and methodology. The historic debate has been over whether prescriptions or precedents should be understood as validation or refutation. A more recent question is how we should look at the phenomenon—that is, whether we should look at *satī* as a voluntary act or a coerced one and how we should proceed in either case. The battle over interpretation goes back a long way, and, as I have tried to show, it forms the necessary background. But the methodological problem of what conditions might explain or even justify *satī* is an insidious one. One of the self-justifying claims of modern promoters of *satī* is that it is exclusively a woman's choice whether she wishes to die as a *satī* and that her right in the matter must not be denied. This argument, which in effect seeks to sanction at least the principle of *satī*, is unconsciously accepted by those who counter by saying that no woman ever wants to become a *satī* and dies as one only when drugged or forcibly held down to the pyre. This argument concedes that *satī* is acceptable if it is voluntary. The point I must insist on is that there is no such thing as a voluntary act of *satī* if by "voluntary" we mean autonomous. Because Roop Kanwar is known to have been a devout worshiper at a *satī* temple, let us grant that she was neither drugged nor held down to the pyre but voluntarily chose to die with her husband. Yet, how autonomous is a woman whose entire life is appropriated by an ideal? Veena Oldenburg reports what an eloquent campaigner against *satī* said to the editors of the influential feminist journal *Manushi*: "How many women have the right to decide anything voluntarily?" Oldenburg asks, if a woman cannot choose her husband or take decisions about her own education or career, can the decision to die "really be called voluntary and self-chosen?"[19] Indoctrination is as coercive as brute force, which is why we have to look at the nature of the ideology that hangs over the heads of Indian women and, for that matter, women everywhere else.

The so-called choice that the promoters of *satī* claim for women seems particularly delusional when we find that often a woman has no understanding of what *satī* involves. In a recent interview, a village woman expressed her utter shock when she found out that to be regarded as a *satī* a woman has to die with her husband. She told the reporter that she had always wanted to become a *satī* because she had been told from childhood that a *satī* is worshiped as a goddess. However, she had never realized that she actually had to die! While this may be an example of exceptional simplemindedness, it does emphasize how an ideology has manipulated women into a falsified perception of the world and even the self.

In pondering the ideological domination of women, it is particularly important not to deny or trivialize a woman's (or a man's, for that matter) inconsolable grief on losing a life partner, a grief that may make life insupportable. This grief is not to be confused with the issue of *satī*, which we have every reason to see as a drama of dominance that benefits every player except the central one. The role that idealized constructions play in that drama is obvious in the personal fate of the individual *satī*, but that role begins to expand far beyond the individual when we return to my original question: Why now? Why has the ideal of *satī* been rejuvenated after more than a century and a half of irrelevancy? The murderous greed of Roop Kanwar's in-laws is easy enough to recognize as a motive, but what made thousands of unrelated watchers jump on the *satī* bandwagon? What drove seventy thousand people, mostly young men but also many women, to march in defense of *satī*? Why did even greater numbers organize, almost overnight, to "defend" their religion against the secular justice system of India? My answer in brief is that today *satī* has nothing to do with religion, self-definition, or even personal gain and everything to do with a political struggle that uses women as chips in a power play. Let me summarize my argument as follows:

- The promotion of *satī* in present-day India has gone beyond family, self-interest, and religious orthodoxy.
- It is a political move, a bid to mobilize support by forging a common identity.
- This identity must claim the moral authority of tradition and principle to command obedience.
- The affirmation of such an identity requires a dramatic event as a revelation.
- *Satī* is such an event.
- Therefore, questions of religious and legal validity are immaterial and have been superseded by political expediency, which is capitalizing on an available ideology with a proven record of ensuring women's consent to subjugation.

My thesis is that the phenomenon of *satī* shows an ideological manipulation of women—and, in many cases, of men as well—and that this ideology has now been seized on as an effective propaganda tool for achieving political ends. Even in a populous and politically volatile country such as India, enormous organizational skills and resources are needed to mobilize hundreds of thousands of supporters. Like the Ayodhyā mosque issue, *satī* is the key to turn on that mobilization, and it cannot be mere coincidence that the same political groups have taken leadership on both issues. The purpose behind *satī* is no longer only the subjugation of women but the subjugation of an entire nation.

Ultimately, it is irrelevant whether there is authority in the ancient books of sacred law. In the past 150 years or more, every piece of such authority has been sifted, interpreted, and reinterpreted. It is equally irrelevant today to try to balance the degree of voluntary motivation against coercion. Academic and legal debates of this kind succeeded in abolishing *satī* 150 years ago because the religious orthodoxy of the time, ponderous and often hard-hearted as it was, was open to reason and scholarly values. The establishment that now promotes *satī* is different. No matter how convincingly you prove that the scriptures do not sanction *satī* or that no woman wants to be burned alive, you will not deflect those who stage-manage *satī*. Burning a woman is not their goal but a mere prologue to the grander action of capturing political power.

If, then, a discussion of the present kind has any meaning, it is a wake-up call to the wife bound to the stake of an imposed ideology. Political action by Indian feminists to protect putative *satīs* is obviously necessary, but the limited value of imposing a solution from above can be greatly strengthened if the ideals that enslave women at risk can be exploded and the women themselves armed for resistance. Helping the victim achieve autonomy is a necessary condition of enduring empowerment, and, because power does come to a large degree through knowledge, finding and affirming that knowledge is the least an academic can do.

Notes

1. To name a few: Ashis Nandy, "The Sociology of Sati," *Indian Express* (October 5, 1987); Romila Thapar, "In History," *Seminar* 342 (February 1988); Rajeswari S. Rajan, "Subject of Sati: Pain and Death in the Contemporary Discourse on Satī," *Yale Journal of Criticism* 3:2 (1990); Lata Mani, "Cultural Theory, Colonial Texts: Reading Eyewitness Accounts of Widow Burning," (1992); Sharada Jain, et al, "Deorala Episode: Women's Protest in Rajasthan," *Economic and Political Weekly* 22:45 (November 7, 1987), pp. 1891–94; Veena Talwar Oldenberg, John S. Hawley, Arvind Sharma, Katherine Young, and Julia Leslie.
2. Kane, 1968, 2:625.
3. *imānārīrvidhavāḥ supatnīrāñjanena sarpiṣā saṁviśantu/*
   anaśravo anamīvāḥ suratnā ārohantu janayo yonimagre//
   Ṛg.Veda x.18.7–8, vol.7, pp. 435–36
   Let these women, who are not widows and who are good wives, sit down with clarified butter used as collyrium. May the wives who are tearless, free from disease and wearing fine jewels enter home first.
4. *udīrṣva nāri abhijīvalokaṁ gatāsumetamupaśeṣa ehi/*
   hastagrābhasya didhiṣoḥ tava idaṁ patyuḥ janitvam abhisambhūtha//
   O woman, arise to the world of the living! Come, this man near whom thou sleepest is lifeless. Thou hast enjoyed this state of being the wife of thy husband, the suitor who took thee by the hand.

5. Cited by Manjushree, 1990, pp. 158–59.
6. *Bṛhaddevatā* 8.13.
7. Vincent Simith, *The Oxford History of India*, p. 86.
8. *mṛte bhartari yā nārī samārohed hutāśanaṁ/*
sārundhatī samācārā svargaloke mahīyate//
Śuddhitattva in *Aṣṭāviṁśatitattva*, pp. 345–48
After the death of the husband that woman who ascends the fire [=funeral pyre] she, proper like Arundhatī, is praised in heaven.
9. *Vaśiṣiṣṭha Dharmasūtra* xvii.72.
10. *Yājñavalkyasmṛti* 1. 81.
11. An almost identical verse appears in the *Manusmṛti* in the context of the remarriage of women, which draws Manu's disapproval (*Manusmṛti* v. 158).
12. *Mahābhārata* vol. i. Adi 95.65; vol. xviii. Mauṣala 7.18.
13. *Harṣacarita*, chap. 5.
14. *yadetadanumaraṇaṁ nāma tadatiniṣphalam.*
Kadambarī paragraph 177, pt. 1 (Kane ed.)
This so-called [practice of] following [one's husband] in death is entirely fruitless.
15. Hawley, 1987, pp. 163–64.
16. Once the husband dies, the torture of his wife begins, as if the messengers of the death god Yama themselves have come to take away her soul . . . . It is the custom that a widow should eat only once a day for a year after her husband's death; apart from that, she also has to fast completely on several days . . . . A woman whose husband is dead is like a living corpse. She has no rights in the home . . . . Thousands of widows die after a husband's death. But far more have to suffer worse fates throughout their life if they stay alive. Tharu and Lalitha, 1991, pp. 358–63.
17. Leslie, 1991, pp. 184–85.
18. *Mahānirvāṇtantra* 10.80.
19. Veena Talwar Oldenburg, "The Roop Kanwar Case." In Hawley, 1994, pp. 101–30.

References

Śruti and *Smṛti* Texts

Aśvalāyana. *Aśvalāyana Gṛhyasūtra*. With the commentary of Haradattacarya. T. Ganapati Sastri, ed. Repr. Delhi: Satguru Publications, 1985.

Aśvalāyana. *Aśvalāyana Gṛhyasūtrabhāṣyam of Devasvāmin*. K. P. Aithal, ed. Madras: Adyar Library and Research Centre, 1980.

AtharvaVeda. With *Sāyanabhāṣya*. Paṇḍit Ramswarup Sharma Gaud, ed. Varanasi: Chowkhamba Vidyabhavan, 1990.

Bhaṭṭācārya, Raghunandana. *Aṣṭāviṁśatitattvaṁ*. Shyamakanta Vidyabhushana Bhattacharya, ed. Calcutta: Bholanath Deva Sharma, 1900.

Bṛhaspati. *Brhaspati Smṛti*. K. V. Aiyanger, ed. (reconstructed text). Baroda: Gaekwad Oriental Series lxxxv, 1941.

Mahanirvanatantra. Baldeo Prasad Mishra, ed. Bombay: Shrivenkateswar Steam Press, 1985.

Manu. *Manusmṛti*. With the *Manubhāṣya* of Medhātithi., vols. 1–2. Ganganath Jha, ed. Delhi: Parimal Publications, 1992.

Paraśara. *Parāśarasmṛti*. Alaka Sukla, ed. Delhi: Parimal Publications, 1990.

ṚgVeda. With *Sāyanabhāṣya*. Ramgovinda Trivedi, ed. Varanasi: Chowkhamba Vidyabhavan, 1990.

Vaśiṣṭha. *Vaśiṣṭha Dharmasūtra*. G. Buhler, tr. Oxford: Sacred Books of the East, 1882.
Yājñavalkya. *Yājñavalkyasmṛti* of Yājñavalkya with Vijñāneśvara's *Mitākṣarā*. Bombay: Nirnaya Sagara Press, 1936.
———.*Yājñavalkyasmṛti* with commentaries of *Vijñāneśvara*, *Bālambhaṭṭa*, *Śrīkara*, *Viśvarupa* and *Aparāka*. Narayan Ram Acharya, ed. Delhi: Nag Publishers, 1985.
———.*Yājñavalkyasmṛti* with Jīmūtavāhana's *Dāyabhāga*. Bombay: Nirnaya Sagara Press, 1936.

Classical Literature

Aśvaghoṣa. *Saundarānanda*. Varanasi: Krishnadas Akademi, 1992.
———.*Saundarānanda*. Delhi: Motilal Banarsidass, 1975.
Bāṇabhaṭṭa. *Kādambarī*. Varanasi: Chowkhamba Vidyabhavana, 1985.
———.*Harṣacarita*. Varanasi: Chowkhamba Vidyabhavana, 1985.
Mahābhārata, vols. 1–18. V. S. Sukhtankar, ed. Poona: Bhandarkar Research Institute, 1968.

Secondary Sources

Altekar, A. S. *The Position of Women in Hindu Civilization*, 2d rev. ed. Delhi: Motilal Banarsidass, 1959.
Hawley, John Straton. *Sati: The Blessings and the Curse*. New York: Columbia University Press, 1994.
Jain, Sharada, Nirja Misra, and Kavita Srivastava. "Deorala Episode: Women's Protest in Rajasthan." *Economic and Political Weekly* 22:45 (November 1987).
Kane, P. V. *History of Dharmaśāstra*, vols. 1–5 Poona: Bhandarkar Oriental Institute, 1968.
Kishwar, Madhu, and Ruth Vanita. "The Burning of Roop Kanwar." *Manushi* 42–43 (1987), pp. 15–25.
Leslie, Julia. *Roles and Rituals for Hindu Women*. London: Printer Publishers, 1991.
———.*The Perfect Wife: The Orthodox Hindu Woman according to the Strīdharmapaddhati of Tryambakarājan*. New York: Oxford University Press, 1989.
Mani, Lata. "Contentious Traditions: The Debate on Sati in Colonial India." In *Recasting Women: Essays in Colonial History*, ed. K. Sangari and S. Vaid. New Delhi: Kali for Women, 1988, pp. 88–96.
———. "Cultural Theory, Colonial Texts: Reading Eyewitness Accounts of Widow Burning." In *Cultural Studies* eds. L. Grossberg, C. Nelson, P.A. Treichler. New York: Toutlege, 1992, pp. 392–408.
Manjushree. *The Position of Women in Yājñavalkyasmṛti*. New Delhi: Prachi, 1990.
Matilal, Bimal K. "Sati." *Illustrated Weekly of India* (October 1987).
Nandy, Ashis. "The Sociology of Sati." *Indian Express* (October 5, 1987).
Narasimhan, Sakuntala. *Sati: Widow Burning in India*. New York: Anchor, 1992.
O'Flaherty, Wendy Doniger. *Textual Sources for the Study of Hinduism*. Chicago: University of Chicago Press, 1988.
Rajan, Rajeswari R. "Subject of Sati: Pain and Death in the Contemporary Discourse on Satī." *Yale Journal of Criticism* 3:2 (1990), pp. 1–23.
Ray, Ajit Kumar. *Widows Are Not for Burning*. New Delhi: ABC Publishing, 1985.
Roy, Mohit, ed. *Satidaha* by Kumudnath Mallik. Calcutta: J. N. Chakravarti, 1991.
Sharma, Arvind, ed. *Sati: Historical and Phenomenological Essays*. Delhi: Motilal Banarsidass, 1988.
Singh, Santosh. *A Passion for Flames*. Jaipur: RBSA Publishers, 1989.
Smith, Vincent. *Oxford History of India*, 3rd ed. Oxford: Clarendon Press, 1958.
Spivak, Gayatri Chakravorty. "Can the Subaltern Speak? Speculations on Widow Sacrifice." *Wedge* (Winter-Spring 1985), pp. 120–30.
Thapar, Romila. "In History." *Seminar* 342 (February 1988), pp. 14–19.
Tharu, S., and K. Lalitha. *Women Writing in India*. New York: Feminist Press, 1991.

JAYATRI GHOSH

Satyavatī

The Matriarch of the *Mahābhārata*

The *Mahābhārata* is, in a sense, a poetic narration of India's history or, as mythography, perhaps something greater; as the noted nineteenth century scholar Ramendra Sundar Trivedi said, "The history narrated in the *Mahābhārata* is the history of humankind," a judgment repeated by Vyāsa in Peter Brook's *The Mahābhārata*. That this most universal of epics describes, analyzes, ponders, and judges every imaginable human experience, both private and public, is a commonplace of Indian cultural history. Less common is the perception that, in pursuing its central moral enquiry into the nature of dharma or righteousness, the *Mahābhārata* holds up alternatives to social norms to the point of subverting convention. The most basic of such reappraisals, given the apparently male orientation of the narrative, is the consistent projection of women's perceptions of their predicaments in terms both of gender and class. We find in Mahābhāratian society not only extraordinary men but also women of exceptional character, whose strength has few parallels, even in the liberalized twentieth century. Women like Gāndhārī, Kunti, and Draupadī stand out, sometimes opposing the injustice of the male world, sometimes determined to claim their rights even while remaining under male authority. But behind the screen of these well-born Aryan women, who are cast ultimately in the heroic mold of the male heroes, stands one intriguing woman made unique as much by the circumstances of her birth as by her life. She is Satyavatī, the so-called *śūdrāṇī*, a woman raised in the peripheral *śūdra* caste.

The central importance of this woman is easy to test: the events of the *Mahābhārata* would simply not have happened, had there been no Satyavatī. The focal point of the principal storyline of the *Mahābhārata* is the *Kuru-Pāṇḍava* war. This is fought between two branches, the *Kauravas* and the *Pāṇḍavas*, of the single dynasty that ruled over the vast *Kurujāṅgāl*, and these branches issued from the one female progenitor, Satyavatī, who was the paternal grandmother of the *Kauravas* and the *Pāṇḍavas*. But beyond this biological instrumentality lies the thematic significance of Satyavatī's encounter with the world, a significance not always recognized. To explain this significance is the purpose of this essay.

Myths surrounding Satyavatī's birth are shrouded in mystery. More than one story is told about her origins. One version tells of a king named Uparicara who loved hunting.[1] He kicked a mountain named Kolāhala, and from the crevasse he created, a river emerged. The mountain had procreated his son and daughter in the womb of the river. Freed by the king, the pleased river offered her children to the king. The sage-like king Uparicara Vasu, the great slayer of foes, made the boy his general and took the maiden named Girikā to wife. One day while hunting, the king recalled the Lakṣmī-like beauty of the exquisite Girikā, and ejaculating in the heat of his desire he collected his sperm on a leaf. Well-versed in the finer points of dharma, the king purified the sperm with mantras and gave it to a hawk to carry it to his wife Girikā. As the hawk flew to her carrying the sperm on the leaf, it was attacked by another hawk, who mistook the sperm for a piece of meat. The two hawks fought and the sperm fell on the waters of Yamunā, where the *apsarā* (nymph) Adrikā sporting in the form of a fish swallowed the sperm and became pregnant. She was caught by a fisherman in her tenth month. When the fisherman opened the belly of the fish, he found to his surprise two children, a boy and a girl. The king was informed of this strange tale and was offered the babies. The king refused to take the girl but adopted the boy as his son. That son later became King Matsya. The rejected girl, born with all possible virtues and attributes of beauty, was Satyavatī.[2]

In a slightly different version of the tale, we are told that King Uparicara Vasu ruled the kingdom of Cedi and was of the Puru dynasty. He married Girikā, the daughter of a mountain dweller (Girikā's father is described as a mountain in the text). Another difference is that the *apsarā* Adrikā had become a fish as a result of a Brahmin's curse. Finally, in this version of the tale, the king gives away his daughter Satyavatī to a fisherman, who brings her up as his own daughter.[3]

Taken literally, the tale defies rational judgment. As a metaphorical representation, it makes sense as the validation of an embarrassing situation: evidently, King Uparicara was attracted to a fisherwoman, had children by her, and to spare Queen Girikā's feelings, the event was transformed into fantasy. Such escapes into fiction to legitimize questionable births are a common feature of the *Mahābhārata*, especially as a miraculous birth is a convenient device to lend supernatural powers or special status to the person born. No less than the Sun-god himself was said to have fathered Karṇa with the unwed Kuntī (although the divine nature of the liaison was not enough to prevent Kuntī from concealing the birth and abandoning the child). The generation of the five *Pāṇḍava* brothers in Kuntī's womb by various gods is an equally famous example. In closer parallel to the legend of Satyavatī, the historical social reality of India offers many instances of children of royal personages borne by *śudra* women and accepted into royal families and even becoming kings. The induction of such a child into a royal family, which we see in the case of the son of the supposed river in the story of King Uparicara, is paralleled in its sequel in the *Mahābhārata* when Vidura, himself a socially marginal figure as the son of Satyavatī's son Vyāsa by a maidservant, marries the daughter of a king borne by his *śudra* wife. That such legends were not unfounded in fact is proved by the history of the founder of the historic Maurya dynasty, Candragupta, who was the son of a *śudṛa* maidservant.

One exception to this pattern of assimilation was Satyavatī. Because her father rejected her, she found no place in the royal household and grew up in a fishing community, which, we are told, caused such a distinctive body odor that she became known as Matsyagandhā. Although her adoptive father was known as the king of the fishers, he was still a *dāśa*, which further distanced Satyavatī from the center of Aryan power. Her only capital was her beauty:

atīvarūpasaṁpannāṁ siddhānāmapi kāṅkṣitāṁ/

Mbh. 1.57.57

She was extremely beautiful [and deserved] to be desired by even those who had attained true knowledge.

She received no instruction in Aryan ways and lived a hardworking life by ferrying people across the river.[4] That is how she met the two men who changed her life radically. The first was the great sage Parāśara and the second, the powerful king of Hastināpura, Śantanu. One after the other, both of these Aryans, each preeminent in his world, were moved by Satyavatī's beauty and desired her. The story of her compliance in both cases is one of transformation of social and sexual subordination into far-reaching personal and political advantage. Still more remarkable is that the matriarchal ascendency she gained is recognized in the *Mahābhārata* as a moral supremacy that lent to her political decisions unquestioned validity. Her story thus inverts the conventional power relationship: rejected by her father at birth and forced into the underclass, she became the arbiter of the fate of *Kurujāṅgāl*. Nor is her success fortuitous because the narrative is careful to mark the shaping intelligence that underwrote her progress.

The story of Satyavatī as an adult began when Parāśara stepped into her boat:

sā tu Satyavatī nāma matsyaghātyabhisamśrayāt/
āsīn matsyagandhaiva kañcit kālaṁ śucismitā //
śuśruṣārthaṁ pitur nāvaṁ tām tu vāhayatīṁ jale/
tīrthayātrāṁ parikrāmannapaśyadvai Parāśaraḥ//

Mbh. 1.57.55–56

This Satyavatī was also known as Matsyagandhā for some time since she was sheltered by fisherman. She was rowing a boat in the water to help her father when the sage Parāśara who had set out on a pilgrimage saw her.

The great sage was at once smitten by her exquisite beauty and asked who she was. She answered:

anapatyasya dāśasya sutā tat priyakāmyayā/
sahasrajanasaṁpannā naur mayā vāhyate dvijaḥ//

Mbh. 1.58.87 (Cal. ed)

O *brāhmin*, I am the daughter of the sonless *dāśa*. I row this boat capable of carrying a thousand passengers for his pleasure.

Later, in answer to King Śantanu's question:

kasya tvamasi kā cāsi kiṁ ca bhīru cikīrṣasi?

Mbh. 1.94.43

Who are you? Whose daughter (are you)? What do you want (to do)?

Satyavatī replied:

sābravīd dāśakanyāsmi dharmārtham vāhaye tarīṁ/
pitur niyogād bhadraṁ te dāśarajño mahātmanaḥ//

Mbh. 1.94.44

That (maiden) said, I am the daughter of a *dāśa* and I am rowing this boat for dharma's sake under my father, the great souled *dāśa* king's instruction. May god bless you!

Parāśara was wise, calm, in control of his reason, and in possession of the knowledge of Brahman. Not one to be moved easily, he was fascinated by Satyavatī at first sight:

dṛṣṭaiva ca sa tāṁ dhīmāṁścakame cārudarśanāṁ/

Mbh. 1.57.57.

Immediately upon seeing the beautiful [maiden], that wise one (*ṛṣi* Parāśara) was overcome by desire.

On the boat in midriver, Parāśara begged Satyavatī for her love. But there were other sages waiting to be ferried across to the other bank. What will they think, asked Satyavatī:

sābravīt paśya bhagavan pārāvāre ṛṣīn sthitān/
āvayor dṛśyatorebhiḥ kathaṁ nu syānsamāgamaḥ//
evaṁ tayokto bhagavān nīhāramsṛjat prabhuḥ/
yena deśaḥ sa sarvastu tamobhūta ivābhavat//

Mbh. 1.57.58–59.

She (Satyavatī) said, Lord! behold the *ṛṣis* standing on the opposite bank. How will our union be possible under their gaze? When she spoke thus, the powerful master (Parāśara) created a mist which darkened the entire region.

Satyavatī was astounded by this revelation of the *ṛṣi*'s power. Yet, she obviously retained her presence of mind, for she realized that this powerful Brahmin should not be repulsed, that his satisfaction might grant her something normally unobtainable, and that his displeasure might cause great harm. Besides, the suitor was a holy man, and his touch, like sandalwood paste, would leave her untainted and pure. Still, she was a virgin, under the authority of her father, and this Brahmin versed in the Vedas would not stay with her but would leave for pilgrimage in search of knowledge; so she would have to retain her virginity. This condition of her submission to the *ṛṣi* is the obvious subtext of her response:

biddhi māṁ bhagavan kanyāṁ sadā pitṛvaśānugāṁ/
tvasaṁyogācca dūṣyeta kanyābhāvo mamānagha//
kanyātve dūṣite cāpi katham śakṣye dvijottama/
gantuṁ gṛhaṁ gṛhe cāhaṁ dhīmanna sthātumutsahe/
etat sañcintya bhagavan vidhatsva yadanantaraṁ
evamuktavatīṁ tāṁ tu prītimān ṛṣisattamaḥ/
uvāca mat priyaṁ kṛtvā kanyaiva tāṁ bhaviṣyasi//

Mbh. 1.57.61–63.

Satyavatī said—Lord, know that I am a virgin, always subservient to my father. My maidenhood will be tainted if I consort with you. O greatest of all Brahmins, wise one, how will I go home with my maidenhood tainted? I will not even be able to live. O great ṛṣi, do what you must after you have thought about all this. When she spoke thus, the ṛṣi (Parāśara) was pleased and assured her that she would remain a virgin after fulfilling his desires.

Having made this reparative promise, Parāśara told her to ask for an additional boon:

vṛṇiṣva ca varaṁ bhīru yam tamicchasi bhāmini/
vṛthā hi n prasādo me bhūtapūrvaḥ śucismite//
evamuktvā varaṁ vavre gātrasaugandhamuttamaṁ/
sa cāsyai bhagavān prādān manasaḥ kāṅkṣitam prabhuḥ

Mbh. 1.57.64–65.

O loving follower, timid one, you may enjoy whatever boon you desire. O sweet smelling one, my blessings have never failed before. When (Parāśara) spoke thus (Matsyagandhā) asked for a pleasant fragrance for her body and the powerful ṛṣi granted her desire.

Only the smell of fish had marred Satyavatī's beauty and now she had overcome that weakness. She now gave herself to the ṛṣī. With the sky, wind, and water as witnesses, the sage was united with the daughter of the fisherman on the floating boat.[5] The smell of fish was eradicated forever, and her body took on the fragrance of the lotus. Matsyagandhā became sweet-smelling Padmagandhā. Her fragrance could be sensed from as far as a *yojana* (eight miles), which is why she became famous also as Yojanagandhā.[6]

Again, seen in the light of common sense, this change in body odor is a powerful metaphor. Satyavatī had native intelligence and beauty, but her mind was untouched by the benefits of Aryan education. Those were the benefits that the *dāsa* woman Matsyagandhā obtained by her union with the Aryan sage. The lotus metaphor, common to the Hindu view of the progress of the psyche, denotes the opening of her mind, which prepared her for her march toward personal power. The next step was even more decisive. It came about when King Śantanu, wandering in the forests by the Yamunā, suddenly smelled an indescribable fragrance. Investigating its source, he saw Satyavatī:

sa kadācid vanaṁ yāto yamunāmabhito nadīṁ/
mahīpatiranirdeśyamājighrad gandhamuttamaṁ//
tasya prabhavanvicchan vicacāra samantataḥ/
sa dadarśa tadā kanyāṁ dāsānām devarūpiṇīṁ//

Mbh. 1.94.41–42.

Once he (Śantanu) went into the woods by the river Yamunā and there (he) smelled a fragrance of indescribable excellence. While searching for the source of that fragrance (he) saw the divinely fair daughter of a *dāśa*.

The key to this event is the fragrance, which is a clear signal that the narrative is building up Satyavatī's career on the platform of her gains from her previous encounter. This cumulative plot structure raises the expectation that her next move could be only upwards, which was just what happened. In contrast to the ṛṣi, the king wished to make Satyavatī his companion for life. It was, of course, entirely within the social practice of the time for a king to take a woman of lower status for his consort, so Śantanu solicited her *dāśa* father for Satyavatī's hand:

rūpamādhuryagandhaistāṁ saṁyuktāṁ devarūpiṇīṁ/
samīkṣya rājā dāseyīṁ kāmayāmāsa śantanuḥ//
sa gatvā pitaraṁ tasyā varayāmāsa tāṁ tadā/
sa ca taṁ pratyuvācedaṁ dāśarājño mahīpatiṁ/

Mbh. 1.94.45–47.

On seeing this daughter of a *dāśa* endowed with beauty, sweetness, and fragrance, King Śantanu desired her. He immediately went to her father and prayed for her hand. The *dāśa* king replied to the ruler of the earth.

Surprisingly, this glittering opportunity did not seem to sweep Satyavatī off her feet. Displaying a rare consciousness of her own needs and rights, she expressed no eagerness to become a royal bride upon her first meeting with Śantanu. Evidently, she was well aware of the implications of her position. In that age, many brides entered the royal family, but only she whose son became king would receive true respect and wield power. Some such calculation, whether on her part or that of her family, led her father, the *dāśa* king, to insist that Śantanu must promise to make Satyavatī's son king of the *Kuru* dynasty. The *dāśa* said,

yadīmāṁ dharmapatnīṁ tvaṁ mattaḥ prārthayase'nagha/
satyavāgasi satyena samayaṁ kuru me tataḥ//
āsyāṁ jāyeta yaḥ putraḥ sa rājā pṛthivīpatiḥ/
tvadūrdhvamabhiṣektavyo nānyaḥ kaścana pārthiva //

Mbh. 1.94.48, 51

If you pray for her as your wife in true dharma then, O pure and truthful one, swear this to me in truth that her son will be king. It will be he who will have to be named crown prince after you. No one else.

It was impossible for Śantanu to make such a vow, as he already had a son, Devavrata, by his elder wife Gaṅgā, who was matchless in appearance, ability, and might; as the older son, he was the rightful heir to the throne. To deprive him of the right to the kingdom of the *Kuru* dynasty was unthinkable, and Śantanu could not take this unjust vow:

nākāmayata taṁ dātuṁ varam dāsāya Śantanuḥ/
śarīrajena tīvreṇa dahyamāno'pi bhārata//
sa cintayanneva tadā dāśakanyām mahīpatiḥ/
pratyāddhāstinapuraṁ śokopahatacetanaḥ//

Mbh. 1.94.52–53.

Though burning with intense desire, Śantanu did not wish to grant the *dāśa* king this promise. But he returned to Hastināpura thinking of the *dāśa* maiden and stupefied with grief.

Noticing his father's despondency, Devavrata discovered the true reason for his sorrow from the courtiers. To dispel his father's gloom, Devavrata himself went to pray for Satyavatī for his father. This brought about that great event, unique in literature and history, the vow of Devavrata that set the benchmark for self-sacrifice in the Hindu tradition.

Satyavatī and the *dāśa* king wanted Satyavatī's son to be king. Even if Śantanu accepted that, would the future of that son or the succeeding generations be safe and secure? Would a valiant prince such as Devavrata not be desirous or capable of regaining the kingdom by the strength of arms? What if in the future Devavrata begot sons who claimed their right to the throne? Satyavatī and her father thought far into the future. It was necessary to be absolutely certain that only the descendants of Satyavatī would rule over Hastināpura. Therefore they were not satisfied when Devavrata promised Satyavatī's spokesman the *dāśa* king that if Satyavatī had a son then that son would become the king of Hastināpura. Devavrata said:

evametat kariṣyāmi yathā tvamanubhāṣyase/
yo'syāṁ janiṣyate putraḥ sa no rājā bhaviṣyati//

Mbh. 1.94.78

I will do as you say—the son born of Satyavatī's womb will become our king.

But the *dāśa* king said:

yat tvayā satyavtyarthe satyadharmaparāyaṇa/
rājamadhye pratijñātamanurūpaṁ tavaiva tat//
nānyathā tan mahāvāho saṁśayo'tra n kaścana/
tavāpatyaṁ bhaved yattu tatra na saṁśayo mahān//

Mbh. 1.94.83–4

O one who is devoted to truth and dharma, among all kings, the vow you have taken for Satyavatī befits you. We have no doubt that you will not break your promise. But O valiant one, we suspect the son who will be born to you.

What the *dāśa* king was, in effect, asking for was Devavrata's celibacy. Devavrata now made that unique and terrible vow:

Dāśarāja nivodhedaṁ vacanaṁ me nṛpottama/
śṛṇvatāṁ bhūmipālānāṁ yad bravīmī pituḥ kṛte//
rājyaṁ tāvat pūrvameva mayā tyaktaṁ narādhipa/
apatyahetorapi ca karomyeṣa viniścayaṁ//
adya prabhṛti me dāśa brahmacaryaṁ bhaviṣyati/
aputrasyāpi me lokā bhaviṣyantyakṣyā divi//

Mbh. 1.94.86–88

O *dāśa* king, hear my words spoken for my father in the midst of all the *kṣatriyas* who wish to hear. O king, I relinquished the kingdom before, now I make a firm resolution not to have a son.
Brahmacarya will be my goal from today onward. In this way, even though I will have no son, I will in future have an eternal life in heaven.

Devavrata accepted *brahmacarya* till death so that the possibility of his progeny might not stand in the way of his father's marriage to Satyavatī. He was lauded for his unique promise and became known as Bhīṣma, the utterer of a terrible vow:

tato'ntarikṣe'psaraso devāḥ sarṣigaṇāstathā/
abhyavarṣanta kusumairbhīṣmo'yamiti cābruvan//

Mbh. 1.94.90

After this *apsarās*, gods and ancestors rained flowers from heaven and said, he shall now be called "Bhīṣma."

Satyavatī now came to Hastināpura and became the queen of the entire *Kurujāṅgāl*. Remarkable as this elevation was, her subsequent history is even more impressive. To this point, she had been obviously helped, perhaps even guided, by her *dāśa* father, and the actions that led her to Hastināpura smell of self-seeking.

But her actions as queen of the *Kurus* at once demonstrate her independence, her decisiveness, and her commitment to putting institutions above individuals.

Satyavatī became the mother of two sons, Citrāṅgada and Vicitravīrya, by the aging Śantanu, who died before the younger son attained his youth. Acting on Satyavatī's wishes, Bhīṣma placed her elder son, Citrāṅgada, on the throne:

svargate Śantanau bhīṣmaścitrāṅgadamarindamaṁ/
sthāpayāmāsa vai rājye satyavatyā mate sthitaḥ//[7]

Mbh. 1.95.5

After Śantanu's death, Bhīṣma placed Citrāṅgada in the kingdom following Satyavatī's wish.

But Citrāṅgada was killed in battle soon after. Because Vicitravīrya was still a minor, Bhīṣma became regent, again in deference to Satyavatī's wishes:

hate citrāṅgade bhīṣmo bāle bhrātari cānagha/
pālayāmāsa tad rājyaṁ satyavatyā mate sthitaḥ//

Mbh. 1.96.1

When his younger brother was killed, Bhīṣma, in accordance with Satyavatī's wishes, began to rule the kingdom.

When Vicitravīrya came of age, Bhīṣma busied himself with preparations for his brother's marriage, first consulting with Satyavatī:

bhrātur vicitravīryasya vivāhāyopcakrame/
satyavatyā saha mithaḥ kṛtvā niścayamātmavān//

Mbh. 1.96.59 (Cal. ed.)

After mutual consultation with Satyavatī, (Bhīṣma) took great care over the preparations of his brother Vicitravīrya's wedding.

All of these key decisions were made according to Satyavatī's wishes. The narrator's reiteration of the phrase *satyavatyā mate sthitaḥ* underlines the acknowledgment of her decision-making role. But her greatest need for self-assertion arose when her younger son, Vicitravīrya died, too, leaving behind two young wives. We are given to understand that none of the calamities she suffered affected Satyavatī's calm judgment:

pretakāryāṇi sarvāṇi tasya samyagakārayat/
rājño vicitrivīryyasya satyavatyā mate sthitaḥ/
ṛtvigbhiḥ sahito bhīṣmaḥ sarvaiśca kurupuṅgavaiḥ//

Mbh. 1.96.59

According to Satyavatī's instructions, Bhīṣma joined with the priests and the chiefs of the *Kuru* clan to perform the last rites of Vicitravīrya perfectly.

tataḥ satyavatī dīnā kṛpaṇā putragṛddhinī/
putrasya kṛtvā kāryāṇi snuṣābhyām saha bhārata//

Mbh. 1.97.1

Then the very sad, upset Satyavatī, desiring sons, joined her daughters-in-law in performing the last rites of her son.

samāśvāsya snuṣe te ca bhartṛśokanipīḍite/

Mbh. 1.97. 2 (Cal. ed.)

The daughters-in law, who were plagued by their sorrow for their husband, were consoled (by her).

Her own grief was limitless, but Satyavatī was in firm control of the necessities of family and state as she directed Bhīṣma over the last rites of her own son and consoled her grief-stricken, widowed daughters-in-law. As the reigning queen of the vast *Kurujāṇgāl*, Satyavatī set duty above sorrow, the institution above the individual.

The need to set aside personal loss, at least for the moment, and protect the integrity of the empire was urgent. Because Vicitravīrya had died childless and Bhīṣma was a *brahmacārī* (celibate), Śantanu's line was faced with extinction. *Kurujāṅgāl* would be rulerless, and according to contemporary *smārtavidhāna* (following the codes of *smṛti*), the *Kuru* clan would be left with no provision for *piṇḍa* (offerings to ancestors by the rightful descendant). With Bhīṣma's leadership precluded by his vow, an impasse had been reached, the resolution of which fell exclusively into the hands of Satyavatī, on whom alone the fate of *Kurujāṅgāl* depended. This situation is unparalleled in the *Mahābhārata* both in the statement of the problem and, as we shall see, in its resolution. Equally unique is the narrative's choice of a woman as the singular cause both of the crisis and of its resolution. As I noted at the beginning of this essay, had there been no Satyavatī, there would have been no story; now we shall see that, without her intervention, the story would not have ended the way it does—namely, in the *Kuru-Pāṇḍava* war.

The problem was to carry on the male line. Satyavatī's solution was to bring about the birth of one or more *kṣetraja* sons—that is, sons begotten in the wombs of her daughters-in-law by a man engaged solely for that purpose. This decision could not have been easy for a mother whose own son's wives were involved, especially as the *kṣetraja* option was a measure of desperation with no more than grudging support from the lawgivers of *smārta dharma*.[8] But Satyavatī's priority was the preservation of the *Kuru* dynasty and the empire of *Kurujāṅgāla*. So she approached the most deserving man she knew—namely, Bhīṣma:

śantanor dharmanityasya kauravasya yaśasvinaḥ/
tvayi piṇḍśca kīrtiśca santānañca pratiṣṭhitaṁ//

Mbh. 1.97.3

(O Bhīṣma), the *piṇḍa*, deeds and family of the just and renowned *Kuru* king Śantanu are now bestowed upon you.

tasmāt subhṛśamāśvasya tvayi dharmabhṛtāṁ vara/
kārye tvāṁ viniyokṣyāmi tacchrutvā kartumarhasi//

Mbh. 1.97.7

Therefore, placing great reliance on your just self (I) will engage you in a deed. Do what you must after listening to this.

ime mahiṣyau bhrātuste kāśirājasute śubhe/
rūpayauvanasaṁpanne putrakāme ca bhārata//
tayorutpādayāpatyaṁ santānāya kulasya naḥ/
manniyogān mahābhāga dharmaṁ kartumihārhasi//

Mbh. 1.97.9–10

O descendant of Bharata, these two are your brother's wives. The two daughters of the king of Kāśī have all auspicious traits, are young, beautiful, and desirous of sons. Therefore acquire dharma by producing children in their wombs for the continuation of our dynasty according to my instructions.

In her quest for the preservation of the *Kuru* dynasty, she was ready to sacrifice self-interest. Fearing that Bhīṣma might balk at producing children in the womb of someone else's wife, she tried to release Bhīṣma from his vow and requested him to marry in accordance with dharma and to ascend the throne in order to preserve the ancestral line:

rājye caivābhiṣicyasya bhāratānanuśādhi ca/
dārāṁśca kuru dharmeṇa mā nimajjīḥ pitāmahān//

Mbh. 1.97.11

Be thou crowned king, rule over the descendants of Bharata and take a wife according to dharma, but do not immerse your forefathers in hell.

Obviously, if Bhīṣma agreed and had his own children, Satyavatī would lose her sovereign powers, which was exactly the fear that had led to her prenuptial dealings with King Śantanu and Bhīṣma's *brahmacarya.* In urging Bhīṣma to take a wife, Satyavatī was thus renouncing her self-interest irreversibly. When Bhīṣma declined this proposal, as his vow required him to do, Satyavatī argued that the demands of social duty must override personal considerations:

jānāmi caiva satyaṁ tanmadarthaṁ yadabhāṣathāḥ/
āpad dharmamavekṣasva vaha paitāmahīṁ dhuraṁ//
yathā te kulatantuśca dharmaśca na parābhavet/
suhṛdaśca prahṛṣyeraṁstathā kuru parantapa//

Mbh. 1.97.21–22

I know your vows, I also know what you had said for me, but look to your duty in the time of distress and bear this great weight. Act so that the line of descent and the thread of dharma are not destroyed and friends remain satisfied.

The principle invoked here is typical of the moral scheme of the *Mahābhārata* as revealed in the epic's common narrative device of leading up to the dilemma of choosing between two equal and mutually exclusive necessities, as seen in Arjuna's response to the need for killing his dearest friends or in Yudhiṣṭhira's need for lying to his teacher Droṇa. In our passage, Satyavatī is thus made the locus of ethical perception. At the same time, the passage also shows that her motivation went well beyond the bounds of self-interest. Bhīṣma accepted her solution in principle but, because he considered his vow unbreakable, he proposed a modification:

brāhmaṇo guṇavān kaścid dhanenopanimantryatāṁ/
vicitrivīryakṣetreṣu yaḥ samutpādayet prajāḥ//

Mbh. 1.99.2

Let a virtuous Brahmin be invited with the promise of wealth to produce children in the wombs of Vicitravīrya's wives.

Satyavatī's response to this proposal revealed yet again her courage, practical judgment, and absolute truthfulness, a combination of moral traits that is central to the epic's concept of right conduct. Agreeing with Bhīṣma, Satyavatī declared that if a Brahmin had to be brought in, then it should be the great *ṛṣi* Kṛṣṇa Dvaipāyana Vyāsa, who was her own son by the sage Parāśara. Here again, we see the circularity of narrative structure typical of the *Mahābhārata* as it takes us back to Satyavatī's youth to resolve the dynastic crisis. In addition, this recall of her liaison with Parāśara replays the theme of an unconventional birth and, looking forward, validates the exceptional measure she is about to take to ensure the continuation of the *Kuru* line. That Vyāsa was the author of the *Mahābhārata* creates a sense of symmetrical closure on yet another level.

This is how Satyavatī related the story to Bhīśma:

tataḥ satyavatī bhīṣmaṁ vācā samsajjamānayā/
vihasantīva savrīḍamidaṁ vacanamabravīt//
satyametan mahābāho yathā vadasi bhārata/
viśvāsāt te pravakṣyāmi santānāya kulasya ca//
na te śakyamanākhyātumāpaddhīyaṁ tathāvidhā//
tvameva naḥ kule dharmastaṁ satyaṁ tvaṁ parā gatiḥ/
tasmānniśamya vākyaṁ me kuruśva yadanantaraṁ//

Mbh. 1.99.3–5

After that Satyavatī, the speaker of just words, told Bhīṣma these words with a little smile. What you say is true. I will tell you something in order to preserve the line because I trust you. I cannot refrain from telling what happened in that time of great danger. Because you are now the protector of dharma and truth of our clan, our sole path (to preserve). Therefore, do what you have to after listening to me.

She revealed:

jajñe ca yamunādvīpe pārāśaryaḥ sa vīryavān/

Mbh. 1.57.69

Parāśara's son was born on an island in the Yamunā and grew up valiant.

Having been born on an island (a *dvīpa*), the child came to be known as Dvaipāyana. Parāśara had left after restoring Satyavatī's maidenhood, but she had not abandoned her illegitimate child, who grew up devoted to his mother, whose commands were law to him. Like his father, he had set out to meditate and acquire knowledge, but only with his mother's permission, promising that he would come whenever his mother called:

sa mātaramupasthāya tapasyeva mano dadhe/
smṛto'haṁ darśayiṣyāmi kṛtveṣviti ca so'bravīt//

Mbh. 1.57.70

He [=Dvaipāyana] told his mother, I will come whenever you remember me and concentrated upon his meditation with his mother's permission.

A striking feature of Satyavatī's narrative is her total lack of embarrassment in acknowledging an illegitimate child and the enduring relationship between mother and son. We have noted Bhīṣma's habitual deference to her; now we observe Vyāsa's when he arrives at her command:

bhavatyā yadabhipretaṁ tadahaṁ kartumāgataḥ/
śādhi māṁ dharmtattvajñe karavāṇi priyaṁ tava//

Mbh. 1.99.25

O one who is well-versed in dharma, I have come to do what you desire. Advise me, and I will do what pleases you.

The passage is marked, on the one hand by the learned Vyāsa's recognition of his mother's knowledge of dharma and, on the other, by his total submission to her judgment. She states the principles on which her commands rest:

mātāpitro prajāyante putrāḥ sādhāraṇāḥ kave/
teṣāṁ pitā yathā svāmī tathā mātā na saṁayaḥ//
vidhātṛvihitaḥ sa tvam yathā me prathamaḥ sutaḥ/
vicitravīryo brahmarṣe tathā me'varajaḥ sutaḥ//
mayaiva pitṛto bhīsṃastathā tvamapi mātṛtaḥ/
bhrātā vicitrivīryasya yathā vā putra manyase//

Mbh. 1.99.28–30

O learned one, sons are born with equal portions of their mother's and father's selves; hence just as father is the master of his sons so does a mother have similar rights. There is no doubt about this. O *brahmarṣi*, according to laws, just as you are my first son so is Vicitravīrya my youngest son. Just as Bhīsṁa is Vicitravīrya's brother because of the (common) father, so are you, because of the (same) mother.

This part of Satyavatī's argument is an interesting extension of what she had said before. So far, she has invoked dharma. Now she extends dharma to a genetic principle that enshrines a mother's rights. Remarkable as this claim by a woman is in an age of supposedly unquestioned patriarchal determinism, it is still more remarkable in being held up by the text as a validating principle of dharma. By accepting this argument, the learned Vyāsa in effect puts the imprimatur of the establishment both on Satyavatī as the source of political stability and on matriarchal rights, for he admits:

vettha dharmaṁ satyavatī paraṁ cāparameva ca/
yathā ca tava dharmajñe dharme praṇihitā matiḥ//
tasṁdahaṁ tvanniyogādardhamuddiśya kāraṇaṁ/
īpsitaṁ te kariṣyāmi dṛṣṭaṁ hyetat purātanaṁ//

Mbh. 1. 9.36–37

Mother Satyavatī, you know the dharma of both this world and the next and your intellect is always immersed in dharma. Therefore I will do as you desire with only dharma as my goal, having observed such past (acts).

As we reflect on this episode of succession, Satyavatī increasingly emerges as the embodiment of principles that seem to run counter to the general social conventions of the epic. First, she, rather than any male figure in her circle, is the decision maker; second, the customary ignominy of bearing a child out of wedlock is reversed in her case to lend power to her decisions; third, she anchors the dharma of her decisions in a biological observation that lays claim to gender parity. All of these reversals of the norm have serious implications for the nature of the moral discourse in the *Mahābhārata* that demand attention.

As we ponder Satyavatī's actions, a comparison with the famous confession of Kuntī becomes inescapable. As a maiden, Kuntī had received a boon from *ṛṣi* Durvāsā, which enabled her to invite any god to have a child by him (*Mbh*. 1. 105. 7–8. Cal. ed.). Kuntī invited Sūrya, who appeared and said:

vyapayātu bhayaṁ te'dya kumāraṁ prasamīkṣase/
mayā tvañcāpyanujñātā punaḥ kanyā bhaviṣyasi//

Mbh. 1.105.19 (Cal. ed.)

Let your fear be dispelled. You will soon see (your) son and according to my command you will become a maiden once more.

Kuntī retained her virginity exactly like Satyavatī, but, unlike her, Kuntī abandoned her son Karṇa, setting him afloat in water.

> *gūhamānāpacāraṁ sā bandhupakṣabhayāttadā/*
> *utsasarja kumāraṁ taṁ jale kuntī mahābalaṁ//*
>
> *Mbh.* 1.105.25 (Cal. ed.)

To hide her misdeed, Kuntī set her son afloat in water in fear of her friends.

A comparison between the two stories carries moral as well as narrative implications. First, Kuntī obviously lacked Satyavatī's courage. Second, Kuntī's action cost her Karṇa's love and devotion, for as he grew up in ignorance of his origin, he developed an implacable hate for Kuntī's five sons, the *Pāṇḍavas*, Arjuna in particular. Accordingly, when Kuntī revealed their relationship to Karṇa just before the battle and appealed to him to desist from taking the *Kuru* side against the *Pāṇḍavas*, she had neither moral nor emotional capital with which to win him over. She realized that the price of her secrecy would be the loss of at least one son. Where Satyavatī's truthfulness had led to love, mutuality, and the preservation of the family, Kuntī's deceit led to alienation, rejection, and fratricide. Again to be noted is the structural strategy of *entrelacement*, whereby the narrative's circularity reflects a moral balance of rights and wrongs.

The contrast between Kuntī and Satyavatī is not easy to explain. To see them, respectively, as representatives of the Aryan and non-Aryan cultures is tempting but not altogether persuasive. Even if we discount Satyavatī's biological origins, she was, after all co-opted into the Aryan ethos and recognized as one learned in the ways of dharma, an Aryan construct that is also the transcendent category in the *Mahābhārata*. Satyavatī's preeminence in the knowledge of dharma is attested by the respect she commands from the two figures of male authority in this part of her story—namely, Bhīṣma, the scion of the *Kuru* dynasty, and Vyāsa, the revered sage. In that Satyavatī and Kuntī make opposite choices in identical circumstances, should we take their stories as illustrations, respectively, of what dharma does and does not mean? But Kuntī is not charged with violating dharma when she abandons her child, which seems to be regarded as a venial act because bearing an illegitimate child is recognized as a matter of shame; at the same time, if that is the norm, then that is precisely why it seems extraordinary that Satyavatī should receive such positive endorsement in the epic for rearing and acknowledging an illegitimate child. At the very least, then, the contrast between the two stories seems to turn dharma into an ambivalent if not inconsistent category.

There seems to be little room for doubt that the *Mahābhārata* is using the Satyavatī story to support an alternative view not only of dharma, but also of the hierarchy of power. That it does so by electing for the central figure of the discourse an embodiment of powerlessness as an abandoned child, a woman—and a woman from the underclass, at that—and an unwed mother underlines the departure from the norm. Satyavatī's rise from outcaste to revered matriarch is a unique transformation, but its significance is not so much a success story as a reversal of social relationships that sees the woman's assumption of the role of the nation's savior.

Yet, in its final outcome, the story of Satyavatī leads us back to the common basis of dharma. No matter how exceptional a social identity this particular practitioner of dharma may represent, the fundamental principle that drives her actions—namely, subordinating private interests to the public—underlies every moral example in the epic. It is precisely because Satyavatī's life and character are so contrary to the dominant models of virtue that her subscription to the common laws of dharma affirms them as universal and immutable. Ultimately, dharma is not ambivalent, despite the ambivalence of the social structure in which its play is experienced. By acknowledging that dharma finds its seat irrespective of class or gender identities, the *Mahābhārata* creates a humanist perception rare in studies in power.

Notes

1. *Rājoparicaro nāma dharmanityo mahīpatiḥ/*
Babhūva mṛgayāṁ gantuṁ sa kadācid dhṛtavratah//
Sa cediviṣayaṁ ramyaṁ vasuḥ pauravanandanaḥ/
Indropadeśājjagrāha grahaṇīyaṁ mahīpatiḥ//

Mbh. 1.57.1–2

There lived a religious *mṛgayā*-loving ruler of the world called Uparicara. This King Uparicara Vasu of the Puru dyanasty lived in the beautiful land of Cedi, which was desirable in every way.

Passages quoted from the *Mahābhārata* are taken from the edition by Vishnu S. Sukthankar (1933) or, where noted as Cal. ed., from the edition by Haridas Siddhantavagish Bhattacharya (*Vaṅgāvda* 1338, i.e., 1931 C.E.).

2. *Mbh.* 1.57.33– 55.
3. *tayoḥ pumāṁsaṁ jagrāha rājoparicarastadā/*
sa matsyo nāma rājāsīd dhārmikaḥ satysaṅgaraḥ/
yā kanyā duhitā tasyā matsyā matsyagandhinī /
rājñā dattātha dāsāya iyam tava bhavatviti/
rūpasattvasamāyuktā sarvaiḥ samuditā guṇaiḥ//
sā tu satyavatī nāma matsyaghatyābhisaṁśrayāt/

Mbh. 1.57.51, 54, 55

King Uparicara accepted the male child as his own, who later became known as Matsya, a just and truth-loving king, and the fishy-smelling daughter of the fish he gave the fisher, saying, "Let this maiden be yours." This girl endowed with all possible beauty and good qualities was Satyavatī.

4. Satyavatī's unique fate becomes all the more striking when we compare her life with that of another heroine of the *Mahābhārata*, Śakuntalā, who was similarly born of an irregular liaison and abandoned by her parents. However, Śakuntalā, so named because as an infant she had been protected by birds (*śakunas*), was raised by a great sage in his idyllic hermitage and received all the advantages of a well-born girl. Although she suffered rejection from her royal husband, it was temporary, and her story ends happily (*Mbh.* 1.84.41–42; 86.8–16).

5. Those familiar with Peter Brook's film version of the *Mahābhārata* should be able to remember the scene. The director faithfully followed this story as given in the Bhandarkar edition.

6. *tato labdhavarā prītā strībhāvaguṇabhūṣitā/*
jagāma saha saṁsargaṁ ṛṣiṅādbhūtakarmaṇā//
tena gandhavatyeva nāmāsyāḥ prathitaṁ bhuvi/
tasyāstu yojanād gandhamājighranti narā bhuvi/
tato yojanagandheti tasyā nāma pariśrutaṁ//

Mbh. 1.57.55–56 (Cal. ed.)

After this, pleased with the boons granted, and adorned with feminine graces (Satyavatī) consorted with the *ṛṣi* who performed such strange acts. (By Parāśara's blessings) the name Gandhavatī became famous all through the world. Since people could smell her from a *yojana* distance, her name also attained fame as *Yojanagandhā*

7. My emphasis here and in following extracts.
8. Manu, in particular, held the practice in disfavor (Manu, vol. 2, ix. 64–66).

References

The Mahābhārata. Ed. Vishnu S. Sukthankar. Vol. 1. Poona: Bhandarkar Oriental Research Institute, 1933.

Mahābhārataṁ: Ādiparva. Ed. Shrimad Haridas Siddhantavagish Bhattacharya. Calcutta: Visvabani Prakashani, *Vaṅgāvda* 1338 [1931].

Manusmṛtiḥ: Medhātithiracita Manubhāṣya sametā. Ed. Ganganath Jha. Vols. 1–2. Delhi: Parimal Publications, 1992.

MADHUSRABA DASGUPTA

Usable Women

The Tales of Ambā and Mādhavī

The *Mahābhārata* is well known for the moral dilemmas it explores. The most notable example is, of course, Arjuna's anguish over his duty as a warrior and his affection for those he may have to kill in battle, but there are many others, such as Yudhiṣṭhira's choice between heaven and his faithful dog. The frequency of these tales of moral choice suggests that these narratives function as exemplars of ethical problem solving, providing in each instance a rationale for the choice made and ultimately correlating the separate rationales to an uniform underlying moral code. Not surprisingly, Hindus have been exhorted through the ages to consider the *Mahābhārata*'s stories both as historical precedents and as ethical methodology. Yet the validity of precedents and methodologies depends on certitude. Many if not most of the *Mahābhārata*'s stories, however, are so deeply etched by moral incertitude that their problems are solved only by the forced imposition of arbitrary rules or assumptions and the suppression of countervailing principles. This ambiguity seems particularly located in the legends of women, good and bad.

The portrayal of women in the epics, both the *Mahābhārata* and the *Rāmāyaṇa*, brings to our attention the ambivalent position of women in ancient India. The claim that women of that period enjoyed a relatively free life, as proven by their participation in intellectual discourses, is perhaps true but only marginally so.[1] Women philosophers such as Gārgī or Maitreyī are very few in number. Rather, the literature of the age testifies to the subordination of women's interests to those of their male relatives or to social power structures such as dynasty or government in which they had no decision-making roles, to the point of silencing women's voices or even erasing them from the narrative. This becomes particularly clear when we examine the *dharmaśāstras* or codes of conduct. These codes of conduct, all formulated by men, are strict rules supposedly designed to govern the lives of both men and women. However, in practice, women's lives were bound much more inflexibly by the requirements of subservience to men laid down in the *dharmaśāstras*.

pitā rakṣati kaumāre bhartā rakṣati yauvane/
rakṣanti sthavire putrā na strī svātantryamarhati//

Manusmṛti. 9.2[2]

Father protects [her] in [her] childhood, husband protects [her] in [her] youth and sons protect [her] in [her] old age: a woman never gains independence.

That these were not merely theoretical injunctions but reflections of a social reality is clearly indicated in the epics, which, being inclusive by their very nature, afford us a close look at the actual world. While reading these narratives, we come upon many situations in which the characters are confronted with moral dilemmas. These moral and ethical issues have been discussed and debated since very early times and continue to hold our interest to this day.

Many of these issues are implicit in the legends of women in the epics and reflect, perhaps unintentionally, certain ambiguities in the depiction of women. Often, what seems to be a woman's free choice, one for which she is lauded, such as Gāndhārī's decision to bandage her eyes shut permanently in emulation of her husband's blindness, turns out to be a disempowering submission to another's interests. Then again, sometimes a woman's apparent compromise with male authority, such as Satyavatī's surrender to two successive lovers, puts power into her hands. Nonetheless, the assumptions that underlie the idealization of women in the epics always advance male interests or confirm male superiority. These assumptions are not always overt in the epics, but close studies of the narratives bring them out and alert us to meanings that are contrary to the surface message. As examples, we shall examine here the legends of Ambā and Mādhavī, two of the lesser heroines of the *Mahābhārata*.

The Tale of Ambā

The king of Kāśī had three beautiful daughters, Ambā, Ambikā, and Ambālikā. When the king proclaimed a royal tournament to give the princesses in marriage to whosoever won them in battle, Prince Bhīṣma decided to win the princesses for his younger brother Vicitravīrya. Having defeated all other princes, Bhīṣma set out for Hastināpura with the three princesses. On his way, he was challenged by a young king, Śālva, who claimed that Ambā, the eldest princess, had been betrothed to him. In the ensuing fight, Bhīṣma defeated Śālva, who withdrew in shame and anger. When Bhīṣma reached Hastināpura, the younger princesses were duly married to Vicitravīrya, but Ambā steadfastly refused because she loved Śālva. When she reproached Bhīṣma with trying to force a woman betrothed to one man to marry another, he attempted to undo the wrong by sending her to King Śālva. But the very sight of Ambā reminded Śālva of his disgrace at the hand of Bhīṣma; he refused to accept a maiden won by another prince and turned her away in anger and shame.[3]

Ambā had to return to Bhīṣma, who was greatly troubled, for he knew that he was to blame for her plight. He took her to Vicitravīrya, who had already married her younger sisters, and asked him to accept Ambā as his bride. But Vicitravīrya declined, and Ambā had to swallow her pride and beg Bhīṣma to take her as his bride. Bhīṣma, though sympathetic toward the princess, was bound by his oath of celibacy and could not marry her. She refused to return to her father, who had given her away. Betrayed and humiliated by everybody, Ambā came to hate Bhīṣma, whom she held as the sole cause of her misery. Seeking revenge by bringing about Bhīṣma's death, she tried to incite other princes to kill him, but no one dared to face him. She then appealed to the sage Paraśurāma for help. Paraśurāma agreed and commanded his former disciple Bhīṣma to help Ambā become one of the queens of Hastināpura. Although Bhīṣma was respectful to his preceptor, he refused to relent. This led to a fight between the two, which was eventually stopped by the ancestors of Paraśurāma. Ambā was unable to get any further help from the sage. But with each failure she grew more vengeful and determined.

Ambā then sought help from the gods and engaged herself in penances and severe austerities for twelve long years. She first lived on roots and berries, then lived on water, and finally immersed herself in meditation and ate nothing. Eventually, Śiva appeared before her and promised her that one day she would bring about the death of Bhīṣma—but not in her present life and not as a woman. She would have to be reborn as the daughter of King Drupada of Pāñcāla and obtain manhood to fulfill her mission. She was assured that her desire for revenge on Bhīṣma would be passed on to her new body and that she would remember everything. Ambā was happy at the prospect and, to hurry the process, she set a fire and leaped into the flames on the bank of Yamunā, in front of a group of sages. Ambā left her mortal body, but her desire for revenge continued, as Śiva had promised, into her next birth.

Born as King Drupada's daughter, Ambā was named Śikhaṇḍinī but presented to the world as his son Śikhaṇḍin to protect her from the envy of her mother's cowives. Childless until now, Drupada had been granted a boon by Śiva that a child would be born to him who would be both a female and male. Introduced as a male child, Śikhaṇḍin was trained in arms and weapons under Droṇa and was later married to the daughter of King Hirṇyavarman of Daśārṇa. When Śikhaṇḍin's wife realized that he was a woman, she reported it to her father, who challenged Śikhaṇḍin. Śikhaṇḍin, ashamed, left for the forest and resolved to put an end to her life. But she chanced to meet in the woods a *yakṣa* (a demigod) called Sthunākarṇa, who took pity on her and offered his manhood as long as she needed in exchange for her womanhood. Śikhaṇḍin returned to Pāñcāla and proved his manhood to a group of courtesans sent by Hirṇyavarman. Thus convinced and pleased, Hirṇyavarman gave Śikhaṇḍin gifts, rebuked his daughter, and returned to his own kingdom. Meanwhile, on hearing that Sthunākarṇa had given his manhood away to Śikhaṇḍin, Kubera, the lord of the *yakṣas*, laid a curse on the *yakṣa*, decreeing that he would remain a woman as long as Śikhaṇḍin lived. Because of this curse, Śikhaṇḍin remained a man for the rest of his life, and Śikhaṇḍin-Ambā's dream of vengeance was fulfilled on the battlefield of Kurukṣetra. He took part in the battle against the Kauravas as an ally of the Pāṇḍavas. He was brought and placed before Arjuna's chariot on Kṛṣṇa's advice on the tenth day of the battle, when Arjuna found it impossible to fight Bhīṣma any longer. Kṛṣṇa knew that, as a strict follower of kṣatriyadharma (code of the warrior class), Bhīṣma would never lift his arms against a woman or one who had been born female. Śikhaṇḍin was thus the only hope for the Pāṇḍavas to confront Bhīṣma and to defeat him. When Bhīṣma saw Arjuna was shooting his arrows from his chariot crouched behind Śikhaṇḍin, he put down his arms and stopped fighting. He had earlier learned from Nārada Śikhaṇḍin's history and remembered the vengeance Ambā had sworn against him many years ago. Arjuna continued to strike Bhisma with his arrows until he fell to the ground. Bhīṣma awaited his death patiently, lying on his arrow bed, and died a few days later. Śikhaṇḍin-Ambā's mission of revenge, borne through two lifetimes, was finally fulfilled through Arjuna's hands. Eight days later, Śikhaṇḍin-Ambā was slain, along with the other Pāñcāla warriors, by Aśvathāmā, the son of his preceptor Droṇa, in a treacherous nighttime raid.[4]

A Gendered Destiny

The story of Ambā and her sisters is a double-edged example of women's powerlessness—though hardly intended as such—in its complementary portrayal of the good princesses and their intransigent sister. Ambā's defiance and resistance and her subsequent plight offer exact contrasts to her sisters' compliance and submissiveness. Ambikā and Ambālikā are model women who follow the dictates of custom without question. They obey their father's wishes and later are content to fall in with the wishes of the man who wins them, only to pass them on to his half-brother Vicitravīrya. When their husband, the king, dies soon after their marriage, the young widows obey the family's wish to ensure the continuation of the dynastic line by bearing children by levirate, as allowed under the prevailing social code,[5] the progenitor of their sons to be chosen by the family and not by them. They had control over neither marriage nor motherhood. But total submission had its advantages because they bore sons and secured prestige. By contrast, Ambā's resistance disrupted the social norm and brought her nothing but trouble and unhappiness. The legend consistently notes Ambā's vengefulness but spares no thought for her humiliation at being given away by her father, refused by the man who won her, and rejected by Śālva, whom she loved, and even by Vicitravīrya. She was treated like a piece of merchandise that, according to Kṣatriya practice, could be won or lost or passed along. When Śālva failed to win her in battle, his pride was hurt; when Bhīṣma later sent her to him, his vanity put an end to his love for Ambā and blinded him to her plight after his rejection. Throughout her two lives, she was at the mercy of the men around her. She could not even pursue vengeance as a woman. As a powerless woman, she had to go through penance and meditation to receive a boon, which again was a denial of her capabilities as a woman. Her defiant individuality was never approved by society. Even the reward for her penance had strings attached, and she was promised success only as a man and in another life. The implication here is that as a woman she was a lesser human being who could not be a man's equal in will, strength, and power. She had to sacrifice her life in the hope of attaining her goal by being reborn as a man in her next life. Here, too, she was disappointed, for she was reborn as a woman and had to borrow masculinity from Sthunākarṇa. Even this was not the end to her humiliation. Because Śikhaṇḍin had not been born male, the male identity she had acquired did not count, and Bhīṣma refused to fight with a member of the weaker sex. As a final irony, the ambivalently gendered Śikhaṇḍin did not even kill Bhīṣma but served as Arjuna's puppet; the very name of Śikhaṇḍin has survived not as a model but as a common label for a powerless front man. For all her single-minded efforts, Ambā did not, after all, have the satisfaction of exacting vengeance on her own.

The story has more than one moral to preach. If you are a woman and are submissive, you can become a queen and win the appropriate prizes as determined by the men around you. This point is clearly shown by the plight of Ambā, who lost every material reward of life, whereas her sisters became mothers and queens. To drive home the idea of the inestimable value of masculinity, as well as the rashness of attempting to alter one's destined identity, we are told the *yakṣa* Sthunākarṇa's story. His story thus resonates against the framing legend of Ambā-Śikhaṇḍin's "unnatural" attempt to overturn her gender-mediated destiny.

Whereas passivity, patience, and obedience are ideals exemplified obliquely in Ambā's story, they are directly and overtly extolled in the legend of Mādhavī, the heroine of our next story. She was a princess who, unlike Ambā, sought neither to shape her own life nor to avenge her sufferings but to win merit by unquestioning obedience and eventually dedication to an ascetic life.

The Tale of Mādhavī

The story begins with Gālava, a young disciple of the sage Viśvāmitra, who wished to offer a gift (*gurudakṣiṇā*) to his preceptor at the end of his novitiate. Reluctant at first, Viśvāmitra eventually yielded to Gālava's persistence and asked him to bring eight hundred white horses, each with one black ear. When this task appeared to be beyond Gālava's power, his friend Garuḍa took him to King Yayāti Nahuṣa of the *candravamśa* (the lunar race) in Pratiṣṭhāna for help, in exchange for which Gālava promised Yayāti a portion of his merit as an ascetic. Yāyāti himself had no horses of that particular kind, but he counseled Gālava to get them from those who had. As barter against the horses, Yāyāti gave Gālava his beautiful and virtuous daughter, Mādhavī, who had already received a boon from a *brāhmaṇa* that she would always remain a virgin, even if she gave birth to a child. Gālava took her to Ayodhyā, whose king, Haryaśva of the Ikṣāku race, gave him two hundred horses of the kind needed in exchange for Mādhavī, with whom the king begot a son, Vasumāna. This trade accomplished, Gālava took Mādhavī away from Ayodhyā and her child to repeat the same arrangement with King Divadāsa of Kāśī for another batch of two hundred horses. Again Mādhavī bore a son, Pratardana, and once again she had to leave her son to be traded for another two hundred horses to King Uśīnara of Bhoja, to whom she bore a son, Śibi. Gālava now had six hundred horses of the particular breed demanded by Viśvāmitra but was still short by two hundred more, and time was running out. A final trade was made, and Viśvāmitra forgave the shortfall in exchange for Mādhavī, who bore him a son, Aṣṭaka. As Gālava's mission was now complete and Mādhavī had carried out her duty, she was free to go back to her father. Unfortunately for her, she had fallen in love with Gālava, who did not reciprocate her love. He remained an ascetic and left for his forest abode while Mādhavī was returned to her father, Yayāti. Yayāti now decided to give away his daughter at a *svayambarā* (selection of a husband by the bride herself) ceremony, so that this time she could choose her own husband. But Mādhavī declined and became an ascetic instead. She renounced the material world and chose the life of a *mṛgacāriṇī* (a woman who adopts the deer's mode of life). At this point, she disappears from the *Mahābhārata*. Much later, we come across her illustrious sons, Vasumāna, Pratardana, Śibi, and Aṣṭaka, who volunteered their accumulated merit to their maternal grandfather, Yayāti, so that he could regain his right to enter heaven, but their mother sinks into oblivion.[6]

The treatment of Mādhavī is so repulsive that it is hard to contemplate with detachment. The key elements of the story are equally offensive. Her father orders her into sexual bondage so that he may earn merit. She is dispossessed of every single son she bears. The man she loves and for whose success in keeping his vow and earning merit she alone is responsible turns her down once his ends have been met. When her use as sexual and reproductive coinage has ended, she is returned to her father, who sets about arranging her marriage as if nothing had happened. Finally, the story erases her from the dynastic chronicles that memorialize her four sons as the illustrious progeny of their respective fathers, not hers. What morals does the story draw? An obvious one is the value of keeping a pledge. Another, equally obvious, is the virtue of a daughter's absolute obedience to her father and her commitment to his interests. But the pursuit of these ideals not only takes the woman's compliance for granted but also altogether ignores the possibility that she might have some goal of her own. More disturbingly, the story ignores the claims of fundamental human affections and bonds that are so powerfully evoked elsewhere in the *Mahābhārata*, as, for instance, in Arjuna's horror at having to fight his kinsmen or Yudhiṣṭhira's decision to stay in the underworld to which he thinks his brothers and their wife, Draupadī, have been consigned. Even sexual purity, that sacred cow of a male-oriented ethic, is abandoned. The whole idea of virtue is, in effect, recast here, turned from an immutable absolutism to social contingency. Mādhavī is prostituted by the men who have control over her life and who save their own honor by declaring that, despite the systematic sexual consumption of this woman, she remains a virgin and retains her pristine virtue. This miracle transparently anticipates accusations of using the woman as sexual currency; virtue as understood in their jurisdiction is demonstrated to be not an immutable category but an arbitrary one, its definition depending on the power of the man who defines it.

In this story, a woman is nothing but a commodity created for men's convenience. This construct requires that silence, submission, and obedience be seen as qualities to be valued over all others in a woman—indeed, the qualities that Mādhavī is seen to possess. Yet the uniformity of her submission becomes questionable at the end, when, in her one act of autonomy, she refuses to obey her father's attempt to marry her off and chooses the ascetic life. The narrative thus leaves a breach between Mādhavī's habitual compliance and her new self-assertion. It is in that space that we may situate questions about the apparently seamless moral program and utilize the story as an ethical puzzle rather than as a straightforward model.

The readings of these two stories do not assume that their narrator(s) imagined them as structures of ambiguity. On the contrary, the stories seem to lend support exclusively to one well-defined set of ideals. Nevertheless, I would argue that these ideals do not add up to the harmonious moral economy that seems assumed in the representation of the world in the *Mahābhārata*. Instead, I believe it is possible and necessary to see in these stories countertexts that lead to alternative readings of that world itself. When we stop viewing the lives of these women strictly from the narrator's point of view, the question of morality pales beside that of gain: whom do the events in either story benefit? Not the women, by any means. That Mādhavī is the loser in every sense hardly needs to be argued. Ambā's case is less clear because the narrative focuses on her singleness of purpose and thus counts Bhīṣma's death as a triumph for her. Yet no celebration of her "success" is allowed into the narrative. Rather, as the slightest awareness of the political and military context will show, the real winner is the Pāṇḍava party. Bhīṣma was the one insurmountable obstacle to their victory, as much because of his prowess as because he was indestructible—unless he chose not to fight, which could be achieved only by the encounter with Śikhaṇḍin. In this high-stakes contest, Ambā-Śikhaṇḍin looks like the best thing that could have happened to the Pāṇḍavas. Yet, for a party that took the high moral road to everything, killing the greatest man of the era by trickery would look bad. So the responsibility was transferred to Ambā-Śikhaṇḍin, along with the whiff of shame that has clung to her name through the centuries.

The political reality of the tales of Ambā and Mādhavī is that both are tools of male ambition. The customary subordination of women to men takes on a particularly dark tone in these stories, for unlike the great heroines of the central strand of the story, such as Kuntī or Gāndhārī, who enjoy a mutuality of interest and emotional gain with their husbands or sons, neither Ambā nor Mādhavī is ever allowed to enter into real relationships. The needs of the men around them confine them to solitary lives. In the terms set in the narratives, they are important only because they are useful creatures. Once we uncover the true function of these women, the acts of their handlers—the glorified heroes of the epic—stand revealed as bare self-interest. Given the ways of their world, what tool could bend better to their use than women?

Notes

1. A. S. Altekar (1962) has cited examples of educated women from the ancient world of the Hindus.
2. Chapter 9 of *Manusmṛti* is entirely devoted to women's roles and duties in society.
3. Those who have had the opportunity to watch the movie or read Peter Brook's version of the *Mahābhārata* will remember the incident.
4. *The Mahābhārata*, Sukhthankar, ed., 1933–69; Udyogaparva: 5.170–197; Bhīṣmaparva: 6. 103–114; Sauptikaparva: 10.8.
5. *The Mahābhārata*, van Buitenan, ed., 1973, Intro. p. xiv; Sukhthankar, ed., 1933–69, vol. 1, chapter 104; Simha, ed., 1990, vol. 1, chapter 104. *Manusmṛti*, 9. 69–70; *Yājñavalkyasmṛti*, 1.68–69.
6. *The Mahābhārata*, Udyogaparva, 5.104–121.

References

Altekar, A. S. *Position of Women in Hindu Civilization, from the Prehistoric Past to the Present Day*, 3d ed. Delhi: Motilal Banarsidass, 1962.

The Mahābhārata, vols. i–xviii. Ed. V. S. Sukthankar. Poona: Bhandarkar Oriental Research Institute, 1933–69.

The Mahābhārata, vols. i–vii. Ed. Kailiprasanna Simha. Calcutta: Modern Book Agency, 1990 (originally published in 1860).

The Mahābhārata, vols. i–iii. Trans. J. A. B. van Buitenen. Chicago: University of Chicago Press, 1973.

The Mahābhārata. Trans. from Jean-Claude Carriere's French rendition of the text by Peter Brook. New York: Harper and Row, 1989.

Manusmṛti. Ed. M. M. Ganganatha Jha. Calcutta: Royal Asiatic Society of Bengal, 1939.

O'Flaherty, Wendy. *The Laws of Manu*. London: Penguin Books, 1991.

Sorensen, Soren. *An Index to the Names in the Mahābhārata: With Short Explanations and a Concordance to the Bombay and Calcutta Editions and P. C. Roy's Translation*. Delhi: Motilal Banarsidass, 1978.

Yājñavalkyasmṛti. With commentary *Mitākṣarā* of Vijñāneśvara and *Bālambhaṭṭi* on *Mitākṣarā* by Bālambhaṭṭa. Ed. Narayana Rama Acharya. Delhi: Nag Publishers, 1985.

5

VIDYUT AKLUJKAR

Anasuya

A *Pativratā* with Panache

Like holy rivers, great myths travel through time and region to acquire volume and substance. Some currents undergo total transformation, some disappear in the course of time, and others survive with remarkable consistency, coupled with creativity. Myths about *pativratās*—virtuous women faithful to their husbands—are a unique feature of Indian mythology. The names of five *pativratās* are woven together in a *śloka*[1] to be recited at the beginning of the day in order to remember their stories daily. Some stories are connected with ritual practices or *vratas*[2] to rejuvenate them by constant retellings and ritual rememberance. Even without such mnemonic aids, the portrait of a powerful ancient *pativratā*, Anasūyā, has enjoyed longevity and veneration in the pan-Indian memory. The present paper focuses on her story. There are three interrelated strata noticeable in the myths connected with Anasūyā: epic, *purāṇic*, and folkloric or vernacular. Roughly speaking, these cover a time span of more than two thousand years. I propose to explore the evolution of the Anasūyā myth through all three lores. My plan is to analyze the composite character of Anasūyā as it emerges from the myths in order to understand the dynamics of the myth's resilience. In the process, I shall highlight traditional interpretations of the role of a *pativratā* to delineate the tenacity of the myths about *pativratās* and their attraction for the Indian psyche. The concept of *pātivratya*,—faithfulness to husband—has recently received a lot of flak as a passive, negative one crystallizing women's subjugation through centuries. I do not deny the negative potential of the concept or its age-old manipulation by the interested parties toward mindless indoctrination of the female, but I would like to investigate actual portraits of a *pativratā* in literature to analyze the complexity of the concept and the implicit traditional interpretations of it that often go unnoticed.

The *Vālmīki-Rāmāyaṇa* narrates an account of the meeting between two *pativratās*, one renowned and one as yet to be tested—namely, Anasūyā and Sītā. The epic encounter with Anasūyā occurs in three chapters at the end of the Ayodhyā kāṇḍa,[3] right after Rāma sends Bharata back to the kingdom with his own *pādukā*, or sandals, and decides to leave Citra-kūṭa, which is a constant reminder of the life he has left behind. The first stop on his onward journey is the hermitage of sage Atri and his renowned wife, Anasūyā. Atri is an ancient sage who has visualized many hymns, collected along with others "seen" by his descendants in the fifth *maṇḍala* of the *Ṛgveda*. He is famous for having understood the secret of the solar eclipse for the first time and is held in high regard by the other sages.[4] He is also given a permanent celestial position among the seven most venerable sages, the *saptarṣayaḥ*. Anasūyā is his one and only wife,[5] just as Sītā is of Rāma.

This incident is depicted with the utmost tenderness and sensitivity by Vālmīki,[6] although its significance is not immediately apparent.[7] Against the background of the emotionally wrenching meeting of the two brothers, Rāma and Bharata, Rāma and Sītā's meeting with the sage and his wife is very peaceful. At the outset, nothing much happens: the younger couple arrives and is received fondly by the older couple; after exchanging pleasantries and spending the night in their hermitage, the younger couple departs for further travel.

I believe that in the account of this meeting, extending over three chapters of the Ayodhyā kāṇḍa in the epic, we get the first glimpses of the fame and charm of Anasūyā. Therefore, I invite you to look at it more carefully. The meeting centers on the two women and their conversation. The narrator describes Anasūyā as aged, frail, wrinkled, and adorned with white hair. While walking, she shakes like a plantain in strong wind.[8] This description furnishes for us only a silhouette of the lady. The warm colors in the picture are fondly filled in by her husband. Unlike the typical Indian husband, who is reluctant to praise his wife in front of visitors, Atri dwells on Anasūyā's virtues, praises her creativity, uses hyperbole to describe the immensity of her penance, and instructs Rāma to send Sītā[9] to visit her. Here is what Atri says:[10]

> When life was being constantly parched due to lack of rain for ten years, she produced the roots and the fruits, and reverted the course of the river Jāhnavī. Such is this Anasūyā, equipped with harsh penance and adorned with her self-restraint. She has practiced the tapas, the penance, for tens of thousands of years. Due to Anasūyā's observances, my dear, all obstacles are removed. In order to accomplish the goal of the gods, she had once hurried and created one night out of ten. Such is she. O innocent one, consider her like your own mother. Send Vaidehī to her, to this famous, old woman, who is never angry, and who is always eligible to be respected by all beings.

Rāma is impressed by this honest appraisal of Anasūyā by her venerable husband. He acknowledges this rare opportunity for Sītā to visit someone so celebrated and urges her to appear in front of Anasūyā. Sītā approaches Anasūyā with folded hands, asks about her health, and is received fondly. Anasūyā has heard that Sītā has chosen to follow young Prince Rāma into the forest on his exile for the duration of fourteen years, and she praises Sītā for that. Such self-restraint and resolve in one so young is remarkable, indeed. She discourses to Sītā on the general admonitions as to how a woman should behave. In six simple verses,[11] we get the gist of the prevalent concept of a *pativratā*. Anasūyā says:

> Whether he lives in the city, or he lives in the woods, whether he is evil, or he is inauspicious, the woman who loves her husband attains the best regions. Whether he behaves badly, is devoted to desires or is devoid of wealth, the husband is the

> supreme deity for the women whose nature is civilized. Even as I think critically, I cannot see anyone who is superior to him as a relative, who is the proper person everywhere, like a penance performed which is undiminishing.
>
> Evil women whose hearts are dictated by passion and who behave as superior to their husbands do not understand the merits or demerits in this manner. Maithilī, such women who have been overpowered by wrong actions indeed destroy their own code of conduct, and attain disrepute in addition. But women like you, who are well-qualified, and who can visualize the later regions, good or bad—such women will attain to heaven just as well as the ones who have done meritorious deeds.

Sītā has heard these general principles before from both her mother and her mother-in-law. She finds them easy to follow. She says to the older woman, "I would have followed my husband even if he were to be devoid of character. But he is sensitive, self-controlled, steady in love, dutiful, mindful of his mothers, and fond of his father. He treats all his mothers with the same respect, so why would I not follow him?" Atri's earlier praise of his aged wife is balanced here by Sītā's wholehearted praise of her young husband. Anasūyā is secure in her married life and has many well-known accomplishments, while Sītā, although self-assured, is inexperienced. Sītā then praises Sāvitrī and Anasūyā as two women who have followed such a code of conduct and have secured their place in heaven. Anasūyā is appreciative of the proper conduct of the young princess. She kisses the forehead of Sītā, praises her, and says, "I am so pleased with your speech. What can I do to please you?" Sītā politely replies, "You have already done so."[12] Anasūyā is very pleased with the young heroine's tact, and she bestows upon Sītā divine garments, garlands, and fragrant ointments. Sītā respectfully accepts them and sits patiently near Anasūyā with folded hands.[13] Anasūyā would like to hear more from this delightful youngster so full of life and says, "I have heard that this successful hero won you as a prize at your bridegroom choice. How did it all happen? Tell me the whole story."[14] Sītā complies and relates the entire story, from King Janaka's finding her in his fields, his adoption of her as his own daughter, and his announcement of her bridegroom choice with the condition of stringing the divine bow, to Rāma's bending and breaking the bow and winning her. Anasūyā pays full attention to her brief account and praises Sītā for her clear, colorful, sweet, succinct narration. Now the day is almost over. Anasūyā says, "Sītā, the night adorned with stars has approached and the moon clad with moonlight is seen arising in the sky. You may go now, with my consent, and follow Rāma."[15] Coming from an aged woman, this gentle acknowledgment of the propriety of the young couple's needs is sensitive and pleasing. Although she is old and wrinkled, Anasūyā's senses are not withered. Having satisfied her sense of hearing, Anasūyā wants to satisfy her vision. So just before retiring, she says to Sītā, "You pleased me by telling me your sweet story. Now I would love to see you adorned with the divine ornaments I gave you. Please put them on here in my presence, and let me feast my eyes." Sītā fulfills her wishes. Adorned like the starlit night, Sītā gratefully takes her leave, returns to Rāma, and relates to him her experience. He is happy to see her thus adorned and rejoices in her rare fortune. Then they retire to the hermitage for the night and the next morning take leave of their aged hosts to go to the Daṇḍaka forest.

This incident acquaints us with the old lady in all her splendor. Everyone refers to her as a great *pativratā*. She, too, opens her conversation with Sītā by elaborating on the virtues of a praiseworthy woman. However, it is not just her faithfulness to her husband that constitutes her greatness. It serves as a solid foundation for the other specific and positive qualities for which she is respected. We realize not only how great a *pativratā* she is but also how everyone, including her husband, is in awe of her various hardships and her manifold accomplishments. His words are full of admiration for her. The reciprocity in their relationship shows their life to be full of wedded bliss.[16] We also realize that Anasūyā, secure in her own virtue is full of admiration of other women's virtues and that she encourages younger women in their chosen path. She has a great sense of beauty and propriety. She is poetic in her description of nature and charming in her behavior toward young and old. She has no trace of malice or jealousy (*asūyā*) hence her name Anasūyā—that is, one who has no *asūyā*. Her name is her character. Having no jealousy seems to be a passive characterization of a person. However, Anasūyā has more to her character than just this mild, passive trait. The positive trait for which she is famous in the epic is her extraordinary creativity. Three of her creative deeds that are mentioned by Atri at the outset seem to point to certain myths already well known by the time of the epic. While the earth is barren for the want of water, she is able to produce fruits and roots. She is also able to revert the course of a famous river. Perhaps these two were complementary acts, in that the river water was used in the absence of rain to produce abundant crops. These acts show her capable of transformations and adaptations. Confronting an adverse situation and overriding it by generating transformations and suggesting adaptations is a mark of a creative mind. Such creativity is the hallmark of this ancient *pativratā*; as we shall see later, it is this thread that has survived in all the other myths associated with her by successive generations.

To come back to the epic passage, we notice that she uses her creativity to aid others. Her aquatic maneuvers and her production of food in difficult times must have helped people around her. She has even helped the gods, we hear, which brings us to consider Anasūyā's third act of creativity. We are told that she hurried in order to fulfill the goals of gods and that she "created one night out of ten."[17] The myth associated with "making one night out of ten" must have been well known in the epic times because in the *Rāmāyaṇa* we get only a mention of it in one verse. For us, it is like finding a fossil of a tiny leaf without having a clue as to the size and nature of the entire tree. The exact significance of this line is not apparent in the present context alone. If we have no other textual help, then we may take it metaphorically to mean that she compressed the darkness in the world, physical or moral. Fortunately, however, we do have references elsewhere that explain this cryptic remark. The commentator Govindarāja[18] glosses over it by merely saying, "This story is found in the *purāṇas*."[19]

That leads us to the second stratum in the myths associated with Anasūyā. Search through the older *purāṇas* indeed reveals another colorful myth in which Anasūyā has a significant role to play.[20] In fact, we notice an amalgam of three separate myths to create one composite myth regarding Anasūyā, as found in a shorter version in the *Garuḍa purāṇa*,[21] and in a more detailed version in the

Mārkaṇḍeya purāṇa.[22] Other *purāṇas* give only one or two of the three stories. One of the three tales is a story of another *pativratā*, who is sometimes called by her own name Śāṇḍilī[23] and sometimes referred to as the "wife of a Brahmin called Kauśika."[24] The second story is of an ill-treated sage called Māṇḍavya or Aṇīmāṇḍavya,[25] who somehow[26] ends up being victimized and impaled for someone else's fault. Finally, in two *purāṇas*—namely, *Garuḍa* and *Mārkaṇḍeya*—both these stories are wrapped in the myth of Anasūyā. In fact, the *Garuḍa purāṇa* provides us with the contextual link of this composite story with the *Rāmāyaṇa*, as the myth occurs in the *Garuḍa purāṇa* in the context of Sītā, and is told to exemplify how Sītā was a *pativratā* like Anasūyā. I shall first give here a full translation of the passage in the *Garuḍa purāṇa*, which gives the summary of the composite myth, and then deal with the larger version from the *Mārkaṇḍeya purāṇa*.

> While staying in the house of Rāvaṇa, Sītā did not surrender to Rāvaṇa. With deeds, with mind, and with speech she was always attuned to Rāghava (Rāma). Sītā was indeed a *pativratā*, just as Anasūyā was one. Listen to the greatness of a *pativratā* that I will relate to you.
>
> Long ago, a Brahmin called Kauśika who suffered from leprosy lived in Pratiṣṭhāna. His wife worshiped him like a God, even though he was thus afflicted. Even as she was criticized by her husband, she still considered him her deity. Instructed by her husband, she took him to a prostitute, carrying also a lot of money. On the path was the sage Māṇḍavya, agonized in pain, as he was impaled on a stake, taken for a thief, when he was not a thief. In the dark, the Brahmin Kauśika, who was being carried on the shoulders of his wife, stirred the impaled sage by his foot. Insulted by his foot, and angry, Māṇḍavya cursed him by saying, "He who stirred me by foot will die at the sunrise." When she heard this, the wife of Kauśika said, "The sun shall not rise." Then due to the absence of sunrise, a constant night resulted for many years, and the gods were terrified. They took recourse to the Creator, Brahmā, the Lotus-born, who spoke to them thus, "Only the brilliance of penance can pacify this brilliance. The Sun cannot rise due to the greatness of a *pativratā*. Due to its not rising, the mortals and you both will suffer. Therefore if you desire to have the sun rise, then you must propitiate Anasūyā, the great ascetic, who is the faithful wife of Atri."
>
> When she was thus propitiated by gods, *pativratā* Anasūyā went and facilitated the sunrise, and also revived the woman's husband.[27]

This account in the *Garuḍa purāṇa* sheds some light on the myth about the third deed of Anasūyā, as it relates the important aspects of the composite myth of Anasūyā. We come to know here which work of the gods she accomplished for them. We have to analyze the story in detail to better understand the role of Anasūyā in it. Here is a story of mistaken identity and misuse of power on many levels. The innocent sage Māṇḍavya is mistaken for a thief and wrongly punished. The wife empowered because of her virtue, whose speech can stop the sun from rising, is mistaken to be a submissive wife, and her sick husband mistreats her as a vehicle to go to a prostitute. The creator Brahmā is mistakenly thought to have power over a *pativratā* and is approached in vain by the terrified gods.

The misuse of power is just as varied. The authorities who have impaled the innocent sage without thorough investigation have misused their civil powers. The sage who curses an inadvertent passerby to die but does not try to enlighten the wrongful authorities has misused the power of his penance. The abused *pativratā* who obstructs the course of the sun rather than setting her husband on the right course has also misused the power of her virtue to generate the misery of mankind.

It is also a story in which the abused person, in turn, abuses someone else, compounds misery with revenge and curses with counter curses, and generates a mudslide of wrong deeds, resulting in total darkness, until Anasūyā comes on the scene. The sage who is maligned by the authorities curses an afflicted leper. The afflicted leper abuses his faithful wife. The sage's curse, in effect, will inflict more misery on the leper's wife, who is already oppressed by her lecherous husband. She, in turn, because of her double oppression, obstructs the rise of the sun and oppresses the entire universe. Thus the story highlights the misdirection taken by virtue when oppressed by an unfortunate turn of events.

In this woeful tale of darkness, Anasūyā's presence brings in a ray of hope. She is endowed not only with the power of her virtue but also with her tactful and just handling of a difficult situation. She can create life out of chaos, generate light out of darkness, and lead the virtuous blind with insight. Earlier in the epic account, we read about her changing the course of the river Jāhnavī to save the drought-ridden public. She uses similar skills to deal with the present situation, as she removes the obstruction to sunrise and changes the course of wasteful and stifling events to let life flow in the right direction. Her presence generates manifold accomplishments. She sets free the captive sun, which restores the universe to life, and then appeases the faithful wife by bestowing the gift of life on her husband.

The *Garuḍa purāṇa* does not tell us how she accomplishes all this. For that, we turn now to the larger version of the myth that appears in the *Mārkaṇḍeya purāṇa*. The *Mārkaṇḍeya purāṇa* devotes the entire sixteenth *adhyāya* (chapter) of ninety verses to elaborate on this story. Basically, the outline there is similar to the one just discussed, with details added to explain how the affairs of the universe came to a standstill and, later on, how Anasūyā restored the balance. I offer here a partial translation.

When the gods approach Anasūyā and request her to make the days and nights as before, she replies:

> "O Gods, so as to not diminish the greatness of a faithful wife in any manner, I shall create the day as before only after properly honoring that good wife. I shall act as to reestablish the stability of day and night, and see to it that the good wife and her husband are not led to destruction."[28]

So she goes to the Brahmin's wife and says to her,

> "Blessed woman, I hope you rejoice at the sight of your husband's face. I hope you consider your own husband to be even greater than all gods.
>
> "I have achieved the greatest rewards by merely serving my husband. All my desires are thereby fulfilled and all obstructions removed.
>
> "Good wife, a man has to repay five debts forever. Similarly, he has to acquire wealth in accordance with his own class and rightful duties, and then use the acquired wealth in accordance with law for the benefit of the righteous. A man has to strive forever to become endowed with truth, straightforwardness, penance, generosity, and kindness. A man has to perform the actions prescribed by the scientific texts as duties every day with great faith and effort and by being devoid

of anger and malice. Then, eventually, with great efforts, O good wife, does one attain to the regions such as the *Prājāpatya*, etc., prescribed in accordance with one's own dharma. Of all that a man thus achieves by great efforts and hardship, a woman obtains half simply by serving her husband. There is no other sacrifice prescribed for a woman—neither oblations to the departed nor any other observances. Merely by serving the husband, women pass on to the desired regions. Therefore, O blessed woman, good wife, you should always concentrate on serving your husband, as a husband is the last resort.

"Whatever good deeds the husband performs to honor the gods and the ancestors who arrive to accept them, the half of all those a woman enjoys simply by being single-mindedly devoted to her husband."[29]

The oppressed but stubborn *pativratā*, when thus advised by Anasūyā, assures her that she follows this way of life and asks her what she and her husband can do to serve her. Anasūyā then describes to her the misery of all gods as follows:

"Because of your speech, the division of days and nights got destroyed, and thereby all gods became devoid of (the offerings from) the sacrifices. All these gods along with Indra are very sad and have approached me, begging me to restore the order of day and night intact as before. That is why I have come to you, so please listen to what I have to say.

"Due to the absence of days, there is a total absence of all sacrificial acts, and due to the absence of those, O virtuous woman, the gods are not getting any nourishment. Due to the destruction of the days, all actions are destroyed, and due to that destruction, there is the absence of rain,[30] and thus the entire world faces destruction. So if you wish to save this world from such a calamity, then, good woman, be appeased, let the people have the run of the sun as before."[31]

The Brahmin's wife replies by saying that the sage Māṇḍavya, in a fit of anger, has cursed her lord husband to die as soon as the sun rises. At that, Anasūyā bargains with her and offers her something she cannot refuse:

"If you like, good woman, then just say so, and I will restore your husband's body just as before (affliction) and make him a new man too. Beautiful woman, I am totally devoted to the greatness of the faithful women, and therefore, I am going to honor you."[32]

The text then narrates the final episode, which I offer here in literal translation:

When the woman consented to this, righteous Anasūyā took the blessed waters in her hand and in that night going on for ten nights long she invoked the sun. Then the blessed sun (Bhagavān Vivasvān), who is of the shape of a fully opened red lotus, rose and shone with his full discus on the king of the mountains.

Right on that cue, the woman's husband lost his life and fell to the ground, while she held him as he was falling.

Anasūyā said:

"Good woman, you should not be sad. Now witness my power, which is acquired by serving my husband. Why wait longer?

"As I have never seen in any other man his beauty, virtue, intelligence, or other adornments such as sweetness in speech, etc., as I have in my own husband, with that truth, may this Brahmin become a young man, free of affliction again, and may he obtain a life of a hundred winters in the company of his wife.

"As I have never seen any other god like my husband, with that truth may this Brahmin live again free of disease.

"As all my efforts, with deeds, mind, and speech have been forever devoted toward the worshiping of my husband, so may this Brahmin live.[33]

In this account in the *Mārkaṇḍeya purāṇa*, we get a possible explanation of the earlier opaque phrase from the *Rāmāyaṇa*, "She made one night out of ten." The context of this phrase in the epic is Anasūyā's rush to do the work of gods. The *Mārkaṇḍeya purāṇa* story supplies us with the details of the myth by describing the incident when the sun could not rise because of the curse of the oppressed *pativratā*, and the resulting dark night lasted for the length of ten nights. Anasūyā was successful in ending that catastrophe on account of the powers of her virtue and her creativity in finding solutions that please everyone. We see how the accounts of the two *purāṇas* complement the account of the epic, in depicting a consistent character of Anasūyā. She is a faithful wife and also a fortunate one, as her single-minded devotion is reciprocated fondly by her husband. She is ingenious, knows how to confront a catastrophe, and uses the strength of her character to aid others, restore the order of the universe, or return joy and harmony in the life of a discordant couple. In all these situations, we find her at peace with herself and always ready to honor and help other women who are following the right path, however blindly they may have followed it. Anasūyā's awareness and open advocacy of the need to honor the virtue of a faithful woman sets her apart from the other celebrated *pativratās*, most of whom are solitary figures struggling to overcome adverse situations to preserve their own virtue. Anasūyā alone is a *pativratā* who hastens to acknowledge the worth of other *pativratās* and to aid them in their adversity, so that harmony is reestablished in the universe.

The chapter in the *Mārkaṇḍeya purāṇa* narrating this account is called *Anasūyā-vara-prāptī*, or "the attainment of a boon by Anasūyā." The account ends by telling us how the gods were pleased with Anasūyā for what she did and how they conferred on her a boon of her choice. Anasūyā asked that the three gods—Brahmā, Viṣṇu, and Maheśa—be born as her children. The gods granted her wish, and thus Viṣṇu took birth as Anasūyā's son Dattātreya, Śiva as her son Durvāsā, and Brahmā as her son Soma. This ending transforms Anasūyā, the faithful wife, into Anasūyā, the mother of gods. It also signifies yet another link with the later cluster of myths associated with Anasūyā that focus on the birth of Dattātreya. This transition brings us to consider the last but not the least of Anasūyā's qualifications, as celebrated in the medieval vernacular folklore and religious texts of India. Although there is a progression noted here from the role of Anasūyā as a faithful wife or *pativratā* to her role as the mother of gods, the two are inseparably linked. As we shall see shortly, it is against the background of her virtue as a faithful *pativratā* that her next role as the mother of gods is highlighted in Marathi Sant poetry.

Throughout the *purāṇic* accounts and the vernacular religious texts, especially the bhakti texts in Marathi, we find the birth of Dattātreya associated with Anasūyā. However, the *purāṇic* and the vernacular accounts differ on at least two significant points. One is the identity of Dattātreya, and the other is the actual event of his birth. As we saw above in the account from the *Mārkaṇḍeya purāṇa*, the *purāṇas* mostly describe the three gods as three different children born to Atri and Anasūyā.[34] The regional tradition in Maharashtra recognizes Dattātreya as an incarnation of all three gods combined in one.[35] The iconographic representation of Dattātreya in Maharashtra is in the form of one person, with three faces and six hands. The myths of Dattātreya common in Maharashtra reveal his composite character to be a remarkable mix of the traits of all three gods. Accordingly, the stories as to how Dattātreya was born to Anasūyā also differ from time to time and from region to region. The most popular myth from the bhakti tradition in Maharashtra is a story told by Eknāth of the birth of Dattātreya.[36] It is a myth consistent with the progression of the mythic character of Anasūyā as we have seen it so far. Here I offer a summary:

> Anasūyā, the wife of sage Atri, is renowned for being the most virtuous *pativratā*. The three goddesses, Sāvitrī, Lakṣmī, and Pārvatī are jealous of the praise of Anasūyā's untarnished wifehood. At Nārada's behest, they send their husbands, the three Gods, Brahmā, Viṣṇu, and Śiva to test the virtue of Anasūyā.
>
> The gods arrive as guests at Atri and Anasūyā's hermitage and demand that their hostess should strip first in order to serve them. Anasūyā complies with their demand without hesitation. She puts her palm on each God's head, and turns each one into an infant. She then strips, puts them to her breast, nurses them, lays them down for a nap into a cradle, and sings lullabies to them.
>
> Many days pass in this manner. The gods are missing. Nārada relates what has happened to the three goddesses. They believe even then that they can rescue their husbands from the hands of this sage's wife. They arrive at Anasūyā's door and demand to see their husbands. She brings them out, places them in front of the goddesses, and says, "Pick your own." The goddesses are nonplussed. The three helpless infants look exactly alike. Finally Pārvatī, Lakṣmī, and Sāvitrī fall at Anasūyā's feet and implore her to restore their husbands to their original forms. She complies, and turns them back into their "divine forms." All heavenly creatures shower her with flowers, and the three gods restored to their normal state offer her a boon. She says, "In all these days of your infancy, I have grown fond of you, so stay with me in that form." They grant her that request and remain united with her in the form of her one son, who becomes known as Dattātreya.

There are several retellings of this specific myth about Anasūyā's trial at the hands of the gods and the birth of Dattātreya. An analysis of this myth reveals the reasons for its popularity.[37] Most *purāṇic* accounts of Anasūyā's motherhood are simpler. Usually it is depicted as an outcome of Atri's and her own desire to have progeny. Either it is a reward of Atri's penance,[38] a reward of Anasūyā's penance,[39] or, as we saw in the account from the *Mārkaṇḍeya purāṇa*, it is conferred upon her as a reward by the gods when she helps restore the order of the universe. In the myth at hand, however, her motherhood is a product of her faithfulness to her husband and her well-known creativity in dealing with a difficult situation.[40] The myth as told by Eknāth utilizes both elements together to create a story that highlights Anasūyā's character as understood by the earliest epic and *puraṇic* accounts.

The three gods have come to test whether she really is the great *pativratā* that she is said to be. They try to trap her into a dilemma. With her presence of mind, her resourcefulness, and her faith in her good-wifehood, Anasūyā resolves the dilemma confronting her. She does not reject the wish of her guests, however outlandish or immoral it may seem, nor does she unmindfully follow their wish and get blamed for her irresponsible conduct. Secure in her wifely virtue, she sees the wish of her divine guests for what it is. To her, it is no more than a childish prank, so quite appropriately, she turns them into children or, to be more accurate, into infants, who alone are eligible to be served without clothes on. When gods forget their divinity and behave like little rascals, a mature woman can only treat them like babies and humor them.

This story illustrates the context-sensitive logic Anasūyā employs to ride over her trial. It also crystallizes a mature woman's response to an insulting demand as different than that of a man's. The male sages or gods in Indian myths, when insulted, get enraged and usually burn the offender to ashes. Śiva burned Kāma, Durvāsas burned his own wife to ashes, and sixty thousand sons of Sagara were burned to ashes by the enraged sage Kapila. Sage Atri's wife, Anasūyā, in our story is no less powerful. However, her power is used to create, to generate, rather than to burn to ashes or destroy. Earlier myths tell us how she could produce food in times of drought or revert the course of River Jāhnavī or, again, how she could remove obstructions to sunrise and restore order in the universe. When confronted with divine guests out to test her virtue, she reacts with similar ingenuity and remarkable composure. Instead of taking offense in a violent way and destroying the offenders, she transforms them into helpless infants. In a sense, she destroys the gods' divinity and distinctive characters by her act, but it is not a total destruction, as in the outburst of male wrath; rather, we witness a gentler transformation most suitable to the role of a woman as a nurturing mother. The motif of transformation, which we saw earlier in Anasūyā's changing the course of a river or in making ten nights into one, is used again in the present myth in a novel context.

Anasūyā's name suggests her character, and Eknāth uses this to add spice to the myth. Whereas the three goddesses act out of jealousy and send their divine husbands to violate her virtue, Anasūyā, the one who is not jealous, behaves to suit her name and fame. Therefore, instead of burning or destroying the offenders, she regenerates them. They demand that she strip for them; instead, they are stripped of their conniving stance by Anasūyā's sagacity, and in their rebirth as babies, they are rendered innocent again. They get a new name, Dattātreya, a new lease on life, or divinity, as it were. Ironically, although it is a story about the birth of a god, in effect, it celebrates the triumph of a woman over god. It shows how a mere woman can outwit not one, not two, but three scheming gods.

When we carefully analyze the character of Anasūyā through all these myths, we find her to be a *pativratā* with panache. If we understand a *pativratā* to be a passive, docile woman, then Anasūyā certainly does not fit the bill. Let me summarize her character as it emerges from the three strata examined so far. She is innovative and creative and does not hestitate to adapt to her advantage a situation in which she finds herself. Often, her adaptations and innovations are directed to help those around her. She is never jealous and never angry. This trait of hers, of course, allows her to think calmly and overcome her trials, no matter how difficult.

She is extremely self-reliant; in all her deeds mentioned in her myths, nowhere is she aided by another person, divine or human, not even by her husband. She is, of course, devoted to her husband, but this devotion is, happily, reciprocated by him. She is appreciative of other women, is generous toward them, and freely offers help to uplift them in the times of their trials. However, she is not averse to the other sex either; in fact, she is friendly to all—male, female, human, and divine. She has no envy or malice. She is just and fair, calm and efficient; therefore, she is able to break through impasses by her conciliatory powers of convincing others. She is also very feminine in her sensuality, loves to hear stories of weddings, loves to see beautiful young brides, and loves to have babies, however divinely mischievous they may be.

This brings me to the concluding part of my excursion through time-honored myths related to Anasūyā. I hope that my analysis so far shows the attraction of the myths associated with a *pativratā* like Anasūyā. She is remembered and loved for the remarkable qualities of her multifaceted character, not just for her devotion to her husband. Although the clusters of myths associated with Anasūyā center on totally different stories and different accomplishments across more than two thousand years, they are remarkably consistent in developing those positive traits of her character that make her a symbol of feminine strength. Only when we see these myths in their own comprehensive context can we begin to understand how complex they are and why they attract many generations of thinkers. It is possible to interpret these myths in the manner of the literary tradition of magical realism, as I have done so far, and see their import as suggestive of deeper truths. Interpreted thus, the myths celebrate the triumph of female productivity and context-sensitive creativity. Granted, they also offer standard traditional panegyrics to the virtue of faithfulness in wifehood, but that virtue serves as a means for the woman's ultimate triumph and is not the end in itself.

Notes

1. Ahalyā draupadī sītā tārā mandodarī tathā /
pañcakanyā smarennityaṁ mahāpātakanāśanam //

2. For example, the *vaṭa-sāvitrī-vrata* connected wtih the myth of Sāvitrī.

3. *Vālmīki-Rāmāyaṇa*, Ayodhyā kāṇḍa, ch. 109–111. The numbering refers to the 1962 Baroda critical edition of the *Rāmāyaṇa* by G. H. Bhatt.

4. *Ṛgveda*, 5.40.5–9

5. In the entire *puraṇic* and epic literature, Anasūyā is the only wife of Atri, with the exception of the *Vāyu-purāṇa*, where he is said to have ten good wives, and the one who gave birth to his sons Dattātreya, Durvāsas, and Soma is called Bhadrā.

6. While acknowledging the industry of successive generations of bards in generating a composite authorship of the epic through the time span for its creation i.e., (200 B.C.E. to 200 C.E.), I have chosen to refer to Vālmīki as the core author; that is the traditional practice, and it is simpler.

7. Perhaps this is why some *purānic* summaries of the Rāma story mention this visit en passant, e.g., rāmo vasiṣṭhaṁ mātṝñśca natvātriṁ ca praṇamya sa˙/ anasūyāṁ ca tatpatnīṁ śarabhañgaṁ sutīkṣṇakaṁ// agastya-bhrataraṁ natvā agastyaṁ tatprasādataḥ/ dhanuḥ khaḍgaṁ ca saṁprapya daṇḍakāraṇyam āgataḥ// *Agnipurāṇa*, 7.1–2. Even the *Padmapurāṇa*

version of this visit is pale in comparison with Valmīki's. It succeeds in capturing the mood of their reception because Atri and Anasūya's actions are described by adjectives such as *mudā* and *prītya*, which are repeated several times. *Padmapuraṇa*, Uttara khaṇḍa, 242, 212–220.

8. śithilāṁ valitāṁ vṛddhāṁ jarāpaṇḍuramūrdhajāṁ / satataṁ vepamānāñgīṁ pravāte kadalī yathā // *Vālmīki Rāmāyaṇa*, Ayodhyā kāṇḍa, ch. 109, 18.

9. Also known as Vaidehī and Maithilī.

10. *Vālmīki Rāmāyaṇa*, Ayodhyā kāṇḍa, ch. 109, 9–13.

11. Ibid., 23–28

12. Ibid., ch. 110, 15.

13. Ibid., 21.

14. Ibid., 24.

15. *niśā* (night) is feminine and *candra* (moon) is masculine in Sanskrit. The image of the starlit night and the moon wrapped in moonlight is suggestive of Sītā and Rāma, as can be seen by Anasūyā's next action.

16. In this respect, Anasūyā seems to be unlike those five other *pativratās* (Ahalyā, Draupadī, etc.), who had to undergo adversities and abuse, even at the hands of their own husbands, to prove their faithfulness. Perhaps that is why her name is not included in the list of five memorable *pativratās* (see note 1). Later on in the *Rāmāyaṇa*, too, another list of eleven *pativrātās* (Sundara kāṇḍa, sarga 24, 9–13) does not include Anasūyā. This might seem puzzling as the list of great *pativratās* is given by none other than Sītā. We may wonder why Sītā, who was so honored by Anasūyā, forgets to mention her name along with all the others. The reason there seems to be contextual. Sītā is reminding Rāvaṇa of all those women who have not left their husbands, even when the husband is impoverished or devoid of kingdom. Because Anasūyā did not have to go through such circumstances, perhaps her name is omitted from that list.

17. Anasūyā, Ayodhyā kāṇḍa, ch. 109, 12.

18. His time is c. 1600 C.E., as noted in the critical edition of the *Vālmīki rāmāyaṇa* (*VR*).

19. iyaṁ kathā purāṇeṣu draṣṭavyā. Govindarāja, in *VR*, 1935A.

20. The other commentaries of the *Rāmāyaṇa* such as the Muni-bhava-prakāśika and the Tilaka, which follows the Kataka, refer to this very myth in their summaries when they gloss over the *VR*, Ayodhyā kāṇḍā, ch. 109, 12.

21. *Garuḍa purāṇa* 1.142

22. *Mārkaṇḍeya purāṇa*, 16–17.

23. *Skanda purāṇa*, 5.171.

24. *Garuḍa purāṇa*, 1.142; *Mārkaṇḍeya purāṇa*, 16–17.

25. *Garuḍa purāṇa*, 1.142; *Mahābhārata*, Ādi parvan, 101; *Mārkaṇḍeya purāṇa*, 16; *Padma purāṇa*, 1.53; *Skanda purāṇa*, 5.169–172.

26. There are various versions of how he ends up being wrongly victimized. His main fault seems to lie in not responding to a question about the whereabouts of the real thieves, and his untimely silence leads the authorities to classify him as a thief, abductor, or culprit.

27. *Garuḍa purāṇa*, 1.142, 17–28.

28. *Mārkaṇḍeya purāṇa*, 16, 51–52.

29. *Mārkaṇḍeya purāṇa*, 16, 54–63.

30. The cycle of interdependent actions described here is corroborated in the *Bhagavad* Gīta, 3.14, as Kṛṣṇa declares, "Creatures are sustained by food, rain sustains food, sacrifice sustains rain, and actions sustain sacrifice" (annādbhavanti bhūāni parjanyādannasaṁbhavaḥ/ yajñyādbhavati parjanyo yajñyā karmasamudbhavāḥ//).

31. *Mārkaṇḍeya purāṇa*, 16, 69–73.

32. *Mārkaṇḍeyapurāṇa*, 16, 75–76.

33. *Mārkaṇḍeyapurāṇa*, 16, 77–84.

34. *Agnipurāṇa*, 20.11–12, *Bhāgavata purāṇa*, 4.1.15; *Skanda purāṇa*, 5.103; *Viṣṇupurāṇa* 1.10.8 etc.

35. R. C. Dhere believes that this transformation in the conception of Dattātreya from being an incarnation of only Viṣṇu to being an incarnation of the trinity of Brahmā, Viṣṇu, and Śiva must have taken place between 1200 and 1500 C.E. See Dhere (1964).

36. Dattātreya-janma ākhyāna, by Eknāth in *Sakala santa gāthā.*, vol. 3, p. 631; also in *Bhāvārtha Rāmāyaṇa*, Āraṇyakāṇḍa, ch. 41–59.

37. I have analyzed this myth in the context of the trial stories told about the generosity of guests in a forthcoming article, "Queer Guests and Gracious Hosts."

38. *Bhāgavata purāṇa*, 4.1.15–33.

39. *Skanda purāṇa*, 5.103.1–109.

40. The only *purāṇic* version of the myth of the birth of Dattātreya that resembles Eknāth's version is the one in the *Bhaviṣya purāṇa*, Pratisarga parvan, adhyāya 17, verses 67–82. The context of Anasūyā's trial by the three gods occurs there: Atri is absorbed in meditation when the gods approach, so he does not take note of them; they approach Anasūyā and demand that she fulfill their passion. She does not respond either, so they proceed to force her, at which point she curses them to be born as her babies.

References

Bhāgavata Purāṇam, 9th ed. Bombay: Nirnayasagara Press, 1950.

Datta Saṁpradāyācā Itihāsa. Ed. R. C. Dhere. Pune: Nilakantha Prakashan, 1964.

Garuḍa purāṇam. Ed. Khemraj Shrikrishnadas. Bombay: Venkateshwar Steam Press, 1906. Repr. Dehli: Nag Publishers, 1984.

Padma purāṇam (uttarakhaṇḍa), pt. 5. Gurumandala Granthamala, 18. Calcutta: Mansukhray Mor, 1962.

The Mahābhārata: The Text as Constituted in Its Critical Edition, vol. 1, Ādi, Sabhā, Āraṇyaka and Virāṭa-parvans. Poona: The Bhandarkar Oriental Research Institute, 1971.

Sakala santa gāthā (gāthāpañcaka). A compendium of major Marathi saints' works based on the Sakhare tradition of manuscripts. Ed. R. C. Dhere. Volumes 1–5. Pune: [1908] Varada Books, 1983.

Skanda purāṇam, vol. 5, uttarardham Avanti khanda with Rewakhanda by Maharshi Vedavyas. Gurumandala Granthamala, 20. Calcutta: Mansukhray Mor, 1962.

Śrī Mārkaṇḍeyamahā purāṇam, pt. 1, ch. 1–45. Trans. and ed. Satyavrat Singh. Adhyayan Mālā, 5. Naimisharanya, Sitapur: Institute for Pauranic and Vedic Studies and Research, 1984.

The Vālmīki-Rāmāyaṇa, vols. 1–7. Ed. G. H. Bhatt. Baroda: Oriental Institute, 1960.

The Vālmīki-Rāmāyaṇa, text with four commentaries: Govindarājīya, Rāmānujīya, Taniślokī, Maheśvaratīrthīya, and two glosses: Munibhāva-prakāśikā and satya-tīrthīyā. Bombay: Venkateshwar Steam Press, 1935. Repr. Dehli: Nag Publishers, 1990.

The Rāmāyaṇa of Vālmīki with the Commentary Tilaka by Rāma, vols. 1–2. Ed. Wāsudev Laxman Śāstrī Paṇśīkar. Dehli and Varanasi: Indological Book House, 1983.

6

CHAPLA VERMA

"The Wildering Gloom"

Women's Place in Buddhist History

The position of women in Buddhism, especially during its early days, has always been a source of great debate. The written records of Buddhism, including authoritative Buddhist texts, have in general presented a negative image of women—for instance, in that the *saṅgha* places nuns at a lower level than the monks. However, this kind of portrayal in Buddhist literature is in conflict with the philosophy propounded by the Buddha and appears to be a reflection of contemporary social relationships rather than a philosophical justification of the patriarchal control of women.

This chapter argues that the Buddha's philosophy is universal in nature and makes no distinction between the genders. However, when scholars attempted to draw up rules to regulate society in accordance with the Buddha's philosophy, they incorporated an imbalance in the positions of men and women into the texts, all of which, we may note, were written long after the Buddha's death. Situating women so negatively appears to have proceeded from the personal opinions of the writers, all of them men, reflecting the patriarchal values of the age. We have no evidence to attribute to Buddha the belittling of women and the low status accorded them over the centuries in Buddhist literature. Rather, the negative position of women is a result of the compilation of texts by men who introduced words and stories that do not reflect the emphasis on universal equality inherent in the Buddha's philosophy.

At first glance, Buddhist texts may appear to altogether silence women. However, a careful analysis of Buddhist historical and philosophical discourses gives us information about female voices that have survived over the centuries. These voices are few but significant because most of the literature that has been written and commented on has been the product of male viewpoints in which the man's role was highlighted whereas the woman's role was deliberately ignored and omitted. Similarly, some incidents in the Buddha's personal life that have been adduced to prove his dislike of women need to be reexamined in the sociocultural context in which the Buddha existed. An interpretation based on that context makes it easier to understand what he did and why he did it, without accepting the notion that the Buddha entertained a bias against women or that he considered them to be inferior to men. This attitude toward women does not seem consistent with his teachings, which are universal in nature and display no gender bias.

In this chapter, I examine the negative portrayal of women in the *Jātaka Kathā* and the references to "historical facts" whereby the Buddha's personal life has been protrayed from a patriarchal point of view. These representations, I argue, are alterations of the actual views of the Buddha and the circumstances of his life. These alterations appear to have been made to project the Buddha as an ideal and perfect human being, to confer on his followers a halo of superior status by association, and to secure for them personal benefits from kingdoms that were increasingly influenced by Buddhist teachings and in which Buddhist scholars enjoyed preeminence. By historically examining the prescriptions, overt and implied, regarding women, we can see that the position of women has been negatively set not by the Buddha's own dictates but by the social bias against women hardening through the centuries after the Buddha and that writers of Buddhist scriptures were influenced by the patriarchal values of their societies.

We may note in passing that such alterations are seen not only in Buddhist writings but also in Christianity, where Christ's teachings were subtly altered to reflect the dominant Jewish and Roman patriarchal attitudes. The early Christian doctrines taught that "although the deity is essentially indescribable, the divine can be imaged as a dyad consisting of both the female and male principles."[1] This doctrine not only threatened the supremacy of the "fathers of the church" within the existing social order but also directly challenged the male-dominated family. Professor Bartchy has pointed out that one reason why Jesus and his followers were perceived as dangerously radical was that they called into question the existing family traditions, treating women as individuals in their own right.[2] This radicalism, however, was lost when the history and ideas of Jesus came to be rewritten to fit the pattern that patriarchal society set for the world.

In similar fashion, the history of the Buddhist way of life shows systematic alterations to the sources from which it draws authority. In general, Buddhist teachings are based on the material that Buddhist scriptures and *Sūtras* attribute to the Buddha himself. However, the accuracy of the information they provide, especially their factual contents, is open to question. The transmission of the Buddha's teachings is complicated by the fact that the history of Buddhism is vast, not only because of its antiquity but also because of its spread over so many Asian cultures. Most of its early history is based on oral tradition in legend form, transmitted from one person to another, which is likely to have been colored by the customary distortions of reportage or the attitudes of particular periods. No scholar can help doubting the authenticity of this kind of history. The root problem is that no documentation was done during the Buddha's own lifetime. A few weeks after the Buddha's death (circa 483 B.C.E.) the first Buddhist council was held at Rājagṛha to establish the canon of the Vinaya, the discipline of the order. After about a century, there arose a violent controversy over certain points of the Vinaya, which led to a schism and divided the Buddhists into Sthaviravādins and Mahāsaṅghikas. The second Buddhist Council was held at Vaiśālī to do away with the ten controversial points of the Vinaya. Finally, the third Buddhist Council was summoned by Aśoka the Great at Pāṭalīputra (circa 249 B.C.E.); about one thousand monks participated. According to Sharma, "Its object was to compile a canon of the Doctrine of the Elders (Sthaviravāda) and the present Pali Canon was probably compiled by this Council."[3] Most of the standard Buddhist commentaries have been based on the literature compiled by this third Buddhist Council.

Thus, the texts that are taken today as the earliest sources of Buddhist thought were compiled at least two hundred years after the Buddha's Parinirvāṇa and represent a reinterpretation of the Buddha's teachings in the light of social developments through those two centuries. Because those responsible for this recasting of the original prescriptions for the conduct and organization of Buddhist society were men, the rules that came to dominate Buddhist life were framed from the male perspective. It is not surprising, then, that the place of men has been elevated in Buddhist society while that of women has been debased. These texts are therefore unreliable guides to understanding both how the Buddha himself thought of women and what the place of women really was in early Buddhist society. It is essential that we supplement these texts with whatever meager literature is available about the female voices of that era so that we may work toward an accurate reconstruction of the Buddha's teachings and their implications. We would be providing a balance against the patriarchal trend of the later, exegetical texts instead of uncritically accepting them as the fountainhead of this universal philosophy. In this process, we need to be objective and understand the culture in the specific time frame. Doing so may help to reanalyze the texts from a feminist point of view by considering the voices and images of the nuns in the *saṅgha* and also of the laywomen of that period who committed themselves to Buddhism and played an important role as donors. In uncovering the history of women within Buddhist life, we must recognize the filters through which they have been viewed in the past; as Gross says:

> Since history is always a selection from the past, it can only be more or less accurate and complete. What is selected and what is omitted, the reasons for including or excluding certain data, always coincide with certain uses of the past. Feminist history is concerned both with the uses to which an androcentric past has been put and what would constitute a usable past for women. The uses to which one would want to put the past reflect one's current values.[4]

Incidents in the Buddha's Life

In this context, we need to examine some incidents in the life of the Buddha that have been cited to suggest that Siddhārtha himself maintained that women were not equal to men. The Buddha was born in a period when Hinduism was already a highly advanced religion that promoted an elaborate social order structured hierarchically. His father, Śuddhodhana, was king of a small kingdom, and his mother, Mahāmāyā, is said to have died seven days after his birth. He was brought up in great splendor and luxury by his aunt, who was also his stepmother. Buddhist texts tell us that a priest told King Śuddhodhana that the boy would become either a great king or a homeless wanderer, and, like all ambitious kings, Śuddhodhana wanted his son to become a great king when the boy succeeded him to the throne. Therefore, he filled Siddhārtha's life with great luxury and had three palaces built for his son, one for winter, one for summer, and one for the rainy season. He also got him married at a young age to Yaśodharā, and the couple had a son named Rāhul.

The texts narrate how Siddhārtha made some journeys outside the palaces and how on such occasions he saw an old man, a sick man, and a corpse. These experiences of the human condition made him wonder why pain and misery seemed to be the ultimate facts of human life and set him on his search for overcoming pain and misery. Most texts suggest that Siddhārtha left home in search of his quest when his wife and son were sleeping, and this incident has been widely criticized for Siddhārtha's inconsiderate abandonment of his family, which appears to suggest that he regarded women and family life as obstacles to a spiritual life. Another important incident that has often been censured is related to his aunt Mahāprajāpati, who wanted to join the *saṅgha* but was discouraged by the Buddha because she was a woman. He is also said to have declined women's attempts to leave their domestic responsibilities and to fulfill their own spiritual needs for liberation. These "life" episodes have been used by later Buddhist clergy as precedents set by the Buddha to deny women an equal place with men in Buddhist society and to impose a patriarchal order.

The Buddha's abandonment of his wife and infant son has been criticized as a sign of his disregard for women, which has led to the total erasure of his wife from Buddhist hagiography. Hira Bansode, a Maharashtrian Buddhist woman, laments:

> The faithful wives of Hindu tradition, Sītā and Sāvitrī, are honoured by all as ideal women. The wives of the great gods, Pārvatī, Durgā, Kālī, Lakṣmī, Sarasvatī, and, in Maharashtra, Rukminī appears in temples. Only the Buddha's wife is ignored, her sacrifice unacknowledged, her influence not even considered.[5]

In this passage Yaśodharā is being compared with Hindu goddesses, such as Sītā and Lakṣmī, who are worshiped with their husbands. But the comparison is incorrect for there are major differences between Yaśodharā and the goddesses. First, Sītā, Lakṣmī, and the other goddesses are mythological figures; they are divine but imaginary beings. In contrast, Yaśodharā and Siddhārtha are part of verifiable history and real people, human figures just like us. Because mythology is constructed according to what people want to believe, the gods and goddesses whose legends we hear are idealized figures. But as human beings Siddhārtha and Yaśodharā were not perfect but rather were seeking perfection. In their lives, we find incidents that are common to most human beings, and therefore their actions need to be interpreted differently from the incidents in the mythologies.

Second, the mythological figures in Hinduism were placed in the *gṛhastha āśrama* (the state of being a householder, that is, a family person), whereas the Buddha renounced that position and chose *sanyāsa* (renunciate), a common practice at that time for those embarking on the quest for the deeper meanings of life. All those who tried to seek spiritual insight had to leave worldly life and live as hermits, to "kick away gold, women and fame, the three universal fetters for man,"[6] exactly as Siddhārtha did, following the traditions of Hinduism in renouncing the world to seek knowledge. This stage in his life preceded his enlightenment, and his actions at this stage cannot be extrapolated to force a meaning upon his views and actions at the stage of enlightenment.

In the Buddha's defense, some historians have cited the ethos into which he was born:

> Given the social and cultural context of sixth century B.C. India and the importance of celibacy to the early Buddhist monastic organization, it is not surprising that women quo women would have been devalued in some of the early literature. In India as in China, women were subservient to three masters: to their parents when young, to their husbands when mature and to their children when old.[7]

The Buddha may appear to subscribe to these views, despite his greater liberality in gender attitudes than other men of his time, but it is necessary to place his actions within his milieu rather than to judge them from a twentieth century perspective.

The Buddha is also said to have resisted women's attempts to renounce their domestic life and to join the Buddhist *saṅgha*. Mahāprajāpati, who was the Buddha's aunt and also his stepmother, wanted to join the *saṅgha* and become a nun, but the Buddha is said to have been lukewarm to the idea. Initially, Mahāprajāpati did approach the Buddha and even suggested that it would be good for women if they could join the *saṅgha*. The Buddha apparently refused permission. Mahāprajāpati later approached Ānanda, who then became her advocate and tried to advance the women's cause by using different arguments. Finally, it is said that the Buddha gave his consent, to which he attached the condition that nuns would have to follow the so-called eight *gurudharma* rules. Mahāprajāpati Gautamī accepted this condition willingly. When the Buddha received Mahāprajāpati's answer and realized that he was now bound by his own word to allow women into the *saṅgha*, he is said to have declared in despair that as a result of this move the dharma would survive for only 500 years rather than the expected 1000 years. To indicate the emasculation of the dharma, he used the analogy of robbers who attack a household that has few men and many women. This story, too, is cited as proof of the lower status prescribed for women in Buddhist society and mentioned to reproach its philosophy.

Indeed, the eight *gurudharmas* given to Mahāprajāpati Gautamī are so degrading to women that they do not even pretend to fit women's duties within the overall context of Buddhist philosophy. It is difficult to imagine that the Buddha himself would have laid down these rules as he was preaching the equality of all living beings and denouncing Hinduism's rigid caste system. A review of these rules makes the argument obvious:

1. A *bhikṣuṇī*, even though she has been ordained for a hundred years, on meeting a *bhikṣu* who has newly entered the Order, must rise, venerate, and pay obeisance to him.
2. A *bhikṣuṇī* shall study for two full years prior to the Upasampadā Ordination and shall inform the Order of *bhikṣuṇī* and make arrangements for the ordination.

3. A *bhikṣuṇī* cannot admonish a *bhikṣu* for either real or unreal offenses, but a *bhikṣu* can admonish a *bhikṣuṇī* for real offenses.
4. A *bhikṣuṇī* should not receive donations before *bhikṣus*. A *bhikṣuṇī* must not receive food, lodging, bedding, and cushions before a *bhikṣu* does.
5. If a *bhikṣuṇī* violates these rules, she ought to perform penance for half a month in both the Orders, the Order of *bhikṣus* and the Order of *bhikṣuṇīs*.
6. On observance day, either all the *bhikṣuṇīs* in the Order or else a representative should go to the monastery of *bhikṣus*. At first, they should worship the stupa, and go to the cell of a *bhikṣu* they are acquainted with to declare their purity. Whenever a *bhikṣu* instructs *bhikṣuṇīs*, he must think of them as daughters; and *bhikṣuṇīs* for their part, must think of their preceptor as the Buddha.
7. A *bhikṣuṇī* should not pass the rainy season by living alone without relying upon a *bhikṣu*.
8. When the rainy season is over, the *bhikṣuṇīs* should observe the (ceremony) of repentance of their offenses in the two orders.[8]

These *gurudharmas* clearly place the *bhikṣuṇīs* in an inferior position and appear to be an attempt at establishing a hierarchy in which men can be guaranteed domination over women. The rules are blatantly biased, for they prescribe that a *bhikṣuṇī* cannot protest, even if a *bhikṣu* has committed an offense. The fourth *gurudharma* prescribes that even when society is ready to pay *bhikṣuṇīs* equal respect, the *bhikṣuṇīs* themselves should take a back seat and give precedence to the *bhikṣus*. The difference in status is taken as a reflection of a fundamental difference in nature, for every *bhikṣu* who instructs is considered equal to the Buddha, but not so a *bhikṣuṇī*. Furthermore, these *gurudharmas* demand that *bhikṣuṇīs* must depend on *bhikṣus* for their survival, whether they need their help or not. It is reported that Mahāprajāpati gladly accepted the eight rules and "took them as a garland of lotus flowers."[9] If women, even one enjoying the status of Mahāprajāpati, were willing to join the *saṅgha* despite such unfair requirements, their social position must, indeed, have been deplorable. No wonder that, reflecting on so unjust a society and a monastic order that upheld its injustices, the Buddha should have declared that the *saṅgha* would not last for more than 500 years.

Authenticity of *Gurudharmas*

Though there was a deliberate downgrading of women's position in Buddhist texts, the same texts tell us that many women became widely renowned as teachers and that a number of *bhikṣuṇīs* attained enlightenment. If we read these accounts carefully, we realize that the capability of women to achieve enlightenment was not in doubt but that there was nonetheless concern over their position. The anxiety was not directly related to gender relationships but arose from the perception of the hidden threat that women were thought to pose to the institution of the *saṅgha*. Given that the patriarchy was already entrenched in society and that the Buddha himself had not created any reformist institution despite his obvious hold on the people, it would be most inexpedient for his followers to take the revolutionary step of allowing women anything more than a subordinate role. They must have been apprehensive about their own position because they had to carry the mantle of the Buddha without his presence to command the allegiance of the people. Whether the acceptance of women into the *saṅgha* would be appreciated by society, upon which the *saṅgha* largely depended for donations and support, may have been a major concern of the Buddhist priests who were preaching the teachings of the Buddha. When we look at the eight *gurudharmas* for women, it seems difficult to believe that the Buddha whose teachings were based on asserting the equality of all human beings would create rules that systematically debased women. These rules and the legends of Buddha connected with them appear to be later additions invented to perpetuate the prevalent patriarchal constitution of society and to counter any suggestion of immorality in the *saṅgha* brought about by the first-ever admission of women into any powerful organization in India.

Because the texts available to us today and historically used as authoritative sources of conduct for Buddhists were not written during the Buddha's lifetime, there are no grounds for thinking that the rules of the *saṅgha* arose out of the Buddha's own injunctions. On the contrary, they appear contradictory to the main tenets of the Buddha's teaching. The Buddha taught that everything is in a state of flux, that nothing is permanent, and that Nirvāṇa is the ultimate truth, which itself is *Śunya* (void) in character. In fact, his eightfold path, which is accepted as the central doctrine of Buddhism by most scholars, tends to eschew extreme positions. The Buddha himself renounced strict observance of penance and propounded the middle way as the guiding principle of life. It appears incongruous that at the same time he would insist on the extreme measures for women that were specified by the *gurudharmas* of his own institution.

We must also note that he left many metaphysical questions unanswered because his main aim was to relieve people from suffering. He repeatedly told his disciples:

> "Two things, my disciples, do I teach—misery and the cessation of misery. Human existence is full of misery and pain. Our immediate duty, therefore, is to get rid of this misery and pain. If instead we bother about barren metaphysical speculations, we behave like that foolish man whose heart is pierced with a poisonous arrow and who, instead of taking it out, whiles away his time on idle speculation about the origin, the size, the metal, the maker and the shooter of the arrow."[10]

It seems unlikely that the Buddha would have said much about the position of women because his major concern was to relieve human beings of misery. The rules governing the lives of nuns, which unquestionably degrade them, make them suffer for being women, and above all confirm their inferiority to monks simply on the basis of gender, appear to be founded on later interpretations that have been presented as if they were uttered by the Buddha. This presumption would be easy to promote, for in the social world of the Buddha patriarchy had taken deep roots, a fact supported by many texts of that period. For instance, *Manusmṛti*, the *Mahābhārata*, and the *Rāmāyaṇa*, texts that had been compiled much before the Buddha's time, speak and approve of the inferior status of women in Indian society. Therefore, it is not surprising to find textual evidence of negative attitudes toward women in Buddhist literature. As an example, we may consider the fact that Ānanda was attacked for having brought women into the Buddhist *saṅgha*. On the occasion of the first gathering of Buddhist scholars after the Buddha's demise, at the famous council held at Rājagṛha, Ānanda was accused by the venerable Mahākāśyapa of having induced the Buddha to admit women into the order. Ānanda is said to have defended himself by referring to Mahāprajāpati Gautamī's merits as the foster mother of the Buddha.[11] At the least, this prosecution of Ānanda shows a hardening of attitudes among the followers of the Buddha after he was no longer there to guide or control them.

Yet the subordination of women in the Buddhist community might not have been universal. While women were, indeed, reduced to lowliness by both precept and practice, history also offers examples to the contrary. Bartholomeusz tells us, "According to the Mahāvaṁśa, the bhikkhuni saṅgha was introduced to Lanka by Sanghamitra, the daughter of the Indian king Ashok."[12]. Aśoka was a powerful monarch who was responsible for the establishment of Buddhism as the state religion in his empire and for its propagation in other parts of Asia. That he himself sent his daughter to start a *saṅgha* for nuns is a definite indication of the high position that a woman might attain in the Buddhist hierarchy and suggests that, at least in Aśoka's time, nothing in Buddhist doctrine prevented women's position from being considered equal to that of men. On the contrary, in the Buddha's lifetime, there would have been reasons militating against the subordination of women in Buddhist spiritual life, as Bartholomeusz points out:

> Due to the Eight Chief Rules that Mahāprajāpati Gotamī accepted when she established the order of nuns, the bhikṣuṇī saṅgha fell under the control of the monks, a position many of the dasa sil matavo do not desire for several reasons. They would resent such a subjugation, in view of their feeling that they are at least equal to the monks in regard to the purity of their practice. Others claim that the Eight Chief Rules would be undesirable for other reasons. Scholarly das sil matavo suggest that the Buddha never proclaimed them—they are the addition of the editor of Cullavagga.[13]

Unfortunately, even today the Buddhist order has not been able to reconcile its philosophical principles with its practice of the social customs shaped by the other religions of the Indian subcontinent. For this reason, many women in Sri Lanka today, who have embraced Buddhism and have completely left the lay life, have refused to follow the *bhikṣuni saṅgha*. They feel by doing so they might lose the independence they gained by renouncing the lay life. They fear that they would fall from one oppressive situation into another by becoming ordained members of the *saṅgha*.

The Buddha's Reluctance to Allow Women into the Buddhist Hierarchy

Many scholars have accepted the hearsay that the Buddha was reluctant to take women into his *saṅgha* and that he considered women's position to be inferior to that of men. For these scholars, the Buddha's act represented the patriarchal viewpoint that admitting women into the sacred and venerated society of the *saṅgha* would corrupt its sanctity and destroy the Buddhist order. But this conclusion has been drawn hastily without considering the social context of Buddhism in India, which would have placed the Buddha in the kind of dilemma that Bartholomeusz sees: "Though the dialogue with Buddha suggests that he may be reluctant to establish the bhikṣuni saṅgha, he none the less regarded it as an essential support of the religion."[14]

The Buddha's concern was not unique. In other Indian sources, similar ideas appear. In the opening chapter of the *Bhagavad Gīta*, Arjuna expresses his concern to Kṛṣṇa: "We should not slay our own kinfolk . . . [for] upon the destruction of the family, the immemorial holy laws of the family perish, . . . the women are corrupted . . . and [thereby] eternal family laws [are also corrupted] and then for men, dwelling in hell certainly ensues."[15] The reluctance by the Buddha to take women into the *saṅgha*, if true, probably reflected similar concerns that their entry might endanger the family unit or that life in and for the monastic order would simply become more complicated if women joined it. Many Teravāda scriptures have portrayed women as a monk's most dreaded threat. Moreover, monks may have felt that rules would have to be created to regulate the interactions of male and female renunciates and that undoubtedly these relationships would have to be stricter and more complicated than those for only monks or for only laywomen. The likely spread of gossip among lay members and non-Buddhists concerning how these male and female renunciates actually interacted might have been perceived as a major threat to the Buddhist order. After all, it was known at that time that Rāma, too, had been forced to renounce his wife Sītā on the gossip of a mere washerman. Rumors were rife: "There are also stories about men trying to seduce or raping nuns."[16] The fear that women renunciates would be vulnerable to male violence may also have been realistic; the humiliations suffered by Draupadī as described in the *Mahābhārata* were well known in that era. This fear of male violence against nuns may have been a more compelling reason to design the regulations of the *gurudharma* than a need to assert the superiority of men over women. That these regulations also prevented women from solitary travel and practices reflects the same situation as today, when we often try to prevent male violence against women by warning women not to be in the wrong place at the wrong time.[17] These measures, disempowering for women as they were, should be seen against the background that male violence against women was not unknown in the Buddhist community, which suggests that these regulations were a practical way of dealing with the social concerns of contemporary society.

In addition, as I mentioned earlier, Buddhist *saṅghas* depended on public donations for their survival. They were not in a position to take any kind of action that would be disapproved by society at large. Buddhism was not a radical revolutionary movement in Indian society that challenged established institutions. The Buddha never took the role of a reformer; his emphasis was rather on the middle path. He therefore sought to curb social malpractices by self-reflection, whereby a person would strive to see if an action was the right one in a global context. Clearly, decisions regarding the admission of women to the Buddhist *saṅgha* were thought to belong to the realm of social customs that needed to be taken into consideration. The apprehension that the *saṅgha* might get a bad name if a monk and a nun got involved with each other might have been the main concern that prompted later Buddhist leaders to impose such stringent rules. In a patriarchal society, it was natural that these rules would work more against women than against men, who dominated the power structure. Moreover, monks were greater in number and received the benefit of rules favoring them. Another reason for the stricter rules for women was that they entered the *saṅgha* much later in life, so that the austere discipline required for the renunciates would not be diluted by the shorter time women had to adjust to the life of renunciation. Many scholars of the time might have genuinely believed that "the real struggle is between monastics and lay people."[18] These social constraints could not be ignored. If the Buddha did, in fact, discourage women from joining the *saṅgha,* then the practical needs of the *saṅgha* would have been more important to his stand than any belief in the inferiority of women to men.

The Negative Image of Women

The *Jātaka* stories, written long after the Buddha's time, are other examples of Buddhist texts that portray women negatively. *Anadabhuta-Jātaka,* a typical story of the innate wickedness of women, tells of a girl who from infancy grew up without seeing any man till her marriage. The story then revolves around her intrigue and liaison with a lover and the deceits she practices upon her husband. Toward the end, the poet condemns her actions in the following words:

> A sex composed of wickedness and guile,
> Unknowable, uncertain as the path
> Of fishes in the water,—womankind
> Hold truth for falsehood, falsehood for the truth!
> As greedily as cows seek pastures new,
> Women, unsated, yearn for mate on mate.
> As sand unstable, cruel as the snake,
> Women know all things; naught from them is hid![19]

The sole purpose of such tales, it seems, was to tarnish the virtuous image of women so assiduously cultivated by stories woven around Sītā and Sāvitrī. To imagine a situation where a girl grew up without ever seeing a man is very difficult. The other aspect of the story—namely, that a nobleman secluded and confined the girl to ensure her virtue and then married her despite their great age difference—offers clear proof of the misogyny inherent in the story. Apparently, the nobleman's power over the girl, his lust, and his control over her whole life do not seem odd or unusual to the author. Both the plot of the story and the fact that it was invented exemplify the male need to exert total control over women—and the extremes to which women may be driven to recapture a sense of selfhood.

Asatamanta-Jātaka is a similar story about the wickedness of women. It tells about the endeavor of a woman to kill her virtuous son to facilitate an intrigue with a youth. The narration describes her lust so luridly that the purpose seems to be something other than merely the narrative:

In the lust unbridled, like devouring fire,
Are women,—frantic in their rage.
The sex renouncing, fain would I retire
To find peace in a hermitage.[20]

Such *Jātaka* tales have effectively damaged the image and position of women in Buddhism. However, there is no evidence that this denigration of women was propounded or countenanced by the Buddha himself, and there is substantial contextual evidence that it was read into the Buddha's teachings at a later time by Buddhist men who took women to be slaves to men. They were the ones who constructed a body of literature that gives the impression that the Buddha himself believed in these notions. Quite to the contrary, a careful examination of other Buddhist sources suggests that such statements do not constitute the sole voice of Buddhism.

A New Interpretation of the Buddha's Departure and Teachings

It is remarkable that, at a later period, those who sought relief from persecution and the promise of a better life outside the oppressive regulations of Hindu society saw even the "facts" of the Buddha's life in a radically different way. An example is B. R. Ambedkar's *The Buddha and His Dhamma*, written to educate his followers, whom he wanted to convert from Hinduism to Buddhism. Ambedkar worked very hard for the revival of Buddhism in India, especially in Maharashtra. As the undisputed leader of Dalits (the oppressed castes and casteless people) in India, he felt that his community could rise from their submissive position and improve their social status if they left the Hindu order. To achieve this, he looked for a religion that was close to the Hindu religion but with a philosophy and social order that sought to promote equality, and undoubtedly Buddhism was an attractive alternative. He therefore encouraged thousands of Dalits to embrace Buddhism and thereby attempt to escape their misery. For his efforts, he became known as Baba Saheb and won the hearts of Dalits and of these neo-Buddhists in particular. A Marathi village folk song referring to Ambedkar as Bhim, the Herculean hero of the *Mahābhārata*, correlates his strength with the potency of Buddhism:

I am daughter of Bhim
and the granddaughter of Gautama.[21]

These Buddhists are the followers of Bhim—that is to say, Dr. Bhimrao Ramji Ambedkar, whose conversion to Buddhism in 1956 capped a long battle for civil rights and human dignity for India's untouchables.[22] Whatever he said had great influence on the Buddhists in Maharashtra. Whatever he has written is and will be believed by millions of his followers. He has given a version of the story about how and why Siddhārtha left home that is completely different from the usual version that tells of his leaving surreptitiously at night. According to Ambedkar's version, Siddhārtha performed a great sacrifice in leaving his home and that Yaśodharā willingly gave him permission to leave. She also showed a keen desire to go with him but could not because of their young son, Rāhul. Ambedkar describes this "history" in the following manner:

> The Śākyas had a saṅgha into which every youth above twenty had to be initiated. Siddhārtha too was initiated in this saṅgha when he turned twenty and had to follow the following rules and duties as a member of the saṅgha:
>
> 1. You must safeguard the interests of the Śākyas by your body, mind and money.
> 2. You must not absent yourself from the meetings of the saṅgha.
> 3. You must without fear or favor expose any fault you may notice in the conduct of a Śākya.
> 4. You must not be angry if you are accused of an offence but confess if you are guilty or state if you are innocent.[23]

For eight years, Siddhārtha remained a devoted member of the *saṅgha* who followed the rules devotedly and unquestioningly. Now, on the border of the Śākya kingdom was the state of Koliya, and the two kingdoms were separated by the river Rohiṇī. The water of this river was used by both and so became a cause of dispute. When Siddhārtha was twenty-eight years old, there was a major clash between the two kingdoms over the water, and both sides suffered injuries. The Senāpati (the chief of the army) of the Śākya *saṅgha* proposed war against Koliya, but Siddārtha opposed this move. Following the democratic convention, their resolution was put to a vote, but the amendment moved by Siddhārtha lost by an overwhelming majority. Next day, the Senāpati proclaimed an order that every Śākya between twenty and fifty would have to participate in the war. At this point, Siddhārtha refused to obey because he did not believe in war in the first place. As a consequence, he had to consider three alternatives as his punishment for disobeying the *saṅgha*.

1. To join the forces and participate in the war
2. To consent to being hanged or exiled
3. To allow the members of his family to be condemned to a social boycott and confiscation of property.[24]

Siddhārtha chose the second alternative and offered to become a Parivrājaka, leave his country, and go into exile. He faced opposition from his parents, who wanted him to postpone his *parivrajā*, but Siddhārtha declined to oppose the democratic ruling or the laws of his land.

Later, Siddhārtha went to meet Yaśodharā and asked for her opinion on this matter. He expected her to vehemently oppose his plan, too, and perhaps collapse with grief. However, nothing of the kind happened, and, with full control over her emotions, she replied:

> What else could I have done if I were in your position? I certainly would not have been a party to a war on the Koliyas. Your decision is the right decision. You have my consent and my support. I too would have taken Parivrajā with you. If I do not, it is because I have Rāhul to look after. I wish it had not come to this. But we must be bold and brave and face the situation. Do not be anxious about your parents and your son. I will look after them till there is life in me. All I wish is that now that you are becoming a Parivrājaka leaving behind all who are near and dear to you, you will find a new way of life which would result in the happiness of mankind.[25]

This is a radical account of Siddhārtha's departure from his home; if it is believed, then all criticism of the Buddha over his desertion of his wife must cease. Perhaps Ambedkar's account is an attempt to make Siddhārtha an ideal man who would not do anything wrong. This account is certainly not consistent with other accounts about the Buddha's departure from his home, which are largely accepted by most scholars.

Yet, Ambedkar's "history" is important in that it shows that facts do get twisted or are interpreted according to what people want to believe rather what actually happened—exactly what may have been done in the case of the eight rules for *bhikṣunis* or the popularization of the *Jātaka* stories. Even if the Buddha was initially reluctant to allow women into his sect, his reluctance had nothing to do with any concept of their inferiority to men but rather with practical social needs. Though patriarchal, the social world of the Buddha was less hostile to women than later times proved to be, as historians of this period have shown.[26] Only later were the Buddha's purely pragmatic considerations converted into moral imperatives, at once accelerating and being accelerated by the downgrading of women throughout later ages.

Other instances of radical interpretations of the Buddha's teachings undertaken to serve the times are not hard to find. Paul Gordon Schalow in "Kukai and the Tradition of Male Love in Japanese Buddhism" talks about homosexuality in Japanese Buddhism. In his analysis, he says:

> For our purposes, the most interesting point made in the preface is the connection between the supposed origins of male homosexuality in Japan and the Buddha's injunction forbidding priests to have sexual relations with women. It gives evidence of a generous view of human sexual need in the Japanese religious tradition, that "need"—in the unnatural situation where relations with the opposite sex are forbidden—supersedes the "natural" legitimacy of male and female relations."[27]

Evidence of this kind suggests that the Buddha's teachings have been changed and interpreted to fit the needs of particular social situations.

The Positive Image of Women in Buddhism

To offset the negative image of women we have found so far in Buddhist literature, we may look at Buddhist texts that accept and even appreciate the presence of women. Considering the fact that only a very small portion of the vast body of Buddhist literature is available today, such references become even more important for the reconstruction of the position of women in Buddhism. When Buddhism reached China, the Bodhisattva, originally a male figure, came to be described differently as the female Kuan-yin. Even though in the earlier Buddhist texts the Buddha was always male, toward the late fourth century the female Bodhisattva forms had become acceptable in China. According to these scriptures (Lotus Sūtra), Kuan-yin appeared in thirty-three forms, and seven of them were feminine: a nun, a Buddhist laywoman, an elder's wife, a householder's wife, an officer's wife, a Brahmin woman, and a young girl.[28] Clearly, women had a positive image in Chinese Buddhism. Though their work and influence were not highlighted in the way the work of men was, it was evidently acceptable to the Buddhist scholars of that period and place that females could be the great Buddha. As Rita Gross comments, "One of the more popular and long-standing Buddhist attitudes regarding gender is the evalution that female incarnation is an unfortunate existence and a result of inferior karma . . . . Women often concurred in this judgment that female rebirth is difficult and unfortunate."[29] Most of the time the celestial Bodhisattva was depicted as male, and even the stories that centre on a female protagonist tell us that she changed her sex just before enlightenment and acquired the male organ. This plot component has been interpreted as discriminatory against women because it implies that no enlightenment is possible for the female body. This interpretation is debatable, however; it seems that the female body is actually not constituted of gross matter but possesses elements of dharma that allow the female to change form of her own free will. She exists in a world of magic in which her sex transformation happens easily and frequently. "Therefore, for this women to change her sex on the spot drives home even more forcefully the point that this woman is indeed already an advanced Bodhisattva."[30]

This concept of a female who changes her sex to become a male is also in accordance with Buddhist philosophy: everything is in a constant state of flux; there is nothing permanent; everything is changing. Thus, the female—or, for that matter, the male—has no inherent reality in itself. It has only relative existence and is subject to change. Male and female bodies are merely appearances, and nothing is fixed or definite because everything in this world is subject to change. Besides, with no set goal driving the change, these women changed their sex at will and appeared to change their sex simply because they were capable of doing it. The main tenet of Buddhist philosophy maintains there should be no goal, even for the realization of Buddhahood, nor should a person strive for it. If they desire it, they will not be able to realize it; rather, it will happen on its own. In the stories of sex change, the women reached the level where they achieved powers by which they could change their sex, but not because they had to. If they started with a desired goal, they would never have achieved it. In thus acknowledging that women had achieved very high levels of understanding of dharma and were in no way inferior to men, these stories testify to women's elevated positions in at least some traditions of Buddhism.

There are positive references to women scattered through Buddhist literature, though they are not systematically highlighted in the texts. A few such have survived remarkably intact through the long period of male domination. The Buddha himself had a very positive opinion about women, and there is a reference to the Buddha telling a king who was disappointed by the birth of a daughter that a girl might prove a better offspring than a boy.

In *Therigāthā*, verses indicate that women enjoyed a high status and were respected. For example, there is the story of the nun Khema, who, after many births, was born in a king's family and later on also became the consort of King Bimbisāra. On a visit to the *vihāra*, she was instructed by the master himself. According to the legend, when he had finished, she attained *arhantship* (perfection), together with a thorough grasp of the norm in form and meaning. Thereafter, she became known for her great insight and was ranked high by the Exalted One himself and given a seat in the conclave of Aryans at the Jeta Grove Vihāra.[31] Clearly, women were not prohibited from joining the Buddhist order as equals to men and were considered no less than men in their achievements and understanding of the dharma. That their legends have not been discussed or highlighted in the texts shows more of the influence of patriarchy on the scholars who wrote them than of the Buddha's actual teaching.

We may also note the story of the nun Sujātā, who, having accumulated merit over many births, was born into an affluent family, married, and led a happy domestic life. One day while coming back from a festival, she stopped at Anjana Grove and listened to the Enlightened One's discourse. The Master, finishing his discourse and knowing the sound state of her mind, expounded the norm to her in an inspiring lesson. Because her mind was fully ripe, even as she sat listening, she attained *arhantship*, together with a complete grasp of the norm in form and meaning.[32]

Yet another example is that of Kisā-Gotamī, who, on losing her son, became disoriented and came to the Buddha for help. Listening to her, the Buddha asked her to get a little mustard seed from a home where nobody had ever died. She could not find any such home, understood the meaning of the lesson, and became a nun. Then one day she listened to the Buddha when he was teaching. He said:

> The man who, living for an hundred years,
> Beholdeth never the Ambrosial Path,
> Had better live no longer than one day,
> So he behold within that day the Path.[33]

When he finished, she understood the dharma and attained *arhantship*. All these examples clearly show that the Buddha respected women as equals and personally bestowed his teachings on many of them. Many of his women disciples also became worthy teachers themselves.

Despite the disdain for women that marks the *Jātaka Kathās*, the nun Muttā could still say:

> O free, indeed! O gloriously free
> Am I in freedom from three crooked things:
> From quern, from mortar, from my crookback'd lord.
> Ay, but I'm free from rebirth and from death,
> And all that dragged me back is hurled away.[34]

The Buddha's favorite disciple, Ānanda, always maintained the tradition of gender equality. The nun Samā is said to have listened to the preachings of Ānanda and thereby attained *arhantship*. Reflecting on her achievement, she expressed herself in this psalm:

> Four times, nay, five, I sallied from my cell,
> And roamed afield to find the peace of mind
> I sought in vain, and governance of thoughts
> I could not bring into captivity.
> To me, even to me, on that eighth day
> It came: all craving ousted from my heart.

Mid many sore afflictions, I had wrought
With passionate endeavor, and had won!
Craving was dead, and the Lord's will was done.[35]

The nun Cittā was ordained by Mahāprajāpati Gautamī. She later won *arhantship* and, reflecting on her enlightenment, said:

Though I be suffering and weak, and all
My youthful spring be gone, yet have I climbed,
Leaning upon my staff, the mountain crest.
Thrown from my shoulder hangs my cloak, o'er-turned
My little bowl. So 'gainst the rock I lean
And prop this self of me, and break away
The wildering gloom that long had closed me in.[36]

These voices, infrequently heard, attest that in the reality of early Buddhist life the nuns were not behind the monks in any way. They were achieving *arhantship* and accorded status equal to their male counterparts. Some were taught by the Buddha himself, who obviously did not discriminate between the sexes, and many more followed his teachings and attained the enlightenment. My argument finds support in Rita Gross's observation:

> When the roles and images of women throughout Buddhist history are studied as part of a feminist revalorization of Buddhism, the quest for an accurate past intertwines with the quest for a usable past, and each enhances the other. An accurate record, corrected for the omissions of androcentricism, demonstrates two things very clearly. It demonstrates that women have participated in the Buddhist discourses in varied and significant ways, and that their roles and images have been discussed relatively frequently in Buddhist texts. On the other hand, looking specifically at women's roles and images throughout Buddhist history also demonstrates quite clearly the patriarchal inadequacies of that past.[37]

Precisely because the majority of Buddhist historical sources demean, silence and erase women, whatever meagre references to women we do find become very important. These are clues to the value of the work done by women and the role they played as teachers in the saṅgha. That these testaments to women's very real share in the spiritual capital of the faith in the Buddha's own time and for some time thereafter have been overlooked in the texts subsequent to the Third Buddhist Council reveals the entrenchment of a minority establishment, the Buddhist saṅgha in this case, behind the dominant patriarchal bulwarks of mainstream public life rather than continuing with a liberalization that only a person of the Buddha's stature could achieve. The history of Buddhist community and monastic life reveals, as I have attempted to argue, different attitudes towards women at different periods of time and the impress of contemporary social structures and values. As the founder of Buddhism, the Buddha himself saw no reason to treat women as less than equals to men but in later centuries his teachings were interpreted for the benefit of power seekers. Clearly, a feminist re-interpretation of the Buddha's life and teachings is called for to establish that the Buddha truly propounded a universal message, one meant for all human beings rather than for one favoured gender.

Notes

1. Pagels (1979), pp. 52–53.
2. Cited in Eisler (1987), pp. 128–129.
3. Sharma (1983), p. 70.
4. Gross (1993), p. 20.
5. Zelliot (1992), pp. 103–104.
6. Sharma (1983), p. 69.
7. Willis, (1985), p. 61.
8. Hirakawa (1982), pp. 50, 51, 83, 84, 86, 93, 95.
9. Willis (1985), p. 63.
10. Sharma (1983), p. 70.
11. Roth (1970), p. 12.
12. Bartholomeusz (1992), p. 38.
13. Ibid., p. 51.
14. Ibid., p. 49.
15. Paul (1979), p. 81.
16. Horner (1975), p. 155.
17. Gross (1993), p. 36.
18. Ibid., p. 45.
19. Chalmers (1960), p. 155.
20. Ibid., p. 150.
21. Zelliot (1992), p. 91.
22. Ibid.
23. Ambedkar (1974), p. 19.
24. Ibid., p. 23.
25. Ibid., p. 26.
26. Horner (1975), p. 71; Falk (1974), p. 105.
27. Schalow (1992), p. 222.
28. Reed (1992), p. 160.
29. Gross (1993), p. 43.
30. Ibid., p 69.
31. Rhys Davids and Norman (1989), p. 67.
32. *Ibid.* p. 69.
33. Ibid., p. 89.
34. Ibid., p. 11.
35. Ibid., p. 25.
36. Ibid., p. 36.
37. Gross (1993), p. 21.

References

Ambedkar, B. R. *The Buddha and His Dhamma.* Bombay: Siddhartha Publication, 1974.

Bartholomeusz, Tessa. "The Female Mendicant in Buddhist Sri Lanka." In Cabezon, *Buddhism, Sexuality and Gender*, 1992.

Cabezon, Jose Ignacio, ed. *Buddhism, Sexuality and Gender*. New York: State University of New York Press, 1992.

Chalmers, Robert. *The Jataka*. London: Pali Text Society, 1969.

Eisler, Riane. *The Chalice and the Blade: Our History, Our Future*. San Francisco: Harper & Row, 1987.

Falk, Nancy Auer. "An Image of Woman in Old Buddhist Literature: The Daughters of Mara." In *Women and Religion*, ed. Judith Plaskow and John Arnold Romero. Missoula, Mont.: Scholars Press, 1974.

Gross, Rita M. *Buddhism after Patriarchy*. New York: State University of New York Press, 1993.

Haddad, Yvonne Yazbeck, and Ellison Banks Findly, ed. *Women, Religion and Social Change*. New York: State University of New York Press, 1985.

Hirakawa, Akira. *Monastic Discipline for the Buddhist Nuns*. Patna: Kashi Prasad Jayasawal Reasearch Institute, 1982.

Horner, I. B. *The Book of Discipline* (Vinaya-Pitaka), volume 5 (Cullavagga). London: Routledge & Kegan Paul, 1975.

Pagels, Elaine. *The Gnostic Gospels*. New York: Random House, 1979.

Paul, Diana Y. *Women in Buddhism*. Berkeley, Colif.: Asian Humanities Press, 1979.

Reed, Barbara E. "The Gender Symbolism of Kuan-yin Boddhisattva." In Cabezon, *Buddhism, Sexuality and Gender*, 1992.

Rhys Davids, C. A. F., and K. R. Norman, *Poems of the Early Buddhist Nuns (Therīgāthā)*. Oxford: Pali Text Society, 1989.

Roth, Gustav. *Bhiksuni-Vinaya*. Patna: K. P. Jayaswal Research Institute, 1970.

Schalow, Paul Gordon. "Kukai and the Tradition of Male Love in Japanese Buddhism." In Cabezon, *Buddhism, Sexuality and Gender*, 1992.

Sharma, Chandradhar. *A Critical Survey of Indian Philosophy*. Delhi: Motilal Banarsi Dass, 1983.

Willis, Janice D. "Nuns and Benefactors: The Role of Women in the Development of Buddhism." In Haddad and Findly, *Women, Religion and Social Change*, 1985.

Zelliot, Eleanor. "Buddhist Women of the Contemporary Maharastrian Movement." In Cabezon, *Buddhism, Sexuality and Gender*, 1992.

SAMJUKTA GOMBRICH GUPTA

The Goddess, Women, and Their Rituals in Hinduism

The *Mārkaṇḍeya purāṇa* (MP) narrates the story of Saraṇyū just before its famous description of the Great Goddess's repeated triumphs over the powerful demons. Saraṇyū was a daughter of the god Tvaṣṭṛ, and she married the sun (Vivasvat), who in this myth was considered to be a mortal—that is, part of the created world, which is ultimately transient. Their son Vaivasvata Manu, who is thus half god and half mortal, is the forefather of humankind. As Wendy Doniger has pointed out, Saraṇyū was never venerated as a goddess or as the original mother of humankind.[1]

Her refusal to behave like a good wife or a good mother may have offended the traditional image of a good woman. She took recourse to deception to sneak away from her home, husband, and children and left behind a look-alike woman to act out her wifely and motherly duties. Moreover, she lacked power and was afraid of her husband's concentrated energy. In fact, her father, Tvaṣṭṛ, to persuade her to go back to her husband, had to cut out most of the sun's energy, leaving him only one-sixteenth of his original energy.[2]

Thus the mother of humankind, Saraṇyū, because of her unwifely and unmotherly behavior was ignored as a goddess while the *MP* narrated the glory of the Great Goddess, the divine energy, Mahāmāyā (cosmic illusion), who from that time onward gradually rose to eminence as the mother of the universe.[3] In the *purāṇas*, she transcends the social roles of both mother and wife and often functions autonomously. Therefore, she cannot be a role model for women in the broader Hindu society, even though some Hindu communities worship very young girls in the family as the image of the goddess, and sometimes women become possessed by a goddess and turn into oracles.[4] However, generally speaking, the paramount importance of the roles of wife and mother for Hindu women cannot be exaggerated. Hence, while the Great Goddess is supremely important in Hindu theology, women's position is society is still rather uncertain in a basically patriarchal and caste-oriented society, where caste is transmitted through the male line of a family. A woman certainly does not possess the goddess's sovereign authority or her divine power. In this society, the role models for women are such epic and *purāṇic* characters as Sītā, who followed her husband to his forest exile, leaving behind the luxury of the palace of Ayodhyā, and Sāvitrī, who followed her dead husband when the god of death was taking him to the land of the dead and tricked the god into returning her husband alive and well.[5]

In this chapter, I examine how Hindu women, by employing the means they find in Hindu religious systems, are able to transcend the restricted position in the family hierarchy and the passive role in Hindu religions that are seemingly accorded them by the law books of Hindu dharma—for example, the *Manusmṛti*. First, I discuss the image of women in Hindu society; second, I briefly sketch the theology of a divine power who is feminine and its effect on the social position of women; thrid, I show how, in spite of her adverse situation in society and her ambivalent position in theology, the Hindu woman has created for herself a gloriously important position in society through her special religious practices (*vrata*).[6]

Dharma

Broadly speaking, every religious-minded Hindu has some idea of dharma, both social and personal, and the doctrines of karma and *saṁsāra*—the transience of life and the endless transmigration of individual selves from life to life. Popular mythology and philosophical thought current among Hindu women try to give structure and a coherent exposition of dharma, and undoubtedly every person within the religion possesses a basic grasp of it. In its various contexts and applications, this dharma has at least three basically different functions and dimensions: dharma is (1) a principle of causal explanation (of factual events), (2) a guideline to ethical orientation and (3) the counterpart and stepping stone to final liberation attained by renunciation and asceticism. These three functions are balanced, reconciled, and integrated in various manners; they do not form a simple and unquestioned unity. Historically, it is possible to see changes, differences, and tensions between older and later levels of thought and also processes of adjustment of prekarmic and extrakarmic ways of thinking to the theory of karma and *saṁsāra*. As official Hinduism explains, the causality of human station in society and its ranking in the social hierarchy and the notions of karma and their retributive effects of good or bad fortune seem to make sense.

Dharma enjoins each person to follow a set of social and religious duties appropriate to that person's individuality (*sva-dharma*)[7] and social station that is usually in harmony with his or her religious and social duties (*jāti-dharma*) as a member of a particular *jāti*—that is, natal community. This dual meaning of dharma is crucial in understanding Hindu social religion. The meaning and scope of dharma have been elaborately discussed in ancient brahmanical law books. All members of brahmanical society must model their actions according to the injunctions of these law books so that the results accrued should be universally beneficial and elevating for active people. A woman's dharma is designated as *strī-dharma*. Note that the universal law of ethics known as the truth (*ṛtam* or *satyam*) transcends both types of dharma and is often referred to simply as dharma. Yudhiṣṭhira, the hero of the

Mahābhārata, was a paragon of this third and universal type of dharma and is distinguished by the epithet *dharmarāja*, king of dharma.

Dharma, *Strī-dharma*, and Ritual Acts

Ritual acts can counterbalance the bad results of one's karma. These rituals give the ritualist certain powers even to remedy some previous wrongdoing that has resulted in some calamity in this life. Sāvitrī rebelled against karma and released Satyavān from the noose of death, Yama, but before that she rigidly followed the dharma of a loyal wife. Thus, she established her personal integrity and purity. She chose her husband without knowing that his fate was to die within a year of their marriage, yet, when informed about his fate, she remained firm in her conviction that, once she had decided to give herself to Satyavān, it would be a breach of her dharma not to keep her promise, even though it had never been uttered. In this instance, she followed the third type of dharma (i.e., *satya-dharma*, dharma which is the truth) and paved her way to winning Yama's approval. Yama is the lord of dharma and is called by that name.

As each individual has a special basic nature (*sva-bhāva*) that determines that person's duties, a woman has to determine her basic nature (*strī-dharma*).[8] Ideally, Hindu dharma advises all people to follow their own (*sva*) dharmas. By strictly adhering to her preordained nature and duties, a woman can function in the socially sanctioned dharmic way. She is the mistress of the house and plays a great supporting role as the custodian of the family dharma; she knows the rituals, teaches her children the basic dharma, and is thus responsible for the dharmic structure of the next generation. Accepting the *śāstras'* criticism of the naturally fickle nature of women and the pollution inherent in the female body, women make themselves utterly subservient to the voice of family authority and frequently engage in acts of ritual purification. I shall soon make this point clear.

Enjoined by God, the cosmic ruler, the prime mover, karma functions as the principle of causal relations of factual happenings. For instance, it explains the causality of human station in society and also supplies a guideline for ethical orientation, the concept of individual responsibility for every intentional act and its future result, ensuring the inevitability of *saṁsāra*, even when a person carefully follows both *sva-dharma* and *jāti-dharma*. Nevertheless, ancient brahmanical religion has taught individuals how to transcend their *sva-bhāva* and thus reduce the importance of their *sva-dharma* by (1) meticulous adherence to religious duties, coupled with strict self-control, which is sometimes close to asceticism; (2) total renunciation of attachment and greed, together with removal of all physical, emotional, and moral weaknesses, thereby leading to purity of body and mind, followed by deep meditation on the real nature of oneself and the phenomenal world; and (3) reception of God's grace through perfect devotion.

The first of these ways really means the correct performance of all the rituals prescribed by the religious system. It associates such rituals with a program of self-restraint and certain ascetic practices whose main purpose is to purify a person's physical, mental, and emotional flaws.[9]

The second way—that is, the way of yoga—is universally accepted by all Hindu religious systems to be the basis of all religious endeavor. The preliminary step for practicing yoga is to control emotion and passion by cultivating calmness (*śama*) and self-restraint (*dama*). The practice of calmness and self-restraint leads a person to renounce the attractions of greed and passion. People are not always required to really renounce their station in life, but the spirit of renunciation (*vairāgya*), going hand in hand with deep meditation on the chosen deity, is highly valued as the basic moral and spiritual requirement for anybody who is seeking God's favor through devotion.

The third way is what underscores all such sects and religious systems that, together with traditional Brahminism, have been called Hinduism. God is supreme and the ultimate authority, whose grace alone can save a person from *saṁsāra*. God's pleasure, then, forms the main goal of all religious practices. People can aspire to it through selfless devotion and constant loyal service to God.

In the real world of the believers in the religions collectively called the Hindu religions, however, these ways are not at all exclusive. There are countless permutations and combinations of these ways to produce a multitude of religious systems and sects. Every pious and religious-minded Hindu believes in the existence of a supreme god, who subsumes all other deities, including a specially chosen beloved deity (*iṣṭadevatā*). Thus, the paradox of monotheism and polytheism functioning simultaneously in Hinduism poses no problem in a Hindu's religious awareness. Sectarian theology amalgamates all three ways mentioned of escaping karma and its result, *saṁsāra*.

In the patrifocal brahmanical tradition, women were systematically excluded from ritualistic religious duties because they were deemed unclean and impure. Hence, they were classed alongside the other impure social group, *śūdra*. This impurity is inherent in women because of their basic capacity to bear children, which sounds paradoxical, especially in the context of *jāti*-dominated Hindus. Let me expand on it. *Jāti* is determined by birth as a son to a man who belongs to a specific *jāti*. The transmission of *jāti* is from father to son. It is the most important factor in arranged marriage and inheritance. Women may belong to a lineage (*kula*) but cannot transmit it. A man needs a wife to beget children to perpetuate his *jāti* and lineage (*kula*). Obviously, a man has to be sure of his own paternity. Hence, early lawgivers betrayed their anxiety on this point by setting up an elaborate system of manipulating women's sexuality. *Manusmṛti*, the most famous ancient Indian treatise on ritual, social and ethical laws, and the system of penalties, did not consider women fit to be free individuals; they should be under the control of their male protectors—that is, their fathers, husbands, and sons. Note that these lawgivers, who were male and of the Brahmin *jāti*, indicated only the spirit of the social values rather than the actual situation.[10]

Not only did the age of marriage for women sink lower and lower until it was normal for a female child to be given in marriage before puberty but also her menstrual flow came to be regarded as polluting and dangerous. A woman in her period used to be avoided by all males, and she was treated as virtually untouchable. Because of this recurrent event in their lives, women came to be branded as basically impure and in need of the most elaborate regimen of fasting and other ritual penance to regain their ritual purity. Somehow, the menstrual blood and women's sexuality were held to be violent and dangerous for males. Even though the advent of a girl's puberty was often celebrated as a happy event and she was feasted and decorated, for the first few days she was required to avoid even meeting male members of her family. This mistrust of a woman's menstrual blood, which established her fertility and hence her usefulness to family and society as a future mother, influenced even childbirth. Like death, birth was associated with blood, destruction, and violence, and so it inflicted impurity on those associated with the event. The mother, the midwife, and everything else associated with childbirth were considered polluting. The special birth chamber was a temporary hut outside the residential area, where the new mother had to spend her period of isolation (six days) with only the midwife looking after her. Other female relatives could visit her but had to ritually purify themselves before entering the household, and all rites of passage were postponed in the family to counteract the effects of pollution during those days. This association of women, blood, and danger is an ancient idea to be found even in the earliest Vedic scriptures. In a myth related in the *Taittirīya Saṁhitā* (*TS*), Indra cut off the heads of Viśvarūpa, the son of Tvaṣṭṛ.[11] Indra thus incurred the great sin of brahminicide. He transferred one-third of his sin to women, and they got their menstruation cycle. Because of this myth, a woman was systematically barred from her ritual duties. Vedic rituals were mostly for progeny and increased grain and cattle, but the principal source of fecundity was banished from the rituals. More and more officiating priests usurped the women's position. It appears almost certain that, as the caste system grew in rigidity, women became the focus of male mistrust as a source of danger for their social status, and hence male domination increased.

The *strī-dharma* enumerated by the lawgivers also lists the elements of a woman's innate nature and clearly reflects society's mistrust of female sexuality and its apprehension of a woman's disloyalty to her husband.[12] In one calendrical Vedic sacrifice, there is a ritual in which the wife of the sacrificer is required to publicly confess the names of her lovers. If she lies, the noose of Varuṇa, the cosmic protector of the universal moral order, would punish her.[13] By contrast, a woman's power of childbearing was always highly valued. As the nurturing female, she not only bore and nurtured her own children but also nurtured her husband. His health, wealth, and longevity depended on her auspicious power derived from her abiding loyalty to her husband. The outward evidence of a woman's chastity and loyalty to her husband was demonstrated by her total submission to her husband's authority. She must accept her husband to be her only deity and spiritual teacher; her greatest virtue lay in serving him with her body and mind. She needed nothing else to secure a position in heaven and to redeem herself. The power of an unequivocally loyal wife was taken to be immense, as expressed in numerous legends. For example, a virtuous wife could stop the natural movements of the sun and the moon or, like Sāvitrī, conquer death.[14]

Just as the Vedic ritualists' gradual removal of women's participation led to the pattern of later Hindu rituals, so also the ancient mythological role model of a virtuous, faithful wife fixed her social position in the Hindu family. Her value in the family depended on her having a socially and economically prosperous husband blessed with health, who lived long after her own demise. Her most important function was to produce and nurture healthy sons to perpetuate her husband's lineage. The welfare of the family depended on her virtue and religiosity.

Thus, women's ritual activities became confined to some locally practiced rites observed during life cycle rituals such as birth and marriage, which were exclusively performed by women. They are called *strī-ācāra*, and ancient lawgivers prescribed them for women. But these rites were not in the same category as other brahmanical religious rites, in which women's participation was seriously undermined.[15] Here, local religious tradition came to women's rescue in the form of an entire corpus of women's rites (*vrata*). I shall presently focus my attention on this form of religious practice.

Now let me turn to the topic of the worship of the Great Goddess and its effect on the social position of Hindu women. Of the two most important roles of women in society—wife and mother—the highest respect and appreciation are reserved for the mother. Mothers are more sacred. In motherhood, women achieve symbiosis with the earth and nature on the one hand and with the Great Goddess, the cosmic mother, on the other. The greatest respect that can be shown to a woman is to call her "mother". A young married woman as a potential mother is deemed to be greatly auspicious, as her controlled sexuality promises to bring great prosperity to the family. If she is also the mother of a male child, she is marked as the luckiest woman. Marriage is the main event in a woman's life. A wife is welcomed in her marital family as an embodiment of their future prosperity. Marriage is her only major life cycle rite. A widow has no position in this society. Daughters are treated as beloved temporary members of their natal family but are most unwelcome as permanent members. In her marital family, unless she has mature male children, a widow's position is unenviable. She is held responsible for her husband's death by failing to secure his long life. Her sexuality becomes once again a source of danger. Because a woman is married into the husband's family, if she commits adultery, it brings sin upon the whole family. Hence, as a social safeguard, a widow must remain in a permanent state of mourning, observing strict asceticism to expiate the sin that took her husband from her. Ancient Hindu law did not allow women to inherit any significant patrimony, and often a widow could not inherit from her husband if she had no male child. No provision was made for her to follow any profession except that of servant. Thus, high-caste Hindus, following traditional brahmanical religion, did not show much kindness to a woman as an individual in her own right. Respite came from the bhakti movement and from tantric religion.[16]

The majority of pious Hindus worship some goddess or goddesses as protecting, nourishing, wealth-giving, and motherly deities, though some of them may also be awe-inspiring and destructive, punishing and wielding divine powers, violent and gruesome. The idea of a divine mother who is the source of creation is an ancient notion, found in various contexts in the early scriptures of India, the Vedas (1500–300 B.C.E.). Although at Mohenjo-Daro and other ancient cities archaeologists have discovered indications of goddess worship in an even earlier period of Indian civilization (circa 2000 B.C.E.), the lack of recorded evidence makes it impossible to know the nature of that religion. During the fourth and fifth centuries C.E., a number of religious texts known as the *purāṇas* and *āgamas* glorified the Great

Goddess. Foremost among them was the *Mārkaṇḍeya purāṇa*.[17] Thereafter, the cult of the Great Goddess developed its theology and rituals in a great number of exegeses. This written tradition is backed up by a rich tradition of plastic art and cult objects. Thus, it is not difficult to achieve an understanding of the nature and ideology of the worship of the Great Goddess since the early medieval period.

What difference did it make to Hindu social concepts and the Hindu worldview if the Supreme Reality, the ultimate divine, is female and not male? Did it change the character of their faith, their attitude toward the divine, or their attitude and conduct toward their fellow human beings, both male and female? Was it an anomaly that Hindu theology—a theology basically oriented to masculinity—developed a feminine theology? Other questions include when the transition occurred, how Hindu society adjusted its attitude toward its women—a daughter, wife, or mother—in the patrifocal family system, and how the women reacted. These and many other questions confront us as students of Hindu ideas of gender and Hindu religions.[18]

During the second quarter of the first millennium C.E., India saw the rise of various religious systems that developed a theology of what I will call inclusive monotheism. The supreme deity is seen as the creator and the savior and as possessing divine indomitable power and potentiality, the cosmic creative energy. However, this Supreme Divine, who is usually identified with either Śiva or Viṣṇu, both male gods, is also regarded—because of the influence of the monistic idealism of the *Upaniṣad*—as totally transcendent, such that nothing can be predicated of him. The *Upaniṣad* (circa 800–300 B.C.E.) speculated on the existence of a unitary, unique, and transcendental truth or reality, which is the essence of all phenomena (*brahman*) and at the same time the irreducible center or self (*ātman*) of all living beings. For theologians, the supreme god is this transcendental reality, eternal and unchangeable, yet he is the creator and sovereign controller of the cosmos as well as of living beings. Although unique and impersonal, this divine entity can be conceived as Śiva, Viṣṇu or any of their various manifestations.

To relate the divine with the creation within the sphere of epistemology, one needs *sakti*, the feminine principle. *Śakti* cannot be adequately translated by a single word. The concepts of power, potency, and potentiality are all present. God has the potentiality to be everything in the world, the power to do everything in the world—if he did not, he would not be God. At the same time, *śakti* represents sovereign, divine authority. She is seen as the concentration of divine and human prowess, the embodiment of glorious victory and of righteousness in the world arena of the struggle between good and evil. She is also the divine consciousness and wisdom. The divine will is expressed through her, and at the same time that will is translated into action by her. Although she carries out the divine will, on the cosmic level she is autonomous and rules creation through the multifaceted powers or energies that emanate from her. Everything in the world, from souls to stones, is an aspect of *śakti* because it is a manifestation and effect of divine power, and just as *śakti* is a hypostatization of the divine essence, an adjective made noun, and an attribute regarded as principle, so everything else can be referred to as if it were a separate entity. Thus, she is the supreme active godhead and wields her divine power through a myriad of secondary powers or goddesses, each of whom represents one special divine area of cosmic activity. It is always the autonomous power, *śakti*, that is the only true agent, as no one can tell her what to do. Here we come to two distinct philosophical ideas—power and authority. Ultimately, *śakti*'s power and potency are derived from the authority of the supreme divine. There is still no paradox here, only personification, because *śakti* is the divine authority and can be regarded as the divine personality. To move to the still more concrete level of myth, *śakti* is God's wife. Because she is related to God as personality is related to a person, their inextricable connection is symbolized by her being half the body of God. The goddess can be one or many, but the local names or forms of the divine feminine principle make no difference to its function as the repository of power and embodiment of God's cosmic force, potency, power, and energy.

This is, in fact, a form of idealism, in that the world is the content of God's thought and the divine power is the thought of God at the primal moment of creation. God's thought is the moment when the plenum of God's pure and contentless awareness is disturbed by God's will to create, which moves divine awareness to the condition of differentiated apperception of experience and its content. This slip from pure self-awareness to will and knowledge and its content is the vibrating point of primal creation. *Śakti* is both God's will and God's omniscience, as well as the content of that knowledge. It is thus the divine feminine principle that is deemed to be the creatrix. She embodies all empirical experience, being both the components of such experience—that is, the signifier and the signified (*vācya* and *vācaka*). Creation is simultaneously both a limitation of the ultimately transcendent awareness and the transformation of the pure spirit into gross material things. The progressive creation is seen in three ranges or gamuts: from conscious to unconscious, subtle to gross, and simple to complex. All three are coordinate and in reality just aspects of *śakti*. Deluded by *śakti*'s *māyā* dimension, human beings take the end result of these processes as absolutely real. Salvation lies in the knowledge or realization penetrating these processes and understanding the basic unity of all experiences, all objects, and all awarenesses. Then the delusion (*māyā*) is gone, establishing a lasting realization of the essential unity between the microcosm and the macrocosm. There are five divine acts on the cosmic level: creation; sustenance; destruction or involution, taking creation to be a process of evolution; delusion; and grace leading to salvation. Delusion is the situation when the microcosm is experienced as totally limited by time, space, and karma, making them fragmented and suffering from transience. This, too, is an act of *śakti* concealing the true nature of human beings. Gross matter is seen as the source of creation both in the biological model and in the evolutionary model. It is matter (*prakṛti*) that evolves into all gross objects, all forms. *Prakṛti* also means Mother Nature.

But in tantric theology there also developed the idea of the cosmic feminine principle as Goddess and sexual partner of God, giving birth to creation. This divine sexuality of the Goddess is equated with divine power. This divine power that carries out the divine will is the beneficial power, the nurturing Mother Goddess. But as Māyā the deluder, she is also the great divine aggressive force, which represents divine righteous anger bringing justice and punishing the unjust, the transgressor against cosmic moral laws. Māyā is also called the seducer, here recalling the aspect of her feminine uncontrolled sexuality. She seduces humankind into the bondage of transitoriness, but side by side with her seductive personality is her natural motherly aspect. Full of love for her children, she provides them with the ways and means of receiving her grace, which is the only way to salvation and bliss. This is her fifth cosmic function. The path is expressed in the scriptures, liturgy, and exegeses. All she demands is total faith in her and dedication to her.

Thus, we see that the paradigm of femaleness is reflected on all the different levels of the cosmic principle of *śakti*. Her nature is motherly[19] and wifely.[20] She performs cosmic functions on the authority of God, seen as her husband, and she procreates as the cosmic mother, but her sexuality has the dangerous quality of seduction and even deception. She not only dims humankind's proper awareness of reality and truth, thereby creating the world of complex diversities, but also could at any moment delude their intelligence and derail them from the path of righteousness. At the same time, she is seen as the nemesis that brings down divine punishment.

The concept of the Goddess reveals the central understanding of feminine nature in a society dominated by the brahmanical idea of a caste-oriented community. She is *prakṛti*, the mother or source of all; *śakti*, the indomitable potency and fecundity; and finally *māyā*, the seductress. All three aspects of the Goddess deal with her sexuality and reflect the two accepted roles of women in society—namely, wife and mother. A virtuous wife is she who is sexually loyal to her husband as long as he lives and even after his death. Once married, her sexuality is under the total control of her husband, and any breach of it drives her out of the status of wifehood forever. In Brahminism, there are strictures against the remarriage of women. This is normal in a society where caste membership is entirely dependent on patrilineality. Motherhood within this normative condition is highly extolled as the fulfillment of a woman's social life. She is the nurturing *prakṛti*. In fact, a sexually active woman as a married wife is considered to be the source of all good fortune, and she is deemed to be immensely auspicious (*sumaṅgalī*). A girl is groomed from her childhood to be a good wife and mother. All social life cycle rites for women overtly deal with her sexuality. As a child, she is often worshiped as an image of the goddess, her purity then unbroken by puberty. At puberty, a symbolic marriagelike ritual is often held to provide her with a surrogate bridegroom, often an affine girl or a divine image, and she is made aware of her loss of purity and taught caution in relationships with male members of the family. She is then married as soon as possible to bring her sexuality under her husband's control. Finally, her motherhood is greeted with several rites.

Her widowhood, by contrast, is stamped on her by her dress, demeanor, and lifestyle. She is the most inauspicious human being. She has the potency but no proper way of fulfillment, no controller. Uncontrolled potency is like uncontrolled divine potency, dangerous and violent, like Bhadrakālī. The harsh treatment of widows stems from this fear and the desire to control her by other, often cruel means.

The reason for Hindu women's subsidiary position in the family should be evident from the material presented so far. I have also made clear that the fact that certain sections of Hindu society worship the Goddess as the active creatrix and even as the saving godhead did not radically change women's position in the Hindu social structure. In fact, as noted before, the feminine paradigm conditioned the view of the devotees about their adored Goddess.[21] The same can be said about the view of the followers of devotional Hinduism concerning their womenfolk although the situation of women in the bhakti movements varies considerably in different parts of South Asia and at different strata of society.[22]

Vratas of Hindu Women

Having given two somewhat pessimistic accounts of the position of women in the Hindu worldview, I shall now give an account of their position in the same society that suggests they are far more powerful in real life than they would appear to be from the religious records. In a real sense, the control of the family usually remains in the hands of the mistress of the house. In the family, little girls get lessons in social behavior that enable them to improve their position in their own society. It is her impurity that makes a woman dangerous to a society in which male ideology prevails. In the case of the Goddess, her sexuality is inseparably entwined with her divine spouse, whose *śakti* she is. But in women such sexuality is viewed as dangerous, and women are taught from childhood to be modest and to suppress their sexuality. Moreover, perfect chastity and loyalty to her husband accords a woman moral superiority over other members of her family.

However, the most important means to derive real moral superiority lies in conducting a spotless religious life and thereby acquiring spiritual power and efficacy, which remove women's impurity. From the teachings of her religion, as outlined earlier, a woman learns how to remove all negative elements from her innate nature (*sva-bhāva*) and overcome her alleged impurity by intensively practicing religious acts (*vratas*) available to her. It is not easy. Living within the family and fulfilling their social duties, women have little opportunity for ostentatious spirituality. Moreover, traditional *vratas* prescribed in brahmanical religious literature are not always available to women.[23] What has evolved out of the utter necessity for self-assertion is a huge parallel religious culture specially followed by women. They are collectively called religious vows (*vratas*) of women.[24] From early girlhood, a woman is encouraged to take up several vows aimed at producing a desirable husband, an affectionate mother-in-law, or long life and prosperity for her brothers. As soon as she is married, vows are taken up for the prosperity of her marital home and family, a good harvest, long life for her husband and children, and safety for her marital and natal families. As soon as she becomes a mother, the welfare of her children is to be safeguarded by taking up yet another vow.

These vows have certain common features: total or partial fasting for the period, voluntary restriction of certain daily habits of food and dress, rigorous purificatory rites, and abstention from sexual acts. We can group them as ascetic abstention, self-mortification, and meticulous physical purity. In these aspects, women's *vratas* do not much differ from the general religious *vratas* mentioned in brahmanical sacred treatises. Instead of the mantras or religious formulas in Sanskrit that are uttered in brahmanical practice, there are metrical compositions in the vernacular that tell the name of the deity and the purpose of the vow, together with recitation of a balladlike narrative in which the deity of the *vrata* rescues her devotees from dangerous situations and bestows on them great prosperity and fulfillment of their wishes. Women who observe these vows often get together and perform them collectively, which develops a certain feminine solidarity. The freehand drawings of diagrams and symbols and the compulsory requirement that participants attentively recite and listen to the narration reveal the underlying element of magic in these rites. The narrative always emphasizes the power of the deity in whose name the vow is taken and who is worshiped. The story emphasizes the efficacy of the ritual practice to fulfill the wishes of the performer, and most important of all, no male priest is needed—in fact, no officiating ritual agent is allowed in. It is entirely a women's affair. In traditional families, women members undertake vast numbers of such vows, and clearly these women are dedicating a great part of their lives to these auspicious religious observances. Because the prayers are always for the longevity and prosperity of their menfolk, in the latter's eyes, the purity and auspicious nature of these women are greatly enhanced. By the constant practice of *vrata*, which combines both the first and second methods of redeeming *karma-phala*, women in traditional Hindu families become great ritual specialists; in fact, the religious duties of male Hindus often totally depend on their wives' active assistance. Far from being a hindrance to male religiosity and a source of danger because of her impure nature, a woman in the family is held—thanks to her voluntary ascetic practice—to be morally, ritually, and spiritually pure. Instead of being cast out of religious practices, women in this sphere of religious activity are the principal actors. All the rites revolve around women as the center of gravity.

To illustrate my point, let me describe a few *vratas*.[25] First, a married woman commonly observes the Lakṣmī *vrata*. Lakṣmī is the benign and compassionate goddess of wealth, grains, and beauty. As soon as a woman is married, her mother-in-law teaches her to perform the Lakṣmī *vrata* every Thursday or Friday. She fasts on that day, takes her morning bath and wets her hair, and then worships Lakṣmī, whose presence is invoked in a full water pot that is covered with a five-leaf spray of mango. A banana is placed on the leaves, and the water pot is placed on a metal plate that holds a few cowries (an older form of money). A pān leaf, a whole areca nut, fruits, and sweets are offered. The worshiper purifies every object of offering by marking it with the sacred red *sindur* (vermilion) paste. Then she and other married women of the family, who have all fasted, take part in the worship. They offer flowers, *vilva* leaves and *kuśa* grass,[26] a lamp, and incense to Lakṣmī in the water pot. After worshiping the deity with lamps (*ārati*), all the women sit in a circle around the chief worshiper, who recites the story (*kathā*) of the *vrata*. On completion of these steps, the women are free to eat their normal meal.

The *vrata-kathā* usually follows a set pattern: some person falls into adversity and then meets either the deity whose *vrata* story is being recounted or worshipers of that deity. The suffering person undertakes the *vrata*, overcomes the misfortune, fully recovers a former happy life, and gains material prosperity. Some relative or friend witnesses the *pūjā* and derides it and its deity. The latter punishes the scoffer by calling down great calamities. Finally, at the request of a close relative (daughter, wife, or mother-in-law) or as a result of the deity's appearance in disguise or in a dream, this person repents and humbly worships the deity in the proper manner.

The person's sins are forgiven, reparation of losses is made, and great prosperity is bestowed. Honesty, faith, and humility are the qualities extolled. Above all, an unflinching faith in the deity's power and the efficacy of the meticulously performed *vrata* are strongly advocated.

A married woman usually takes the weekly Lakṣmī *vrata* for life. The annual Lakṣmī *vrata*, also taken for life, is a very important event, especially in the eastern rice-growing areas of Bengal. It occurs on the first full-moon evening after Durgā's annual worship in early autumn. The goddess is clearly related to the rice grain, and this is the time when, after the monsoon, the rice grain ripens in the fields and the peasants' and farmers' wives worship the grain goddess in anticipation of a good harvest. She is primarily represented by a new terra-cotta plate filled with rice, fruit, and other products of the land that is covered by a round, convex earthen plate. This second plate is painted with figures in red, green, yellow, blue, and black. The figures include the goddess Lakṣmī, her attendants, her vehicle the owl, and ears of rice grain. On the day of the annual *vrata* performance, all performers must fast the whole day and prepare as much food as possible as an offering. They must observe strict purity rules. The house is cleaned and then decorated with line drawings made with thin rice paste. The designs consist of lotus diagrams, rice plants with ears of rice, and small footprints on which Lakṣmī steps to enter the house. The altar, a low table, is decorated with drawings of small lotuses, a comb and a mirror, ornaments, and a pair of small footprints in the middle of the front border. The sacred water pot is placed in the center.[27] The Lakṣmī plate is set just behind it. Sometimes a small mock boat is made of the outer casing of the banana plant, containing little cylinders made of the same, which are filled with various lentils and beans to indicate the later event of the harvest coming home.

After the evening worship and the recitation of the *vrata* story, the worshipers break their fast (*pāraṇa*) by taking a little bit of the offered food, but they do not take rice. Then all of the adult women keep vigil the entire night, by playing dice or card games, awaiting Lakṣmī's arrival. The day before, the worshipers must observe celibacy and eat only once, at noon, rice and vegetables boiled together. On the following day, they must observe the same restrictions, breaking their fast only at noon. This is called keeping the *vāra*,[28] which is essential for all annual *vratas*. The main purpose of the Lakṣmī *vrata* is to keep the family economy in good shape.

Another *vrata* for life is that of Vipattāriṇī, she who removes all calamities. This annual event is observed on any day between the third and the ninth day of the bright fortnight of Āṣāḍha (June–July) to remove bad luck and sudden calamity. It must be observed on a Saturday or a Tuesday. The deity is Durgā or Caṇḍī, who is very popular in Bengal as the remover of all life's dangers and misfortunes. Besides the ordinary ingredients of the offering, the worshiper must get thirteen types of fruit, thirteen types of flowers, thirteen leaves of pān and areca nuts, and thirteen thread bracelets, each consisting of thirteen strands of red thread bunched together with thirteen knots, each knot being stuck with a *kuśa* tip. Thirteen little baskets are offered, each containing one of the special offerings. Apparently, thirteen is a magic number. From the day before the ceremony, the worshiper starts keeping the

FIGURE 1. Decorative motifs and designs for women's rituals.

vāra. She must fast completely on the day of the *vrata*. After the worship of the goddess, she recites or listens to the recitation of the *vrata-kathā*. Then, having prostrated herself before the goddess, she puts on one of the red thread bracelets on her own right hand and ties others on the right hands of other family members. She completes her *pāraṇa* the next day at noon by taking a fruit, after which she can eat her usual meal of rice.

Although the *Śivarātri vrata* is observed by all devout Hindus, it has special significance for unmarried girls. This *vrata* brings them merit in the form of a suitable husband. Girls under the guidance of older women of the family fast the whole day. They observe *vāra* the day before. Late at night on the *Śivarātri* (the fourteenth of the dark fortnight of Māgha, i.e., January–February), the girls start preparing Śiva *liṅgas* (the phallic symbol of Śiva) with clay collected the day before from a pond or lake. Then they put four *liṅgas* on a metal plate and worship one of these with flowers, fruits, 108 *vilva* leaves, the juice of *vilva* fruit, milk, and coconut milk. The important rite is to pour milk, water, and *vilva* fruit juice on top of the *liṅga*, which has a drop-shaped clay bead on it. They keep a vigil, and at the start of each of the remaining three watches of the night, one of the remaining Śiva *liṅgas* is worshiped in the same way as before. The worship of the last *liṅga* finishes with the reciting of the *vrata-kathā*. In the early morning, sacred water is poured over the *liṅgas*, which breaks their form. Then the clay and most of the *pūjā* ingredients, except the food, are thrown into a river. The worshipers then take a bath and break their fast (*pāraṇa)* by drinking *vilva* fruit juice.

What are the important features of these *vratas*?

1. *Vratas* are undertaken either for a limited period or for life. They are not compulsory rituals, but for women in traditional families some *vratas* are so normal that they have become almost compulsory. It is quite normal for married women to observe two weekly *vratas*. If a woman is menstruating, she can still observe the fast while another suitable family member performs the actual *pūjā*.
2. The sense of group solidarity is really noteworthy. Women living in the same neighborhood tend to perform *vratas* together. Older women or experienced women not only teach other women how to perform a *vrata* but also perform it together, often crossing their caste thresholds. There are many *vrata* stories in which Brahmin and cowherd women are great friends and observe the same *vratas*; even an outcaste woman may see the power of a *vrata* and undertake it, or sometimes an outcaste woman performs a *vrata* and teaches a higher-caste woman in distress how to perform it. It is also a requirement of a *vrata* ritual that the recitation of its story must have an audience, and even a friend from a low caste may help a *vrata* observer by listening to the recitation. In the world of *vrata* stories, women seem to join in each other's lives without bothering about caste or class barriers.
3. Bathing, donning freshly washed clothes, and then fetching pure water in the water pot are important features. The goddess, who is worshiped in most *vratas* in some form or other, is always worshiped in the water

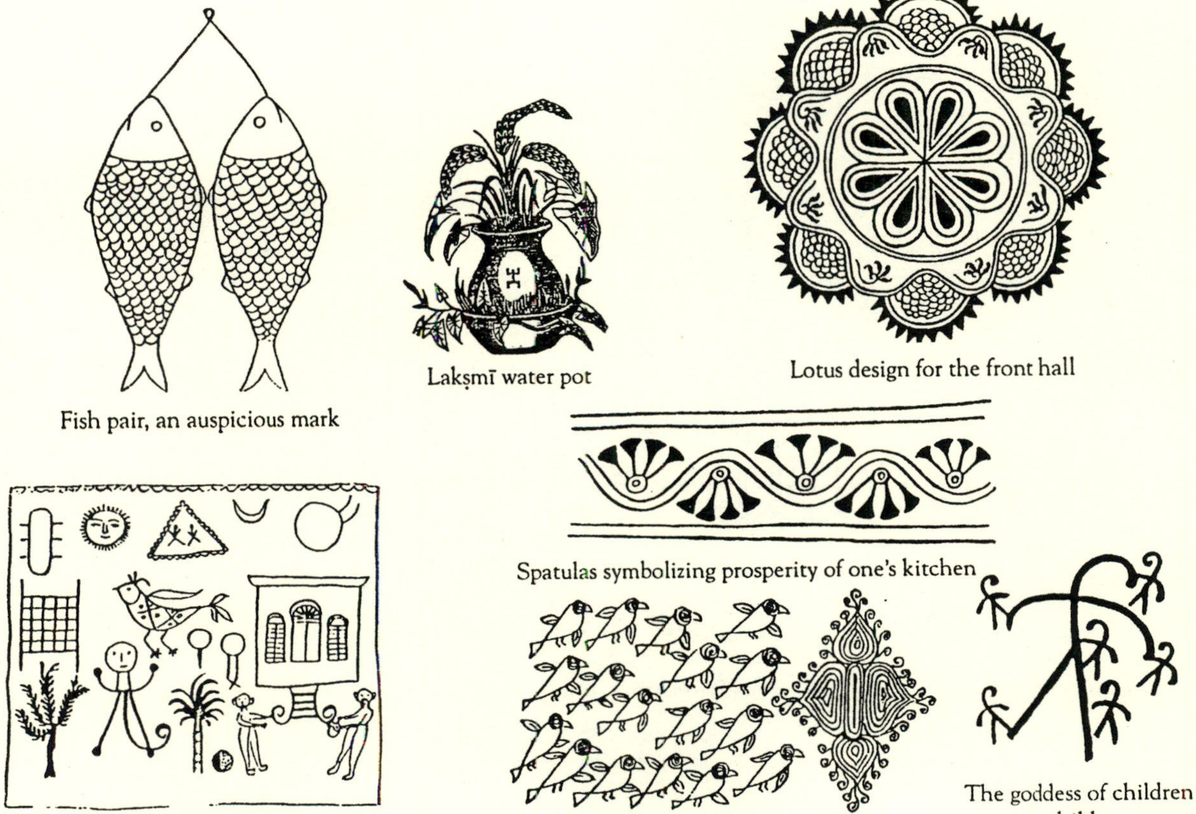

Fish pair, an auspicious mark

Lakṣmī water pot

Lotus design for the front hall

Spatulas symbolizing prosperity of one's kitchen

Senjuti *vrata* designs showing sun and moon, children and palace with guards

Ducks of Suvacani *vrata*

The goddess of children carrying children

FIGURE 2. More decorative motifs and designs for women's rituals.

of the water pot (*ghaṭa*). In some cases, the performers must go to a body of water, but *vratas* are usually performed at home, either on specially consecrated ground or inside the family shrine.

4. These rituals are almost entirely outside the domain of men. If the invoked deity belongs to the official Hindu pantheon, a priest may be employed for the central *pūjā* rites, but for the majority of the *vratas* male priests are not needed, and women perform all the rites themselves. Nevertheless, in almost all cases, the beneficiaries of the *vrata* are the male members of the family. There are, of course, *vratas* observed for the benefit of the worshiper, for instance, to get a suitable bridegroom or to obtain a husband's love and attention.
5. The paraphernalia (*upakaraṇa*) of worship (*pūjā*) often involve magical symbolism. Diagrams are drawn with special materials, such as rice powder, red *sindur*, and cow dung, to ensure the purity of the auspicious site of the ritual and to safeguard it. Sacred designs like the lotus or conch shell are employed to enhance the purity of sacred space. Objects within the boundary of a diagram acquire magical value. For example, a performer may draw some jewelry inside the diagram in the hope that the deity will give them to her. Sometimes important points of the *vrata* story are drawn inside the diagram.[29] Magical numbers, special sorts of fruit and flowers for specific deities, and compulsory attendance for all women to some *vrata* performance to listen to the narration of myths attached to the *vrata*, point toward the use of magic to propitiate a deity who has power to manipulate human destiny.
6. *Vratas* for a husband's protection and prosperity are almost always finalized by inviting, decorating, and feeding a married woman, often a Brahmin, and giving her presents and money. In some special *vratas*, often related to the goddess Gaurī, the daughter of Himālaya and spouse of Śiva, little girls are treated in the same way.
7. Above all, strict purity rules, fasting, and uninterrupted performance of the *vrata* are emphasized. A *vrata* observation must never be interrupted until the final ritual is successfully completed. Similarly, certain food taboos and other special rites, such as keeping strict silence, are of crucial importance. Any lapse in such matters brings dire consequences. When fasting, the observer may not even drink water. Some *vratas* require total abstinence from a special fruit during the period of the *vrata* observation; for instance, the goddess Santoṣī does not approve of sour fruits, vegetables, or pickles, which Indian women in particular are reputed to like. Some *vratas* demand that the performer should observe total silence during her *pāraṇa*; others stipulate difficult postures for eating the ritual meal. These regulations point to a strict notion of asceticism held and observed by women. They observe these ascetic rules with great care and willingness. Asceticism purifies and elevates their spirits and even supplies them with a great sense of spiritual power and astuteness. They acquire a religious stature honored by all members of society, male and female.

Conclusion

By observing such arduous *vratas* with great care and devotion, the Hindu woman overcomes her branding as a sinful, impure person. Their *vratas* are modeled on the brahmanical religious rites and sectarian rituals and follow the general Hindu religious value system. Women also follow the ethos and practices of the renouncer yogins. On top of all these, their natural affinity for the values of the religion of bhakti has helped them to follow their own ways with confidence. The ecstatic bhakti religion does not condemn passion—even sexual passion. In that religion, women have found religious freedom and dignity. Historically, with the help of that religion, they rose above their debilitating "innate nature" and became spiritual equals to the best of the religious personalities in the ancient and modern history of the Hindu religions. Instead of being a source of danger and degradation to her family, a woman is looked on as the repository of family welfare and spirituality. The equal of Sāvitrī and Sītā, she is endowed with the beneficial feminine power of the goddess, which commands both respect and awe.

The mythological role models present few options for women. They can be virtuous and suffer like Sītā, the virtuous wife of the righteous King Rāma of the epic *Rāmāyaṇa*, and mutely or perhaps not so mutely accept their destiny. Innumerable *vrata* legends narrate how a virtuous and uncomplaining sufferer finally triumphs; that is, indeed, a bhakti concept that shows total dependence on God's will. They can be virtuous but assertive and aggressive, like the dangerous goddesses, as in the story of Kaṇṇaki-Paṭṭini in *Cilappatikāram*,[30] or the wife of the leper.[31] Virtuous elderly widows also follow that pattern and obtain respect. The third option is to turn to religion and leave one's family. I have shown why this is not an easy option.[32] It is available in some Śaiva sects, and, at their inception, many great women saints adorn the Nayannārs, Vīraśaivas, and Tantric Śaivas. In eastern India, the Tantric Śaivas have continued to uphold the special position of women saints and spiritual leaders. Sometimes the status of a woman guru is higher than that of men.[33] In some esoteric sects of Bāuls, for instance, a woman is considered the most suitable of all gurus. Their strict sectarian ethic requires the Tantric Śaivas to show special respect to women.

For ordinary women in Hindu families, however, the practice of *vrata* and the strict maintenance of the purity and honor of the family enable a woman to enhance not only the family's prosperity and social respectability but also her own spiritual progress. It enhances her power as well. For women who stay in family life, *vratas* are the most important religious practices for redemption, spiritual elevation and even release from *saṁsāra*. What the renouncers achieve by leaving family life, women achieve within the family by practicing austerity and the self-restraint required for the observance of the rituals of countless *vratas*.

Notes

1. Doniger (1996), pp. 157ff.
2. *Mārkaṇḍeya purāṇa*, ch. 80–81, describing the reigns of Vaivasvata Manu and of Sāvarṇi Manu, when the goddess appeared to kill the buffalo demon.

3. Coburn (1991); Brown (1974).
4. Gupta (1991), pp. 193–209; Erndl (1996), pp. 173–94.
5. *Mahābhārata*, Vanaparva, 3.277–83; *Rāmāyaṇa*, passim.
6. *Vrata* consists of a corpus of female religious practices that exist parallel to traditional brahmanical and sectarian religious practices. See McGee (1991), pp. 71–88; Robinson (1985), passim.
7. One's *sva-dharma* is determined by one's innate nature, *sva-bhāva*.
8. Leslie (1989), passim. See also Gupta (1991). A woman is by nature (*sva-bhāva*) not only polluted but also potentially dangerous because of her excessive sexuality. Therefore, in her family her sexuality should always be controlled, and she should always be subservient to male authority. Her sexuality is a source of prosperity when it is active but controlled by her husband; in any other situation, she must totally repress it.
9. Most important Hindu ritual acts for rectifying one's bad *karma-phala* are called *vratas*. The performer of a *vrata* declares an intention to follow a special ritual program of a certain deity or deities over a fixed span of time. The period can be any length of time. The program includes elements of austerity and ritual expiatory acts meant to purify the performer's body, mind, and spirit.
10. Leslie (1989), p. 328.
11. Smith (1991), pp. 23–26, 42–45; Viśvarūpa had three heads (*TS*, 2.5.1).
12. Leslie (1989), pp. 246–49, 318–21.
13. Kane (1941), ch. 31, pp. 1091–1106.
14. *Mārkaṇḍeya purāṇa*, xvi, 14–90.
15. For example, in the *Bṛhaddharma Purāṇa* (Uttarakhaṇḍa, ch. 8, 7), married women are prohibited from observing religious rites involving fasting and the like because their only religious rite is to act in accordance with their husbands' wishes. See also Robinson (1985), pp. 190–93.
16. Gupta (1991). See also McGee (1991), pp. 74–76. In sectarian religions, a great number of rites called *vrata* are prescribed for sect members, which are often performed by both sexes. See also Robinson (1985), pp. 195–99.
17. Agarwala (1963), preface, pp. iv–xiii; Gupta (1979), pp. 8–10, 159–60.
18. McDermott (1996), pp. 294–304.
19. As indicated by the idea of *mātṛkā* and the epithet *jagajjananī*—that is, the mother of the universe.
20. As seen in the conception of Umā-Pārvatī and Lakṣmī.
21. In all visual representations of Viṣṇu lying on the couch, made by the body of Ananta, the cosmic serpent, the goddess Lakṣmī is portrayed as massaging the feet of her divine spouse, Viṣṇu. In Bengal, the most popular form of Umā-Pārvatī is the mother of Gaṇeśa.
22. Gupta (1991).
23. Robinson (1985), p. 192; see also Gupta (1991).
24. McGee (1991), pp. 71–88; Robinson (1985), pp. 195–211.
25. For a fuller description, see Kayal (1969), pp. 177–200; and Tiwari (1991), passim.
26. Pan is betel leaf; vilva is *Aegle* marmelos, a tree whose fruit and leaves both possess medicinal value; *kuśa* grass is always used in ritual worship as a purifying object.
27. See figures 1 and 2; and Thakur (1956).
28. *Vāra* is a Bengali term meaning restriction of food and drink, observed by the performers of a *vrata* on the day(s) before and after the *vrata*.
29. See diagrams on figures 1 and 2.
30. Zvelebil (1975), p. 112.
31. *Mārkaṇḍeya purāṇa*, ch. 80–81.

32. Gupta (1990), pp. 50–59; (1991), passim.
33. Personal discussion with a Bāul lineage head. See also Vidyālaṅkāra (1820).

References

Agarwala, Vasudev S. *Devī-māhātmyam: The Glorification of the Great Goddess*. Ramnagar, Varanasi: All India Kashiraj Trust, 1963.

Babb, Lawrence A. "Indigenous Feminism in a Modern Hindu Sect." In Ghadially, *Women in Indian Society*, 1988.

Bennett, Lynn. *Dangerous Wives and Sacred Sisters: Social and Symbolic Roles of High-Caste Women in Nepal*. New York: Columbia University Press, 1983.

Bṛhaddharma Purāṇa. Bibliotheca Indica Series. Calcutta: Asiatic Society of Bengal, 1888–97.

Brown, Cheever Mackenzie. *God as Mother: A Feminine Theology in India*. Hartford, VT: C. Stark, 1974.

———. "Kālī, the Mad Mother." In Olson, *The Book of the Goddess*, 1985.

Brubaker, Richard L. "The Untamed Goddesses of Village India." In Olson, *The Book of the Goddess*, 1985.

Coburn, James B. *Encountering the Goddess*. Albany: State University of New York Press, 1991.

Doniger, Wendy. "Saraṇyū/Saṃjñā: The Sun and the Shadow." In Hawley and Wulff, *Devi*, 1996.

Erndl, Kathleen M. "Serāṅvālī." In Hawley and Wulff, *Devi*, 1996.

Fruzzetti, Lina M. *The Gift of Virgin: Women, Marriage and Ritual in Bengali Society*. New Brunswick, NJ: Rutgers University Press, 1982.

Fuller, Mrs. Marcus B. (Jenny). *The Wrongs of Indian Womanhood*. Edinburgh: Oliphant Anderson and Ferrier, 1900. Repr. New Delhi, Inter-India Publications 1984.

Ghadially, Rehanna, ed. *Women in Indian Society: A Reader*. New Delhi: Sage, 1988.

Gross, Rita M. "Hindu Female Deities as a Resource for the Contemporary Rediscovery of the Goddess." In Olson, *The Book of the Goddess*, 1985.

Gupta, P. L. *The Imperial Guptas*. Varanasi: Vishwaridyalaya Prakashan, 1974–1979.

Gupta, Samjukta Gombrich. "Divine Mother or Cosmic Destroyer: The Paradox at the Heart of the Ritual Life of Hindu Women." In Joseph, *Through the Devil's Gateway*, 1990.

———. "Women in the Śaiva/Śākta Ethos." In Leslie, *Roles and Rituals of Hindu Women*, 1991.

Haddad, Yvonne Yazbeck, and Ellison Banks Findlay, eds. *Women, Religion and Social Change*. Albany: State University of New York Press, 1985.

Hawley, John Stratton, and Donna M. Wulff, eds. *Devi: Goddesses of India*. Berkeley: University of California Press, 1996.

Joseph, Allison, ed. *Through the Devil's Gateway: Women, Religion and Taboo*. London: SPCK, 1990.

Kane, P. V. *The History of Dharmaśāstra*. Poona: Bhandarkar Oriental Research Institute, 1941.

Kayal, Akshay Kumar. "Women in the Folklore of West Bengal." In Sen Gupta, *Women in Indian Folklore*, 1969.

Leslie, Julia. *Perfect Wife: The Orthodox Hindu Woman according to the Strīdharmapaddhati of Tryambakarājan*. New York: Oxford University Press, 1989.

Leslie, Julia, ed. *Roles and Rituals of Hindu Women*. London: Pinter, 1991.

Mahābhārata. Ed. Vishnu S. Sukhthankar. 18 vols. Poona: Bhandarkar Oriental Research Institute, 1933–69.

Mani, Lata. "Contentious Traditions." In Sangari and Vaid, *Recasting-Women*, 1989.

Manusmṛti. With Medhātithibhāṣya. Ed. G. N. Jha. 3 vols. Bibliotheca Indica Series 210. Calcutta: Asiatic Society of Bengal, 1932–39.

Mārkaṇḍeya Purāṇa. Bibliotheca Indica Series 29. Calcutta: Asiatic Society of Bengal, 1862.

McDermott, Rachel Fell. "The Western Kālī." In Hawley and Wulff, *Devī*, 1996.

McGee, Mary. "Desired Fruits: Motive and Intention in the Votive Rites of Hindu Women." In Leslie, *Roles and Rituals*, 1991.

O'Hanlon, Rosalind. "Issues of Widowhood." In Sangari and Vaid, *Recasting Women*, 1989.

Olson, Carl, ed. *The Book of the Goddess: Past and Present*. New York: Crossroad, 1985.

Parikh, Indira, and Pulin K. Garg, eds. *Indian Women: An Inner Dialogue*. New Delhi: Sage, 1989.

Rāmāyaṇa. Ed. G. H. Bhatt. Baroda: Oriental Institute, 1960.

Robinson, Sandra P. "Hindu Paradigms of Women: Images and Values." In Haddad and Findlay, *Women, Religion and Social Change*, 1985.

Sangari, Kumkum, and Sudesh Vaid, eds. *Recasting Women: Essays in Colonial History*. New Delhi: Kali for Women, 1989.

Sāradātilakam. Ed. M. M. Pandit Shri Mukunda Jha Bakshi. Varanasi: Kashi Sanskrit Granthamala 107, 1963.

Sen Gupta, Sankar, ed. *Women in Indian Folklore*. Calcutta: Indian Publications, 1969.

Smith, Frederic M. "Indra's Curse, Varuṇa's Noose, and the Suppression of the Woman in the Vedic Srauta Ritual." In Leslie, *Roles and Rituals*, 1991.

Thakur, Abanindranath. *Banglar Vrata*. Calcutta: Visva Bharati Publications, 1956.

Tiwari, Laxmi G. *The Splendour of Worship: Women's Fasts, Rituals, Stories and Art*. New Delhi: Manohar Publications, 1991.

Vidyālaṅkāra, R. *Prāṇatoṣiṇī*. Calcutta: Basumati Sahitya Mandir, 1820.

Zvelebil, K. V. "Tamil Literature." *Handbuch Der Orientalistik*. Zweite Abteilung, Indien, Zweiter Band, Erster Abschnitt. Leiden: E. J. Brill, 1975.

PART TWO

WOMEN AND POWER

The disintegration of the Gupta empire, which at its height held most of India in its sway and attained a high plateau of social, political, and economic stability, initiated a period of turmoil from about the ninth century until the Mughal conquest of India in the fifteenth. In the intervening centuries, waves of invaders from the north—the Scythians, the Huns, the Mongols, and the Afghans—broke the cultural unity of India achieved under the imperial Guptas. The dissolution of central authority forced the predominantly Hindu social ethos to seek survival regionally, which led to the growth of different powerful traditions in religion, social customs, art, and literature, often drawing upon regional folk cultures. In religion, this medieval era in India witnessed a growing plurality, seen in several trends of lasting impact. Because of the attenuation of the state power that had patronized the brahmanical religion, folk religions became firmly established, often by amalgamating with brahmanical principles and practices. Buddhism, the major alternative to Brahminism, also became stronger in certain regions. In response to these developments, Brahminism sought to affirm its identity through an increasingly rigid regimen. Another development was tantra, an esoteric system of spiritual advancement by cultivation of physical and psychic resources that is rooted in the ancient Hindu philosophical concept of *śakti*, the feminine principle of energy. The most influential trend, however, was the rapid spread of bhakti, a spectrum of faiths asserting the inalienable and all-absorbing relationship of love between the human and the divine that became the most popular religious movement of the era. Outside these Hindu belief systems and their derivatives, Islam, too, made its appearance in the later part of the medieval period. These religious developments were to affect the lives of the people of India, including their social customs and art forms, through the succeeding centuries to the present.

Like earlier Indian history, religion provided the ideology that molded the lives of women in the medieval period. Therefore, the majority of the chapters in this part address the religious life of women in this period. Whether in the home, in the community, or in the temple, women were expected to follow and did follow the dictates of religion as laid out by a paternalistic establishment. These times saw the deepening contradiction between the glorification of goddesses as forms of *śakti* and the subordination of mortal females to male rule, an inconsistency inherited from earlier times, as noted by Samjukta Gombrich Gupta in part I and further explored in this part in Madhu Khanna's study of the goddess-woman equation in the *śākta* tantras. The ambivalence inherent in goddess worship and what the ascription of power to a female deity meant to her women votaries are discussed in two complementary studies of the cult of Manasā, the goddess of snakes. Despite the influence of the *śakti* cults, women's lives were undoubtedly coming under increasingly greater constraints. In this era, the growth of women's self-expression became evident, as much in literature and art as in religious practice. An examination of Tamil inscriptions leads Leslie Orr to the double conclusion that women of this era, whether Hindu, Buddhist, or Jain, were, indeed, denied key religious roles as defined in normative religious texts and in popular understanding and that they nevertheless occupied central positions in the actual practice and organization of worship.

Three essays in this part look at the burgeoning of women's imaginative life in music, poetry, and philosophy, as attested by the wealth of women's writings and the artistic traditions set by them. Nancy Martin-Kershaw argues that the conflicting life stories of Mirābāi, the Rajput princess poet-saint whose songs still form the core of Hindu devotional music, show how she transcended her role of good wife to achieve a personal identity by her resolute pursuit of spiritual freedom. Nabaneeta Dev Sen's essay on the sixteenth century Bengali woman poet Candrāvati, ignored in conventional histories of literature, not only affirms her imaginative originality in rewriting the epic *Rāmāyaṇa* from a woman's point of view but also uncovers her sustained demand for justice for women and the feeling of sisterhood that can vindicate their rights. The breadth of women's spiritual quest and its poetic expression is the subject of Eleanor Zelliot's survey of the women "sant" (i.e., holy) poets of Maharashtra, who, she points out, advanced the creed of every individual's capacity for the love of god against the false contraints of caste and gender and who, she further demonstrates, gained at least some limited parity as "sants" in their male-dominated world.

The medieval age, then, was a contradictory era in which the tightening grip of social restraints on women was counterbalanced by the sustained efforts of women to find their own places in the world of the spirit and the imagination, which they often self-consciously valorize over the social. A very different but equally persuasive portrayal of women's initiative appears in the alien world of politics in Mriducchanda Palit's study of women of the Mughal dynasty. Granted no position of public power by formal social dispensation, a succession of these women nonetheless became major power brokers and influenced both policy and government; at the same time, this chapter recognizes the irony that the often superior political wisdom of the women did not lessen the fragility of their positions which depended entirely upon the goodwill of their domineering menfolk.

These studies in no way claim that in medieval India women played any but the most definitely subordinate roles in private and public life. Then again, there does seem to be reason to see the founding of a still inchoate but accelerating women's culture that was responding in new ways to the captivity that was women's man-made lot.

MADHU KHANNA

The Goddess-Women Equation in *Śākta* Tantras

Women have been kind to religion, but religion has not been favorable to them. Feminist critiques of classical Hinduism unequivocally assert that Hinduism betrayed women. Study of the early scriptures, the Vedas, amply proves that women could not become priestesses, run religious institutions, or have direct access to spiritual liberation. These criticisms are often framed in the context of the great divide between the exalted image of the divine feminine and her inferior status on the social plane.

Several myths and legends illustrate the idealizations for women. The characterizations of the two—epic heroine and the goddess, Sītā and Pārvatī—provide exemplary role models for women. Sītā in the *Rāmāyaṇa* embodies the ideal Hindu wife who forsakes all the luxuries of life to live with her husband in exile for fourteen years. She is abducted by Rāvaṇa and held captive in a grove, where she spends her days worshiping and waiting for Rāma to rescue her. Finally, she is made to undergo *agni-parīkṣā* (fire ordeal), a test to prove her fidelity. When she can bear no more, she entreats mother earth to take her back into her womb. The earth cracks and swallows Sītā into her womb. The ideal woman is selfless and has no desire of her own. She is only a passive instrument of others. Another central character is the goddess Pārvatī, whose only aim in life was to win Śiva as her husband. To achieve this end, she performs fierce austerities for sixty thousand years. Next, she desires sons, lives happily with her husband, and spends a life of devotion and self-sacrifice. The suffering heroines of the Hindu epics are celebrated for their wifely self-effacing virtues, and young girls are traditionally taught to emulate the exemplary traits of these two heroines. The portrayals of Sītā and Pārvatī are supported by the theology of subordination of the feminine, which expounds the notion of male superiority over the female. In the social cosmos, this view amounts to the sovereign authority of men as fathers and husbands over women. Alongside the role-model legends is a vast body of literature dealing with *strī-dharma*, or the normative dharma, outlining the conduct and postures of good and evil to be followed by Hindu women, reinforced in the *dharmaśāstras* and the *smṛti* literature. The *Manusmṛti* or the Laws of Manu, for example, which were compiled from the second century C.E., expound the Brahminic attitudes on caste, theology, and law. The Laws of Manu laid the foundation of their social, legal, and moral code and introduced several innovations that concerned women. It eulogized the eternal nature of *dhārmic* marriage and introduced a husband-deifying ideology, according to which the spouse must be worshiped as a god by a faithful wife. *Manusmṛti* was also instrumental in abolishing female property rights and prohibiting widow remarriage. Girls were disqualified from performing *śrāddha* rituals in favor of their fathers. Marital restrictions placed on women decreased their authority considerably and introduced an era of sexual double standards that perpetuated the theology of subordination and weakened the autonomy of women.

The bulk of myths linked to Sītā and Pārvatī give us only one paradigm of the goddess-women equation. The sources provide but one perspective in the continuum of history. Another viewpoint on the ideal feminine and the corresponding images of women come from the *Śākta* Tantras. Outside mainstream Hinduism, such as some forms of Tantra, several traditions attempted to create a distinct "world of their own" setting beside the patriarchal ethos of brahmanical religion. Moreover, given the diverse and culturally pluralistic environment of India, different interpretations can be applied to images of women. If we follow a diachronic analysis, we find that texts emerging from a different textual milieu present a significant departure from the dominant tradition and that certain key images of the feminine get recast within women's views of the ontology of the feminine. Running alongside these sources is a significant body of material on *Śāktācāra*, rules of conduct followed by the *Śāktas*. The *ācāras* have a much broader frame of reference as they exemplify a reverential attitude toward the women. Note that in the Hindu context there is no such category as an absolute dharma. Even the views of the dominant tradition that appear to be absolute are displaced or transformed by an endless series of expropriations and reappropriations of meaning. We frame our discourse in the context of this very flexible interpretation of gender dharma.

This chapter then locates itself in the *Śākta* Tantras and addresses the relationship between the idealized image of the feminine, the Great Goddess of the *Śāktas*, conceived to be the primal energy of the cosmos, and secular women on the human plane. The chapter explores women's attempts to promote a positive and constructive alternative to the "sexist" image of the feminine of the past. The first section of the chapter summarizes the "reconstruction" of the feminine principle in the *Śākta* worldview; the second section traces the form in which the goddess-women equation is expressed.

References abound on *Śākta* attitudes toward women, sexuality, body and senses, and religious roles. It is generally held that women are mere passive copartners who are "used" as instruments by men to promote their religious ends. This generic view has gone unquestioned. Few attempts have been made to identify areas within *Śākta* Tantra that have a positive value for women. Unfortunately, much of the debate in the context of women and Tantra has centered on women's roles in sex-yogic ritual, whereas the role of women has to be viewed in the context of the larger issues of *Śāktācāra*, which in some areas may alter our perception of the tenuous relationship of *dharma* and gender in Hindu thought.

The Goddess in *Śākta* Tantras

The goddess's flowering took place in the context of the heterodox movement within Hinduism called Tantra. Tantra embodied a critical and controversial attitude toward women, sexuality, their relationships with their bodies and senses, social classes, and traditional notions of purity and impurity. The emergence of *Śākta* Tāntrism was characterized by several distinct features. It gave rise to a scriptural corpus that dealt exclusively with the goddess cult. The textual sources codified and "rewrote" goddess theology and descriptions of her nature, her cosmic functions, and her relation to the male deity. Goddess theology introduced a female pantheon and cosmology. These inventions transfigured the image of goddess icons. To mark their superiority over male gods, the Tantric goddesses are often depicted seated, standing, or in copulation with their male consorts. Although by 600 C.E. the goddess begins to rival male deities and acquires a distinctive position in her independent cult, with the resurgence of the Tantras (900–1600 C.E.) she has made a sweeping victory and has both "feminized" and energized Hinduism.

Any discussion on the Tantric goddess should begin with the goddess Durgā, whose mythology has been discussed in the *Devī-Māhātmya*. According to Coburn, "the *Devī-Māhātmya* must be judged the classic text of Hindu goddess worship, and one of the major religious documents produced in the subcontinent. Its conception of the Devī as singular and unique *Śakti* makes it intelligible to most monastic Tantric tradition."[1] The text is sprinkled throughout with Tāntric elements. The most celebrated story of the goddess is recounted in a myth that centers on the conflict between the gods and demons. It describes in detail the defeat of Mahiṣa, a demon who had earned a boon that he would be invincible to all beings save a woman. Mahiṣa became so powerful that he defeated the gods and drove them out of their celestial paradise. Angry and powerless, the gods emitted a flood of energy. A radiant substance spewed forth like streams of flames, which combined into a cloud that grew larger and larger until it congealed into a body of a woman. The divine woman, with parts formed by the gods, was given weapons and a lion vehicle. She was created to contain the *śakti* of the cosmos and so had an edge over the gods to delude and defeat the demons. The *Śākta* imprint of the text is obvious from the myth of the origin of the goddess. The gods empowered her with their potency and invested the most difficult task of restoring the balance of the cosmos to a woman. The compilers of the text have adapted the narrative to accommodate the all-pervasive feminine principle in mythic context. Through the narrative, the text reverses the role of the Hindu woman and violates the model ascribed to her. Quite contrary to the model set out for women, to be submissive and subordinate to males, Durgā holds forth her own and needs none to support or empower her. She is not portrayed in a domestic context, nor is her beauty exploited to win a husband. As a battle queen, she is shown playing a "male" role and assumes an independent and autonomous status. In one episode, the demon Mahiṣa, seeking Durgā's love, sends his emissary to her. He reminds her of her unprotected status.[2] Rather than complying with his endearing proposal, Durgā challenges him and tells him that she will marry the one who defeats her in battle. Throughout the encounter, she remains unperturbed and sees through the "male" game.

The legend describes in great detail the fierce battle that ensues with the demon. Durgā defeats the demons one by one. When the encounter with her adversary becomes uncontrollable, she splits into her most terrible form as Kālī. She also creates innumerable sister helpers who assist her in battle. On the battlefield, the emaciated Kālī, wide-mouthed with a red, lolling tongue, destroys the army of demons not with her weapons but by devouring them. Laughing terrifyingly, she "flung the elephants into her mouth," crunched horses and chariots with her teeth, crushed others with her feet, and licked the blood from the battlefield until the demons were destroyed.

In the closing scene, the gods acclaim her as the highest principle of the cosmos, as "the power of creation; preservation and destruction, the ground of Being." The goddess herself explains that her function is to "intervene" like an *avatāra*, an incarnation, and to restore the balance of the cosmos. In the *Devī-Māhātmya*, Durgā's cosmic role is recast through her myth. Although all the goddesses of the Hindu pantheon embody the *śakti* of the male gods, rarely do they manifest their power so openly and powerfully. They are partial *śaktis*. In contrast, Durgā's characterization contains the full blossoming of the *śakti* concept in its totality.

Another figure of great significance who claims an exclusive status in the *Śākta* Tantras is the goddess Tripurāsundarī. Widely known as Lalitā, Kāmeśvarī, Ṣoḍaśī, Rājarājeśvarī, Śrīvidyā (after her esoteric, fifteen-syllable mantra), or simply Tripurā, she is one of the most sublime personifications of the goddess. A unique feature of the goddess is that she is worshiped in an iconic symbol, the *Śrīcakra*, which is composed of nine interlacing triangles, two rings of lotus petals, and a square, centered around a *bindu*. The *Śrīcakra* is the goddess in form as the fullness of creation. It embodies the most sophisticated theology of the goddess and describes the two dynamic flows of the cosmos—emanation and involution—explained in her theology. The philosophical addition of Tripurāsundarī is traced to the *Pratyabhijñā*-based *Trika* school of the Kashmirian *āgamas*.

The essence and the character of the goddess are expressed in the triple nature of her name. All-pervasive and all-inclusive, she presides over the categories of the cosmos recognized as a triad. Her triadic nature has been interpreted by Bhāskararāya: "There are three gods, three Vedas, three fires, three energies, three notes, three worlds, three abodes, three lotuses, three categories of Brahman and three letters of mantra. Whatever in this world is three fold, as the three objects of human desire, O goddess, your name is in accordance with all these."[3]

The sophisticated ontology of the *Śaivādvaitavāda* of Kashmir is absorbed in the feminine theology of the Tripurā cult. The theology of the goddess defines her cosmic role and function and her relation to Śiva, her consort, and to the objective world. These sources represent one of the most sophisticated models of *Śākta* tantra. In the worldview of Tripurās the universe is composed of the union of two principles: *Parama Śiva* and *Vimarśa Śakti*. Śiva identified as pure consciousness is the all-inclusive transcendent essence; *Śakti* or primal energy as his vibrant, creative power is personified as the great goddess, his consort. These two principles are the ultimate cause of creation; they are distinguished in all composite things but are in essence one. Thus, all the polarities of life—such as body and mind-soul, subject and object, truth and falsehood, inertia and activity, light and dark, male and female, purity and impurity—can be subsumed under these two principles. The most fundamental teaching of this school is that the entire universe is composed of these two opposite but complementary categories: male and female principles. From the minute atom to the galaxy, everything has an androgynous kernel and is an amalgam of the two. Śiva, the male principle, is the static or inert principle, and Śakti is the dynamic aspect of creation. She is the energetic principle that sustains creation. *Śakti* is the creative power of the cosmos and the prime mover of creation. Without her, nothing can stir or be imbued with life. The potent energy of the goddess empowers her male consort: "Śiva devoid of energy is unable to accomplish anything but he is empowered . . . when he is united with his Śakti."[4] Several sources reiterate that the power and strength of the holy trinity come from the goddess alone. Before her presence, the might of the male deities is humbled: "The rumour goes that Brahmā is the creator, Viṣṇu is the Preserver, and Maheśvara is the Destroyer! Is this true? O Goddess, through Thy force, that we create, preserve and destroy."[5]

Although the entire universe is sustained by the divine bounty of Śiva and Śakti, the Great Goddess has claimed greater recognition in the Tantras. This great Śakti is represented as goddess Durgā, Kālī, Tripurāsundarī, Cāmuṇḍā, Bhairavī, and the goddess Kuṇḍalinī, who dwells in the subtle body of the adept.

If we follow her cosmic role, we find that the *Śākta* goddess is no longer idealized as merely a wife of the male god but is conceived of as his creator. She is the transforming power of creation and in that cosmic role, appropriates the powers and attributes of the holy trinity.[6] What is noteworthy is that the goddess not only contains the functions of the trinity within her but also transcends them.

In the *Śākta* Tantras, the goddess reclaims her supremacy by combining polymorphous traits in her characterization. The comely, husband-obeying figure of earlier periods is replaced by a powerful autonomous personification. In the Tantras, the goddess combines the dynamic polarity of contrasting traits: benign and terrific, erotic and demure, motherly and virginal, saintly and heroic, ferociously powerful yet calm and silent:

> At the time of giving birth she is a mother,
> at the time of worship, she is a divinity,
> at the time of union, she is a consort,
> and at the time of death she is Kalikā herself.[7]

The goddess is re-created to accommodate contrasting traits and is conceived of as an apocalyptic fusion of benign (*saumya*) and terrific (*raudra*) qualities. These two traits are well represented in the mythology of Durgā. Durgā is propitiated as a protector and preserver of the cosmos when she assumes a peace-loving, benign form as mother of the universe, bestowing beneficence, compassion, and mercy. Her auspicious form grants boon and fortune. In this role, she embodies the perfection of human qualities. Although this is the most sublime of her personifications, she also veils another identity of guarding and protecting the cosmos from antidivine forces. She is approached by the gods at an hour of cosmic crisis, when the demons are intent on disturbing the stability of the world. In her destructive role as a demon slayer and a battle queen, her benign features are transfigured into fierce ones. In the legend of the *Devī-Māhātmya*, when the confrontation with the demon army becomes uncontrollable, the goddess creates her terrible aspect in Kālī and assumes a frightful visage. The golden-complexioned, three-eyed goddess is instantly transformed into a dreadful and ferocious goddess, Kālī, whose complexion is black as ink. In contrast to the radiant and comely Durgā, Kālī is emaciated, with sunken eyes, a lean body, and a lolling tongue. She stands in the battlefield as an ultimate image of fury and a condensation of the power of annihilation. As an apocalyptic fusion of dynamic polarities, the goddess embodies the fullness of complementary categories of the cosmos: of life and creation and of death and destruction. The terrifying forms of the goddess are portrayed very vividly in her myths, but this portrayal can be understood and expressed in purely abstract and philosophical terms. Some goddesses, like Tripurāsundarī, assume a creative and destructive role, but the destructive role is not overtly imminent in a terrible manifestation and, instead, latent in her cosmic function.

Beyond these extreme all-embracing embodiments, the goddess has been portrayed as an omniscient and omnipotent deity transcending limitations of space and time (*deśakālānavacchinna*), as partless (*niṣkala*) and qualityless (*nirguṇa*). In this highest state (*parā*), she is looked on as an ungendered deity, transcending the distinctions of empiric existence. We may then summarize that in the *Śākta* Tantras, epiphany is never a single creation but contains a total, all-inclusive vision of the whole. In this total vision, there is no room for fragmentation, and her association with her physical counterpart, the real woman on earth, is conceived to be *actual*.

The Goddess-Women Equation

One of the most interesting features of *Śākta* Tantra is that women share with the goddess a continuity of being. All women, irrespective of their caste, creed, age, status, or personal accomplishment, are regarded as the physical incarnation of *Śakti*, the divine cosmic energy, the Great Goddess. All women at birth are the bearers of an intrinsic *Śakti*. This *Śakti*hood is not extrinsic to their female experience as something to be acquired from the outside of their own selfhood, but a spark that inheres naturally as a part of their being at birth. For this reason, respectful sayings and tributes are paid to women exalting their *Śakti*hood and their inseparable connection with the divine counterpart in the goddess. Thus, the women-goddess equation is echoed throughout the *Śākta* texts:

> Every woman in this world is, indeed, my [human] form.[8]

> All women are Thee, and all men are Myself, O beloved.
> Merely by knowing this, the devotee attains spiritual powers.[9]

> Every woman is born into the family [*Kula*] of the Great Mother.[10]

Śākta Tantras do not make any gender evaluations in that they do not consider that women are subordinate to men. They claim that at birth all women, of all cultures, naturally assume the power and divinity of cosmic energy and that they are to be looked on as the goddess's physical counterpart on earth. An inseparable body unites the physical women with the cosmic as they both reflect one another.

The *Tripurārṇava* Tantra says, "Even outside the sacred circle, all women are born of thy parts"[11] because "it is the great goddess alone who having assumed the form of the physical women created this world."[12] It is for this reason that a volume of hymns in praise exalt the nature and attributes of women. Thus, we read in the *Śaktisamāgama Tantra*:

> Woman is the creator of the universe
> The universe is her form:
> Woman is the foundation of the world,
> She is the true form of the body,
> Whatever form she takes
> is the superior form.
> In woman is the form of all things,
> of all that lives and moves in the world.
> There is no jewel rarer than woman,
> There is not, nor has been, nor will be;
> There is no kingdom, no wealth,
> to be compared with a woman;
> There is not, nor has been, nor will be,
> any holy place like unto a woman.
> There is not, nor has been, nor will be,
> any holy yoga to compare with woman,
> no mystical formula nor asceticism to
> match a woman.
> There are not, nor has been, nor will be
> any riches more valuable than her.[13]

The uniqueness of Tantra lay in that the elaborate praises exalting women are not empty of content. A genuine and sincere attempt is made in the Tantras to develop a code of ethics and rules of conduct, which are entirely in favor of women. These prowoman codes are described in chapters on *Kuladharma*, the rules for *Śākta Tāntrikas* who follow the *kula* path, and passages dealing exclusively with the norms of ethics for goddess worshipers (*Śāktācāra*). The true *Śākta* devotee has to honor all women and look upon them with great reverence. Some examples from the sources show the sensitivity, and respect accorded to women: "Whenever he observes a group of women, the devotee should bow down with respect."[14] "If by mere chance the gaze of the devotee falls on a woman, he should imagine in his contemplation that he is performing her worship."[15] "Women are not to be censured or angered."[16] The *Tripurārṇava* Tantra says, "Even outside the sacred circle, all women are born of thy parts"[17] because it is the great goddess alone who, having assumed the form of the physical women, created this world.[18]

Tantra also attempted to take a strict stand against wife beating and sexual abuse of women. Thus, the *Kulārṇava Tantra* states, "One should not beat a woman even with a flower, even if she is guilty of a hundred misdeeds, one should not mind the faults of women, and should make known only their good points."[19] Men are advised "to desist from hating or hurting women, rather they should honour them in special ways"[20] Men should not be angry at women, "even if they [prove to be] wicked".[21] Extreme sensitivity is shown to women who are socially vulnerable. Even widows, low-caste women, and prostitutes are worthy of respect.[22] The *Parānanda* Tantra equates "a young courtesan with Brahmā."[23]

In *Śākta* circles, all women—be they young maidens or mature women—are addressed as *Mā* or *Devī* or *Vīrā*. This title protects women from being looked on in sexual terms. As it is rightly pointed out, "To call a woman 'mother' is a classic way for an Indian male to deflect a woman's hint at marriage or a courtesan's proposition."[24] What is noteworthy in these texts is that here, for the first time in Hindu religious history, an attempt is made to actualize the divinity of women on the social plane and thus introduce an ethos of equality and reverence for them. In this respect, Tantra stands apart from other orthodox traditions in India, for here we find more than a mere triumph of the divine feminine, as energy of the cosmos. We get a glimpse of prowomen codes for ordinary and secular women who are at par with their male partners.

Body and Senses

The *Śākta* Tantras highly value the body and the senses. The woman's body and her five senses are made into a locus of purity, a view that is radically different from orthodox perceptions, in which a woman's body is safe and pure only when pregnant or barren with age and too old to procreate. Both a woman's body and senses and her latent or manifest spiritual energy are equated with consciousness (*cit*). All the physical processes such as her breath, her physical acts such as her postures and gestures, and her biological processes such as her menstrual cycle and bodily substances are considered to be sacred and manifestations of the goddess. Thus, hair and menstrual flow, traditionally conceived to be impure, unclean, and polluting, are said to be pure, clean, and energy bestowing. To do justice to the Tantric view on the sacredness of the female body, it must be contextualized in relation to the Tantric concept of the divinity of the body. The human body is conceived as a miniature cosmos (*kṣudra brahmāṇḍa*). Behind the corporeal frame is an "etheric" double that manifests subtle form as pulsations of cosmic energy, technically referred to as the *Kuṇḍalinī Śakti*. This *śakti* resides in the divine body (*sukṣma-śarīra*), which symbolically mirrors all the elements and astral planes of the outer universe. Whatever forces govern the outer cosmos also govern the inner planes of the body cosmos. It is held in the Tantras that we do not experience our consciousness as external to our bodies. The subtle aspects of consciousness of the unity of creation manifests in, and through, the subtle channels of the body cosmos. Tantra has evolved a very elaborate symbolic code of the *cakras*, energy vortices, and subtle channels, together with a yoga to unfold the mysteries of creation. In addition, the *Śākta* Tantras also absorbed the traditional knowledge system on the biological basis of a women's biorhythms, which govern her body. Since very early times, it has been accepted that the rays of the full moon regulate the pineal gland to cause ovulation at full moon and menstruation at the new moon in the dark fortnight of the month. Recognition of the empathy between the menstrual cycle and moon phases enhanced the understanding of female sexuality and led to the development of what modern feminists would call lunaception, a natural method of birth control. The menstrual cycle, governed by the moon, also guided the rhythms of daily survival to determine the right time for planting seeds. Perhaps based on these views, it was determined that moon phases are intimately connected to certain parts of the female body. The deity Kāma travels over the woman's body through the entire moon cycle. Consequently, each phase of the moon is equated with certain energy zones of the woman's body in its waxing and waning aspects. The energy points marked zones for contemplation during the sex-yogic ritual.

Tantra accords value to the body and the senses in the service of spiritual liberation, not as a form of sacrifice but as yoga, which refines the senses into the sublime experience of cosmic unity. Rather than degrading the female body, it celebrates the sacredness of a woman's body and her senses in several forms of non-procreative yogic rituals for spiritual liberation.

Cultural attitudes toward the female body and reproductive system are inextricably linked to the attitude toward female sexuality. Although in the abstract a woman is valued for her fertile powers, the attitude toward menstruating women remained oppressive. In orthodox brahmanical tradition, a woman is unclean (*aśuci*), defiled, and impure (*apavitrā*) during menstruation. The idea of menstrual pollution is linked to the symbolic codes of brahmanical religion. The origin of the polluting act is traced to a myth of Indra's slaying of the demon Vṛtra.[25] Vṛtra is a vicious demon of drought, a withholder of the waters of heaven who wields immense power over lightning, mist, hail, storm, and thunder. He is figured as a shoulderless serpent, a dragon like monster whose abode is the rivers, clouds, and celestial water or the bowels of the earth. He is a symbol of danger and loss. Indra wages a war against him with his thunderbolt and slays him. By this act, Indra, the supreme victor, thereby releases the water of plenitude which symbolically denote wealth, prosperity, cows, and progeny. The texts of the *Dharma Śāstra*, borrowing a fragment, weave the story into their myth that describes the reason for women's menstrual flow. In the later version of the myth, Indra is punished for the crime of killing Vṛtra, who has assumed the status of a learned Brahmin. Aware of the heinous crime, he ran helter-skelter for protection and asked the women to take upon themselves the third part of this guilt of Brahminicide. The women agreed to do so, and the guilt of Brahminicide appears every month as menstrual flow:

> For it has been declared in the Veda, "When Indra had slain (Vṛtra) the three-headed son of Tvastṛ, he was seized by Sin, and he considered himself to be tainted with exceedingly great guilt. All beings cried out against him (saying to him), "O Thou slayer of a learned Brāhmaṇa! O thou slayer of a learned Brāhmaṇa!" He ran to the women for protection (and said to them), "Take upon yourselves the third part of my guilt (caused by) the murder of a learned Brāhmaṇa." They answered, "What shall we have (for doing thy wish)?" He replied, "Choose a boon". They said, "Let us obtain offspring (if our husbands approach us) during the proper season, at pleasure let us dwell (with our husbands) until (our children) are born". He answered, "So be it". Then they took upon themselves (the third part of his guilt). That guilt of Brāhmaṇa-murder appears every month as the menstrual flow.[26]

Although menstruation removes the stain of sin inflicted by Vṛtra, it is also a punishment that keeps women subservient to the mechanics of patriarchal manipulations. As Indra frees himself, his guilt is transferred onto womankind, who remain in eternal bondage because of the guilt. It is not surprising, therefore, that the pollution of women during menstruation became a major theme of discourse. A woman during her menstrual courses is compared with a fallen woman who is sinful and corrupt:

> On the very day a lady's menstrual course begins, she assumes the character of a Caṇḍālinī. On the second day [of the menstrual course] she is entitled as a sinful woman. On the third day her character amounts to that of a corrupt woman, and on the fourth day she becomes like an anchorite woman. On that day [i.e., fourth] she gets pure when she has performed her ablutions.[27]

Prescriptions and rules for the modes of the behavior outlined in the brahmanical sources reflect male control of purely feminine functions:

> [During that period] she shall not apply collyrium to her eyes, nor anoint [her body], nor bathe in water; she shall sleep on the ground; she shall not sleep in the day-time, not touch the fire, not make a rope, nor clean her teeth, nor eat meat, nor look at the planets, nor smile, nor busy herself with (household affairs), nor run; she shall drink out of a large vessel, or out of her joined hands, or out of a copper vessel.[28]

Tantra honors both the physical woman of flesh and blood and her energy in bestowing bodily fluids. In direct contrast to the orthodox view, menstrual blood is seen as a natural extension of the body and as a pure substance by the *Śāktas*:

> The menstruation of women
> emanates from her body,
> How can it be impure?
> [It is a substance] through which [the devotee]
> attains the supreme state.[29]
> Feces, urine, menstruation, nails and
> bones—all these are,
> O beloved, considered to be pure by
> the Master of mantras.[30]

Tantra considers the time of menstruation to be suitable for performing the ritual of union. At that time a woman's real sexual energy is at its peak.[31] The menstrual blood consists of ova—energy-containing properties with large amounts of estrogen substance. It has been scientifically validated that "in its idle state in the body, it is the purest form of blood."[32] Therefore, no shame or guilt is attached to the menstruating woman. By contrast, the *Śāktas* celebrate the sacredness of a woman's body and her senses. Her body is the repository of bodily fluids, which are the physical representation of a deity, worth offering to the gods. Throughout the sources, menstrual blood is described in a coded word, such as *puṣpa*, *svāyambhū*, and *kuṇḍagola*.

The brahmanical ideology links menstruation to sin, guilt, murder, punishment, and fear and, by extension, regards a woman's body senses and sexuality as dangerous and threatening. The *Śākta* Tantras challenge the orthodox conception and invert the orthodox values to their advantage. To do justice to the Tantric view on the sacredness of the female body, it is necessary to contextualize it in relation to the Tantric concept of the divinity of the body.

Śakti Pūjā

The affirmation of the women-goddess equation is actualized fully in ritual worship, where women of all ages and social classes receive worship as goddesses. On innumerable occasions, the physical woman is adored as a goddess. There are three important forms. The first is *Kumārī Pūjā*, in which young virgins or chaste, premenstrual girls receive worship. The young girl is represented as a powerful mother goddess. The *Kumārī Pūjā* usually takes place on certain auspicious days dedicated to the goddess. The young girl is made to sit on a special pedestal (*pīṭha*) like the image and offered five or sixteen ritual offerings. After the worship, she gets up and blesses the devotee who has performed the ceremony. Usually, unmarried girls of a Hindu household also go through this worship for a period of nine days during the autumn festival of the goddess Durgā, the *navarātra* festival. For those nine days, they are looked on as incarnations of the weapon-wielding goddess Durgā. After the festival, they are again ordinary mortals.

In the second major form of worship, the *Suvāsinī Pūjā*, married and unmarried women are worshiped by their husbands or *Śākta* devotees as living incarnations of Tripurāsundarī or Lalitā. They receive worship either individually or collectively on certain auspicious occasions. After the image of the goddess has been honored, the power of the goddess is visualized as symbolically transferred to the women, who are designated as *Suvāsinī*. The women incarnated then receive ceremonial worship, are empowered by the goddess, and then, in that mental state, bless the worshiper. The short spell of goddesshood empowers their lives with sacred meaning.

The third type of *Śakti Pūjā*, practiced exclusively by the Left-Hand *Tāntrikas*, takes the form of the sex-yogic ritual of union, observed by only an extreme *kaula* sect. In the *kaula* rite of the five Ms (*pañcamakāra*), offerings of wine, meat, fish, parched grain, and ritualized sex are made to the goddess. In this ritual, the physical woman is looked on as the human incarnation of the goddess on the earthly plane. A very elaborate code of ritual practices has been built into this secret ritual. The main focus of the ritual is to use the senses and the body as an instrument of liberation. The ritual consists of the arousal and sublimation of latent sexual energy by uniting the twin ideal of the enjoyer and renouncer in a *bhogātmakam yoga*, a form of yoga unique to Tantra, centered on the enjoyment of the sublime senses.

These *pūjās* can be performed on girls and women of any caste group. As a matter of fact, the tradition of women's worship in *Śākta* celebration or in the secret circles was an attempt to break the impervious boundaries set by caste-ridden hierarchies. Women from widely separated classes, including low-caste virgins or women from the lowest rung of the social ladder, were included in the worship. These rituals do attempt to rend asunder the rigid norms of social identity.

It is accepted in *Śākta* circles that the goddess power uses her human vehicle for insightful communication before and during the ritual. The holy communication may exist in the form in the form of a blessing. It may appear in a dream or in a code language (*sāṁketika-bhāṣā*). The women who undergo the ritual are said to express the pure truth and, as they say, assume an alternative identity during the worship.

Guruship and Transmission of Traditional Knowledge

Women have the authority to become priestesses and gurus, initiate disciples, run their own respective *āśramas*, and hold positions of power in the religious sphere. The texts claim that women are the purest source of transmission of sacred revelation. Knowledge of the Tantras must be transmitted through *yoginīmukha*, "the lips of the self-realized female *yoginīs* and spiritually accomplished women." The *āgamas* and the Tantras are often cast in the form of a dialogue in which the goddess Pārvatī or Bhairavī assumes the form of a guru or teacher as the source of revelation. It is evident from the list of the masters of several sects and from an impressive range of textual sources that many men received their first inspirations and subsequent initiations from female ascetics or *yoginis*, self-realized female ascetics. It is held that, to be valid as revelation, a doctrine must be revealed from the *yoginī*. The author of *Mahārthamañjarī*[33] has traced how a *yoginī*, who is an invisible transmitter of traditional knowledge and authority, revealed the text to him in a dream. Such *yoginīs* generally appear in a disembodied form, in a dream, or in a state of semitrance.[34] The text of the *Kaulajñāna Nirṇaya* speaks of the *yoginī kaula* sect. This text embodies an orally transmitted tradition by a line of female ascetics who were accomplished (*siddha*) in *kaula sādhanā*. This tradition has its origin in Assam in northeastern India and was popular there. It was transmitted by women who were also designated as *yoginīs* (*Kāmarūpe idaṁ śāstraṁ yoginināṁ gṛhe gṛhe*).[35] We also know that the first recipients of the tantric wisdom in the *krama* sect of Kashmir were the tantric ascetics, who also received the knowledge from the "lips of the *yoginīs*". (*yoginīvaktra sambhūta*). Although not every female aspirant assumes this role, the tradition of female saints in not uncommon. We read of the semidivine legendary heroine Lopāmudrā, who is credited with having started her own lineage and is known as the legendary figure who transmitted the knowledge to her husband, sage Agastya. The divine lineage of female saints also finds a physical counterpart in earthly women, such as Muktakeśinī, a highly accomplished seeress of the *Hadimata sampradāya* of the cult of goddess Tripurāsundarī in the eleventh century, who was regarded as a living guru of this tradition. The Tantras state several times that women have the authority to impart initiation (*dikṣā*). Initiation given by a woman is considered to be more efficacious than initiation given by a man.[36] Initiation by one's mother is considered to be the best form of transmission.[37] This authority is the preserve only of women and not of men: "No rules apply to women, since all women are regarded as gurus; merely by receiving the principal mantra, she assumes the form of a guru. A woman-guru may initiate [others] by reading out the mantra from an authoritative text. Men have no authority to do this; only women are permitted to do so, because they are identical with the supreme deity."[38] Few examples of this tradition have survived in our day. At the advent of this century, Śrī Rāmakṛṣṇa Paramahaṁsa had passed on his spiritual prowess to his wife, Sāradā Devī, who is universally regarded as divine embodiment. In my exploration, I have also come across a *Tāntric yoginī* of a very high caliber. Her Holiness Mādhavī Mā had five male gurus, and they passed their spiritual mantle to her, a woman disciple. She belongs to the *Śākta* tradition and initiates disciples, both men and women of all castes, through *Śaktipath*. She is regarded as a living human icon of goddess Kālī and Tārā. Her prowess spread through many disciplines. She is many things: a guru, a healer, a ritualist, and a divine spiritual personality who has mastered the disciplines of Tantra. This is a dramatic shift for a culture in which women by and large are not empowered to play such roles.

Tantra gives prominence to the female principle and recognizes women's ritual role at each state of *sādhanā*. Men and women share the same metaphysical performative and social space. Several elements of *Śākta* dharma help women take this path. The tradition does not discriminate by caste or gender, as far as the quest of spiritual *sādhanā* is concerned; the householder married with children and unmarried *yoginīs* or female ascetics have access to tāntric practice. The precepts of *Śākta* Tantra are applicable to men and women alike. In some cases, there are fewer restrictions for women than men.

Conclusion

This chapter has given a broad overview of the image of the feminine principle and some prowoman precepts found in the local *dhārmic* codes of the *Śāktas*. These stipulations appear in male-authored texts and were therefore legitimized through the pens of men. We also looked at some ways in which a woman shares unity of being with a goddess in a variety of ritual contexts—as an object of adoration in *Śakti pūjā*, as guru, and as a transmitter of esoteric knowledge. Some radical attitudes of the *Śāktas* about the body and senses and the normative prescriptions on purity and impurity not only subvert and undercut certain dominant brahmanical values but also go to show that the *Śākta* tradition is relatively open and free and speaks directly to women's experience. This is a rare instance of gender-inclusive dharma in Indian religious history.

In contrast to the orthodox view, the vision of the Tantric goddess is supported by a theology of male-female equivalence. Here the male and female are equal and coeval, and the goddess's autonomy is taken for granted as a necessary condition for her survival. The archetype significantly alters our perception of male-female relationships and our view of ourselves in several dimensions: physical-erotic, intellectual, social, and cosmic. The goddess traditions in India—one that portrays goddesses as wives of the masculine deity and another in which the goddess represents the energetic counterpart of the male consort—invite more complete understanding of our personhood and also reveal to us what feminine nature is all about. I make no exclusive claim that the *Śākta* women are not or were not under the influence of the patriarchal structures of Brahmin orthodoxy. What I have explored is that the *Śākta* attitude toward women appears to be relatively more consistent and in harmony with the lofty abstractions of the image of the feminine principle who is both divine and mortal, transcendent and immanent, ideal and real simultaneously. Despite the constraints imposed by orthodoxy, the women who fearlessly trod this path with devotion claimed their rightful positions as teachers, saints, mystics, and accomplished *yoginīs*.

Notes

1. Coburn (1984), p. 6.
2. *Devī-Māhātmya* 5.120ff.
3. *Bhāskararaya, Saubhāgya bhāskara* 2, p. 254.
4. *Nityaṣoḍaśikārṇava* 4.6.
5. *Devībhāgavata Purāna* 34.39–40.
6. *Kālikā Purāṇa*, Book 1, IV.55–61, 64–67.
7. *Mahārthamañjari Parimala*, p. 7.
8. *Durgāsaptaśatī* 6.2
9. *Niruttara Tantra* 6.4
10. *Kulārṇava Tantra* 11.64.
11. *Tripurārṇava Tantra* 14.86.
12. *Niruttara tantra* 2.12a.
13. *Śaktisamagama Tantra*, Chapter 2, 13.43–49.
14. *Tripurārṇava Tantra* 14.80a.
15. *Kālī Tantra*, chap. 8.
16. *Parānanda Sūtra* 16–17.
17. *Tripurārṇava Tantra* 14.86.
18. *Niruttara Tantra* 2.12a.
19. *Kulārṇava Tantra* 7.97–98.
20. *Kaulāvalī Nirṇaya* 16–33.
21. *Tantararāja Tantra* 5.80.
22. *Kaulāvalī Nirṇaya* 21–96
23. *Parānanda Tantra* 16–17.
24. McDaniel (1992), p. 36.
25. *ṚgVeda* 1.32.
26. *Vaśiṣṭha Dharma Sāstra* v.7.
27. *Rati Śastram*, pp. 50–51.
28. *Vaśiṣtha Dharma Śastra* v.6.
29. *Jñānanava Tantra* 22.31.
30. Ibid., 22.26–27.
31. Rawson (1978), p. 88.
32. Dudley (1982), p. 115.
33. *Mahārthamañjari*, p. 191.
34. *Śivasūtra*, p. 4.
35. *Kaulajñāna Nirṇaya*, 22.10.
36. *Śāktānanda Taraṅginī* 2.31a.
37. *Śāktānanda Taraṅginī* 2.31b; *Tripurārṇava Tantra* 1.20a–21.
38. *Tripurārṇava Tantra* 1.196–97.

References

Primary Sources

Devībhāgavata Purāṇa. Ed. B. M. Pandey. Varanasi, [n. p.]963.

Devī Māhātmya (Durgāsaptaśatī). Gorakhpur: Gita Press, n.d.

Durgasaptaśatī. Ed. Rameshwar Bhatta. Bombay: Kshemaraja Krishnadasa, 1972.

Jñānārṇava Tantra. Ed. Ganapatarāya Yadavaraya Natu. Poona: Anandasrama Sanskrit Granthamala 69, 1977.

Kālikā Purāṇa. Ed. Viswanarayanan Shastri. Varanasi: Chowkhamba Sanskrit Series 1972.

Kālī Tantra. Ed. Ramakrishna Shukla. Prayag: Kalyana Mandira Prakashana, 1972.

Kulārṇava Tantra. Ed. Arthur Avalon and Taranath Vidyarnava. London: Tantrika Texts 5, 1917.

Kaulajñāna Nirṇaya. Ed. P. C. Bagchi. Calcutta: Calcutta Sanskrit Series 3,1934.

Kaulāvalī Nirṇaya by Jnānānandanātha. Ed. Arthur Avalon. Calcutta: Tantrika Texts 14, 1907.

Mahārthamañjari. Varanasi: Acharya Krishnanad Sagar, 1985.

Manusmṛti: The Laws of Manu. Tr. G. Buhler. Delhi: Motilal Banarsidass, 1975.

Niruttara Tantra. Ed. Ramakrishna Shukla. Prayag: Kalyana Mandira Prakashana, 1979.

Nityaṣoḍaśīkārṇava. Ed. V. V. Dwivedi. Varanasi, 1968.

Parānanda Tantra. Ed. Ramakrishna Shukla. Prayag: Kalyana Mandira Prakashana, 1977.

Rati Śāstram: or the Hindu System of Sexuality. Tr. Abinash Chandra Ghose. Calcutta, 1921; Delhi: Nag Publishers, 1977.

Śaktisamāgama Tantra. Ed. Binaytosh Bhattacharya. Baroda: Gaekwad Oriental Series 61, 1978.

Śāktānanda Taraṅginī by Brahmanandagiri. Ed. Ram Kumar Rai. Varanasi: Tantra Granthamala Series 19, 1993.

Śāktānandataraṅginī by Brahmanandagiri. Ed. S. P. Upadhyaya. Varanasi: Sampurnanada Visvavidyalayasya Yogaratnagranthamala. 11, 1987.

Tantararāja Tantra by Subhagananda. Ed. Arthur Avalon and Lakshmana Shastri. London: Tantrika Texts 8, 1919.

The Devī Upaniṣad. Ed. and tr. Alain Danielou. Madras: Adyar Library Bulletin 19, parts 1–2, 1995.

Tripurārṇava Tantra. Ed. S. P. Upadhyaya. Varanasi: Sampurnanada Visvavidyalayasya Yogaratnagranthamala. 12, 1992.

Vaśiṣṭha Dharma Śāstra. Tr. G. Buhler. In *The Sacred Books of the East*, vol. 14. Repr. New Delhi, 1984.

Secondary Sources

Coburn, Thomas B. *Devī Māhātmya: The Crystalization of the Goddess Tradition*. New Delhi: Motilal Banarsidass, 1984.

Dudley, Rose Mary J. "She Who Bleeds, Yet Does Not Die." *The Great Goddess, Heresies: A Feminist Publication on Art & Politics*, Issue 5, 1982, pp. 112–16.

Khanna, Madhu. *The Concept and Liturgy of the Śricakra*. D. Phil. thesis, Oxford, 1986.

McDanial, June. "The Embodiment of God Among the Bouls of Bengal." *Journal of Feminist Studies in Religion*, 8, 2, 1992

Mookerjee, Ajit. *Tantra Asana: A Way to Self-Realization*. New York: George Wittenborn, 1971.

Mookerjee, Ajit, and Madhu Khanna. *The Tantric Way*. London: Thames & Hudson, 1977. Repr. 1993.

Rawson, Philip. *The Art of Tantra*. Greenwich, Conn.: New York Graphic Society, (1973); London, 1978.

9

LESLIE ORR

Women's Wealth and Worship

Female Patronage of Hinduism, Jainism, and Buddhism in Medieval Tamilnadu

South Asian scriptural norms—and popular stereotypes—have led us to believe that women in the subcontinent have not had a public presence and that their participation in religious activities has been less important and less "official" than that of men. *Dharmaśāstra* literature, which is widely considered to have shaped the behavior of Hindu women, defines women primarily as wives within the framework of the patrilineal family, represents women's economic capacity and autonomy as severely restricted, and, in part because of her lack of personal resources, regards a woman's religious activity as dependent on the support and permission of her husband. Although dharma literature and sectarian literature, such as the *āgamas*, carefully describe the qualifications and procedures for men to take up the roles of sacrificer, renouncer, teacher, or priest, we search in vain in these texts for official sanction for women to occupy such publicly recognized and formally defined religious roles.[1] Jain and Buddhist normative texts, by contrast, do provide means through which women may enter onto the renunciant's path—a path depicted as most conducive to attainment of the highest spiritual goal—and detail the organization of female monastic orders as officially constituted elements in the structure of the religious community as a whole. But these same texts require that Jain and Buddhist nuns be subject to restrictions above and beyond those applying to their male counterparts, that nuns be excluded from certain types of activities in which monks may engage, that nuns show deference to monks, and that the nuns' orders be dependent on and subordinate to the authority of male monastic institutions.[2]

These normative texts may, however, be misleading. The images they provide of women's religious lives—as dependent Hindu wives confined to the domestic realm or as marginalized Buddhist and Jain nuns—need to be compared with historical evidence that reveals something of the actuality of women's religious activities and roles. We are fortunate in possessing such evidence for medieval South India in the form of inscriptions. This evidence is especially relevant to the issue at hand, inasmuch as these inscriptions were designed to be public and permanent documents and were sanctioned by local religious authorities. Thus, they tell us a good deal about the character of "official" religion. In this chapter, I investigate the activities of women in medieval Tamilnadu as supporters of Hindu, Jain, and Buddhist institutions and practices, based on an examination of the Tamil inscriptions between C.E. 700 and 1700 that record their gifts. The evidence of these inscriptions challenges the idea that women conformed to scriptural norms and were therefore outside the mainstream of public religious life. The inscriptional evidence also raises questions about the extent to which the normative texts are capable of providing us with a complete or accurate view of how religious life was actually organized in a particular time and place, in terms of the definition of central religious values and practices.

Because I propose to consider activities related to three different religious traditions—Hinduism, Jainism, and Buddhism—it is first necessary to describe the nature of the inscriptional evidence available to us in each case. Brahmanical, Jain, and Buddhist ideas and institutions have coexisted and interacted in Tamilnadu since before the beginning of the first millennium. In this milieu, the three religious traditions developed certain distinctively "Tamil" features and appear to have shared, in many ways, a common religious culture.[3] In the course of the last thousand years or so, however, the history of each of the three traditions has had a different character, and the material evidence associated with each has been preserved in a different manner. The most abundant material remains can be considered to belong to the Hindu tradition, and the vast majority of the twenty thousand Tamil inscriptions that have been found are associated with Hindu institutions.[4] One of the reasons for this is that many of the temples dedicated to Śiva and Viṣṇu that were important centers of religious life in medieval times continue in use. These temples have been renovated and expanded, and frequently considerable care has been taken to ensure that the inscriptions on the temple walls were recopied or preserved. Although a few older Jain temples in Tamilnadu are still active, many medieval Jain centers fell into disuse, particularly after the thirteenth century, when the number of supporters of Jainism seems to have declined and the Jain population became concentrated in the northern part of Tamilnadu. As a result, many of the stones bearing records of Jain patronage and worship in the medieval period were destroyed or displaced. Many of the Jain inscriptions that remain are engraved below images of Tīrthaṅkaras and deities that were sculpted on the rock faces of remote hillsides; most evidence of Jainism's presence in the villages and towns of medieval Tamilnadu has been erased. The situation is similar but worse for Buddhism, which appears to have survived in Tamilnadu until about the sixteenth century and subsequently disappeared. There are Buddhist texts in Tamil and Buddhist images fashioned in the Tamil style—but, surprisingly, scarcely a single Buddhist shrine or monastery has been thus far identified or unearthed in Tamilnadu.[5] There are no Buddhist inscriptions in situ or even on stray stones that may have been dislodged or removed from Buddhist structures. The only Buddhist inscriptions we have are those engraved on images of the Buddha.

In the three tables of Hindu, Jain, and Buddhist inscriptions, I show the extent to which women and men are represented as donors in the inscriptions of each of the three traditions. The available information is handled differently in each case. Because of the overwhelmingly large quantity of Hindu inscriptional data, I have surveyed only those inscriptions in eight small study areas in various parts of Tamilnadu to generate the figures in table 9.1.[6] Even within these limits, this study involved examination of 2,990 inscriptions. For the much smaller corpus of Jain inscriptions, I attempted to examine all available inscriptions, which amounted to 397 (table 9.2). The still smaller group of Buddhist inscriptions discussed in this chapter was gleaned from T. N. Ramachandran's *The Nāgapaṭṭiṇam and Other Buddhist Bronzes in the Madras Museum*, which catalogues the bronze Buddhist images whose provenance appears to be Tamilnadu (most are a part of the massive trove of Nāgapaṭṭiṇam, in Tanjavur district) and that are today housed in museums in Madras and elsewhere.[7] Of the 277 images Ramachandran described, most of which represent Gautama Buddha, 85 are inscribed (table 9.3).

In the case of each of the three bodies of inscriptional evidence, the vast majority of records describe a religious gift, and the vast majority of religious gifts were made in support of worship. In all three of the religious traditions, women are well represented as donors. In the eight study-areas, 326 Hindu inscriptions refer to women as donors, a figure that is 14.3% of gift-recording inscriptions on which it is possible to discern the identity of the donor (see table 9.1). Hindu inscriptions mention men as donors in 80.5% of these inscriptions and corporate groups, such as "assemblies" (*sabhaiyār*) or "townspeople" (*nakarattār*), in 5.2%. The proportional figures for Jain inscriptions are very similar: forty-four inscriptions mention female donors, which means that 16% of the inscriptions with identifiable donors record women's gifts, and the percentages are 81% and 3% for men and corporate groups, respectively (see table 9.2). In the case of the Buddhist inscriptions I examined, women are proportionally represented at even higher levels: women are responsible for 30% of the gifts of images, where we can discern the identity of the donor, and men for the other 70% (see table 9.3).

In certain periods, women are especially prominent as donors. As patrons of Jain institutions and worship, women have a strong presence in the eighth century, at the beginning of the period I am surveying, when a large proportion of the extant Jain records were inscribed. In this century, women are featured in close to a quarter of donative inscriptions. For women who made gifts in support of Hindu temples, the earlier part of the period under review is equally significant: throughout the period of the eighth to the eleventh centuries, women are mentioned in more than 20% of all donative records, and in the tenth century—when a very large number of Hindu inscriptions were made—women figure in a 25% of them. With the small number, uncertain dating, and more localized provenance of the Buddhist inscriptions, we cannot make too much of the fact, but, like the Hindu and Jain inscriptions, the single century in which most inscriptions were made had the highest proportion of female donors. For the Buddhist inscriptions, this peak comes in the thirteenth century, a century when there is not a single reference to a female donor in the Jain inscriptions and when female donors to Hindu institutions seem to be less and less in evidence. But, as I have argued elsewhere,[8] tracking women's "status" through the ages is not a simple matter. What is worth noting in this case is that—within the Hindu, the Jain, or the Buddhist context—whenever there are particularly large numbers of religious gifts, women are prominent as donors.

This finding suggests that women were active participants in mainstream

TABLE 9.1 Hindu Inscriptions by Century and Type of Donor

Donor	8th	9th	10th	11th	12th	13th	14th	15th	16th	17th	?	Total
No donor	11	22	121	108	73	173	57	20	60	14	28	683
Donor = ?	3	6	58	25	17	28	5	5	19	4	7	177
Corporate donor	1 7%	6 7%	36 6%	29 11%	18 6%	31 7%	5 6%	3 4%	4 2%	1 3%	1 3%	135 5.2%
Female religious donor		1	4	2	8	15					3	33
Queen donor	1	1	54	19	4	10			1		1	91
Other female donor	2	17	80	37	34	20	3	2	10		3	208
Total Female	3 21%	19 23%	137 24%	54 20%	46 14%	44 10%	3 4%	2 3%	11 6%		7 18%	326 14.3%
Male religious donor		1	5	4	10	12	2	2	18	11		65
King donor	2	11	14	15	25	61	9	17	38	3	1	196
Other male donor	9	53	393	175	230	312	63	46	123	25	29	1458
Total Male	11 79%	64 78%	412 72%	194 73%	265 82%	383 85%	74 90%	65 93%	178 93%	39 98%	30 79%	1715 80.5%
Total Inscriptions	28	110	748	398	414	651	144	95	271	58	73	2990

The inscriptions in this table are all the published inscriptions, written in Tamil or Sanskrit, that fall into the period under analysis and are found in one of the eight study areas, excluding those I have considered to be "Jain" inscriptions. The eight study areas are Kanchipuram taluk (Chingleput district), Tirukkoyilur taluk (South Arcot district), Chidambaram taluk (South Arcot district), Kumbakonam taluk (Tanjavur district), Tiruchirappalli taluk (Tiruchirappalli district), Kulattur taluk (Tiruchirappalli district–former Pudukkottai State), Madurai and Melur taluks (Madurai district), and Kovilpatti and Ambasamudram taluks (Tirunelveli district). (Taluk and district boundaries are those used by the Archaeological Survey of India and reflect pre-Independence political administration.)

In this table, the row of "no donor" figures refers to inscriptions that are not records of donations or inscriptions in which the intent of the record is not clear. "Donor = ?" refers to inscriptions that record gifts where the identity or sex of the donor is not clear.

The numbers in this table represent inscriptions rather than individuals. Percentages represent the proportion of inscriptions where the identity of the donor is clear (i.e. the "total inscriptions" minus "no donor" and "donor = ?") that belong to a particular category. For example, in the eighth century, 21% (3 of 17) of the inscriptions where the donor's identity is clear refer to a female donor, in the nineth century the figure is 23% (19 of 88), etc. In some cases, a single inscription records the gifts of several types of donors (e.g., a queen and her female attendant, a husband and wife, a male temple servant and a nonreligious man); therefore, the figures in each column add up to more than the total number of inscriptions. In calculating the number and proportion of inscriptions that refer to female (or male) donors, care has been taken to adjust for this multiple representation.

TABLE 9.2 Jain Inscriptions by Century and Type of Donor

Donor	8th	9th	10th	11th	12th	13th	14th	15th	16th	17th	?	Total
No donor	6	15	8	5	6	10		1	11	1	8	71
Donor = ?	5	7	3	3	6	7	1	2	2		8	44
Corporate donor	2 2%	1 2%		1 7%	2 13%	1 5%	1 13%				1 9%	9 3%
Female religious donor	21	3	1									25
Queen donor		1	1	1								3
Other female donor	4	5	3	2	1		1					16
Total Female	25 23%	9 16%	5 17%	3 21%	1 6%		1 13%					44 16%
Male religious donor	21	25	6	2		2			1	1	1	59
King donor	1	1				2		1	6			11
Other male donor	58	21	18	8	13	17	6	2	4	3	9	159
Total Male	80 75%	47 82%	24 83%	10 71%	13 81%	21 95%	6 75%	3 100%	11 100%	4 100%	10 91%	229 81%
Total Inscriptions	118	79	40	22	28	39	9	6	24	5	27	397

The inscriptions in this table are a subset of those listed in A. Ekambaranathan and C. K. Sivaprakasam's *Jaina Inscriptions in Tamilnadu* (Madras: Research Foundation for Jainology, 1987), including only those inscriptions whose texts have been published and where enough of the text remains to determine the intent of the inscription, inscriptions written in Tamil or Sanskrit that fall into the period under analysis, and those that can, by virtue of their location or content, be considered "Jain" inscriptions. I follow Ekambaranathan and Sivaprakasam in dating these inscriptions.

In this table, the row of "no donor" figures refers to inscriptions that are not records of donations. "Donor = ?" refers to inscriptions that record gifts where the identity or sex of the donor is not clear.

The numbers in this table represent inscriptions rather than individuals. Percentages represent the proportion of inscriptions where the identity of the donor is clear (i.e. the "total inscriptions" minus "no donor" and "donor = ?") that belong to a particular category. For example, in the eighth century, 2% (2 of 107) of the inscriptions where the donor's identity is clear refer to corporate donors, 23% (25 of 107) refer to female donors, and 75% (80 of 107) refer to male donors.

TABLE 9.3 Buddhist Inscriptions by Century and Type of Donor

Donor	8th	9th	10th	11th	12th	13th	14th	15th	16th	17th	?	Total
No donor			1	1	2	7	3	8	1		14	37
Donor = ?					1	1					3	5
Corporate donor												
Female religious donor						1						1
Queen donor												
Other female donor			1			6	1	1			3	12
Total			1			7	1	1			3	13
Female			100%			41%	100%	25%			19%	30%
Male religious donor					1	1						2
King donor												
Other male donor					3	9		3			13	28
Total					4	10		3			13	30
Male					100%	59%		75%			81%	70%
Total Inscriptions			2	1	7	25	4	12	1		33	85

The inscriptions in this table are those reported in T. N. Ramachandran's *The Nāgapaṭṭiṇam and Other Buddhist Bronzes in the Madras Museum* (Madras: Government Press, 1954). All the inscriptions are found on Buddhist images. Dates; based on art historical style and paleography, are those provided by Ramachandran.

In this table, the row of "no donor" figures refers to inscriptions that evidently supply the name of the Buddha on which they are inscribed, rather than the donor. "Donor = ?" refers to inscriptions where the sex of the donor is not clear.

The numbers in this table represent inscriptions rather than individuals. Percentages represent the proportion of inscriptions where the identity of the donor is clear (i.e., the "total inscriptions" minus "no donor" and "donor = ?") that belong to a particular category. For example, in the 10th century, 100% (1 of 1) of the inscriptions where the donor's identity is clear refer to a female donor; for the whole corpus of inscriptions, 30% (13 of 43) of the inscriptions where the donor's identity is clear refer to a female donor.

religious practice and not marginal to public religious life or subordinate to or dependent on male kin or male religious authority. The records of women's gifts almost always refer to them as autonomous agents, capable of acquiring, possessing, and alienating property without permission or interference from others.[9] The manner in which women's gifts are made and recorded, the substance of their gifts, and the object of them find exact parallels in the inscriptions that record the gifts of men. The evidence for female patronage of Hindu institutions and worship in medieval Tamilnadu clearly indicates that women's religious behavior was not constrained by the norms enshrined in the *Dharmaśāstra* texts, in which women's limited rights to property and their dependent religious identity effectively preclude the possibility of this extensive and autonomous gift giving on the part of women.

The lack of fit between scriptural prescriptions and women's activities is also apparent for Jain and Buddhist evidence. In this case, the normative texts provide considerable encouragement for women to offer material support, in the form of alms given to mendicant monks and nuns or more substantial donations; indeed, such charitable giving, or *dāna*, is regarded as an extremely important religious activity. The medieval Tamil inscriptions show that both women and men were, in fact, involved in this activity but they also indicate departures from the normative pattern in several respects. First, although the primary focus of the Jain and Buddhist texts concerned with *dāna* is on patronage of monks and nuns, the gifts recorded by the inscriptions are almost entirely in support of worship, for the most part donation of an image. In the case of the Buddhist evidence, this can be clearly be attributed to the character of the extant inscriptional material, but it is striking that the Jain inscriptional evidence, too, indicates much greater support of devotionalism than of asceticism.[10] This parallels what is found for the Hindu inscriptions. Thus, for all three religious traditions, the inscriptional evidence suggests that shrines, and not monasteries or maths, received patronage and that gods (or Tīrthaṅkaras or Buddhas), and not ascetics or gurus, were receiving offerings. Second, the Jain and Buddhist texts exhort members of the laity to engage in religious giving, while monks and nuns are always depicted as the recipients of *dāna*, but the Tamil inscriptions tell a different story, in which religious patronage is not an exclusively lay activity. The evidence for the involvement of monks and nuns (or "religious" men and women) is stronger for Jainism than for Buddhism, at least in the Tamil country, but it is also more surprising, given the insistence on nonpossession (*aparigraha*) as a central feature of the Jain mendicant life.[11] Finally, the Jain and Buddhist texts (and particularly those in the Digambara tradition, which is likely to have been the dominant form of Jainism in medieval Tamilnadu) impose a series of restrictions on nuns that would seem to have the effect of diminishing their public authority and activity relative to that of their male counterparts[12]—yet Jain and Buddhist "religious women" are present in the medieval Tamil inscriptions and represented as having a status and access to material resources comparable with those of "religious men."

An examination of the various types of donors referred to in the inscriptions will fill out our picture of the actuality of women's participation in religious life and help us to see how it differs from the image projected by normative texts, how it may differ from men's involvement, and how patterns of female patronage to Hindu, Jain, and Buddhist institutions may have taken different shapes. Within each inscriptional corpus, I have classified individual female donors as "religious donors" "queens," or "other female donors" and individual male donors as "religious donors," "kings," or "other male donors."

Among the Buddhist inscriptions, there seem to be three records of gifts made by "religious donors"—people termed, in this case, *ciramana* (= Skt. *Śramana*)—two men and a woman (see table 9.3).[13] All three have donated images of standing Buddhas, which are datable to the twelfth or thirteenth centuries. The Buddhist inscriptions provide no evidence of royal patronage, although, given the small size of this inscriptional corpus, it is unwise to draw very definite conclusions. Apart from the three "religious donors," all of the other sponsors of Buddhist images are "other donors," male or female, and, from the records of their gifts that we can date, the bulk fall in the thirteenth century, when, as we have seen, female donors are well represented. Because of the nature of these Buddhist inscriptions, as very short "labels" engraved on bronze images, we are provided with virtually no information about the donors other than their names. It is interesting to note, however, that the women's names are not distinctively "Buddhist"; in fact, in many cases they are identical to the names of female donors mentioned in Hindu inscriptions—including names of Hindu goddesses (e.g., Umai = Umā, Tukkāi = Durgā)—and a few of the men's names have a more Buddhist flavor (e.g., Cīriputtira = Sāriputra, Tarmmasenan = Dharmasena).

"Religious donors" are more prominent in Jain inscriptions than in Buddhist and Hindu records. Of the 282 Jain inscriptions in which the donor's identity is evident, 25 (9%) record gifts of "religious women" and 59 (21%) record gifts of "religious men." Thus, "religious donors" are mentioned in almost a third of all Jain donative inscriptions, whereas the comparable figures are 7% for Buddhist inscriptions and less than 5% for Hindu inscriptions. I use the rather vague terms "religious women" and "religious men" not only to provide a basis for comparison among the different religious traditions but also because the ways in which the inscriptions identify these people are not in conformity with the terminology and clear-cut definitions of "religious" status (in terms of ordination or initiation, for example) that are presented in the normative texts. For example, Jain "religious women" are not called "nuns" in the Tamil inscriptions, but are referred to as *kurattis* ("teachers," from Skt. *gurus*) or *māṇākkiyār* ("students," related to *Ta. māṇi*, found in the Hindu inscriptional context referring to *brahmacārins*, or male celibate students). For Jain "religious men," we find the parallel terms *kuravar* and *māṇākkan*, as well as *āciriyikar* ("teacher," from Skt. *ācārya*) and terms meaning "ascetic" (e.g., *tapasikal*, *vairāgiyar*).[14] Jain religious women are particularly prominent as donors in the eighth century, when they are mentioned in twenty-one (20%) of all donative inscriptions (see table 9.2). Jain religious men are present in equal numbers in the eighth century and also constitute a very substantial presence among ninth century donors, mentioned in more than 40% of donative inscriptions, whereas the number of female religious donors drops off abruptly after the eighth century. Even though they make a relatively brief appearance, religious women outnumber other types of female donors. We find a few queens—the daughters and wives of Chola rulers—mentioned as patrons in the Jain inscriptions of the ninth to eleventh centuries. There are more references to kings than to queens, but most of the kingly donations were rather late in the medieval period, in the sixteenth century. Among "other female donors" in the Jain inscriptions are women who are identified as daughters or wives, including the wives of chiefs and merchants. After the eleventh century, the Jain inscriptions scarcely mention any female donors, but the numbers of male donors—and the number of Jain inscriptions—also dwindle in the later medieval period.

In the case of the Hindu inscriptions, the classification of "religious donors" includes people of a somewhat different character from those mentioned in Jain or Buddhist inscriptions, who, even if they are not referred to as "nuns" and "monks," appear to be renunciants of some sort. The female patrons of Hindu institutions classed as "religious women" are those whom I term "temple women" and who are frequently referred to as *devadāsīs*.[15] In the medieval Tamil inscriptions, the term used most often for these women is *tevaraṭiyār*, "devotee of god." I include in the category of Hindu "religious women" women referred to by this term (or *tevaṉār makaḷ* "daughter of god") and women who are described in the inscriptions as being "of the temple" or as performing some function in the temple. "Religious men" in the Hindu context are referred to by a different range of terms (some of which, bearing the meanings of "teacher" or "ascetic," overlap with those used for Jain "religious men"), but they, like their female counterparts, are also classed as "religious" by virtue of being "of the temple" or active in various roles (e.g., as priest, drummer, or gardener) in the temple. Vastly more religious men than religious women are mentioned in Hindu inscriptions, but, through the thirteenth century, religious women are at least as numerous as religious men as donors (see table 9.1).[16] Although religious women are not as numerous as other types of female patrons to Hindu institutions, as we saw in the Jain case, Hindu temple women are particularly prominent among female donors in the thirteenth century. In earlier centuries, queens were very much in evidence as donors. In the tenth and eleventh centuries, the wives and daughters of Chola rulers made up more than a third of all female donors, and their gift-giving activity overshadowed that of kings. After this period, male royal patronage became relatively significant only in the thirteenth and subsequent centuries, particularly in the fifteenth and sixteenth centuries in the era of the Vijayanagara and Nayak rulers. The majority of female supporters of Hindu institutions and Hindu worship were neither temple women nor queens, but were "other female donors"—including members of local chiefly families, the wives of landowners and merchants, Brahmin women, and palace women.[17] These "other" women were especially active as donors in the period of the ninth through twelfth centuries.

When we compare the patterns of women's religious patronage revealed in the Hindu, Jain, and Buddhist inscriptions, we see the involvement of a variety of types of women in all three donative contexts. The only category of female donor whose gift giving is directed exclusively toward the support of one or another of the three traditions is the category of "female religious donor": the Hindu temple woman patronizes only Hindu institutions, the Jain religious woman only supports Jain worship, and the only reference to a female *ciramana* that we find is on an image of a Buddha. Apart from this, there is no evidence that particular types of women, or women generally, felt especially drawn to provide support for one or another of these religious traditions.

Not only is the range of types of female donors similar in the case of each of the three traditions but also the kinds of religious activities that women's gifts were designed to support in each case. These activities are, in the great majority of cases, associated with worship—with producing images and building shrines, with bathing and adorning images, with arranging for offerings of lamps, food, and flowers, and with employing service personnel who were charged with preparations for and officiation of worship.[18] This focus on the patronage of worship was characteristic of women of all types—queens or commoners, "religious" or not—and of men, and it was characteristic of donation whether in the Hindu, Jain, or Buddhist context. I have discovered only one difference in donative style and purpose among the three traditions, among different types of donors, or between male and female donors. This difference relates to the expression, in a small proportion of the Hindu and Jain inscriptions, of the wish that the merit generated by the gift be transferred to another.[19]

Among the 208 inscriptions recording gifts by "other female donors" to Hindu institutions, we find such a transfer of merit in 16 cases. In 14 of the 16 cases, the woman specifies that the spiritual benefit arising from her gift be transferred to a relative—6 times to a son, 4 times to her husband, twice to her mother, once to a daughter, and once to a brother. Expressions of the desire to transfer the merit of a gift are not found in inscriptions recording the gifts of temple women or queens to Hindu institutions. We do find such expressions in the case of male donors—although, again, not in the case of Hindu religious men or kings—in 94 of the 1,458 records of the gifts of "other male donors" in support of Hindu worship. But the transfer of merit is, in two-thirds of these cases, directed toward the benefit of nonrelatives, particularly the king and other men.[20] Although male and female patrons of Hindu institutions express the desire to transfer the merit of their gifts with about the same frequency (in the case of 6% to 7% of the donations recorded), we see a striking difference with respect to the beneficiary they name.

The pattern of gifts that support Jainism is, once again, different. Jain religious women and religious men were involved in the transfer of the merit of their gifts in a way that is not seen in their Hindu counterparts. Three of the 59 inscriptions that record gifts made by Jain religious men express the wish that the merit be transferred to another (in two cases, male relatives, including a brother and a nephew). But it is among Jain religious women that the frequency of such expressions is at its highest: 7 of the 25 records of these women's gifts (28%)—transfer the merit of the gift to another. It is also noteworthy that none of the beneficiaries of the merit of Jain religious women's gifts is said to be her relative, and all of the beneficiaries are male. Even if we consider that Jain religious women might have renounced connections with their families (although, as we have just seen, Jain religious men did not), we would expect that they would honor their preceptors—most of whom, according to the inscriptions, were female—by bestowing on them the merit of their donations. Indeed, one of the beneficiaries of the merit of a Jain religious woman's gift is a religious man, who may have been her teacher, but no inscriptions register the transfer of merit to a Jain religious woman. Among the Jain inscriptions recording the gifts of "other female donors," only 1 (of 16) mentions a transfer of merit: a woman, the wife of a shepherd, makes her husband the beneficiary. "Other male donors" to Jain institutions transfer the merit of their gifts at a greater rate (although not as often, proportionately, as Jain religious women). Twenty of the 159 inscriptions that record their gifts express the wish that merit be transferred, and only twice is the recipient of the merit a relative—in both cases, the donor's father.

The notion of the transfer of merit as an aspect of religious donation is shared by patrons of both Jain and Hindu institutions, although we see differences between the two communities of patrons, and within each community, especially in terms of nonreligious women's greater concern, relative to their male counterparts, to bestow merit on their family members. The fact that this notion of merit transfer is found in inscriptions that record the gifts of Jain religious women and men indicates that it is a concept of relevance not only to the "laity" but also to members of religious elites in medieval Tamilnadu. And, even though it is explicitly expressed in only a fraction of the Jain and Hindu inscriptions, this shared notion provides us with an idea of the spiritual significance of religious patronage in general.[21]

In medieval Tamilnadu, making gifts to support worship was an extremely important religious activity. It is the religious activity most in evidence in the official and public inscriptional record, and involves the participation of members of every religious community and virtually every type of person represented in the inscriptional record—shepherds, merchants, landowners, Brahmins, queens and kings, teachers, priests, and ascetics. In many descriptions and interpretations of Indian religious life, gift giving is deprecated as mere merit making, part of the inferior religious path followed by those without the opportunity or attainments that would allow them to pursue a higher spiritual way. I believe that this judgment results in an extremely narrow view of the meaning of actual religious practice and experience and misleads us into thinking of those who engage in gift giving—including women—as figures who, at best, play supporting roles while the central religious drama is enacted by others.

This image and assessment of Indian religious life have taken root for a number of reasons. First, of course, there is the very heavy reliance on textual evidence that has characterized the study of Indian religions. This pattern of scholarship is found even among anthropologists. Louis Dumont, for example, whose understanding of the character of Indian society has been extremely influential, has based his interpretation on the normative texts and concludes, therefore, that the economic realm—the realm within which patronage is of necessity based—can have no religious significance or even social importance.[22] A second and related reason for the devaluation of religious patronage grows out of the complex history of comparative assessments of India and the West, in terms of the polarized categories of the "material" and the "spiritual," which were important in the development of colonial, Indological, and Indian nationalist thought.[23] The emergence in the course of the nineteenth century of the notion that India's cultural genius and identity wore wholly "spiritual" had the effect of focusing attention on the "inner truths" of India's religions. This notion inspired, on one hand, such scholarly productions as Max Weber's analysis of India's religious history and, on the other, reform movements within Hinduism, Jainism, and Buddhism that sought to retrieve an original and authentic religious essence. In both cases, the "other-worldly" life of the renunciant was idealized; the externals of religious practice, such as the worship of images, were deprecated as latter-day accretions; and the relationships, including economic ones, that linked the religious virtuoso to the world were decried as unfortunate, if inevitable, signs of spiritual decline.[24] When we have such ideas as these in the background and turn our gaze on medieval India's religious practice, we are likely to fail to find what we are looking for or will regard what we do see with little appreciation, as we focus on what we perceive as the self-interest of patrons—seeking local fame, personal welfare, and gain—or the manipulation and greed of those who accepted gifts on behalf of the temple, shrine, or monastery.[25]

Gift giving is not ignored in the normative texts, but the transactions described in the earlier texts are almost invariably gifts made to people—to Brahmins and ascetics, monks and nuns—and these gifts always flow from the person of lower religious status toward him (or, very occasionally, her) of superior status. The later textual traditions betray ongoing tensions and adaptations linked to the activity of gift giving as they attempt to resolve such issues as whether a gift to a temple can, in the absence of a recipient, be considered *dāna* in the strict sense, whether a gift whose substance or whose donor is of questionable purity can be accepted, or whether a gift to a recipient who is unworthy can nonetheless be meritorious.[26] In the context of these discussions, two problems seem perennially resistant to resolution: the first is that the most worthy donee is the person who is most loath to accept gifts, and the second is that the greatest benefit is realized by the donor who makes a gift in the spirit of complete relinquishment of benefit. One solution to these problems, which emerges in the literature of all three traditions considered here, as well as in scholarly analyses of religious patronage, centers on the notion of the king as paradigmatic patron. Because it is the dharma, or religious duty, of the king to promote and protect religious institutions, the difficulties associated with self-interest in gift giving are dissolved; meanwhile, such patronage is regarded as appropriate on the part of its beneficiaries, inasmuch as the mutually supportive alliance between king and Brahmin or king and monk can provide a framework within which religious virtues and behaviors are encouraged.[27] But there still seems to be a gap between these systems of ideas about gift giving and the ways that gift giving works in practice. The ideals and meanings related to religious patronage that are found in the normative texts cannot fully explain the religious significance of donative activity in medieval Tamilnadu, where institutions and not individuals are being patronized, where the king does not act as the premier patron, where Jain and Buddhist "religious" figures act not only as recipients but also as donors of gifts, where donors do not entirely relinquish their gifts but as worshipers are able to continue to enjoy the use of what has been given, and where women are prominent as sponsors of worship—a female role about which the normative texts are silent.[28]

Perhaps because of the radical definition of renunciation within the Jain tradition and the apparent incommensurability of Jain ascetic values with the wealth of pious lay Jains, the gift giving of contemporary Jains in western India has recently attracted scholarly attention. In the works of Reynell, Banks, Babb, Cort, and Laidlaw, an effort has been made to examine Jain religious goals and religious meanings from a perspective other than that of the renunciant in order to take seriously the apprehension of laypeople that they are, indeed, "real" Jains, whose religious activities are not inferior to those undertaken by the nun or monk, or necessarily dependent on the presence and authority of members of the mendicant orders.[29] Here we begin to see the possibility of a positive evaluation of the religious significance of gift giving, including the building of temples, the consecration of images, and the sponsorship of worship. Such patronage does not have to be regarded as auxiliary or incidental to more fundamental religious practices and can, indeed, be viewed as embodying the highest Jain values and conducing to the highest spiritual goals, inasmuch as giving *is* renunciation.[30] Furthermore, providing, through the establishment of shrines and images and services, the opportunity for others to reap the benefits of worship surely cannot be regarded as wholly self-serving.[31] These perspectives on the religious meanings of the patronage of worship would seem useful in our efforts to understand the patterns of religious activity that we have discerned in medieval Tamilnadu.

Gift giving, because it is a social transaction or because it takes place within an institutional framework, is almost by definition a public act and one that may be highly ritualized.[32] Certainly the donative activity recorded in the Tamil inscriptions has an extremely public character. At the same time, gift giving can and should also be regarded as a private, individual, and interior religious matter.[33] The public nature of the religious gift does not exhaust its significance or reveal its motive. We have already seen how religious giving can be experienced and considered as an act of renunciation and an act of selflessness. In the context of the religion of devotion of medieval Hinduism, Jainism, and Buddhism, patronage of worship expresses the core religious values of service, honor and reverence, and dedication of oneself. If the past resembles the present, it is likely that private or domestic ritual—about which the inscriptions are silent—had many points of similarity with the worship activities conducted in temples and that similar religious values were embodied in both the public and private spheres. Thus, religious gift giving may be regarded as an activity that bridges the public and the private, the exterior and interior aspects of religious self-expression. It is significant that women were among those who had the ability to participate, through gift giving, not only in private but also in public religious life.

The medieval Tamil inscriptions document one particular field of religious activity; they do not reflect the totality of religious life. They do not give us access to the religion of the household or to the religion of the poor, nor do they tell us very much about the particular activities of ascetics and religious teachers, whose lack of visibility is rather surprising, given their prominence in later accounts of this period and their apparent embodiment of authoritative and traditional religious ideals. But, with respect to the field that the inscriptions do document—a public and "official" territory—they indicate that the major feature of Hindu, Jain, and Buddhist religious life was patronage of worship. If we accept that this donative activity was, indeed, central and that it was, as I have previously argued, religiously meaningful, then it is impossible to view women as marginal.

The normative texts of Hinduism, Jainism, and Buddhism and scholarly understandings of the character of Indian religion, as well as contemporary standards for evaluating the assignment of gender roles, have encouraged us to look for women in particular types of religious roles. For example, in a quest for evidence of women's "official" participation in Hindu religious life, we might try to seek out women who played roles equivalent to those of the renunciant or priest that are authorized for men in the *Dharmasūtras* or the *āgamas*, or we might attempt to discover if there were women who fit into the "official" category of nun, as described in the Jain texts. But when we look at the medieval Tamil inscriptions, we do not find such women; instead, we discover other types of women active in religious life. We do not find female priests, but we do find temple women; we do not find women who seem to be "real" nuns, but we do find female Jain teachers. These women, as they are represented in the inscriptions, bear titles and various other markers of their publicly acknowledged religious status, but they do not necessarily have the same roles as men do. Indeed, if we focus on women's exclusion from the roles that men have played in religious life—roles that loom large in the normative texts and that men, according to the testimony of the inscriptions, have, in fact, filled—we have the strong impression that women had only a marginal religious status.[34]

But marginality depends on how the territory is defined. If, instead of considering the religious activities that Hindu, Jain, and Buddhist "religious women"—and other women in medieval Tamil society—were *not* engaged in, we look at what they actually *were* doing, the picture is completely different. If, instead of seeking evidence for women's participation in what we regard as key religious roles—priest, ascetic, and monk—we are open to seeing that a number of keys can unlock the meanings of religious activity, we will discover that there were many people playing other sorts of roles, people whose significance we are just beginning to appreciate. If we disengage from the assumption that the normative texts, authored by male members of particular religious elite groups, represent what is essential and authoritative for their traditions and for all time, we can begin to draw another type of map that represents religious life as it has existed in real time and space. This map, which has religious patronage at its center, shows that women were far from marginal.

Notes

I am grateful to my colleagues and students in the Department of Religion at Concordia University for their very useful suggestions and insightful comments on an earlier version of this paper. I would also like to thank Ellison Banks Findly for sharing with me her unpublished work, "Women's Wealth and Styles of Giving" (forthcoming), and for discussing with me various issues related to women's religious patronage; these exchanges have been of considerable help to me in working out the ideas presented in this paper.

1. Kane (1930–1962), pp. 2:427–639, 3:543–661; I. Leslie (1989), pp. 41–43, 110–15, 318–21; Olivelle (1993), pp. 184–90; Orr (1994), pp. 107–41; Jamison (1996), pp. 36–38, 116–18, 194–95; Orr, "Women in the Temple" (forthcoming).

2. Deo (1956), Shanta (1985), Jaini (1991), Horner (1975 reprint, 1930), Falk (1980), Orr "Jain and Hindu 'Religious Women' in Early Medieval Tamilnadu" (forthcoming).

3. Most accounts of the history of South Indian religions have stressed the antipathy and conflict between "Hindu" and "heterodox" traditions in the early medieval period. In these accounts, heterodox religion became dominant in Tamilnadu in the fifth and sixth centuries, during a shadowy period known as the "Kalabhra interregnum," but gave way to a Hindu "revival," which ultimately triumphed over Jainism and Buddhism. These accounts seem to be influenced by the negative attitude toward Jains and Buddhists expressed by the Vaiśṇava and Śaiva poet-saints of the sixth to ninth centuries, the Āḻvārs and the Nayanmārs, who are taken to be leaders in the victorious struggle against heterodoxy. But there is little evidence that Hindu and "heterodox" religious ideas and practices were so radically opposed

to one another, that Hindu and "heterodox" forces formed embattled camps, or that Jainism and Buddhism suffered defeat. The fact that the devotional poetry of the Āḷvārs and the Nayanmārs has parallels in the very similar work of contemporary Jain and Buddhist authors demonstrates both the resemblances among the traditions and the survival of heterodox religion. As I will show in this chapter, the material evidence bears similar testimony.

For brief descriptions of the Jain and Buddhist devotional literature in Tamil, see Nagaswamy (1975); Vijayavenugopal (1979), pp. 93–97; and Kandaswamy, (1981). On the works of the Āḷvārs and the Nayanmārs, see, among other works, Hardy (1983) and Peterson (1989).

For other descriptions of the character of Jainism and Buddhism in medieval Tamilnadu and discussions of the interactions of these traditions with Hinduism, refer to Desai (1957); Chakravarti (1974); Rao (1979); Arunachalam (1979); Pillai (1980); Richman (1988); Orr, "Jain Worship in Medieval Tamilnadu" (forthcoming); Orr, "Jain and Hindu 'Religious Women" (forthcoming); Davis, "The Case of the Disappearing Jains: Retelling the Śaiva-Jain Encounter in Medieval South India" (forthcoming); and Peterson, "Śramaṇas against the Tamil Way: Jains and Buddhists in the Hymns of the Tamil Śaiva Saints" (forthcoming); and Monius (1997).

4. The differences among inscriptions I am classifying as "Hindu," "Jain," or "Buddhist" are very minor. In most cases, my classification is based entirely on the context of the inscription—the setting in which it was engraved—because neither the terminology of the inscription, the name of the donor, nor the record's object (the religious activity to be supported and name of the being to be worshiped) is distinctively Hindu, Jain, or Buddhist. I am equally anxious to avoid giving the impression that the chapter's discussion is centered on "Hindu women," "Jain women," and "Buddhist women," inasmuch as I believe that our contemporary understandings of these identities will mislead us in our efforts to comprehend the activities of most of the types of women in medieval Tamilnadu with whom we are concerned. In other words, patronage is not necessarily a marker of sectarian identity, which may be particularly true when sectarian distinctions are as indistinct as the medieval Tamil inscriptions suggest.

5. Tamil-Brāhmī inscriptions dating from the second century B.C.E. to the fourth century C.E., which record the gifts of cave shelters and rock beds to monks, have been found in the far south of Tamilnadu; although there has been scholarly debate about the identity of these monks, they are now generally considered to have been Jains rather than Buddhists (Mahadevan, 1995, pp. 173–88). In the midnineteenth century, there were some remains of a Buddhist "pagoda" at Nagāpaṭṭiṇam, but this structure seems, judging by the style of its construction, to have been sponsored by a non-Indian Buddhist. This site has subsequently yielded a very large number of bronze images but not, evidently, any architectural remains (Ramachandran, 1954, pp. 13–25). There has been more success at the site of Kaveripattinam, where excavations have uncovered a Buddhist monastery and temple that seem to date from the period of about the third to the eighth centuries; no inscriptions are associated with these structures (Soundara Rajan, 1994). Further north, in Kanchipuram, in the vicinity of the Kāmākṣī temple, archaeologists have found a pottery shard inscribed with Brāhmī characters that "may represent the name of a Buddhist monk," some structures "possibly forming part of a Buddhist shrine," "a *stupa*-like structure" dating from the early centuries of the first millenium, and "a small circular structure, perhaps serving as the basement of a votive *stupa*," dating from the period of the fourth to ninth centuries (Lal, 1973, pp. 34–35; Deshpande 1974, pp. 32–33). The identification of these materials as Buddhist seems rather speculative, although we know that Kanchipuram was an important Buddhist center in medieval times and that the Kāmākṣī temple, built in the fourteenth century, contains a huge cache of Buddhist images (Srinivasan, 1960).

6. The eight study areas are—from north to south—Kanchipuram taluk (Chingleput district), Tirukkoyilur taluk (South Arcot district), Chidambaram taluk (South Arcot district), Kumbakonam taluk (Tanjavur district), Tiruchirapalli taluk (Tiruchirappalli district), Kulattur taluk (Tiruchirappalli district–former Pudukkottai State), Madurai and Melur taluks (Madurai district), and Kovilpatti and Ambasamudram taluks (Tirunelveli district). In the case of these "Hindu inscriptions," as also for the Jain and Buddhist ones, I have used only those inscriptions that have been published so that I could refer to the full text of the inscription. I would like to thank Steven Engler, Paul Hammett, Philip Moscovitch, and Michelle Folk for their assistance in my work with the inscriptional material on which this chapter is based.

7. I have relied on Ramachandran's work—although it is more than fifty years old and heavily weighted toward the representation of activities at a single site—because it is still the most comprehensive and systematic documentation of Tamil Buddhist material evidence available. A great deal of further work remains to be done, which would be of considerable value; there are, for example, a large number of Buddhist stone images from Tamilnadu, scattered in museums around the world, that could be catalogued and examined for inscriptions (see Dehejia, 1988, pp. 53–74).

8. Orr, "Women in the Temple, the Palace, and the Family" (forthcoming).

9. In some inscriptions of the twelfth and thirteenth centuries, women's involvement in buying and selling land is mediated by an agent (*mutukaṉ*), but this lack of independence in property transactions is not typical of women's donative activity even in these centuries and virtually absent in other periods (Orr, "Women in the Temple, the Palace, and the Family," forthcoming). There is, in my view, no reason to accept the suggestion of Vijay Nath that the identification in inscriptions (e.g., in Jain records from Mathura) of female donors as wives, mothers, and daughters indicates "the general economic dependence of women on their menfolk, especially in matters of giftmaking" (Nath, 1987). In medieval Tamil inscriptions, both men and women are identified with reference to kin (including female relatives); although these forms of identification may have considerable significance with respect to social and family organization, I do not believe they have much to tell us about economic relationships.

10. In this connection, we can contrast the focus on support of worship that characterizes the Jain inscriptions of medieval Tamilnadu with earlier Tamil inscriptions, which were exclusively concerned with donations to monks (see n. 5) or with medieval Jain inscriptions from neighboring Karnataka, which refer a great deal more frequently to ascetic practices, such as the Jain fast to death, and to the support of Jain ascetics (Orr, "Jain Worship in Medieval Tamilnadu," forthcoming).

11. Although the picture of Buddhism in medieval Tamilnadu is so far very sketchy, there is considerable inscriptional evidence from outside Tamilnadu that Buddhist monks and nuns acted as patrons of religious gifts, as well as recipients (see, e.g., Schopen, 1984, pp. 110–26; Schopen, 1988–89, pp. 153–68; Moscovitch, 1995, pp. 54–67; Singh, 1996, pp. 1–35. Individual ownership on the part of Jain "religious" seems to be a long-standing feature of Tamil Jainism: the early Tamil-Brāhmī inscriptions indicate that the donated dwelling places were transferred into the possession of individual renunciants, who were most likely Jains (see n. 5). We seem not to find evidence for religious giving by Jain monks and nuns outside Tamilnadu (Orr, "Jain and Hindu 'Religious Women,'" forthcoming). In the context of Tamil Jainism, I prefer to use the expressions "religious women" and "religious men"—rather than "nuns" and "monks"—because the inscriptions do not use these latter terms.

12. For the Digambara position on women's (minimal) eligibility for pursuing the path of the true mendicant, see Jaini (1991). Digambara "nuns" are not, in fact, admitted to full ordination. The Śvetāmbaras are much more open to women's participation in the renunciant life; in fact, Śvetāmbara nuns outnumber monks in India today (Laidlaw, 1995, pp. 56–58).

It is Falk (1980) who first argued that the extra restrictions on Buddhist nuns and their subordination to the authority of monks had the effect over time of preventing them from gaining public standing as teachers and of receiving adequate material support, so that the nuns' order in India eventually died out.

13. Of the three inscriptions, the one referring to a female *ciramana* is most definitely indicative of the "religious" status of the donor. Her name is *Ciri* (= Skt. *Śrī*). In the other two inscriptions, the term *ciramana* cannot be so clearly made out, and in one of these two, as well, the sex of the donor is not obviously male.

14. For a more complete description and discussion of the character and activities of Jain religious women and men in medieval Tamilnadu, see Orr, "Jain and Hindu 'Religious Women'" (forthcoming).

15. For details on "religious women" and "religious men" in the Hindu context of medieval Tamilnadu, see Orr (1995), pp. 109–36; Orr (1994); Orr, "Jain and Hindu 'Religious Women'" (forthcoming); Orr, *Donors, Devotees and Daughters of God*.

16. Although the area study whose findings are represented in table 9.1 shows male religious donors as more numerous than female religious donors, this obscures the fact that, *proportionately*, religious women were much more likely to act as donors than were religious men; in an earlier study, I calculated that close to half of the inscriptions referring to Hindu temple women record their activity as donors, but only 2% of those referring to religious men do so (Orr, "Jain and Hindu 'Religious Women,'" forthcoming).

17. Orr, "Women in the Temple, the Palace, and the Family" (forthcoming).

18. Orr, 1995; Orr, "Jain Worship in Medieval Tamilnadu" (forthcoming).

19. I suspect that if we are able in the future to uncover more medieval Tamil Buddhist materials, we will find evidence of the transfer of merit in the Buddhist donative context as well. Outside Tamilnadu, Buddhist inscriptions provide ample documentation of this notion and practice (see, e.g., Schopen, 1984). Like these Buddhist inscriptions, the Tamil Jain inscriptions show us that in practice, actions may be motivated by religious notions whose possibility is not admitted by the normative texts, which hold, for both the Buddhist and the Jain, that a person's karmic condition and spiritual destiny are matters of individual responsibility alone (for the doctrinal Jain position, see Jaini, 1983). In the Tamil inscriptions of the early medieval period, we do not encounter the use of terms (e.g., *puṇya*) explicitly denoting "merit," which are more in evidence in the second half of the period under review; the earlier inscriptions indicate the transfer of merit by stating that a gift was made that was "connected to" (*cārtti*) the recipient of the benefit of the donation. In a few of the inscriptions, it is clear that the recipient of merit is deceased, but this is certainly not the case for all transfers of merit.

20. Of 94 cases of the transfer of merit, male donors named nonrelatives as recipients of the merit in 63 inscriptions (the king in 22 cases, another man in 31 cases, the queen in 4 cases, another woman in 3 cases, a preceptor twice, and a guild once). Of the 31 inscriptions in which relatives were named as recipients by male donors, we find fathers mentioned 12 times, mothers 5 times, sons 5 times, brothers 4 times, "ancestors" twice, an uncle once, a sister once, and a wife once. The differences between the kinds of relatives named by men as beneficiaries and those named by women are rather interesting: for example, women never mention their fathers as recipients of the merit of their gifts, although the father is the relative most frequently named by men, and there are more transfers of merit from wife to husband than vice versa. But given that the numbers of examples of transfers of merit found in the area study are rather small, it is premature to draw any conclusions.

21. The vast majority of medieval Tamil inscriptions that record religious gifts do not indicate a rationale or motivation for the gift. The expression of the wish to transfer the merit of the gift is the most frequently encountered indicator of the significance of the gift

to the donor. Another way in which inscriptions may refer to religious merit is in the context of the formulaic expressions that are on occasion appended to the record of a gift, including imprecations against those who would obstruct the terms of the grant and phrases that describe the merit attaching to donors and to the protectors of endowments. A very small proportion of medieval Tamil inscriptions include such expressions. Apart from these types of references to religious merit, in a dozen or so cases in the corpus of Hindu inscriptions surveyed here a gift is said to have been made as expiation for inadvertently causing someone's death, and in two cases a male donor had made a donation as a thank offering for the birth of a son.

22 "No doubt there is in India today a distinct sphere of activity which may properly be called economic, but it was the British government which made this possible. . . . One can say that just as religion in a way encompasses politics, so politics encompasses economics within itself. The difference is that the politico-economic domain is separated, named, in a subordinate position as against religion, while economics remains undifferentiated within politics. Indeed, one can study kingship in the Hindu texts, even if it receives less careful treatment than priesthood. But if we go one step further and raise the question of the merchant, the normative texts are silent" (Dumont, 1972, pp. 210–11). Dumont goes on to say that, despite his generally negative assessment of Weber's ideas, he approves of Weber's notion of a link, in the Indian context, between mercantile activity and "heresy" and between the emergence of trade and the rise of Jainism and Buddhism. This idea of a dichotomy in the religious culture of the agriculturalist and the merchant, the man tied to the land and the city dweller, conceptualized in terms of the dichotomy of adherence to Hindu or "heterodox" traditions is, in my view, much less useful than might be suggested by its frequent occurrence in scholarship on the history of Indian religions. See Stein (1980) and Reiniche (1985) for the application of this idea in the context of Tamilnadu. It should be clear, even from the brief summary of patronage patterns presented here, that merchant or urban groups were not especially drawn to the patronage of Jainism, nor that those dwelling in villages and engaged with the agrarian economy were exclusively "Hindu" (see also Orr, "Jain Worship in Medieval Tamilnadu," forthcoming).

23. Waghorne (1994), pp. 85–103, 255–62.

24. Ivan Strenski has urged a reassessment of this type of negative view in the case of scholarly analysis of the bureaucratization and "domestication" of the Buddhist *saṅgha* (monastic order) in the course of its development in ancient India. He points to the fact that donations to the *saṅgha* are recirculated in the community in a system of "generalized exchange" and emphasizes the idea that the increase of economic and political interest focused on the *saṅgha* is a natural and normal development, rather than a deviation from Buddhism's "purpose" (Strenski, 1983, pp. 463–77). On Jain attitudes toward the "domestication" of the Jain monastic orders and for an account of some of the reform movements that sought to sever the ties between Jain renunciants and society and property, see Dundas (1987–88), pp. 181–94.

Jonathan Parry outlines the contrast between Indian and Western attitudes toward acquisition of wealth:

> Nothing I have ever heard would suggest that trade is regarded as *intrinsically* bad, or that traders see themselves as confronted by. . . moral peril. . . . In Hinduism it is by no means easy to find parallels for such Biblical notions as the love of money being 'the root of all evil,' or as camels having an easier time getting through needles' eyes than rich men getting to heaven. . . . Hindu thought has elaborated almost every conceivable explanation for suffering and evil. Yet by comparison with our own cultural heritage the striking thing is that [there is] . . . hardly a mention of money and avarice. Indeed the whole thrust of the most characteristically Indian solution to the problem of theodicy—the doctrine of

> *karma*—is that the rich deserve and have earned their good fortune. . . . Far from being an outsider to society, as was the Jew in medieval Christendom, the financier tends rather to be a paragon of religious orthopraxy. (Parry and Bloch, 1989, p. 78; see also Rudner, 1994, pp. 133–35; Laidlaw, 1995, pp. 5–7).

I find Parry's argument quite convincing on this point and would therefore reject Vijay Nath's interpretation of the motivations of donors mentioned in North Indian texts and inscriptions of 600 B.C.E.–300 C.E.:

> There is a preponderance of those who belong to the affluent ruling and mercantile classes. This naturally suggests that it was perhaps a sense of guilt produced by the exploitative nature of their economic pursuits as well as the increasingly impersonal and unscrupulous manner of their social dealings which induced them to make *dāna*. A similar motive may also be discerned in the case of gifts made by members of such professional groups as that of courtesans [and] usurers. (Nath, 1987, p. 31)

25. In Nath's treatment of the motives and causes for religious gift giving, self-interest is declared to be the dominant motive, and this type of motivation is regarded as having grown up in the post-Vedic period in a climate of "a growing spirit of individualism," in contrast to the context of gift giving in the preceding Vedic period, which "would not appear to reflect an overwhelming egotistical concern for oneself" (Nath, 1987, pp. 28–34).

There are many representations of medieval Indian religion that focus on the self-serving nature of the recipients of gifts, from Jain caricatures of portly Buddhist monks to contemporary descriptions of the evolution of Hinduism, which frequently seem to be influenced by Weber's interpretation of religious developments in India. In Kosambi's view, for example, Brahmin priests, in their efforts to incorporate tribal and peasant communities into the Hindu fold, accommodated and preserved a great variety of local traditions, resulting in "an incredible proliferation of senseless ritual." In addition, of the large amount of property controlled by the temple, "most of the cash was locked up in precious images or jewels for the gods; or just pocketed by the priesthood and their parasites" (Kosambi, 1969, pp. 172–73, 196; cf. Weber 1922, reprint1964, pp. 77–79). These ideas have been applied to the specific case of medieval Tamilnadu by several authors. Narayanan and Veluthat consider early medieval temples as centers for the economic domination of Brahmins; in their view, temples were instrumental in establishing a feudal and highly stratified society (Narayanan and Veluthat, 1978, pp. 45–58). Jha maintains that cash donated to temples in the Chola period was converted into unproductive deposits and did not circulate in the economy, and that the terms of land grants to temples tended to oppress the peasantry by increasing taxation (Jha, 1974, pp. 207, 212–13). These interpretations of the character of medieval society and economy in Tamilnadu are not supported by the findings of scholars who have based their studies on the inscriptional evidence and who find that donations to temples resulted in the recirculation of wealth and the development of agricultural, artisanal, and mercantile enterprise (Appadorai, 1936, pp. 274–301; Stein 1960, pp. 163–76; Heitzman, 1985, pp. 227–40).

26. It is beyond the scope of this chapter to review the whole of the vast literature on religious giving in each of the three religious traditions. In the present discussion, I mean by "early" literature the so-called canonical texts of Jainism and Buddhism, which concern themselves especially with the conduct of the renunciant, and, within the Hindu scriptural corpus, late brahmanical, *dharmaśāstra*, and epic literature. The "later" literature includes commentaries and digests based on the texts just mentioned, *purāṇas* and ritual texts such as the *āgamas*, and various forms of narrative and didactic literature. Phyllis Granoff has suggested that Jain literature of the "later" strata presents a more detailed portrayal of the realities of temple patronage than do the Hindu texts, which treat this aspect of religious life only

incidentally (Granoff, "Patrons, Overlords, and Artisans: Some Comments on the Intricacies of Religious Donations in Medieval Jainism," forthcoming).

On the problem of gifts to temples, in the Hindu tradition, see Kane (1930–62), vol. 2, pp. 157, 889, 915–16; and Sontheimer (1964), pp. 45–100. On the "contentiousness" of *dāna* in Jainism, see Laidlaw (1995), pp. 294–301.

27. In the Hindu context, the concept of the king as the premier patron of the temple—and as drawing his legitimacy from his alliance with the Brahmin, sectarian guru, or temple deity—is discussed with reference to Tamilnadu by Appadorai and Breckenridge (1976), pp. 187–211; Dirks (1987); and Reiniche (1985).

28. Among those who have questioned the centrality of royal patronage for the growth of religious institutions are Singh (1996) and Kaimal (1996), pp. 33–66. On Buddhist and Jain mendicants as donors, see n. 11. David Rudner discusses the way in which colonial British legislation, based on the understanding of religious patronage as disinterested "philanthropy," rode roughshod over Indian notions in which private and public interests in gift giving coexisted (Rudner, 1994, pp. 145–47). I contrast the reality of women's donative activity in medieval Tamilnadu with the rather remarkable neglect on the part of the *Āgamic* texts of the notion of women's patronage of worship in "Women of Medieval South India in Hindu Temple Ritual" (1994).

29. Reynell (1991); Banks (1992); Babb (1996); Cort (1991), pp. 391–420; Laidlaw (1995). The contemporary anthropological work on Jains generally stresses a sexual division of labor in which, among the laity, men's primary religious activity is gift giving, whereas women engage more in ascetic activities such as fasting. There is no evidence in medieval Tamil inscriptions of such distinctively gendered religious roles.

30. For instance, Babb discusses "giving as giving up" and proposes that, for lay Jains, gaining merit (through gift giving, for example) is not regarded simply as a route leading toward worldly reward but as a means whereby karma could be "shed," and it is therefore conducive to the highest spiritual goal (Babb, 1996). Laidlaw discusses the generous gift as a form of renunciation (*tyāga*) (Laidlaw, 1995, pp. 314–23). Paul Dundas sees religious gifting by Jains as an extension of the ideal of the frugal and disciplined life and as a religious activity in which the layperson is relatively autonomous because gift giving is not necessarily linked to interaction with ascetics (Dundas, 1992, pp. 168–71).

31. Schopen describes the religious significance of donations made in support of Buddhist worship, on the basis of his analysis of inscriptions of the early first millennium C.E. in India: "The laymen and monks who made these gifts. . . were giving objects of worship, objects which in fact made worship possible. They were, then, really giving to any of their fellow beings who ritually approached those objects both the means and the opportunity to make merit, they were providing for all both the opportunity and the means to further their religious life. . . . The initial gift of the actual object only marked the first moment in the donor's act of giving. . . which in a very concrete sense made each consecutive act of worship possible. It was because the donor's act was continually repeated over time, because it took place again and again long after the donor himself had disappeared, that it was necessary to clearly record the donor's name, the moment of the initial act, and. . . the donor's intentions" (Schopen, 1984, pp. 125–26). I believe that these ideas are extremely important for our understanding of religious gifting in medieval Tamilnadu. The Tamil inscriptions, like the Buddhist inscriptions discussed by Schopen, record gifts whose impact is meant to be felt long after the passing of the donor; indeed, ensuring this continuity is a major purpose of the recording of the gift and the engraving of the record.

32. On the ritual aspects of gift giving and recording the gift in an inscription in medieval Tamilnadu, see Stein (1980), pp. 358–61, and Heitzman (1995), pp. 73–109.

33. I am grateful to have had the opportunity—in discussion, in teaching together,

and in reading her work—to share ideas about the question of public and private spheres of women's religious activity with my colleague Norma Baumel Joseph. Her forthcoming chapter, "Celebrating Women: A Jewish Profile," makes an important theoretical contribution to this issue.

34. Kersenboom, in her treatment of the roles of temple women, goes to some lengths in her effort to demonstrate that the roles of these women were as ritually significant as those of men and that the women occupied a structurally symmetrical position to their male counterparts in temple ritual (Kersenboom, 1987). I think that it is unrealistic to expect to find exact parallels, or even complementarity, between male and female roles in any particular ritual context or religious institution. My own investigation in medieval texts and inscriptions into the representations of women in ritual roles seems to indicate that women's presence and activity in temple ritual were regarded as optional and incidental (Orr, 1994). But, as I try to demonstrate in this chapter, participation in temple ritual is merely one of several types of religious activity to which women, and men, might have access.

References

Appadorai, A. *Economic Conditions in Southern India (1000–1500 A.D.)*. Madras: University of Madras, 1936.

——— and Carol Breckenridge. "The South Indian Temple: Authority, Honour and Redistribution." *Contributions to Indian Sociology* 10, 1976.

Arunachalam, M. *The Kalabhras in the Pandiya Country and Their Impact on the Life and Letters There*. Madras: University of Madras, 1979.

Babb, Lawrence A. *Absent Lord: Ascetics and Kings in a Jain Ritual Culture*. Berkeley: University of California Press, 1996.

Banks, Marcus. *Organizing Jainism in India and England*. Oxford: Clarendon, 1992.

Chakravarti, A. *Jaina Literature in Tamil*. New Delhi: Bharatiya Jnanapitha, 1974.

Cort, John E. "Two Ideals of the *Śvetāmbar Mūrtipūjak* Jain Layman." *Journal of Indian Philosophy* 19, 1991.

Davis, Richard H. "The Case of the Disappearing Jains: Retelling the Śaiva-Jain Encounter in Medieval South India." In John E. Cort, ed. *Open Boundaries: Jain Communities and Cultures in Indian History*. Albany: State University of New York, forthcoming.

Dehejia, Vidya. "The Persistence of Buddhism in Tamilnadu." *Marg* 39/4, 1988.

Deo, S. B. *The History of Jaina Monachism from Inscriptions and Literature*. Poona: Deccan College, 1956.

Desai, Pandurang B. *Jainism in South India*. Sholapur: Jaina Sanskriti Samarshak Sangha, 1957.

Deshpande, M. N. *Indian Archaeology 1970–71: A Review*. New Delhi: Archaeological Survey of India, 1974.

Dirks, Nicholas B. *The Hollow Crown: Ethnohistory of an Indian Kingdom*. Cambridge: Cambridge University Press, 1987.

Dumont, Louis. *Homo Hierarchicus: The Caste System and Its Implications*. London: Paladin, 1972.

Dundas, Paul. "The Tenth Wonder: Domestication and Reform in Medieval Svetambara Jainism." *Indologica Taurinensia* 14, 1987–88.

———. *The Jains*, London: Routledge, 1992.

Ekambaranathan, A., and C. K. Sivaprakasam. *Jaina Inscriptions in Tamilnadu (a Topographical List)*. Madras: Research Foundation for Jainology, 1987.

Epigraphia Indica. Calcutta: Director General, Archaeological Survey of India, 1892–.

Falk, Nancy Auer. "The Case of the Vanishing Nuns: The Fruits of Ambivalence in Ancient

Indian Buddhism." In Nancy Auer Falk and Rita M. Gross, eds. *Unspoken Worlds: Women's Religious Lives in Non-Western Cultures*. San Francisco: Harper and Row, 1980.

Findly, Ellison Banks. "Women's Wealth and Styles of Giving: Perspectives from Buddhist, Jaina, and Mughal Sites." In D. Fairchild Ruggles, ed. *Women, Patronage, and Self-Representation* (forthcoming).

Granoff, Phyllis. "Patrons, Overlords, and Artisans: Some Comments on the Intricacies of Religious Donations in Medieval Jainism." In V. N. Misra, ed. *Sir William Jones Bicentennary of Death Commemoration Volume, Bulletin of the Deccan College Post-Graduate and Research Institute* (forthcoming)

Hardy, Friedhelm. *Viraha-Bhakti: The Early History of Kṛṣṇa Devotion in South India*. Delhi: Oxford University Press, 1983.

Heitzman, James. "Gifts of Power: Temples, Politics and Economy in Medieval South India." Ph.D. dissertation, University of Pennsylvania, 1985.

———. "Networks of Social Control in Early South India." *Journal of Asian and African Studies* 50, 1995.

Horner, I. B. *Women under Primitive Buddhism*. 1930; Reprint, Delhi: Motilal Banarsidass, 1975.

Inscriptions (Texts) of the Pudukkottai State Arranged according to Dynasties. Pudukkottai [state], 1929.

Jaini, Padmanabh S. "Karma and the Problem of Rebirth in Jainism." In Wendy Doniger O'Flaherty, ed. *Karma and Rebirth in Classical Indian Traditions*. Delhi: Motilal Banarsidass, 1983.

———.*Gender and Salvation: Jaina Debates on the Spiritual Liberation of Women*. Berkeley: University of California Press, 1991.

Jamison, Stephanie W. *Sacrificed Wife, Sacrificer's Wife: Women, Ritual, and Hospitality in Ancient India*. New York: Oxford University Press, 1996.

Jha, D. N. "Temples as Landed Magnates in Early Medieval South India (C. A.D. 700–1300)." In *Indian Society: Historical Probings*. New Delhi: People's Publishing House, 1974.

Joseph, Norma Baumel."Celebrating Women: A Jewish Profile." In Diane Edwards and Phyllis Senese, eds., *The Feminization of Ritual*. Victoria, B.C: Centre for Studies in Religion and Society, forthcoming.

Kaimal, Padma. "Early Cola Kings and 'Early Cola Temples': Art and the Evolution of Kingship." *Artibus Asiae* 56/1–2, 1996.

Kandaswamy, S. N. "Jainistic and Buddhistic Literature." In S. V. Subramanian and N. Ghadigachalam, eds., *Literary Heritage of the Tamils*. Madras: International Institute of Tamil Studies, 1981.

Kane, P. V. *History of Dharmaśāstra*. Poona: Bhandarkar Oriental Research Institute, 1930–62.

Karashima, Noboru, et al. *A Concordance of the Names in the Cola Inscriptions* (3 vols.). Madurai: Sarvodaya Ilakkiya Pannai, 1978.

Kersenboom, Saskia C. *Nityasumangali: Devadasi Tradition in South India*. Delhi: Motilal Banarsidass, 1987.

Kosambi, D. D. *Ancient India: A History of Its Culture and Civilization*. New York: Meridian Books, 1969.

Kutantaik Kalvettukkal. Ed. N. Markciyakanti. Madras: Tamil Nadu State Department of Archaeology, 1980.

Laidlaw, James. *Riches and Renunciation: Religion, Economy, and Society among the Jains*. Oxford: Oxford University Press, 1995.

Lal, B. B., ed. *Indian Archaeology 1969–70: A Review*. New Delhi: Archaeological Survey of India, 1973.

Leslie, Julia. *The Perfect Wife: The Orthodox Hindu Woman according to the Strīdharmapaddhati of Tryambakayajvan*. Delhi: Oxford University Press, 1989.

Mahadevan, Iravatham. "From Orality to Literacy: The Case of the Tamil Society." *Studies in History* 11/2, 1995.

Mahalingam, T. V. *A Topographical List of Inscriptions in the Tamil Nadu and Kerala States* (8 vols.). New Delhi: Indian Council of Historical Research, 1985–.

Misra, V. N., ed. *Sir William Jones Bicentennary of Death Commemoration Volume, Bulletin of the Deccan College Post-Graduate and Research Institute* (forthcoming).

Monius, Anne E. "In Search of 'Tamil Buddhism': Language, Literary Culture, and Religious Community in Tamil-Speaking South India." Ph.D. dissertation, Harvard University, 1997.

Moscovitch, Philip. "Buddhist Monasteries Real and Imagined: Monks, Wealth, and Community in Medieval Sri Lanka," *Journal of Religion and Culture* 9, 1995.

Nagaswamy, R. "Jaina Art and Architecture under the Pallavas." In U. P. Shah and M. A. Dhaky, eds., *Aspects of Jaina Art and Architecture*. Ahmedabad: L. D. Institute of Indology, 1975.

Narayanan, M. G. S. and Kesavan Veluthat. "Bhakti Movement in South India." In S. C. Malik, ed., *Indian Movements: Some Aspects of Dissent, Protest and Reform*. Simla: Institute of Advanced Study, 1978

Nath, Vijay. *Dāna: Gift System in Ancient India (c. 600 B.C. –c. A.D. 300): A Socio-Economic Perspective*. New Delhi: Munshiram Manoharlal, 1987.

Olivelle, Patrick. *The Āśrama System: The History and Hermeneutics of a Religious Institution*. New York: Oxford University Press, 1993.

Orr, Lesile C. *Donors, Devotees, and Daughters of God: Temple Women in Medival Tamilnadu*. New York: Oxford University Press, forthcoming.

Orr, Leslie C. "Jain and Hindu 'Religious Women' in Early Medieval Tamilnadu." In John E. Cort, ed., *Open Boundaries: Jain Communities and Cultures in Indian History*. Albany: State University of New York, forthcoming.

———. "Jain Worship in Medieval Tamilnadu." In N. K. Wagle and Olle Qvarnstrom, eds. *Proceedings of the International Conference on Approaches to Jaina Studies: Philosophy, Logic, Rituals and Symbols*. Toronto: Centre for South Asian Studies, University of Toronto, forthcoming.

———. "The *Vaiṣṇava* Community at Śrīraṅgam: The Testimony of the Early Medieval Inscriptions." *The Journal of Vaiṣṇava Studies* 3/3, 1995.

———. "Women in the Temple, the Palace, and the Family: The Construction of Women's Identities in Pre-Colonial Tamilnadu." In Kenneth R. Hall, ed. *New Horizons in South Indian Studies: Papers in Honor of Noboru Karashima*. New Delhi: Oxford University Press, forthcoming.

———. "Women of Medieval South India in Hindu Temple Ritual: Text and Practice." *Annual Review of Women in World Religions* 3, 1994.

Parry, J., and M. Bloch., eds. "On the Moral Perils of Exchange." In *Money and the Morality of Exchange*. Cambridge: Cambridge University Press, 1989.

Peterson, Indira V. *Poems to Siva: The Hymns of the Tamil Saints*. Princeton, N.J.: Princeton University Press, 1989.

———. "Sramanas against the Tamil Way: Jains and Buddhists in the Hymns of the Tamil Saiva Saints." In John E. Cort, ed. *Open Boundaries: Jain Communities and Cultures in Indian History*. Albany: State University of New York, forthcoming.

Pillai, A. Velu. *Epigraphical Evidences for Tamil Studies*. Madras: International Institute of Tamil Studies, 1980.

Ramachandran, T. N. *The Nagapaṭṭiṇam and Other Buddhist Bronzes in the Madras Museum*. Madras: Government Press, 1954.

Ramesh, K. V. "Jaina Epigraphs in Tamil," appendix to A. Chakravarti, *Jaina Literature in Tamil*. New Delhi: Bhāratīya Jñānapīṭha, 1974.

Rao, T. N. Vasudeva. *Buddhism in the Tamil Country*. Annamalainagar: Annamalai University, 1979.

Reiniche, Marie-Louise. "Le temple dans la localit: Quatre examples au Tamilnad." In Jean-Claude Galey, ed. *L'Espace du temple I: Espaces, itineraires, mediations*. Paris: Editions de l'Ecole des Hautes Etudes en Sciences Sociales, 1985.

Reynell, Josephine. "Women and the Reproduction of the Jain Community." In M. Carrithers and C. Humphrey, eds. *The Assembly of Listeners: Jains in Society*. Cambridge: Cambridge University Press, 1991.

Richman, Paula. *Women, Branch Stories and Religious Rhetoric in a Tamil Buddhist Text*. Syracuse, N. Y.: Maxwell School, Syracuse University, 1988.

Rudner, David West. *Caste and Capitalism in Colonial India: The Nattukottai Chettiars*. Berkeley: University of California Press, 1994.

Schopen, Gregory. "On Monks, Nuns and 'Vulgar' Practices: The Introduction of the Image Cult into Indian Buddhism." *Artibus Asiae* 49/1–2, 1988–89.

———. "Filial Piety and the Monk in the Practice of Indian Buddhism: A Question of 'Sinicization' Viewed from the Other Side." *T'oung Pao* 70, 1984.

Shanta, N. *La voie jaina: Histoire, spiritualit , vie des ascètes pèlerines de l'Inde*. Paris: O.E.I.L., 1985.

Singh, Upinder. "Sanchi: The History of the Patronage of an Ancient Buddhist Establishment." *Indian Economic and Social History Review* 33/1, 1996.

Sontheimer, Gunther-Dietz. "Religious Endowments in India: The Juristic Personality of Hindu Deities." *Zeitschrift fur vergleichende Rechtswissenschaft* 67/1, 1964.

Soundara Rajan, K. V. *Kaveripattinam Excavations 1963–73*. New Delhi: Archaeological Survey of India, 1994.

South Indian Inscriptions, vols. 2–26. Delhi: Director-General, Archaeological Survey of India, 1891–1990.

South Indian Temple Inscriptions. Ed. T. N. Subrahmaniam. Madras: Government Oriental Manuscripts Library, 1953–57.

Srinivasan, P. R. "Buddhist Images of South India." In A. Aiyappan and P. R. Srinivasan, eds. *Story of Buddhism with Special Reference to South India*. Madras: Government of Madras, 1960.

Stein, Burton "The Economic Function of a Medieval South Indian Temple." *Journal of Asian Studies* 19, 1960.

———. *Peasant State and Society in Medieval South India*. Delhi: Oxford University Press, 1980.

Strenski, Irvan. "On Generalized Exchange and the Domestication of the Sangha." *Man* 18, 1983, pp. 463–77.

Swaminathan, K. D. *Early South Indian Temple Architecture: Study of Tiruvalisvaram Inscriptions*. Trivandrum: CBH Publications, 1990.

Tirumalai, R. *Rajendra Vinnagar*. Madras: Tamil Nadu State Department of Archaeology, 1980.

Vijayavenugopal, G. "Some Buddhist Poems in Tamil." *Journal of the International Association of Buddhist Studies* 2, 1979.

Waghorne, Joanne Punzo. *The Raja's Magic Clothes: Re-Visioning Kingship and Divinity in England's India*. University Park: Pennsylvania State University Press, 1994.

Weber, Max. *The Sociology of Religion*. Tr. Ephraim Fischoff. 1922; Reprint, Boston: Beacon Press, 1964.

MANASI DASGUPTA AND MANDAKRANTA BOSE

The Goddess-Woman Nexus in Popular Religious Practice

The Cult of Manasā

A striking cultural phenomenon of medieval eastern India, most notably Bengal, was the rise and spread of a variety of *śakti* cults—that is, beliefs and rituals centered on the idea of powerful female deities. Grounded in esoteric Hindu philosophical systems, these cults gained their largest following among the masses, dominated popular religious life for centuries, and are still in evidence in some locations and among some communities, though in a greatly debilitated form. The practice of these regimens of worship is of particular interest as the domain of women. The women of a family or a neighborhood rather than an official priest would organize and perform the ceremonies, an essential part of which was the recitation of the story of the particular deity worshiped. The following two-part chapter—the first by Manasi Dasgupta, the second by Mandakranta Bose—discusses aspects of the narrative of one of the most awe-inspiring of these deities and one of the most intriguing, Manasā, the goddess of serpents.

Faces of the Feminine in the *Manasā Maṅgala*

One of the most popular and enduring narrative types in medieval Bengali literature was the *maṅgala kāvyas*, verse tales celebrating the power and munificence of divine beings, prevalent in Bengal from the thirteenth century till the time of the poet Bhāratacandra—that is, the midseventeenth century.[1] The most striking of the many features distinguishing these tales from the older myths of gods and goddesses is that the deities at their center are all female. The narrative pattern of conflict, retribution, and reconciliation common to the tales is striking as well, particularly in that each tale forms around the life of a male authority figure who either scoffs at a goddess or, although he receives her favors, at the height of his fortune begins to neglect her. Her vengeance follows swiftly until, persuaded by his wife or some other female relative, he propitiates the goddess and regains all. These tales are thus founded on the twin themes of (1) the sovereignty of *śakti* or feminine energy conceptualized in Hindu religious thought and (2) women's powers of moral persuasion as exemplars of patience, submission, and self-sacrifice. These qualities are thrown into relief against the conviction of the irresistible power of the goddess, allegiance to whom is grounded in the hope of receiving her boons and in the fear of her wrath. Nominally from the regular Hindu pantheon, these goddesses are relics of older belief systems grounded in folk culture. Their cults have eroded with time but not disappeared, especially from rural India. However, their attenuation requires the present discussion to locate the worship of these deities, of which an essential part is the telling of their tales, in premodern times.

One tale stands out from the rest because of the extremes to which the pattern of retribution and reward is pushed in it. This is the *Manasā Maṅgala*. The reigning deity in this tale is unique as much in her ferocious self-assertion as in her own tormented background and compromised status as a deity. One of the most popular of the *maṅgala kāvyas*, this tale appeared throughout Bengal and even Assam and Bihar in many different versions, although the basic plot remained unaltered. The cult of Manasā commanded a very wide following, especially in East Bengal, where, as Ashutosh Bhattacharya points out, the tales of Manasā were known as Padmā-Purāṇ or Manasā Bhāsān. He argues for its antiquity by citing the well-known poetess of *Mymensingh Gītikā*, Candrāvatī, who recalls that her "father sang Manasā Bhāsān."[2] The term *Manasā Bhāsān* seems also to fit D. C. Sen's picturesque description of *Bhāsān-Yātrā* performed in the month of Śrāvaṇa (July–August) in Sylhet, Buckergunge, and other districts: "There are sometimes a hundred oars in each of the long narrow boats, the rowers singing in loud chorus as they pull them with all their might . . . . These festivities of Manasā Pūjā sometimes occupy a whole month during which men keep vigil and recite the songs before the goddess."[3]

The festival of Manasā Bhāsān did not last long, but the worship of Manasā in the form of the sij plant (*Euphorbia nivulia*) did,[4] and the ritual narration of her story by women during July and August continued into the twentieth century. Manasā's image still appears on pottery and scrolls, its form uniting the two conflicting aspects of beauty and fear inherent in the way she is conceived. Commenting on this opposition, Edward C. Dimock notes that "Manasā has control of snakes, and though her actions are somewhat snake-like, she herself is a goddess who has human form."[5] Shashibhushan Dasgupta considers the human interest of the tale to be its primary content but content that is often submerged in an "undercurrent of religious tone—by the fact that it really represents the struggle of decaying Śaivism of Bengal against the growth and spread of Śaktism, represented by the Śakti-cult."[6] The story exists in several versions, but as the following outline shows, all of them agree as to Manasā's own unhappy history, her vindictive nature, and the redemption of human beings, who live under willful gods, through women's heroic love.

Manasā was born out of the erotic imaginings of Śiva,[7] whose seed fell on a lotus leaf and trickled down into the underworld kingdom of serpents, where it was given the shape of a girl. Because she was born from a lotus leaf, or a *padma* leaf, she was called Padmā, but because her true origin was in Śiva's mind, or *manas*, she came to be known as Manasā. Abandoned in childhood, she grew up to be a beautiful young woman who possessed magic powers. Not recognizing her when he saw her later, Śiva lusted after her; learning of her identity, he was remorseful and took her home as his daughter.[8] But his wife Caṇḍī refused to accept her as a dependent and, suspecting her to be a rival, treated her cruelly and blinded her in one eye by throwing a stick at her. Angered by this, Manasā killed Caṇḍī but, on Śiva's command revived her. Caṇḍī remained unappeased even by this favor and unimpressed by her display of power, so Manasā had to seek her place in the world by herself, accompanied only by her servant Netā, also a woman with magic powers, and with all the serpents of the world for her to command. She found no human being to worship her, and Śiva declared that nobody would until his own devotee Cānd, the great merchant of Campaknagar, offered her worship. This made Manasā take up the conversion of Cānd as her single aim. When Cānd refused to worship her, jeering at her blindness and calling her *kānī*, the one-eyed female, she was furious and vowed vengeance on him. This she exacted swiftly by appearing to Cānd in the shape of an alluring courtesan to trick him out of Śiva's gift of *mahājnāna*, his "great learning"—namely, the art of reviving the dead. She also killed his closest friend, the great doctor Śaṅkar Gāḍuria, sank his ships, and caused the death of six of his sons. Determined to protect his youngest son, Lakhindar, from her, Cānd placed him inside an iron chamber, where Lakhindar was to be married to Behulā. But Manasā managed to have a tiny hole left in the wall, though which she sent one of her snakes to sting Lakhindar to death on his wedding night.

The story now moves on to the heroic efforts of Behulā to win back her husband's life. Placing his dead body on a raft, she floats down the river in search of Manasā, whom she wishes to propitiate. Overcoming many obstacles in the form of hungry beasts and lustful men and helped by a sympathetic Netā (Manasā's servant), Behulā finds her way into the assembly of the gods, whom she pleases by dancing for them, and through Śiva's intercession wins Manasā's acquiescence in restoring Lakhindar on the condition that Behulā persuades Cānd to worship Manasā. This last proves difficult, but eventually Cānd grudgingly obliges; thus propitiated, Manasā restores Cānd's wealth and the lives of his six older sons and his friend. This rapprochement signals the founding of her cult in human society, celebrated in the month of Śrāvaṇa on the eleventh day of the waning moon, which marks the day of Cānd's surrender. As for Behulā and Lakhindar, it now transpires that they are actually the divine pair Uṣā and Aniruddha, forced to take mortal shapes under a curse.[9] Having expiated their offense by their sufferings, they now return to heaven. It appears that Manasā has been the instrument of their redemption.

This basic plot appears in many versions with additions, alterations, and embellishments by as many as eighty poets. Manasā even makes an appearance in the *Mahābhārata* story of the churning of the ocean, in the course of which Manasā appears as Viṣahari (taker and remover of poison) and asserts her right of place among powerful gods and goddesses. In that episode, she saves Śiva himself, who, in his bid to prevent the poison that spews out of the ocean from destroying the world, drinks it, falls dead, and is revived by Manasā. The different versions of her story appear in manuscripts scattered over many regions of eastern India, some full, some mere fragments, which have been gathered into several collections, each generically known as *Bāiśā Kavir Manasā Maṅgala*—that is, the tale of Manasā by twenty–two poets. The number twenty-two is not quite accurate but simply means several, nor are the same poets included in each collection because the choice of poets depends on geographical provenance. Ashutosh Bhattacharya states that the "bāiśā" of Mymensingh do not include any composition of the *maṅgal* poets from Barisal and vice versa, whereas collections from West Bengal give preeminence to Kṣemānanda Ketakadāsa.[10]

Like other *maṅgala-kāvyas*, the *Manasā Maṅgala* shows affinities with the *purāṇa* tales, although it remains firmly rooted in the folk imagination.[11] Apart from the common narrative core of heroic struggle leading to rewards both in this life and in afterlife, the *purāṇas* and the *maṅgala-kāvyas* depict the sufferings of women. Perhaps not surprisingly, this focus on women's sufferings seems to be a common element of folk belief in many regions of India. David Kinsley notes that "an important theme in myths concerning the origin of village goddesses is the injustice done to women by men,"[12] drawing upon the myths of Māriāmman, Ambābāru, and other popular South Indian village deities, who, according to some scholars, may have traveled as far as riverine Bengal to take the form of Manasā during the reign of the southern Sen Burmans.[13] Dinesh Chandra Sen compares Behulā in *Manasā Maṅgala* to Sītā in the *Rāmāyaṇa*, placing Behulā in the same position of cultural centrality for Bengal that Sītā holds for the larger tradition of Hindu culture. Sen identifies Behulā's principal and most memorable virtue as that of utter devotion to her husband, who "appeared to her as a priceless treasure."[14] The moral and social lesson drawn from the figures of both Sītā and Behulā is that it is a privilege for a virtuous wife, not a mere duty, to suffer selflessly for her husband. But it is noteworthy that the poets of *Manasā Maṅgala* ascribe a greater agency to women by viewing them as protectors of men. They suggest that, as soon as a woman becomes a wife, she assumes the role of the protective mother of her husband, responsible not only for his comforts but also for his physical survival. A man lives in safety because his wife protects him with her active love. This is a significant departure from the model of passive virtue that Sītā represents.

The gender relationship is significantly different in the *Rāmāyaṇa*, where Rāma is responsible for Sītā's protection and not the other way round. In fact, calamity strikes when Sītā tries to reverse roles and acts to protect Rāma, who, of course, is never in danger. Sītā's concern for Rāma's safety is needless, and her attempt to assume the role of Rāma's protector results in her own abduction by Rāvaṇa when she compels Rāma's brother Lakṣmaṇa to go to his help. By contrast, Behulā has the role of her husband's protector and savior forced on her, and she rises to the task with courage and determination that belie the traditional image of the wilting female. She actually performs the duty of looking after Lakhindar far better than her father-in-law, overconfident about his own powers, who can only rant at Behulā at his son's death but will not, because of his pride, accept the obvious solution of surrendering to Manasā to save his son.

Lakhindar's death thus becomes the turning point in the tale's representation of gender identities. Whatever the version of the tale, Cānd is arrogant, wrathful, and stubborn. The various men who try to seduce Behulā as she journeys with her dead husband are all sexual predators. If this seems to be a conventional profile of the masculine psyche, it is interesting that the profile does not include the virtue of heroic initiative. Whatever action is taken, the female personalities take. The action is initiated by Manasā. The response to it comes from Behulā. Behulā also breaks out of her father-in-law, Cānd's, power by unilaterally venturing outside the home, the woman's traditional sphere, to seek Manasā's help in bringing Lakhindar back to life. At the same time, this role reversal is counterbalanced by reminders of the traditional framework of gender identities in the submissiveness of Cānd's homebound wife, Sanakā, who cannot even pray to Manasā for fear of her husband's disapproval, and in the authoritarianism of Śiva, who, in laying down the law for an intransigent Manasā, enforces the condition of patriarchy. A similar ambiguity—it is hard to tell whether it is intended—marks the happy ending, which can be read either as Cānd's surrender to a triumphant Manasā or as a pyrrhic victory for her, insofar as she has to be content with Cānd's contemptuous, token *pūjā*, which he performs by turning his back on her and throwing a flower at her. While the reciters of the tale and their listeners celebrate Manasā's power, they cannot ignore the fact that she was elevated to the status of a deity to be worshiped in the world only because Śiva decided to confer on Cānd the power to so recognize her.

The story thus seems at once to uphold the patriarchy and to acknowledge the power of the feminine. But the latter is the more interesting because although the celebration of the Great Goddess in a variety of forms is certainly an established tradition, the *Manasā Maṅgala* gives it new twists. The power that is ordinarily accorded the goddess is here extended to the mortal Behulā, and even if it is not the magical force that goddesses possess, it is equally effective as moral strength. Still more intriguing is the representation of Manasā as a fearsome being, half-goddess and half-demon, whose vindictiveness merely confirms her self-seeking nature, teaches no moral lesson, and only verifies the reality of supernatural malevolence.

Thus, the figure of Manasā repudiates the two common paradigms of the feminine—namely, the woman as the protecting mother and the woman as devoted wife, both of which are embodied in Behulā. The conception of Manasā reveals an entirely different face of the feminine. Although *śakti* literature does recognize—indeed, glorify—the terrifying and destructive aspects of the feminine, it does not associate vindictiveness with it. Narratives of the Great Goddess of *śakti* belief systems celebrate her as the protector of humanity and the upholder of righteousness. *Manasā Maṅgala* shows a deity of alluring female shape but incapable of loving anyone, whose worship is moved by fear of her anger rather than hope for her protection. Although several poets call her *mātā* (mother), it seems a propitiatory gesture produced by fear, for Manasā does not nurse feelings of motherly love for anyone on earth or in heaven. It is difficult to accept Dimock's view that, though vengeful by nature, "Manasā has a strange and equally wanton compassion. She has the power to bring her victim back to life."[15] She does bring her victim back to life, but she does so to show her power, and power can hardly be a synonym for compassion. Compassion and pride do not go together. Manasā is intensely self-centered in her pride. She is readily angered, sometimes fears for the safety of her retinue, but is relentlessly cruel and self-serving in her fight for authority and recognition. That she stands outside the pantheon of deities in the tale is thus an appropriate sign of her alien nature.

But it is in this portrayal of Manasā that the story achieves its subtlest ambivalence. Because the narrative does not allow us to forget the injustices she suffers, it seems to make allowance for her as a wronged person driven to ruthless self-assertion. A piece of psychological perception, this explanation of Manasā is also sociological, for much of Manasā's suffering arises out of the fact that she is a female dependent upon the goodwill of males, both divine and human, and even has to resort to seductive behavior to gain a small victory. In this, her plight is not all that different from that of Behulā, whose absolute virtue cannot save her from being blamed for her husband's death and pursued by lustful men. This gendered perception of Manasā goes deeper still in the mystery with which the story surrounds her power. It is not a power similar to that of the commoner deities of *śakti* religions but derives from Manasā's birth in the land of snakes and is expressed through the coupling of frequent deaths with frequent resurrections. Her power is myserious because she is the goddess of snakes. Dimock believes that the "regenerative power of Manasā is not . . . wholly separable from the snakes themselves. The snake simultaneously represents life and death. It regenerates itself periodically in the shedding of its skin. It is immortal."[16] When the story projects this fearful reverence on to a female being, it adds up to an acknowledgment of a primal awe at the mystery of the feminine, of immeasurable power as the source of life, which needs to be contained if social structures as conceived within patriarchy are to be maintained. We may note here that Behulā is as much a life-giver in the story as Manasā. She is not an alien like Manasā to a stable community, but she, too, breaks out of her society's bounds. The primary concern, then, of the story is with the nature of the feminine and the social ideology that must control it. That is why, while the *Manasā Maṅgala* vests ultimate authority in male figures such as Śiva and Cānd, what it focuses on are faces of the feminine, faces that can be both wrathful and compassionate.

Faith, Justice, and the Feminine in the *Manasā Maṅgala*

Maṅgala kāvyas are narratives of the boons that worshipers receive from the gods and goddesses to whom they prove their devotion. Ironically for tales purported to celebrate the beneficence of divine beings, the stories are intimidating in their portrayal of deities who are as overwhelming in their gifts when pleased as in their vengefulness when dissatisfied. Reward and punishment are the two poles between which the perception of the spirit world grows in these tales. As discourses for the masses, the formulations of these perceptions are not arguments of abstract reasoning but models of concrete, worldly action. Grounded as they are in felt experience, it is hardly surprising that these perceptions should be organized into a literary format and their rhetoric molded in terms of human interactions on social and emotional levels. This lends particular interest to the genre when we see the importance they accord to women or female deities, making these stories preeminently women's narratives. Although this aspect of the genre has been generally recognized,[17] the complexity of the perception of the feminine remains to be thoroughly explored as a key to the understanding of power, status and, conduct; to questionings of the idea of faith and justice; and to the conceptualization of the unknown in the world of the *kāvyas*, in an era long past but still exerting an imaginative force on present times.

Within the genre, the earliest text is the *Manasā-Maṅgala*, which enjoyed wide popularity for centuries from the thirteenth till the eighteenth. Through its long history of transmission, it appeared in many versions, although the story line did not change substantially. Rather, the alterations reflected the differing sympathie of different storytellers. The account here rests on the incidents on which th texts are in general agreement. The story begins with the life of Manasā, her origin as a divine figure and reigning deity of snakes, and her efforts to obtain a following among humankind by winning the devotion of a merchant, Cānd, whose loyalty to Śiva proves to be an insuperable obstacle and who therefore needs to be forced into submission by intimidation. But he proves recalcitrant despite the sinking of his ships; the killing of his six sons and his friend Śaṅkara Gāruḍī, who knew how to revive the dead from snakebites; and Manasa's tricking him out of his own magic power, *mahājñāna*, the knowledge of reviving the dead. Nor can the importunities of his wife Sanakā move him. The tragic action reaches its height when the youngest son, Lakhindara, is bitten by one of Manasā's snakes and killed on the night of his wedding to Behulā. But the reversal of the action begins at this point, when Behulā refuses to accept her husband's death and sets out with his corpse to win back his life from the gods. After overcoming many dangers, she finds a patroness in Netā, a powerful companion of Manasā, and, making her way to the court of the gods, Behulā pleases them by her dancing. After examining Behulā's appeal, Śiva forces Manasā to restore Lakhindar to life on the condition that Behulā persuades her father-in-law, Cānd, to worship Manasā. Moved at last by Behulā's appeal, Cānd does so, although only with his left hand and with his face averted from the goddess. Satisfied with this doubtful victory, Manasā restores Cānd's fortune and all his sons. As an envoi to the story, we are told in most versions that Behulā and Lakhindara are, in fact, heavenly beings, Uṣā and Aniruddha, who had been cast into their earthly life as a result of Manasā's trickery, again aimed at using them to gain a foothold in human society. The course of events thus turns out to be an elaborate plan to create an exemplar of human conduct both within the human world and in relationships with gods and goddesses, with Uṣā and Aniruddha providing the didactic keys.

What we see here, then, is a multiple-contest plot. Beginning with an unresolved conflict between Manasā and Pārvatī, the plot moves on to the hostility between Manasā and Cānd and then to the main action of the story, Behulā's struggle to revive her dead husband, which becomes a contest between her and Manasā. This constitutes the bulk of the action, and Manasā and Behulā emerge as the two main characters. Their mutual opposition also represents opposed idealizations of the feminine in the story. But as the story unfolds and the characters take shape, a third character appears as a third idealization of the feminine, an exemplification of womanly qualities on an exclusively domestic level. This is Sanakā, the wife of Cānd and the mother who lost all her children to Manasā. Her reaction of love and helplessness as she struggles with her loss and her husband's adamant attitude shows her as the idealized mother-wife of her time and also sets an example for later times. Whether the model is followed today or not, as an ethical idea it remains a powerful ideal for a Bengali woman. For almost six hundred years, from the thirteenth to the early nineteenth century,[18] the ideals represented by the three central female figures in *Manasā Maṅgala* influenced the later *maṅgala kāvyas* as well as other early Bengali literature. Although the portrayals of these three characters vary somewhat in the different versions, their central roles in the plot and the scheme of ethical instruction never change.

Because the tale appears in different versions, it would be useful to take note of the principal variations. Of the more than twenty extant texts, besides a number of oral versions,[19] three stand out. These are by Nārāyaṇadeva, Vijayagupta, and Ketakādasa, each of whom takes a different stand about the events without altering the basic plotline. For instance, in theirs as in other versions, Manasā (a goddess) appears as an envious, cunning female who can hardly draw respect from human beings. The difference lies in what each poet chooses to emphasize. Nārāyaṇadeva presents Cānd as an almost flawless character whose stubborn hostility to Manasā proves his devotion to Śiva and Caṇḍī. Manasā is of small account in this text. An unique note is struck by Vijayagupta, who is alone in his sympathy for Manasā, whom he portrays as a victim of rejection and ill treatment, which makes her entire behavior psychologically pardonable. She has no mother and is rejected both by her stepmother, Caṇḍī, and by Jaratkāru, to whom she had been married off as a matter of convenience. Furthermore, although she is the daughter of Śiva, she is denied the regard due to her birth. In this version, Cānd is a stubborn, egotistic, and arrogant character who tyrannizes his wife and daughter-in-law. Taking a different aim again, Ketakādāsa portrays Behulā as a beautiful girl who is capable of winning everyone's heart through faith, love, courage, loyalty to her husband, chastity, and determination. He develops the divine origin of Behūlā and her husband Lakhindara at great length. Behūlā's performance as a great dancer and the entire dance scene in heaven are also carefully presented. Ketakādāsa's interest seems to be a romantic celebration of beauty that is strong enough to mute, though not erase, Manasā's meanness and Cānd's stubbornness.

These versions are distinguished by their different emphases, rather than major redirections in plot or characterization. Even Vijayagupta, who attempts to elicit sympathy for Manasā, does not exculpate her actions or redesign her character. Still more important, the ethical framework remains unaltered, suggesting an enduringly monolithic social base of norms. The implied praise of Cānd's intransigence as evidence of masculine strength and the systematic subordination of female characters are equally substantial components of that base. And yet, accepting the status quo, as the story in its many versions does, it is difficult to reconcile the opposite ideas about the feminine or the understandings of faith and justice contradictorily invoked by humans and gods.

To readers of *Manasā Maṅgala*, the arbitrary and vindictive self-seeking of the divine figures is only too apparent. The gods and goddesses are characterized by the worst kind of passions imaginable. Also apparent is the use of the feminine as the dominant trope for power to create both suffering and happiness, metaphorized as life and death. Commentators on the *maṅgala kāvyas* in general and *Manasā-Maṅgala* in particular have noted the central importance of the women in the story[20] and pointed out how a mother's love, grief, anxiety, and protectiveness toward her children and a wife's resolute dedication to her husband both reflect the social values of the time and act as models for later idealizations of women. Accurate as these readings are, they need to be supplemented with recognition of other aspects of the feminine that are perhaps less comforting and suggest other layers within the feminine as an imagined construct. The story and the cult for which it serves as the text clearly are a narrative of the feminine. But more interesting than this obvious characteristic of the story is the ambivalent understanding of the feminine it creates, rendering the female characters in it, both human and superhuman, as at once autonomous and subjugated.

The importance of women is built into the ritual itself. The primary responsibility for its performance, including the vital reading of the tale, belongs to women. The plot itself is laden with—indeed, moved by—gender values marked by sexual motifs. Manasā is born when Śiva's (in one version the *ṛṣi* Kaśyapa's) ejaculation, caused by uncontrollable lust at the sight of an *apsarās*, is swallowed by a fish, in whose womb she is then conceived. Not only is her origin the result of illicit masculine sexuality but also she is herself the object of it in at least in one version of the story, when Śiva, failing to recognize her when she grows up, lusts after her. Pārvatī torments her cruelly because she is seen as a sexual rival. Even this last action is rooted in the primacy of the male, for Pārvatī's cruelty is a desperate move to retain her status with her male consort. The compromised condition of the female whose survival depends on the pleasure of the male affects even the powers that females in the story possess. On the one hand, Manasā holds the powers of life, death, and transformation—occult abilities that no male in the story is shown to possess. Yet, endowed as she is with such powers, she still has to employ stereotyped feminine wiles, which run from sexual seduction to blackmail. When she needs to rob Cānd of his *mahājñāna*, the knowledge of reviving the dead, she has to stoop to posing as a courtesan. Ironically, too, the end she pursues turns out to be no more than acceptance by a male devotee. In Behulā, the true heroine of the story, we see the moral opposite to Manasā, for Behulā acts entirely out of dedication to another and that is what gains her the gods' approval and help. Yet even this paragon of womanhood, lauded for her resolute service to her marital identity and her chastity, must please the gods as a woman rather than as the model of devotion she is and dance alluringly—indeed, seductively, if we are to believe her husband's subsequent (and boorishly ungrateful) complaint that she has stained his and her honor by dancing lewdly:

> *nāṭinī haiñā bāpāra jāta majāili* |
>
> . . . .
>
> *debasabhāya uluñgu kāpaṛa kene para* | *Visṇu*.23
> By becoming a dancer you have ruined your father's caste
>
> . . . .
>
> Why do you wear revealing clothes in the assembly of gods?

The forces that define women's lives act as much on this female warrior against death as on any ordinary woman at the mercy of convention. During her long travels fraught with many dangers, the one constant threat she faces is from a succession of libidinous men, who try to seduce her by bribery or force. One of them, the gross Godā, promises her infinite wealth. Another, a self-proclaimed shaman, presses her to spend three nights with him, promising in return to bring her husband back to life:

> *marā jīyāiba yadi satya rākha* ।
> *tina dina tina rātri mora saṅge thāka* ।
> I will bring him back to life if you keep one promise:
> Stay with me for three days and three nights.

In a final demonstration of the fragility of women's status, the story relates how, after her long struggle to snatch life back from death and reverse fate itself, when she does succeed, she faces rejection from her social world, which demands proof that she did not lose her chastity in six months of unchaperoned wandering.

Manasā Maṅgala's essential contradiction in evaluating womanhood is located in the question of power. On the one hand, the story consistently reinforces the subordination of the feminine to the overarching control of masculine norms. On the other, there runs throughout the story an undercurrent of awe at the mysterious powers of the feminine. Not only Manasā but also her companion Netā possess powers of life and death. As Behulā floats down the river with the corpse of her husband on a raft of banana stalks, she sees a washerwoman on the river bank. Pestered by her child, the woman kills it but after finishing her chores she revives the child. This woman is Netā, whose friendship Behulā gains as the first step toward placating Manasā. Behulā herself is not without magical strengths. Throughout her travels, she protects herself from man and beast by powers she inexplicably possesses. Her aura of purity repels serpents and crocodiles. One look from her blinds a man who dares to look on her lustfully.

The story thus holds at its center irresoluble contradictions created by concepts of the feminine. The reader is driven to question, What constitutes the feminine? The story shows that it is at once the life-destroying Manasā and her polar opposite, the loving, life-giving Sanakā. Sanakā herself is placed opposite Behulā, the mother-in-law dutiful and submissive to convention while the daughter-in-law is energetic and self-defining in rising above custom. No dominant requirement for the ideal female can be claimed. Behulā's position in her world is rendered uncertain because she has to satisfy more than one requirement of a model woman: even as she meets the ideal of wifely dedication, she fails the ideal of submission to family authority, even when specifically required to do so by Cānd, who holds her responsible for not being able to prevent his son's death:

> *badhūr ṭhāṅi jijñāsā karo ki āche sāhas* ।
> *lakhāir saṅge puḍiyā maruk ghucuk apayaś* ।
> Ask my daughter-in-law if she has the resolution
> To burn to death with Lakhai and dispel her infamy

Instead of falling in with this custom, Behulā sets out on her own. In addition, she also fails to display conspicuous chastity as one of the prime womanly virtues. The greatest contradiction is that exclusively female figures wield power but they need endorsements specifically from males. Manasā cannot take her place in the pantheon of deities worshiped by humankind unless a man consents to offer her *pūjā*. Sanakā's devotion will not do; her husband's grudging, left-handed offerings will.

By recognizing the contradictions to which women's existence is subjected, in the *Manasā Maṅgala* we find a richly layered construction of the feminine. This construction begins with the contrast between the vicious female deities against the loving women but proceeds on the social level toward identifying the forces that determine women's lives and on the emotional level toward acknowledging the mystic power of the feminine over life and death. Thereby, the feminine becomes not only the central theme of the tale but also, in its multiple, often oppositional qualities, an idea that commands wonder, which may account for the sustained popularity of the narrative over such a long time.

The irreconcilable ideas of the feminine as a moral category expose tensions in concepts of social categories as well. Here again, the feminizing of the narrative is the instrument of perception. The gendered attribution of power calls into doubt the ideas of faith and justice on which the integrity of social organization is founded. We can legitimately see the plot as a series of violations of justice, beginning with the cruel treatment Manasā receives from birth onward. The injustice she suffers is replicated in her own treatment of Cānd, who is no more just toward his family, Behulā in particular. When we consider her life, injustice appears to be the rule rather than the exception, for she is blamed by all—her in-laws and their neighbors—for her husband's death. Injustice pursues her even into her triumph, when she has to pass an ordeal by fire to prove her chastity. Blind custom, expediency, and cunning rather than faith in a just and single standard of conduct seem to be the motive forces in the world of the story. Behulā does succeed, but not by rights. The contrast with the classical lesson of the *Rāmāyana* is striking: Sītā is explicitly protected by an universal moral order. No such systematic scheme is at work for Behulā. She wins the contest against Manasā simply because she manages to obtain the patronage of a stronger god, who forces her enemy into accommodation. Can faith in righteousness flourish in Behulā's world or, indeed, survive the reading of her story?

If humankind is fated to live under arbitrary gods "as flies to wanton boys" who kill for sport, to cite old Gloucester in *King Lear*, can any idea of human worth emerge from the story? In answer, the only comfort comes from turning to those emotional responses that are unmediated by social injunctions. An obvious example is Behulā's faith in herself, which she asserts in direct contradiction to regulations. But more illustrative of human worth is the love that characterizes Sanakā. A creature of custom, she blames Behulā for her son's death, as well as for her unwomanly and possibly dishonorable independence. Yet, when Behulā really sets out on her dangerous voyage, Sanakā becomes a mother whose unconditional love breaks free of the prejudices she has been taught. Behulā is now her daughter, whom she cannot let go, even if it means she has to give up the hope of regaining her son:

sonā bale badhū tumi āmār kathā rākha ।
lakhāir badale more mā baliyā dāka ।
Sanaka says, daughter-in-law, listen to me,
Instead of Lakhai you call me mother.

The anxiety for a loved child here transcends the customary hostility toward a daughter-in-law and preference for a male child. At this point, the story moves away from the wonders of the occult, as well as its fearful reverence for terrible gods, to establish an emotional base upon which the definition of humanity can be founded. That such human feelings are, indeed, the ultimate transforming agents within the human world is indicated still more persuasively by that apparently irredeemable slave to custom, Cānd himself. Neither fear nor argument makes him yield to Manasā; what does is his compassion for Behulā and his other daughters-in-law. Their grief breaks through the walls manufactured by his religion and liberates his instincts.

These assertions of human worth are muted but not feeble. Indeed, they are more persuasive because they arise out of moments of powerlessness to effect reversals of mood, as well as action. Particularly worth noting in this context is that the instruments of these assertions are the women in the story, precisely those who are denied autonomy in social practice. Their lives are lived in an arena of competing definitions of the female nature—the stereotype of the female as weak and grasping pitted against that of the female as strong and self-sacrificing. The juxtaposition of such definitions, essentialist constructions of the feminine in one way or the other, confirms nothing but the enslavement of humanity to unjust gods. Yet, countervailing this gloomy perception, the instances of common human affection claim dignity and worth for humankind. These opposite messages build an ambivalence into the heart of the narrative that can be resolved by none of the social or religious imperatives enshrined in it. Perhaps it was this ethical indeterminacy that drew so many poets over so long a time to the retelling of the story.

Notes

1. As dated by Bhattacharya (1939), p. 1. The location "Bengal" is taken here as a cultural entity historically mediated by the Bengali language rather than a political jurisdiction.
2. Bhattacharya (1939), p. 1.
3. Sen (1911), pp. 252–76.
4. Raychoudhuri (1953), p. 139.
5. Dimock (1989), pp.154–55.
6. Dasgupta (1946), Introduction, p. xiv. Noting Manasā's power as the goddess of serpents or Viṣahari, Dasgupta (1977, p. 172) explains that the "mother-goddess could stir the life and intellect of the people of the country mainly through the philosophy of Śakti."
7. Tarafdar (1965), pp. 241–42. In some versions, Śiva is Manasā's mentor and imparts to her the mysterious powers of life and death; see "Manasā" in Sarkar (1963), pp. 413–14.
8. *Manasā Maṅgala*, p. 120.
9. Sen (1911), pp. 252–76.
10. Bhattacharya (1939), p. 1.
11. Ibid.
12. Kinsley (1986), p. 186.
13. Ray (1970), p. 304.
14. Sen (1911), pp. 252–76.

15. Dimock (1989), p. 163.
16. Ibid.
17. Chaudhuri (1978).
18. Dinesh Chandra Sen, Sukumar Sen, Ashutosh Bhattacharya.
19. Tarapada Bhattacharya (1962, p. 186) lists the following authors of *Manasā Maṅgala*: Kāṇā Haridatta, Vijaygupta, Vipradāsa Pipilāi, Nārāyaṇadeva, Tantravibhūti, Asamīyā poets: Manakar and Durgāvar, Dvijavaṁśī, Ketatkādāsa Kṣemānanda, Viṣṇupāl, Kālidāsa, Sītārāmadāsa, Rasika Miśra, Kavivallabh, Kavicandra, Ratideva, Kṣemānanda 2, Jagajjīvana Ghoṣāl, Jīvankṛṣṇa Maitra, Rājā Rājasiṁha, Rāmajīvana Vidyābhūṣaṇa, Vaidya Harināth, Kṛṣṇānanda, Jānakīnātha, Jagannātha, Kavi Karṇapūra, Rāmavinoda, Gaṅgādāsa Sen, ṣaṣṭhīvara, Vāṇeśvara, Haragovinda, Madhūsūdana, Chirāvinoda, Kālīprasanna, and Jagamohana. D. C. Sen, Sukumar Sen (1968), and A. Bhattacharya mention 20 poets. Not all of them are well known, and some may have been oral poets.
20. Chaudhuri (1978) and Smith (1980).

References

Bhattacharya, Ashutosh. *Bāṅglā Maṅgalakāvyera Itihāsa*. Calcutta: Calcutta Book House, *Vaṅgābda* 1346 [1939].

Bhattacharya, Ashutosh. *Bāṅglā Sāhityer Itihāsa*. Calcutta: Calcutta Book House, 1939.

Bhattacharya, Hamsa Narayan. *Bāṅglā Maṅgalkāvyer Dhārā*. Calcutta: House of Books, 1970.

Bhattacharya, Tarapada. *Banga Sāhityer Itihās*. Calcutta: S. Gupta Bros., 1962.

Chaudhuri, Bhudev. *Bāṅglā Sāhityer Itikathā*, vol. 1. Calcutta: Dey's Publishing, 1978.

Das, Ashutosh, and Surendrachandra Bhattacharya. *Manasāmaṅgala: Jagajjīvan viracita*. Calcutta: Calcutta University, 1984.

Dasgupta, Shashibhushan. *Obscure Religious Cults*. Calcutta: Firma K. L. Mukhopadhyay, 1946.

Dasgupta, Shashibhushan. *Aspects of Indian Religious Thought*. Calcutta: Firma K. L. Mukhopadhyay, 1977.

Dimock, Edward Cameron, Jr. "The Goddess of Snakes in Medieval Bengali Literature." In *The Sound of Silent Guns and Other Essays*. Delhi: Oxford University Press, 1989.

Gupta, Ksetra. *Bāṅglā Sāhityer Samagra Itihāsa*. Calcutta: Granthanilaya, 1992.

Kayal, Akshay, and Chitra Dev, eds. *Manasāmaṅgala: Ketakādāsa Kṣemānanda viracita*. Calcutta: Lekhapara, 1978.

Kinsley, David. *Hindu Goddesses: Visions of the Divine Feminine in the Hindu Religious Tradition*. Delhi: Motilal Banarsidass, 1986.

Manasā Maṅgala. A selection from Ketakadāsa Kṣemānanda's works, selected and edited by Bijan Bihari Bhattacharya. New Delhi: Sahitya Akademi, 1987.

Poddar, Aravinda. *Bāṅglā Sāhitya: Saṁkṣipta Itihāsa*. Calcutta: Indiana, 1962.

Ray, Nihar Ranjan. *Bāṅgālīr Itihāsa: Ādi Parva*. Abridged and ed. by J. Sinha Ray. Calcutta: Lekhak Samavay Samiti, *Vaṅgābda* 1373 [1966].

Raychoudhuri, Tapan. *Bengal under Akbar and Jahangir: An Introductory Study in Social History*. Calcutta: A. Mukherjee, 1953.

Sarker, S. C., compiler. *Paurāṇika Abhidhāna* (Dictionary of the *Purāṇas*). Calcutta: M. C. Sarkar & Sons, *Vaṅgābda* 1370 [1963].

Sen, Dinesh Chandra. *History of Bengali Language and Literature*. Calcutta: Calcutta University, 1911.

Sen, Dinesh Chandra. *Baṅga Sāhitya Paricay, or Typical Selections from Old Bengali Literature*, part 1. Calcutta: Calcutta University Press, 1914.

Sen, Dinesh Chandra, ed. *Behula*. Calcutta: Jijnasa Publishers, *Vaṅgābda* 1370 [1970].

———. *Bānglā Sāhityer Itihāsa*, vol. 1, part 1. Calcutta: Eastern Publishers, 1963.

———. *Vishnu Pala's Manasāmaṅgala*. Bibliotheca India Series. 289, issue no. 1587. Calcutta: Asiatic Society, 1968.

———. *History of Bengali Literature*. New Delhi: Sahitya Akademi, 1971.

Smith, William. *The One-Eyed Goddess: A Study of the Manasāmaṅgala*. Stockholm: Almqvist and Winkell, 1980.

Sen, Uma. *Prācin O Madhyayuger Bānglā Sāhitye Sādhāraṇ Mānuṣ*. Calcutta:

Tarafdar, Mamtazur Rahman. *Hussain Shahi Bengal 1494–1534* A.D.—*A Socio-Political Study*. Dacca: Asiatic Society of Pakistan Publication, 16. 1965.

11

NANCY MARTIN-KERSHAW

Mīrābai in the Academy and the Politics of Identity

A fifteenth or sixteenth century rebellious woman poet-saint, who pursued her devotion to Kṛṣṇa with complete dedication, composed exceptionally beautiful songs of love and longing for God, and endured severe persecution because she did not behave as a member of the royal household should or because she crossed caste boundaries, seems a likely candidate for those who would look to the past for exemplary women of power and independence. Mīrābai is such a saint, but as soon as we begin to try to uncover the precise details of her life, we encounter multiple Mīrās. People have told her story in myriad ways, making her over in their own image and sometimes trying to appropriate her absolute devotion for their own purposes.[1] Her story of struggle and perseverance is compelling, but was she a good wife who turned to serious devotion only after her husband's death, suffering unjustly at the hands of her in-laws, as some would have it, or was she a woman who knew her own mind and risked her life, disregarding hierarchies of gender, caste, and religion, in her shameless passion for God, as others claim? No single image of Mīrā wins universal acceptance, and a stubborn multiplicity remains. Her devotion to none but God, coupled with the resistance so fundamental to her character, appears to inhibit her complete incorporation into any political and social agenda (or institutionalized religious sect, for that matter). Many people also speak in her name—of their own suffering, of dignity and resistance in the face of oppression, of love fulfilled or denied.[2] No authentic original body of works attributable to an individual woman of medieval Rajasthan has yet been reliably identified either, and stories and songs continue to multiply around her.[3]

One particular family of tales emerges in the late nineteenth century as Mīrā becomes the object of historical study, and it is this narrative line that we will examine in detail. These tellings of Mīrā's story differ considerably from the devotionally inspired hagiographies and even more radically from those tales told and sung among members of low castes in rural Rajasthan.[4] However, they have come to dominate popular portrayals of Mīrā in films, novels, and comic books, as well as school lessons in Hindi literature. Although they ostensibly reflect an objective pursuit of the historical "facts" of Mīrā's life, historical inquiry in her homeland of Rajasthan has been intimately tied to the development of Hindu nationalist and revitalized Rajput identities, and traditional historical sources provide little information about her.[5] A careful examination of the tales of Mīrā will reveal a conscious "Rajputization" of Mīrā (making her over into a good Rajput woman and wife) and the influence of stories of Rajput heroines on their narrative structure, lending support to the argument first advanced by Parita Mukta that Rajput appropriation of Mīrā is a recent phenomenon.[6]

Further, the source of these related tales appears to be a very small group of men related to Mirā's natal family and the court of Mewar (into which she married). A clear ideological agenda underlies their narrative, and I will endeavor to show that the emerging academic "biography" has no greater claim to authority, when it comes to who Mīrā was and is, than the tales told by hagiographers, who seemingly lived much closer to Mīrā's time and shared her devotion, or by low-caste singers of Rajasthan, who may have been singing about this well-loved saint for centuries. Though they offer us considerable insight into the political and social context in which Mīrā must have lived, scholars, no less than the folk singers and other narrators of her life, actively engage in a creative process when they shape their data into a coherent life story and speak of her individual actions and motivations and those of the people around her. There is no reason, therefore, to privilege their view of Mīrā over other. What proves interesting, in the absence of hard "facts" about her, is who is telling her story in what way and why.

The foundation of the academic reconstructions of Mīrā's life lies in the earliest records we have of her—the *Bhaktamāl* or "garden of devotees," recounting of the lives of the saints in short verse and the commentaries on them, which fill in narrative detail. Such hagiographies laud Mīrā's devotion and speak of the opposition she encountered from members of her marital household. She appears rebellious, ecstatic, and without shame before God and human society alike. Priyadas's 1712 C.E. commentary on Nabhadas's earlier verses (ca. 1600 C.E.) sets the tone and plotline for almost all subsequent narratives.[7] The story Priyadas tells is the following:

Mīrā of Merta (in the kingdom of Marwar) was a devotee of Kṛṣṇa from childhood but was forced to marry a ruler of the kingdom of Mewar—the *rāṇā*. She did so unwillingly, her mind on Kṛṣṇa, and the only wedding gift she wanted from her parents was her beloved image of her Lord. She immediately got into trouble in her marital household for her refusal to worship any but Kṛṣṇa. When she was isolated in a separate palace as punishment for her insolence, she thrived there, worshiping God and meeting with holy men, again enraging her new in-laws with what they perceived as her shameful behavior in conversing with men outside the family.

Her sister-in-law tried to reason with her, but she would not listen, and the *rāṇā* sent poison to her under the guise of holy water, which he knew she would never refuse to drink. If anything, she looked more radiant after consuming it. He then sent people to spy on her, hoping to catch her in a compromising situation with a man, but when he was informed that she could be heard conversing with a lover within her chambers, he found only her image of Kṛṣna before her and backed away in confusion.

Three encounters with men outside her family follow. A supposed holy man tried to take advantage of her by telling her that Kṛṣṇa had ordered him to make love to her. She defeated him by erecting a bed in the midst of the community of devotees and saying that, if such was the Lord's command, then there would be no shame in carrying out the act publicly. He became her disciple and begged her forgiveness. The emperor Akbar and his court poet Tansen are said to have visited her and, through her intercession, depending on one's interpretation of the passage, to have been vouchsafed a vision of Kṛṣṇa, the form she adored. She is also said to have gone to Vṛndāvan, where she met Jīva Gosvāmī, a disciple of Caitanya and the central figure in the formative stages of the *Gauḍīya* sect of Kṛṣṇa devotion.[8] The latter broke his vow not to speak to women in order to converse with her (in other tellings, only after Mīrā reminded him that all devotees are female before this decidedly male God).

The tale ends with her going to Dvaraka and the *rāṇā's* sending a delegation of Brahmins to bring her back to Mewar—perhaps because he had finally seen the light, perhaps because she was still bringing shame on the family; Priyadas does not tell us, though others will.[9] She refused to come; they threatened to fast to the death if she did not. She cried out to Kṛṣṇa, and he drew her to him. When the Brahmins came looking for her, they found only her clothing draped across his image. She had merged into her Lord and was finally beyond their grasp.

The basic narrative is hagiography rather than history, but if Mīrā actually lived, we might hope to confirm elements of the story and fill in additional details by consulting traditional historical sources. We find such sources largely silent with respect to Mīrā's existence. Indeed, the closer we get to her probable lifetime, the colder the trail of evidence becomes. Records from the fifteenth and early sixteenth century consist mainly of inscriptions capable of withstanding the ravages of time and political turmoil, but among those relating to the royal families of Merta and Mewar, Mīrā is not mentioned.

Few women find a place in such records, with the notable exception of Ramā Bāi, daughter of Rāṇā Kumbha, praised in the Javar inscription (1497 C.E.) as a highly educated woman in both literature and music, who was responsible for the construction of a tank and a temple at Kumbhalgarh fort and a reservoir at Javar.[10] She is hailed not only for her intellectual and artistic talents and her devotion to God but also for her great love for her husband and his for her. No similar tribute to Mīrā has been found, although academic tellings of her life story, as we shall see, suggest that she shared these qualities and also built lasting structures of that type. Perhaps the political chaos of sixteenth century Mewar left no leisure for such inscriptions, or perhaps Mīrā was not related to such a famous man. But there may have been other reasons for Mīrā's absence, especially if she was, indeed, perceived as considerably less than an ideal wife and as one who brought shame to her Rajput family through her unorthodox behavior, as other accounts of her life (including Priyadas's) suggest.

The only known reference to Mīrābāi before the nineteenth century in traditional historical sources is a single line in the seventeenth century writings of Muhnot Nainsi (1610–1670), chief minister under Maharaja Jasvant Singh of Jodhpur.[11] *Nainsī rī Khyāt* chronicles the history of the Rajputs back to their mythic origins, though it focuses primarily on the history of Marwar (Mīrā's natal kingdom) and contains a wealth of detail about life and culture in seventeenth century Rajasthan. Mīrā merits passing mention in this work in connection to Rāṇā Saṅgha's son Bhojrāj: "it is said that Mīrābāi Rāṭhor was married to him."[12] The names of Saṅgha's other sons' wives are not given, and generally only the names and lineages for wives of rulers who are also the mothers of their heirs are listed. That Mīrā appears here at all suggests that she was sufficiently well-known to both author and audience that this bit of information would have been interesting, even though the marriage appears to be a genealogical dead-end without particular historical ramifications. The date of Bhojrāj's marriage (1516 C.E.) is a part of the historical events surrounding Mīrā's life.[13] This is a very thin thread with which to begin to weave a historical biography, however.

Why do we find this silence in traditional historical sources? We might expect to find Mīrā mentioned in the family records and histories of her natal and marital kin, especially if they held her in high esteem, but for the most part we do not. In general, the available sources deal with battles, administrative concerns, economic transactions, and genealogies, in which women had little place except as wives and mothers to rulers and as the means for political alliances through marriage. Extraordinary women do find their way into oral traditions and legends, however, and in this sense, Mīrā seems to belong more to the ranks of Padminī, Pānnā, and other legendary women of Mewar (though their sacrifice and devotion were for the sake of the kingdom and to uphold Rajput honor rather than for God). There is so little evidence that Mīrābāi's existence as an actual historical person might even be questioned, as Padminī's has been by those who argue that she was the creation of poets rather than a woman of flesh and blood. [14] That Mīrā lived and lives in the popular imagination, however, cannot be denied.

Outright suppression of Mīrā's story by the royal family of Mewar has been asserted by Parita Mukta.[15] Mukta cites five examples drawn from field interviews in 1986 and 1987 to support her claim: a puppeteer who in 1971 inadvertently enraged members of a Sisodiya Rajput village by singing Mīrā songs to gather an audience for a performance; Mukta's own experience of hostility when she asked some Bhatti Rajput women in a village near Chittor if they would name their daughters Mīrā; the testimony of a librarian in Udaipur, who assured her that Mīrā was reviled by the rulers and that no records would be found; the disparaging remarks of a Rajput man in Chittor; and the claims of a former employee of the princely state in Chittor that in past times no one would dare mention Mīrā for fear of losing his or her job, so despised was she.[16] Other evidence beyond that given by Mukta can also be marshaled. In 1938, M. L. Menaria wrote to Purohit Harinarayan Sharma of the Maharana [Bhupalsingh]'s opinion of Mīrā: "Even the Maharana Sahib believes that Mīrā has been a black-blot on the fair page of the Mewar History and musicians are not allowed to sing the Padas of Mīrā Bāi in the Palace."[17] Menaria asked Harinarayan not to mention this in any published work, but the correspondence has now been made public.

Are these examples sufficient evidence of an active attempt to repress the memory of Mīrā maintained for four centuries? I myself ran into no such overt hostility during my field research in Rajasthan in 1992 to 1993, though I did encounter some ambivalence about her behaviour as woman and wife, and elsewhere my inquiries were met with indifference. Mukta's informants suggest that, in the recent past, hostility may have been greater. Mīrā's absence from the historical records cannot be definitively attributed to intentional suppression, given the paucity of references to other women in this type of documentation. It is true, however, that if her natal or marital kin had thought very highly of her (as later members of her family claim), a saint of such great popularity for their lineage surely might have merited greater attention. At the very least, this silence suggests indifference and makes every retelling of Mīrā's life story necessarily something less than historical biography.

The academic study of Mīrābāi began in the early nineteenth century, when she caught the interest of Europeans who were writing about Indian religion, literature, and history. In 1828, H. H. Wilson wrote of her, along with other saints, in "The Religious Sects of the Hindus."[18] His information was drawn primarily from hagiographic accounts, but he also mentioned a sect of Mīrābāi's (though no subsequent scholar has been able to confirm the existence of such a sect). Price, in his *Hindee and Hindustanee Selections* (1827), offered translations of several poems attributed to Mīrā (also drawn from a hagiographic text, Nagridas's *Padaprasaṅgamālā*), and Wilson and Price became references for Colonel James Todd's account of Mīrā in the *Annals and Antiquities of Rajasthan* (1829–1832).[19]

Todd had been appointed as the political agent to Mewar by the East India Company in 1818, when a treaty was ratified between Mewar and Britain, though his tenure was short, ending in 1822. The kingdom was apparently in disarray at his time, torn apart by war and debt.[20] Todd wrote of the glorious deeds of Rajput heroes and is credited with ushering Rajasthan onto the national and world stage and with initiating modern historical writing on the region. With respect to Mīrā, he writes of her being the wife of Rāṇā Kumbha (the grandfather of Bhojraj, with whom Nainsi had associated her) and reports information drawn from conversations with devotees about the temple in Chittor he supposedly built for Mīrā.[21]

These accounts of Mīrā's life, as well as those of Garcin de Tassy (1839), Shiv Singh Sengar (1876), G. A. Grierson (1988), and G. M. Tripathi (1892), are fragmentary narratives, drawn from hagiography, songs attributed to Mīrā, and popular legendary materials.[22] Nainsi's reference was unknown to the authors. Mīrā's husband and the details of her life remain vague, although Rāṇā Kumbha is often reported as the one to whom she was married. She is romanticized as a swooning, pious, beautiful devotee, who perhaps learned her devotion from her husband (according to Todd) or tried with innocent purity to convert him (according to Tripathi). As portrayed by these authors, she lacks the strength and shamelessness of the devotional accounts and, instead, is sentimentalized and relegated largely to the world of women. [23]

As the history of Rajasthan grew to be a nationalist concern in the late nineteenth century, a new, more complete portrait of Mīrā emerged in the construction of Hindu nationalist and revitalized Rajput identities in response to colonial domination. The academic portrayal of Mīrā is squarely situated in this nationalist and Rajput discourse and must be understood in this context. The late 1820s, when Todd and Wilson first wrote of Mīrā, was a transitional era in British rule. Ashis Nandy, in his study of the psychology of colonialism, suggests that before

1830 the idea of empire had not yet taken hold in the minds of the British, nor had "homology between sexual and political dominance . . . [become] central to the colonial culture."[24] After this time, however, both became operative as the British middle class entered colonial administration and as British political and cultural dominance over India became more complete. Justification for colonial rule had to be constructed by generating a rhetoric of hypermasculinity that put the British in the role of dominant male, both rescuing vulnerable Indian women, who were perceived as victims of Indian male barbarism and ignorance, and taking care of those same men, who were alternately characterized as womanly, weak, childlike, and in need of guidance and discipline.[25] Nandy suggests that within this characterization a "manly man" (read "British man") was better than a "womanly man" (read "Indian woman"), and an "effeminate man" (read "Indian man") ranked below them both.[26]

The nationalist response to this rhetoric was a counternarrative to the British one.[27] Drawing on the British conception of the martial races (used in military recruitment) and on history and legend, they told an alternate story of military heroism with the Sikhs, Rajputs, and Marathas valiantly resisting foreign domination (primarily portrayed as Muslim). The works of Todd on the Rajputs, J. D. Cunningham on the Sikhs, and Grant Duff on the Marathas offered a wealth of raw material for this project, and the emerging identity was decidedly Hindu, though transregional.[28] This glorification of *Kṣatriya* (warrior and ruling caste) ideals was in full swing in the latter half of the century, with their origins traced back to the epic traditions of the *Mahābhārata*. The Rajputs, in particular, were portrayed as having never bowed to foreign domination, preferring to die rather than submit.

The new identity was forged in narrative; consciously constructed through the reshaping of myth, legend, hagiography, and history; and exercised in fiction. Heroes from the more distant past merged with those of the present, and even the deities were not privileged in this process.[29] Kṛṣṇa was transformed under the pen of Bankimchandra Chatterji, a novelist and key figure in this nationalist endeavor to reshape Hindu identity.[30] In the words of Nandy, Bankimchandra:

> tried to build a historical and historically conscious Kṛṣṇa—self-consistent, self-conscious and moral according to modern norms. He scanned all the ancient texts of Kṛṣṇa, not only to locate Kṛṣṇa in history, but to argue away all references to Kṛṣṇa's character traits unacceptable to the new norms relation to sexuality, politics and social relationships. . . . His Kṛṣṇa was respectable, righteous, didactic, "hard" god, protecting the glories of Hinduism as proper religion and preserving it as an internally consistent moral and cultural system. Bankimchandra rejected as latter-day interpolations—and hence unauthentic—every trait of Kṛṣṇa that did not meet the first requirement for a Christian and Islamic god, namely all perfection. His goal was to make Kṛṣṇa a normal, nonpagan male god who would not humiliate his devotees in front of the progressive Westerners.[31]

The transformed Kṛṣṇa mirrors the ideal Hindu Indian man, combining qualities of the military hero and the spiritual renouncer.[32] I would argue that the historians of Rajasthan performed the same exercise on Mīrā: transforming her into a Rajput heroine and ideal wife and disregarding as historically inaccurate or "mere folk stories" any tellings that might suggest otherwise.

Mīrā enters this process of identity construction in part because a new Hindu woman was needed to stand beside the new Hindu man, and the search was on for exemplary women from the past. The Hindu woman had to be both heroic and self-disciplined, ready to step out of the home in defense of the motherland yet also to remain within it, preserving Indian superiority over the British in the spiritual realm as the embodiment of all that was best in Indian culture.[33] Indian history and legend included stories of heroic women or *vīrāṅganās*, many of whom were Rajputs (though not the Rani of Jhansi, whose battles with the British during the so-called mutiny of 1857 made her an ideal figure to rally the independence movement).[34] These heroines moved beyond the normative gender constructions of their high-caste birth and were known for their martial skills and valor in battle. They took roles normally available only to men in administering kingdoms and, in times of crisis, leading armies, even dressing as men in many cases, riding horses, and wielding swords in defense of their homeland.

Such strong women offered a stark contrast to the British portrayal of Indian women as victimized, passive, helpless, and in desperate need of rescue. The bounds of this independence and strength were circumscribed, however, and never allowed to undermine the masculinity of the Hindu man reclaimed in the face of British hypermasculinity. In *Ānandamaṭh*, Bankimchandra portrayed this Hindu woman as an everyday *vīrāṅganā*—one who in a time of crisis could transcend both her sexuality (his heroine Śānti dresses as a male renouncer) and domesticity (she fights at her husband's side in defense of the nation).[35] Still, crisis made this type of action acceptable, and in most nationalist constructions women were generally expected to continue to adhere to the ideals embodied by Sītā—the long-suffering, self-sacrificing, virtuous, absolutely devoted wife of Rāma—and instill in others the same sense of integrity, devotion, and self-sacrifice in the service of the nation. In this middle-class reformulation, women who dared to challenge notions of *strīdharma* (women's religious and social duty) were seen as betraying not only their men but also the nation. The other side of participation in this rhetoric of hypermasculinity was that "woman" had to remain the measure of the masculine by contrast and complementarity.

The nationalist embrace of Rajput martial culture and the search for exemplary Indian women focused attention on Mīrābāi, in addition to the more traditional *vīrāṅganās*. Mīrā's popularity extended across the subcontinent and made her a likely candidate for a pan-Indian Hindu cultural heroine with universal appeal. Her extreme dedication and willingness to undergo suffering in the name of truth led Gandhi and others to draw on her as an example for resistance against the British and a symbol of Indian women's strength and courage.[36]

In the face of such widespread admiration and the identification of Mīrā with Rajasthan, the Rajput elite could hardly ignore her, though she, like Kṛṣṇa, might need to be rehabilitated and though alternate tellings of her story might be denounced as erroneous. As she appears in hagiographic accounts, Mīrā does not precisely fit the *vīrāṅganā* model or the mold of an ideal wife. Her story must be retold and is—with the *vīrāṅganā* narrative structure used as a template. This transformed Mīrā emerges as a part of the conscious self-representation of Rajputs through the medium of historical writing.

The first official recognition of Mīrā in a historical document associated with the royal family of Mewar is in Kaviraj Shyamaldas's monumental *Vīr Vinod*, completed in 1886.[37] Nationalist interest in Rajasthan had been fueled by Todd's tales of Rajput warriors, and Bengali intellectuals took up the task of writing Rajasthani history, with Harimohan Mukherjee's *Rājasthaner Itihāsa* published in 1884 and Gopal Chandra Mukherjee's *Rājasthāna* in 1885 in Bengali.[38] Todd's work inspired rulers in Rajasthan to commission the writing of their own history, seemingly as much to recover a Rajput identity of honor and valor as to forge a new national Hindu one. Shyamaldas was assigned this task by the ruler of Mewar. Similar moves were being made in other regions to take back Indian history from foreign scholars and political agents. Serious investigation of available historical records was undertaken (though these histories served nationalist and regional ideological needs as well).[39] Unfortunately, Shyamaldas's enemies in the court somehow convinced the Mahārāṇā that his work would undermine the ruler's authority, perhaps because he wrote of weakness and excess as well as heroism. All but a few copies of the text were locked away and sealed in a palace room from 1892 until 1945.[40] A few copies remained in the hands of those who worked with him on this project, however, and these men disseminated and continued his work.

Shyamaldas was clearly influenced by Todd in his approach to writing history. He took a more objective stance in writing the history of a kingdom than might be expected of someone sponsored by the rulers, but he also took on the task of correcting Todd's many "errors" and presenting the "true" history of Mewar.[41] With respect to Mīrā, he denied Todd's assertion that she was married to Rāṇā Kumbha.[42] She was, in fact, the wife of Rāṇā Saṅgha's oldest son, Bhojrāj, granddaughter of Duda, daughter of Ratan Singh, niece of Virāmdev, and cousin of Jaymal of Merta. He gives his source for Bhojrāj as Mīrā's husband as the histories of the Mertiya Rathors and Jodhpur (the center of Marwar). He also makes it very clear that Mīrā lived during the reigns of the brothers-in-law Vikramāditya and Udaisingh and that it was they who honored devotees and holy men and composed and sang songs of renunciation (*virāg*).

A more complete telling of her life story appears for the first time in Munshi Deviprasad's *Mīrābāi kī Jivan Caritra* (1898).[43] Deviprasad's purpose is explicit: both to increase awareness about Mīrābai because people do not know her story and to correct mistaken notions about her. These goals mark much of the academic study of Mīrā. He constructs his account by taking the episodes related in the hagiographic narratives and the marriage date to Bhojrāj of 1516, searching for all available historical facts that might impinge on Mīrā's life, and weaving them together with the threads of legend and hagiography. He cites his sources, specifically stating that he has consulted Shyamaldas and his assistant Gaurishankar Ojha and the archives of Mewar.[44] The emerging tale differs markedly from Priyadas's.

Deviprasad begins by clarifying the lineage of both Mīrā and Bhojrāj. He details the long history of political squabbles and alliances forged through marriages between the Rathor and Sisodiya families, of which Mīrā's marriage to Bhojrāj in 1516 is but one example. As Deviprasad tells the story, when Mīrā was a child, she had an image of Kṛṣṇa that she treated as a playmate. Duda, her uncle Virāmdev, and her cousin Jaymal—all known to be great Vaiṣṇavas—imparted their devotion to her.

Her mother died when she was very young, her grandfather called her to Merta, where he saw to her education; and her father arranged her marriage to Bhojrāj when she was twelve years old. Deviprasad is silent about her married life and moves immediately to the death of her husband. Her father-in-law was killed shortly thereafter, as was her father while fighting as his ally. Mīrā is portrayed as turning to God as a result of the loss of so many people near and dear to her and as only at this point developing the devotion that began with her childhood games.

Her brother-in-law, whom Deviprasad calls Ratan Singh, came to power, and there was considerable turmoil within the kingdom during those years, from both internal strife and external threats. After Ratan Singh's short reign, the younger Vikramaditya came to the throne, and Deviprasad says specifically that it was he who persecuted Mīrā because her association with saints and holy men led people to slander the family. The Rana's sending of poison is recounted, after which Mīrā returned to Merta to her uncle Virāmdev and her cousin Jaymal. This move proved to be only a temporary solution to her problems, however, as her family was forced to flee from place to place after successive losses to Maldev of Jodhpur.

With respect to Mīrā's death, Deviprasad recounts the devotional tradition of her merger with Kṛṣṇa's image in Dvaraka. He also give her death date as 1546 based on the oral records of a traditional genealogist of the Rathors. Beyond this, he reports that people say she went to Vrindavan and had her well-known encounter with a celibate (Jīva Gosvāmī is not mentioned by name) and that she was supposed to have met Akbar and Tansen and corresponded with Tulsidas, both of which Deviprasad doubts because of the discrepancy of dates. Of Mīrā's poetry, he adds that many songs were composed later in her name, and he closes with three famous ones.

The Mīrā who emerges from Deviprasad's telling is a woman whose life was marked by sorrow and loss and whose devotion flowered out of this soil of suffering—a very different image from that in the hagiographic accounts. She turned fully to Kṛṣṇa only after she had been forced to realize the illusory nature of this world and its pleasures. In this way, her devotion is rationalized, and her rebellion becomes renunciation. Further, she was a widow, whom fate and the world had renounced, rather than a young, beautiful woman who renounced the world. Her behavior was somewhat extreme for a Rajput widow, but the edge is taken off her infractions. Figuratively, draped in white, she is an ideal for widowed women, strong in the face of opposition and absolute in her devotion to God after the path of wifely devotion was closed to her. Though almost every point in this version of Mīrā's story—her birth and death dates, her place of birth, and so on, continued to be contested across the century of scholarship that followed, a consensus view (with various disputed details) eventually emerges, with the narrative structure laid down by Deviprasad as its foundation.

This version of Mīrā's life seems to emanate from a very small group of men who acknowledge each other in their published works and in their correspondence with Harinarayan Sharma (who himself spent 40 years investigating Mīrā's life and songs).[45] Shyamaldas's assistant, Ojha, became the preeminent historian of Rajasthan, publishing a number of volumes on various kingdoms from 1924 to 1940.[46] He mentions Mīrā, giving the same general story as Deviprasad, who, in turn, had acknowledged his own debt to Shyamaldas and Ojha.[47] Jagdish Singh Gahlot provides further details, noting that the low-caste leatherworker-saint Raidas must have been Mīrā's guru (because he is mentioned in songs attributed to her) but that a Brahmin named Gajadhar was her childhood teacher.[48] Another historian, Har Bilas Sarda, acknowledges that his information about Mīrā (reported in his 1818 work, *Mahārāṇā Saṅgha)* came from Shyamaldas's *Vīr Vinod* and from *Caturkul Caritra*, composed by Chatur Singh of Rupaheli in 1902.[49] Chatur Singh and Gopal Singh of Badnor were both members of Mīrā's family line through her cousin Jaymal. The latter mentions Mīrā in his *Jaymal Vansh Prakash*, following the same line as Deviprasad's tale by adding the detail that Mīrā's wedding to Bhojrāj was accompanied by great celebration and that the Mertiya Rathors are proud of her.[50]

These men were clearly in conversation with each other. Chatur Singh reports to Harinarayan that Deviprasad, Ojha, and Gahlot had visited both him and Gopal Singh to discuss Mīrā.[51] This particular story of Mīrā was first given full form by Deviprasad, Gahlot, Chatur Singh, and Gopal Singh. They apparently were drawing primarily on sources from Mīrā's natal kin, in addition to more widely known hagiographic and legendary material. Beyond *Nainsī rī Khyāt*, no written sources that specifically mention Mīrā have been confirmed, so presumably the unique details of this narrative of Mīrā's reflect oral traditions, and the resulting tale corresponds to these men's notion of what might be "appropriate," "natural," and "rational" when choices had to be made about what to include or what gaps to fill in.

Why they might be interested in presenting their version of Mīrā's story is also clear from Chatur Singh's correspondence with Harinarayan. He writes that people in even the smallest villages throughout the land do not know the names of Mewar and Marwar or even Rajasthan but everywhere are familiar with "*Mīrā ke desh*" (Mīrā's country) and the towns of Merta and Chittor.[52] When the great leaders of the nation "sing the praise of the jewels of Indian womanhood," they inevitably mention Mīrā: Vivekananda, Bal Gangadhar Tilak, Lajpat Ray, Chitta Ranjan Das, Madan Mohan Malavya, Motilal Nehru, Rabindranath Thakur, and Gandhi all offered her the highest praise, he reports to Harinarayan.[53] His pride in Mīrā is clear, as is the seeming necessity and efficacy of Rajputs in reclaiming her as one of their own.

The particular story they tell was not well-known. In fact, it appears to have required considerable research to uncover. Lindsey Harlan's work among Rajput women in Udaipur gives weight to the suspicion that even among other Rajputs it may not have been familiar and suggests further that the unmitigated admiration for Mīrā expressed by these men might also not be shared by all Rajputs (even as the unmitigated condemnation suggested by Mukta may not be).[54] Elements of the academic account of Mīrā's life are present in these women's tellings of her story, but they could have been exposed to this as easily through external sources as through family traditions. Given the discrepancies between their accounts and the academic ones and the deep ambivalence toward Mīrā's behavior that runs through their tellings, the former is as likely as the latter, if not more so.

As Harlan reports, the Rajput women she interviewed unequivocally stated that Mīrā's behavior enraged her marital family, although her husband was alternately portrayed as angry or supportive by different narrators. In every case, Mīrā refused to be a proper wife to the *rāṇa*, denied her marriage to him by refusing to consummate it, and claimed to be already married to Kṛṣṇa. When she left her home and became a famous devotee after her husband's death, her marital family continued to be shamed by her behavior . They sent men to bring her back, but when they entered the temple where she worshiped she was already gone, having merged with her lord. The story of the lascivious holy man, largely excised from the academic accounts, was included by these women, but the denouement occurred in private before the image of Kṛṣṇa, and the *sādhu* ran away rather than becoming Mīrā's disciple.

Theirs is definitely not the same story told by Chatur Singh and the others. Mīrā's behavior was an insult to the Sisodiya Rajputs of Mewar until she died and perhaps beyond, and there was no reconciliation. In Harlan's analysis, the women telling this tale admire Mīrā's courage and dedication in facing social sanction and her in-laws' cruelty, and they question Mīrā's behavior as *pativratā* (proper wife), suggesting that because she was married she should not have taken up *bhakti* (devotion to God) and renounced the world. Further, they focus on Mīrā's death, which somehow vindicates her life choices because she was willing to die for them even as a Rajput heroine or *satī* would be and because Kṛṣṇa seemed to affirm in this fine embrace the divine marriage that Mīrā claimed had invalidated her earthly one. The miraculous nature of her demise separates her forever from ordinary women, and there is no suggestion that she was ever a *pativratā* of her earthly husband.[55]

The differences between the tellings of these Rajput women and those of the early scholars (though perhaps in part related to the gender of the narrators) suggest that there is not widespread standard Rajput remembrance of Mīrā. Mīrā's story seemingly was not kept alive across the centuries in any exclusive way by Rajputs or in the form presented by the scholars. The active traditions among devotees and low-caste communities seem to be much more fertile ground for ensuring the continuity of the tradition over time and for Mīrā's far-reaching and ongoing popularity, as Mukta's groundbreaking study of the traditions of Mīrābāi among low-caste groups in Rajasthan and Gujarat suggests.[56]

Although the narrative line of Mīrā's story put forth by Deviprasad and the others has never been universally accepted, it received further elaboration by later scholars and with time became widely propagated as "truth" about Mīrā, especially among educated members of the middle and upper classes and castes, who were only too willing to dismiss the miracle-filled tales of devotees and folk renditions, with their embedded critiques of social, religious, and gender hierarchies. Certain elements received particular attention in these elaborations: Mīrā's education, her relationship with the men of her marital household, and the political awareness underlying some of her actions.

For example, Harinarayan reports the following additional details from his conversations with Chatur Singh and Gopal Singh. According to the *Gurjargaui* Brahmins' *khyats*, Mīrā was well educated by her guru Gajadhar in reading, writing, music, and religious matters, and she was so intelligent that she was soon recognized for her wisdom.[57] Further, based on their conversations, she appears to have lived happily with her husband for five to six years until he died, and only then, overcome with sorrow, did she turn completely to devotion. Saṅgha (her father-in-law) is portrayed as fully supporting her religiosity, providing her funds to worship as she chose and to care for religious mendicants, and giving her a great entourage, including elephants, servants, and soldiers for her pilgrimages. A temple was built for her by Udaisingh in Dvarka after her death, demonstrating that she had the uniform support of the male members of her marital family. Harinarayan further reports that, according to Chatur Singh, Mīrā never wore the saffron clothes of a renouncer, and Raidas was not associated with her in any way.[58] Mīrā thus appears to challenge neither caste barriers nor the institution of marriage, and she never steps out of the signification of a woman's identity in terms of marital status marked by dress.

Three other authors stand out as particularly significant in giving final shape to this family of tales: Bankey Behari (1935) in his explicit incorporation of Rajput honor and ideals and Hermann Goetz (1956) and Kalyan Singh Shekhawat (1974) in their politicization of Mīrā's actions.[59] Bankey Behari was a former advocate and recognized theologian and philosopher who was a great devotee of Mīrā. He makes it clear that he writes a "truth" about Mīrā that is (in his estimation) higher than that revealed by historical and academic investigation (though his narrative structurally and ideologically belongs to this same family of tales). Like the hagiographic accounts, it turns on Mīrā's triumph over opposition of various kinds. Some previously reported conflicts are reduced to mere appearance—although Mīrā's mother-in-law feigned anger at her refusal to bow down before the goddess, she was, in fact, deeply impressed with the girl's piety. Nowhere in Behari's retelling is Mīrā anything but the perfect wife with the single exception that "she stood adamant in her virgin glory, guarding her rights with meticulous care," and spent her nights worshiping Kṛṣṇa rather than with the *rāṇā*.[60] He portrays her as very popular with the court as well as the people. Bhojraj is also a sympathetic character—a paragon of Rajput virtue who has nothing to do with Mīrā's persecution.

When Rajput honor was threatened after a Muslim man, the emperor Akbar, dared to approach and converse with a Rajput woman, the wife of a prince no less, Bhojrāj rightly had to defend that honor, ordering Mīrā to drown herself. She went willingly, upholding that same honor and obedient to her husband's command. Only Kṛṣṇa's direct intervention stopped her. Releasing her from the bonds of her earthly marriage, he sent her to Vrindavan, where she dreamed of her former life as Rādhā. The way was full of hardship and privation, but Mīrā was uncomplaining, entirely immersed in God and mindless of difficulties of the journey, even as Bhojrāj was on military campaigns according to Behari.

As her fame grew, news of her reached Bhojrāj. Disguising himself as a holy man, he went to see her (in an inversion of the "lustful *sādhu*" episode). He asked her to return to Chittor, and ever the good wife, she went willingly. Unfortunately, he died soon thereafter, and his brother Ratan Singh, at the instigation of her sister-in-law Udābāi, began to torment Mīrā. Distraught at the interference with her devotion, she wrote to the poet-saint Tulsidas to ask him what she should do. His response was that her true family was the community of devotees, so she should leave Chittor and live among them. She then encountered her true guru, Raidas, and finally merged with Kṛṣṇa's image in Dvarka in a state of ecstasy and in the midst of the community of devotees rather than in isolation and as a result of coercion.

How far this telling has come from that of Nabhadas and Priyadas! Bhojrāj and Mīrā together uphold both Rajput ideals and devotion, and Mīrā is the embodiment of feminine virtue and strength. She remains always obedient to men, who make her decisions and control her destiny: to her father in accepting her arranged marriage without question, to her husband in conforming to his every request (except perhaps one), to Kṛṣṇa in going to Vrindavan, to Tulsidas in finally leaving Chittor, and to Raidas, who is credited with leading her to a higher experience of her Lord. Within Bankey Behari's narrative, she manages to remain both a wife and a disciple, obedient to social and religious institutional control, as well as to God, who seems to reinforce these structures. It was this version of Mīrā's story that was selected for the widely distributed *Amar Chitra Kathā* comic book series on Hindu saints and deities.[61]

Hermann Goetz gives final form to the academic narrative by combining a careful study of history with rational explanations for the seemingly miraculous elements of the tale. Goetz was born in Germany in 1898, lived in India from 1936 to 1955, and was a scholar of Indian archaeology, precolonial history, and art history, with an interest also in mysticism across religious traditions.[62] His devotion to Mīrā is also unquestionable—the only person he deems worthy of comparison with her is Jesus Christ. Goetz is admired by many for his meticulous attention to historical details, though in their absence he does not hesitate to weave a probable (or improbable) tale that reconciles a variety of narrative fragments.

In his attempt to understand the motivations of the characters in her life story, he turns to politics as the most compelling explanation of events. He details the turbulent history of Mīrā's marital family in the years after Bhojrāj's death and suggests that perhaps Mīrā earned her father-in-law's favor by warning him of an impending coup. But she may also have made enemies in the process. Further, he suggests that the persecution of Mīrā was motivated by political rather than religious concerns stemming from this incident. This is the only reasonable explanation for Ratan Singh's opposition to her, according to Goetz. Mīrā had no interest in politics or sectarian matters, but her integrity led her to speak the truth when she saw something unethical. Describing the lives of women in Mīrā's position, Goetz suggests that there was nothing unusual about her behavior except the intensity of her devotion—even taking care of wandering mendicants would have been a common activity.

When Saṅgha and her own father died, she lost her protection, and Ratan Singh went after her without anyone to stop him. He was suspicious of Mīrā's fraternization with holy men because spies often took such a guise (clearly not an issue of honor or possible sexual impropriety here). Attempts were made on her life, but she survived, not because of miracles but because she had supporters within the palace who replaced the poisonous snakes sent in the fruit basket with nonvenomous ones and diluted or switched the poison said to be holy water.

When Vikramaditya came to power, he continued to torment Mīrā and ordered her decapitation. When no one would carry it out, he told her to drown herself.

She escaped somehow and joined her uncle Viramdev in Merta. Goetz's description of Vikramaditya is as degrading as he can possibly make it; the young ruler's unmanliness is portrayed in decidedly homophobic terms as "a wanton and coward, fond of strong young men, and subservient to older men who knew how to take him" and as despised by the rest of the court.[63] His nobles defected right and left, and his downfall was inevitable, according to Goetz. What more appropriate persecutor could there be for Mīrā than this man whom other historians agree was a despicable aberration in an otherwise noble line?

Goetz goes on to speak of Mīrā as revolutionary simply in the sense that she ignored the rules of the social order in the interest of spreading religion to the lower classes and to women. Her behavior was not tolerated by her relatives in Merta either, and she became a wandering mendicant, eventually reaching Dvaraka. Kṛṣṇa of Dvaraka, Goetz assures us, was a mature warrior prince rather than a cowherding, youthful lover, and Mīrā's attraction to him was based on her embrace of "the philosophy of duty and courage combined, in the Gītā, with the message of Divine love and surrender," in a characterization that seems to echo Bankimchandra's Kṛṣṇa.[64] Her disappearance when Brahmins were sent by Udaisingh to fetch her is also rationalized—she must have left the temple by some hidden exit and continued to live out her life as an anonymous wandering devotee.

Goetz's Mīrā is intelligent, strong, politically astute, and decisive; she upholds social convention even as she pursues devotion. A religious reformer and active missionary (of a rather Christian-sounding sort), she preaches a gospel of love and of individual access to the divine to the disenfranchised. She is no *devadāsī*, no intoxicated dancing lover of the Divine Cowherd. Rather, she is one who, like Kṛṣṇa in Dvaraka, combines duty, courage, and devotion in a dignified religious calling.

Kalyan Singh Shekhawat (1969) tells the tale yet again, with a few new details gleaned from the *kulguru* (hereditary family priest) of the Mertiya Rathors, but it is his further politicization of Mīrā's motives for leaving Chittor that is of greatest interest for our purposes. As Goetz had mentioned, Mīrā was suspect because spies often took the guise of holy men to enter an enemy's territory undetected. Shekhawat suggests that when Mīrā learned that her actions might be endangering Chittor, she chose to leave to protect the kingdom, even as her uncle Virāmdev called her to him when he heard of her suffering at the hands of Vikramāditya. Her actions in leaving Chittor thus become heroic, worthy of praise rather than condemnation.

This family of tales told by the scholars from Shyamaldas and Deviprasad to Goetz and Shekhawat differs significantly from the hagiographic accounts of Mīrā's life, as we have seen. Mīrā has been thoroughly "Rajputized" to uphold and embody Rajput ideals and values. Some of the details are puzzling, however. Why is Mīrā's mother said to have died when she was young, for example, when most other tellings of Mīrā's story have her present at the time of her daughter's marriage? An examination of the narrative structure of the tales reveals that this set of stories of Mīrā conforms not to the usual pattern of the stories of women *bhakti* saints lives but rather to that of *vīrāṅganā* narratives.[65] In such tales, heroic Rajput and Brahmin queens, including Durgavatī, Tārābāi, Ahalyābāi, and Lakṣmībāi (the Rāṇī of Jhānsī), are broadly educated in the same way it is suggested in academic narratives that

Mīrā was, well-versed in war and statecraft, as well as literature and religion.[66] They are trained by older males—fathers and fathers-in-law—and there is no place for mothers in their tales, even as there is no place in Mīrā's story in this form.

Crises force these women to take positions of leadership usually reserved for men; either they fight side by side with fathers or husbands, or they take over when their husbands die and their sons are too young to rule. Though Mīrā does not engage in such activities, her turn to extreme devotion is motivated by crisis, and Goetz and Shekhawat politicize her actions. She emerges as a strong and willful woman who exhibits a similar fearless courage in the face of death, has many characteristics of a man, and moves in the world of men (though more often in the company of holy men than of soldiers—a kind of masculinity defined by self-control rather than aggression, epitomized again by Bankimchandra's Kṛṣṇa). No mere victim, she acts decisively and involves herself in the affairs of state in the name of truth. In Shekhawat's telling, she even willingly gives up everything to leave Chittor for the good of the kingdom.

In general, the *vīrāṅganās* are portrayed both as having the strength, courage, and skills of men and as being good wives as long as their husbands are alive. Ahalyābāi decided to commit *satī* when her husband died but was deterred by her father-in-law and went on to rule the kingdom and lead armies into battle; Tārābāi fought side by side with her husband to win back her father's kingdom and later immolated herself on his funeral pyre after he was poisoned. Mīrā, too, takes on masculine traits in her independence and strength but exhibits characteristics of the *pativratā* during her husband's lifetime. This "manly woman" stands in contrast to a "womanly man," Vikramāditya, identified as the very opposite of the "manly man" Bhojrāj and reviled by Goetz as an effeminate homosexual, the worst possible characterization in the larger discourse of hypermasculinity, of which such stories are a part. Yet Mīrā herself does not challenge the manhood of Bhojraj and acts as the perfect wife—in some tellings, living in blissful marital union until his death; in others, offering him every wifely service while maintaining her chastity absolutely and thus transcending sexuality. Her husband cannot be said to have opposed her in any way because as a *pativratā* she would have been bound to obey him. Mīrā's transformation into a Rajput heroine is complete, and the logic of various elements of this family of tales is revealed.

Do these scholars then have the real truth about Mīrā? I would suggest not. They do give us considerable information about her probable lifetime, and further study will undoubtedly provide additional contextual richness. However, the "truth" they tell is only one among many: Mīrā's story has clearly become a second-order language to speak about things other than the life of a saint from the past. To dismiss Mīrā because of the way they have told her story is a mistake.[67] She remains immensely popular and stubbornly beyond our ability to pin her down to a single image, a single story, or a single repertoire of songs. Her traditions are a powerful resource to voice resistance among members of lower castes, and her example is an interpretive category that facilitates the choices made by some women to live lives outside marriage in a society where such options are severely limited.[68] There are other far different "Mīrās," and I see no reason to surrender her to those who are more comfortable with a Mīrā who is a good Rajput wife than with one so devoted to God and so sure of her own calling that she would disregard every rule of social behavior in pursuit of her goal, dance out her love, and laugh in the face of death. It is this latter Mīrā who might have sung:

I am dyed in the colour of my Dark Lover, Rana,
  dyed in the colour of my Dark Love.
Beating out the rhythm on a drum,
  In the presence of holy men, I danced.
People thought me mad with desire,
  raw for my Dark One's love.
I am dyed in the colour of my Dark Lover, Rana,
  dyed in the colour of my Dark Love.
The poison cup that Rana sent,
  I drank without a second thought.
Mīrā's Lord is the clever Mountain Bearer,
  He stays true in life after life.[69]

Notes

1. This essay is based in part on fieldwork carried out in Rajasthan from August 1992 through November 1993, funded by the American Institute for Indian Studies, and is drawn from a chapter of my dissertation on Mīrābai entitled "Dyed in the Color of Her Lord: Multiple Representations in the Mīrābai Tradition" (Graduate Theological Union, 1995). Considerably more detailed information is available there for the interested reader.

2. Parita Mukta (1994), provides translations and interpretations of songs attributed to Mīrā sung by women and low-caste singers in Rajasthan and Saurashtra, Gujarat.

3. Winand Callewaert. (1991), pp. 201–14.

4. I have chosen to follow A. K. Ramanujan in using the term "tellings" rather than "variants" to refer to different versions of the story because "variants" implies an original form, compared with which all others are variations, and no such original or standard telling of Mīrā's life exists. See Ramanujan (1991), pp. 24–25.

5. The Rajputs are the castes to which Mīrā and the hereditory rulers of Rajasthan belong. Mīrā was born into the Rathor branch (centered in Merta, a part of the kingdom of Marwar) and married into the Sisodiya line (the rulers of the kingdom of Mewar, centered first in Chittor, then in Udaypur).

6. Mukta (1994), pp. 12–16, 49–70, 173–81.

7. Nabhadas (1969), pp. 712–13. Hawley and Juergensmeyer have translated Nabhadas's verse and paraphrased Priyadas's commentary on Mīrā (1988), pp. 122–28. These passages are also discussed by Mukta and numerous authors in Hindi literature.

8. Vṛndāvan is the place where Kṛṣṇa spent his childhood and adolescence, sporting with the cowherding women of the village. A popular pilgrimage site, its geographic location is in Uttar Pradesh, an eternal realm where Kṛṣṇa engages in love play with every soul.

9. Dvaraka, on the seacoast of Gujarat where Kṛṣṇa later established his kingdom, is another important pilgrimage site for his devotees.

10. G. N. Sharma identifies Ramabai as the only woman meriting mention in such records, although he notes that more women appear in Jain inscriptions in this time period. Sharma, personal communication, April 30, 1993. Information about the inscription can be found in Agarwal (1958), pp. 215–25.

11. Bhatnagar (1992) pp. 10–21. This reference to Mīrā is discussed by a number of authors writing about Mīrā in Hindi literature.

12. Nainsi (1981), p. 21.

13. H. S. Bhati (1987, p. 14, n. 37) cites *Mertīya Khāp Khulāsā* (100/1) 850, Abhliekhgarh, Bikaner, as the source for this date.

14. Ahluwalia (1992), pp. 142–43.

15. Mukta (1994), pp. 69–70; 178–81.

16. Mukta also cites the fact that Mīrā's name is sometimes used in a derogatory way to refer to a woman who is overly religious, not sufficiently concerned about domestic matters, and/or too independent-minded, but it is not clear that this is strictly a Rajput phenomenon. My own research suggests this use of Mīrā's name crosses caste boundaries.

17. This passage is translated and discussed by Callewaert (1991), p. 201.

18. Wilson (1828), pp. 98–100; also in vol. 1 of Wilson's collected works edited by Ross (1861) and reprinted in Calcutta (1958).

19. Price's translations appear in Wilson's text, and Wilson's editor, Ernest R. Ross confirms in a footnote that they came from Price (vol. 1, pp. 99–100); also Wilson (1958), p. 79; and Todd (1990).

20. Somani (1985), pp. 159–70.

21. Todd (1990), pp. 337–38, 951, 1818.

22. Tassy (1870); Grierson (1888); Sengar (1876); Vrajaratnadas (1948), pp. 59–61; Tripathi (1916).

23. Tripathi and Todd are also discussed by Mukta (1994).

24. Nandy (1983), pp. 4–5.

25. In addition to Nandy, see also Metcalf (1994).

26. Nandy (1983), pp. 7–8.

27. The following description is drawn from Uma Chakravarti (1990), pp. 47–48. See also P. Chatterjee (1986, 1993).

28. Todd (1990); Cunningham (1849); Duff (1826).

29. Rajani Kanta Gupta (1876), cited by Chakravarti (1990), p. 48.

30. Bankimchandra Chatterji (1886, in *Racanavali*, 1958, vol. 2, pp. 407–583), cited by Nandy (1983), p. 23. See also P. Chatterjee (1986), pp. 54–84.

31. Nandy (1983), pp. 23–24.

32. Chakravarti (1990), p. 49.

33. P. Chatterjee, *American Ethnologist 16*, 1989 pp. 622–33.

34. The Rani of Jhansi was a Brahmin married to a Maratha. For her story in detail, as well as those of other heroines set in the context of gender construction on India, see Kathryn Hansen (1992), pp. 20–52.

35. Chakravarti (1990), p. 53, drawing on Jasodhara Bagchi (1985), pp. 60–61.

36. For further discussion of Gandhi's use of Mīrā, see Mukta (1994), pp. 182–200; and Kishwar (1989), pp. 86–87.

37. Somani (1985), p. 275; Sharma (1987), pp. 57–70.

38. Majumdar (1961), p. 423; Mallick (1961), p. 451.

39. Mallick (1961), pp. 446–59.

40. Sharma (1987), pp. 33–34.

41. Ibid. pp. 62–63.

42. Shyamaldas, *Vīr Vinod*, part 1, pp. 362, 371; part 2, vol. 1, pp. 1–2.

43. Munshi (1954).

44. Ibid., p. 2 (notes). Munshi (1954), pp. 1–2, mentions an earlier text by Babu Kartikprasad (1893) specifically as having reported in error that Mīrā was born in 1418 as the daughter of Jaymal Rathor. An alternate citation given by Callewaert (1991), p. 209, is to Khatri (1893). I was unable to locate a copy of this text.

45. A portion of Sharma's correspondence has been published, and the original documents are available at the Rajasthan Oriental Research Institute, Jaipur. See N. S. Bhati (1982).

46. K. S. Gupta (1992), pp. 71–80.

47. Ojha, *Udaipur Rājya kī Itihās*, p. 358; *Rājputāne kī Itihās*, vol. 2, p. 672. These texts are given (with some ellipsis) by Padmavati Shabnam (1973), pp. 36–37.

48. Shabnam (1973), pp. 75–76, gives J. S. Gahlot's edited version of Kavivar Umardan's *Umar Kāvya* as the source for his real contribution to the conversation on Mīrā (rather than his *Rājputāne kī Itihās*). Shabnam (1973), pp. 37–38. Harinarayan Sharma identifies further information from Gahlot's *Mārwār kā Itihās*, p. 255, in his discussion of these materials found in Bhati (1982), p. 68.

49. Sarda (1918), pp. 95–96, 148. The date and the author of *Caturkul Caritra* are not given by Sarda but can be found in a letter from Chatur Singh to Harinarayan, dated January 21, 1940 (Bhati 1982, p. 84). It appears from the correspondence that Harinarayan may not have been able to obtain a copy of this text for examination, and I certainly could not.

50. Rathor Mertiya (1932), vol. 1, pp. 71–73. For more detailed information on this text, see Shabnam (1973), pp. 37–38.

51. Chatur Singh, letters to Harinarayan dated January 21, 1940 (p. 85) and February 28, 1940 (p. 89), in Bhati (1982), p. 78.

52. Ibid., p. 85, and Harinarayan's notes from his conversation with Chatur Singh and Gopal Singh in the same text, pp. 72–73.

53. Ibid. p. 78.

54. Lindsey Harlan (1992), pp. 205–22.

55. Ibid., pp. 209–11.

56. Mukta (1994).

57. This information is found in a report by Harinarayan (Bhati, 1982, pp. 66–83).

58. Ibid., p. 91.

59. Bankey Behari (1935); Goetz (1966), pp. 87–113; Shekhawat (1974).

60. Bankey Behari (1935), p. 38.

61. Chandrakant, *Amar Chitra Kathā*, 36. See also Kishwar and Vanita (1989), pp. 85–87; Hawley (1995), pp. 107–34.

62. Correspondence of Roy and Goetz from 1967 in Roy (1983), pp. 63–67.

63. Goetz (1966), pp. 22–23.

64. Ibid., p. 29.

65. Ramanujan delineates the stages in women saints' lives (1982), pp. 316–324.

66. Hansen gives the stories of each of these *vīrāṅganās* (1992), pp. 28–34.

67. Samjukta Gupta seemingly accepts this story of Mīrā and thus dismisses her (1991), pp. 193–209.

68. Mukta (1994) and my article (1995), pp. 5–44.

69. Chaturvedi (1989). English translations of this song were previously published by Alston (1980), p. 49; and by Hawley and Juergensmeyer (1988), p. 134. I am particularly indebted to Hawley and Juergensmeyer's translation of the first and second verses.

References

Agrawala, R. C. "An Inscription from Javar, Rajasthan." In *Indian Historical Quarterly* 34, 1958, pp. 215–25.

Ahluwalia, M. S. "Modern Writers on Early Medieval Rajasthan." In G. N. Sharma and V. S. Bhatnagar, eds., *The Historians and Sources of History of Rajasthan*. Jaipur: University of Rajasthan, 1992.

Alston, A. J. *Poems of Mīrā*. Delhi: Motilal Banarsidass, 1980.

Bagchi, Jasodhara. "Positivism and Nationalism: Womanhood and the Crisis Nationalist Fiction: Bankimchandra's *Ānandamaṭh*." In *Economic and Political Weekly* 20, p. 43 (October 1985).

Bankey, Behari. *The Story of Mīrābāi*. Gorakhpur: Gita Press, 1935. Reproduced in *Bhakta Mīrā*. Bombay: Bharatiya Vidya Bhavan, 1961.

Bhati, Hukam Singh. *Mīrābāi: Itihāsik va Sāmājik Vivecan*. Jodhpur, Rajasthani Sahitya Samsthan, 1987.

Bhati, Narayan Singh, ed. *Vidyābhuṣaṇ Purohit Harinārāyaṇ, Paramparā* 63–64. Caupasani, Jodhpur: Rajasthani Shodh Sansthan, 1982.

Bhatnagar, V. S. "Munhata Nainsi." In G. N. Sharma and V. S. Bhatnagar, eds., *The Historians and Sources of History in Rajasthan*. Jaipur: Centre for Rajasthan Studies, University of Rajasthan, 1992.

Callewaert, Winand. "The 'Earliest' Songs of Mīrā (1503–1546)." In *Orientalia Lovaniensia Periodica* 22, 1991, pp. 201–214.

Chakravarti, Uma. "Whatever Happened to the Vedic Dasi?" In Kumkum Sangari and Sudesh Vaid, eds., *Recasting Women: Essays in Indian Colonial History*. New Brunswick, N. J.: Rutgers University Press, 1990.

Chandrakant, Kamala. "Mīrābāi: The Touching Tale of a Great Devotee of Kṛṣṇa." In *Amar Chitra Kathā* 36. Bombay: India Book House, n.d.

Chatterjee, Partha. "Colonialism, Nationalism, and Colonized Woman: The Contest in India," *American Ethnologist 16*, 1989, pp. 622–33.

———. *Nationalist Thought and the Colonial World: A Derivative Discourse?* London: Zed Books for the United Nations University, 1986.

———. *The Nation and Its Fragments: Colonial and Postcolonial Histories*. Princeton, N. J.: Princeton University Press, 1993.

Chatterji, Bankimchandra. "Kṛṣṇacaritra" (1886). In *Racanavali*, vol. 2. Calcutta: Sahitya Samsad, 1958.

Chaturvedi, Parashruram. *Mīrābāi kī Padāvalī*. Prayag: Hindi Sahitya Sammelan, 1989.

Cunningham, J. D. *A History of the Sikhs*. London: John Murray, 1849.

Duff, Grant. *History of the Marathas*. London: Longmans Green, 1826.

Gahlot, J. S. "Mārwār kā Itihās." In N. S. Bhati, ed. *Vidyābhuṣaṇ Purohit Harinārāyaṇ, Paramparā* 63–64.

Goetz, Hermann. *Mīrābāi, Her Life and Times*. Bombay: Bharatiya Vidya Bhavan, 1966 (first published in the *Journal of the Gujarat Research Society* 18, April 1956).

Grierson, G. A. *The Mediaeval Vernacular Literature of Hindustan*. Vienna: Alfred Holder, 1888.

Gupta, K. S. "Dr. Ojha as a Historian." In G. N. Sharma and V. S. Bhatnagar, eds. *The Historians and Sources of History of Rajasthan* Jaipur: University of Rajasthan,1992.

Gupta, Rajani Kanta. *Sipāhī Yuddhera Itihāsa*, 1876, cited by Chakravarti, "Whatever Happened to the Vedic Dasi?" 1990.

Gupta, Samjukta. "Women in the Śaiva/Śākta Ethos." In Julia Leslie, ed. *Roles and Rituals for Hindu Women*. Delhi: Motilal Banarsidass, 1991.

Hansen, Kathryn. "Heroic Modes of Women in Indian Myth, Ritual and History: The *tapasvinī* and *vīrāṅganā*." In Arvind Sharma and Katherine K. Young, eds. *Annual Review of Women in World Religions, Volume 2: Heroic Women*. Albany: State University of New York Press, 1992.

Harlan, Lindsey. *Religion and Rajput Women: The Ethic of Protection in Contemporary Narratives*. Berkeley: University of California Press, 1992.

Hawley, John Stratton. "The Saint Subdued: Domestic Virtue and National Integration in

Amar Chitra Kathā." In Lawrence A. Babb and Susan S. Wadley, eds. *Media and the Transformation of Religion in South Asia*. Philadelphia: University of Pennsylvania Press, 1995.

Hawley, John Stratton, and Mark Juergensmeyer. *Songs of the Saints of India*. New York: Oxford University Press, 1988.

Hawley, John Stratton, and Donna Marie Wulff, eds. *The Divine Consorts: Rādhā and the Goddesses of India*. Boston: Beacon Press, 1982.

Kartikprasad, Babu. *Mīrābāi ka Jīvan Carit*. Bhujjapaharapur: Narayan Press, 1893.

Khatri, K. P. *Mīrābāi kī Jīvanī*. Calcutta: Thakur Prasad, 1893.

Kishwar, Madhu. "Gandhi's Mīra."*Manushi* 50–52, 1989, pp. 86–87.

Kishwar, Madhu, and Ruth Vanita, "Modern Versions of Mīrā." *Manushi* 50–52, 1989.

Majumdar, R.C. "Nationalist Historians." In C. H. Philips, ed. *Historians of India, Pakistan and Ceylon*. London: Oxford University Press, 1961.

Mallick, A. R. "Modern Historical Writing in Bengali." In C. H. Philips, ed. *Historians of India, Pakistan and Ceylon*. London: Oxford University Press, 1961.

Martin-Kershaw, Nancy. "Dyed in the Color of Her Lord: Multiple Representations in the Mīrābai Tradition" paper read at the Graduate Theological Union, 1995.

———. "Mīrābāi: Inscribed in Text, Embodied in Life." *Journal of Vaiṣṇava Studies*, Fall 1995 pp. 5–44.

Metcalf, Thomas R. *The New Cambridge History of India: Ideologies of the Raj*, vols. 3 and 4. Cambridge: Cambridge University Press, 1994.

Mukta, Parita. *Upholding the Common Life: The Community of Mīrābai*. Delhi: Oxford University Press, 1994.

Munshi, Deviprasad. *Mīrābāi kī Jivan Caritra* [1898]. Calcutta: Bangiya Hindi-Parishad, 1954.

Nabhadas. *Śrī Bhaktamāl*, with the *Bhaktirasabodhinī* commentary of Priyadas. Lucknow: Tejkumar Press, 1969.

Nainsi, Munhata. *Munhatā Nainsī rī Khyāt*. Jodhpur: Rajasthan Oriental Research Institute, 1981.

Nandy, Ashis. *The Intimate Enemy: Loss and Recovery of Self under Colonialism*. Delhi: Oxford University Press, 1983.

Ramanujan, A. K. "On Women Saints." In John Stratton Hawley and Donna Marie Wulff, eds. *The Divine Consorts: Rādhā and the Goddesses of India*. Boston: Beacon Press, 1982.

———. "Three Hundred Ramayanas: Five Examples and Three Thoughts on Translation." In Paula Richman, ed. *Many Rāmāyaṇas: The Diversity of a Narrative Tradition in South Asia*. Berkeley: University of California Press, 1991.

Rathor Mertiya, Thakur Gopal Singh. *Jaymal Vansha Prakasha or the History of Badnore*, vol. 1. Ajmer: Vedic Yantralaya, 1932.

Ross, Ernest R. *A Sketch of the Religious Sects of the Hindus*. London: Trubner, 1861; reprint: *Religious Sects of the Hindus*. Calcutta: Sushil Gupta, 1958.

Roy, Dilip Kumar. *The Rounding Off*. Bombay: Bharatiya Vidya Bhavan, 1983.

Sangari, Kumkum, and Sudesh Vaid, eds. *Recasting Women: Essays in Indian Colonial History*. New Brunswick, N. J.: Rutgers University Press, 1990.

Sarda, Har Bilas. *Mahārāṇā Saṅgha, the Hindupat, the Last Great Leader of Rajput Race*. Ajmer: Scottish Mission Industries, 1918.

Sengar, Shiv Singh. *Sivsimh Saroj* (1876). In Vrajaratnadas, Mira Madhuri. Varanasi: Hindi Sahitya Kutir, 1948, pp. 59–61

Shabnam, Padmavati. *Mīrā: Vyaktitva and aur Kṛtitva*. Calcutta: Hindi Pracharak Sansthan, 1973.

Sharma, G. N. "Kavirāja Śyāmaladās aur unkā *Vīr Vinod*." ed. N. S. Bhati Chaupasani, *Parmparā* 82–83. Jodhpur: Rajasthani Shodh Sansthan, 1987.

Sharma, G. N., and V. S. Bhatnagar, eds. *The Historians and Sources of History of Rajasthan*. Jaipur: University of Rajasthan, 1992.

Shekhawat, Kalyan Singh. *Mīrābāi kā Jīvanvṛtt evam Kāvya*. Jodhpur: Hindi Sahitya Bhavan, 1974 (Ph.D dissertation, 1969).

Somani, Ram Vallabh. *Later Mewar*. Jaipur: Current Law House, 1985.

Tassy, Garcin de. *Histoire de la Literature Hindouie et Hindoustanie* [1839]. Paris: Adolphe Labitte, 1870.

Todd, James. *Annals and Antiquities of Rajasthan*, 1829–1832. Ed. William Crooke. Reprint, Delhi: Low Price Publications, 1990.

Tripathi, G. M. *The Classical Poets of Gujarat and Their Influence on Society and Morals*. Bombay: N. M. Tripathi, 1916. Paper originally read for the Wilson College Literary Society in 1892.

Vrajaratnadas. *Mīrā Mādhurī*. Varanasi: Hindi Sahitya Kutir, 1948.

Wilson, H. H. "The Religious Sects of the Hindus." In *Asiatic Researches* 16, Calcutta, 1828. Republished in vol. 1 of Wilson's collected works, ed. Ernest R. Ross as *A Sketch of the Religious Sects of the Hindus*. London: Trubner, 1861; reprinted as *Religious Sects of the Hindus*. Calcutta: Sushil Gupta, 1958.

NABANEETA DEV SEN

Candrāvatī Rāmāyaṇa

Feminizing the Rāma-Tale

Prelude

"My name is Kamalama. I come from the village Mainla in Manikota Taluk. It is painful to tell the story of my life. My mother was a slave in the house of some landlords. By then three generations had existed like this. My mother, her mother and grandmother had all been slaves in the landlords' house. They say my grandmother's name was Venkattamma."[1]

"Where the river Phuleśvarī flows by, Yādavānanda used to live. Born in a Bhattacharya family, married to Añjanā, he lived in a thatched hut with bamboo posts. They were worshippers of Manasā Devī. Hence Lakṣmī abandoned them out of spite. By the grace of Manasā, a son, Dvijavaṁśī, was born to them, the poet, famous for *bhāsān* songs (in praise of Manasā). But they had no rice to feed themselves with, no straws to thatch their roof. When it rained their home was flooded. To add to their tale of woe, Candrāvatī, the luckless was born to them. My father wandered from place to place, singing the song of Manasā and brought home the rice and money he could get. Manasā appeared in a dream and requested us to sing her praise, which would remove our poverty.

"I worship Devī Manasā, it was she who removed our distress. I worship my mother a million times, for it is she who has shown me this world. I worship Śiva and Pārvatī, I worship river Phuleśvarī, who has quenched my thirst, I worship mother Sulocanā and father Dvija Vaṁśīdās, who taught me the *Purāṇas*. Having worshipped one and all as demanded by custom, Candravatī now sings the *Rāmāyaṇa* by her father's orders."[2]

I do not know who my parents were, who were my brothers/
I am just a bunch of moss in the current of the river/
floating from bank to bank/
floating I have come to this Tapovana/
and where I shall be tomorrow, nobody knows.

(Sītā to Lakṣmaṇa)[3]

> I have heard the lamentations of millions of women/
> the lamentation of millions of women who have lost their husbands and sons.[4]

I am about to narrate three tales. All three were written down to be orally narrated to different audiences at different times and places.

The first was written in the seventeenth century, in East Bengal, in ballad form; the second was written in the sixteenth century, in eastern Mymensingh, (East Bengal) in epic form; and the third was written recently as a paper in Calcutta. The prologue is a bit long. I shall start with the ballad *Candrāvatī*, by Nayanchand Ghosh, a village bard of Mymensingh. He was singing the life story of a Brahmin girl, Candrāvatī, in love with a Brahmin boy, Jayānanda (or Jayacandra), and the two were formally engaged. During the period of engagement, Jayānanda suddenly becomes infatuated with a Muslim girl, Aṣṭamī, and writes her a love letter. On the day of Candrāvatī's wedding, Aṣṭamī goes to the village *kazi* with the letter and files a complaint. As a result, Jayānanda is converted to Islam (Jaynul) and forced to marry Aṣṭamī instead of his childhood sweetheart, Candrāvatī. The betrayal breaks Candrāvatī's heart, but, being the courageous woman that she is, she decides never to marry and to devote her life to the worship of Śiva. Her father, Dvija Vaṁśīdās, a famous poet himself, permits her to act according to her own will but advises her to follow his own profession and write poetry. "Worship Śiva and write the *Rāmāyaṇa*," he tells her. So she does, as a good girl should.

One night, a repentant Jayānanda returns to Candrāvatī when she is deep in meditation within her temple. A great storm is raging outside, and Jayānanda's piteous appeals do not reach her ears. Jayānanda repeatedly begs her to open up, waiting almost all night, and then he writes a good-bye note on the temple door with the red juice of crushed *sandhyā-mālatī* flowers, telling her that he had come only to take one last look at her face and to apologize before punishing himself for what he had done to her.

On reading that note in the morning, Candrāvatī reacts in a rather weird manner. Her major worry is that a Muslim had entered her temple premises and had contaminated it (*jāt nāś koireche nāgar*). So she takes the temple utensils to the river to wash them clean. There she finds Jayānanda's body floating in the river. Candrāvatī stood still on the river bank, a lost woman (literally, a woman without a mind).

Chandra Kumar De, the first collector of the ballad, tells us that the real Candrāvatī had lived about fifty vears before Nayanchand Ghosh composed this ballad about her and that she, too, was a renowned poet, a greater one than Nayanchand, who has turned her into a legend. Our first narrative is over. Now we shall move toward our second narrative.

This legendary Candrāvatī is supposed to have written two of the three best known Mymensingh ballads, *Molua Sundarī* and *Dasyu Kenārām*. But she had also written a *Rāmāyaṇa*, supposed to be her first attempt at poetry inspired by her poet father, whom she had assisted in composing his famous songs on Manasā, *Padma-Purāṇa*, *Manasā Maṅgala*, or *Manasā Bhāsān*. *Candrāvatī Rāmāyaṇa* is the next narrative we are going to read. All the histories of Bengali literature that mention Candrāvatī's work seriously judge this text as the worst and the weakest of her works. Sukumar Sen even seems to think it is a fake; in fact, he thinks most

Mymensingh ballads—and all of Candrāvatī—is faked.[5] Others do not agree, and even in 1966, long after Sukumar Sen had aired his views, fresh versions of Candrāvatī's works were found in Mymensingh by Khitish Moulik and published by Suniti Kumar Chatterjee in 1976.

However, all scholars agree that what is called *Candrāvatī Rāmāyaṇa* is an incomplete text, an incomplete *Rāmāyaṇa*. All the collectors, the editors, and the historians of Bengali literature agree that the whole of the Rāma tale is not to be found in it. It is only a fragment. Besides, it differs heavily from both Vālmikī and Kīrtivāsa, the two pillars of the great tradition and the little tradition, the standard Sanskrit text and the standard Bengali text of the *Rāmāyaṇa*. Instead, it shows strange similarities with the southern *Rāmāyaṇas*, the *Jain Rāmāyaṇa* and *Adbhūta Rāmāyaṇa*—apart from showing distinct influences of the folk *Rāma Kathās*, the *Maṅgal Kāvyas*, and *Vrata Kathās* in its text and language. Here we have our second narrative, the *Candrāvatī Rāmāyaṇa*.

Though for her *Manasā Bhāsān*, *Moluā Sundarī*, and *Dasyu Kenārām*, Candrāvatī is regarded as a great ballad poet, it is not her strong point. Having been thus discouraged by the literary historians who are now the custodians of our literature, I had read only her ballads. Candrāvatī is also hard to find. Recently, quite accidentally, I came across the seventh volume of K. Moulik and was going through it, curious to inspect how weak and how incomplete the *Rāmāyaṇa* was, when I discovered that I was holding in my hand a unique text, a woman's retelling of the Rāma tale. It is the Rāma story retold by a Bengali Hindu village woman who had known suffering, a woman who had the courage to choose the lonely intellectual life of a poet, in sixteenth century rural Bengal.

Sukumar Sen, when he mentions the life of Candrāvatī in his history of literature in connection with Nayanchand's ballad on Candrāvatī, says—after telling us about her unrequited love—that "she remained a virgin all her life. This is the sum total of the ballad." This is not the sum total of the ballad. The ballad mentions that she wrote the *Rāmāyaṇa* and worshiped Śiva for the rest of her life. For our literary historian, this information is irrelevant, he never mentions anything about her writing the *Rāmāyaṇa*, and he stops at her oath of virginity. The positive, active part of the future plan remains unmentioned.[6]

Are we to take this as a silencing tactic? It is no wonder that this text had been silenced by the urban male mediators who are literary historians. We cannot blame them either. In this rather unusual *Rāmāyaṇa*, Rāma himself is gently pushed back to a corner where he is hardly visible, except in relation to Sīta. The narrative pattern clearly and unmistakably follows the storyline of Sītā's life, and the tale as it stands is unabashedly a Sītā tale under the traditional guise of a Rāma tale. The only episodes of the *Rāmāyaṇa* depicted here are the episodes of Sītā's life, beginning with the supernatural birth of Sītā, going through her tales of woe, *Sītā's Bāromāsī* (which mentions her childhood, her marriage, and her life as an abducted woman), and describing her pregnancy, childbirth, exile, humiliation, and entry into mother earth. In a *Rāmāyaṇa*, you would expect the *janmalīlā* section of Rāma, would you not?

The supernatural birth scene is supposed to tell us all about Rāma's birth and the purpose of his appearance on earth to destroy the evil Rāvaṇa. In any case, in a patriarchal social system, that ought to be the traditional pattern of storytelling. But the order is reversed here, as Moulik notes: "According to the rule, Rāma's birth story should come first and Sītā's should come next. The song-books that I have seen have it that way. But, in D. C. Sen's earlier edition, Sītā's birth comes first. I am following D. C. Sen's footsteps here".[7]

Candrāvatī breaks the accepted pattern by beginning her epic with Sītā's birth story. Khitish Moulik, in his later search for material, found that the order had been "corrected," but he preferred to keep the earlier order and followed D. C. Sen's edition in his own. We are grateful for that, because it makes a great deal of sense with regard to the total structure of the epic. Candrāvatī begins her epic by giving us Sītā's birth story in great detail: the first six long sections are devoted to describing the complex tale of the conception and birth of Sītā. Sītā is born of sorrow, the blood of tortured ascetics and the death wish of a neglected Mandodarī mingle to create her, and she comes to destroy Rāvaṇa and his clan. The evil Rāvaṇa, strengthened by the boon of Brahmā, was tyrannizing all the three worlds, and had collected the blood of the ascetics in a box as a poison to destroy the immortality of gods. Now, Candrāvatī tells us how his wife, Mandodarī, felt neglected and heartbroken, as Rāvaṇa was spending all his time making love to the divine females he had abducted from heaven. So she decided to take the poison strong enough to kill the deathless tribe. She took the poison. But, lo and behold, what happens to her? Being a woman has its mysteries. Instead of dying, she gives birth. Sītā is born in the form of an egg. Soothsayers in Laṅkā predict that this egg would produce a dangerous daughter who would cause the total destruction of the demon dynasty. Hearing that, Rāvaṇa wants to destroy the egg, but mother Mandodarī cannot allow that. She manages to make him throw the egg, protected in a golden casket, into the ocean. It floats across the Bay of Bengal, and a very poor but honest fisherman, Mādhava Jāliā, finds it. He brings it home to his very poor but honest wife, Satā, who has nothing to eat, nothing to wear, and nothing to complain about. She performs various auspicious rituals and receives the egg worshipfully. Hence Lakṣmī, the goddess, hiding in the egg as Sītā, showers her with favors. The poor fisherman becomes rich. In the meantime, his wife, Satā, gets a dream message that Lakṣmī wants her to deliver the egg to King Janaka. Satā immediately follows the divine instructions. The only reward she wants from the queen is that the daughter, when born, should be named Sītā, after her own name, Satā. The consonants and the last vowel are the same in both names; only the first vowel differs. So with the name of a poor fisherman's wife, Sītā was born out of an egg in Candrāvatī's text—not found by the king while tilling the soil, as in the classical legend. King Janaka, in fact, has no role to play here. It is his wife who takes care of the egg that produces Sītā. This is the supernatural birth of the heroine, to destroy evil. Sītā is born to bring about the total destruction of Rāvaṇa and his clan. The story, echoing *Adbhūta Rāmāyaṇa* and *Jaina Rāmāyaṇa*, reminds us of the Oedipus tale—Rāvaṇa desires Sītā without knowing that she is Mandodarī's child. She is not Rāvaṇa's child, only Mandodarī's. The story also reminds us of Kṛṣṇa and Kaṁsa and also of the Prahlāda legend—each for a different reason.

Candrāvatī devotes only two comparatively shorter, later sections to the births of Rāma, his three brothers, and one sister, the evil Kukuya, who has the Bengali-Sanskrit term for evil (*ku*) twice in her name.

In the next section, book 2, the narrator changes, and a subnarrative appears within the main narrative. Sītā herself is now the narrator. She sits in the inner apartments of Rāma's palace and talks to her girlfriends, who ask her all kinds of questions about her personal experiences. Having returned from Laṅkā, Sītā is now at ease and talks freely about her childhood, her marriage, her life with Rāma as a bride and in exile, and her life in Laṅkā as an abducted woman. As for Rāma's achievements, the breaking of *Haradhanu* and the entire epic battle are only summarily referred to and not described, through Sītā's *Bāromāsī* (the song of twelve months, relating the incidents of one's life to the seasonal changes). The heroic code is thus gently broken. There are no gory battle scenes, no details of heroic achievements. Most of the epic actions are referred to through the conceit of dream, as dream messages.

This section is most interesting because, in an epic, the epic battle is of central importance. But in *Candrāvatī Rāmāyaṇa*, twice mediated by feminine sensibility—once by Candrāvatī's, as a composer, and once by Sītā, as the narrator—the epic battle loses its glory and gets only a few dull lines to itself. All of Rāma's grand exploits are briefly and colorlessly reported, if at all, by Sītā to her girlfriends. Rāma's initiation is not referred to because it was not Sītā's experience, so we do not hear of Tāḍakā, Mārīca, and Śabara. *Haradhanubhaṅga*, coronation and exile, the golden stag, *akālabodhana*, the worship of the Mother Goddess, bridge building, and the killings of Rāvaṇa, Indrajit, and Kumbhakarṇa are all lightly touched upon. Maximum color and space are spent on the romantic exploits of Sītā and Rāma in the forest. Sītā and Candrāvatī make exile sound most attractive.

After her return from Laṅkā to where she had been abducted, there are four more important episodes of Sītā's life: pregnancy, betrayal and exile, childbirth, and humiliation and voluntary death or entry into mother earth. All these experiences are described in great detail. Mother nature seems to appear in the form of mother earth to put an end to the human injustice that Sītā was subjected to by Rāma.

Candrāvatī Rāmāyaṇa most logically ends here, with the death of Sītā, and it is here that our third narrative begins. It is our story, yours and mine, the reader's story. Does the narrative I have just related to you sound like an incomplete text? Another fragmentary epic like Homer's or even the *Song of Roland*? We could perhaps, with a little courage, call it a heroic epic—if heroism is taken to signify man's superhuman ability to stand and overcome human suffering—because that is what Sītā displays here. It is not an epic battle with visible special weapons of moral values. And this is where we hear the battle by fighting with the traditional weapons of the values supplied by the dominant ideology of Candrāvatī's time, whereas Candrāvatī herself, as the narrator-composer, challenges the same values in the very structure of the narrative.

We have here a narrative about a woman, narrated by a woman—by two women, in fact—meant for women narratees. Yes, the text was originally intended for a female audience, as the recurring formula here is *śuno sakhijana* ("listen, girlfriends") not *śuno sabhājana* ("listen, members of the court") or *śuno sarvajana* ("listen, one and all"), as the regular formulae go.[8] The producer of the text is a woman, the product depicts a woman's life, and the intended recipients are also women.

Therefore, it is not surprising that the story of Rāma is insignificant here, except in relation to Sītā's life story. Rāma is not an ideal man in this text, in any case, not even according to the patriarchal values, because he stoops to listen to the evil counsel of a woman, the Alakṣmī, his sister Kukuya, who shares all the consonants of her name with her mother, Kaikeyī. There is no concept of *Rāma-Rājya* at all in this text. Instead, Rāma brings death and destruction to Ayodhyā by sending Sītā, the Lakṣmī, the good luck of the city, into exile. Finally, in book 3 he loses her for good, again by listening to the evil counsel of his jealous sister and some of his evil-minded subjects. Candrāvatī scolds him openly for his weakness and lack of judgment and holds him responsible for the fall of Ayodhyā.

In book 3, the narrator changes once again. Candrāvatī returns as the narrator, but a male character finds his way in, too, Lakṣmaṇa. He strongly voices the general patriarchal values and even reminds us once of Rāma's superhuman quality, of which there are no visible signs anywhere in the text. It is in that sense a secular *Rāmāyaṇa*.

Interestingly enough, I think Lakṣmaṇa and a great part of book 3 (sections four to nine) have been introduced because of the mediation of male performers. In the first edition of the epic (collected before 1914 but published in 1926), this section is absent. In the second version (collected between 1934 and 1966), this portion is found. Clearly, the poem had become the property of the bards of East Bengal long ago and was sung to a mixed audience. To suit them, in the second (later) version, we also find that the regularized form of the earlier address, *śuno sakhijana*, becomes *śuno sarvajana* from time to time. The editor notices this and draws our attention to it. The intended audience remains female, and in Sītā's own narrative about Rāma—she is privately conversing with her girlfriends (*sāt pāñc sakhijane basiyā*), who are in the inner chambers.

The patriarchal voice is clearly audible in the last section of the second version, where Lava, Kuśa, and Hanumāna interact heroically and the ascetics Vaśiṣṭha and Vālmikī appear in their full brahmanical splendor. Before the last two (probably interpolated) sections of book 3, so many males are never seen together in the epic song. Hence, we can read it today as a silenced text of yesterday.

Rāmāyaṇa is a misnomer for our narrative. It should have been called *Sītāyaṇa*, the route of Sītā. Rāma is not at the center of the narrative. He is only a foil against whose false steps Sītā's actions and character are highlighted. Candrāvatī often intrudes into the text and directly addresses her characters herself. She warns them, rebukes them, sympathizes with them, laments for them, and finally tells Rāma that he has lost his mind and that the whole country will have to pay for this sad lack of wisdom:

> *Parer kathā kāne loile go nijer sarbonāś* /
> *Candrāvatī kahe Rām go tomār hoilo nāś*.
> You will bring disaster upon yourself if you listen to others/
> Candrāvatī says, O Rām your disaster is near./

The *Candrāvatī Rāmāyaṇa* does not tell us about the route of Rāma, but it does tell us all about the life journey of a woman—a complete, biological life cycle of birth, marriage, pregnancy, childbirth, maturity, and death. It is a woman's text for the selection of episodes, for the highlighting and detailing of intimate feminine experience like the pregnant woman's craving for chewing burnt clay, like pregnancy and childbirth (Mandodarī's description), maternal feelings ("*antar jvalilo māyer go jeno jvalanta aguni*") the woman's desolation and desperation at being neglected, worship of local goddesses (Maṅgal Caṇḍī, Manasā, Vanadurgā, Sulocanī, Śitalā, Ṣaṣṭhī), and performance of religious rituals. Candrāvatī even uses *vratakathā*-style formulaic language to describe Satā's ritualistic performances. Lastly, *Candrāvatī Rāmāyaṇa* is crying out as a clear woman's text from its obvious silences. Candrāvatī is silent about Rāma's valor, silent about Rāma's battle skills, and silent about Rāma's wisdom. The only aspect of Rāma stressed here is lover: *nayane lāigyā rahilo go śyāmal varaṇ*, "my eyes are filled with his (beautiful) brown complexion". But he turns out to be a traitor in love, banishing his pregnant wife unjustly. We find Rāma in this *Rāmāyaṇa* a poor husband, a poor king, a poor brother who bullies his loyal brother into acting against his own conscience, and a poor father who does not carry out his parental responsibilities. He is also a jealous husband; sending Sītā into exile is partly because of his jealousy of Rāvaṇa. The description of the jealous Rāma runs like this:

unmatta pāgal prāy go hoilen Rām/
raktajavā āṅkhi Rāmer go, śire rakta uṭhe/
nāsikāy agniśvās go, brahmarandhra phuṭe/ (book 3)
Rāma almost turned mad/
The eyes of Rāma became red and blood reached his head/
His nostrils breathed fire and the top of his head turned boiling hot/

This is far from the balanced, moderate, *sthitadhī* (level-headed) Rāma we have known through classical epics.

As we have noticed before in this sixteenth-century woman's song from rural East Bengal, two parallel voices are heard in the voice of the narrator herself: her own dissenting authorial voice and the voice of the dominant ideology that she had interiorized. As narrators, Sītā and Candrāvatī differ in that one is a character and the other an outsider. With two different standpoints, they also differ in their worldviews. Sītā is an ideal representation of dominant ideology, but Candrāvatī is a dissenter. She openly questions, challenges, and punctures the ideology of her times in her personal intrusions and also in her selection of episodes, depth of detail, and silences. Though she criticizes Rāma every now and then, she does not criticize Sītā for acting according to the dominant ideology.

Whatever Candrāvatī's intentions, the text shows, apart from the authorial ideology, its own ideology, the dominant one. Therefore, in the portrayal of Sītā and Kukuya, Lakṣmī and Alakṣmī, good and evil, she reiterates the dominant ideology in the two opposite figures. There is a clash of interests here in that her own interest is at odds with the interests of her times. In Indian epics, the epic battle is between good and evil; in a patriarchal system, which produces epics, both are represented by male characters. In *Candrāvatī Rāmāyaṇa*, also, there is this war of good and evil—but both are represented by women, Lakṣmī and Alakṣmī again, Sītā and Kukuya. Both have supernatural births; both bring disaster to their parental clans, Sītā to Rāvaṇa and Kukuya to Rāma.

Furthermore, in an epic narrative, curses and blessings often regulate the main epic actions. Here Rāma and Sītā both admit to Lakṣmaṇa, separately, that their great misfortunes were brought on them by the great suffering that they had caused the women of Laṅkāpurī and Kiṣkindhyā. Rāma mentions: (1)*Tārā Mandodarīr abhiśāp go* (this happened because of) the curse of Tārā and Mandodarī,; (2) *satīr abhiśāper āgun go*" (this is the result) of the fiery curse of a chaste woman. Sītā mentions the nameless millions who had lost their sons and husbands in the war:

> *āmi to śuniyāchi go lākh lākh nārīr hāhākār/*
> *patihārā putrahārā go lākh lākh nārī/*
> *abhiśāp diyeche more go baḍo dukhe paḍi*. (book 3)
> I heard the cries of millions of women/
> Millions of women who lost their husbands, sons/
> They have cursed me in their immense suffering/

Hence the root cause of the epic actions, the powerful words, are also attributed to women, to suffering women in this text. We could look at it from the opposite angle, however, and say that once again the dominant ideology has been interiorized here: it is always women who are made to cause all the distress in the world, irrespective of the circumstances.

Candrāvatī Rāmāyaṇa seems important to me for two more reasons. Candrāvatī foretells the "pioneering" approaches of two of our finest poets in Bengali, Michael Madhusudan Dutta and Rabindranath Tagore. By mentioning Saramā as the only friend of Sītā in Rāvaṇa's Aśoka Kānan (*sāntvana kariyā rākhe ek Saramā sundarī*), Saramā consoles her—a theme that is developed by Michael in his *Meghnādvadh Kāvya*, Candrāvatī shows the sisterhood of women. She also requests Lakṣmaṇa to end the troubles of the neglected wife Ūrmilā: *Ūrmilār dukha tumi go koiro samādhān* "(Please) wipe away Ūrmilā's sorrow." This was the very topic on which Tagore had written his famous essay "Kāvye Upekṣita." Yes, Lakṣmaṇa's wife Ūrmilā is neglected by all the male narrators of the Rāma-tale, but not so by the female narrator of sixteenth century Bengal.

Similarly, *Candrāvatī Rāmāyaṇa* has been neglected and rejected for years by our male custodians of Bengali literature as an incomplete work. This is what we call a silenced text. The editors decided it was a poor literary work because it was a *Rāmāyaṇa* that did not sing of Rāma. Its eccentricity confused not only the editors but also the historians of Bengali literature to such an extent that they could not even see the complete epic narrative pattern clearly visible in it. It got stamped as an incomplete text. Today, a rereading of the narrative exposes an obvious failure of the male critics and historians: to recognize *Candrāvatī Rāmāyaṇa* as a personal interpretation of the Rāma-tale, seen specifically from the wronged woman's point of view.[9]

Notes

1. Lalitha (1989), p. 45 (life stories of women from Telengana people's struggle).
2. Autobiographical note to *Candrāvatī Rāmāyaṇa*, quoted by Moulik (1970), vol. 1, p. 207.
3. Moulik (1975), vol. 7, p. 334–35.

4. Ibid., p. 334.
5. Sukumar Sen (1963).
6. Sukumar Sen (1963), vol. 2, p. 279.
7. Moulik (1975), vol. 7, p. 278.
8. Ibid., p. 247; books 1 and 2, passim; book 3, p. 320.
9. Even when a feminist collection of *Women's Writing in India* was published, *Candrāvatī Rāmāyaṇa* was entered as an incomplete and weak text, although the feminine voice is best heard in her *Rāmāyaṇa*. Historians of literature have thus misguided readers and scholars alike. To my delight, I found in Paula Richman's *Many Rāmāyaṇas* an article by Narayan Rao on women's *Rāmāyaṇa* in Telugu, whose approach seems similar to mine. When the late A. K. Ramanujan attended my lecture in February 1990 in Delhi, he informed me about Dr. Rao's ongoing work, but it was yet to be published. This article was written and presented at Oxford University and also at the International Conference of Comparative Literature in Tokyo, before *Many Rāmāyaṇas* came out. Hence, there is no reference to the book here.

Since then, I have extended my study into other Indian regional language versions of women's *Rāmāyaṇas* (Telugu and Mārāthī) and collected contemporary women's Rāma saga from Mymensingh, Bangladesh. The second phase of this work is in progress.

References

Candrāvatī. *Ramāyana*. In *Prācīna Pūrvavaṅga Gītikā*, vol. 7, ed. Khitish Moulik. Calcutta: Firma K. L. Mukhopadhyaya, 1975.

Candrāvatī. *Ramāyana. In Mymensingh Gitika*, ed. D. C. Sen, Calcutta: Calcutta University, 1923.

Ghosh, Nayanchand. "Candrāvatī." In *Mymensingh Gītikā*, ed. D. C. Sen. Calcutta: Calcutta University,1923.

———. "Candrāvatī." In *Prācīna Pūrvavaṅga Gītikā*, vol. 1, ed. Khitish Moulik. Calcutta: Firma K. L. Mukhopadhyaya, 1970.

Lalitha, K., et.al. (*Stree Shakti Sangatana*), eds. *We Were Making History*. New Delhi: Kali for Women, 1989.

Moulik, Khitish, ed. *Prācīna Pūrvavaṅga Gītikā*, vols. 7. Calcutta: Firma K. L. Mukhopadhyaya, 1970–1975.

Richman, Paula. *Many Rāmāyaṇas*. London: Oxford University Press, 1991.

Sen, D. C. *The Bengali Ramāyāṇas*. Calcutta: Calcutta University, 1920.

———, ed. *Mymensingh Gitika*. Calcutta: Calcutta University, 1923.

———, ed. Purvavanga Gitika. Calcutta. Calcutta University, 1926.

——— Introduction. *Bāṁlā Bhāṣā O Sāhitya*. Calcutta, 1926.

Sen, Sukumar. *Baṅglā Sāhityer Itihās*. 2 vols. Calcutta: Eastern Publishers, 1963.

Tharu, Susie, and K. Lalitha, eds. *Women's Writing in India*. New York: Feminist Press, 1991.

ELEANOR ZELLIOT

Women Saints in Medieval Maharashtra

The Bhakti movement, the spread of devotional religion in medieval India, seems to have been the most inclusive and open of all facets of Hinduism. Saint-poets of all classes and castes, women as well as men, were recorded in the song literature in Tamil, Kannada, Marathi, and Hindi especially; in Maharashtra, an extraordinary number of women sang their devotional songs in Marathi. Their householder and family situations were also extraordinary. Most women saint-poets in other areas left husbands or never married and found that their devotion could flower only if they had no household responsibilities. In contrast, the women saint-singers of Maharashtra, with one exception, found ways to be close to the god of the Marathi Bhakti movement, Viṭṭhal or Viṭhoba, while remaining close to brothers, husbands, and sons.

Beginning with Muktabai in the thirteenth century and ending with Bahina Bai in the seventeenth, the voices of some dozen women saints are recorded in the collected songs of all the saints. The eighteenth-century collection of the lives as recorded in the legends of the saints collected by Mahipati tells of the struggles, the miracles, and the family situations of these women saints. Each woman seems to have a personality, a character, to be a religious devotee of exceptional dedication, even though in most cases her life is depicted as part of her husband's or her brothers'.

To begin with Muktabai, we see her as the sister of three brothers, all outcaste Brahmins because their father had returned to his wife, even though he had entered the *sannyāsī* state, at the behest of his guru, and the four subsequently born children suffered the brahmanical penalty of loss of caste. None of the four married, but all supported each other as if in a close family. Muktabai was especially close to Dnyaneshwar, author of the most popular religious book in Marathi, a commentary on the *Bhagavad Gītā* and an exposition of Maharashtrian values. A very recent plaster image of Alandi, the town where Dnyaneshwar took his *samādhi*, or self-chosen removal from this world, shows a strange domestic scene. The Brahmins had forbidden the outcaste children from building a cooking fire, so Dnyaneshwar with his spiritual power heated his back so that Muktabai could cook chapatis as if over a fire.

The poem of Muktabai, or Mukta, however, which has been translated in a very modern way by a modern poet, Arun Kolatkar, is not at all domestic. Using the Marathi love of colorful irony and equal love of puzzles and riddles, Muktabai put her sense of the wonderful mystery of life in these words:

the zoom art
swallowed the sun
the barren woman
begot a son
a scorpion went
to the lower depths
sesha bowed to him
with a thousand heads
a pregnant fly
delivered a kite
having seen it all
mukta smiled[1]

A slightly later woman saint, Janabai, lived in the family of Namdev. According to legend, Namdev, a saint from the tailor community, traveled north to Hindi territory with Dnyaneshwar, and subsequently his Hindi poetry has become part of the Sikh holy book, the *Guru Granth Sahib*. His main book of songs and most of the legends about him, however, are in the Marathi language and the Maharashtrian world. Namdev is credited with beginning or at least popularizing the annual pilgrimage to Pandharpur, the site of the chief temple of Viṭhoba. He is also credited with writing more than two thousand *ābhaṅgas* or songs in the informal meter of the saint-poets. One of these credits all the members of his large family with being devotees:

Gonai-Rajai, both mother and her daughter-in-law
Dama and Nama, the father and his son
Nara, Mhada, Gonda, Vitha—four sons
Born in this holy lineage,
Ladai, Godai, Yesai, Sakarai—look, Nama's daughters-in-law
Nimbai his daughter, Aubai his sister,
Crazy Jani his servant—
Every one has sung ābhaṅgas—Nama says
God has fulfilled us all.

This list of medieval names includes Namdev's mother, father, sister and wife, his sons and their wives, and a surprising name, Jani or Janabai, his maidservant. Next to Namdev himself, Janabai is the best-known poet in the family, although six of the women's voices are recorded in the collection of *Bhakti* hymns. There is an amusing and very human exchange of verses between Namdev and his wife and his mother, both of whom are very critical of his ecstatic states, which leave them without household support![2] But what is important for us here in this discussion of the extraordinary voices of women saints is the poetry of Janabai, an orphan taken in as serving maid for Namdev and all her life a valued member of the family. There are many stories of Janabai's closeness to the god Viṭhoba. She often calls him Viṭhabāi, or Mother Viṭhoba, using the Maharashtrian convention of considering gods and gurus as female figures. She also addresses Dnyaneshwar as a woman friend or mother. Her *ābhaṅgas* tell of Viṭhoba's coming to help her gather cow dung, grind grain, wash clothes, even wash her hair and remove lice! But in the midst of all these homey things, Janabai sings songs of great imagination and religious understanding. Using the poetry of Arun Kolatkar again, here are two of the most imaginative of Jani's songs. Again, the punctuation is that of the poet, perhaps in emulation of Marathi script, which traditionally had neither capitals nor periods.

Jani 1
i eat god
i drink god
i sleep
on god
i buy god
i count god
i deal
with god
god is here
void is not
devoid of god
jani says:
god is within
god is without
and moreover
there is god to spare

Jani 2
see the void
above the void
on the top of it
there's a void
the first void
is red
it's called
the lower void
the higher void
is white
the middle void
is gray
but the great void
is blue
it contains
only itself
jani was struck
with wonder
when she heard
the silent bell [3]

Of all the women saint-poets of Maharashtra, the most unusual are two women of the untouchable Mahar caste, the wife and sister of the Mahar saint Cokhamela, friend of Namdev, and honored member of the circle of saints who danced and sang their way to Pandharpur in the annual pilgrimage to the town and temple of Viṭhoba. There are many stories about Soyrabai, wife of Cokhamela, and Nirmala, his sister (who probably was married to Soyrabai's brother.) There are tales of the birth of her son after she protestingly fed a Brahmin medicant at her door—protesting because she felt her caste did not allow her to offer food to a Brahmin. There is a story of the god Viṭhoba, who came to her in the guise of her sister-in-law when her son Karmamela was born; Cokhamela had run off to escape the trauma of the birth (and in the legend she forgives him unquestioningly when he returns). There are stories of Brahmins who harass them but also stories of all castes joining with them in joyful worship. There are also many recorded *ābhaṅgas* credited to Soyrabai. Although the text may have become a little corrupted through the centuries, her voice comes across as authentic. One song that seems to be from a very bleak period in her life as a housebound woman also contains the remedy for days of pessimism—the recitation of the Name of God, a form of meditation still practiced by devotees.

House and home are meaningless: *saṁsār* is meaningless,
the body is meaningless.
Your Name is meaningful, all else is meaningless;
if people don't drown in this world, it's only because of the Name.
All things are meaningless, ideas are meaningless,
great wisdom is meaningless. Who cares?

That last note is a sarcastic reference to brahmanical wisdom, which she castigates along with the married life, *saṁsār*, and even the body. In another of the "sad" *ābhaṅgas*, Soyrabai talks to God as if he were a superior person, but one she is familiar with and can reproach:

Why have you saddened me so?
Who would call you the just?
We sit at your doorstep
asking for alms, saying, "give, give"
And you have taken from so many —
How can you feel good about it?
This is not decent conduct
says the Mahari of Cokha.

But Soyrabai is by no means always so scornful of the life she lives in this world. In an *ābhaṅga* that reveals she knows quite a few of the classical *Puranic* stories of gods and heroes, she tells the god, using the Vaiśṇava names Gopāla and Nārāyaṇa:

O Gopāla, I will present incense, lights and garlands to you,
I'll place a leaf before you and serve you family food.
O God, it's not fit for you, but imagine it sweet and accept it.
Vidhur served watered broken rice, O Mother and Father, O Lord.
O Narayana, Draupadi's one leaf smeared with leftover food satisfied you—
It's just like that here, says the Mahari of Cokha.

One of the most moving of Soyrabai's *ābhaṅgas* contains the most explicit reference to the condition of pollution that marks her untouchability. Although she is by no means a rebel in her *ābhaṅgas*, this poem certainly indicates that she does not accept the idea of pollution as determining caste status. She protests the very idea of heredity pollution.

A body is unclean, they say,
only the soil is untainted.
But the impurity of the body
is born with the body.

By which ritual does body become pure?
Not a creature in the world has been born except in a bloody womb.
This is the glory of God: defilement exists within.
The body is polluted from within.
Be sure of it, says the Mahari of Cokha.

Soyrabai does not deal with the problems of her untouchable status very specifically in terms of social interaction. She does call out, "O God, I am lowly," and in perhaps a reference to the difference between her spiritual and her social status, she sings, "The great river flowed, but my body is still not pure." And she does rejoice in the loss of caste and indeed in the fourfold *varṇa* system in the spiritual world:

After seeing you, O Nārāyaṇa, I have no more worldly desires.
Differences and distinctions no longer exist. My mind is pure.
The net of pollution is broken with the strength of the Name.
The rope binding the four bodies is discarded, says Cokha's Mahari.

Although Soyrabai never quite reaches the imaginative heights of Muktabai or Janabai, she does play with language, rhythm, and the strangeness of the world around her in several *ābhaṅgas*. For instance:

So many die, so many cry, so many laugh for no reason.
Think about this: those creatures long in vain to know what is real,
what is false.
What is death? What is grief? What is laughter? Laughter at what?
Who died? Who is left behind? I don't know why they laugh or cry.
But this amazes me says Soyra: no one is mindful of God.

At times, she uses mystical language that reflects the Maharashtrian belief that the God with qualities and the God without qualities (*saguṇa* and *nirguṇa)* are one; that is, the very sight of Viṭhoba at Pandharpur (here called Pandhari) gives one a total understanding of the formless *brahman*.

All colors have merged into one. The Lord of Color himself is immersed
In that color.
When I saw the Lord of Pandhari, the I-you feeling also disappeared . . .
You who have a body are not embodied . . .
I who look and the looking itself are one, says Cokha's Mahari.

Cokhamela's sister, Nirmala, refers so often to him as her ideal, and Soyrabai refers so often to Nirmala with affection and respect, that we have a real sense of family closeness. It is to Soyrabai that Cokhamela runs when he hears that the time for the birthing of his son has come, and Nirmala tells him that he is wrong to do this! But it is also Cokhamela to whom Nirmala turns when she has a period of "the dark night of the soul, " and she calls him by the affectionate diminutive of his name:

There is not a drop of happiness in *samsār*. I am full of sorrow day and night.
I cannot, I cannot meditate on the Name, nor can I worship the saints.

My mind cannot stay in one place, on one thought; I am restless
Night and day.
Nirmala says, Cokha knows; he keeps the King of Pandhari in his heart.

Even in her unhappiness, it is clear that Nirmala knows the technique of meditation. In another *ābhaṅga*, she makes us understand that she can become very close indeed to God.

I am certain of you; I surrender to your feet.
Now do what you think is right; I have put down my burden.
I have put my head in your lap, knowing what the future holds.
Nirmala says, save me or kill me; now the burden is yours.

Nirmala's image of putting her head in the lap of Viṭhoba is not nearly as graphic as some of Janabai's images, such as having her hair combed and oiled by Viṭhoba. In fact, the household and duty images that almost all the other saint-poets use do not occur in the poetry of Cokhamela's wife and sister, except for the story of Soyrabai's giving birth to her son.

There are several especially interesting feminine touches in the poetry of these women. For instance, Soyrabai speaks of "man and woman" almost always, never of man alone. Although she often refers to herself as "Cokha's Mahari" she also signs herself simply Sorya from time to time. Nirmala never refers to her husband, Banka, only to her brother, even though there also are *ābhaṅgas* by Banka in the collection of all the saints' songs. This practice is more in keeping with the Maharashtrian practice of a wife's never referring to her husband by name.[4] One wonders what prompted Soyrabai to take her husband's name so often, although that may simply be legitimacy by association with a well-known and honored saint. And Janabai calls out triumphantly, "Let me not be sad because I am born a woman."

The stories of two more women are more interesting than their own words. Kanhopatra, a contemporary of Namdev and Cokhamela and their families, was the daughter of a courtesan. Rather than go to the palace of the sultan, who admired her beauty, she fled to Pandharpur, where she merged with the image of Viṭhoba. She is the only example of a Maharashtrian woman who was not in some sort of family, and she is the only person whose *samādhi* is in the temple at Pandharpur itself.

The last in the line of woman saints was the seventeenth-century Bahina Bai, whose status is clear in the title of an article by Anne Feldhaus, "Bahina Bai: Wife and Saint." A Brahmin, Bahina Bai's poem as recorded in Feldhaus, paints a dismal portrait of her situation:

The *Vedas* cry, the *Purāṇas* shout
That no good can come of a woman.
I was born with a woman's body—
How am I, now, to attain the Goal?
They're foolish, selfish, seductive, deceptive—
Any link with a woman brings harm.
Bahina says, "If a woman's body's so harmful,

How in this world will I reach the goal?"
What sin did I do in an earlier life
That I'm now removed from God?
My body's a man's, with the shape of a woman.
Sins without number have borne their fruit.
I haven't the right to hear the *Vedas*:
The Brahmans keep secret the *Gāyatrī mantra*
I may not say "Om,"
I may not hear *mantras*' names.
Must not speak of these things with another.[5]

One wonders if Bahina Bai feels a greater sense of oppression than Soyrabai and Nirmala because of her later time period or her Brahmin status. I would judge the latter, that untouchable women were by all accounts freer than those of the upper classes, and all untouchables, not only women, were deprived of Sanskritic knowledge. In spite of her sense of deprivation, Bahina Bai became a disciple of the greatest of all saint-poets, the *śūdra* Tukaram, and her husband, after years of abusing her, through a sort of miracle realized in the midst of an illness that he should learn Bahina Bai's sense of devotion to God. As Feldhaus states, Bahina Bai "was able to practice at once both devotion to her god and service to her husband. But this did not come about until, forced to choose between them, she had placed her husband ahead of her god." [6]

What conclusions can be drawn from this chapter on the woman saints of Maharashtra? For one thing, it stresses their difference from other women saint-poets in other language areas in their adherence to husband and household, a difference possibly caused by the rural nature of the *bhakti* movement in Maharashtra and the necessity for all family members to deal with the harshness of the land. Possibly the lack of a strong *sanyāsī* tradition in the Marathi-speaking area enters into the conundrum. It is also possible that a sort of egalitarian tradition made it possible for women to be honored *bhaktas* (if they did not forsake all the duties of the household!). The problems of Bahina Bai also make us wonder if the fact that the movement was not attached to brahmanical orthodoxy in any way allowed for greater freedom for women. Clearly the women find the life of the household, *samsār*, difficult to reconcile with intense meditation, but it does not seem to occur to them to do more than find the way of the Name to mitigate the problems of *samsār*.

There is another large and most interesting question. Can we conclude that the presence of so many women poets in pre-British times is connected to the presence of many women writers from all walks of life in Maharashtra in the modern period? Or to the many women involved in reform movements since the early pioneers of women's rights, Pandita Ramabai and Tarabai Shinde? Or to the remarkable poetry of a peasant woman, also called Bahina Bai, and the poetry of ex-untouchable (now Buddhist) women who are part of the Dalit literary movement today? We can only speculate and report that contemporary women do refer to *Bhakti* women's writings as they themselves struggle for full rights and opportunities for creativity.[7]

Notes

The Hindi and Marathi term *sant* is translated here as "saint," which carries almost the same meaning in English. *Samsār* refers to the life of an individual in the world, which for women is assumed to be married life and household and family duties.

Translations have been done with the help of Vijaya Deo, Jayant Karve, and S. G. Tulpule.

1. Kolatkar (1982), p. 114. The punctuation is Kolatkar's own; *shesha* is a snake; a kite in this context is a hawk.
2. I have detailed a little of this in "The Householder Saints of Maharashtra."
3. Kolatkar (1982), p. 114.
4. A twentieth-century autobiography of the wife of a well-known nationalist is titled simply *Himself*, and the author never refers to her husband by name.
5. Feldhaus (1982), p. 594
6. Ibid, p. 598.
7. See *Manushi* and Bhagwat in the References.

References

Bahina Bai. *Bahina Bai: A Translation of her Autobiography and Verses* by Justin E . Abbot. Pune: Scottish Mission Industries, 1929.

Bahinabai (Chaudhari). "Four Poems" translated by Philip Engblom, Maxine Bertsen and Jayant Karve. In *Journal of South Asian Literature* 17 (1982), p. 102–8.

Bhagwat, Vidyut. "Janabai" and"Bahinabai." In Susie Tharu and K. Lalita, eds., *Women Writing in India: 600 B.C. to the Present*. Vol 1: 600 B.C. *to the Early Twentieth Century*. New York: Feminist Press, 1991.

——— "Man-Woman Relations in the Writings of the Saint Poetesses." *New Quest* 82(1990), pp. 224–32.

——— "Marathi Literature as a Source for Contemporary Feminism." *Economic and Political Weekly*, April 29, 1995, pp. 24–29.

Bhavalkar, Tara. "Women Saint Poets' Conception of Liberation." In Anne Feldhaus, ed., *Images in Maharashtrian Literature and Religion*. Albany: State University of New York Press, 1996.

Deleury, G. A. *The Cult of Vithoba*. Poona: Deccan College, 1960.

Feldhaus, Anne. "Bahina Bai: Wife and Saint." *The Journal of the American Academy of Religion* 50: 4 (1982), pp. 591–694.

Feldhaus, Anne, ed. *Images in Maharashtriam Religion and Society*. Albany: State University of New York Press, 1996.

Kolatkar, Arun. "Translations from Tukaram and Other Saint-Poets." *Journal of South Asian Literature* (1982), pp. 109–14.

Kosambi, Meera. *At the Intersection of Gender Reform and Religious Belief: Pandita Ramabai's Contribution*. Bombay: Research Centre for Women's Studies, S.N.D.T. Women's University, 1993.

Mahipati. *Nectar from Indian Saints*. Trans. Justin E. Abbott and N. R. Godbole. Poona: United Theological College of Western India, 1934. Repr. Delhi: Motilal Banarsidass, 1982.

Manushi. Nos. 50–51 (1989). Also printed separately as *Women Bhakta Poets*. See especially Ruth Vanita, "Three Women Sants of Maharashtra: Muktabai, Janabai, Bahinabai," pp. 45–61.

O'Hanlon, Rosalind. *A Comparison between Women and Men: Tarabai Shinde and the Critique of Gender Relations in Colonial India*. Madras: Oxford University Press, 1994.

Sellegren, Sarah. "Janabai and Kanhopatra: A Study of Two Women Sants" In Anne Feldhaus, ed., *Images of Women in Maharashtrian Literature and Religion*. Albany: State University of New York Press, 1996.

Shah, A. B. "Pandita Ramabai." *New Quest* 2 (August 1977), pp. 11–26. See also Pandita Ramabai's own writing.

Zelliot, Eleanor. "The Householder Saints of Maharashtra." In Alan Entwistle, Carol Salomon, Michael Shapiro and Heidi Pauwels, eds., *Proceedings of the Sixth International Conference on Early Literature in New Indo-Aryan Languages, 1994* (forthcoming).

———. "The Religious Imagination of Maharashtrian Women Bhaktas." In Shrikant Paranjpe, Raja Dixit, and C. R. Das, eds. *Western India: History, Society and Culture. Dr. Arvind Deshpande Felicitation Volume*. Kolhapur: Itihas Shikshak Mahamandal, 1997.

———. "Stri Dalit Sahitya: The New Voice of Women Poets." In Anne Feldhaus, ed., *Images in Maharashtrian Religion and Society*. Albany: State University of New York Press. 1996.

———. "Women in the Homes of the Saints." In Irina Glushkova, ed., *House and Home in Maharashtra*. Papers from the 1995 Maharashtra Conference in Moscow. In press.

MRIDUCCHANDA PALIT

Powers Behind the Throne

Women in Early Mughal Politics

The importance of the Mughal era in the history of India rests not only on the unification of virtually all of India under an elaborately centralized administration but also on the complexity of its political culture. The finely nuanced character of the power games that shaped the fortunes of the dynasty are nowhere better illustrated than in the lives and acts of the great ladies at the Mughal court, who often exerted an influence far beyond the limits granted them by their male-dominated polity. Although in principle the Islamic faith acknowledges the equality of men and women in both ability and intelligence, in practice in the Mughal world, as in others, women were relegated to a subordinate position. Yet despite the constraints on women, many of the mothers, daughters, and wives of the Mughal emperors were the driving forces behind them, who protected and advanced them by their own will, talents, and ambitions. This is a steady but often overlooked pattern of achievement, even though the cultural sophistication of these women is common knowledge by virtue of their literary and artistic work. The diaries and autobiographies of Babur's daughter Gulbadan Begum, Shahjahan's daughter Jahanara, and Aurangzeb's daughter Zebunnisa are well known as both historical and literary documents. But the political content of Mughal women's perceptions remain neglected even as examples of their acumen in politics and commerce abound; for instance, Nurjahan Begum, Emperor Jahangir's queen, played a pivotal role in the administration of the empire during his reign and was the only Mughal queen to have her face inscribed on a coin of the realm.[1] Materials for a history of these women are at best sketchy, but some sense of their abilities and careers may be recaptured from the sometimes anecdotal references and tributes to them in contemporary records. This chapter reviews the contribution of women to Mughal politics during the founding and consolidation of the dynasty.

The story of the Mughal dynasty begins with the rise of Zahirud-din Mohammed Babur, the founder of the Mughal empire, but the diplomatic maneuvers of Aisan Daulat Begum, his maternal grandmother, contributed substantially to his extraordinary success. When Babur became the ruler of Farghana at the age of eleven in 1494, he also inherited the legacy of Chengiz Khan through his maternal grandfather, Yunus Khan, the Grand Khan of Mughlistan.[2] But the independence of Farghana was soon endangered by the onslaughts of his paternal and maternal uncles. Had Babur not had the armed support of some loyal emirs and the active intrigues of his grandmother at this critical moment, it is doubtful whether he could have survived.[3]

Aisan Daulat Begum is known in Mughal history for her courage and integrity. The story of her encounter with Sheikh Jamal-ud-din Khan illustrates her strength of character in extreme adversity. At one point in her eventful life, she and her husband, Yunus Khan, were taken prisoner by Sheikh Jamal-ud-din Khan. Yunus was forced to surrender her to one of the Sheikh's officers, with no apparent protest by Aisan Begum, who received the officer in her apartment at night. But within moments the man was overpowered by her and her maidservants, stabbed to death, and his corpse flung on the street. To the agent of Jamal-ud-din who came to enquire about this ghastly murder, she responded, "I am the wife of Yunus Khan, and only his. Sheikh Jamal thought it fit to give me to another. He knows whether this is in accordance with religion and law. I have killed the man; let Sheikh Jamal kill me, if he chooses." The sheikh was impressed by her courage, and she was allowed to return with honor to her husband.[4] It was with this resolute and high-spirited lady that Babur lived from the age of five and under whose tutelage he grew up when his grandfather died. He acknowledged her influence in his memoir in the following words: "She was very wise and far-sighted, and most affairs of mine were carried through under her advice."[5] She died in 1505, not fortunate enough to see her grandson become emperor of Hindustan, but it was she who sowed the seeds of courage and ambition in Babur.

The history of early Mughal expansion often surprises us with the contribution of Mughal women to the task of empire building and the position women held in the power elite. Babur's grandmother was not the only female influence on him. Both his mother, Qutlugh Nigar Khanam, and his elder sister Khanzada Begum were close advisors during his years of struggle.[6] After the conquest of Hindustan, ninety-six women of the Mughal clan who came from Kabul to Delhi at the invitation of Babur received *jagirs* (land grants) and other valuable gifts from him.[7] His eldest son, Humayun, was no less fortunate in finding a mentor in his mother, Maham Begum, the third wife of Babur, daughter of a noble Shia family of Khorasan, who helped him in building his career. She was highly educated, intelligent, and broad-minded. "Maham was the chief lady of the royal household . . . . She was supreme, and had well-defined rights over other inmates."[8] When Humayun received his first assignment as governor of Badakshan at the age of twelve, his mother stayed with him and not only looked after his comforts but also helped him form his strategies during the days of his apprenticeship.[9] At his succession after Babur's death, it was again Maham Begum who guided him.

Women's life at the Mughal court was relatively free of restraints. Purdah was less strictly observed in the harems of the first two Mughal emperors than enjoined by custom. Gulbadan Begum states that the ladies of the royal harem mixed freely with their male friends and visitors. They often dressed in male attire, played polo, and engaged in music.[10] They were free to remarry after divorce, and some did so more than once after divorce. For instance, Aiysha Sultan Begum, the first wife of Babur, left him within three years of their marriage[11] and married twice more. Babur's elder sister Khanzada Begum married at least three times. Gulburg Begum, daughter of Nizam-ud-din Khalifa, married at first Mir Shah Hussain Arghun in 1524 and, after separation, married Emperor Humayun sometime before 1539.[12] Mughal women enjoyed a large degree of freedom in choosing their partners, and marriage was not devoid of personal choice. A celebrated example is that of Hamida Banu.

Hamida Banu Begum, who was to bear Akbar, was the Persian Shia wife of Humayun. After his defeat at the hands of Sher Khan in the battle of Kanauj, Humayun took refuge with Hussain, Sultan of Thatta. Humayun first saw Hamida Banu at a banquet given in his honor by his stepmother Dildar Begum at Pat, a town in Sehawan, a district of Thatta.[13] Humayun indicated his desire to marry the beautiful Hamida Banu, daughter of Mir Baba Dost, a Shia Maulavi who was the spiritual preceptor of Dildar Begum's son Hindal. Initially, Hamida Banu refused to marry Humayun, declaring, "Oh, yes, I shall marry someone, but he shall be a man whose collar my hand can touch and not one whose skirt it does not touch."[14] Humayun courted her for a period of forty days, which convinced Hamida Banu of his sincerity, and she eventually gave her consent to the marriage, which took place in 1541, when Humayun was thirty-three. Hamida Banu came to be known as Maryam-Makani after her marriage.[15] Their marriage went through in spite of Hindal's disapproval; his mother, Dildar Begum, organized the wedding.[16] Maryam-Makani remained devoted to her husband through her life. She never left Humayun during the dark spell of fourteen years when he was ousted from his kingdom and kept on the run by Askari. She was not only his constant companion but also his only source of inspiration. She did not even hesitate to leave her eighteen-month-old son, Akbar, to be with her husband.[17] Humayun reconquered his throne in 1555 but died only a few months later in 1556. Maryam was not even thirty at that time.

To Maryam-Makani's wifely devotion, we may add political ability, which was amply demonstrated when her illustrious son, Akbar, ascended the throne as the third Mughal emperor at the age of fourteen in February 1556, with Bairam Khan as his guardian. She played an important role during the initial years of her minor son's rule. When Bairam Khan became the first Vakil-us-Sultanate—that is, the prime minister of Shahinshah Akbar—and assumed the reins of government on behalf of Akbar during the period of his minority (1556–60), he became an autocrat.[18] Not only did Bairam chastise Akbar but also he even prevented Akbar from maintaining any relation with the emirs who had been close to Humayun. Anticipating the danger inherent in this isolation of Akbar, which could perhaps lead to his overthrow, Maryam-Makani kept her son informed of every turn in the situation. Later, after the Second Battle of Panipat (1556), Maryam-Makani made a political alliance against the wishes of Bairam Khan by arranging Akbar's marriage to the granddaughter of Munim Khan, who had been a trusted emir of Humayun. A group of her own trusted emirs helped her forge this alliance.[19] This was the first move against Bairam Khan's growing power orchestrated by Maryam-Makani, who was always by her son Akbar's side. He was becoming increasingly impatient with

Bairam's high-handedness, and eventually at the age of eighteen in 1560, he decided to take the reins of power in his own hands. In planning his strategy to secure his empire, Akbar confided "his closely hidden secret"[20] to his foster-mother Maham Anaga, her son Adham Khan, son-in-law Shihabuddin, and Munim Khan, a trusted lieutenant of Humayun, all of whom were close and trusted followers of Maryam-Makani. Her preeminence was due to the political sagacity and determination with which she used her position as dowager queen in the Mughal harem and the respect and affection she received from her son the emperor. For example, during one of her trips from Lahore to Agra, her palanquin bearers were Akbar and some of his emirs.[21] Whenever his mother returned from a visit, Akbar would invariably go out of the city to receive her and pay his respect.[22] Maryam-Makani retained her commanding position till the last days of her life, although there were other ladies at court who were active players in Mughal politics. When her grandson Salim revolted against his father, Akbar, a rapprochement was eventually brought about by Salim's stepmother, Salima Begum,[23] of whom we shall hear more later, but Salim went first to Maryam-Makani and obtained her pardon before he went to anyone else.[24] She died in 1603 only two years before Akbar's death in 1605.

A striking feature of women's political position at the Mughal court was that personal ability rather than blood relationship legitimated their participation. A good example is the career of another lady who exercised considerable influence in the early years of Akbar's life. This was Maham Anaga, one of Akbar's wet nurses.[25] Because of Humayun's political vicissitudes, Akbar had been separated from his mother in his childhood and breast-fed by several wet nurses.[26] These wet nurses or foster mothers were mostly ladies of rank and were called *anagas*. The most important among them was Maham Anaga.

Maham Anaga not only risked her life to save the child Akbar's life from his uncle's plan to kill Akbar but also dedicated her life to his well-being and was totally committed to his welfare, toward which she applied herself with active interest and political shrewdness. In the years of Humayun's adversity, which continued even after Akbar's birth, when most of his associates deserted him, including his younger brothers Askari and Kamran, and he had to flee to Persia, his Queen Maryam-Makani fled with him, leaving the infant Akbar in the camp with his nurses.[27] The child was seized by his Uncle Askari as a hostage and taken to Kandahar where he was lodged in the servants' quarters. Fortunately, Askari's wife took a fancy to the infant and made suitable arrangements for his upbringing under women of the nobility, as Abul Fazl has recorded: "Maham Anaga, Jiji Anaga and Atka Khan were made fortunate by serving him."[28] From 1545 to 1547, Humayun underwent many changes of fortune; he invaded and captured lost territory and won and lost battles in his effort to regain his kingdom. To force him into submission, his brothers moved young Akbar to Kabul, where he was held captive by his uncle Kamran. Although Akbar was freed and reunited with his father in November 1545, Humayun was overpowered again by Kamran, and Akbar was recaptured. Two years later, when Humayun mounted his second invasion of Kabul in November 1547, Kamran placed Akbar on the rampart of the main gate of the fort to expose him to the gunfire of Humayun's artillery. Maham Anaga risked her life to save Akbar by protecting him with her person on the rampart at that crucial moment.[29]

It is remarkable how frequently Akbar's survival, both physical and political, depended upon Mughal women. Akbar went on to mount his father's throne, but in the first four years of his reign, Bairam Khan controlled the administration, and Akbar was merely a figurehead. By 1560, Akbar was trying to assert his desire to become a "king in fact as well as in name."[30] Grave conflict seemed imminent when the enemies of Bairam Khan set afloat rumors that he was hatching a conspiracy to dethrone Akbar and place Abut Quasim, son of Mirza Kamran, on the Mughal throne. Akbar and his well-wishers felt alarmed and decided to strike against the conspirators before they could execute their plan.[31] The faction that organized the coup and won over sections of the nobility envious of Bairam's power was the "harem party." In the political machinations, Maham Anaga, the foster-mother of Akbar and "a marvel for sense, resource and loyalty," played a major role. She divulged the plan to her son-in-law Shihabuddin Ahmad Khan Atka,[32] governor of Delhi and a favorite of Akbar, who immediately swung into action and prepared a detailed plan to oust Bairam Khan. Shamsuddin Muhammad Khan Atka, governor of Lahore and the husband of Jiji Anaga, another wet nurse of Akbar; Munim Khan, governor of Kabul; and other prominent Mughal nobles were secretly won over in favor of Akbar.[33]

Dowager Queen Maryam-Makani was already in Delhi. On March 19, 1560, pretending to go on a hunting expedition toward Aligarh, Akbar left Agra with his cousin Abul Quassim as part of a plan to misdirect Bairam Khan's faction. Actually, Akbar joined Maham and her party at Sikandra, from which he sent a message that he was proceeding toward Delhi to see his mother, who was seriously ill. At Delhi, Shihabuddin and some other nobles arranged a royal reception for the young monarch amid great public rejoicing on March 27, 1560. Akbar then secured his position by arresting some agents of Bairam while the rest fled. The defenses of the fort at Delhi were then thoroughly strengthened by Akbar's supporters and the army kept in readiness. Prominent governors and army officers received messages regarding the assumption of sovereign power by Akbar. Abul Fazl states that on the receipt of this information, "right-minded novices and devoted seniors . . . came trooping in from all parts to the sublime Court. . . . Everyone who brought sincerity to the threshold was exalted by fitting offices and title and fiefs."[34] Akbar took the reins from Bairam Khan and expressed his desire that Bairam Khan should leave for Mecca.[35] Bairam agreed and proceeded toward Mecca after being honorably discharged from his office in a manner befitting his position and past services. On his way, however, he was stabbed to death (January 1561) by a Lohani Afghan as a result of a private quarrel.[36] In all of this except the last tragic event, Akbar had the backing of harem politics, and the most important role in removing Bairam Khan from the political scene was played by Maham Anaga as the leader of the harem party. It was her "real capacity for political intrigue which gained for her an important position in the state."[37]

Most contemporary historians refer to the great influence Maham Anaga acquired at the royal court after the fall of Bairam Khan. She acted as the young monarch's principal counselor. The extent of her influence has been judged harshly by Vincent Smith, who comments: "Akbar shook off the tutelage of Bairam Khan only to bring himself under the 'monstrous regiment' of unscrupulous women."[38]

Smith believes that Maham Anaga assumed power herself, bestowed favor on her own relatives, and furthered only her own interests. She became a kingmaker and initiated a petticoat government, of which, in Smith's opinion, Akbar became a puppet. There is no doubt that Akbar loved Maham Anaga like his own mother and had great regard for her and her people. He felt obliged to all those who had stood by him in his trial of strength against Bairam Khan. After the sudden expulsion of Bairam and his men, when state positions and military commands were redistributed by Akbar, the lion's share went to the leaders of the harem party as a reward.[39] Not mature enough to gauge the intricacies of politics all at once, Akbar actively associated the harem party in setting state policy. As the leader of the harem party, Maham Anaga enjoyed great authority at that time. However, Akbar was the master of his own will, and as soon as he felt that anyone was encroaching upon his sovereignty, he acted swiftly to cut that person down to size, although he continued to trust Maham Anaga as a valued advisor.[40]

Maham Anaga's initiatives in securing Akbar's ascendancy did not flag with success. After the fall of Bairam, Akbar appointed as many people as possible, in quick succession, to the office of the prime minister in order to prevent any one person from becoming too powerful. The first prime minister was Shihabuddin Khan Atka, governor of Delhi, who was appointed on March 27, 1560. Soon after, Maham Anaga was entrusted with a *vakalat* to represent his majesty. Thus, Akbar experimented with a dual prime ministership, with both incumbents jointly responsible to him. This experiment, however, did not work well, as Maham Anaga, by virtue of her closeness to the young emperor, attempted to overrule her colleague in matters of state policy. According to Abul Fazl, Maham Anaga, "in her great loyalty, took charge of affairs and made Shihabuddin Ahmad Khan and Khwaja Jahan her tools . . . ."[41] Soon, relations between the two prime ministers became strained. Taking advantage of Turkish nobles disgruntled over the misrule of Shihabuddin, Maham Anaga advised Akbar to remove Shihabuddin from the prime ministership. The prime ministership was then offered in association with Maham Anaga to Bahadur Khan, a distinguished Turkish noble.[42] Bahadur Khan accepted the office and helped foil the conspiracy of the Turk group against Akbar but lost his position because of his incompetence. The real power in this period of Akbar's reign rested with Maham Anaga. Abul Fazl writes, "In those days, Bahadur Khan had the name of Vakil, yet in reality, the business was transacted by Maham Anaga. O ye worshippers of forms, what do you behold? For this noble work, wisdom and courage was necessary, and, in truth, Maham Anaga possessed these two qualities in perfection. Many a woman treads manfully wisdom's path."[43]

Abul Fazl's comment on women's manly abilities is interesting not only as an estimate of notable women of his time but also as a gendering of character values: power and manliness were inseparable. Maham Anaga's "manliness" became the cause of her undoing, for the qualities that earned awe and respect for her also placed her in a transgressive gender role. Her resolute spirit made the young emperor feel that Prime Minister Maham Anaga was overbearing and aggressive. Moreover, the Mughals had no tradition of being controlled by a woman prime minister, however capable that woman might be.

Therefore, Maham Anaga was politely asked by Akbar on September 10, 1560, to hand over the *vakalat* to Munim Khan, who became the fourth prime minister, with the title Khan-i-Khanan. Still, Maham Anaga, who held charge of the royal household, continued to influence the state administration through Munim Khan, also a member of the harem party. Akbar then proceeded to conquer Malwa and chose Maham Anaga's son Adham Khan as the commander of the army, a decision that further underlines the influence of Maham Anaga and the harem party.[44] Adham Khan and Pir Muhammad Khan successfully conducted their invasion.[45] However, Adham Khan's pride over their victory brought his downfall when he sent to the emperor a report of his victory but only a few elephants as booty. He appropriated the rest of the spoils. Akbar was furious at this insolence and personally marched to Sarangapur to punish the delinquent, who, taken by surprise, surrendered to the emperor. Adham Khan was excused through the intercession of Maham Anaga. In her ruthless drive to secure her son's fortunes, Maham Anaga did not hesitate to kill two innocent girls in Baz Bahadur's harem who were witnesses to her son's scandalous conduct. Adham Khan was permitted to remain in Malwa as governor, with Pir Muhammad as his principal assistant. But the pardon was short-lived, and soon Adham Khan was recalled from Malwa.[46] This angered Maham Anaga, "who regarded herself as the virtual lieutenant of the empire."[47] When in November 1561 Akbar summoned Shamsuddin Atka Khan from Kabul to appoint him prime minister, she was extremely annoyed, and so was Munim Khan. By then, the harem party had broken up into two groups: the Maham Anaga group and the faction of Atka Khan.[48] Extreme hotheadedness brought Adham Khan's doom on May 16, 1562, when, accompanied by his followers, he burst in on Shamsuddin Khan and killed him. He then rushed into the inner chamber of Akbar where he was overpowered by Akbar. By Akbar's command Adham Khan was put to death by being twice thrown from the terrace. Akbar himself broke this news to Maham Anaga, who was ill. The sick woman simply said, "Your Majesty did well," and forty days later died of grief for her worthless son. In grateful remembrance of his foster mother, who had once risked her life for his sake and sheltered him from the cradle to the throne, Akbar raised a mausoleum at Delhi, where mother and son were interred.[49] Maham Anaga deserves a special place in Mughal history not only as Akbar's foster mother and protector but also and more important as one of his most capable and faithful political allies. By her political skills and resolute character, she broke out of the limitations of her gender to reach the highest office in the land. Her position was not without its irony, though; she held very great power, indeed, but she held it only by the pleasure of Akbar, who could and did give her free rein or curbed her at will.

We have already had a brief glimpse of Sultana Salima Begum, another woman who stands out in early Mughal history. A granddaughter of Babur, Salima Begum was the senior consort of Akbar. She was the daughter of Gulrukh Begum, sister of Prince Hindal, who was noted in the Mughal family for her beauty and accomplishments.[50] In *Tuzuk-i-Jahangiri*, she is described as a poetess who wrote under the pseudonym Makfi. Her aunt Gulbadan Begum has also eulogized her in the same vein in her *Humayun Nama:* "She creates an impression of herself as a charming and cultivated woman."[51] Akbar gave her in marriage to his guardian, Bairam Khan, to make him a member of the royal family,[52] for even though Akbar eventually got rid of Bairam Khan, he always remained grateful and respectful to Bairam. He acknowledged that it was through the mediation of Bairam Khan that Humayun had secured the help of Tasma Shah, the Safavi emperor of Persia.[53] Bairam was instrumental not only in helping Humayun regain the throne of Delhi in 1555 but also in ensuring Akbar's succession a year later, when he threw his weight as *wazir* or prime minister behind Akbar to save him from falling into the hands of his strongest enemies, the Afghans. It was with his help that Akbar won the Second Battle of Panipat in 1556 against the Surs.[54]

The marriage of Salima and Bairam took place in 1557, but Bairam Khan was killed four years later in 1561. Through these four years, Akbar was emperor only in name, and Bairam Khan actually ruled. Whether Salima Begum shared the power with Bairam would be a matter of speculation. As Bairam's wife, she undoubtedly commanded respect but evidently not the confidence of the political women of the harem, who were, as we have seen, instrumental in overthrowing Bairam. When on his way to Mecca in 1561, Bairam was killed by Mubarak Khan, an Afghan youth whose father had been killed at the Battle of Machhiwara in 1555 by troops led by Bairam Khan, Salima Begum was accompanying Bairam with her infant son. Akbar was shocked to hear the news of the sad death of his former mentor, guardian, and *wazir*. As a mark of respect to the memory of Bairam, Akbar married his widow, Salima Begum, and brought up under his personal care Bairam's infant son, Abdur Rahim,[55] who grew up to be a distinguished military general and scholar and was considered one of the nine jewels of Akbar's court. The emperor honored him by conferring on him his father's title Khan-i-Khanan in 1584.[56] Salima Begum gained as much prestige and influence through being as the mother of her illustrious son as she did through being the senior consort of Akbar. In other words, her power stemmed from her connections with powerful men, first as the wife of Bairam, then as the wife of Akbar, and finally as the mother of Abdur Rahim.

Salima Begum's political talents lay in a direction quite different from those of the other Mughal women we have observed here. Instead of maneuvering for power, she exerted herself to make peace between warring factions, which she did so successfully that contemporary records emphasize her ability to make Akbar's last days peaceful. Akbar was partial to his eldest son, Salim, son of Jodhabai, daughter of Biharimal of Amber, but when Salim revolted against him, Akbar resolved to crush Salim, driven by his commitment to his family's long-term welfare. Educated, well-trained in the arts of government and war, and lover of the fine arts, Salim became addicted to wine and women in his youth. Offended by his imperious attitude, a group of emirs tried to have Khasru, the eldest son of Salim and Manbai, declared heir to Akbar by setting aside Salim's claim.[57] The main figures behind the plan were Man Singh, maternal uncle to the 17-year-old Khasru, and Mirza Aziz Koka, his father-in-law. The move incurred the wrath of Salim, who began to see Khasru as an enemy; to preempt the pro-Khasru faction, he rose in armed rebellion in 1600 to wrest the Mughal throne from his father.[58] At that time, Akbar was engaged in the siege of Asirgarh in the Deccan. Salim marched on to Allahabad, where he proclaimed himself an independent king and struck gold and copper coins in his own name. He also started negotiations with the Portuguese for furthering his designs. All efforts of Akbar to win back his rebel son failed. In

June 1602, Akbar summoned Abul Fazl, his prime minister and most trusted counselor from the Deccan, to help him solve the problem. But Abul Fazl was murdered on the way by Vir Singh Bundela, an agent of Salim, in August 1602. This ghastly murder deeply hurt Akbar's feelings and set him against Salim even more implacably. At this critical moment, Salima Begum stepped into the affair and urged by her fondness for her stepson Salim and her devotion to Akbar's interests, she initiated the process of bringing together father and son.[59] That Salim escaped punishment was due entirely to the intervention of his stepmother. She herself went to Allahabad and persuaded Salim to come to Agra and beg Akbar's pardon. At the same time, Salima Begum also consoled the grieving emperor and prevailed on him to forgive his son. Eventually, she forged a reconciliation between Akbar and Salim and thereby averted a grave threat to the Mughal dynasty.[60] Salim was declared heir apparent to the throne and eventually ascended it under the name Jahangir. Because of Salima Begum's espousal of Jahangir's cause, she enjoyed a special position in the royal household in the opening years of Jahangir's reign as the Padshahi Begum (i.e., chief of the Mughal harem), as the wife of Akbar, as the mother of a famous son, and as the stepmother of Jahangir.[61]

There is little doubt that women of the Mughal court played central roles in the power games, often murderous, that shaped the history of medieval India. Whether at the inception of Mughal power or during its tortuous consolidation, women such as Aisan Daulat Begum, maternal grandmother of Babur; Maryam-Makani, Humayun's wife and Akbar's mother; Maham Anaga, Akbar's foster-mother; and Sultana Salima, Babur's granddaughter and Bairam's wife and later a senior consort of Akbar, all influenced policy and wielded substantive power over the administration. Their full histories remain to be written, but telling elements emerge even from a brief overview such as this. First of all, these were women of high intelligence, determination, and courage. Without these character attributes, they could not have stayed afloat in the political currents of the time. Second, they appear to have worked primarily for the benefit of the male figures around whom they orbited, driven, it seems, by affection and dynastic considerations and never attempting to take the reins of empire in their own hands, let alone actually staking any claims to the throne.[62] Even when they were seated literally next to the throne, as was Maham Anaga, they moved in the shadow of its male occupant.

At the same time, the history of these women reveals an aspect of Mughal society not often recognized for the ambiguity it represents— namely, that this society did not render women as utterly helpless and submissive as the conventional wisdom about women's lives in India holds.[63] Within the constraints of religion and custom, there was enough room for Mughal women to socialize with men on the basis of mutual respect and, more important, to achieve personal development, as demonstrated by the substantial body of their literary, artistic, and musical works. Perhaps the greatest privilege these women enjoyed was the power of literacy, to which we can probably ascribe their self-awareness, aspirations beyond domesticity, and strategic sense, which combined into a diplomatic persuasiveness that compelled attention. Admittedly, a few gifted individuals do not a spring make, but that those few could blossom argues for the availability of sustenance in their world. It would be just as false to claim that in Mughal society *forms* of power were anything but strictly gendered, as to assert that the *substance* of power was a male monopoly. Were Maryam-Makani and Maham Anaga mere accidents? Or was there some idea of freedom inherent in the Mughal world that legitimated crossing gender boundaries? Was it despite the conditions of Mughal society that women acceded to power or because of them? Out of answers to these questions may emerge a reevaluation of Mughal culture, and to answer them a full history must first to be written of the women of the time, if only to bring them out of the shadows cast by Mughal pomp and splendor.

Notes

1. The only other instance of this acknowledgment of a reigning queen in the history of pre-British India comes from the Gupta era: Emperor Samudragupta's coins bear his image with that of his queen.
2. *Babur Nama* (1922), pp. 12–24.
3. Ibid., p. 43.
4. Lane-Poole (1899), p 23.
5. *Babur Nama* (1922), p. 43.
6. Lal (1988), p. 22.
7. *Humayun Nama* (1972), pp. 203–297.
8. Ibid., pp. 8–9.
9. Mehta (1981), pp. 146–147.
10. Ibid., Introduction, pp. 7, 31–32.
11. *Babur Nama* (1922), pp. 35–36.
12. Ibid., p. 230.
13. Stewart (1972), p. 31.
14. *Humayun Nama* (1972), p. 151.
15. *Akbar Nama*, vol. 1(1989), pp. 8–9.
16. Stewart (1972), p. 31.
17. Ibid., p. 52.
18. Majumdar (1984), pp. 108–109.
19. Hussain (1941), p. 141.
20. *Akbar Nama*, vol. ii (1873–87), p. 141.
21. Coryat, in Foster (1921), p. 278.
22. *Akbar Nama*, vol. iii (1873–87), p. 348.
23. Salima Begum was the granddaughter of Babur, who was first married to Bairam and later, after Bairam's death, to Akbar.
24. Elliot (1867–77), p. 112.
25. *Akbar Nama*, vol. ii (1989), p. 134.
26. Ibid., pp. 130–31.
27. Stewart (1972), p. 52.
28. *Akbar Nama*, vol. i (1989), p. 395.
29. *Tabaqat-I-Akbari* (1929), p. 112.
30. Smith (1921), p. 32.
31. *Akbar Nama*, vol. ii (1873–87) p. 145, n. 1.
32. Ibid., p. 141. The husband and other male relations of a wet nurse were called Atka.
33. *Akbar Nama*, vol. i (1873–87), p. 130.
34. Ibid., pp. 142–44.

35. Ibid., p. 153.

36. Ibid., pp. 201–2.

37. Ibid., p. 204.

38. Smith, (1921) p. 35. Smith's allusion to John Knox's misogynist tract (1558) hardly inspires confidence in his impartiality.

39. Majumdar (1984), p. 111.

40. Ibid., p. 112.

41. *Akbar Nama* vol. ii (1989), p. 149.

42. Ibid., p. 150.

43. Ibid., p. 151.

44. Majumdar (1984), p. 112.

45. Led by Adham Khanand Pir Muhammad, the Mughal army invaded Malwa, and the musician king, Baz Bahadur, a well-known voluptuary, was easily defeated by the superior army of Akbar. Baz Bahadur fled, and his women, his treasure, and his elephants fell into the hands of the victors, but his queen Rupamati, who was famous for her beauty, took poison to save her honor (Smith, 1921, p. 37).

46. Ibid., pp. 37, 40.

47. Burn (1987), p. 81.

48. Majumdar (1984), p. 113.

49. *Akbar Nama* vol. ii (1989), pp. 269–75.

50. Ibid., p. 329, n. 2.

51. *Humayun Nama* (1972), p. 279.

52. Mehta (1981), p. 198.

53. Stewart (1972), pp. 54, 59–68.

54. Smith (1921), pp. 29–30, 35.

55. Ibid., pp. 30, 34.

56. *Akbar Nama* vol. ii (1989), p. 204.

57. Smith (1921), p. 231.

58. Mehta (1981), pp. 374–75.

59. Smith (1921), p. 73.

60. Ibid., pp. 219–21, 224–25.

61. Tripathi (1956), p. 421.

62. The only woman ever to ascend the imperial throne was Sultana Rizia of the pre-Mughal Mameluk dynasty in the thirteenth century, but she could keep it only for a short period. Her father Iltutmis "chose for his successor his daughter Razzyya, whom he considered a 'better man' than his sons. This queen was a brave and clever woman, however the warrior chiefs, owing to their Moslem prejudices, saw subodination to a woman as dishonorable" (Antonova, et al. (1979), pp. 203–4. Ceaseless conspiracy by the chiefs brought her down after four years.

63. Histories of India abound in stereotypes in general. A case immediately in point is Antonova et al.'s comment in n. 62, which explains the hostility of the chiefs to Sultana Rizia by invoking "their Moslem prejudices."

References

Akbar Nama. 3 vols. Text, Bibliotheca Indica Series. Calcutta: 1873–87. Tr. H. Beveridge. Calcutta: 1921–48. Repr. 3 vols. Delhi: Low Price Publication, 1989.

Antonova, K., G. Bongard-Levin, and G. Kotowsky. *A History of India*. Tr. Katherine Judelson. Moscow: Progressive Publishers, 1979.

Babur Nama (*Memoirs of Babur*), 2 vols. Ed. tr. A. S. Beveridge.London: Luzac, 1922.
burn, Richard, Ed. "The Mughal Period." In *The Cambridge History of India*, vol. 4. New Delhi: S. Chand, 1987.
Elliot, Henry M. and John Dowson, Tr. *History of India as Told by Its Own Historians*, 8 vols. London: Hertford 1867–77.
Foster, W. *Early Travels in India*. London: Oxford University Press, 1921. With the narratives of Fitch (pp. 1–47) Mildenhall (pp. 48–69); Hawkins (pp. 60–121); Finch (pp. 122–87), Withington (pp. 188–233), Coryat (pp. 234–87) and Terry (pp. 288–332).
Humayun Nama. By Gulbadan Begum. Ed. tr. A. S. Beveridge. London: Royal Asiatic Society, 1902. Indian reprint; Delhi: Idarah-Adabiyat-i-Delhi 1972.
Hussain, Hidyet. *Twarikh-i-Humayun Wah Akbar*. Ed. Bayazid Bayet. Calcutta 1941.
Lal, K. S. *The Mughal Harem*. Delhi: Aditya Prakashan, 1988.
Lane-Poole, Stanley. *Babar*. Oxford: Clarendon Press, 1899.
Majumdar, R. C. ed. *History and Culture of the Indian People*, vol. 7. *The Mughal Empire*. Bombay: Bharatiya Vidya Bhavan, 1984.
Mehta, J. L. *Advanced Study in the History of Medieval India*, vol. 2 (1526–1707), *Mughal Empire*. New Delhi: Sterling, 1981.
Prasad, Beni. *History of Jahangir*. Allahabad: India Press Private, 1962.
Roy Chowdhury, Makhan Lal. *Jahanarar Atmakahini*, 2d ed. Calcutta: Indian Book Concern, 1977.
Smith, V. A. *Akbar the Great Mogul*. Oxford: Clarendon Press, 1921.
Stewart, Charles. *Jouhar, The Tezkareh al Vakiat* (Private memoirs of the Mughal Emperor Humayun). Indian reprint; Delhi: Idarah-i Adbiyat-i Delli, 1972.
Tabaat-I-Akbari. vol. 2, Tr. B. De. Calcutta: Asiatic Society, 1929.
Tripathi, R. P. *The Rise and Fall of the Mughal Empire*. Allahabad: Central Book Depot, 1956.

PART THREE

EMERGING VOICES

The establishment of British power in India in the mideighteenth century marked the beginning of an era unlike any other in India's history. For the first time, vast territories were captured by an alien power that was, in fact, a private trading concern, the East India Company, and one that was determined to remain alien. Unlike previous foreign empire builders, such as the Pathans and the Mughals, the East India Company made no moves to claim India as its home. The key to its presence was not primarily territorial ambition but the need to secure the most advantageous terms for trade and commerce by shutting out competitors, including both Indian merchants and European interests. The aim of the company was to skim as much wealth as possible off a captive production system and market, which had to be guaranteed by seizing political power through military supremacy.

Given the vastness of the conquered land, the variety of peoples and cultures within it, and the complex legal, religious, and economic life of an ancient civilization, the economic imperative could not by itself sustain an alien occupation. The force of arms as the primary control mechanism had to be replaced by a wholesale reorganization of the civil administration, including such social apparatuses as education and the judicial system. The project of managing so enormous a property for endless, preferably accelerating productivity could not be left to private interests, no matter how well organized they might be. In the midnineteenth century, therefore, the control of India passed from the East India Company to the British Crown. The event that triggered this transition was the the Great Indian Mutiny of 1857, also known as the Sepoy Mutiny after the disaffected sepoys or Indian soldiers in the East India Company's army. Queen Victoria became the empress of India. The political and administrative trends set by the East India Company were consolidated under the imperial government's rule, but more decisively and comprehensively.

The coming of the British brought to India the profoundest changes imaginable. Not only politically and economically but also in many parts of civil society, British intervention transformed the lives of the peoples of India. When in the eighteenth century British power had begun to take root in India, the empire of the Mughal dynasty, in the process of unraveling, was allowing the resurgence of various sizes of feudatory principalities throughout the land. By the beginning of the nineteenth century, under the ambitious governor-general Lord Wellesley, not only had the British replaced the Mughals as the single unifying power in India but had also annexed most of the principalities under their direct rule. The smaller principalities were still left under their Indian rulers but their independence was severely limited by treaties that turned them into British protectorates that could be, and often were, swallowed by the British whenever the conduct of their rulers displeased the government of India.

The thrust of British policy in this most productive of British colonial possessions was to lay down a uniform and comprehensive system of civil administration that rationalized land tenure, taxation, civil and criminal codes, law enforcement, communications, and education as a precondition to the efficient running of a colonial economy. Imposing homogeneity on a land of such size and cultural diversity would seem to be an absurd proposition, and, indeed, no absolute standardization ever took place. The British did create a stable administration, however, and it was welcomed by the majority of their subjects, weary as they were of political chaos and civil insecurity in the dying days of the Mughal empire, exacerbated by the East India Company's systematic robbery as it consolidated its power. When the mutiny flared up, the majority of Indians wished for the quick reassertion of British authority. Representations from Calcutta affirmed the signatories' loyalty to the British cause, and a popular versifier, Ishwar Gupta, expressed his plain relief at the defeat of the sepoys.

In the nineteenth century, therefore, the British congratulated themselves on having saved India from anarchy and gained the richest jewel in the imperial crown. The richness of the prize in economic, geopolitical, and cultural terms compelled concentrated attention that drew India ever more decisively into the kind of knowledge project uncovered by Edward Said in *Orientalism*. Reciprocally, the dissemination of Western ideas via English education and of the practical knowledge necessary to get ahead in the colonial state altered forever the political worldview of Indians and their cultural orientation, though it also gave rise, on the part of Indian traditionalists, to fear and misgivings about cultural deracination.[1] Their fears, rooted in a dense orthodoxy and obscurantism, were often justified by the frequent devaluation of cultural modes and practices that seemed improper to British cultural values. Not only were many religious practices and social customs deemed barbaric and immoral but also whole domains of the arts and literature of India shared the blame as enervating if not outright corrupting influences. An example is the proscription against dancing, which was seen entirely as sexual commerce and elicited strong official disapproval.[2] So deep was the impact of Britain's cultural domination that educated Indians felt nothing but embarrassment about the complement of erotic love in the legends of gods and goddesses and the explicit sexuality of temple sculptures. But in the usual irony of history, the cultural domination of the West contained the seeds of resistance to its political domination because Western ideals of democracy and liberty supplanted traditional Indian ideas of social organization and fostered the demand for self-determination that led to the collapse of British power in India in the twentieth century.

A necessary consequence of the British response to India was the impulse for redeeming India from its so-called backwardness. For many Westerners and Indians, the most visible icon of that backwardness was the pitiable status of Indian women, which therefore called for sustained study and corrective social action. In the battle for reshaping India according to the Victorian vision of progress, the Christian missionaries were on the front line, and for them a key element in the idea of progress was the uplift of India's women, viewed as both the victims of an ignorant and oppressive society and the perpetuators of ignorance and superstition. In her study of the efforts of one missionary society to rescue these women from their miserable condition, Sarika P. Bose shows the colonialist maternalism inherent in the missionary initiative, which, however, defeated itself by triggering a nationalist countermove to wean the women targeted by the missionaries into an alternative scheme.

How thoroughly the mindset of colonial ownership affected the colonists' view of Indian women is demonstrated by Karyn Huenemann in the Indian fiction of Flora Annie Steel, the popular Victorian novelist. A self-assured feminist writing to claim strength and independence for her characters, Steel nonetheless took the self-privileging position of speaking for the Indian women she wrote about and fashioning them in the image she decided was right for them. In this case, the stereotype of the passive, cringing Indian woman was replaced by another stereotype, the strong female idealized in turn-of-the-century British feminism.

Given the power that stereotypes have, we need not be surprised that the attributes and position of women in India should have assumed a central importance in the colonial critique of India, as well as in Indian nationalist self-fashioning. Because the state of India's women was being constantly projected as a telling sign of India's decadence, their emancipation was as necessary to the altruistic colonist carrying the white man's burden of civilizing the world as to the Indian nationalist engaged in revivifying India's moral and cultural identity at the core of national life, the home. Indian social reformers made strenuous efforts throughout the nineteenth century to educate women and bring about legislation to benefit them, while the later period of nationalist struggle saw women's co-option into that struggle, though rarely on equal terms with men. Subjected to a multitude of forces, often contradictory, the women of India—not unlike women elsewhere—began to move toward self-perception, self-expression, and self-determination, slowly, indeed, and against tradition. The two world wars, especially the second, not only thrust India into the vortex of global political and economic forces but also brought far-reaching changes to women's lives. The disruption of civil society created opportunities as well as hazards for women. For instance, the insatiable demands of a war economy on the labor market, coupled with the impoverishment of uprooted families, brought great numbers of women into previously closed domains of institutional employment, such as the civil service, though only at ground level. At the same time, by undermining the social institutions that had traditionally insulated women from the buffeting winds of public life, the upheavals of the twentieth century exposed Indian women to unprecedented personal and cultural hazards.

When India gained independence from British rule in 1947, Indian women were no longer contained within the colonial taxonomy. Vast numbers of middle-class women were educated and articulate, many of them in professional careers and a good number in politics; even at lower levels of privilege, some sense of personal rights was percolating into women's consciousness. In the stereotype of the Indian woman as a submissive, homebound, mindless object of pity, women of midtwentieth-century India could see no reflection of themselves. That the stereotype persists for many India watchers underlines the politics of representation. Yet the break from the past is also a contested reading of the present. The enormous weight of tradition continues to bear down on our own contemporaries, as demonstrated by Suma Chitnis, who describes certain features of the traditional base of Maharashtrian culture to explain why development programs aimed at women do not always yield the expected returns.

Tradition is also examined in Doris R. Jakobsh's study of Sikh women, though not so much an albatross around women's necks as a source of silences about women that have determined the construction of gender identities in Sikh historiography. The study shows how frequently the normative ideal of gender parity departs from the actuality of gender relations. Idealizations and stereotypes thus become key problematics of the representation of women from both outside and inside the tradition and national consciousness. Reviewing responses to reports of women's victimization over dowry in India, Matilda Gabrielpillai explains the construction of the feminine in India as a reductionist imaginary produced by the dominant Western readings of India, against which she positions Tamil women's short fiction as a mode of resisting and renegotiating the ideologies of gender and sexuality. Striking a note of stronger personal anguish and speaking as a writer, Nabaneeta Dev Sen comments on the pressures of cultural politics in the form of the dominance of a gender ideology in the literary marketplace, which forces women writers to conform to traditional female roles instead of achieving the liberation of the spirit that is the imaginative writer's right.

While resistance to imposed definitions as a mode of women's self-expression awaits closer historical investigation, two essays in this part review women's movements in the common arena of public action. Tripti Chaudhuri documents women's participation in political movements in Bengal, first as part of the anti-imperialist struggle and then as key actors in the response of radical socialism to the political establishment of independent India, as illustrated by the history of a particular women's organization. A more general account of how women's movements evolved into the feminist movement in Bengal is given by Maitreyi Chatterjee, who situates feminism there in its cultural context and historical background. The success of these movements appears both limited and ambiguous to participants and historians alike.

The essays in this part present complex political and cultural perceptions that appear to render the feminine condition uncertain in the political and cultural economy of India. However, that uncertain position seems to be counterbalanced by the growing presence of women in India's public arenas, even if they wield little power there. Far more empowering is the liberating potential of women's self-representation as embodied in efforts in political organization and imaginative self-expression. Implicit in the act of writing these essays is the potential for women's liberation from the captivity of history.

Notes

1. See Kumar (1991), pp. 59–60.
2. See, for instance, Mandakranta Bose, "Gender and Performance: Classical Indian Dancing" (in press).

References

Bayly, C. A. *Indian Society and the Making of the British Empire*. Cambridge: Cambridge University Press, 1988.

Bose, Mandakranta. "Gender and Performance: Classical Indian Dancing" in Lizbeth Goodman and S. J. de Gay, eds. *The Routledge Reader in Gender and Performance*. London: Routledge, 1998.

Embree, Ainslie T. *Imagining India: Essays on Indian History*. Edited By Mark Juergensmeyer. Delhi: Oxford University Press, 1989.

Featherstone, Donald. *Victorian Colonial Warfare, India: From the Conquest of Sind to the Indian Mutiny*. New York: Cassell, 1992.

Kumar, Krishna. *Political Agenda of Education: A Study of Colonialist and Nationalist Ideas*. New Delhi: Sage, 1991.

Marshall, P. J. *Bengal—The British Bridgehead: Eastern India, 1740–1828*. Cambridge: Cambridge University Press, 1987.

Wolpert, Stanley. *A New History of India*. New York: Oxford University Press, 1993.

SARIKA P. BOSE

For Our Native Sisters

The Wesleyan Ladies' Auxiliary in India

> They are in bitter bondage; chains, stronger than iron, fetter them, and forbid them to rise. Knowing this, shall not we as Christians work more diligently, and pray, more earnestly and believingly, "Thy Kingdom Come"?[1]

Several modern scholars have commented on the imperialist maternalism with which British women in India treated Indian women, a trend that lasted from the nineteenth century well into the twentieth.[2] This maternalism was a complex construct: on the one hand, British women deplored the devouring Indian mother and, on the other hand, posited the Indian woman as a child who needed a (British) mother to set her straight. The Indian woman became a kind of blank subject, who could be visualized in a variety of ways. The thousands of British women who went out to India to serve went ostensibly to take up the "white woman's burden"[3] and to serve the colonial peoples the empire had taken into its protection. They succeeded, at the same time, in reinforcing British self-conceptions of superiority. At every encounter, the Indian woman could be seen as the negative of the "positive" British values. The creation of the female Indian identity by those who were not Indian resulted in a reading of Indian femaleness based on ignorance of the various languages of Indian values. However sympathetic they intended to be, the interpreters of Indian identity were ultimately restricted to their personal value bases.

To acknowledge the maternalist bias of British women toward their female subjects in India is not to deny the good they so frequently did on an individual level. Some of the better-known women activists such as Mary Carpenter, Mary Kingsley, Flora Shaw, and Josephine Butler left important legacies, but many more lived out their lives in service to the empire without leaving similarly recognized marks. Most women served by merely existing as wives or supports for officials of the empire, and many worked among Indian women by holding Sunday schools or doing charity work. Beside these informal acts of benevolence (or perhaps boredom) we must place the far more purposeful and organized charity work of the many women who went to India to serve as missionaries for various British Christian denominations. Missionary work was particularly appealing to women who were fed on myths of the limits of female usefulness, as well as the increasingly spreading myth of the superfluous woman. Although women had done missionary work for years, they had done so in a subordinate capacity—as assistants to officially church-designated missionaries. The female presence at a mission would be that of a wife or sister of a missionary, unless the mission was Roman Catholic, in which case there might be nuns. Later in the century, the formation of church-oriented sisterhoods or female orders in other denominations did bring an increased female presence in missions, but these "sisters," like Roman Catholic nuns and missionary wives, were very much under male authorities.[4] Although women in Indian missions were not uncommon, they had little impact because women had no formal authority in the missions. Still, they gained a recognized place in the missionary framework and began to come to India to fill designated positions when missionary activity began to expand in India both in volume and in kind.

Although the missionaries' specifically religious agenda was regarded with some unease in the days of the East India Company, the replacement of the Company by the British government and its rapid consolidation created greater and more stable support for missionary efforts, which began to embrace not only the religious but also the social metamorphosis of the natives of India. The missionaries' mission, after all, was to transform the unreadable Indian (Hindu, Muslim, Buddhist, etc, with alien customs) into the readable, the unstable heathen into the malleable, Anglicized Christian. That the converted Hindu or Muslim (the main targets of missionary efforts) should be a *British* Christian was of prime importance, as is evident from disgruntled reactions to missionaries from other nations.[5]

Putting the British stamp on the targets of missionary effort in India was particularly important because of the anxieties created by the mutiny of 1857, especially in that the mutiny came at a time when evangelism was enjoying a revival. The year after the mutiny, 1858, was a specially important year for that revival in both England and America because it saw a great surge in the number of missionaries and missions in different parts of the world, including Japan, China, and India. For India, the year marked a new initiative that was to have far-reaching effects. As soon as the English managed to get their breath back after the mutiny, the Wesleyan Mission in London formed a Ladies' Auxiliary[6] specifically designed to send women to educate and minister to their fellow women in the colonies. The formation of the committee was inspired by a Mrs. Batchelor, wife of the Rev. Peter C. Batchelor, who ran the mission in Negapatam, a stronghold of the Methodists in India. Mrs. Batchelor wrote a desperate appeal to the Wesleyan Mission in London for the establishment of a separate Ladies' Auxiliary Branch to minister to the heathen women of the empire. The proposal was warmly received and an organization was so quickly set up that by January 1859 female missionaries were already on the boat to India. The appeal of an organization that was specifically oriented to and administered by women was, not surprisingly, high at a time when there were few choices for respectable and dignified female employment. In the missions, women found avenues for talents other than spiritual, for they were required to be not only missionaries but also secretaries and administrators who had to deal with finances and correspondence. They were also responsible for editing a mission journal launched in 1858 (though the first issue was published in 1859). This was a particularly important responsibility because it brought recognition to these members of the auxiliary branches in print by listing them at the beginning of every issue.[7] In their single-minded devotion to their cause in India, these missionaries were new kinds of activists within the Wesleyan organization. Mrs. Batchelor specified single women who could keep their minds on their missionary work instead of on their families. Most important, these young women were to be missionaries in their own rights, and to be so, they were to be trained at a missionary college.[8] In other words, here was an opportunity for women to become *certified* professionals—paid workers with real credentials.

Because the initiative in forming the Ladies Auxiliary had come from the Negapatam mission, the bulk of the committee's effort was concentrated on India, even though its members managed to gain footholds in Spain, Italy, Africa, China, and Ceylon. The establishment of this and other Christian societies also coincided with the new attitude towards India since the East India Company's rule of commerce had been replaced by Her Majesty's government's rule of duty and responsibility. The religious sparks that had set off the mutiny obviously had to be extinguished decisively, and what better instrument could there be for that than evangelical Christianity to unify and control the wilderness of heathenism?

Even though the first years after the mutiny still required missionaries to step cautiously, they had more power and freedom than previously. Missionaries had been discouraged by the East India Company, whose tolerant attitude toward Indian religions was largely due to a reluctance to jeopardize trade. In the early years of missionary activity, one of the great debates both in India and in Britain was the involvement of the East India Company and, later, of the British government in dealing with local religious customs. Grants to temples or mosques that had been traditional features of royal charters in the kingdoms of India continued, but missionaries and Christian-minded officials saw this practice as directly hampering the spread of Christianity in India. The East India Company had found it easier to go along with local religious customs than to antagonize the natives and thus jeopardize their commercial interests, and the British government's initial desire to create as little disruption as possible coincided with the assurance of non-interference in religious matters contained in the queen's proclamation that extended her jurisdiction and protection over her Indian subjects after the British government had taken control of India after the mutiny. With regard to the religious faiths of India, the queen's proclamation stated:

> We disclaim alike the right and the desire to impose Our convictions on any of Our subjects. We declare it to be Our royal will and pleasure that none be in anywise favoured, none molested or disquieted, by reason of their religious faith or observances, but that all shall alike enjoy the equal and impartial protection of the law.

This guarantee was somewhat weakened by the resolution, added in the queen's own hand, of "Firmly relying ourselves on the truth of Christianity, and acknowledging with gratitude the solace of religion," but it did mark the path to be taken by the British administration. That it was indeed the path taken is shown by the difficulties in every direction—financial, religious or cultural—that missionaries faced during this transitional period in India. The new British administration in India was itself divided in its attitude toward missionary activities so soon after the mutiny, with some officials believing Christian missions would be contravening the noninterference policy and others believing that Christian principles were at the foundation of government and were therefore no tyrannical imposition but a necessary aid to the Indian people. This latter was the position taken by the missions, which looked for help in the government's own regulations. For instance, missions began to take advantage of a premutiny education dispatch from 1854 that offered grants to schools administered by voluntary efforts so long as they accepted government inspection and guidance in respect to the secular part of their curriculum. The dispatch specifically recognized the rights of individual schools to offer whatever religious instruction they wished. These grants were open to any agency, whether religious or secular, and were made also to Brahmin schools, but the missionary schools were the chief beneficiaries, and their numbers, therefore, multiplied rapidly.

The Wesleyans were one of three Protestant groups that had managed to gain a strong influence even during the days of the East India Company (the others were German Lutheran groups and the High Anglican Society for the Propagation of the Gospel in Foreign Parts, these being joined by the Salvation Army in the 1880s). However, not only did the Wesleyans have to compete with the Brahmin schools but also they had to compete against other Christians, most notably the Roman Catholics and the Jesuits and even the Lutherans and the American Methodists. The greatest objection that the proselytizing orders had to the Roman Catholics— and to the government—was their willingness to compromise with the Hindus and Muslims, especially on the issue of caste. For example, the very successful St. Mary's Tope, a special Catholic community of converted Brahmins near Trichinopoly in South India, was successful only because caste was allowed to be retained. This resulted in a larger number of converts who could both support each other and suppress the otherwise inevitable social ostracism. Soon, the families of the converted were visiting them and even eating in their homes.

This compromise was unacceptable to the Protestant groups, who particularly stressed the equalizing force of the various castes taking Holy Communion together. Because the Methodists refused to compromise on this issue, their record for high-caste conversions was practically negligible when compared with the records of the Roman Catholics and other missionary groups. In the last quarter of the nineteenth century, the missionary records show four Brahmins converted to Methodism in the Tanjore district. But even though the Roman Catholics continued to outnumber the Protestant groups by about nine to one, Indians saw the latter as more dangerous to Indian religions and cultural values because of their strong evangelical nature. The Methodists (and Anglicans) were determined to eradicate caste distinctions altogether, so that converted Hindus of various castes would sit together in church or school and eat together at the same table. The cultural tolerance with which the Jesuits and other Roman Catholics regarded caste was nonexistent in the Protestant missions.

The Methodists aimed a large part of their evangelical effort at the women of India, for they identified the women's domain, the home, as the bastion of heathen superstition. Education would wean these women away from their degraded state, and the expansion of missionary activity in India meant that Christian education could reach an ever-widening flock. In the 1860s and 1870s, the Wesleyan Methodist Missionary Society (henceforth the "Society") remained mostly confined to southern India, in the Mysore and Madras districts, especially in Negapatam, Royapettah, Bangalore, Toomkoor, and Goobbee. By the 1890s it had extended its work not only to more schools within those districts but also to other parts of India, such as Bengal, especially the Calcutta region. Education, particularly women's education, was beginning to assume a new urgency. Despite its reasonably long establishment in India, the British Methodists had had no organized missionary system aimed at assimilating women, but in the postmutiny years they began to be recognized as a huge and important part of the Indian population who had been not only unjustly but also *dangerously* neglected by missionary efforts. When it came to the female population of India, the salvation of their souls had rested on only the very uneven quality of the efforts of missionaries' wives to establish Sunday schools and the like. The haphazard system of depending on missionaries' wives, who were untrained and in demand for household and other duties, to perform the same duties as their husbands led to sporadic educational efforts such as schools that often had to be shut down because of illness, overwork, loss of interest in the project, or transfer to a new posting. The radical reorganization of missionary work in India, at least among the Wesleyan Methodists, appears particularly forcefully in the pages of the mission journal that followed in the wake of the Ladies' Auxiliary.

Through its long life of seventy-odd years, the journal changed its title several times. These name changes were not casual but occasioned, as editorials explained, by the Society's constant attempts to accurately define itself and describe its activities. The title became more neutral as the century came to a close and reflected changes in the journal's orientation to India, but its format changed little. It was a quarterly report of the activities of the Society, written mostly in the form of letters from the various mission workers in the field. Although the Society continued well into the twentieth century, the relevance of the journal to the Society's work with women is best seen in the nineteenth century.

With the creation of the Ladies' Auxiliary, the problems of the "native" women began to assume far greater importance and to merit systematic resolution. These problems were seen as enormous and thought to stem from two aspects of Indian culture: Hinduism with its barbaric depiction of godhood, which prompted all sorts of immoral (sexual and social) behavior in women, and the Hindu patriarchal system, which oppressed women on the socioeconomic level. Christianity and the accompanying smattering of Western "practical" learning was supposed to give women the courage to break free of both these bonds. Yet at the same time, women were also seen as the *cause* of heathenism. Mrs. Batchelor's view was that:

> The women of this mighty continent are inveterate idol-worshippers. "They form the stronghold of idolatry, the keep of the castle of superstition;" and they instil, with unremitting endeavours, their own beliefs into the minds of their children . . . when we remember how blessed and holy is the influence of a pious mother, we may draw a concrete inference as to the pernicious influence of a heathen mother. (No. 1, March 1859, p. 8)

This characterization of Indian women continued through the 1860s and peaked in the 1870s, especially during the leadership of two ministers, the Rev. J. K. Kilner and the Rev. J. C. Sowerbutt. In January 1873, Kilner explained the grave dangers posed by the Indian woman to Christianity:

> When we take into account the immense influence of woman, even though Heathen, in the counsels of the household, in the planting and developing the germs of character, in the perpetuation of religious feeling, and usage, and life, we cannot but regard her as nearly omnipotent at home. (J. K. [J. Kilner], No. 55, January 1873, p. 718, *Ladies' Committee for Ameliorating the Condition of Women in Heathen Countries, Female Education, etc.*)

In the next issue, Kilner continues the diatribe:

> It would be an easy thing to show, that woman is the centre of India's most vital interest; that she is the condition on which all real progress depends; the agency that sways the greatest social and moral influence; that on her rests the hope of India's regeneration; that she is the sealed book of India's destiny.
>
> There is nothing which her influence does not, in one way or another, reach: — nothing social or religious, nothing domestic or parental, which she does not cramp or crush or blight! She is the soil of the nation's superstitions, the very life and vigour of the religions that there obtain. The Priests of Hinduism know her value as an instrument to further their ambition of avarice; and consequently they make her needs and susceptibilities prominent elements in their ordinary ritual and public festivals. The most potent personages in the pantheon, and by far the most popular objects of reverence, fear, or solicitude, are the female divinities, Kali, Durgha, &c., &c.
>
> The mother is the germ-planter of heathenism. She it is that perpetuates that baneful system. Her first care is to plant deeply the dread of these goddesses and gods in the heart of her child. This done, then she cherishes all modes and degrees of superstition in her own home, and among her kindred, over whom she sways no inconsiderable authority. She it is that suspects first any falling away of earnestness in her young idolater: she it is that detects the first pulsations in her child towards Christianity: she it is that rises in formidable, yea, even terrible opposition, to the child that expresses a desire to be a Christian: she it is that invents, directs, and applies, with deathless perseverance, and relentless hate all conceivable appliances to shake the faith, damp the courage, and tarnish the reputation of the son who has resolved to be a Christian: she it is that, when she cannot absolutely prevent her child taking the desperate plunge into the new faith, seems to forget her maternal pity, and, with a wrath and fury almost demoniacal, hunts and distresses, pursues and persecutes, the unfriended and, perhaps, homeless young disciple: she it is that, so long as she remains a heathen, will leave no stone unturned to seduce her Christian son back into heathenism! Who can admeasure the keenness and power of her religious antipathy to Christianity? Who can delineate her reckless disregard for everything, if only she

may ultimately carry her purpose? What could she not effect if she were on our side? (J. Kilner, No. 57, July 1873, *Wesleyan Missionary Society. Ladies' Auxiliary for Female Education*, pp. 805–6)

In other words, the "angel in the house" had become the "devil in the house," a neat reversal of the Victorian ideal as articulated by Coventry Patmore in his famous and popular poem of the 1860s. The British mother kept the household straight on its path of living a Christian life. The heathen mother actively turned the household away from Christianity. The strengthening British rhetoric about the mother as the moral guardian, not only of British children but also through them, of the entire British empire, surely influenced the attitudes of Kilner and his colleagues and provided them with an easily comprehensible framework within which to capture the meaning of the Indian female, who was, in reality, far removed from them. Modern scholars have commented on the maternal aspect of missionary work, which saw the Indian as a child,[10] to be weaned away from its false mother, the Indian female, who therefore had to be destroyed by complete reconstitution. If she herself could not be changed, her influence had to be nullified by the missionaries through the refashioning of her children. The missionaries hoped that what they taught the children would be remembered at least by a handful who would then pass on their knowledge to those whom the missionaries could not reach, especially older women. This seemed not an altogether vain hope, for there were, indeed, instances recorded of older women who converted to Christianity (often on their deathbeds) and whose conversion influenced many others around them.

These standard estimates of Indian women were shared by missionaries' wives and male missionaries alike. But in 1881, the first annual report of the Society showed a somewhat different focus in its attitude toward Indian women. There was a long editorial in which the members of the Society were reminded why women's work was so important:

> This [zenana] work is of extreme importance, because it is our only means of reaching the wives and mothers in many parts of India. It is in their minds that the old superstitions of the country are most deeply rooted; it is they who cling so tenaciously to the belief of their ancestors, and yet to them is committed the training of the children for the first few years of their lives. It is therefore necessary, if we would secure the next generation for Christ, that we influence the women of India; and it is only by visiting them in their own homes that we can get at them at all—homes (if such they may be called) in which our sisters are immured like caged birds, beating their tired wings against the prison walls, vainly, yet eagerly, longing to know something of what is beyond, and to hear further of the faint whisper which has been borne in to them of a brighter life somewhere, they know not where;—homes in which women know nothing, therefore care for nothing beyond the present, count and recount their jewels, and listlessly perform their daily routine of duties, at the bidding of mother-in-law or grandmother;—homes in which women exist as mere slaves, only to do the will of him whom they call husband or master; where the iron has entered into their souls, and they curse the day in which a little daughter is born to them, because a similar fate to their own awaits her;—homes where the sick infant is left to die uncherished and unattended, its fevered lip unmoistened, its brow unfanned, the mother looking helplessly on, withheld by fear and superstition from yielding to a mother's instincts.

> Into such homes our agents go, and the weary inmates find their craving and longing met and stilled by that which alone can fill the aching void; the love and sympathy of a Saviour is told to them, they sit at the feet of Jesus and are satisfied. The listless are aroused from their indifference by the charm of the "old, old story;" they crowd around the teacher as she opens her wonderful book; a new interest is created, and they find that there is something really worth living for here, and they learn to hope for a bright hereafter. The depressed and down-trodden captives are told of a love that breaks the strongest fetters, of the yoke that is easy and the burden light, of a life of freedom and liberty. With simple faith they drink in the story . . . death has lost its sting, now that she ears [*sic*] of the victory which Christ has won over death. [11]

This is a view of the Indian woman as the victim rather than the agent of the forces of darkness, doing whatever evil she did because of ignorance. In particular hazard were the younger women and girls, who became the chief targets of missionary effort, for they were victimized not only by men but by older female relatives like mothers-in-law and grandmothers. The Indian attitude (of both males and females) toward women was, of course, seen to be the fruit of heathenism. The missionaries characterized their own work as laying down paths to freedom, a common evangelical trope that seemed particularly apt to the situations missionaries encountered in India. Many of the women who were confined to zenanas were literally "freed" once they admitted to Christian beliefs (if their families did not spirit them away from the missionaries' influence)—freed from family ties and financial and emotional protection, and wholly dependent on the missionaries, who now became their all in terms of financial, emotional, and cultural resources. The missionaries had developed a sort of maternal sisterhood, if there can be such a thing, a kind of superior sisterhood in which there was a constant thankfulness for one's own ethnicity alongside sympathy for the oppressed Indian female.

Important in marking a new stage in the British construction of the Indian woman, this shift in attitude is equally significant as a sign of the feminization of missionary activity itself, for by 1881 most of the writers contributing to the journal were single women who had been trained as professionals and given a great deal of individual responsibility and, consequently, self-respect. They were missionaries in their own right even if they were not ordained. By this time, the rhetoric inculcated in them, through conduct books and similar guides for girls, had created a new set of criteria for self-definition, which made it acceptable and even desirable for women to be independent and educated. Along with Christian instruction, this desire to attain selfhood was what the women missionaries passed on to their female contemporaries in India. Although the suffrage that was coming more and more to the forefront in British public life was not a position deemed proper in missionary discourse or one that missionary women could ever conceivably take (and not once discussed in the society's publication in the 1880s and 1890s), the basic idea of suffrage—of the liberation of women from bondage—seemed to be expressed in the attitudes toward these women's suffering sisters in India.

At the same time, the ethnocentric ideology of the British missionaries continued to guide their efforts. Any alternatives to Western (preferably British) culture was inextricably linked with heathenism and seen as a reversion to a primitive state. Christianity and Britishness had been implicitly equated and placed on the same level in the many guidebooks for British children; the men and women who grew up on this fare found it hard to separate Christianity from Britishness or to see England as anything other than the ideal Christian land.[12] England's culture was Christian culture and therefore was the ideal to be followed by those who wanted to be true Christians. Whether the missionaries acknowledged the political implications of their work or not, the potential of this moral doctrine for legitimizing the subjection of Indians to the British is hard to ignore. Bringing Indians into the fold is thus the double task of redesigning their beliefs and realigning their loyalties. What Christian altruism achieved, consciously or unconsciously, was to transform the politics of domination into a scenario in which the missionaries saw themselves as caring parents to ignorant heathen-children.

Indian women were seen as both victims and perpetrators of heathen religions. That education is the path to Christian felicity is the message we read in the journal; education is the prime strategy for ameliorating the condition of these heathen sisters. Realizing that all efforts would be wasted without continuity and self-replication, the new Ladies' Auxiliary introduced a disciplined school system operated by trained teachers who could teach not only the Bible but also basic school subjects and thus bring a professionalism into the conversion of the heathens by whom they were surrounded. Only trained teachers were going to be accepted, and these teachers were to be specially selected from the Wesleyan Normal College, Westminster. The teachers were going to be single women with their own salaries, missionaries in their own right, even though they were not ordained ministers. In this way, the Wesleyan Methodists encouraged single women's professionalization and, later in the century, extended its professional arena for women into the medical field. By January 1859, the first Wesleyan missionary teachers were off to India to establish proper schools for girls. The formerly untrained teachers had failed in their tasks because, as Mrs. Batchelor observed:

> Many young women in the glow of early zeal are ready to go far hence for Christ's sake: there are but few who, without the incentive of many eyes upon their work, and many tongues speaking their praise, have patience to endure, and strength to persevere, through years of toil, in spite of hardship, disappointed hopes, and failing health. (No. 1, March 1859, pp. 4–5)

The requirements listed for the ideal missionary teacher were:

> True devotedness to Christ, and to His cause, a sound judgment and a cheerful temper, are needful qualifications. The candidate should have made some attainments in elementary knowledge; and she should have rather more than the average power of learning a foreign language. Good health is essential; and, if offering for India, lady-like habits and associations are very desirable. From twenty to twenty-five is considered the most suitable age for entering on this work. It is hoped that among the many young women to whom Christ's Gospel has come . . . some will be found who, constrained by His love, will gladly offer themselves upon this sacrifice and service. (No. 1, March 1859, p. 5)
>
> A pious, kind, active, well-informed, patient, cheerful, motherly body, who can cut out and teach needlework, keep house, manage servants, and maintain neatness and order, is far more useful and likely to be more happy than a young lady with modern accomplishments. (No.2, June 1859, p. 23)

In these profiles of the ideal teacher, we may detect a model also for the teacher's Indian charges: usefulness in the home rather than "modern accomplishments." Even as the Society proposes to lead Indian women from the darkness of heathenism, it denies them access to the world outside the home. It is not hard to understand that education is conceived entirely as an instrument to prepare the women for Christianity rather than for emancipation. Given the missionaries' conviction that Indian women led an abjectly brutish life, their educational strategy had to inculcate the values of civilized domesticity to effect a measure of social progress, but that progress was not to take the students beyond the home. As the December 31, 1881, editorial reveals, the home was where the good fight was to be fought. Battling the forces of darkness was a constant theme for the Society, and its rhetoric kept pace with mission rhetoric—they are soldiers for Christ—which strikes today's secular reader particularly forcefully with its acquisitive and battlefield images. There is often a grasping desperation in the missionaries' tone when they use terms such as "securing" or "getting souls for us."

From the earliest volumes of the journal, Indian women themselves were portrayed as interested in education, although this portrayal was often debatable in that the women's interest was evidently in a way of life that would grant them some escape from what is recorded as the drudgery of their lives. There are frequent references to the grief of girls who were taken away from school against their will either to be married off or because their relatives disapproved. Then again, we hear complaints about severe inattention on the part of schoolgirls and zenana women alike. Although a great number of students were drawn from the poorest villages and the lowest castes, there were students from the Muslim upper class and Hindu upper castes from the beginning. Hindus and Muslims were targeted more or less equally, though Hindu students and Hindu encounters in general are more frequently mentioned. There are isolated references to other Indian religious groups as well, such as a report on a bizarre incident in which a group of Buddhist parents burned down a missionary school in their neighborhood. But such trials are offset by steady gains, and as the century progresses, more and more girls and women, from ever-widening circles, are reported as interested in education and Christianity.

Despite its generally optimistic tone, the journal acknowledges the task of the Society as a difficult one. It also speaks of many specific problems, the most pressing of which is financial. There are constant appeals for funds, as well as for goods that are to be used as both prizes and fund-raisers. Dolls and clothes for bazaars, workboxes, aprons and little dresses, and sewing materials were the most popular of these goods. There were complaints about the higher financial support received by the American Methodists and their subsequent ability to "get" more students, souls and all. It is interesting to see this evident lack of cooperation and fierce competition between different groups of missionaries, even when they are part of the same denomination. Of course, the greatest competition came from outside the Christian community—that is, from the Brahmin schools, which, according to the missionaries, were not above sharp practices when it came to getting students. Indian teachers trained by the missionaries were sometimes lured away from the missionary schools, Indian parents were threatened or bribed to send their children to the Brahmin schools, Hindu landlords of missionary school buildings would become uncooperative with rent agreements or repairs, and schools were sometimes burned down. The quality of education in these schools was seen as suspect by the missionary educators; the teachers were generally seen as untrained or of low moral character. Yet, there are isolated mentions of Hindu schools that are given grudging respect, such as the girls' school established in Mysore as the pet project of the Rani and Raja of Mysore in the 1880s. This school, in fact, became known as the Indian Girton, and its students gained fame beyond its gates. The Wesleyans went so far as to record individual stories of girls from this establishment, which was never done for any other rival establishment.

Frequently, the letter writers express regret at the numbers that appear in the records of conversions. One of the biggest annoyances faced by the missionaries was the reluctance of many of their targets to publicly embrace Christianity. There are innumerable mentions of people who have confided their belief in Christ or Christianity in secret to missionaries but who are afraid to acknowledge their conversion in a formal, public ceremony[13]. There was a financial incentive behind the push for numbers: the more converts were recorded, the more willing their supporters in England were to continue sending funds, and the more evidence that the missionaries were doing their jobs. Although many of the missionaries acknowledged the problems of social ostracism for their converts and even the more potent dangers of virtual imprisonment within the family, forced marriages, and kidnaping of girls who showed too much interest in Christianity, they still believed that the community they had to offer in exchange was compensation enough for every loss and danger suffered by their converts. They baptized them with new names, encouraged even more interest in British culture (as far as possible), arranged marriages between young converts, all of whom became missionary teachers or preachers, and often provided lodgings for them.

Education was thus the battlefield on which the fight for British spiritual and social progress was to be won. In pursuit of that progress, the Christian content and goal of missionary education remained unaltered through the Society's life in India, although the kind of competencies proposed for the students changed. In June 1859 (No.2), Mrs. Jenkins from Madras wrote that "these girls cannot learn much, and they belong to poor parents, and will marry poor men." For such potential students, the aim of education could not be very high because they were seen as belonging to a serving class, much like the village girls in the Dame and Rag schools in England, or the working class girls in the cities. The kind of education proper to their station in life would first of all instill the "*feeling of God*, of sin, of Christ," and on that basis teach Indian women:

> to read thoughtfully and with understanding; to clearly and readily, perhaps in English, if they exhibit any talent for it, certainly in their own language; to use easily the simpler rules of arithmetic; to work neatly; to fix, and, if they can, cut out expertly; to be cleanly, civil, well-behaved, and kindly. (No. 2, June 1859)

What was envisaged was a thoroughly domestic education. Mrs. Batchelor echoed from Negapatam that English would be useless after marriage; the essential task was to teach them in their own language so that they could read the Bible. The missionaries themselves spent a great deal of effort in learning to read, write, and speak the languages of the regions to which they were assigned, which gave them the confidence to teach in these languages. Because they could do so and because there were translations of the Bible available in many Indian languages, Mrs. Batchelor was right in asserting that English was less a priority than the native languages. Learning in their own languages also made schooling easier for the learners.

Ease of learning was an important consideration because, as the excerpts from the journal show, there was little confidence in the intellectual or moral capacity of the students. As a result, education could only be a very limited program, especially if conducted solely in Indian languages. Although the girls and women so educated might indeed become better homemakers, their lack of English confined them to the home and prevented any possible foray into the public world. The education they received from the missionaries did not, then, offer them any liberation from their incarceration by the rigid rules of both Hindu and Muslim society that determined women's lives in India.

The situation, however, changes slowly but surely through the Society's existence. As the century rolls to its end, the journal begins to record a widening range of training provided by the missionaries. The details of the process are somewhat wearisome, but in summary it can be said that the Society's policy moves its students from the domestic to the public arena. The students did not come to be trained in public life, but they were increasingly brought in contact with it and trained to be legitimized by public tests. The domestic education so desirable to Mrs. Batchelor is replaced by the range of subjects required by the regulations of public instruction, complete with public examinations. A further departure from the past is the altered approach of later missionary educators to their duties and their charges. They are far less filled with the spirit of proselytization and take their educational tasks as complete in themselves without the ulterior function of effecting conversions to Christianity. Not surprisingly, their emphasis shifts from religious conversion to social uplift, to which education is seen as the only available path. The professional identity that the educators themselves enjoy as a mark of their own autonomy is what they ideally want for their students.

The life of the journal shows how, through the course of the century, the focus of education changed, progressing from its purely domestic orientation to an intellectual and professional instrumentality. By the end of the century, the female students of the Society's schools were regularly writing board exams and passing matriculation exams, often with honors. The kinds of missionary educators sent out were obviously more qualified to teach at higher levels than the first educators, who merely required basic elementary and domestic science training. The attitude toward education of both the British missionaries in this Society and of the Indian men (who claimed to want educated wives and daughters) had changed from that of condescension on one side and fear or outrage at the erosion of tradition on the other, to one of acknowledgment of the potentialities of female minds (even Indian ones) and the enhancement of their moral agency. The missionaries' change in attitude seems to parallel the changes British women themselves were experiencing in their social and intellectual situations in England. But it may also have been caused by the tug-of-war created when indigenous groups (mostly Hindus, Muslims, and Buddhists) decided to fight the encroachment of Christian teachings and values by setting up rival educational establishments. In the process, the Indian groups managed to formulate a nationalist discourse in which education and religion became bound up with Indianness. The intensity of the rivalry is evident in the constant complaints in the journal against the Brahmin schools set up by the Hindu Tract Society in particular. The missionaries' dismay at the growing power of schools set up by Brahmins and other Indian religious groups went beyond religious concerns. The Indian culture reinforced by the various Indian groups negated or altogether erased the effect of missionary efforts to spread a British Christian culture in India. Ultimately, then, the role of missionaries in co-opting the women of India into British cultural imperialism became ambiguous at the very least. Even while the advancement of females (no missionary would ever see herself as a feminist or suffragist) was embraced and celebrated as a triumph by the Society that had begun as the Ladies' Committee for Ameliorating the Condition of Women in Heathen Countries, their initiative resulted in triggering intense Indian nationalism within the religious arena and unwittingly subverted the cultural basis of British imperialism in India.

Notes

1. Wesleyan Methodist Missionary Society, Women's Auxiliary. *Woman's Work as Conducted by the Ladies' Auxiliary* (July 1891), no. 129, p. 676.

2. See Burton (1994), and Midgley (1995), pp. 247–76.

3. This was a term used by the suffragist Hester Gray ("The White Woman's Burden," *Common Cause*, November 27, 1914, pp. 565–66, quoted in Burton [1994] p. 10) who used it to speak of the white woman's duty to help "the less priviledged women of the East."

4. Martha Vicinus (1985) mentions one such sisterhood, "Wesleyan Sisters of the People," formed in 1887 under Mrs. (Katherine) Hugh Price Hughes so that "devout and educated" women could work more systematically for the Methodists. Vicinus has no more information about this society other than the fact that their records do not seem to have survived. Although there is no mention of any sisters during the period of our study, after the union of the three Methodist churches in 1935, the Methodist Missionary Society (as the new unified society came to be called) appears to have incorporated some Methodist sisterhood, as its following records include names of women missionaries with the title of "Sister."

5. See the reaction against American missionaries in the 1890s, for example, in, the January 1891 issue (no. 127, p. 552).

6. The Society underwent several title changes through the course of its history, eventually becoming part of an unified Methodist missionary order called the Methodist Missionary Society in the 1930s.

7. There were auxiliary branches in all parts of England, though the headquarters of the Society was in Bishopsgate, London.

8. The missionary women were trained at the Wesleyan Normal College, Westminster.

9. Queen Victoria's Proclamation of November 1858, in C. H. Philips, *The Evolution of India and Pakistan, 1858–1947. Select Documents*. London: Oxford University Press, 1962, pp. 10–11.

10. For example, Susie Tharu, "Tracing Savitri's Pedigree: Victorian Racism and the Image of Women in Indo-Anglian Literature," in Sangari and Vaid (1989), pp. 245–68.

11. *Report of the Ladies's Auxiliary of the Wesleyan Methodist Missionary Society for the Year Ending December 31st, 1881*, pp. 19–20.

12. See Rowbotham (1989) on the influence of children's books and moral tracts and guidebooks aimed at young people in the creation of the Christian-British identity.

13. Both men and women were afraid to acknowledge Christian beliefs, but this Society's focus is women, and thus information about male converts and their reasons for reluctance are often incidental and, at most, secondary.

References

Burton, Antoinette. *Burdens of History: British Feminists, Indian Women, and Imperial Culture, 1865–1915*. Chapel Hill: University of North Carolina Press, 1994.

Chaudhuri, Nupur, and Margaret Strobel, eds. *Western Women and Imperialism: Complicity and Resistance*. Bloomington: Indiana University Press, 1992.

Copland, Ian. "The Black Hole in the Historiography of Colonial India." *Asian Studies Review* 19:3 (April 1996) 58–62.

Coward, Harold, ed. *Hindu-Christian Dialogue: Perspectives and Encounters*. Maryknoll, N Y.: Orbis Books, 1990.

Jayawardena, Kumari. *The White Woman's Other Burden: Western Women and South Asia during British Colonial Rule*. New York: Routledge, 1995.

Kopf, David. *The Brahmo Samaj and the Shaping of the Modern Indian Mind*. Princeton: Princeton University Press, 1979.

Krishnamurty, J. *Women in Colonial India: Essays on Survival, Work and the State*. Indian Economic and Social History Review. Delhi: Oxford University Press, 1989.

McDermid, June. "Women and Education," in J. Purvis, ed. *Women's History: Britain, 1850–1945, an Introduction*. London: UCL Press, 1995, pp. 107–130.

Methodist Missionary Society [Women's Auxiliary]. *Women's Missionary Service: Annual Report*. London: Methodist Missionary Society, 1932–1934.

Methodist Missionary Society [Women's Auxiliary]. *Women's Work: Annual Report*. London: Methodist Missionary Society, 1935–1965.

Midgley, Claire. "Ethnicity, "Race" and Empire," in J. Purvis, ed. *Women's History: Britain, 1850–1945, an Introduction*. London: UCL Press, 1995, pp. 247–276.

Neill, Stephen. *A History of Christian Missions*. Rev. ed., Owen Chadwick. Harmondsworth: Penguin, 1986.

Oddie, Geoffrey A. *Hindu and Christian in South-East Asia*. London Studies on South Asia 6. London: Curzon Press, 1991.

Oddie, Geoffrey A. "Old Wine in New Bottles? Kartabhaja (Vaishnava) Converts in Bengal, 1835–1945." *Indian Economic and Social Review* 32:3 (1995) 327–343.

Philips, C. H. The Evolution of India and Pakistan, 1858 to 1947, Select Documents. London: Oxford University Press, 1962.

Purvis, June, ed. *Women's History: Britain, 1850–1945, an Introduction*. London: UCL Press, 1995.

Rowbotham, Judith. *Good Girls Make Good Wives: Guidance for Girls in Victorian Fiction*. Oxford: Blackwell, 1989.

Sahay, Keshari N. *Christianity and Culture Change in India*. New Delhi: Inter-India Publications, 1986.

Sangari, Kumkum, and Sudesh Vaid, eds. *Recasting Women: Essays in Colonial History*. New Delhi: Kali for Women, 1989.

Studdert-Kennedy, Gerald. *British Christians, Indian Nationalists and the Raj*. Delhi: Oxford University Press, 1991.

Trollope, Joanna. *Britannia's Daughters: Women of the British Empire*. London: Hutchinson, 1983.

Vicinus, Martha. *Independent Women: Work and Community for Single Women 1850–1920*. Chicago: University of Chicago Press, 1985.

Webster, John C. B. *The Dalit Christians: A History*. Delhi: Indian Society for Promoting Christian Knowledge, 1992.

Wesleyan Methodist Missionary Society. *Ladies' Committee for Ameliorating the Condition of Women in Heathen Countries, Female Education, &c*. London: Wesleyan Methodist Missionary Society, 1859–1873.

Wesleyan Methodist Missionary Society. *Woman's Work as Conducted by the Ladies' Auxiliary*. London: Wesleyan Methodist Missionary Society, 1885–1893.

Wesleyan Methodist Missionary Society. *Woman's Work as Conducted by the Women's Auxiliary*. London: Wesleyan Methodist Missionary Society, 1893–1899.

Wesleyan Methodist Missionary Society. *Report of the Women's Auxiliary of the Wesleyan Methodist Missionary Society*. London: Wesleyan Methodist Missionary Society, 1893–1915.

KARYN HUENEMANN

Flora Annie Steel

A Voice for Indian Women?

Feminism and Colonial Discourse Analysis

One of the more interesting trends in literary criticism today is the application of discourse analysis and feminist critical theory to the investigation of colonial literatures. By considering the literary representations of women's history in light of these two approaches, some recent feminist critics attempt to unravel the complexities of women's involvement in British imperial history. Implicit in this attempt is the comparison of Western literary (mis)representation of the Orient with male literary (mis)representation of women, a comparison complicated by some Victorian women's concomitant involvement in both British imperialism and the feminist political battles of the late 1800s.

Critics such as Barbara N. Ramusack and Antoinette Burton illustrate that the motivation for Victorian feminist involvement in Indian women's lives appears to have been predominantly ethnocentric: Victorian women (in social organizations and the feminist press, as well as in literary representation) appropriated the voices of Indian women to articulate their own social messages. The complications some critics perceive in Victorian Anglo-Indian[1] novels (such as Flora Annie Steel's)[2] are echoed in current feminist criticism. The ease with which Victorian feminists assumed their right to speak *for* Indian women, ostensibly for their exclusive benefit, illustrates the lesson that modern feminists and critics must learn from historical texts: we must remain aware, as the Victorians did not, that the heterogeneity of women's lived experiences cannot be addressed appropriately by feminist political strategies that assume a "universal sisterhood."

The notion of heterogeneity raises the issues of "representation" and "authorial authenticity" that plague postcolonial critics today: "only a black can speak for a black; only a postcolonial subcontinental feminist can adequately represent the lived experience of that culture."[3] These issues, familiar through their continued pertinence to studies of gendered representation, both contemporary and historic, are compounded when *white* women construct literary images of *black* women. In discussing Mulk Raj Anand's *Untouchable*, Arun Mukherjee reminds us that,"as readers, we must examine and remain aware of the difference between 'a voice for' and 'a voice of.'[4] Flora Annie Steel's representations of Indian women require readers to remain cognizant of this distinction. In Mukherjee's terms, the "voice of" a subject requires an authorial authenticity many other critics demand, but that was obviously unattainable for Victorian Anglo-Indian women who were writing about their Indian counterparts. By portraying fictional Indian women through the filter of Western ideology, Steel has constructed a "voice for" Indian women that is fuel for the ongoing debate regarding the positive and negative ramifications of representation.

As Vron Ware recognizes, the "tension among feminists" regarding authorial authenticity and representation of others, which complicates current feminist discourse, had its genesis in "the relationship between white and Indian women" in the late 1800s.[5] To begin to understand the relationships between women of different ethnicities today, it is productive to consider the ideological assumptions and narrative manipulations that earlier British female authors employed in their own ethnocentric feminist battles. One conscious practitioner of such narrative manipulations is Flora Annie Steel, one of the best-known female Anglo-Indian authors. In addition to her autobiography, two biographies have been written,[6] and she is often the only female author discussed in critical surveys of Anglo-Indian literature. Most important, in terms of her ability to "re-present" Indian women to the British public, Steel was greatly admired during her lifetime for her "success in the portrayal of native types and modes of thinking."[7] Her "extraordinary wealth of descriptive power and a masterly insight into character"[8] were accepted as being firmly based on "her close acquaintance with Anglo-Indian life"[9] and her "intimate knowledge of Indian life,"[10] and she was considered "the female Kipling,"[11] not in style or attitude, but in her ability to reveal India to the untraveled British population. According to one reviewer, Steel had the ability "to adjust our ethnological perspective" with "an insight unsurpassed by the best of Mr. Kipling's work."[12] This unself-conscious acceptance of Steel's right to speak for Indians is indicative of much of the Victorian response to Steel's work, and it has hitherto placed her novels under censure from postcolonial feminist critics. But if we accept the possibility of a consciously feminist agenda in Steel's works, the complexity of her relationship to (suspension between) imperialism and feminism becomes clear.

Sara Suleri, in her discussion of *The Rhetoric of English India*, claims that Anglo-Indian women's writing (specifically the "feminine picturesque") begins to establish "lines of contiguity between the position of both Anglo-Indian and Indian women and the degrees of subordination they represent."[13] Flora Annie Steel's explicit attempts to portray this contiguity are not so much an illustration of a pancultural feminist agenda as a pointed attempt to reflect the position of British women within Victorian patriarchy through depiction of a strong, even feminist, Indian woman. Although Steel employs "the idea of a common sisterhood in oppression as a basis for a common women's struggle"[14] against which some feminist postcolonial critics argue so strongly, her more positive representations of Indian women are an attempt to create an image of Indian womanhood in which Victorian women could recognize themselves and their own social and political possibilities. Steel could easily have felt justified in her appropriation of Nurjahan's story for the British feminist cause, in response to her society's ongoing involvement with issues of Indian womanhood.

The historic relationship between British women's representation of Indian women and Indian women's right to self-representation is complicated by the assertions of organizations such as the Brahmo Samaj, established in 1830 by a high-caste Indian man, Rammohun Roy, with the intent of reforming Indian society along essentially Western lines, as noted by Ware: "eradicating idolatry, polytheism and caste." According to Ware, Roy's "commitment to Indian women's rights won him a wide reputation" in Britain, and his successor, Keshub Chandra Sen, reasserted the demand for British women's involvement in Indian social and educational affairs, "not for one, not for fifty, but for millions of Indian sisters." By heeding the call of a "native," British feminists felt justified for what seemed a completely altruistic intervention in their "Indian sisters'" lives: Ware comments that "Sen's plea was well-received" essentially *because* "it accorded with the idea that British women had a unique duty to bring civilisation to the uncivilised."[15] Ramusack comments that, similarly, "in response to a request from Keshub Chandra Sen," the social reformer Mary Carpenter (who had spent a total of six months in India, upon which brief experience she based numerous publications and years of metropolitan involvement with Indian women's issues) "founded the National Indian Association to spread knowledge of India in England and understanding of English culture among Indian visitors."[16] Like Mary Carpenter and many of her contemporaries, Flora Annie Steel imbibed the rhetoric of the Brahmo Samaj, laced it with her own feminist ideals, and attempted to fortify the British feminist cause through her involvement with Indian women. It is perhaps unfortunate that in achieving her aims as a feminist author for her female *British* audience, Steel unconsciously fell into the trap of constructing a voice for *Indian* women that was not their own.

The distinction Gayatri Chakravorty Spivak draws between "representation as 'speaking for,' as in politics, and representation as 're-presentation,' as in art or philosophy,"[17] is readily apparent in Steel's two contrasting narrative constructions of Indian women, which can be separated neatly into two of the fictional subgenres Steel employs: the "historical novel" and the "social novel." Between 1908 and 1928, Steel wrote four Indian historical novels, of which *Mistress of Men* (1916) is the third,[18] in addition to *On the Face of the Waters* (1896), her famous Anglo-Indian historical novel dealing with the 1857 Indian mutiny, or first Indian war of independence. In her historical fiction, Steel claims to have "adhered in all matters of importance to the evidence of contemporary witnesses" and to have "done nothing save fill up with trifling incidents the gaps which history and tradition have left between the major occurrences."[19] In cases such as these, when Steel's intention was explicitly an interpretation of history, her female Indian character construction shows strong indication of an attempt at more "representation" than "re-presentation."

In addition to her historical novels, however, Steel wrote five other novels set in India: *Miss Stuart's Legacy* (1893), *The Potter's Thumb* (1894), *The Hosts of the Lord* (1900), *Voices in the Night* (1900), and *The Law of the Threshold* (1924). These novels, which I have termed her "social novels," are primarily concerned with social and romantic relations within the Anglo-Indian community and for the most part are not attempts at faithful representation of "Indian reality."

In neither her historical nor her social novels is Steel averse to using her Indian characters to further her ideological statements demanding Anglo-Indian social progress, but her methodology differs drastically in the two cases. In the social novels, where Steel's primary intent was to portray her *Anglo-Indian* female characters as strong, independent women, her Indian female characters are "re-presentations" of the negative stereotypes firmly entrenched in Anglo-Indian literature: caricatures, self-sacrificing narrative tools, or foils for the purer, stronger, Anglo-Indian female characters. In the historical novels, where Steel more often felt herself to be "representing" *Indian* women (in a sociopolitical sense), she imbues her female Indian characters with a strength and nobility usually reserved for self-representations of "white western women" within the empire. In *Mistress of Men*, Steel does create a successful, strong Indian woman in her reconstruction of Nurjahan (wife of the Moghul Emperor Jahangir); yet Nurjahan, however strong, is nonetheless an ideological construct Steel employs in asserting an ethnocentric feminist message to her British reading audience.

Critical Response to Steel's Life and Works

Despite Steel's popularity during her lifetime, there is insufficient critical work attempting to reconcile her proclaimed feminist attitudes (in her autobiography she states unequivocally that she "had always been a vehement Suffragette")[20] with her complicity in the patriarchal imperialism of the British Raj. The most critically interesting investigation of this issue is Nancy Paxton's 1990 article "Feminism under the Raj," which, while revealing the imperialist attitudes that are at odds with Steel's proclaimed feminism, does not, perhaps, sufficiently examine the sociopolitical motivations behind Steel's varying representations of Indian women. Following Adrienne Rich's claim that feminists historically expressed their marginal position by "disloyalty to civilization," Paxton holds Steel accountable as a feminist for her "'loyal', racist, elitist and politically conservative analysis of British and Indian society"[21] and carefully supports this opinion through Steel's own account of her life.

Paxton's reading of Steel's autobiography, *The Garden of Fidelity* (1929), is interesting, yet the elitism and authoritarianism Paxton detects in the text, while present, are constantly mitigated by humor and compassion that are not revealed by Paxton's article. To focus on Steel's "gynephobia," to use Adrienne Rich's phrase, does her an injustice; although Paxton is right is perceiving the conflicts between many of Steel's attitudes, she fails to observe that Steel herself recognized the inconsistencies between her version of feminism and Indian women's real needs.

Quoting Steel's opening admission of her "inborn dislike to the sensual side of life,"[22] Paxton perceives in Steel—as in Annie Besant, with whom she is compared—"what Rich calls 'internalized gynephobia,' that impulse to despise the feminine in the self and to see the feminine Other as the 'rejected part,' as the 'anti-self.'"[23] Yet Steel's autobiography and fiction go beyond this "inborn dislike" to an understanding of the relationship between male control of female sexuality and male social oppression of women. Steel's answer, echoed through her characterizations of strong Indian women (although not all her female Indian characters) was very much that "every woman be self-identifying and self-defining, with the right to determine how, when, and for whom she will exercise her reproductive powers."[24]

Although Steel could write that, as she left Bombay for England after twenty-two years, "India loomed homogenous, and so looked a lie"[25] and was careful in her autobiography to distinguish between Moslem and Hindu, rural and urban Indian women, she nonetheless fell into the Victorian feminist trap of assuming that Western feminism was the most appropriate response to any male oppression, much as white Western feminists are accused of assuming today. Her constructions of Indian women are either stereotypically negative or strongly Westernized creations. Some of Steel's representations leave her open to a charge of racism, but the two critics who have written at length on Steel's works echo Steel's contemporaries' opinions that the strength of her novels lies in her *faithful* representation of the Indian people and "the breadth of [Steel's] sympathy for both the Indian and the British point of view."[26] Contemporary biographies report on "the practical service she gave to the many thousands of native Indian women with whom she lived,"[27] and Maud Diver, in *The Englishwoman in India*, comments that "in whatever district Fate placed her, [Steel] made a point of interesting herself in its women, their lives and their work."[28] Even Benita Parry, whose chapter on Steel in *Delusions and Discoveries* is little more than a categorical castigation of the "racism" of Steel's novels, notes the extent of Steel's involvement with Indian women and observes that "clearly her experience of India was less vicarious than that of most Anglo-Indian women."[29] According to many sources, including her autobiography, Steel's personal involvement with Indian women *was* greater than many Anglo-Indian women's; as a result, she has often been heralded as the "voice of" Indian women in the same way that Kipling has been considered "the bard of empire." The Indian author and critic, Mulk Raj Anand, recognizes that Steel "developed a sympathy with Indian life far in advance of her time and greatly in excess of the other Anglo-Indian writers" and that "her interest in the suffragette movement gave her deeper affinities with the women of India."[30] Daya Patwardhan similarly declares that "the life of the Indian women of various classes is a special feature of Mrs. Steel's novels" and (surprisingly) that "a reader not knowing the novelist's name, may be persuaded to believe that she is an Indian."[31]

Despite her personal involvement with Indian women and the compassion that is obvious in her autobiography, in her novels Steel remains a Victorian British "voice for" Indian women: a voice with its own ethnocentric feminist agenda. It is illuminating, in light of the observations previously noted, to relate an anecdote from Steel's personal history. In 1899, as Antoinette Burton notes, "an Indian woman named Marie Bhor attended the International Council of Women . . . but at the introductory session said nothing while the famous Anglo-Indian novelist Flora Annie Steele [*sic*] spoke on her behalf."[32] Such an appropriation of the Indian woman's voice directs concern for Indian women's actual position to a focus on the position of British women as reflected in the plight of their "Indian sisters."

The attention lavished on India and its women in periodicals like the *Women's Penny Paper* had the effect of stripping Indian women of their foreignness and their exoticism and thereby domesticating them for a British audience. But because Indian women rarely spoke for themselves in these controlled textual spaces, British feminists robbed them of their power to name themselves, effectively silencing them in the name of feminist "sisterly" protectiveness.[33] Not only in her fiction but also in reality, Steel became a self-appointed "voice for" Indian women, who, as Burton later points out, were probably sufficiently articulate on their own behalf.

Indian Women in Steel's "Social Novels"

In her social novels, Steel subscribes (for the most part) to the stereotypic images of native women, constructed by Victorian Anglo-Indian male authors such as Rudyard Kipling and Philip Meadows Taylor, which bear a striking resemblance to the madonna-whore dichotomy pervading Victorian literary images of women in general. Kipling and Balestier's Sitabhai (*The Naulahka*, 1892) and Philip Meadows Taylor's Seeta (*Seeta*, 1872) are exemplary illustrations of these opposites: Sitabhai resorts to sexual persuasion in her attempts to blackmail (and murder) the American hero of the tale; in the opening scenes of Taylor's novel, Seeta leaves purdah to bear witness against her Indian husband's murderers in the Anglo-Indian court and, at the close of the novel, dies defending her new Anglo-Indian husband during the 1857 uprising.

In Flora Annie Steel's social novels and the historical novel *On the Face of the Waters*, these literary types (predominantly that of Sitabhai) are repeated. In *Miss Stuart's Legacy*, the manipulative Kirpo becomes embroiled in John Raby's dishonest dealings and has her nose cut off by her husband in "traditional" punishment for reputed dishonor at the hands of the Englishman. In *The Potter's Thumb*, the courtesan Chandni is openly malicious, connives for power within a corrupt native state, and resorts to blackmail of a British memsahib in an unsuccessful attempt to gain her personal ends. In *The Hosts of the Lord*, the aged Mumtaz Mahal encourages her soldier-grandson, Roshan Khan, in his excessive pride of race. Her goading insinuations ultimately cause his "passionate native nature" to overcome his (Western-taught) sense of duty and result in his organizing a revolt against his British regiment. As in *On the Face of the Waters* (when the impetus of the 1857 uprising in Delhi is attributed to the taunting of courtesans), the manipulative Indian female is held explicitly responsible for the aggressive actions of the weak Indian male. In *Voices in the Night*, the female members of the pensioned royalty in Nushapore are not as manipulative or devious as Mumtaz Mahal or Chandni, but they are nonetheless depicted as petty and narrow-minded. To these social ills are added Khadjee's excessive "native superstition" and the young Sobrai's descent from royal respectability to regimental prostitution. In *On the Face of the Waters*, the women of the palace—especially the power-hungry queen, Zeenut Mahal—are depicted as malicious and sexually preoccupied. These characteristics, Steel insisted in her autobiography, were the unavoidable result of women being "confined to twelve feet square of roof" where "every little incident [relating to sexuality] is magnified a thousand times."[34]

Azizan, in *The Potter's Thumb*, is cast in an antithetical mold. Like Seeta, she is the native woman faithful unto death—faithful, that is, to the obviously superior British male whom she can attract but could never marry. Her source of personal strength is her worship of the civil engineer George Keene and, following Victorian literary conventions, the only possible outcome of her fictional life is death. In *On the Face of the Waters*, the dead Zora and her servant Tara are equally indicative of the idealized literary version of Indian womanhood; their lives are devoted (and ultimately sacrificed) to the comfort, service, and preservation of the hero, Jim Douglas.

Maya Day in *The Law of the Threshold* and Kohjee in *Voices in the Night* are slightly more complex but ultimately as disappointing. The tantric-feminist Maya Day exhibits a marked degree of personal strength and devotion to her cause, but Steel ultimately fails to utilize Maya's potential as a politically active character. In this novel, Steel illustrates the schism between Western materialism and Eastern spirituality and the inner conflict that arises in the "spiritual native" who is trained in "Western" logic. Maya, instead of resolving her dilemma in any politically significant way, resumes the stereotypic role of faithful, devoted native woman, offers herself as a human sacrifice to secure the safety of her Anglo-Indian lover, and thus frees him to return to the more suitable Anglo-Indian woman. Maya is ultimately mistress of her own fate, but her decisions support the ideals of British materialist-imperialist culture: her suicidal end consigns her to the realm of the expendable narrative tool. The conflict between East and West that Steel sets up in her text dissolves into a stereotypic positioning of the native as less socially and politically capable (and therefore less worthy) than the British characters.

Kohjee, in *Voices in the Night*, is used for a similar narrative purpose. Although she leaves purdah and actively speaks out against native superstition and dishonesty, Kohjee is nonetheless articulating the message of her British masters: when rumors attribute the plague to the "devilish treachery" of the British, Kohjee proclaims that "God knows what happened was not the fault of the *Huzoors*."[35] Although Kohjee takes pride in her honesty and faithfulness, her activity (like that of Azizan, Taras, and Maya Day) is inspired by her devotion to an Anglo-Indian man and not by any sense of personal emancipation. In Flora Annie Steel's literary repertoire, possibly the only exceptions to these two basic Indian female "types" are Nurjahan in *Mistress of Men* and Newasi Begum in *On the Face of the Waters*.

Indian Women in Steel's "Historical Novels"

The different constructions of "Indian woman" in Steel's Anglo-Indian social novels and her historical novels reflect Steel's conflicting attitudes and suggest an agenda that is not directly involved with *Indian* women's needs. Steel's blending of historical account and fictional narration is a powerful vehicle for her argument: history (accepted by readers as "fact") and the novel ("fiction" accepted by readers as psychological verity) combine to present the authorial attitudes as a priori reality. Yet despite her claim that she did "not allow fiction to interfere with fact in the slightest degree,"[36] Steel's ethnocentric feminist attitudes and intentions have invested her work with an inescapably Westernized portrayal of Indian women.

In support of Nancy Paxton's claim regarding Steel's complicity in imperialism, for the modern reader, the tone of *On the Face of the Waters* leaves much to be desired. The superficial objectivity of the story—the focus on both Indian and British perspectives of the uprising—masks a racial arrogance that Steel's Victorian readers would not have necessarily detected. In fact, Steel was commended for being "no partisan" [37] at the same time the novel was revered for its "note of heroic passion."[38] Despite her explicit intent to try "to give a photograph—that is, a picture in which the differentiation caused by colour is left out,"[39] Steel succeeds only in showing that there *was* a second side to the story: "differentiation caused by colour" underlies the moral judgments made by the authorial voice in no uncertain terms. Although the subliminal messages of Steel's tale of the mutiny did nothing to disturb the Victorian perception of moral and cultural superiority, neither did they advance her call for women to assume the right to control their own lives. The characters previously mentioned are blatant counterexamples of Steel's explicitly feminist attitudes, but even Newasi, the most autonomous Indian woman in *On the Face of the Waters*, falls short of Steel's own demands for women's emotional independence as the foundation of physical and financial independence.

Of these three forms of personal independence, Newasi is described as having achieved a modicum of the latter two. Physically, she had separated herself from the petty intrigues of the palace, preferring "a religious and celibate life," "under the clear sky in her scholar's dress," to "easeful idleness and luxury, the dim, scented, voluptuous light" of the palace.[40] Financially, she maintained her independence through her status as "the widow of one of the King's younger sons" [41]; emotionally, however, Newasi was bound to her nephew-by-marriage, Prince Abool-Bukr. In recreating their historical relationship, Steel encounters the difficulty she predicted in her introduction, that "in attempting to be at once a story and a history, [the book] probably fails in either aim"[42] In attempting to remain faithful to historical accounts of Newasi's emotional thralldom, Steel manipulates the situation and expounds her belief in the necessity of women's emotional and psychological independence (even within the physical constraints of purdah, which Steel disagreed with but saw as a separate issue).[43] Newasi "read the London news with great interest, in the newspaper Abool-Bukr used to bring her regularly" and is articulate in her denigration of suttee, "prevented by the *Huzoors*. And rightly." [44] Although these traits suggest a parallel between Newasi and Steel's "more enlightened" British readers (as does repeated reference to Newasi's similarity to the British character, Kate),[45] Newasi's less favorable characteristics are brought to the fore in her final confrontation with British culture.

Placed in a situation where she can either protect Kate from discovery by the enraged Abool-Bukr or surrender her to him, Newasi stands firm against her lover's impassioned demands for admittance to her apartment. On the surface, this appears to illustrate a solidarity between women that later suffragettes heralded in song—"one nation,/ Womanhood" [46]—but Steel makes explicit that Newasi's motivation was the passionate protection of a woman for her lover. Newasi is "a born coward,"[47] and her real motivation is neither an altruistic sense of justice nor solidarity but a fear that Abool-Bukr's intended violence will bring unwelcome retribution on him at a later date: "For his sake this strange woman must not be seen—he must not, should not guess she was there!"[48] Once Abool-Bukr has departed, Newasi's assistance abruptly ends. "She turned towards where Kate cowered, and dragged her by main force to the stairs where, a minute before, she had sacrificed everything for her. No! not for her, for him! 'Go,'she said bitterly. 'Go! and my curse go with you!'"[49]

No universal feminine understanding in this exchange! Newasi's sexual passion prevents her from affirming Steel's authorial demand for emotional autonomy, in a way that Nurjahan's hunger for power does not.

The statement that I believe Steel was making through Newasi's failure was not primarily that *Indians* were inherently weak and controlled by their passions (although this is one obvious interpretation of the situation), but rather that *any woman* who was controlled by emotional or sexual considerations was thus opening herself to oppression and placing herself in a position of subalternity shared by natives and women alike. No woman, Indian or British, should consider it acceptable—as Newasi did—to "risk all; her pride, her reputation," for the sake of a man.[50] This suggestion is supported by other of Steel's female characters, British rather than Indian: Belle in *Miss Stuart's Legacy*, Lucy Morrison in *The Law of the Threshold*, and both Eve and Lillian in the British novel *The Curse of Eve* (1929). The strongest assertion of this stance against women's emotional subjugation is Steel's reconstruction of Nurjahan, who functionally controlled India through her marriage to the Moghul emperor Jahangir.

Steel's intention is ostensibly to portray Nurjahan's "extraordinary personality and power—which even in those days would raise criticism in a woman."[51] That Steel chooses as a historical subject a legendary *Indian* woman is significant. Steel's representation of Nurjahan as strongly feminist helped to justify her own position regarding the education and forced emancipation of Indian women in accordance with the entreaties of both the Brahmo Samaj and the Victorian militant feminist appropriation of the right to speak for "women all over the world, of whatever race, or creed, or calling, whether they be with us or against us in the fight."[52] Antoinette Burton succinctly describes the racial-political hierarchy accepted by many Victorian feminists, including Steel herself:

> Throughout contemporary middle-class feminist discourse "the Indian woman" served as evidence of British feminists' special imperial "burden." Despite both their genuine concern for the condition of Indian women *and* the feminist reform activities of prominent Indian women during this period, many middle-class British feminists viewed the women of the East not as equals but as unfortunates in need of saving by their British feminist "sisters."[53]

Through accepting the "burden" of Indian women's plight and assuming the "knowledge" of Indian womanhood that such a task necessitated, Victorian feminists empowered themselves in the battle against patriarchal oppression. Steel's fictional reconstruction of Nurjahan provided part of her British readers' "knowledge" of Indian women.

Steel's assumed knowledge of Indian women empowers her argument for universal female strength and autonomy at the same time that it disenfranchises the Indian women she purports to represent. Steel assumes her right—as a woman and a European—to draw back "the veil of the East" for her readers to reveal not the expected allure of difference and exoticism but a reflection of British strengths (male *and* female, conflating gender and race identities by refuting *all* of the negative stereotypes of "Indianness") in an Indian woman. By so doing, Steel inflates her readers' own sense of self-worth and social accomplishment. An inherent sense of superiority over Indian women (generally perceived as uneducated, emotionally downtrodden, and physically trapped behind the purdah) is used to suggest the advantages women in Britain (even the uneducated, downtrodden, and socially trapped) had over their Indian sisters. Although in reality Nurjahan was upper-class Persian and therefore in a position of privilege if not power,[54] Steel casts her as an Indian woman from a middle-class background. If, despite this disadvantage, the fictional Nurjahan could achieve the powerful position she purportedly held, Steel's British women readers are asked to believe that female suffrage and equal rights should not be seen as beyond the scope of their capabilities. In illustrating the success of an *Indian* woman (using images already familiar to her readers through the British feminist press), Steel was showing how much more was possible for a *British* woman. Like the "Illustrious Indian Women" described in the *Woman's Suffrage Journal*, Nurjahan was "proof of what *even* Indian women, with all their disadvantages, can become."[55] In this way, Nurjahan can be seen as doubly constructed: a strong Indian woman competing successfully in the male Indian political arena (suggesting that Indian women, desired emancipation—and by implication British assistance), and an Indian feminist, fighting alongside the British feminists, who were still struggling to achieve that emancipation for themselves.

Many critics have observed that the Victorian response to empire was rife with this dichotomy between—and conflation of—self and other: while the natives were "other," foreign, unknown, and unknowable, they were nonetheless the objects of a psychological projection of the "self." Rana Kabbani, for example, considers the Orient a "pretext for self-dramatisation,"[56] and Homi Bhabha employs Lacan's model of the "mirror-phase" in his introduction to Fanon's *Black Skin, White Masks*, the title of which is in itself indicative of the inescapable connections Bhabha perceives between colonizer and colonized: "Man as his alienated image, not Self and Other but 'Otherness' of the Self inscribed in the perverse palimpsest of colonial identity."[57] Thus the uncharted "blank page" of empire becomes colored with the fictional representation of "unacceptable" male fantasies played against the feminized landscape: eroticism, domination, cruelty. In *Mistress of Men*, however, Steel is using this literary method of self-projection in a far more constructive way.

In *The Colonial Rise of the Novel*, Firdous Azim succinctly describes the Lacanian model on which Bhabha draws:

> The child recognises itself in the mirror and this recognition is, of necessity, split. The child becomes the subject and the object: gazing (the subject) at its image (the object), and the identity it acquires is split into the recognition of "je/moi."The mirror becomes the Other site which affirms the child's identity, while alienating it (by projecting it elsewhere) from its own self.[58]

In recognizing the mirror image as "other," the child is also forced to recognize the image as "self." It is this "self-in-other" conflict that Steel is utilizing in her creation of a fictional "Indian suffragette." Steel's Nurjahan *cannot be* a faithful representation of the Indian woman who married Jahangir (in fact, as Said suggests,[59] it is pointless to insist on such a representation); she is nonetheless a far less negative representation than many female Indian characters in male Anglo-Indian literature. While Steel is creating a voice *for* Nurjahan, and through it articulating a stance that is decidedly that of the British feminist movement in the early 1900s, she is also creating a female character that her readers would concur is a powerful, motivated, and fundamentally reasonable human being. Steel is imbuing Nurjahan with an abundance of positive female character traits and creating an acceptable, feminist mirror image for her British reading audience.

In *Mistress of Men*, Flora Annie Steel attributes to Nurjahan the qualities that generally distinguish Anglo-Indian heroes and heroines from their peers and, more important, from the natives they rule: duty to God, physical prowess in the fight for right, and intellectual and moral superiority. Nurjahan is in many ways a typical "hero of empire," but these admirable qualities are combined with Nurjahan's femininity and race to create an interesting psychological vehicle for Steel's own vision of the ideal feminist woman. Nurjahan has not only physical strength and intellectual ability but also a highly developed sense of honor (missing from other Indian characters, such as Roshan Khan in *The Hosts of the Lord*). These traits cause a male admirer to proclaim that "had thou but been a man . . . thou wouldst have ruled India well" (despite fictional indication that Nurjahan did rule India well *as a woman*).[60] That a supportive male character makes such a chauvinistic statement indicates the depth of the prejudice that Nurjahan (and, by implication, British feminists) fought against.

Nurjahan's femininity is seen as both a pathway and an obstacle to greatness. Her comments on "the crime of being a woman," which culminate in a recognition of the true powerlessness of her position, further reflect Victorian women's experiences of chauvinism. Despite her almost arrogant self-esteem and despite attaining significant political power in India, Nurjahan was at the mercy of social laws and attitudes that remained decidedly patriarchal: "she lived solely by reason of the beauty which had captivated a King."[61] Yet the foundation of Nurjahan's power was her cunning intelligence and physical courage. At her birth, she is described as "a lusty one indeed," who does not die from the overdose of opium her nurse administers in an attempt at female infanticide. As her political power grew, her physical prowess became a necessity that saved her life when enemy factions kidnapped the emperor and allowed her to lead her men into battle to rescue their ruler.[62] In the final stages of her reign (as Jahangir neared his death), Nurjahan assumed political control in no uncertain terms. Establishing her own army, she was responsible for many successful political decisions and at least one significant military victory.[63]

From birth, Nurjahan exhibits the strains of feminist assertion that later develop into functional control of the Moghul empire. Although her male playmates "held, naturally, that as male creatures they should have all the best of everything," Nurjahan "denied this; her baby fingers held fast to her own."[64] In a fight with the young Jahangir over possession of her cup, she resorts to violence against the royal person. Having achieved her goal through force, Nurjahan reverted to her female nature, "offering [her cup] to him with a complacent smile which converted the outrage into an honour,"[65] thus extricating herself from a potentially fatal situation.

This childhood pattern is repeated, although reversed, by the adults: it is through her femininity that Nurjahan attains her power over Jahangir; it is through qualities traditionally perceived as masculine (intelligence, strength, determination) that she holds that power.

This pattern illustrates Steel's view that women should not be dictated to or forced against their will to submit to the stronger physical power of men but also enforces the Victorian sense of women as nurturers and caregivers. Although Nurjahan is always portrayed as a powerful woman, she is at the same time cast as a nurturing woman, who uses her caregiving as power over others. After her marriage to Jahangir, she asserts this power by usurping the position of the court doctor and replacing native superstition with a British-Victorian sense of self-control and moderation. By permitting Jahangir only a certain amount of wine per night and controlling his use of opium, Nurjahan ensured that he maintained a respectable—imperial—presence in his court. (Once again we see how Steel's Victorian ideology imbues her "Indian" woman with very British attitudes.)

The matter of Nurjahan's marriage, too, can be seen as an authorial insistence on women's control over their own lives. Brought before Jahangir's father, Akbar, Nurjahan is given a choice between her affianced husband and the prince. The exchange is interesting, as one doubts whether Akbar—even in the benevolence Steel ascribes to him in all her writings—would ever have asked the opinion of a middle-class girl whom his royal son desired.[66] Akbar's decree that "the maiden must be given her freedom of limited choice" can be seen as an example of Steel's feminist desire more than as an adherence to historical verity. Steel's own personality shines through in Nurjahan's decision: in choosing to marry her cousin rather than Jahangir, she asserts that it is because he is "the better man"and admits that "I love no one; but love is not all."[67] Steel herself asserts in her autobiography: "Why I married I cannot say. I do not think either of us was in love. I know I was not; I never have been. That is a sad fact, but it has to be faced. It has not made life any the less entrancing."[68]

Steel's experience of marriage—without passionate love but with a great deal of personal satisfaction—is replicated in her reconstruction of Nurjahan's life. Whereas Nurjahan's first marriage is based on a Victorian sense of idealism (marriage to "the better man" if married one must be), her subsequent marriage to Jahangir is a distinctly political decision. After years of hating him as the suspected instigator of her first husband's murder, she determines that the most effective method of revenge is control and sets out to rule through him, her power vested in his need of her:

> Revenge she wanted, and revenge she must have, but it must be of a different kind from that of the past. For the last four years she had lived, rejoicing in the gradual decadence of the man who had done her so grave an injury. Now, if it were still possible, she would make that man the slave of her will. He should, as it were, live through her; her vitality should overbear his apathy and indolence. She would at last be Queen not only of Women but of Men![69]

Nurjahan's success in this endeavor illustrates Steel's belief that control of one's emotional and sexual responses was essential in maintaining social autonomy: in contrast to Newasi's passionate attachment to Abool-Bukr, Nurjahan's sexual and emotional self-control, combined with Jahangir's obsessive love, enables her to obtain ultimate power through—and over—him. Although she terms love "life's greatest gift," Nurjahan recognizes that it is her very inability to love completely—her natural tendency to respond like men, who "reserved something [of themselves] always"—that enables her to retain her autonomous power.[70]

In Nurjahan, Steel does not create a woman shaped in an unfamiliar mold, "disloyal to civilization." Her ideal feminist creation is very "feminine" yet imbued with many of the "masculine" character traits admired by her society. Although feminism today has progressed to a stage that demands society's acceptance of women *as women*, Flora Annie Steel and her contemporaries were still trying to force their way into a man's world by playing the game according to men's rules. Nurjahan is a delicately balanced portrayal of a beautiful woman, with a great deal of feminine charm, who has physical and intellectual abilities that enable her to overcome patriarchal oppression and succeed in the very masculine world of seventeenth-century India. Such a utopian creation cannot be taken as a faithful representation of the historical Nurjahan, but comprehension of Steel's use of Nurjahan as a didactic construct provides a fascinating insight into the dialogue between colonialism and feminism in the early 1900s.

Conclusion

Chandra Talpade Mohanty's claim that no criticism can be apolitical but is "a directly political and discursive *practice* insofar as it is purposeful and ideological"[71] can be extended to literary production. Flora Annie Steel's fiction is patently didactic and must be considered both in light of her own articulated attitudes and within the context of feminist and imperialist history. Although Steel asserts a personal compassion for the Indian women she knew, many of her fictional re-presentations of historical Indian women replicate negative constructions of the East. Controlling the "object" of her investigations through her assumption of knowledge, Steel appropriates Indian women's identities and defines "Indian Woman" to her less-informed British reading public. As Mohanty observes, "such objectification (however benevolently motivated) needs to be both named and challenged."[72] Although Flora Annie Steel deserves little credit for the characterizations of Indian women in her social novels, she must be recognized for her attempt, in the case of Nurjahan, at providing an image of Indian womanhood that she undoubtedly felt to be as empowering for Indian women as it so obviously was for her own feminist cause.

Her *own* feminist cause was, after all, her primary concern. Despite her attempt to correct the image of Nurjahan as "ambitious and without shame," Steel chose her topic in response to her anger at any woman's being denied her historic voice merely because she was a woman, "destined to be judged by male standards throughout the years."[73] That she chose to portray a great Indian woman is partially circumstantial and largely fortuitous. Through engaging in the discursive construction of Indian women that was dominant in the British feminist press, Flora Annie Steel located an excellent site upon which to portray the social possibilities of British womanhood. Through her unavoidable immersion in imperialist ideology, Steel could in all fairness have done nothing other than "re-present" Nurjahan in a very Western way. Yet, by the creation of any image of Indian womanhood that moved forward, away from the negative stereotypes inflicted on literary representations of natives and women alike, the metropolitan image of Indian women was altered for the better. We must not look for *exclusively* positive messages, in our modern ideological terms, from authors embedded in a different temporal (and therefore ideological) position. As Paxton observes,[74] even Annie Besant, now famous for her political work with the Indian National Congress, was not immune to patriarchal ideological manipulation.

Flora Annie Steel was undoubtedly, self-assuredly, feminist. That she was unable to extricate herself from the imperialist ideology within which she lived complicates critical appreciation of her work. Yet within the larger debate between feminism and imperialism, the questions Steel's texts suggest still remain unanswered by modern critical analysis. Spivak claims that the subaltern woman today still cannot speak.[75] When this is the case, do other women have the moral right to speak *for* her, even toward their own ends? Can creating a "voice for" an "other" woman constitute a *positive* political act? Although these questions remain at the forefront of feminist and postcolonial critical investigation today, many Victorian feminists—Flora Annie Steel among them—felt that their answer was in all ways affirmative.

Notes

1. I use "Anglo-Indian" in the Victorian sense, meaning British men and women living in India.
2. See, for example: Rosemary Hennessy and Rajeswari Mohan, "The Construction of Woman in Three Popular Texts of Empire: Towards a Critique of Materialist Feminism"; Nancy Paxton, "Feminism under the Raj: Complicity and Resistance in the Writings of Flora Annie Steel and Annie Besant"; and Jenny Sharpe, *Allegories of Empire: The Figure of Woman in the Colonial Text.*
3. Suleri (1993), p. 247.
4. Mukherjee (1991), p. 36.
5. Ware (1992), p. xiii.
6. Patwardhan (1963) and Powell (1981).
7. Payne, review of *The Hosts of the Lord* (1900).
8. Review of *On the Face of the Waters* (*Academy*, 1896).
9. Review of *Miss Stuarts's Legacy* (*Atheneum*, 1893).
10. Review of *The Potter's Thumb* (*Academy*, 1894).
11. Review of *On the Face of the Waters* (*Academy*, 1896).
12. Payne, review of *The Potter's Thumb* (1894).
13. Suleri (1990), p. 78.
14. Ramazanoglu (1989), p. 117.
15. Ware (1992), pp. 121–27.
16. Ramusack (1992), p. 122.
17. Spivak (1993), p. 70.
18. The others are *A Prince of Dreamers* (1908), a fictional biography of Steel's favorite Indian historical figure, Akbar; *King Errant* (1912), the story of Akbar's predecessor, Babar;

and *The Builder* (1928), which deals with Shahjahan, on whose command the Taj Mahal was built.

19. *Mistress of Men*, pp. vii–viii.
20. *The Garden of Fidelity*, p. 222.
21. Paxton (1990), p. 333.
22. *Garden*, p. 1.
23. Paxton (1990), p. 335.
24. Rich (1986), p. 279.
25. *Garden*, p. 191.
26. Powell (1981), p. 3.
27. Review of *Garden* in *Quarterly Review* (1930).
28. Diver (1909), pp. 153–54.
29. Parry (1972), p. 101.
30. Anand (1971), p. 19.
31. Patwardhan (1963), pp. 219, 229.
32. Burton (1992), n. 60.
33. Ibid., p. 48
34. *Garden*, pp. 246, 245.
35. VN 283, 281
36. *OFW*ūv
37. Rev. of *OFW. Academy*
38. Payne, rev. of *OFW.*
39. *OFW*ūvi.
40. *OFW*ū91, 260, 237.
41. *OFW*91.
42. *OFW*ūv.
43. Although Steel blamed purdah for many of Indian women's social problems, her fiction does not address this question as strongly as it does more British feminist issues. In her depiction of Newasi and Nurjahan, the issue of purdah is glossed over: in Newasi's case, purdah is seen as a social situation that does not inhibit expression of her independence; in Nurjahan's case, purdah does not exist in any inhibiting degree at all. To Steel, physical emancipation was the result of, not a precursor to, emotional autonomy, especially in projecting a feminism appropriate to her *British* readers: they did not suffer under purdah, so such issues become less important in Steel's fiction.
44. *On the Face of the Waters*, p. 93.
45. Ibid., pp. 148, 343.
46. Qtd. in Burton (1992), n. 60.
47. *On the Face of the Waters*, p. 260
48. Ibid., p. 344.
49. Ibid., p. 346.
50. Ibid., p. 414.
51. *Mistress of Men*, p. vii.
52. Qtd. in Burton (1992), p. 148.
53. Burton (1992), p. 137.
54. Kulke and Rothermund (1990), p. 204.
55. Burton (1992), p. 147, my emphasis.
56. Kabbani (1986), p. 11.
57. Bhabha (1993), p. 116.
58. Azim (1993), p. 24.
59. Said (1991), p. 11.

60. *Mistress of Men*, p. 170.
61. Ibid., p. 204.
62. Ibid., p. 311.
63. Ibid., p. 340.
64. Ibid., p. 40.
65. Ibid., p. 43.
66. Ibid., pp. 76–78.
67. Ibid., p. 77.
68. *Garden*, p. 27.
69. *Mistress of Men*, pp. 56–57.
70. Ibid., p. 127.
71. Mohanty (1993), p. 197.
72. Ibid., p. 201.
73. *Mistress of Men*, pp. 367, 368.
74. Paxton (1990), pp. 341–42.
75. Spivak (1993), p. 104.

References

Anand, Mulk Raj. "Anglo-Saxon Attitudes: Twentieth-Century English Fiction About India." In M. K. Naik, S. K. Desai and S. T. Kallapu, ed., *The Image of India in Western Creative Writing*. Madras: Karnatak University Press and Macmillan, 1971.

Azim, Firdous. *The Colonial Rise of the Novel*. London: Routledge, 1993.

Bhabha, Homi K. "Remembering Fanon: Self, Psyche and the Colonial Condition." In Williams and Chrisman, eds., *Colonial Discourse and Post-Colonial Theory*, 1993.

Burton, Antoinette M. "The White Woman's Burden: British Feminists and 'The Indian Woman,' 1865–1915." In Chaudhuri and Strobel, eds., *Western Women and Imperialism*, 1992.

Chaudhuri, Nupur, and Margaret Strobel, eds., *Western Women and Imperialism: Complicity and Resistance*. Bloomington: Indiana University Press, 1992.

Diver, Maud. *The Englishwoman in India*. Edinburgh: William Blackwood, 1909.

Hennessy, Rosemary, and Rajeswari Mohan. "The Construction of Woman in Three Popular Texts of Empire: Towards a Critique of Materialist Feminism." *Textual Practice* 3 (1989), pp. 323–359.

Kabbani, Rana. *Europe's Myths of Orient: Devise and Rule*. London: Macmillan, 1986.

Kulke, Hermann, and Dietmar Rothermund. *A History of India*. London: Routledge, 1990.

Mohanty, Chandra Talpade. "Under Western Eyes: Feminist Scholarship and Colonial Discourse." In Williams and Chrisman, eds., *Colonial Discourse and Post-Colonial Theory*, 1993.

Mukherjee, Arun. "The Exclusions of Postcolonial Theory and Mulk Raj Anand's *Untouchable*." *Ariel* 23.3 (1991), pp. 27–48.

Parry, Benita. *Delusions and Discoveries: Studies on India in the British Imagination, 1880–1930*. London: Allen Lane Penguin, 1972.

Patwardhan, Daya. "Flora Annie Steel: A Lover of India." In M. K. Naik, S. K. Desai, and S. T. Kallapu, eds., *The Image of India in Western Creative Writing*. Madras: Karnatak University Press and Macmillan, 1971.

———. *A Star of India: Flora Annie Steel, Her Works and Times*. Poona: A.V. Griha, 1963.

Paxton, Nancy L. "Feminism under the Raj: Complicity and Resistance in the Writings of Flora Annie Steel and Annie Besant." *Women's Studies International Forum* 13.4 (1990), pp. 333–346.

Payne, William Morton. Rev. of *On the Face of the Waters*, by Flora Annie Steel. *Dial* 22 (1 March 1897), pp. 153–156.
———. Rev. of *The Hosts of the Lord*, by Flora Annie Steel. *Dial* 29 (16 December 1900), p. 496.
———. Rev. of *The Potter's Thumb*, by Flora Annie Steel. *Dial* 17 (1 September 1894), pp. 121–122.
Powell, Violet. *Flora Annie Steel: Novelist of India*. London: Heinemann, 1981.
Ramazanoglu, Caroline. *Feminism and the Contradictions of Oppression*. London: Routledge, 1989.
Ramusack, Barbara N. "Cultural Missionaries, Maternal Imperialists, Feminist Allies: British Women Activists in India, 1865–1945." In Chaudhuri and Strobel, ed., *Western Women and Imperialism*, 1992.
Rev. of *Miss Stuart's Legacy*, by Flora Annie Steel. *Atheneum* (18 November 1893), p. 693.
Rev. of *On the Face of the Waters*, by Flora Annie Steel. *Academy* (5 December 1896), p. 488.
Rev. of *The Garden of Fidelity*, by Flora Annie Steel. *Quarterly Review* 255 (1930), pp. 198–199.
Rev. of *The Potter's Thumb*, by Flora Annie Steel. *Academy* (28 July 1894), p. 63.
Rich, Adrienne. "Disloyal to Civilization: Feminism, Racism, Gynephobia (1978)." *On Lies, Secrets, and Silence: Selected Prose, 1966–1978*. London: Virago, 1986.
Said, Edward. *Orientalism: Western Concepts of the Orient*. 1978. London: Penguin, 1991.
Sharpe, Jenny. *Allegories of Empire: The Figure of Woman in the Colonial Text*. Minneapolis: University of Minnesota Press, 1993.
Spivak, Gayatri Chakravorty. "Can the Subaltern Speak?" In Williams and Chrisman, eds., *Colonial Discourse and Post-Colonial Theory*, 1993.
Steel, Flora Annie. *Miss Stuart's Legacy* [1893]. London: Heinemann, 1900.
———. *Mistress of Men* [1916]. London: Heinemann, 1917.
———. *On the Face of the Waters* [1896]. London: Heinemann, 1897.
———. *The Garden of Fidelity: Being the Autobiography of Flora Annie Steel, 1847–1929*. London: Macmillan, 1929.
———. *The Hosts of the Lord* [1900] London: Nelson, n.d.
———. *The Law of the Threshold*. London: Heinemann, 1924.
———. *The Potter's Thumb* [1894]. London: Heinemann, 1904.
———. *Voices in the Night*. London: Heinemann, 1900.
Suleri, Sara. "Woman Skin Deep: Feminism and the Postcolonial Condition." In Williams and Chrisman, eds., *Colonial Discourse and Post-Colonial Theory*, 1993.
———. *The Rhetoric of English India*. Chicago: University of Chicago Press 1990.
Ware, Vron. *Beyond the Pale: White Women, Racism and History*. London: Verso, 1992.
Williams, Patrick, and Laura Chrisman, eds., *Colonial Discourse and Post-Colonial Theory: A Reader*. Hemel Hampstead, UK: Harvester Wheatsheaf, 1993.

SUMA CHITNIS

Exploring Tradition and Change among Women in Marathi Culture

The Exploration of the Vernacular Subcultures

In India today, efforts to fathom the traditions in which women's attitudes and values are rooted and to identify the influences that shape their behavior and their consciousness have led to the exploration of all kinds of source materials in the vernacular languages. Mythology, folklore, folk songs, oral and documented history, different forms of literature, and other wirtings in the regional languages are being avidly explored. Administrative and judicial records, historical archives, newspapers, and magazines in the regional language are being researched and studied. There is a related effort to examine and understand the meanings of local and regional forms of recreation, festivals, custom, ritual, and practices.

To an extent, this is the feminist dimension of the postcolonial explosion of interest in recovering connection with indigenous life and culture. It is an aspect of the attempts made by independent India's Western-educated, English-speaking elite to return to the traditional culture from which they have been distanced through a century and a half of colonial rule and European education. The same impulse has generated the country's spectacular renaissance of indigenous art, craft, music, dance, and theater. The same quest has brought about the renewal and reinstatement of indigenous systems of medicine such as yoga, *āyurveda*, and *unāni* and indigenous sciences such as *Vāstu Śāstra*—that is, the science of architecture.

However, a more pressing practical concern has stimulated these explorations into vernacular culture. Postindependence efforts to improve the status of women, including legislation aimed at eradicating practices such as female infanticide; measures to advance women's rights in marriage, divorce, adoption, and inheritance; and moves toward improving their access to education, employment, and health care have failed to produce the results expected. As our experience of development has grown and the failures more courageously confronted and rigorously examined, it is evident that, as with many other programs for development, programs for the advancement of women fail because they are neither adequately informed about nor sensitive to the ground realities of their target group. Analyses reveal that many of the programs for change are based on the somewhat simplistic assumption that the new values, new ideals of gender justice and equity, and new concepts of appropriate roles for women will be accepted because they are good. The programs ignore the fact that the overwhelming majority of Indian women, whose role concepts, self-images, and notions of what is right and wrong are shaped by traditional values, are genuinely reluctant to change.

Consequently, strategies for change must be based on an understanding of traditional ways, values, customs, and practices— and why these continue to be respected. They must be fully aware of and purposefully counteract the powerful mythology, processes of socialization, religious and semireligious observances, and rituals by which traditional values are inculcated and reinforced. Efforts to change the situation of women are not new to Indian society, and those who design and administer change must examine this history and learn from it. Finally, it may not be wise to reject tradition altogether. Working through traditional ways and practices, where this is possible may be more productive. In fact, those who are responsible for change must be so well acquainted with traditional beliefs and convictions that they can, on occasion, turn them on their heads to make an effective point in favor of change.

As feminists, development workers, and others measure up to these challenges, they discover that the oral and the written source materials that they need to explore for this purpose are available only in the vernacular languages. Strongly motivated, they have plunged into exploring the vernacular subcultures through the vernacular languages. This phenomenon, triggered by the immediate needs of development, has a significance far beyond this immediate need.

To appreciate this larger significance, it is necessary to recognize that understanding India's vernacular cultures is the first step toward understanding the Indian culture at an unprecedented depth. India is a country of almost a billion people who speak sixteen officially recognized languages, each with several dialects. Each language is spoken over a well-defined territory, which, because of its geographical location and historical circumstances, has its own distinctive culture. What some believe to be a single Indian culture is, in fact, a conglomeration of several such subcultures. It is impossible to describe Indian customs and practices with any detail or authenticity or to adequately explain seemingly uniform features of Indian society such as the caste system without taking cognizance of India's subcultural pluralities. The challenge is to develop a composite picture that accommodates the pluralities and is therefore not only authentic but also as rich as the variegated fabric of Indian life. So far, this challenge has never been met satisfactorily, because the vernacular cultures are not adequately studied or understood by the well-educated Indians who are generally called upon to speak for India. Women's studies in India can be proud that feminist research and development research pertaining to women should have triggered a much needed move toward research in the vernacular subcultures and toward sharing findings and perceptions from this research across these subcultures.

This chapter describes some features of the Maharashtrian culture and presents some materials from the Marathi language that are pertinent to understanding tradition and change as they affect Indian women. The presentation touches on four points. First, it describes how games, fasts, rituals, and narratives from mythology have traditionally been used as instruments for the socialization of young girls and for the reinforcement of traditional role concepts and values among women. Second, it describes the space available to women for personal expression in the traditional Marathi culture. Third, it provides information on the movements involving women, and on behalf of women, that have occurred in Maharashtra. Fourth, it touches on the traditional culture of silence and indicates how important it is for those who are interested in understanding the situation of women to be able to understand and interpret this silence.

The Process of Socialization

Games

The games children play often function as a mechanism for their socialization, particularly games that simulate adult roles—for instance, when little girls play at homemaking or teaching school or, little boys play cops and robbers. As children try to play an allocated role to perfection, they understand what is expected from that role. Simultaneously, they understand what to expect of others in the set of roles involved in the game that is being played. The following describes some of the games that young girls in Maharashtra have traditionally played. It is easy to see how traditional norms and values pertaining to the roles of women are communicated and reinforced through these generations.

BHATUKALI

By far the most popular pastime for little girls all over the world is to play at homemaking. The traditional version of this in Maharashtra is the *bhatukali*. The players in a *bhatukali* are all girls, generally from the neighborhood. However, very young brothers who promise to behave, may be included to function as men in the household. A short *bhatukali* session takes two to three hours. An elaborate *bhatukali* can start early in the morning, run through the whole day, and replicate all that happens through the day in an ordinary household.

Cooking and the distribution of responsibilities in the kitchen are the core elements of a *bhatukali* session. Ordinarily, the cooking is make-believe. Leaves, flowers, petals, pebbles, and even mud are used as ingredients for the make-believe meals. Sometimes girls are given peanuts, jaggery, puffed rice, and other dry ingredients that can be eaten raw. When mothers, grandmothers, and aunts decide to treat the little girls in the family to a very special *bhatukali*, they provide proper ingredients. Coal or kerosene stoves are allowed, and girls are helped to prepare real meals. The miniature stoves, pots, pans, and kitchen implements, as well as the plates on which the food is served, are fashioned out of brass, copper, or stainless steel. They are careful imitations of what is actually used in Maharashtra homes.

In addition to cooking, a *bhatukali* session simulates several other aspects of the daily routine in a home. *Bhatukali* players take on the different roles in the family and enact their roles with meticulous precision. The little girls may take on male roles as part of the game, but they generally concentrate on the different roles of grown-up women in a household. Not only do the players simulate the routine within a household but also they simulate some of the crises that occur. The crisis imitated may be relatively simple—for instance, the unexpected arrival of a guest. Enterprising players may venture into simulating some of the more complicated crises that occur in Indian families as women try to balance the hierarchies of age and gender or to maintain the order of importance of the various consanguineous and in-law relationships in terms of which their lives are structured.

BAHULICHE LAGNA

Events such as weddings or religious festivals are routinely celebrated in a *bhatukali*, but sometimes girls are treated to a more elaborate *bahuliche lagna* or doll wedding. For these weddings, the bride doll and the bridegroom doll belong to girls from different families. The bride's jewelry and trousseau, the bridegroom's attire, the gifts exchanged between the two families, the wedding music and the wedding feasts are close imitations and truly elaborate, as also the finery in which the players are dressed, the mock rituals, and the behavior of the girls in their roles as the family of the bride or bridegroom. The bridegroom's father, mother, brothers, sisters, and other relatives are allowed to be demanding, condescending, and difficult to please. In contrast, the bride's father, mother, sisters, brothers, and other relatives are expected to be submissive and respectful. They are expected to skillfully steer the wedding through the tantrums that the bridegroom's family are expected to throw.

Both *bhatukali* and *bahuliche lagna* underline the centrality of marriage, motherhood, and homemaking in the life of a woman. As they play at homemaking and get their dolls married, little girls are put through their paces for their adult roles as mothers, wives, and homemakers. Playing house and homemaking continues to be a popular pastime for little girls in Maharashtra. However, it is being rapidly overtaken by other games. Moreover, the substance of the roles played is visibly changing. It would be interesting to observe the changes in play and see what they reflect of the changes that are taking place in the role and status of women and in the structure of gender relationships in Maharashtrian society. It would also be useful to explore the possibility of consciously using this game to promote new concepts about the role of women and new values in gender relationships.

Rituals, Fasts, and Group Songs

A more direct and disciplined socialization for the traditional values of womanhood is accomplished through a rigorous schedule of fast, rituals, and other religious practices that girls are required to follow. These are spread through the course of the year and provided for in the Hindu calendar. A particular fast or ritual centers around an important event in the life of a girl. For instance, the Hartalika fast and its accompanying rituals center on marriage and are, in essence, a young girl's prayer for a good husband. Many of the rituals are observed and celebrated together, in groups, by girls from the joint or extended family or from the neighborhood, which provides more solidarity in the commitment to the values that the events are designed to inculcate and support.

Group games, and songs are an important feature of these events. Almost invariably the songs either talk about the sufferings that a girl has to face at the home of her in-laws or about the love and warmth of her parental home. Their catchy tunes, simple rhythm, and poignant words go straight to the heart. The songs about the home of the in-laws prepare girls to face the difficulties that they almost invariably encounter in the joint family of the husband. They convey the message that these difficulties must be borne with dignity; they particularly emphasize that this must be done to maintain the honor of the parental home. The songs about the mother's home prepare a girl to accept the break from her maternal home after her marriage at a tender age. They also advise her to seek comfort in happy memories of her parents and her siblings and to remember how much they love her—whenever she feels unloved and oppressed in the home of her in-laws.

The pertinence of these songs is difficult to appreciate without familiarity with what a woman often has to suffer in the home of her husband and her in-laws in a traditional Indian family. Nevertheless, the following example should provide some idea of what is typically said.

About the In-Laws

The road to my in-laws is stony and thorny,
Now what messenger's come, oh my friend?
Brother-in-law messenger's come, oh my friend,
What gift has he brought me, friend?
He's brought you a bracelet, friend.
Say I won't take it , say I am not coming
Close all the doors and let loose the dog!
The road to my in-laws is stony and thorny,
Now what messenger's come, oh my friend?
Father-in-law messenger's come, oh my friend,
What gift has he brought me, friend?
He's brought you a sārī, friend.
Say I won't take the sārī, say I am not coming
Close all the doors and let loose the dog!
The road to my in-laws is stony and thorny,
Now what messenger's come, oh my friend?
Your husband himself has come, oh my friend,
What gift has he brought me, friend?
He's brought you a whip, friend.
Say that I will take it , say I'm coming
Open all the doors and tie up the dog!

It is revealing to read these sad lines about the home of the in-laws in juxtaposition to the following lines that are typical of the many songs that express a girl's sentiments about her mother's home.

> Oh these Karanjis I have made have come out so good
> They deserve to be put in the very best tray.
> Now the tray with the Karanjis looks so good
> It deserves to go to the very best home
> Mother's home is the very best home
> That's where I will send them—if I can
> Yes mother's home is the best
> There I am allowed to play
> That is the home that deserves this very special tray.

Kathās from Mythology

The conditioning for traditional values that is done through fasts, rituals, group games, and songs is further firmly reinforced by narratives from the epics or from mythology. These narratives, called *kathās*, are primarily a part of the oral tradition of Maharashtra. However, some *kathās* are also available in texts handed down through the generations in families of professional *kathākārīs* or storytellers. The beauty and the power of a *kathā* lie in that a narrator can add to and embellish it suitably for a particular gathering or audience. Generally, a gifted storyteller from the gathering may come forward or be requested to narrate a *kathā*, but it is possible to engage a professional *kathākar* or a storyteller. Although *kathās* are routinely part of ritual get-togethers for young girls, special *kathā* sessions, generally conducted by professionals, may also be organized. They are major events in which women of all ages participate. In educated, middle- and upper-class, urban India, the *kathā* has almost disappeared, but it continues to be an integral part of life in rural areas. Feminist groups and development workers have found that the *kathā* is a powerful instrument for communication of new values in programs for the empowerment of women. The following example illustrates the efficacy of the *kathā* as an instrument for the inculcation and reaffirmation of values.

In the traditional Indian value system, a wife is expected to serve her husband as her lord and her master, with selfless devotion, till the end of her life. In the brahmanical value system, this expectation generated the ideal of the *pativratā* or the devoted wife. A *pativratā* is expected to be willing to do anything for her husband. On his death, she goes with him as *satī*, by voluntarily immolating herself on his funeral pyre. The courage required for the performance of this act is believed to come from grace bestowed upon the true *pativratā*. For more than a century now, the practice of *satī* has been firmly prohibited and illegal, but the ideal of a *pativratā* as a wife who serves her husband to her last breath continues to prevail. In Maharashtra, as in some other parts of India, the ideal of a *pativratā* is reaffirmed and reinforced by an annual fast and the ritual worship of Sāvitrī, a mythological figure who is deified as an ideal wife. Sāvitrī's *kathā*, which is central to the spirit of this annual event, is narrated on this occasion. The essence of the story follows.

Sāvitrī is the wife of Prince Satyvān. The couple is childless. Satyavān is the only son of his father. The father, a ruling king, is dispossessed of his kingdom and hit by blindness. As tragedy thus hits the household, Satyavān dies. At Satyavān's death, his blind father is left without any heir to fight for and regain the kingdom.

Sāvitrī, devoted to her husband Satyavān, follows him to death. Yama, the god of death, asks her to turn back, as her time has not yet come. But Sāvitrī refuses, saying that she is only doing her duty and following her husband to serve him wherever he goes. Impressed by her devotion as a *pativratā*, Yama grants Sāvitrī a boon. Surprisingly, Sāvitrī does not ask for her husband to be returned to life. She asks only that her father-in-law see his grandson on the throne. The boon is granted. But because *pativratā* cannot bear a son by a man other than her husband, Yama has to bring Satyavān back to life for Sāvitrī to bear a son, and he has to restore sight to Sāvitrī's father-in-law so that he can see his grandson on the throne. Thus Sāvitrī uses a single boon to restore her husband's life, gain a son, get back her father-in-law's vision, and regain the lost kingdom.

Traditionally, the story has been used to illustrate a *pativratā*'s devotion to her husband. It is also used to support the practice of *satī*. It underlines Sāvitrī's willingness to follow Satyavān into death. Sāvitrī's courage, her quick wisdom, and her capacity to outwit none less than the god of death are never brought out. Those who work at programs aimed at empowering women can use the *kathā* to emphasize Sāvitrī's courage, strength, wisdom, and capacity to outwit Yama. They can point out that Sāvitrī is to be revered not because she was willing to die with Satyavān but because she was courageous enough to confront Yama and wise enough to ask for a boon that not only brought her husband back to life but also simultaneously accomplished three other ends.

Women's Own Space

While the *bhatukali*, *bahuliche lagna*, songs about the mother-in-law and the mother, and the *kathā* have served as instruments for socialization of girls in traditional Maharashtrian society, the *palna* and the *owi* provide women with privacy and space within which to express their thoughts and feelings. In a culture that allowed very little personal indulgence, this space was very special.

The Palna

Traditional culture did not permit mothers, particularly young mothers in joint families, to indulge in playing with their children. It did not allow them to kiss, fondle, admire, or praise their offspring or in any other way demonstrate their affection for them in the presence of others, particularly the elders. As a routine chore, however, mothers were allowed to rock or pat their little ones to sleep and to sing lullabies as they did so. Women use these lullabies in full measure for the expression that they were otherwise denied.

The oral tradition of Maharashtra is rich with *palnas* that enable the mother to retreat into a world of her own with her child. The imagery of some of these *palnas*, passed down from generation to generation, is so rich and powerful that their capacity to create magic moments between the two is almost palpable. For instance, the verses describe cradles fashioned from ivory, ebony, sandalwood, silver, or gold, lined with gossamer, satin, or silk, and decorated with hangings fashioned out of rubies, emeralds, pearls, and other precious stones. They refer to the babe in the cradle as the infant Lord Kṛṣṇa, and to the mother as Kṛṣṇa's mother, queen Yaśodā. Allowing free expression to a mother's pride, hopes, and dreams for her little offspring, they talk of how fair the infant sleeping in the cradle is and how brave, wise and famous the baby will grow up to be. In some *palnas*, the mother commands the clouds not to thunder and frighten her child or warns the blossoms on the trees to open softly so that they do not disturb the little one's sleep. In others, the mother invites the morning sun to breakfast with her child. Sensitive to nature, *palna* verses bring in the clouds, the moon, and the stars. They capture the freshness of dawn, the splendor of sunrise, and the brilliance of the setting sun. They resound with the music of the elements—the soft murmur of summer breeze, the gentle gurgling of brooks, and the lashing of wild storms and angry seas. They engage in imaginary conversations with birds, flowers, tigers, elephants, and other creatures big and small, and they help the mother to bring the child some very special company.

The Owi

The *owi* is the song sung by women as they grind grain into flour in the wee hours of the morning. Generally, only the woman who sings the *owi* is awake and at work at that hour. The rest of the household is fast asleep. Her solitude is very private and belongs to her alone.

Owis have a sweet, soulful refrain that blends rhythmically with the smooth, steady humming of the grinding stone. Often sad and always intensely moving, the mood of an *owi* is very different from that of a *palna*. So is the substance of its text. In an *owi*, a woman reminisces about her childhood, lovingly remembers her parents and her siblings, and expresses her yearnings for her parental home. She reflects on her relationship with her husband and her in-laws, muses over her problems, and meditates on her blessings. In some *owis*, women engage in conversations with God, generally with Viṭhovā, the popular folk deity of Maharashtra. They put questions to Viṭhobā—and often offer their own answers to the questions they have asked. *Owis* can be highly philosophical and reflective, but even the simplest is pregnant with wisdom and rich with feeling drawn from women's continuing struggle with life. Sung in the privacy of darkness before dawn and in communion with the rhythm of the grinding stone, they create a warm and secure space for women to recoup from the pressures of domestic life, to reflect, and to seek resignation and peace.

Movements Involving Women and on Behalf of Women

The Bhakti Movement and the Saint Poetesses

Many of the *owis* commonly sung are compositions by saint poetesses who belonged to the *bhakti* movement. Within the limits of this chapter, it is not possible to go into the genesis of this movement or even describe its salient features. The basic point is that the movement was a nonviolent but firm and effective protest against the brahmanical canon, which first decreed that *jñāna* or knowledge through the study of sacred texts is the only means to *mokṣa* or spiritual salvation, and then denied women and Śudras (who rank low in the cast hierarchy) the right to seek or acquire such knowledge. From the sixth century onward, persons from the Śudra castes had started to claim that spiritual salvation could also be achieved through devotion and true love for God. In keeping with their conviction, many of them dedicated themselves to the *bhakti mārga*—the path of devotion and prayer. Some of them expressed their devotion through the composition of music and verse.

The movement, which seems to have started in South India, occurred at different points of time in the different regions of the country. In Maharashtra, it was most active between the thirteenth and the seventeenth centuries. One of the most distinctive features of the movement in Maharashtra was the large number of women who were involved in it. Even more distinctive was the fact that several of these women came from high-caste Brahmin families and chose gurus (spiritual teachers) from among Sudra disciples. Most of these gurus, such as Sant Tukaram and Sant Ramdas, were looked upon as saints and highly respected for the depth of their wisdom, integrity, courage, and humility. Nevertheless, in taking Śudra men as their gurus, the Brahmin women made an extraordinarily bold, autonomous, and radical move. The women who joined the *bhakti* movement in Maharashtra were not only courageous but also highly competent. Many of them rose to eminent positions of leadership and responsibility in their sects. Several composed devotional poetry that, to this day, is considered outstanding, both for its literary excellence and for the profundity and sensitivity of its thought.

The participation of women in a movement that forged an alternate path to spritual salvation and thus cleverly combated brahmanical oppression without frontally opposing it, their autonomous move to take Śudra gurus, and the capability with which women served the leadership positions they reached have had a strong and lasting influence on the status of women in Maharashtra. The compositions of the saint poetesses, particularly their verse, are still extensively recited, sung, and quoted. A study of the genesis, growth, and decline of the *bhakti* movement, of the lives of some of its eminent women, and, above all, of the verse and other compositions by these women should therefore be valuable to understanding the psyche and the situation of Maharashtrian women today.

THE COMPOSITIONS OF THE SAINT-POETESS

The *bhakti* verse is not composed for an audience—real or imaginary. In fact, most of it is in the form of soliloquies. Some of these soliloquies are hymns in praise of God. Others are intense conversations and sometimes single-person dialogues with God. In these conversations and dialogues, God is seen and addressed as father, mother, friend, or lover. Regardless of the image in which God is seen and addressed, the relationship as expressed in the verse is always warm, open, and intimate. It is without barriers and, considering the limitations placed on women in those days, surprisingly bold. Some *bhakti* verse fantasizes about the romantic relationship between Rādhā and Lord Kṛṣṇa or about other deities. Such verse, as well as the verse in which saint poetesses address God in an intensely personal, romantic vein, is referred to as *madhura-bhakti* or romantic devotion.

Bhaktas came from diverse backgrounds. Although all of them were basically deep into devotion and prayer, each *bhakta* had a distinctive personal agenda. *Bhaktas* who established sects made this the agenda of the sect. Apart from this, the concerns that are expressed in the compositions of the *bhaktas*, the language, and the style of these compositions invariably reflect the background and the personality of the composer. This individual makes a rich diversity and for universal appeal. In the legacy of verse, pithy sayings, and records of dialogues between *bhaktas*, everyone can find something that is particularly appealing and close to the heart. This variety is one of the major strengths of the *bhakti* tradition. Following are brief descriptions of the lives and work of four of the most eminent women in the *bhakti* movement. They offer a glimpse of the diversity of backgrounds from which the women came and the range of issues in a woman's life that their compositions touched and covered.

Mahādayesa (1233–1302), the earliest saint poetess on record, was a child widow in a learned Brahmin family. She took Chakradhara, the founder of the Mahānubhava sect, as her guru and later rose to be an eminent *bhakta* in her own right. When Chakradhara knew he was dying, he appointed her the head of the sect. Chakradhara was probably the first advocate of gender justice and gender equity in Maharashtrian history. He insisted on equality between men and women in his sect and treated Mahādayesa a colleague. Convinced that women's own attitudes to their bodies, their self-images as inferior beings, and the image that men hold of women lie at the root of oppression of women, Chakradhara made his mission to fight these sources of gender oppression and inequality. Some of the compositions attributed to Mahādayesa are records of conversations between her and her guru, Chakradhara, on these issues. They are mainly searching questions and equally searching answers. In addition, Mahādayesa composed rich and lively verses about the romantic relationship between Lord Kṛṣṇa and Rādhā.

Muktā (1277–1297) came from a background very different from that of Mahādayesa. She was the only daughter of a Brahmin couple who had been ostracized for a ritual lapse. Although the couple and their four children were considered outcaste and severely marginalized, the father, a highly learned scholar, taught the religious texts to his four children, including Muktā, his only daughter. The Brahmin authorities objected to the outcaste children being thus given *Jñāna* (knowledge), and the family was literally hounded for what was considered another major lapse. Despite this harassment, one of the sons, Jñāneśvara, grew up to be an eminent saint, a profound philosopher, and one of the most distinguished poets in Marathi literary history. At a time when high learning and religious writing were exclusively in Sanskrit he was the first to write a commentary on the *Bhagavad Gitā* and other religious texts in Marathi, the language of the people. To this day, these commentaries are among the most respected. They are also considered to be outstanding in literary quality.

Like the compositions of her eminent brother, the compositions of Muktā are profoundly philosophical. They are also highly sophisticated, both in style and in substance. Many of them are about understanding the self and the search for truth. She probes these issues with remarkable maturity and confidence, particularly considering that she lived to be only twenty years old. Unlike many other saint poetesses, Muktā does not bring any personal life into her compositions. She does not say much on the relationship between men and women either; in the one or two places where she addresses the issue, she brushes it aside with statements to the effect that one must pass beyond mundane concerns about the body by accepting both the male and the female physical body with emotional neutrality.

Jānā (1298–1350) was the daughter of poor low-caste people who were *bhakti mārgīs*. She had been in bonded labor to an upper-caste family who were also *bhakti mārgīs*. Nāmdev, the son of the family to which she was sold, rose to be an eminent *bhakta*. Jānā started as devotee and remained so as long as she lived. However, as she advanced in spirituality, she achieved eminence on her own.

The themes, language, and imagery of Jānā's verse are altogether different from that of the others. She talks to Viṭhovā about her heavy and endless chores as a domestic. She cheerfully sings about how Viṭhovā, her friend and helpmate, helps her carry and heat the bathwater for the family, to sweep the courtyard, to scour the vessels clean—and even to scratch her scalp when the lice bite her. She also talks of Viṭhovā as a companion who comes to keep her company in her humble abode when she is lonely and tired and tells how he drifts off to sleep as their conversations continue through the night. Freely, without inhibition, Jānā questions Viṭhovā as well as Nāmdev on the caste distinctions made by them between their *bhaktas*. With the same freedom, almost with abandon, she declares her boundless and consuming love for Viṭhovā. In one particular highly respected verse she states that she is willing to walk bareheaded through the market place, even sell herself as a slut, declaring her devotion and singing in praise of her lord. This joyous abandon and unrestrained declaration of love remain among the most powerful expressions of devotion in the *bhakti* movement. From among the wealth of *bhakti* verse that is part of the living traditions of Maharashtra today, Jānā's is probably the most widely recited and sung.

As a clue to her times, Jānā's verse is unique in the range of issues it covers and in the quality of the insights it offers into the lives of people in positions such as hers. It portrays the life of a domestic laborer and reveals that caste distinctions existed in what is believed to be an egalitarian movement. It must have required extraordinary courage for Jānā to speak so freely on these issues. Another special feature of Jānā's verse is that she addresses God in several relationships in which she sees him—as a deity, as a close friend, as a companion who shares her work, her joys, and, her sorrows, and as a lover for whom she feels beyond measure. Through her verse, we are able to see the different kinds of relationships that these liberated women had with God.

Bahinā (1628–1700) was a Brahmin girl, attracted to religion and spirituality from her early childhood. She was married at the tender age of three to a man twenty-seven years older. He was a high-caste Brahmin scholar. There were two major crises in Bahinā's life. First, she chose to continue to be a wife and a homemaker, despite the fact that she had no inclination to these responsibilities. Second, she chose a Śudra *bhakta* her guru, despite the fact that her Brahmin husband was a religious scholar. Bahinā's verse expresses the conflicts she herself faced in dealing with these crises. In the process, it provides some deep and sensitive reflection on how one can combine the demands of spirituality with the mundane responsibilities of being a wife and homemaker. It also provides deep insights into human nature and gently exposes the many hypocrisies of the high-caste Hindu religion and life. Again, drawing on her life experience, Bahinā's verse provides valuable insights into the problems faced in a traditional society by women who have the courage and the capacity to think on their own. On a more philosophical plane, Bahinā writes about the journey of her soul through twelve previous lives as well as the present.[1]

The Nineteenth-Century Movement for Social Reform

Although the period from the thirteenth to the seventeenth centuries thus resonates with the compositions of the saint poets and poetesses of the *bhakti* movement, the nineteenth century in Maharashtra stands out as the era of social reform. As in Bengal and Tamilnadu in the same period, much of this reform was on behalf of women. In Maharashtra, it centered on issues such as abolition of child marriage, the establishment of the right of remarriage to upper-caste Hindu widows, and the education of women. Some of the boldest initiatives in the country on each of these three issues were taken in the Bombay-Pune region of Maharashtra.

As is well known, the Indian National Congress was born out of this movement for social reform. Toward the end of the nineteenth century, as nationalism advanced, the social reform movement in Maharashtra was seriously divided. One section was led by Lokamānya Tilak, who had fired the first salvo of the nationalist movement with the slogan, "Freedom is my birthright and I will have it." This section felt that much of the reform, particularly reform relating to women, was "Western" and therefore inconsistent with nationalism. It also believed—and insisted—that nationalism should be given priority over social reform and that the movement for social reform should be slowed in the interests of nationalism. Another section, led by Agarkar and including reformers like Lokahitavādī and Maharṣi Karve, believed that social reform was not inconsistent with nationalism and must be given equal status.

This conflict between political priorities and efforts to advance the status of women continues as a recurrent feature of Indian society. The constitution of independent India, framed in the euphoria of freedom won after a long and tenacious struggle against British rule, firmly provides for gender equality, gender justice, and the empowerment of women. But, with the politicization of religion in postindependence India, political factionalism and politically engineered religious fundamentalism have again and again pushed social reform on behalf of women into the background. In fact, in the name of religion, there has been a reassertion of antiquated religious laws that govern marriage, divorce, adoption, and inheritance—issues that are central to the lives of women. The nineteenth century and early twentieth-century debates on nationalism versus social reform are thus very pertinent to a proper understanding of the current situation. The story of how reformers made their way through the opposition they faced is not only fascinating as history but also valuable from the point of view of learning how to cope with the obstacles that programs for the empowerment of women currently face. Many different sources of information about the nineteenth-century movement for social reform on behalf of women range from Marathi newspapers and magazines to the Marathi cinema.

NEWSPAPERS, MAGAZINES, AND JOURNALS

On March 8, 1832, the eminent social reformer Balshastri Jambhekar established the first Marathi daily newspaper, *Darpan*. For almost ten years, *Darpan* remained the lone Marathi newspaper. Then, in 1841, came the *Prabhākar*, in 1842 the *Jñānodaya*, 1862 the *Induprakāś*, and in 1889 the *Sudhārak*. The *Prārthanā Samāj* was established in 1867. The reformist organization soon started bringing out a monthly journal-cum-newsletter. In 1873, Jyothiva Phule established the Satyaśodhak Maṇḍal, one of the earliest organizations set up to politically contest discrimination against the Śudra castes and against women. This organization brought out its own journal. Other magazines and journals like the *Strī Dnyān Pradīp* (1869) and *Manorañjan* (1890) were set up. These newspapers and journals were active and articulate on women's issues. What is most remarkable is the fairness with which they authentically reported public debates and gave full representation to all arguments in favor of and against the issues reported.

One of the earliest issues of the *Darpan* talks about the education of women as the foundation for a good society. Soon, another issue protests against child marriage by pointing out how little girls are ruined by the practice. A 1869 issue of *Strī Dnyān Pradīp* published a detailed statistical report on the poor state of education of girls in the city of Thane near Bombay. Agarkar's *Sudhārak* ran a special column to voice the opinions of women. Many women wrote under pen names in this column. The issues most commonly dealt with were child marriage, the remarriage of widows, and the education of women. The opportunity for expression provided by the *Sudhārak* gradually encouraged women to write. The *Manorañjan* carried letters, essays, and short stories in which women expressed their ideas and their feelings on issues that touched their lives. Some women seem to have been regular contributors; for instance, the names of Shantabai, Janakibai Maratha, and Kashibai Kanetkar recur. This tradition of active advocacy of reforms in favor of women and of providing information and a forum for dialogue on women's issues has been kept alive by the Marathi press. Today, Marathi newspapers such as the *Maharashtra Times*, *Sakal*, *and Lokasatta* and magazines such as *Miluni Sarya Jani* are particularly active.

TREATISES

As early as 1873, when very few women in Maharashtra were literate, Sakhubai Sangwekar wrote *Candraprabhā Viraha Varṇan*, a treatise that advocates science education for women. The author states that science education equips a person to think clearly and with confidence. She acknowledges that a woman must serve her husband, but she points out that a girl must then have a right to choose her husband.

She also asserts that there should be no child marriage. In 1882, Tarabai Shinde wrote a thirty-seven-page treatise *Strī Puruṣ Tulnā* (comparing men with women). In this treatise, she points to several instances in which men are guilty of the very vices of which they accuse women and questions why behavior that is considered appropriate for men is disallowed for women. She describes herself as a "prisoner within a Maratha household" but writes with fiery freedom. In a scathing indictment of patriarchy in Indian and particularly Hindu society, this treatise advises men to be ideal husbands, deserving of their loyal wives. In 1882, Pandita Ramabai wrote *Strī Dharma Nīti*. In this treatise, addressed to women, the author advises women on how to be companions rather than slaves to their husbands. In 1863, Govind Madgaokar wrote a description of Bombay, and in 1865 N. V. Joshi similarly wrote about Pune. These two treatises provide sensitive descriptions of domestic and public life as it affected women. Finally, the collected writings of reformers such as Lokahitavadi, Jyotiva Phule, Agarkar, and Pandita Ramabai provide a comprehensive understanding of the situation of women in these times and of the movement for reform.

THE NOVEL

In 1865, Baba Padmanji, a social reformer from Bombay, published *Yamunāparyaṭan*, which deals with the issue of child widows and brings in the Christian concept of compassion. Not many other novels were published during the nineteenth century, but from the beginning of the twentieth century onward a rich crop of novels portrayed the lives and problems of nineteenth- and early twentieth-century women. One of the most sensitive and incisive novelists of this genre was Hari Narayan Apte. His sharp and sympathetic portrayal of the oppression of women and the conflicts they faced continues to be relevant. Malativai Bedekar, who wrote under the pseudonym Vibhavari Shirukar, was another sensitive writer of this period. She wrote about how men who claimed to be reformers treated their wives with the same lack of dignity as the diehard orthodox.

BIOGRAPHIES

A totally different and deeply authentic perspective on nineteenth-century social reform is available from the autobiographies written by women who were themselves affected by the movement. For instance, both Anandibai Karve, the wife of the famous reformer Maharshi Dhondo Keshav Karve, and her sister, Parvatibai Karve, wrote their autobiographies in the third decade of this century. From the 1870s on, he had fought for remarriage rights for upper-caste widows, which was unheard of. He married Anandibai, who had been widowed in childhood, and he was severely ostracized for this. Undaunted, he continued to serve the cause by starting a shelter for child widows. He saw to it that the girls who sought refuge in this shelter were taught to read and write, and this shelter gradually developed into a residential school. Stimulated by this success, Karve established, in 1916, what is now the prestigious S.N.D.T. Women's University. Anandibai's experiences as the wife of this social reformer and her own perspective on reform are extremely revealing.

For instance, Anandibai raises an interesting question about her own marriage. "I have never quite understood whether he married Anandi, or whether he married the ideal of widow remarriage," she comments. Anandibai's sister Parvatibai, also a child widow, had helped to raise funds in Africa, England, and the United States for the institutions they set up. She writes about this in her autobiography.

At least two women, wives of two of the most eminent reformers of their times, Ramabai Ranade (1862–1924), wife of Justice Mahadev Govind Ranade, and Yashodabai Agarkar (d.1938), wife of Gopal Ganesh Agarkar, have written their memoirs. These memoirs provide rare insights into the reform related work their husbands were involved in. However, by far the most famous, instructive, and deeply sensitive autobiography was written by Lakshmibai Tilak (1868–1936), the wife of the well-known poet Reverend Tilak, who converted to Christianity. The trauma of her husband's conversion, the chaos it created in her life, and the emotional turmoil she experienced as she herself made the transition from Hinduism to Christianity are delicately yet powerfully conveyed. Written at about the same time and equally powerful is the biography of Anandi Gopal Joshi, the first Maharashtra woman to qualify as a doctor. This biography portrays the compulsive, almost obsessive effort made by Anandi's husband, Gopalrao, to educate her. In the process, it also portrays one of the major paradoxes in Maharashtrian society: a husband so determined to educate his wife that he pushes her, almost ruthlessly. It also portrays Anandi's own resilient struggle and the deep conflicts she faced as she tried to balance her new views and perceptions as an educated woman with her own traditional values, as well as the traditional expectations of her husband.

CINEMA AND THEATER

Plays and films from the 1930s dealt with issues of social reform pertaining to women. For instance, *Śāradā*, a musical play, discussed child marriage, particularly the widespread practice of older men who took child brides; *Manoramā*, another play, portrayed how an alcoholic husband can ruin his wife and his home; and *Kulavadhu*, a play, dealt with the issue of whether women from respectable families should act in films. Parbhat Studio, established by V. Shantaram, produced several movies about the injustices women suffered. Many of these are considered to be all-time classics, such as *Kunku*,which deals with the issue of a girl married to a man several years older.

Silences That Need to Be Heard

As seen from the foregoing discussion, both the oral and the textual traditions of Maharashtra are highly articulate. They speak openly and directly about the situation of women, about their feelings, and about the conflicts and dilemmas they face. However, as anyone with research experience in the suppressed sectors of society knows, there is as much to learn from the unspoken and the unsaid as there is from what has been voiced. The following two examples illustrate silences that are pregnant with meaning.

Women in History

The compositions of the saint poetesses from the *bhakti* movement provide some information about women from the thirteenth century through the seventeenth. The nineteenth and the twentieth centuries are well covered by newspapers, short stories, the novel, biography, autobiography, theater and the cinema. But there is very little information available on women in the eighteenth century. Researchers involved in a program to bridge this gap found it difficult to locate any clues to the lives of ordinary women. Because there was occasional mention of women from the ruling Peshwa and Bhosle families in the documented history of the times, they decided to explore information on this sector.

In the regular historical documents and records, they found nothing more than the marginal mention of these women that they had already observed. It was obvious that historians did not care to take cognizance of what women did. However, at the end of sustained and persistent explorations, the researchers located well-preserved administrative orders, records of land settlement disputes, and masses of family, personal and official correspondence, that mentioned women. As they scanned through these materials and read between the lines, they found some references to women from the ruling families. Laboriously piecing these references together, they found some patterns.

Their preliminary findings indicate that these papers from the Peshwa and the Bhosle records, known as the Peshwa Bakhars, are a virtual mine of information about how royal widows, royal mothers guarding the interests of a son too young to rule, or queens ambitious to advance the prospects of their royal spouses use every opportunity available to them to cleverly steer state affairs in the direction they desired. The findings reveal some interesting patterns of difference between the functioning of the women belonging to the Peshwa, who were Brahmins by caste, and those belonging the Bhosle family, who were Marathas. There are also some amusing findings, which could be the basis for further exploration of the status of women in these ruling families. For instance, one of the Bakhar papers, which documents the monthly expenses in the household of a ruling family, mentions that the allowance of *kimam* (scented tobacco eaten with betel leaf) was not disbursed to the women in that household in a particular month because the men were away at war. This minor record is extremely suggestive of how minutely the comforts of women in ruling families were governed by consideration of the comforts they offered (or were not in a position to offer) their men. Regular historians have made extensive use of the Bakhars for their research, but these documents from the Peshwa rule remain a rich, unexplored source of material for research into involvement of women in the affairs of the state in eighteenth-century India.

The Silence of the Well-Behaved Woman

An even more important and critical silence is that maintained by Indian women in response to the expectation that well-behaved women will not speak in presence of elders and of others they respect. The latter traditionally includes the husband. For those who have learned to decipher it, however, this culturally conditioned silence can be extremely articulate. In fact, it speaks in many voices, each distinctly different. For instance, what the coy silence of the bashful bride says is very different from what is communicated by the nervous silence of the timid new daughter-in-law or by the frightened silence of the ill-treated wife. The defiant silence of an angry woman conveys messages that are altogether different from those conveyed by the resilient silence of the woman who has learned to endure. The eloquence of each of these silences is enhanced by the accompanying body language—for instance, the light steps that convey confidence and joy, in contrast to the entire body cowering in fear, the shoulder drawn in apprehension or slouched in apathy or despair, the lowered gaze, the movements of the feet and of the hands. There are other signals as well: the sound of toe rings on the bare floor, the jingle of glass, gold and silver bangles on the wrist, the way the sari *pallav* is held or draped.

Husbands, lovers, children, and others who have to live with the silence of women in the family have always interpreted these many silences and taken their cues from the accompanying body language. Social workers, counselors and others, who work with women who have been terrorized and traumatized are now learning to listen carefully to the silences of their clients. Often, they have nothing but these silences to go by in handling a case of rape, family violence or threatened dowry death. What a woman under threat, a victim of violence, or even the woman who is the aggressor feels or thinks has to be constructed from her silence. Vijaya Mehta, one of most eminent directors and actresses of the contemporary Marathi stage has used this language of silence to creatively portray some of the most important characters she has directed or played. Only recently has it been generally recognized that a wealth of valuable statements by women remains unheard and unrecorded because those who are educated are themselves highly articulate and unaware of the cultural conditioning that inhibits traditional uneducated women from speaking. Not very long ago, the educated used to dismiss the silence of the uneducated as their inability to speak. Now, as they explore the indigenous culture, they can capture and interpret the silences they face.

Exciting Possibilities

The current interest in understanding indigenous women's traditions and in reaching into the indigenous culture through the vernacular languages is exciting. It should lead to a deeper and more comprehensive understanding of how most Indian women think, feel, and behave and of how they define their roles, construct reality, and view change. Beyond these immediate gains, it should open up new pathways and avenues for research in disciplines such as social and cultural anthropology, sociology, history, psychology, and literature.

Exciting as it promises to be, exploration into traditions will not be easy. Traditions generally operate almost imperceptibly and are difficult to locate. For instance, some of the most educated, supposedly modern men and women are deeply influenced by and function according to orthodox traditions pertaining to what is considered appropriate or inappropriate for women. But this remains masked and invisible under the crust of their modernity.

The effort to learn from movements for social change on behalf of women is likely to run into similar problems. Their impact on Indian culture is difficult to sort out and identify because a unique feature of Indian society is its capacity to co-opt and thus nullify protest and change. This is perhaps nowhere so clearly evident as with respect to the several protestant movements within the Hindu religion. Again and again, such movements have merged with Hinduism and functioned as sects instead of maintaining their identity as break-away movements. The point may be illustrated with reference to the radical statements and exposures made by *bhakti* poets. Allowed to advance in the bold spirit of freedom and reform that they represented, these fiery statements could have created revolutions toward justice and equity in brahminical Indian society. But, quietly absorbed into a tradition in which the capacity to serve and suffer silently is considered a virtue, they have been converted into gentle, soothing, peaceful, relatively blunt devotional verse.

This chapter introduces the reader to the range of sources available to those who wish to explore Indian traditions concerning women through the Marathi culture. It also hopes to make the reader aware of some of the complexities involved in that exploration. Covering the variety of source materials adequately has not been possible; for example, the reference to these materials stops at the beginning of the twentieth century. The entire spectrum of material available could not possibly be accommodated within this brief chapter. Some cut-off point had to be arbitrarily chosen, and the third decade of this century was chosen because most of the seminal elements of tradition and change in Maharashtra society are contained within this period.

Actually, Marathi folk songs, folklore, folk theater, fasts, rituals and *kathās*, and all the other traditional media for the transmission and communication of values and culture remain a live tradition in Maharashtra. They keep evolving as dynamic elements of the culture, but even as they do so they are continuous with a past that goes back many centuries. Even more important, modern Marathi theater, literature, and other expression are also continuous with the past, for tradition does not terminate where modernity begins. What has been presented in this chapter should therefore help the reader to relate more comfortably to modern Marathi writing, theater, cinema, television, and other expression.

As is evident in this chapter, materials in the Marathi language are extremely valuable for understanding the traditions that have influenced Indian women and molded their psyches, the forces of change in favor of women in Indian society, and the current outlook and situation of Indian women. There have been some efforts to bring these materials to those in the English-speaking world who are interested in knowing something about Indian women. For instance, Lakshmibai Tilak's autobiography and Anandi Gopal Joshi's biography were translated into English several decades ago. More recently Marathi translations have appeared in Susie Tharu and K. Lalitha's pioneering *Women Writing in India*. But such efforts have so far been rare. In fact, Marathi-language material of the kind referred to here has not even been adequately explored by feminist scholars who write in Marathi. In 1990, the Women's Studies' Unit of the Tata Institute of Social Sciences at Bombay launched "The Footprints of the Movement for the Liberation of Women in Maharashtra," eight volumes that cover materials from the beginning of the *bhakti* movement in the thirteenth century to the present, but this series is only a beginning. One hopes that as the wealth of resource material in Marathi becomes better known, it will be more extensively and productively used.

Note

1. To understand the full range of women's writing from Maharashtra, see Susie Tharu and K. Lalitha, eds. *Women Writing in India* (1991), especially the selections from Bahina Bai (1628–1700), "Atmanvedana," pp. 107–115; Tarabai Shinde (1858–1910), "Stri purush tulana" (a comparison of men and women), pp. 221–235; Pandita Ramabai Saraswati (1858–1922), " The High Caste Hindu Women," pp.243–253; Kashibai Kantikar (1861–1948), "Palkicha Gonda" (The Silk Tassel in the Palanquin), pp. 256–262; Ramabai Ranade (1862–1924), "Amachya Ayushatil Kahi Athawani" (Memoirs of Our Life Together), pp. 281–290; Cornelia Sorabji (1866–1954), "India Calling" pp. 296–309; Lakshmibai Tilak (1868–1936), "Smriti Chitre" (Memory Sketches), pp. 309–322; Bahinabai Chaudhuri (1880–1951), "Ata Maza Mate Jeeva" (Now I Remain for Myself), pp. 352–354; Anonymous (1881, 1889), "Mumbaitil Prarthanasamajsambandi Striyancha Sabheta Eka Baine Vachlela Nibandha" (A Speech by a Woman at a Women's Meeting of the Prarthana Samaj) and "Hindu Vidwanchi Dukhit Stithi" (The Plight of Hindu Widows as Described by a Widow Herself), pp. 356–358; Indira Sahasrabuddhe (1890–?)," Balutai Dhada Ghe" (Learn a Lesson, Balutai), pp. 385–390; Vibhavati Shirukar (Malatibai Bedekar, b. 1905), "Virlele Swapna" (The Dream That Has Faded), pp. 424–437; Geeta Sane (b. 1907), "Hirvalikhal" (Under the Grass of the Green Lawn), pp. 444–450.

References

Athvale, Parvati. *Hindu Widow: An Autobiography*. Tr. Justin E. Abbot. Repr. New Delhi: Reliance Publishing House,1986.

Desai, Neera. "Women in Bhakti Movement." *Samya Shakti* 1, 2 (1983), pp. 92–100.

Ghadially, Rehana, ed. *Women in Indian Society: A Reader*. New Delhi: Sage Publications, 1988.

Kakar, Sudhir. *The Inner World: A Psycho-Analytic Study of Childhood and Society in India*, 2d ed. Delhi: Oxford University Press, 1982.

Kosambi, Meera. "Women, Emancipation and Equality: Pandita Ramabai's Contribution to Women's Cause." *Economic and Political Weekly* 23, 44 (1988), pp. 38–49.

Mies, Maria. *Indian Women and Patriarchy*. Delhi: Concept, 1980.

O'Hanlon, Rosalind. *Caste, Conflict and Ideology: Mahatma Jotirao Phule and Low Caste Protest in Nineteenth Century Western India*. Cambridge: Cambridge University Press, 1985.

Omvedt, Gail. *Cultural Revolt in Colonial India: The Non Brahmin movement in Western India 1873–1930*. Bombay: Scientific Socialist Education Trust, 1976.

Shah, A. B., ed. *The Letters and Correspondence of Pandita Ramabai*. Bombay: The State Board for Literature and Culture, 1977.

Thapar, Romila. *Ancient Indian Social History: Some Interpretations*. Delhi: Orient Longman, 1979.

Tharu, Susie, and K. Lalitha. *Women Writing in India: 600 B.C. to the Present*. New York: Feminist Press, 1991.

18

DORIS R. JAKOBSH

The Construction of Gender in History and Religion

The Sikh Case

> The status of women was not an issue in Sikhism. Equality was implicit . . . . Women are considered as an integral part of society who must not be excluded by any ritual or doctrinal consideration. Since rituals tend to be exclusive, they cannot be made part of a true faith. In other words, the position of women could be a touchstone for the genuineness of a faith.[1]
>
> To know whether to take speakers seriously is difficult in a society that blurs the boundary between serious and strategic communication. When are promises or statements of intent, for instance, merely the casual talk of everyday life or strategic manoeuvres in compromising situations rather than acts of serious communication?[2]

The role and status of Sikh women in history have not been given a great deal of attention in Sikh studies. Although Sikh apologetics repeatedly insist that men and women are inherently equal in the Sikh worldview, in reality, historical writings say virtually nothing about women, apart from minimal asides about the occasional exceptional woman who has been deemed worthy enough to have *made* the pages of history. They then are typically held up as the standard by which to measure the egalitarian ethos of the Sikh tradition.

Clarence McMullen notes that in speaking of religious beliefs and practices there is the need to make the distinction between what he labels as normative and operative beliefs:

> Normative beliefs and practices are those which are officially stated and prescribed or proscribed by a recognized religious authority, which can be a person, organization, or an official statement. Operative beliefs and practices, on the other hand, are those actually held by people.[3]

Although McMullen uses these distinctions in his delineation of contemporary beliefs and practices of the Sikhs in rural Punjab, they are useful in analyzing the role and status of women from the larger theoretical perspective of history as well. With regard to the inherent egalitarianism of Sikh men and women, one writer asserts: "The Sikh woman has enjoyed superior status compared with her counterparts in other communities. She has earned this by showing the ability to stand by the side of her husband in difficult times."[4] Yet, if women and men are inherently equal in the tradition in terms of roles and status, why are they not given similar representation in the pages of Sikh history? It is a question perhaps best explained in light of McMullen's differentiation; namely, what is officially touted as normative with regard to gender in history is not necessarily the same as the actual and operative aspects of the same Sikh history.

Harjot Oberoi has noted that the principles of "silence" and "negation" are paramount in addressing issues that could be conceived as ambiguous within the tradition.[5] I would add the principles of "accommodation" and "idealization," specifically with regard to the question of gender within the tradition. The focus of the chapter will be to outline and analyze the role and status of women from within each of these four paradigms.

The guiding principle within Sikh history is silence with regard to women. Given the traditional ideology of history being about political and economic development, historians (Sikh or non-Sikh) have been skeptical about women's history as having anything tangible to offer in the production of historical knowledge, in that they are generally perceived as not having played important roles in the businesses of economics, war, or politics. It must also be underlined that, given the fact that women have not generally written their own histories, historical accounts are written through the lens of the male gender.[6] What was and is important to men thus becomes the focus of historical analysis.[7] Needless to say, the overwhelming impression we receive from reading the texts of Sikh history is that women do not have a history. From the silences surrounding women of history, their experiences and lives can be perceived only as inconsequential. Yet, "We know that besides history through mankind there exists a 'herstory.' Many aspects of this herstory have been wiped out so that it is quite difficult to reconstruct its basic elements."[8]

According to some feminist historians, history has less to do with facts than with historians' perception of history. Although traditionally historical writers have operated on the principle of objectivity—that is, pursuing facts, stringing these bits of information together, and thus presenting objective "history"—a new wave of scholarly analysis, including feminist theory, argues that the process is not nearly as objective as was once believed. There has been a slow recognition that "the writing of history [is] a mental activity in its own right, somewhere between natural science and the writing of fiction."[9] The historian thus has an active, creative role in the documentation of the process of history. The specific questions asked are of the essence. Through the questions put to history, a person chooses to attend to certain aspects of history; presumably, what is presented is in the writer's estimation more important than what is left out. When looking to Sikh women's history, we are told as much about the values of the chroniclers of history as about the actual events surrounding women themselves. Consequently, one is faced with the often painstaking task of piecing together aspects of Sikh history that have been either disregarded or interpreted to fit into the dominant male worldview of the time. Ultimately, then, the history of half the Sikh population—namely, male history—is a distorted history. Certainly, integral to the study of women in Sikh history is the principle of stony silence, one mechanism used to deal with the discrepancies between Sikh ideology as egalitarian with regard to women and their exclusion from the process of history.

The second principle noted is that of negation. Harjot Oberoi uses this principle to point out how heterogenous elements in Sikh history—those labeled as deviant, marginal, threatening, or unimportant—are negated to "generate homogeneity and represent the Sikhs as a collectivity which shared the same values and movements."[10] Though this chapter does not deal specifically with the same issues of heterogeneity and homogeneity, the principle of negation is particularly useful in exploring the ways in which ambiguous aspects of women-focused history have been presented. Here I turn initially to M. K. Gill's *The Role and Status of Women in Sikhism.*[11] Though the title denotes a more extensive analysis of the role of women within Sikhism, Gill's primary focus is what she presents as the institution of the guru *mahals*, the wives of the gurus. While giving attention to each *mahal* within the tradition in terms of her achievements and contributions, Gill also addresses the fact that these women are simply not known within or outside of the tradition, in spite of Gill's understanding of the guru *mahals* as integral to the very development of the fledgling Sikh movement. Although she implicity questions the indifference of Sikh historians to them, this point is certainly not the gist of her book. For Gill, "it is the attitude of the Gurus towards women which becomes more important than the availability of material regarding the guru *mahals*."[12] Gill purports that the gurus unequivocally raised the status of women, despite the fact that:

> The guru histories are, by and large, silent about the wives of the gurus. From Guru Nanak to Guru Gobind Singh the wives have been treated as part of the historical background, not as individual in themselves . . . [Yet] man does not communicate by words alone . . . even the silence of later historians all point to a sociological fact. It is the silence of respect that is accorded to womanhood in the Punjabi culture and ethos. It helps surround her with an invisible cloak of dignity . . .The silence that surrounds the Guru's family is an intrinsic feature of Sikh tradition.[13]

Negating the obvious—namely, that women, *even* the guru *mahals* are simply not viewed as consequential to the history of the Sikh tradition—she maintains that the silence surrounding the *mahals* is indicative of the respect given women in Sikhism.

Further, Gill maintains that after the death of the tenth guru, Guru Gobind Singh, it was Mata Sundri, one of his three wives, who for thirty-nine or forty years took over the political and spiritual leadership of the Khalsa. Ironically, this points to Mata Sundri leading the Sikh Panth longer than any of the nine gurus succeeding Guru Nanak, the founder of the Sikh tradition. Though Gill presents Mata Sundri as leading the Sikh Panth through one of its more difficult and divisive periods,[14] she acknowledges that surprisingly little is known of her actual leadership.[15] She notes: "History is silent on this point, but the silence of history is merely a reflection of her personality."[16]

Traditional history, too, maintains that Guru Govind Singh, having no living survivors (read, *male*), ended the living guru succession and decreed the twin doctrines of Guru Granth and Guru Panth as personifying and continuous with the guru.[17] It is clear that Mata Sundri's leadership of the Khalsa was not deemed sufficiently legitimate, either by Guru Govind Singh or by her contemporaries in the Khalsa, to formally initiate her as the principal leader of the Sikhs. To accommodate the lack of male successors to the guru, a doctrinal shift in the institution of the guruship had to be made.

Fitting squarely into the principle of negation, a recent volume presents the Sikh rite of initiation into the Khalsa, established by Guru Gobind Singh in 1699, as particularly indicative of the inherent equality between men and women.[18] Kanwaljit Kaur Singh maintains that Guru Gobind Singh, the tenth guru, initiated both men and women into the Khalsa movement.[19] Yet initiation of women into the Khalsa appears to be a much later development, possibly originating with the Namdhari or Kuka reform movement well after the annexation of the Punjab by the British.[20] Preaching against the prevalent social taboos of the time, particularly those that affected women—the dowry system, *satī* (advocating, instead, widow remarriage), and child marriage—the Namdharis also supported the notion of women initiates into their fold. In 1858, Baba Ram Singh, the leader of the Namdharis, baptized a woman named Khemo of village Siyahar in the district of Ludhiana.[21] Surjit Kaur Jolly maintains that until this point women were not included in the ceremonial baptism of the Sikhs.[22]

Though dealing more specifically with scriptural exegesis than with women of history, Nikki-Guninder Kaur-Singh's contributions, too, tend to fit into the paradigm of negation. Singh purports that "breaking all patriarchal idols and icons, the Sikh sacred literature celebrates the feminine aspect of the Transcendent and poetically affirms the various associations and images that are born from her."[23] Focusing on the feminine grammatical forms and images within the Sikh scripture, Singh suggests that it is the feminine in its myriad forms that is predominant over the male.[24] Yet, this prevalence of the female over the male is contestable, in that the Ultimate in the Sikh scripture, the *Adi Granth*, is almost exclusively conceived in masculine terms, *Akal Purakh*, *Karta Purakh*—*Purakh* referring to "man."

Singh asserts that with regard to female imagery within the *Adi Granth*, "no negative associations belittle her."[25] Yet numerous passages in the scripture associate woman with *maya*, that which is sensual as opposed to spiritual:

> Attachment to progeny, wife is poison
> None of these at the end is of any avail. (AG: 41)[26]

> *Maya* attachment is like a loose woman,
> A bad woman, given to casting spells. (AG: 796)

Further, while women are exalted when obedient and subservient, as wife to her divine husband, men are ridiculed for those same characteristics:

> Men obedient to their womenfolk
> Are impure, filthy, stupid,
> Man lustful, impure, their womenfolk counsel follow (AG: 304).

There is more to be said about the subject, but suffice it to say that Singh's approach fits squarely within the principle of negation previously outlined.[27]

A principle that was used particularly by the Singh Sabha reformers in the late nineteenth century is accommodation. Here a comparison of the effects of French colonialism in Muslim Algeria with the Singh Sabha reformers and British colonists is particularly helpful. Kay Boals writes about a reformist consciousness that developed among educated Muslim men after the colonization of Algeria. She notes the attempt to accommodate the valuable aspects of the dominant culture (colonial) and ground them in the tradition of Islam. It is thus an endeavor to reform and reinterpret the religion and culture of the time:

> This process involves a reinterpretation of that tradition to read back into its past the genesis of ideas which in fact have been absorbed from the dominant culture . . . The reformists, however, must show that what they advocate has long been part of their own culture and is firmly rooted there, when in fact that is usually not the case. It is not hard to see that in such a dilemma one's desire to succeed would promote easy distortion of the tradition, distortion which is probably both conscious and unconscious.[28]

Further, reformers typically were thoroughly educated in Islamic law and culture while highly exposed to Western influences. Boals notes that this type of education was characteristically open only to men, and thus men were at the forefront of reform, especially with regard to gender relations:

> While reformist consciousness is certainly not feminist in any very far-reaching sense . . . in many Muslim countries the theoretical arguments in favor of reforming Muslim practice in the realm of male-female relations were advanced by men . . . Reformist consciousness, by wanting to purify the tradition, takes that tradition very seriously as something of value to be reinterpreted for modern life. It is thus concerned with male-female relations, not directly and in themselves, but rather as they reflect the Koranic prescriptions (rightly interpreted and purified) for relationships between the sexes.[29]

The time and context of the Singh Sabhas in the late nineteenth century presents a similar scenario. Imbued by a liberal Western education, decrying undesirable aspects of the Sikh tradition, yet unwilling to reject it outright, these "new elites" tended to walk the often shaky line of accommodation between two often opposing worldviews.[30] Ultimately, their focus was the reformation and reinterpretation of the Sikh tradition, made possible by their ascendancy into positions of power and prestige. Harjot Oberoi maintains that the development of print culture in Punjab, along with their Western education, gave the Sabha reformers the necessary tools to reinterpret the Sikh tradition armed with "resources towards etching out a novel cultural map for Punjab that would define their aspirations and reflect the changed environment in the province. The canvas for this map was made out of borrowings from the European enlightenment, particularly rationalism."[31]

As in Algeria, the role and status of women became an important platform on which the Singh Sabhas preached their reforms. There were a number of reasons for this focus. Christian missionary activities had begun an active campaign to reach both the outcastes of society and women, groups relegated to the bottom of the Sikh and Hindu societal hierarchy. Missionaries began going into the homes, attracting women from the very bastions of protection, and finding in them converts to Christianity.[32] Alarmed by these conversions, the reformers needed to safeguard the Sikh tradition from the menacing activities of the missionaries. The emancipation of women, particularly female education, became a central issue for the Singh Sabhas.

So, too, was the development of female role models in literature. The prolific writer Bhai Vir Singh wrote numerous novels with female figures in the central roles. The novel *Sundri* is perhaps his most famous, depicting a young woman who is true to the faith, devout and pure, active in battle, and elevated at times to the status of a goddess.[33] While the story is designed to advance the cause of Sikh women, it also attempts to glorify the status of Sikh women as compared with their Hindu and Muslim counterparts, and herein we find an important difference from the Algerian reformers, whose main goal was to accommodate positive aspects of colonial culture by reinterpreting those attitudes into their own tradition. In the Sikh case, reformers concurred with this aim yet had another equally important objective—namely, the need to show the complete separation of Sikhism from the dominant Hindu tradition.[34] Thus, we have Sundri pleading with her fellow Sikhs:

> I entreat you to regard your women as equal partners and never ill-treat them with harshness and cruelty . . . In the Hindu Shastras . . . the woman is treated as Shudra—an outcast. All the Gurus have praised and commended women. In Guru Granth Sahib, woman has been eulogized and she has been given equal right of worship and recitation of the Holy Name.[35]

The need to show that this positive regard of women was integral to the Sikh tradition—as *opposed* to the oppressive Hindu religion and *similar* to the claims of the Christian missionaries and colonizers—was thus of utmost importance for the Singh Sabhas. Much of the revitalization effort must be seen in light of these anti-Hindu, anti-Christian sentiments, particularly with regard to Sikh scripture, for only thus could it be "proven" that this was a long-standing tradition within Sikhism. Given Guru Nanak's absorption in the *bhakti* worldview of the fifteenth century, there was ample evidence with which to empower women.[36] It was Guru Nanak, the founder of the Sikh tradition, who stated:

> Of woman are we born, of woman conceived,
> To woman engaged, to woman married . . .
> It is through woman that order is maintained.
> Then why call her inferior from whom all *Rajas* are born?
> Woman is born of woman;
> None is born but of woman. (AG: 473)[37]

Armed with hymns that supported their claims, the reformers insisted that what they were advocating was very much in line with the original designs of the Sikh gurus, as opposed to the degradation of the Sikh tradition as a result of the dreaded influence of Hinduism, upon which all ills within Sikh society were heaped.

And yet, J. S. Grewal maintains that, upon examination of the hymns of Guru Nanak in particular:

> It appears that Guru Nanak has very little to say about what today are called "social evils." He disapproves of the custom of becoming *sati*, but almost incidentally. He appears to be familiar with the institutions of slavery but he has little to say about it. He has little to say about "child marriage" or about the disabilities of the widow . . . Guru Nanak is most articulate in his social criticism when customs and institutions appear to touch upon religion.[38]

It is not the evils of the caste system or the status of women that occupies the message of Guru Nanak but rather the spiritual domain. One's high or low status, one's sex, one's race—these are totally irrelevant to one's salvation.

It is the principle of accommodation that has characterized almost all subsequent engagement with regard to women and the Sikh tradition, including the present day. Passages from the Granth that show positive regard for women as integral to the very core of the Sikh tradition are quoted and requoted, as are a few choice anecdotes from the lives of the gurus, with regard to the condemnation of *satī*, pollution, purdah, and female infanticide. Yet, this interpretation of Sikh history can perhaps best be captured by Eric Hobsbawm's understanding of "invented tradition." He notes that "insofar as there is such reference to a historic past, the peculiarity of 'invented' traditions is that the continuity with it is largely factitious. In short, they are responses to novel situations which take the form of reference to old situations . . ."[39] In the case of the Sikh reformers, historical and theological "inventions" with regard to the status of women must invariably be understood as innovative responses to the rapidly changing cultural and socioeconomic world within which they had achieved hegemony.

Let me turn briefly, once again to Nikki-Guninder Kaur-Singh, who is very much in line with this principle of accommodation in her analysis of the goddess Durgā in the writings of Guru Gobind Singh.[40] She critiques the way many Sikh historians and writers have attempted to distance the guru from passages celebrating the goddess Durgā and strive to show that they were not actually written by Gobind Singh but by "Hindu" elements within his entourage. Kaur-Singh decries this as a ". . . not fully conscious fear of 'female power'. "[41] Instead, she insists, Guru Gobind Singh's incorporation of the deity is indicative of the positive Sikh attitude toward the feminine, though it can never be understood as goddess *worship*. Accentuating the continuity of the gurus within the Sikh tradition, Singh attempts to accommodate the writings of the tenth guru and the clear rejection of the earlier gurus of the goddess within the Sikh sacred scripture:

> Whoever worships the Great Mother
> Shall though man, be incarnate as woman. (AG:874)

Kaur-Singh maintains that Durgā's great literary merit was recognized by the guru, who utilized the symbolism to "renovate and regenerate an effete society."[42] As opposed to being a devotee of the great goddess, Guru Gobind Singh is posited as an insightful artist. Yet we must wonder where literary license ends and veneration begins. In what appears to be an uncompromising tribute to Durgā, the Dasam Granth states:

The sovereign deity on earth
Enwrapped in all the regal pomp
To you be the victory,
O you of mighty arms. ("Akal Ustati": *Dasam Granth Sahib*, vol. 1, 44)

Historical research has indicated that remnants of the feminine, the goddess, are present in all traditions that are indubitably monotheistic and inadvertently androcentric. The questions that need to be answered are: "Why did monotheism attempt to get rid of the goddess? Could it have anything to do with androcentrism and patriarchy? Feminist studies of the Ancient Near East make it overwhelmingly obvious that such is the case."[43] In the Durgā mythology of the Dasam Granth, Sikhs have the goddess in their midst. To draw an unrealistically rigid line between the recognition of Durgā's literary merit and actual homage to the goddess is to miss an opportunity to explore how and why a system did away with the feminine, which was so obviously and critically integrated into early Sikh society. Indeed, Kaur-Singh's selective endorsement of the writings of Guru Gobind Singh adheres well to the principle of accommodation previously outlined in her attempt to reinterpret aspects of the goddess tradition in a manner that reflects its emancipatory qualities for women, while not fully exploring the implications of Durgā mythology for the Sikh tradition.

The fourth principle utilized in Sikh history with regard to women is idealization. Similar to the principle of accommodation, idealization is an extension of the former, with important differences as well. Positive strains of scripture are again upheld as normative and of ultimate authority, but the dominant need is not so much to *reform* the tradition as to *idealize* aspects of history and scripture as they pertain to women. Glorified examples of Sikh women who lived exceptional lives, mainly as warrior figures, such as Mai Bhago in Guru Gobind Singh's retinue,[44] Sada Kaur, the mother-in-law of Maharajah Ranjit Singh,[45] and Bibi Sahib Kaur,[46] are held up as women whose illustrious deeds are the result of the "transformation of Guru Nanak's philosophy in action that preaches equality among the human beings irrespective of caste, creed, or sex."[47]

Similarly, M. K. Gill, in her treatment of the guru *mahals* notes with regard to the *gurdwara* bearing Mata Sundri's name:

> [It] is not merely a historical monument . . . It is rather, a cherished haven of refuge where the devotee finds inner peace and his sense of emptiness is washed away . . . Mata Sundri has a place among the few who are immortal, ever living. For hundreds of people today it is matter of a daily relationship with her memory.[48]

Given that Gill remonstrates earlier that few Sikhs are even knowledgeable about the basic facts of Mata Sundri's life, this effort to uplift the name and contributions of Mata Sundri must be understood in light of the principle of idealization.

Rita Gross maintains that in traditional historical accounts, when women *are* mentioned in the annals of history, it is only because they deviate from the norm—that is exceptional women who do play a part in what is considered to be "normative history":

> Androcentric thinking deals with them [exceptional women] only as objects exterior to humankind, needing to be explained and fitted in somewhere, having

> the same epistemological and ontological status as trees, unicorns, deities, and other objects that must be discussed to make experience intelligible.[49]

In the paradigms that represent Sikh women's history as outlined in this chapter— specifically the principle of idealization but accommodation as well— unicorns are presented as normative, thus indicative of the romanticizing tendencies of the Singh Sabhas and those who unquestioningly follow in their footsteps. Further, the occasional woman of note was generally situated in the uppermost echelon of society. As wives and sisters of rajas, they certainly did not lead lives that were very much akin to their contemporaries. In many ways, then, they conjure up false images as to the roles and status of women in Sikh society. Returning once more to Clarence McMullen's observations, there is a vast divide between that which is normative and that which is operative in traditional Sikh history as it pertains to women.

In the examples noted in this chapter, it is specifically Nikki Kaur-Singh who situates herself squarely within Western feminist theological traditions. However, many feminist scholars within the study of religion insist that the central challenge in religious studies, as in other fields, is its delineation and critique of androcentrism, which Kaur-Singh has not done. In other words, she has not delved into the ambiguous aspects within the tradition, in relation to scripture. As pointed out earlier, while there *are* women-affirming tendencies within the Adi Granth, there are also those that support the subordination of women. The feminist theologians to whom Nikki Kaur–Singh pays tribute in her book insist that to expose androcentrism within religious traditions means moving beyond sheer affirmation (in Kaur Singh's case, through the unearthing of female principles within Sikh scripture and literature) toward a "hermeneutic of suspicion," following the model of Paul Ricoeur.[50] Indeed, there is a complex interplay between religion and social change. Nancy Falk in *Women, Religion, and Social Change* notes that "religion is among the foremost of institutions which conserve society, encoding stabilizing worldviews and values, and transmitting these from generation to generation."[51] Only upon an unmasking of the androcentric presumptions of writers and their writings, including sacred scripture, and only upon a suspicious reading entailing a thorough evaluation of the *inherent* sexist attitudes and practices within religious and historical works is one enabled to understand the sources and symbols within the tradition that sustain the subordination of women throughout history.

Conclusion: Moving Beyond Description

Much of what has been presented as the construction of women within Sikh history and religion fits largely into what feminist historians have characterized as a descriptive approach—or "her-story" approach—to the history of women.[52] This first wave of feminist history—namely, the resurrection of lost women, as well as a reassessment of activities that have traditionally been deemed unworthy of fulfilling the requirements of important or "real" history—has been a critical aspect of the rewriting of history. Yet, while "her-story" is fundamental in addressing the paucity of historical knowledge about women, it does not confront the issue of *how* the hierarchy of male-female, dominant-subordinate is constructed and legitimated throughout history. As historian Joan Wallach Scott insists, a more radical feminist epistemology is necessary in the study of history.[53] "The emphasis on 'how' suggests a study of processes, not of origins, of multiple rather than single causes, of rhetoric rather than ideology or consciousness. It does not abandon attention to structures and institutions, but it does insist that we need to understand what these organizations mean in order to understand how they work."[54] Michel Foucault's analysis of the domain of the private and, by implication, the feminine, based on an understanding of power as dispersed constellations of unequal relationships, discursively constituted in social "fields of force," is particularly useful in coming to an understanding of how unequal relations are created and sustained.[55]

Advocating a different perspective, Pierre Bourdieu emphasizes another source of power, which he defines as "symbolic relations of power," which "tend to reproduce and to reinforce the power relations that constitute the structure of social space."[56] These go beyond (though are not exclusive of) economic and political spheres and include power located within language, religion, education, art, and ideology—areas where women's participation is more readily accessible.[57]

As well, historians are moving beyond a solely women-centered approach to history to an analysis of the *construction* of identity, specifically gender identity in historical writings. Thus, views of gender identity as "natural" and primordial are challenged. Scott, for instance, advocates an understanding that gender as constructed for *both* women and men has significant consequences:

> The term "gender" suggests that relations between the sexes are a primary aspect of social organization (rather than following from, say, economic or demographic pressures); that the terms of male and female identities are in large part culturally determined (not produced by individuals or collectivities entirely on their own); and that differences between the sexes constitute and are constituted by hierarchical social structures.[58]

This chapter is not of a scope to allow for more than a cursory reference to these theoretical approaches to history, but it does point to possibilities and the need for historical research to go beyond description of Sikh history as it pertains to gender. The historian is challenged not only to analyze the relationships between women and men but also to pursue questions with regard to the correlation between historical knowledge and gender relations on a broader scale. In other words, how does the analytical category of gender function in comprehensive social relations? To move from a descriptive approach in an attempt to resolve these and other questions will necessarily require moving beyond existing histories to engender the *rewriting* of history. With regard to the construction of women in Sikh history and religion, alternative approaches are more likely to scrutinize *all* aspects of the past, without the need to idealize on one hand and relegate to silence on the other.

Notes

1. Suri (1989), p. 112.
2. Fenn (1982), p. 113.

3. McMullen (1989), p. 5.

4. Kaur-Singh (1994), p. 152.

5. With regard to the principles of silence and negation, Oberoi notes, "In the Sikh case, historical texts are virtually silent about religious diversity, sectarian conflicts, nature worship, witchcraft, sorcery, spirits, magical healing, omens, wizards, miracle saints, goddesses, ancestral spirits, festivals, exorcism, astrology, divination, and village deities. When, occasionally, some of these are mentioned in historical texts, they serve to dress up an argument about how Sikhism was rapidly relapsing into Hinduism in the nineteenth century, how its adherents deviated from the 'true' articles of faith and subscribed to 'superstitious' and 'primitive' beliefs. Ultimately, this argument in official Sikh historiography goes on to establish that Sikhs were delivered from the bondage of un-Sikh beliefs by the intervention of the late-nineteenth-century Singh Sabha movement. Scholars who favour such interpretation are backing what I call the principle of negation. They are of the view that Singh Sabha reformers were in line with traditional Sikh doctrines when they opposed a large terrain of Sikh beliefs and practices in the nineteenth century" (Oberoi, 1994, pp. 30–31).

6. There are rare instances of women writers in Sikh history. When they do appear, their contributions have often been interpreted as mere guises for the men who were the "real" voices of authority. Kanwaljit Kaur-Singh notes that Mata Gujri, the mother of Guru Gobind Singh,wrote *Hukamnamas*, letters of instruction written to the Sikh Panth, which are regarded as binding on the whole Sikh community. Kanwaljit Kaur-Singh adds, "In the case of Mata Gujri, who shouldered the responsibility of looking after the affairs of the Singh *Panth* during the minority of Guru Gobind Singh, there were *Hukamnamas* to the *sangat*, written by her and accepted by the community, but the credit is given to her brother, Kirpal Chand. Of course, Kirpal Chand was Mata Gujri's adviser, but she was at the helm of affairs" (Kaur-Singh, 1994, p. 155).

7. Amrita Pritam, the celebrated poet and novelist, was asked to write a poem for the five-hundredth anniversary of Guru Nanak. She produced a work entitled "The Annunciation," which caused considerable uproar in Punjab and in the wider Indian community (Pritam, 1975, pp. 37–40). Focusing on the hopes, dreams, and bodily experiences of the pregnant Tripta, Guru Nanak's mother, it was not typical of the devotional poetry written for this quincentenary. Further, the son is never even mentioned, the focus and silent acclamation for his mother, the lifegiver of Guru Nanak. For Pritam, it was enough, more than enough to become one with Mata Tripta as she awaited the birth of her extraordinary son, yet undeniably one senses Pritam's love and devotion to Guru Nanak. The outcry that followed the publication of the poem was ruthless, demanding that the poem be banned by the government and questioning how a lowly "love's worm" could attempt to write on so elevated a theme (Pritam, 1989, p. 53). It would appear that history, understood and presented from the perspective of the feminine, can only be vilified and postulated as incomparable to *real* history, that of the male perspective.

8. Albrecht-Heide (1988), p. 124.

9. Bosch (1987), p. 48.

10. Oberoi (1994), p. 34.

11. Gill (1995).

12. Ibid. pp. 4–5.

13. Ibid. pp. 52–53.

14. Traditional sources maintain that Guru Gobind Singh passed on the leadership of the Khalsa to Banda Bahadur just before his death in 1708. Although Banda Bahadur has come to be viewed as a rather mythical figure, an honored warrior fighting for justice during a time of fierce persecution of the Sikhs, he was also the source of a tremendous rift in the fledgling Khalsa movement. McLeod notes: "There were evidently disputes between Banda

and his immediate followers on the one hand and the so called Tat Khalsa (the 'true' Khalsa) on the other. These disputes, which concerned the proper form of disagreement first developed between the Bandai Khalsa and the Tat Khalsa, a period much too brief for clear definitions to have emerged on all significant points" (McLeod, 1992, p. 48). Gill presents Mata Sundri as the effective leader of the Tat Khalsa during this time.

15. To illustrate lack of knowledge about the female leaders of the Khalsa, another writer depicts Mata Sahib Devan, another wife of the guru, as the leader of the Sikhs. Joginder Singh notes: "Punjabis venerate Mata Sahib Devan as the mother of the 'Khalsa.' She outlived her husband Guru Gobind Singh. She saved Sikhism from the schism into which it was about to fall after Banda's death. It was at her bidding that the martyr-saint, Bhai Mani Singh, was appointed the head priest of Harimander, now famous as the Golden Temple" (J. Singh, 1983, p. 7).

16. Gill (1995), p. 59.

17. McLeod explains the doctrines in the following manner: "The orthodox doctrine affirms that Guru Govind Singh, immediately prior to his death in 1708, declared that after he had gone there would be no successor as personal Guru. The eternal Guru would remain with his followers, mystically present in the sacred scripture and in the gathered community. The scripture thus becomes the Guru Granth and the assembled community becomes the Guru Panth" (McLeod, 1992, p. 52).

18. Oberoi describes this rite as follows: "By the turn of the seventeenth century, the Khalsa was much more than a semantic category analogous to imperial revenue terminology: *he* [italics mine] was a new person with a concrete identity. His personhood came to be confirmed through an unusual initiation rite called *khande ki pahul*, the like of which had never existed before in South Asia. Most religious sects in the past had initiated their fresh constituents, and this appears to be the case with the Sikh tradition as well, through *charn amrit*: a ritual in which the toe of a guru was dipped into water that was then given to the new initiate to drink. Although we have no contemporary description of the *khande ki pahul*, this much is certain, that it involved the use of a heavy double-edged sword and sanctified water. Whatever its precise form and sequence, this new initiation ritual and its distinctive religious imagery gave the Khalsa a powerful symbolic grid on which to proclaim and affirm their new identity. To this new identity, Gobind Singh gave further shape by commanding the Khalsa always to carry arms on his person, and by making hookah-smoking taboo." It would appear that the rite is clearly male-defined. (Oberoi, 1994, pp. 60–61); see also Oberoi in Lorenzen (1995), pp. 44–45.

19. K. Kaur-Singh (1992), p. 99.

20. Jolly notes that the Namdharis were founded in 1847 by a Sikh named Balak Singh of the Arora caste, though it is Ram Singh who is viewed as the official founder of the Namdharis. Jolly adds that Baba Ram Singh received "spiritual powers from Baba Balak Singh of Hazro and was the twelfth *guru* in succession to the mortal *Gurus* of the Sikhs" (Jolly, 1988 p. 132). Namdharis were also known as Kukas, or shouters, because they fell into states of frenzy during their religious exercises and recited their prayers in loud cries.

21. Ibid., p. 89. Ironically, this reform movement was considered heretical, given its doctrine of spiritual lineage beyond that of Guru Gobind Singh. McLeod notes,"They suffered agonizing exclusion from their own caste brotherhood and from normal intercourse with others; they were banned from the use of wells and cremation grounds; they were deprived of traditional ceremonies, and much more. Repeated efforts were made, in all ways and by all means, to persecute these loyal teachers of the Nirankari faith" (McLeod, 1984, p. 122).

22. Jolly (1988), p. 89. She adds (p. 122) that the Bedis and Sodhis, descendants of the Sikh Gurus, were critical of Ram Singh because he had undermined their monopoly of baptizing people at the major Sikh centers.

23. N. Kaur-Singh (1993), pp. 243–244.

24. Kaur-Singh advocates the belief that the gurus, though male, understood their words, their message, to be female, in congruence with the feminine form of *bani*. "But the Sikh Word is not a masculine *logos*, it is the beautiful and formless *bani*. The Word proclaimed by the scriptures and secular writers of Sikhism is Woman" (N. Kaur-Singh, 1993, p. 252). Yet, this grammatically feminine form of the sacred word is very much in line with the Vedic understanding of sacred speech, deified as the goddess *Vāc*. What is not clear is whether the male gurus, in fact, understood their enunciation to be feminine or whether the representation of sacred speech in the feminine form is simply indicative of their surrounding social, cultural, and religious surroundings. To move from a grammatically feminine form of speech to the theological underpinnings of the gurus' egalitarian ethos is conceivably more a reading *into* the term *bani* as opposed to the actual intent of the gurus.

25. Ibid., p. 4.

26. These quotations are from the English translation of the *Adi Granth* (1987).

27. For a more detailed exploration of some of the issues raised here, see Jakobsh (1996).

28. Boals (1976), pp. 198–199.

29. Ibid. p. 203.

30. Referring to the privileged positions of the educated Sikh reformers, Harjot Oberoi notes that

> "Anglo-vernacular education is emblematic of an educational process which combined a knowledge of vernacular languages with English education that was first imparted at mission and state schools, and later at educational institutions set up by the new elites themselves. It produced men who were at least bilingual, if not polyglot. But even though the colonial machine churned them out by the hundred, these men were still a privileged minority in a society where 93 per cent of the people were illiterate. In 1891 only 19,274 out of an approximate twenty-three million Punjabis could speak and write English. Bilingual skills and western education became a form of capital in a colonial society that could be effectively used to acquire power, privilege and the ability to strike political bargains" (Oberoi, 1994, p. 262).

31. Ibid., p. 277.

32. Kapur (1986), p. 15.

33. B. Singh (1988).

34. Nabha Kahan Singh's book (1914) is indicative of one aspect of the Singh Sabha platform with regard to their absolute insistence on the separation of Sikhs and Hindus.

35. B. Singh (1988), p. 114.

36. Describing the multifaceted world of *bhakti* during the time of Guru Nanak, J. S. Grewal writes: "And there was a good deal of rivalry between the various religious groups. In the midst of this rivalry, many of the contestants had come to believe that salvation was the birthright of every human being irrespectful of his [*sic*] caste, creed or sex. On the whole it was a rich and lively religious atmosphere. And it was this atmosphere that Guru Nanak breathed" (Grewal, 1979, pp. 139–140).

37. Although this hymn has been much touted as indicative of the emancipatory message of Guru Nanak, it can also be interpreted as saying just as much about Nanak's political stance; Guru Nanak does not denounce the political order of his time. Woman should not be reviled because it is she that gives birth to great ones: "Rulership and riches come not as acquisitions of men but as God's gifts. The *raja* as well as the beggar exists because of divine dispensation" (Grewal, 1979, p. 152).

38. Ibid., pp. 195–196.

39. Hobsbawm and Ranger (1983), p. 2. Hobsbawm adds (p. 6) that "[m]ore interesting, from our point of view, is the use of ancient materials to construct invented traditions of a novel type for quite novel purposes. A large store of such materials is accumulated in the past of any society, and an elaborate language of symbolic practice and communications is always available. Sometimes new traditions could be grafted on old ones, sometimes they could be devised by borrowing from the well-supplied warehouses of official ritual, symbolism and moral exhortation."

40. The writings of Guru Gobind Singh, including his odes to the Goddess Durgā were by popular account compiled by Bhai Mani Singh, the celebrated head of Harimandir in 1712–34. There is a great deal of controversy regarding this anthology, given the fact that Sikh theology is avowedly monotheistic, whereas in the *Dasam Granth* there is an unabashed celebration of the goddess as well as the erotic. Khushwant Singh, the noted Sikh writer, states that "the lofty character and the value [Gobind Singh] set on spartan living do not go with prurience of the kind found in some of the passages of the *Dasam Granth*" (K. Singh, 1991, Appendix 4, pp. 314–316). Yet Harjot Oberoi has shown that the *Dasam Granth* was held on par with the *Adi Granth* during the nineteenth century; its displacement as sacred scripture was a fairly recent development (Oberoi, 1994, p. 99).

41. Kaur-Singh (1993), p. 123.

42. Ibid., p. 131.

43. Gross (1994), p. 355.

44. Mai Bhago is a much celebrated woman warrior who is held up by Sikhs as an example of the honor and bravery of Sikh women. Tradition tells of forty Sikh men who had staunchly remained with the guru through the last days at Anandpur yet, finally fearing for their lives, left the battlefield and returned home. Mai Bhago is presented as taunting them for their cowardice and then taking them under her command to return to fight at the side of Guru Gobind Singh in the battle of Muktsar. Macauliffe adds that she donned male attire and "fought heroically in their ranks, disposed of several of her Muhammadan opponents, and transmitted her name as an Indian heroine for the admiration of future generations" (Macauliffe, 1990, p. 213).

45. Sada Kaur is noted as the chief architect of Maharaja Ranjit Singh's remarkable rise to power. She also had considerable influence over the young Maharaja in ruling the rather volatile region. Upon her husband Gurbakhsh Singh's demise, she masterminded the alliance of her own Kanhaya Misal with that of the Sukerchukias Misal, that of young Ranjit, through his union with her infant daughter, Mehtab. After the death of his father, this alliance left Ranjit in a potentially powerful position. Further, Sada Kaur was not about to give up her predominant position with the maturing of Ranjit Singh. It was she who ventured against the Afghans in battle alongside Ranjit Singh. "She is remembered as one of the greatest generals of her time even in the Afghan records" (J. Singh, 1983, p. 7).

46. Bibi Sahib Kaur has been memorialized through the words of General George Thomas, who noted that "she was a better man than her brother" in defending the capital city of Patiala during Thomas's expedition of 1798. On another occasion, this "woman of masculine and intrepid spirit" again defied the wishes of her brother (Raja Sahib Singh) and countered George Thomas in the invasion of Jind. With Kaur's rally of the previously beleaguered Sikh troops, the historian Gupta notes that "this proved to be a turning point in the course of the siege" (Gupta, 1980, pp. 293, 300, 301).

47. G. Singh (1988), p. 43.

48. Gill (1995), pp. 51–52.

49. Gross (1994), p. 333.

50. Paul Ricoeur defines the hermeneutic of suspicion as "sett[ing] out from an original negation, advanc[ing] through a work of deciphering and . . . struggl[ing] against masks, and finally . . . put [ing] in the quest of a new affirmation" (Ricoeur, 1978, p. 217).

51. Falk (1985), p. xv.

52. Joan Wallach Scott notes with regard to the "her-story" approach to feminist history: "As the play on the word 'history' implied, the point was to give value to an experience that had been ignored (hence devalued) and to insist on female agency in the making of history. Men were but one group of actors; whether their experiences were similar or different, women had to be taken explicitly into account by historians" (Scott 1988, p. 18).

53. Scott advocates a poststructuralist approach to history: "Precisely because it addresses questions of epistemology, relativizes the status of all knowledge, links knowledge and power, and theorizes these in terms of the operations of difference, I think post-structuralism (or at least some of the approaches generally associated with Michel Foucault and Jacques Derrida) can offer feminism a powerful analytic perspective. I am not suggesting the dogmatic application of any particular philosopher's teachings and I am aware of feminist critiques of them . . . [yet] the openings they provide to new intellectual directions have proved not only promising but fruitful" (Scott 1988, p. 4).

54. Ibid.

55. Foucault (1980), pp. 97–98.

56. Bourdieu (1989), p. 21.

57. Göçek and Balaghi (1994), pp. 8–9.

58. Scott (1988), p. 25. Cautiously supportive of the understanding of gender as opposed to "women," Ruth Behar notes: "Academic feminism has reached an interesting crossroads . . . Now 'gender' is the burning issue. Have we lost the courage to speak of women, plain and simple? I hope not. I want to think that studying gender is part of the new feminist desire to understand how the construction of identity, for women *and* men, has crucial consequences. At last, we are realizing that we all are in this together. On the female side . . . there is a lingering fear of betrayal. But gender embodies hope: the hope that opening up feminism to include men will not, once again, make women invisible" (Behar, 1994, p. 81).

References

Adi Granth. Tr. Gurubachan Singh Talib in *Sri Guru Granth Sahib*, 4 vols. Patiala: Punjabi University, 1987.

Albrecht-Heide, Astrid. "Women and War: Victims and Collaborators." In Eva Isaksson, ed., *Women and the Military System*. London: Harvester-Wheatsheaf, 1988.

Behar, Ruth. "Gender, Identity, and Anthropology." In Göçek and Balaghi, eds., *Reconstructing Gender in the Middle East* (1994).

Boals, Kay. "The Politics of Cultural Liberation: Male-Female Relations in Algeria." In Berenice A. Carroll, ed., *Liberating Women's History: Theoretical and Critical Essays*. Urbana: University of Illinois Press, 1976.

Bosch, Mineke. "Women's Culture in Women's History: Historical Notion or Feminist Vision?" In Maaike Meijer and Jetty Schaap, eds., *Historiography of Women's Cultural Traditions*. Dordrecht, Holland: Foris, 1987.

Bourdieu, Pierre. "Social Space and Symbolic Power." *Sociological Theory* 7/1 (Spring 1989), pp. 14–25.

Falk, Nancy. "Introduction." In Yvonne Yazbeck Haddad and Ellison Banks Findly, eds., *Women, Religion, and Social Change*. Albany: State University of New York Press, 1985.

Fenn, Richard K. "The Sociology of Religion: A Critical Survey." In Tom Tottomore, Stefan Nowak, and Magdalena Sokolowska, eds., *Sociology: The State of the Art*. London: Sage, 1982.

Foucault, Michel. *The History of Sexuality: An Introduction*, vol. 1. New York: Vintage, 1980.

Gill, M. K. *The Role and Status of Women in Sikhism*. Delhi: National Book Shop, 1995.

Göçek, Fatma Müge, and Shiva Balaghi. "Reconstructing Gender in the Middle East through Voice and Experience." In Fatma Müge Göçek and Shiva Balaghi, eds., *Reconstructing Gender in the Middle East: Tradition, Identity, and Power*. New York: Columbia University Press, 1994.

Grewal, J. S. *Guru Nanak in History*. Chandigarh: Publication Bureau, Panjab University, 1979.

Gross, Rita M. "Studying Women and Religion: Conclusions Twenty-Five Years Later." In Arvind Sharma, ed., *Today's Woman in World Religions*. Albany: State University of New York Press, 1994.

Gupta, Hari Ram. *History of the Sikhs*, vol. 3. New Delhi: Munshiram Manoharlal Publishers, 1980.

Heilbrun, Carolyn G., and Nancy K. Miller, eds., *Gender and the Politics of History*, Gender and Culture Series. New York: Columbia University Press, 1988.

Hobsbawm, Eric, and Terence Ranger, eds., *The Invention of Tradition*. Cambridge: Cambridge University Press, 1983.

Jakobsh, Doris. "Gender Issues in Sikh Studies: Hermeneutics of Affirmation or Hermeneutics of Suspicion?" In Pashaura Singh and N. Gerald Barrier, eds., *The Transmission of the Sikh Heritage in the Diaspora*. New Delhi: Manohar Publishers, 1996.

Jolly, Surjit Kaur. *Sikh Revivalist Movements: The Nirankari and Namdhari Movements in Punjab in the Nineteenth Century, a Socio-Religious Study*. New Delhi: Gitanjali Publishing House, 1988.

Kapur, Rajiv A. *Sikh Separatism: The Politics of Faith*. London: Allen and Unwin, 1986.

Kaur-Singh, Kanwaljit. "Sikh Women." In Kharak Singh, G. S. Mansukhani, and Jasbir Singh Mann, eds., *Fundamental Issues in Sikh Studies*. Chandigarh: Institute of Sikh Studies, 1992.

———. "Sikhism." In Jean Holm with John Bowker, eds., *Women in Religion*. Themes in Religious Studies Series. London: Pinter,1994.

Kaur-Singh, Nikki-Guninder. *The Feminine Principle in the Sikh Vision of the Transcendent*. Cambridge: Cambridge University Press, 1993.

Kohli, Yash, eds. *The Women of Punjab*. Bombay: Chic Publications, 1983.

Lorenzen, David N., ed. *Bhakti Religion in North India: Community Identity and Political Action*. SUNY Series in Religious Studies, Harold Coward, general ed. Albany: State University of New York Press, 1995.

Macauliffe, Max Arthur. *The Sikh Religion: Its Gurus, Sacred Writings and Authors*, vol. 5. Delhi: Low Price Publications, [1909] 1990.

McLeod, W. H., ed. and tr. *Textual Sources for the Study of Sikhism*. Textual Sources for the Study of Religion Series, John R. Hinnells, ed. Chicago: University of Chicago Press, 1984.

———. *Who Is a Sikh? The Problem of Sikh Identity*. Oxford: Clarendon Press, 1989.

McMullen, Clarence Osmond. *Religious Beliefs and Practices of the Sikhs in Rural Punjab*. New Delhi: Manohar Publications,1989.

Oberoi, Harjot. *The Construction of Religious Boundaries: Culture, Identity and Diversity in the Sikh Tradition*. Delhi: Oxford University Press, 1994.

———. "The Making of a Religious Paradox: Sikh, Khalsa, Sahajdhari as Modes of Early Sikh Identity." In Lorenzen, ed. *Bhakti Religion in North India* (1995).

Pritam, Amrita. "The Annunciation." In *Time and Again and Other Poems*. Calcutta: United Writers, 1975.

———. *Life and Times*. Delhi: Vikas Publishing House, 1989.

Ricoeur, Paul. *The Philosophy of Paul Ricoeur: An Anthology of His Work*, Charles E. Reagan and David Stewart, eds., Boston: Beacon Press, 1978.

Scott, Joan Wallach. *Gender and the Politics of History*. Gender and Culture Series, Carolyn G. Heilbrun and Nancy K. Miller, eds. New York: Columbia University Press, 1988.

Singh, Bhai Vir. *Sundri*. Tr. Gobind Singh Mansukhani. New Delhi: Bhai Vir Singh Sahitya Sadan, 1988.

Singh, Gulcharan. "Women's Lib in Sikh Scriptures & Sociology." *The Sikh Review* (March 1988). pp. 38–43.

Singh, Joginder. "The Illustrious Women of Punjab." In Yash Kohli, ed., *The Women of Punjab*. Bombay: Chic Publications, 1983.

Singh, Khushwant. *A History of the Sikhs: volume 1: 1469–1839*. Delhi: Oxford University Press,1991.

Singh, Nabha Kahan. *Ham Hindu Nahin* (We Are Not Hindus), 4th ed. Amritsar, [n.p.]1914.

Suri, Surinder. "Position of Women in Sikhism." In Jyotsna Chatterji, ed., *The Authority of the Religions and the Status of Women*. Banhi Series. Delhi: WCSRC-CISRS Joint Women's Programme and the Willian Carey Study and Research Centre, 1989.

19

MATILDA GABRIELPILLAI

Postcolonial Identity as Feminist Fantasy

A Study of Tamil Women's Short Fiction on Dowry

In Canada in 1996, an Indian man's massacre of almost all of his ex-wife's family in the British Columbia town of Kelowna was immediately misrepresented in the media as a fatal consequence of the Indian system of arranged marriages, so that the incident was portrayed as something other than family violence and as indicating an Indian cultural pathology. The Indo-Canadian community stepped in to correct this misrepresentation and argue that the perpetrator of violence was operating from within patriarchal ideologies common to most cultures, including those of the West. However, for the West, even feminist studies departments, Indian dowry culture continues to function as the vehicle for a Western imperialist epistemology of India as its Third World "other." The Indian nation's central meanings are deliberately and reductively quilted to the experiences of the Indian woman's body to produce an India that is culturally retrogressive and, more particularly, to represent its culture in sexual metaphor as a masculinity that is always-already pathologically inadequate in its greed and brutal perversity and as always-already less than masculine. This discourse has entailed the West's willful refusal to recognize Indian women's response to the dowry system as intending subjects of resistance and also to misrecognize one aspect of Indian culture as the representative of the whole. This burden—the excessive meaning that the dowry system is made to bear as signifier—is also made possible by the West's imaginary perception of the dowry system as present everywhere in India and in the self-same form; in actual fact, dowry practices occur in specific pockets of the country and involve different activities, sometimes generating meanings for women that are other than disempowerment. For instance, in some southern parts of India, as well as in the diaspora, women are given control over their dowry money, and it is not unheard of for them to use this money for additional education. Parminder Bhachu reports that British consumption patterns, ideologies of identity communicated by the British media, British class identities, and regional and subcultural trends have led to the transformation of the traditional dowry *daaj* by Punjabi women in contemporary Britain,[1] whereas Van Willingen and Channa argue that, in India, dowry is more commonly practiced among urban middle-class families and in areas in the north, where dowry demands are inflated because of women's nonparticipation in cultivation because of the use of the plowing method.[2] In addition to overriding the widely dispersed meanings of dowry practices, which vary according to the caste, class, historical, and geographical circumstances of Indian communities, Western imperialist and unhistoricized readings of the dowry system as signifier of sex or gender oppression and national or ethnic meanings have also been made possible by the West's voluntary blindness toward colonial and neocolonial involvement in reconstituting dowry practices and thereby inflating endlessly their potential for female oppression. The Western media's intense interest in the violence linked to the dowry system—of the killing of young brides, female infanticide, selective female abortion, dowry-related suicides of young women—and its lack of interest in representing Indian women's resistance suggests a certain investment of desire in the violence, similar to the salvatory desire Lata Mani traced in colonial reports of *satī*—it is impossible, after all, to take on the role of savior without first ensuring via discourse that a victimization has been practiced. No doubt many in the West would be surprised to learn that dowry has been legislated against in India since the early 1960s, so that it ought rather to be read as an abuse of Indian culture rather than as one of its central signifiers.

As has been noted by Partha Chatterjee and others, the Indian nationalist movement's conceptualization of Indian identity, despite its anticolonialist agenda or perhaps because of it, merely duplicated the colonial gaze, so that Indian ethnicity emerged as what differentiated it from the West in a kind of reversal (the same but backward) of colonial constructions of Indian culture. Hinduism was an important component of this search for an ethnic essentialism, and subject-positions assigned to Hindu women in Indian society came to stand in for this essential Indian national ethnicity. Deniz Kandiyoti's argument that the concepts of nation, citizen, and civil society must be read in the masculine—whereas women "follow a different *trajectory*" from men in their integration into modern nationhood as citizens in a sovereign nation-state[3]— rings true for many women in postcolonial nation-societies who find that their "trajectory" is also often contradictory; they may be, within nationalist projects, both the nation's foremost symbol of modernity (as working, independent women and feminists) while simultaneously the boundary markers of their nation's cultural difference and authenticity. India's insertion into the circuit of the global economy, multinational capitalism, and the modernization drive has only exerted more pressure on India to delineate its "difference," and the Hindu woman has found herself bearing even more of the burden of being the "privileged" signifier of national identity, chiefly in terms of the way, as Kandiyoti puts it, "women's appropriate sexual conduct," as dictated by religious and other traditional, rural or feudal social texts, makes up "the crucial distinction between the nation and its 'others.'"[4]

Do Indian women resist the ways in which meanings of Indian identity are doubly mapped onto their bodies by their own societies and by those of the West? How do they extricate themselves from such a complicated, cross-cultural text, in which it would seem that their female emancipation can be achieved only treacherously, by placing meanings of national identity and the anticolonialist agenda in jeopardy? Bhachu suggests that the reading of Indian women's cultural and gender identity locations within the representative space of the dowry system must involve taking into account the role of women as cultural reproducers who renegotiate their ethnic cultural and gender identities, both in their resistance to dowry as well as through their transformatory participation within the dowry system. Taking a cue from Bhachu, this paper will survey English translations of short stories about dowry written by Tamil women in Tamil, to examine the ways in which dowry practices and their related ideologies provide the cultural ground on which a feminized postcolonial imaginary of national identity expresses itself. Tamil women's writings were selected chiefly because I, a Tamil myself though not of Indian nationality, felt I had better cultural access to it than to writings by women from other Indian cultures. That these stories were originally written in an Indian language also offered an opportunity to engage with postcolonial identity and feminist resistance as imagined from a cultural environment that is often marginalized by Western multicultural studies (said with some awareness of the irony inherent in approaching multiculturalism from a specific cultural center).

These women's stories deconstruct the structural binaries on which Indian masculinist conceptualizations of national identity turn, where the home and the world, tradition and modernity, domesticity and the transnational, and the private and the public are conveniently viewed as separate entities, which are further imagined to correspond exactly with the female and male aspects of national identity. Refusing the possibility of this separation, they argue that the modern circulates through the traditional, Western ideas dialogize native concepts, and capitalism transforms feudal and rural cultural institutions so that "essentially" Indian cultural configurations such as the dowry system no longer exist in their original form. How, then, can these be used as signifiers of Indian cultural authenticity, these women ask. For these women writers, the dowry system is one of the cultural sites where the postcolonial nation's identity is forced into crisis and where the Indian woman transforms herself within a national space from gendered subaltern into intending subject of resistance. I hope in this chapter, through the readings of Tamil women writers' representation of the dowry system, to foreground postcolonial national identity as a semiological terrain that is already fluctuating, already in contestation in terms of gendered meanings, so that Kandiyoti's reading of the nation as masculine is itself to be read as always-already a privileging of the male fantasmatic of nationhood over that of the postcolonial woman's, as itself complicit, in the domination of the male voice that it bemoans. Unwittingly, perhaps, Kandiyoti's reading also involves the postponement of gendered national identity politics from the present into the future.

Many of these stories work toward refusing dominant meanings of the dowry system by recoding it as the (im)possible coming together of essentialized Indian ethnic tradition and the capitalist-modernist-Western liberal system of abstracting value. The dominant meanings of the dowry system by the West and by the Indian nation-as-male, where the dowry system either signifies the pathological lack of Indian culture-masculinity or is viewed as the location of an essentialized national ethnic identity, depend on the conceptualization of tradition and ethnicity as separable from modernity and Western values. In these feminist writings, however, dowry culture is represented as an "undecidable"and hence unrepresentative element in national culture, where tradition is already infiltrated and transformed by modernism and capitalism. The dowry system—read against the grain by dialogizing it with the two contradictory cultural systems, Indian tradition and modernism—becomes the arena where Indian national identity splits apart. The various cultural aspects thus shown to be incommensurate, we see the aporia that exists at the very center of dominant constructions of national identity.

In Chudamani Raghavan's short story, "Counting the Flowers,"[5] the representational systems of the traditional and the modern confront each other and disturb the coherence of each other's meanings. The narrative re-presents the traditional first meeting of the two families involved in a possible marriage and the ensuing dowry negotiation that takes place but reapprehends them through the cultural screens of modern-Western-capitalist culture. Thus, the showing of the prospective bride and the dowry negotiation begin to look like the parading of prostitutes at a brothel for the evaluative gaze of the male customer, who then negotiates the price with the brothelkeeper or pimp. In the process, the structural relations between the actants in a dowry negotiation scene are altered so that the groom's parents and the groom function as the male customers at a brothel, the bride's father is the pimp, and the bride is the sexual object who will enter into a circuit of exchange between the buyer and seller of her body. The scene begins with the assumption that the woman's "value" depends on her ability to signify ethnic and traditional codes of behavior, so that the would-be bride's prowess in the domestic services, such as her turning out of traditional Indian savories such as *bondas* and *soji*, actually earns her a discount in the dowry payable. Gradually, however, it becomes clear that the real "ethnic" value of the female subject, the one that enables her to marry upward into a family of a better class than hers, lies not in her ability to reproduce Indian traditions but rather in her sexual attractiveness. As the protagonist's father realizes that the would-be groom is captivated by his daughter's beauty, he ups the stakes by directing his daughter to change into a georgett (a filmy, transparent, and body-hugging fabric) sari and to display her physical assets by walking around the room.

Indian ethnic culture, as such, is unmasked here as a euphemism for the patriarchy's sexual commodification of women, and it is remetaphorized in gender terms as the betrayal of a daughter by her father. In this narrative, the dowry system's current abuse of women is related to the "new" unethnic meanings it has acquired in the modern and late capitalist era, where a woman's body becomes the surplus value that can be exchanged in the marriage market for a better economic future for her family, especially for her male relations or siblings. The father in this story wants to improve his son's family's social and economic position; in particular, he wants to be able to afford a good education for his son and to improve his son's marriage and career prospects. Though he himself lacks the money to carry this out, his daughter's attractiveness gives him leverage; he trades her beauty for his family's entry into a better class and even manages to extract from the groom's family a promise of financial support toward his son's education. However, given his own inability to offer a good dowry, he has to accept a less-than-ideal, crippled husband for his daughter. Rajam Krishnan's story, "Yellow String,"also narrativizes the intrusion of capitalism into the dowry culture's coding of values, where the latter is represented as the reconstitution of patriarchal power by modernity, which enables a woman's body to be sold in marital exchange for her family's and brother's social and economic gain; the female protagonist in question here is "sold off" to a much older but wealthy man.[6]

Both these stories subvert meanings of Indian ethnicity and reveal their complicity in capital gain and in patriarchal exploitation of the woman. Stained with sexual shame, where the woman's sexuality is exchanged for money, the dowry system thus becomes the negative location of national identity,—that is, where the nation's core values cannot be. Lakshmi Kannan's "India Gate" further deconstructs the quilting of meanings of Indian national identity to ethnic tradition by her linguistic exploration of the dowry system as the nation's site of cultural contradiction, where the nation degenerates into semantic nonsense.[7] Her protagonist, Padmini, a graduate woman who is married to her occupational equal, finds that her experience within the dowry system is incommensurate with all other aspects of her life as an Indian woman. Most significant, Padmini realizes that in the dowry system the language of tradition rubs offensively against that of modernity; it resists translation, resists integration. As in Raghavan's story, the dowry system is the site where the encounter of a traditional subjectivity with a modern subjectivity radically shifts the epistemological ground, so that words in one symbolic code change their meanings through translation into the other symbolic code, revealing a gap of untranslatability. Padmini reflects that the word "daughter-in-law," which in dowry-speak is the signifier of the traditional role of women within marriage, translates into the modernist code as "servant." Realizing that tradition and modernity are antagonists, she decides that she must make a choice between them or suffer the consequences of a divestiture of her subjectivity. As a modern woman who views economic productivity as gender-neutral, Padmini realizes that the dowry culture's delimiting association of "work" with masculinity can be traced to the original blindness of traditional ideological cultural texts to woman as subject, as material being, and as generator of meaning and value. Surprised that she has to pay a dowry even though she is marrying an intellectual, social, and economic equal, that her "work" does not count in the dowry negotiation, she muses to herself: "Ah but those words are attributed exclusively for the work done by men, aren't they? My work is invisible. Because my very being is invisible."[8] Gender role splits from subjectivity and body from mind as Padmini plays traditional wife, serves her husband, and sees to his whims and fancies, while mentally unable to acknowledge Balaraman's masculinity. The trope of travel is used in the story as the process by which the postcolonial national imaginary is feminized as the coming into being of a modern, liberated female subjectivity. The protagonist's movement in the story from her hometown in Madras to Tiruchy, her husband's home, and eventually to New Delhi corresponds with her emergence into national subjectivity as well as into female subjectivity. Padmini identifies New Delhi as the national center of India and quilts the nation's meanings to cosmopolitanism and modernity, where woman, liberated from traditional meanings and the burdens of ethnicity, stands as the nation's already gendered symbol of postcolonialism. It is in New Delhi that Padmini throws off her husband and buys a house for herself, signifying that the home-world split in an incoherent and contradictory national identity has now been corrected and restored to sense by the formerly female aspect of Indian national identity, the "home," relocating itself within the "world," the previously male arena of national identity. The dowry system and its patriarchal code, now consigned to the geographic as well as social, economic, and cultural margins of India (Madras and Tiruchy), can no longer function as signifier of national culture because the nation's center, New Delhi, which has entered into global circulation, cannot accommodate such a reading of India as Hindu, and its modern-day economic realities do not permit the coding of women as men's subordinates.

There is, however, a conspicuous absence in these stories: none of them frames the emancipation of Indian women from patriarchal and familial control in terms of Western feminist notions of the liberation of female sexuality or Western notions of romantic love. Kannan probably comes the closest of these writers to making such a suggestion, but, even then, she shrouds such meanings in metaphor. Padmini's divorce from her husband and her decision to lead a life independent of familial and patriarchal control are appropriate to such a suggestion. The metaphor of India Gate, which carries meanings of India's openness to global cultural influences, is another hint. But at no point does Padmini explicitly codify her break from her husband as a moment of sexual liberation or entertain thoughts of romantic adventures. In Krishnan's "Yellow String," which is concerned with locating the dowry system within a decolonized space of difference from the West, Western feminist norms are directly critiqued. Although the female protagonist here has been married off to an elderly but rich landowner in exchange for his settling of her wastrel brother's debts, she refuses to concede that the cultural and gender ideologies of the dowry system are inferior to those of the West. In this story, even the woman who has been shortchanged by the dowry system is still considered to be better off than many of India's Westernized, corporate-class women, who, though they marry for love, are eventually neglected by their husbands and find themselves displacing their desires for companionship in the erstwhile pleasures of consumerism. The protagonist begins her reflections on the dowry system by considering it an oppression of female desire (her marriage aborted her romantic relationship with a young man) but later decides that the shackles of an arranged marriage, symbolized by the yellow string tied around her ankle, are actually the Indian woman's symbol of security, saving her from being thrown into a Western, modern, alien space of meaning, where Western notions of sexual and romantic freedom are represented as false consciousness, as an ideological cover-up for loneliness, lovelessness, and cultural nihilism. Her husband, though too old for her, loves her and takes good care of her, she decides.

Western feminists need to understand that the rejection of Western models of female liberation is strategic to Indian women's indigenization of their postcolonial feminist struggle and allows them to escape from the cultural deadlock in which their feminist resistance is read as alien or even treacherous to the nation's cultural identity. The foreclosure of Western meanings of female liberation, romantic love, and modern and Western ideologies of marriage shapes the form of the Indian woman's fantasmatic, where not only women's liberation but also postcolonial identity itself is imagined in gendered, feminized terms as the freedom of women from the abuses of traditional patriarchal gender ideologies. Significantly, the majority of the stories do not critique the dowry culture itself, viewing it still as a signifier of Indian difference, but fantasize about a utopian, postcolonial identity, where the modernization and reform of dowry practices and ideologies are metaphors for the general desire for the modernization and reinterpretation of tradition. In these fantasies, which read as imaginary myths of postcolonial subjectivity, female subjects who are hystericized or schizophrenic, the woman-as-outcast as well as abused women, are offered as figures of a consciousness of gendered subalternity that marks the incommensurate in postcolonial subjectivity as that which needs cultural intervention.

In most of these stories, and even to a certain extent in Kannan's "India Gate," the female protagonists' awareness of their gender oppressions either forces them to forsake these by occupying the subject position of social outcasts or leads those who decide to live within the system to do so with desire and subjectivity split off from their existential existence. In "India Gate," Padmini's "liberation" makes her a social outcaste of sorts, whose rejection of the dowry system and traditional gender value systems entail her separation from her family and living her life alone, much like the widows of past eras, who took the only alternative other than committing *satī* offered to them,—that is, living out the rest of their lives as outcasts. With her 'liberation', Padmini's social space in India has significantly become constricted to New Delhi, which, in the story, resonates with the anonymity of modern, urban life. Raghavan's protagonist in "Counting the Flowers" does not have the financial resources to oppose or escape her arranged marriage, but it is understood that a traumatized, hysterical subjectivity will haunt her for the rest of her life. The would-be bride's realization of her gendered subaltern subject-position is metaphorized in the story as the moment when female sexual desire, represented in terms of the protagonist's yearning look at phallus-shaped *nagalinga* blossoms, is refused its phallic object; her look yields, instead, dozens of lame legs, her soon-to-be husband's physical lameness transformed into a hysterical symptom of her blocked desire. The story also represents the heroine's subjectivity as deeply divided from her existential existence, as the latter's contradictory, shadowy, other self.

Raghavan, like other Tamil women writers, focuses on the abuses of the dowry system as metaphor of what is wrong in national culture. But, like them, she offers a critical reformation of dowry practices—the modernization of the traditional as the horizon of a decolonized subjectivity. In another of her stories, "The Strands of the Void,"[9] a Hindu priest has to come to terms with contradictions in Hindu ideologies brought to crisis by the realities of modern life: he is caught in a dilemma where he is duty-bound as a father to protect his daughter from harm but cannot rescue her from dowry violence because doing so would involve removing her from her marital home, something that is forbidden by his culture. Confronting the "question mark of life," the priest-father just barely avoids loss of faith in Hindu scriptures by renegotiating Hindu epistemology and bringing it into alignment with modern-day realities. With the unusual situation here of a woman writer speaking through a male protagonist who also happens to be a priest and father, Raghavan stages postcolonial identity as the feminization of traditional patriarchal codes. The father-priest here fulfills his dharma by taking responsibility for his daughter and by factoring in female interests in his reinterpretation of the scriptures. As priest, his is the authoritative voice that deems dowry violence to be an abuse of traditional dowry culture and of the teachings of sacred, traditional texts, which emphasize the practice of human decency and the recognition of human dignity and frown on material greed. In this story, dowry violence and abuse of women are the site where Indian ethnic meanings cannot be. However, it is clear that the father-priest's new, feminized understanding of Hindu tradition has not moved far enough. The daughter may have been saved from dowry violence and spousal abuse, but her taking refuge in her father's home only positions her as a social outcast: still technically married, it is understood that she will be barred from remarriage or any romantic or sexual liaisons; also, as a woman living apart from her husband, she will have no voice or role in society.

The imagining of Indian postcolonial subjectivity in terms of feminist insurgency and feminist rewriting of ethnic identity is taken even further in Ambai's short story "Mother Has Committed a Murder,"[10] in which patriarchal Indian tradition itself is represented in female terms as the original self-betrayal of female subjectivity and desire. In this story, a close and harmonious relationship between a young girl and her mother ends abruptly when the mother, after failing to negotiate a dowry-marriage for a female relative (who is dark and, according to Indian aesthetic standards, unattractive), returns home to curse her daughter for being dark. In the daughter's eyes, the mother "has committed a murder": by identifying with the dominant patriarchal cultural logic, she destroyed her daughter's female subjectivity, which she herself had, in large part, shaped. Here, women's history is represented in terms of a prior female subjectivity, which is brought to a traumatic end by the patriarchal symbolic code that the female enters upon womanhood. The prepubertal daughter, who has lived a childhood in imaginary identification with her mother, finds that, on attaining age (first menstruation), she has to identify with the codes of the father. What's worse, these patriarchal restrictions of female subjectivity and desire are transmitted to the daughter through other women: her elder system, an elderly female neighbor and her mother. Representing this female identification with male codes as woman's betrayal of herself and her gender, Ambai's story dramatically inscribes female responsibility and guilt at the source of gender oppression. The young girl's indictment of her mother for "murder" is a loaded rhetorical strategy: if a murder charge is read as performing a demand for justice, then this story, as speech act, calls to women to take action, to resist traditional gender ideologies, and to restore an original female identity.

Tamil women's writings expose the reductivism involved in dominant-Western readings of Indian dowry culture as a signifier of Indian ethnicity imagined in terms of a problematic or pathological masculine subjectivity. Rather, these short stories show the complicity of Western culture, especially capitalism, as determinants of contemporary dowry practices, including dowry inflation and dowry violence—that dowry culture as practiced now is so extensively permeated with Western meanings of capital accumulation that it cannot function as a pure signifier of Indian ethnic culture, that it is a cultural site where Indian ethnic identity is being threatened rather than the authentic site of its expression. If the fantasmatic frames our desires and teaches us how and what to desire,[11] then these stories reframe postcolonial desire in terms of the dialecticization of traditional Indian values and modernity. Their postcolonial dream is to offer an "Indian modernity" that is culturally different and capable of contesting the cultural dominance exerted by Western versions of modernity. Resistance against and renegotiation of the ideologies of gender and sexuality that encode current practices of dowry are, thus, not only an important aspect of the forging of contemporary Indian identity but also—and this is important—they are part of a fantasmatic of postcolonial subjectivity that involves a saying no to aspects of Western culture, especially to some of its ideologies of gender and sexuality. If Indian national identity is currently understood in patriarchal terms as a sexual "division of labor"–of the happy combination of modern culture, imagined as masculine activity in economic spheres, and of Indian tradition, conceived in terms of women's conformity to traditional roles assigned to them in premodern social texts—then these women's writings bring this two-part identity into crisis and gender the postcolonial imaginary itself as feminist insurgency, as the invasion of female meanings into patriarchal cultural logic. They implicitly also raise the question as to the circulation of desire in Western dominant representations of Indian women as victims of dowry violence, where Indian women's bodies are looked at as suffering bodies rather than as bodies of resistance, so that the pathology is in the gaze rather than in the spectacle of dowry violence.

Notes

1. Bhachu (1991), pp. 401–12.
2. Van Willingen and Channa (1991), pp. 369–77.
3. Kandiyoti, in Van Willingen and Channa (1991), p. 377.
4. Ibid.
5. Raghavan (1990), pp. 84–86.
6. Krishnan (1963).
7. Kannan (1992), pp. 143–66.
8. Ibid., p. 160.
9. Raghavan (1991), pp. 142–54.
10. Ambai (1978), pp. 188–98.
11. Silverman (1992).

References

Ambai (Laksmi, C. S.). "Mother Has Committed a Murder." K. Subramaniyam, ed. *Tamil Short Stories*. New Delhi: Authors Guild of India, 1978.

———. *The Faces behind the Mask: Women in Tamil Literature*. New Delhi: Vikas, 1984.

Bhachu, Parminder. "Culture, Ethnicity and Class among Punjabi Sikh Women in 1990s Britain." *New Community* 17.3. April 1991.

Harrell, Stevan, and Sara A. Dickey. "Dowry Systems in Complex Societies." *Ethnology* 24.2. April 1985.

Heyer, Judith. "The Role of Dowries and Daughters' Marriages in the Accumulation and Distribution of Capital in a South Indian Community." *Journal of International Development* 4.4. July–August 1992, pp. 419–36.

Kannan, Lakshmi. "India Gate." *Parijata and Other Stories*, Trans. Lakshmi Kannan. New Delhi: National, 1992.

Karin, Kapadia. "Marrying Money: Changing Preference and Practice in Tamil Marriage." *Contributions to Indian Sociology* 27.1, January–June 1993, pp. 25–51.

Krishnan, Rajam. "Yellow String." In K. Swaminathan, et al., eds. *The Plough and the Stars: Stories from Tamil Nadu*. Bombay: Asia, 1963.

Munck, Victor C. de. "Cross Sibling Relationships and the Dowry in Sri Lanka." *Ethnos* 55.1–2, 1990. pp. 56–73.

Parker, Andrew, et al. *Nationalisms and Sexualities*. New York: Routledge, 1992.

Raghavan, Chudamani. "Counting Flowers." *The Slate of Life: An Anthology of Stories by Indian Women*. New Delhi: Kali for Women, 1990.

———. "The Strands of the Void." *Modern Tamil Short Stories*, vol. 1, trans. M. S. Ramaswami. Calcutta: Writers Workshop, 1991.

Rao, Vijayendra. "Dowry Inflation in Rural India." *Population Studies* 47.2. July 1993, pp. 283–93.

Sandhu, M. K. "A Study of Dowry among Working and Non-Working Women."*Indian Journal of Social Work* 49.2. April 1988, pp. 155–64.

Silverman, Kaja. *The Subject of Semiotics*. New York: Oxford University Press, 1983.

———. *Male Subjectivity at the Margins*. New York: Routledge, 1992.

Teja, Mohinderjit Kaur. *Dowry: A Study in Attitudes and Practices*. Women in South Asia Series. New Delhi: Inder-India, 1993.

Upadhyay, Carol Boyak. "Dowry and Women's Property in Coastal Andhra Pradesh."*Contributions to Indian Sociology* 24.1. January–June 1990, pp. 29–59.

Van Willingen, John, and V. C. Channa. "Law, Custom and Crimes against Women: The Problem of Dowry Death in India." *Human Organization* 50.4. 1991, pp. 369–77.

Verghese, Jamila. *Her Gold and Her Body*. Shahibabad: Vikas, 1980.

Zizek, Slavoj. *The Sublime Object of Ideology*. London: Verso, 1989.

NABANEETA DEV SEN

Eroticism and the Woman Writer in Bengali Culture

A woman with ideas and ability to express them is something of a social embarrassment, like a housebroken pet.

Marye Manner, "The Problems of Creative Women," in S. M. Farber and R. H. L. Wilson, eds., *The Potential of Woman* (New York: McGraw Hill, 1963), pp. 116–130

Her raw vocabulary is disturbing precisely because it reminds us that even today a sexual double standard applies to profanity.

New York Times on Karen Finley's "We Keep Our Victims Ready" (1990)

Speaking as a woman writer, I shall try to explore why, in Bengali literature, examples of women writers' treatment of eroticism have been so sparse as to be almost nonexistent. I shall argue this out in five stages.[1]

First, writing is a social gesture; it is a form of self-expression allotted to men. In Bengali culture, most gestures are codified according to gender, and women's gestures are especially clearly codified by the duties and space allotted to them by society.

A close look at the Bengali words for "woman" and "wife" clearly reveals the sociocultural roles imposed upon the Bengali woman. Her actions are predominantly sexual, as the breeder; her duties all household-related, as the nurturer; her character passive, as servant; her space indoors, to limit her powers. She is bound within the kitchen and the bedroom—which really means catering to the senses of menfolk. The woman's ultimate duty turns out to be catering to the senses, and we may stretch it a little further beyond the kitchen and the bedroom to the area of the arts.

And there, another revelation awaits us. The woman who sings is a singer, the woman who dances is a dancer, she who paints is a painter, and she who cooks, a cook. But she who writes? She is a woman writer. In *her* case, the gender identity is added on. What is this? A *woman* dancer or a *woman* cook is an absurd expression, but a woman writer is not. This is probably so because singing, dancing, and cooking are female gestures. These acts appeal directly to the senses, and the intellectual appreciation of these acts comes later. Music goes to our ears, dance to our eyes, food to our tongues. But words? What about words? Eyes and ears can make nothing of them if the mind does not respond. A foreign language will bring the response from our eyes, not from our ears. The primary appeal of language is to the mind.

A writer deals with verbal signs. The act of writing is an act of intellection, and therefore it is regarded as male territory. In Bengali culture, as elsewhere, the area of the mind is allotted to men and the area of the senses to women. Hence, the woman who dances, cooks, or sings is well within her rights, but the woman who writes? She is not. She has stepped out of her area of the senses and has appropriated a male gesture. Her appeal with words is to the mind and not to the senses. The power relationship is reversed. The moment she takes up the pen, the woman commits an act of transgression against the social code. She has trespassed into this male territory and has given rise to silent hostility, to an unconscious resistance among her readers.

By the way, I do not believe that writing is a male gesture because the pen happens to look like the phallus. That's false, because then the modern mode of writing is female gesture: the word processor has a womblike memory and actually produces copies through the printer. So if writing with a pen is a male writer, using a word processor would be a female gesture. In fact, by the same analogy of the phallic symbol as the active agent, cooking would become a definitely male gesture. The pots and pans are female sexual symbols, and the long-handled ladle or the stirrer is the active agent, a phallic symbol as obvious as the knife. Why, then, is cooking not regarded as a male gesture? I give this example only to make us aware of the dangers of being excessively enthusiastic about simple semiosis. However, to get back to the point, writing as an act of intellection is regarded as a male gesture. And no matter what a woman writes, she is always a trespasser.

So, second, let us look into the contract that exists between the reader and the writer. The contract between the male reader and the male writer differs from that with the female writer, depending on cultural attitudes and expectations. When a woman takes up writing, *it* becomes *her own* gestures, and *it* falls a victim to all the codes of conduct that apply to a woman's gestures. Both the reader and the writer accept this system and function within it. Through her repressive education, the woman is taught to be culturally silent. For a woman in Bengali culture, "modesty"and "a sense of shame" are of the ultimate value. They are fundamental virtues for a woman. She is supposed to act, speak, move, look, smile, laugh, and weep in a "reserved" way. Her space is limited everywhere. Her eyes should be lowered, her voice should be low, her steps should be short, her mouthfuls should be small. As her voice, her vision, and her gestures are all extensions of her body, these should not occupy too much space—because space means power.

Similarly, her mental space is also curtailed by limiting her knowledge. In the ancient days of brahmanical Hindu culture, women were not allowed to read the Sanskrit scriptures. They were barred from writing in the elevated language. The classical Sanskrit plays show how women used a broken language, Prakrit, along with the lower castes, while kings and Brahmins used Sanskrit, the language of power. Perfect language, in fact, is a double source of power—as a source of further knowledge and enlightenment and as a tool of self-expression. That might explain why it was traditionally barred to women. In the British period, Indian women were given education in their mother tongue, and English was reserved exclusively for men—another attempt to curtail woman's power.

So when the woman starts using language and actually writes, she is committing an aggressive act, and she knows it unconsciously as well as society does. Hence, she tries to be as docile as possible in order to be subversive: she accepts the codes imposed on her and tries to keep within them.

She encounters two types of male readers. The first type totally rejects women writers, skips over those pages of a journal occupied by a woman writer, and thinks it is beneath his male dignity to stoop to listen to what a woman might have to say. It must be pure gibberish. One way of silencing women is not to pay attention. The second group reads with a great deal of interest—a great deal of unholy, extracurricular curiosity. A woman writer is constantly watched like prisoners in a jail who are made to parade before the warden every morning. The woman writer's private life is under the strict surveillance of society. Her name becomes an essential part of the text that she produces, and with her whole personal life and her body. The whole of Bengali society is the woman writer's moral guardian. Unfortunately, the female readership in Bengal, though very great in number, happens to be the silent majority. The writer gets no feedback from them. All the literary critics are *men*, so the only feedback the woman writer gets is from the male readership. And the contract is therefore virtually between the male reader and female writer.

Third, now that we can see that the male reader treats male and female writers differently, we can perhaps find out how he does it. Among many strategies, the one relevant to us today is that the artistic excellence of a piece of writing by a woman is not judged by art alone. The female writer's personal life is always taken into account. I was surprised to note that this regrettable cultural characteristic is not only true of Bengali, but also sometimes true of advanced, progressive, Western cultures.

In a seminar at the University of Toronto in 1987, a gentleman from Germany, a professor of anthropology, mentioned how a woman, a South American native Indian woman, who had had sexual relations with many men, wrote a love poem, and how it was a very special thing, a most surprising act—because the promiscuous woman must be a superficial woman and therefore incapable of deeper artistic abilities. This approach is objectionable but not new. This attitude does not arise when a promiscuous male poet writes a love poem. How many women he sleeps with is quite irrelevant to the artistic assessment of his work. Here I am tempted to quote a young student friend of mine who remarked on hearing that story: "Byron screwed everything that moved. Well, Byron must have been pretty 'superficial'. How could he ever write poetry?" I agree with my student. How could he?

The public interest in the private life of the woman writer is so great that her every action is morally judged. If I told you about the letters I receive, especially about my personal travelogues! For example, "How come you spent nights in the same bed with as many as six pilgrims, all men? Aren't you afraid of losing your chastity? Or is it a lost cause already? How do you expect to find decent husbands for your daughters after this?" And this is in response to a holy piece of pure pilgrimage, nothing to do with eroticism! Here is another letter: "Are you a crazy woman? Why rush off to the Tibet border hitch-hiking on a ration truck instead of going to a decent place? And how dare you spend nights alone in the same tent with an unknown man in Tawang? Do you want us to believe that nothing happened?" And this comment came after I had taken such pains to explain in my book how hard it was for me to convince the meek gentleman that his chastity was in no danger from me, that I would leave him alone in one piece! If we did not share the tent, one of us would have frozen to death on the Tibet border. Fortunately, not every reader feels like a moral guardian to me. However, not even my correspondents would have bothered to write those letters if I were a man. These very same acts would have seemed quite all right—in fact, quite romantic perhaps—if the writer had been male and the six other occupants of the room female. Here is how the reader's attitude differs according to the gender of the writer.

There was a point in my life when I stopped writing poetry and shifted to humorous prose because my readership had started finding deep personal messages about my private life in my poems, which bothered me. Inevitably, the woman writer's personal life becomes an integral part of her writing, to be analyzed and approved by the reader, which is not something the male writer experiences or suffers.

Fourth, the mother tongue has a very important role to play in this. A young, unmarried girl, Debarati Mitra, wrote a rather beautiful erotic poem about oral sex in a little magazine. Her life was made unbearable by comments and rumors. If she had written the same poem in English, nothing would have happened. The mother tongue stands guard over the woman writer like the mother herself, and to break the taboo of language is not easy.

The mother tongue reinforces all the taboos imposed by the dominant, conservative ideology, but men get society's support to break the rules, to non-conform, to experiment. A man has the artist's "poetic license" from society to defy custom and tradition, to shirk social and even immediate family responsibilities. But the woman writer is not given the license to do as she pleases, either with the language or with her life. She must conform. As it is, she is chiefly a trespasser and a transgressor, a breaker of rules. She has already dangerously reversed the power position by taking up the pen. Enough is enough.

In fact, a Bengali woman writer can break this shackle of language if she shifts to another, preferably Western, language medium. Writing in English will bring her complete freedom, as she does not have to be barred by the Hindu-Muslim taboos, nor does she have to conform to the rules of Western culture. The male writer may use his mother tongue uninhibitedly to suit his artistic purpose but a woman writer may not. She has to think of the extraliterary disadvantages of her gender, of her social image as a woman rather than as an artist.[2]

Fifth, in today's popular Bengali literature, as in popular Bengali films, just as in pornography, there is really a tacit understanding between the male producer and the male consumer, and the basic commodity being sold is woman. However, the situation really becomes difficult when a woman is the producer because she is also the product. When a woman uses the popular genres of fiction or film, she is falling victim to this "male conspiracy," the invincible setup where the male producer and the male consumer have a perfect understanding. The woman writer or woman film director becomes an alien in that setup and is ultimately forced to sell herself unless she can find a new genre, a new device for herself, and make a fresh contract with the consumers. Therefore, when a male writer or film director uses erotic material, it is regarded as art, but when a woman uses the same material, it is regarded as pornography.

This really makes us deviate a little and think about where to draw the line between pornography and literature. Is it really a question of erratic social attitude? As far as I can see, both pornography and popular fiction do their best to reiterate and reinforce the dominant ideology. Pornography does not for a moment challenge it or change it; by showing the aberrations, it only reestablishes the rules that popular fiction openly follows.

In a sense, I feel, pornography is sadistic, antiromantic, and against women—meant to cater to the male readership alone. Pornography is essentially antierotic, as it presents only physical sensations as eroticism. That eros has anything to do with love is forgotten, and the erotic has little to do with love as we understand it—its sole concern is with lust.

Here the question of other arts, like cinema, comes to mind. Like the woman writer, the woman film director is committing a grave violation of male territory. Directing is undoubtedly another male gesture involving power play, and when a woman appropriates that position she creates a resistance among the viewers. The male social attitude begins to work, and the woman director, like the woman writer, is reduced to an object of pleasure inseparable from the text she has produced.

Thus, the text becomes an extension of her body and embarrasses her socially. I shall end with two parallel examples. In 1985, almost simultaneously, two films were released in Calcutta, each dealing with the adulterous relationship of a married woman. Both included some erotic scenes. In one film, the adulteress is made to feel guilty and is punished; in the other, she is not. The first was written and directed by a man. It was highly praised but not highly attended. The other, written and directed by a woman, became a box office hit. People saw it over and over again and said how unspeakably evil it was, as it was also an older woman's affair with a younger man. Rumors and gossip flew through the air that the story was, in fact, the woman writer-director's, own life history, which it was not. But nobody spread any gossip about the other film, which was directed by a man and had a very similar story. It did not even occur to the people who concoct such tales to start gossip about the male director. The two films exemplify two opposite social attitudes. *Piku*, the one made by Satyajit Ray for French television, reiterates the conservative myth of the chaste woman. The unchaste woman is a danger to society, and *Paroma*, written and directed by the actress Aparna Sen, challenges that very position. While no one bothered Ray, Sen was personally harassed and criticized no end for making a courageous statement in the film. The male director's life did not become an erotic text, but the female director's life did.

The same stories of promiscuous adventures that add glamor to a male writer's name prove disastrous for a woman writer's life because the whole society happens to be her moral guardian. Eroticism, with its extraspecial taboo for Hindu women, makes the Bengali woman writer most vulnerable. It disturbs her family peace and public image by turning her into an object of pleasure, along with the text she produces. To protect our privacy, our sanity, and our personal dignity, to avoid ending up as consumer products ourselves, until we discover some new, original genre for self-expression or a new society to work in—we, the timid, the modest of Bengali women writers, do not touch the dangerous area of eroticism with a ten-foot pole! (As I did tell you earlier, I do not believe in phallic symbols!)

Postscript

I read Audre Lorde's "Uses of the Erotic—The Erotic as power" after this paper was presented. Her alternative viewpoint is interesting and very different from the view presented in this paper. According to her:

> The erotic is a resource within each of us that lies in a deeply female and spiritual plane, deeply rooted in the power of our unexpressed and unrecognized feeling. In order to perpetuate itself, every oppression must corrupt or distort those various sources of power within the culture of the oppressed that can provide energy for change, For women, this has meant suppression of erotic as a considered source of power and information with our lives.
>
> We have been taught to suspect this resource, vilified, abused and devalued within Western society. On the one hand, the superficially erotic has been encouraged as sign of female inferiority—on the other hand women have been made to suffer and to feel both contemptible and suspect by virtue of its existence. I speak of it as an assertion of the life-force of women. (p. 53)

I am afraid in India this spirit is yet to be seen in women's writing today. In the sexually explicit novels of Shobha De or Kamala Das, it is used in the conventional way, effectively asserting the power of men over women. Even if it is a relationship of love between women that is depicted, the approach is borrowed from the male market in pornography. The "liberation of the feminine spirit" is not achieved there.

Notes

1. This is a revised version of a lecture delivered at a seminar on "Eroticism in Literature" at the University of Toronto, 1987, but notes were added in 1996. I am sad to say the situation for women in Bengali literature has not improved in nine years, but times are changing and hopefully this chapter will be dated by the time it appears.

2. But the Indian woman writer can cleverly exploit an "exotic Indianness" by using the English language as her medium of expression and avoid the taboos of her mother tongue. Thus she can produce commercially highly successful pieces that are alien to Indian culture but may be used to represent Indian literature, even Indian women's literature, to a worldwide readership. That which is obviously marginal passes as mainstream because of commercial propaganda and finds a readership even within the country. Here the woman writer becomes

an accomplice to the (male) bookseller by catering to the reader of soft porn and by willingly allowing her femininity to form a part of the (extraliterary) erotic appeal of the text. As an example, I can quote an incident that took place at the Melbourne Literary Festival, October 1995. Leaflets and posters were distributed, describing the two writers representing India at the festival. One was Mrinal Pande, "a well-known writer in Hindi and a leading journalist," and the other, Shobha De, "Jackie Collins of India." Not merely that, one leaflet said, "Jackie Collins pales beside Shobha De"! Both are women writers from India, one is a major writer in Hindi, and the other writes best-sellers in English every year but is not a major Indian writer, as her forte lies in soft-porn romances. She also happens to be a professional model and is still quite glamorous, so her photographs were used, too, to draw an audience for this "Jackie Collins of India." This contrast can be noticed more sharply when a woman writer is bilingual. Kamala Das has been writing a lot of controversial stuff, including narratives placing herself in her own person in the erotic text; she writes in English. Though recognized as a good poet, she has achieved fame only as a soft porn writer as far as her English prose goes. But in Malayalam, under the name Madhavi Kutti, she has produced very powerful short stories and has won several literary awards and the respect of her audience. These two split personalities in Das-Kutti prove the point I was trying to make. In her mother tongue, she nurtures the traditional image of a serious writer and does not try to seduce her readership through cheap semipornographic stuff, as she does in English. Writing in English is purely a commercial game for her. Probably it is the same with Shobha De, because she is an excellent columnist with a sharply witty tongue. I do not know of women writing in the regional languages of India who have tried to write like Shobha De or Kamala Das. Even Das and De themselves have not tried it out in their mother tongues.

TRIPTI CHAUDHURI

Women in Radical Movements in Bengal in the 1940s

The Story of the Mahilā Ātmarakṣā Samiti (Women's Self-Defense League)

A woman's movement, as Gail Omvedt defines it, "is the organized effort to achieve the goals of equality and/or liberation for women."[1] It also mobilizes women to motivate them for a change in the system of political, social, and economic equality.

The women's organizations in Bengal from the days of the earlier nineteenth century cultural radicalism of Brāhmo Samāj to the later economic radicalism of the communists have partly justified such a definition. In the beginning, initiative in this regard came from a progressive section of the male patriarchy. In a society that valued modesty and practiced sex segregation, the program was limited. Very many political, economic, and social constraints impeded the growth of an autonomous women's movement in colonial India.

Later, with the advent of the nationalist movement and politicization of women, they tried to organize themselves for achieving the social and economic goal. Some women's associations were formed during the first three decades of the twentieth century. Even then, the associational politics did not achieve much for women. The Indian women's movements, however, unlike their Western counterparts, received male patronage rather than hostility. The nationalist leaders were gradually becoming aware of the importance of women's involvement in the freedom struggle. Still, the improvement of women's status and their deliverance from social exploitation were not their primary concerns. At that time, it was believed that independence from foreign rule would automatically liberate women from all kinds of injustice. Naturally, the autonomous women's associations like Women's Indian Association (WIA, 1917) and All India Women's Conference (AIWC, 1927), which raised important issues of women's rights, could not be integrated into the mainstream of the nationalist politics.

My central argument is that though they continued to work within the broad framework of the Congress-led movement and thought in terms of the compatibility of women's and nationalist aims, the Bengali women leaders were far ahead of the Congress leadership in following a more radical program. I would also like to point out that the new historiography of the feminist movement has not adequately emphasized the radical movements in Bengal in the 1940s. This paper is a study of the activities of the Mahilā Ātmarakṣā Samiti (MARS) or Women's Self-Defense League, a radical left-wing organization of women (1942).

The National Movement and the Bengali Women Leadership

To analyze the background of the women's movements, it would be relevant to note that the nationalist leaders were not totally indifferent to women's questions. In the late nineteenth century, this topic was often treated as a part of the program for social reform. Some considered the inequality of women a social evil to be eradicated by legislation. Because nationalism, not feminism, was their main concern,[2] the liberal (male) nationalists viewed women's agitation for the franchise, legal and social rights, and reform of marital status as part of the larger scheme of the nationalist program. Their apparent sympathy for women's issues impeded the growth of a western-type, militant, gender-based movement. The force of the nationalist movement overshadowed all sectarian considerations.

To avoid issues that could create disunity in the national movement, the early Indian National Congress left the question relating to the status of women to the National Social Conference (1889). Bhārat Mahilā Pariṣad (BMP), one of the premier women's organizations in India, was formed under the auspices of the conference in 1904. Its intent was to establish a communication network among Indian women as merely a supportive organization. We do not know much about the extent of its success in achieving this end.

However, in the same year (1904), a far more active program for encouraging women's interest in political and social issues was undertaken by Sarala Devi Choudhurani, the younger daughter of a well-known Bengali writer, Swarna Kumari Devi, and also the niece of Rabindranath Tagore. She introduced festivals and rituals known as Vīrāṣṭamī (celebration of heroes) and Śaktipūjā (worship of the goddess of energy), as well as *svadesī*, or nationalist festivals, to generate courage among Bengali youth.

Although the ideology of the *svadeśī* movement in Bengal precluded a leadership role for women,[3] Sarala Devi defied the movement by founding Bhārat Strī Mahāmaṇḍal (BSM), a pioneer feminist nationalist organization in 1910. The BSM soon had branches in Calcutta, Lahore, Allahabad, and other north Indian centers.[4] At a period when there were few women leaders or little formalized political association to integrate women in political activities, or little political will to integrate, Sarala Devi's attempt to create a women's organization at the national level was completely novel. The impetus behind the formation of this organization was the determined efforts and the independent spirit of its founder. Sarala Devi herself pointed out that she had established the BSM because of her disputes with the leaders of the National Social Conference regarding the rights of women and the autonomy of the women's movements.[5]

It should be pointed out that the social composition of the leadership of the BSM, like that of the WIA and AIWC, was confined to a tiny sector of urban women. Though the BSM did not last long, it initiated the women's movement for independent political activity on an all-India scale.

The Baṅgīya Nārī Samāj (Bengal Women's Society), an elite women's organization for political lobbying in favor of women's interest, came into existence in 1921. The Samāj was the first women's association to campaign for legislation on women's issues and to secure the voting right for women at the provincial level.[6]

Gandhi's emergence as the supreme leader of the Congress (1920) not only widened the platform of the women's movement but also added a new dimension to it. Mass mobilization under Gandhian leadership brought more women to the national movement and forged a lasting connection between the Congress and women. Though Gandhi made women believe that they were integral to the national movement, women's participation was supported only within the strict framework of Gandhi's program. Women were mobilized for the nationalist movement, but they were assigned supporting roles. Gandhi had a genuine respect for women and sincere desire for their rise, but at the same time he limited women's sphere of action and did not encourage them to question their traditional roles. Admiring women's capacity for self-sacrifice and tolerant disposition, he considered them to be particularly adept at the technique of *satyāgraha*[7] and nonviolent struggle for freedom. In the beginning of the noncooperation movement, he planned his program in such a way that women did not have to abandon their homes and families to join the movement. However, a number of women participants wanted to play a more active role and enlisted as volunteers. In fact, women from Calcutta under the leadership of Basanti Devi [8] joined the street picketing and were arrested on December 7, 1921. The next day, the whole city was in commotion.[9] Calcutta became the main arena of women's activism. Because the arrest created "firm public support," it led Gandhi to recognize the potential of women as freedom fighters in their own right.[10]

It has been argued that Gandhi urged women to support the Congress but did little in terms of women's support from Congress. By popularizing the myth of ideal, Indian womanhood as symbolized by Sītā, the obedient follower of her husband, he also prevented the growth of radical and independent ideas among his women followers.[11] The women's movement in the era of Gandhi hesitated to challenge the legacy of patriarchy and make totally independent decisions. Because this particular milieu of the Gandhian movement impeded the articulation of a radical feminist ideology, the women's groups remained as feeder organizations throughout this period.

The role of these feeder organizations was maintained during the civil disobedience movement, when a vast majority of women supporters of Congress strictly adhered to the Gandhian guidelines. Bengal became one of the most active provinces in terms of women's protest. Nārī Satyāgraha Samiti (women's organization for the search for truth) groups were formed in most districts of undivided Bengal, and about 3,630 women were arrested during the movement. But even in this surcharged atmosphere and despite the existence of the Congress Women's Organization (CWO,1928), Sarala Devi Choudhurani raised the demand for a separate women's congress in Bengal in 1931. Summing up her experience with the Congress, she noted that women's involvement was not accepted at the policy-making stage. Through the CWO, "Congress has assigned to women the position of law breakers only and not of law makers,"[12] hence the necessity for such an independent organization. This, she felt, would be addressed by the development of a separate, independent organization. She presented a charter of radical feminist demands: women's ten fundamental rights, including equal inheritance, equal rights to guardianship of children, birth control, and universal adult franchise.

However, because of the overpowering influence of the civil disobedience movement in Bengal, neither her suggestions nor her plan for organizing a separate women's organization was immediately realized. The volatile political atmosphere made it difficult for her to gain support for such women's issues. The police excesses against the movement created a revolutionary antiimperialist mood in Bengal politics, and by the end of 1931 Bengal was declining as a political center of civil disobedience. A number of women activists frustrated with nonviolent programs joined active revolutionary activities and became famous as rebels against the Gandhian movement. They participated in daring raids, assassinations, and robberies and evoked intense patriotic emotions.[13] But after all these activities, women's aspirations remained unfulfilled. They had neither a political organization of their own nor a separate independent voice in Indian politics. Moreover, attempts at mass mobilization remained a sporadic affair. Women's political involvement to a great extent remained purely the politics of respectability.[14]

Even during the "spontaneous revolution" of the Quit India movement (1942), when an unprecedented mass upsurge crossed the limits of the Gandhian movement, guidelines for women's organizations and involvement did not acquire a separate status. Women's sacrifices and courageous behavior in the face of brutal police attacks were much admired. Ill treatment of women activists by police "surpassed all sense of decorum and decency," particularly in Medinipur, Asti, Chimur, Bardoli, and areas in Assam.[15] But even then, no concrete program was taken by Congress for promoting women to leadership roles.[16]

Of late, criticism of this fundamental weakness of the Indian women's movement has been the central theme of the historiography of women's studies in India. Women's studies as part of Indian historiography is, however, a recent phenomenon. Beginning in the late 1960s, women's studies crystallized as a discipline in 1975, the International Women's Year, when, as Gail Omvedt puts it, the "whole world awoke in an official sense to the consciousness of women's oppression."[17] From the point of view of Third World countries like India, it certainly created a new dimension in women's studies. The process of restoring common women to history as a political force searching for identity has just begun in India. A radical feminist trend has begun to emerge in these studies.

A group of feminist historians, apparently believing that only women themselves can determine how the record of the past can contribute to the present struggle, concentrates on studies of women's movements and organizations. Recent movements such as the Shahada movement in the Adibasi belt of the Dhulia district of Maharashtra (1972–1974) and the Chipko movement of rural hill women in the Garwal district of Himachal Pradesh in the Uttarakhand region (1971–1975) where women proved to be a driving force, have also attracted the attention of these social scientists.[18]

The severe criticism of the "elite women organizations" for their "failure to reach the rural areas" in *Towards Equality: Report of the Committee on the Status of Women in India* on the eve of the International Women's Year (1975) also made women's organizations aware of the necessity of organizing at the grassroots level. But even at this stage, these movements and organizations could not adequately influence the political parties and be free from male political control.

At the end of the Decade of International Women, the Asian Women's Research and Action Network (AWRAN), with representatives from sixteen countries, held a conference in the Philippines on April 12 to 16, 1985, recapitulating the progress of women's movements during the preceding decade. It criticized the Indian women's movement and argued that it had marginalized poor and working-class women and failed to organize them for a struggle against social injustice and exploitation.[19]

But modern feminist scholars also question the effectiveness of the entire process of politicization of Indian women in the preindependence era from the point of view of the distinctive position of women. They emphasize two major arguments. First, Indian women, though much praised for their role in the freedom movement, are not much visible in politics today,[20] and their movements had hardly attempted socio-economic regeneration of women masses.[21]

Second, in spite of their long tradition of politicization, Indian women, even in a highly politically developed state like West Bengal, have not become able to organize a properly autonomous feminist movement. On the contrary, in the leftist regime, "the centralized, party-directed, institutionalized" movements increasingly replaced spontaneous forms of women's militancy.[22] Out of loyalty to the Marxist thesis that the women's movement is inseparable from that of the working class, the leftist leadership ignored the diversity of women's problems and treated gender- based movements as a threat to the unity of the struggle of the working class.[23]

Recently, the validity of the Marxist assumption that separatist "bourgeois feminism" is not relevant to the needs of toiling masses has been challenged.[24] It is also argued that the Marxist theory of class solidarity has hindered the growth of women's protest movements at the grassroot level.[25] Though these arguments refer to present-day movements, it seems that this modern feminist historiography tends to ignore one important chapter in the struggle of Indian women. Within the given framework of the Gandhian movement, they generally conclude that "the Indian Women's movement favoured the politics of elite representation over the mass mobilization."[26] Mass mobilization was crucial to women's success; the Indian women's movement was not able to adapt.

Such a conclusion simply overlooks an important phase in the women's movement in Bengal, the work of the Mahilā Ātmarakṣā Samiti (MARS), in which a small group of dedicated women across the lines of caste, class, and community mobilized women at the grassroots level. Understanding that a genuine mass-based women's movement can grow out of only those organizations working at the grassroots level, they established a network MARS branches from its very inception in 1942.

The following account attempts to show how, from a small but determined beginning, MARS gave a thrust to the women's movement. It was, indeed, a people's movement that greatly stimulated the struggle for women's emancipation, freedom, and rights, including the right of self-defense. From a few activists, the movement soon became a tidal wave of 43,000 members in undivided Bengal (1943). Within a year, the movement spread like wildfire to all the twenty-seven districts of Bengal.

The work of MARS has attracted little scholarly attention. Published accounts (mostly in Bengali) of the participants themselves and oral history based on the interviews of some of the first-generation leaders and rural activists are the main sources of our study. Other sources are eye-witness accounts, police records, newspapers, pamphlets, and organizational records. Fortnightly Confidential Reports of the Government of Bengal on the political situation of Bengal from March 1943 to December 1944 did not even mention the MARS. Most of the leading activists (who had connections with the Communist party) could not keep personal diaries during that period. The party had instructed them not to record day-to-day incidents because their records could help the police.[27]

The Origin of the Mahilā Ātmarakṣā Samiti

MARS was the first mass-based organization of women, mainly under the communist leadership of the 1940s. It was formed in a distinctive cultural climate generated by the antifascist movement. The undivided Communist party of India sensed a need to organize the resistance movement at every level of society. The communist movement at that period closely identified itself not only with students, peasants, and workers but also with a renaissance in Bengali culture, specifically, literature and theatre. The All India Kisan Sabha, Indian People's Theatre Association, All India Progressive Writers Association, and the All India Students Federation—all newly formed organizations (most of them in 1936)—helped the party launch a broad-based movement to infiltrate every stratum of society.

Since its formation in 1936, the Communist-led Kisan Sabha was trying to form a mass base, integrating into it some "marginal" groups, such as sharecroppers, agricultural laborers, tribals, and landless poor for militant action, and thus earning the disapproval of the Indian National Congress. The Kisan Sabha failed to mobilize the peasant women because it had no women's branch. In this context, women came forward to organize the peasant women, the weakest section of rural society. Organizations like MARS, the Andhra Mahilā Saṅgham (1942), and All Kerala Mahilā Saṅgham (1942) were formed to unite and activate the rural women against feudal exploitation. About the beginning of 1943, the call in Kerala was: "Men in the Kisan Sangham, women in the Mahila Sangham and children in the Bal Sangham."[28] Such a broad-based mobilization was also planned for Bengal through establishing links between Kisan Sabha, MARS, and the Kiśor Bāhinī, because of the liberal policy of the undivided Communist party of that period. The party developed a somewhat sectarian character later, but during the 1940s the left leadership thought in terms of dissemination of leftist ideas in society through broad participation of all classes of people. Factional differences were rare during that decade.

The Role of Female Students

The nucleus of the MARS activists was mainly drawn from female students who were being organized under the All India Students Federation (1936). But this student body was dominated by male students. In the existing social order, free mixing was still a taboo, so very few of the female students joined the federation. Keen on having an organization of their own, they formed the Chātrī Saṅgha (Female Students Association) in Calcutta in 1939, which incorporated the progressive elements among the female students of various colleges, as well as Calcutta University. The first of these associations formed a united front in miniature. The members of different leftist parties like the Communist party, Labour party, Congress Socialist party, and the Royist Socialist party (i.e., the followers of M. N. Roy) had their representatives in it.[29] Though it represented diverse shades of the left wing, the committee initially started its work with an antiimperialist program and maintained a pronationalist identity. The Chātrī Saṅgha was not a training center for future communist members, contrary to later suggestions. It wanted to maintain an apolitical character at that time. After the first All India Women Students Congress at Lucknow in 1940, which was inaugurated by Sarojini Naidu, further female student associations were formed in Bombay, Punjab, Delhi, and Patna. But after Russia was attacked on June 22, 1941, and the leftist perception of the nature of the war changed, emphasis shifted to an antifascist campaign during the "People's War" phase.[30] In almost all the districts of undivided Bengal, branches of the Chātrī Saṅgha were formed. The shift of Calcutta Colleges to locations outside Calcutta during the wartime emergency facilitated such formations.

The women students' organization in Bengal played a significant role in building up mass militant organizations throughout 1941 and 1942. The all-pervasive antifascist movement was a decisive influence on these women activists. They thought that during that crisis of civilization, antifascist ideas should be spread in all possible forms to all classes of women. Surrounded by the vast ocean of illiteracy, these girls realized that an endeavor for delivering their fellow countrywomen from ignorance and inequality could make their work lasting and effective. With this aim, they tried to link up the students' movement with a mass women's movement.[31] Students also taught women how to assert their own rights and defend themselves against injustice and exploitation. Above all women were encouraged to overthrow the "subordinate syndrome" and gain confidence through team spirit and class solidarity.

But creating such a consciousness was not at all easy. With the advent of the Quit India movement, the communists were accused of betraying the national interest for not joining this movement and instead supporting the war efforts of the imperialist government. The communist campaign for a national government based on Congress–Muslim League unity was totally ignored by the national leadership. The leftist women had long worked throughout India in collaboration with the AIWC (1927), but with the growing anticommunist feeling, the conference became indifferent toward the antifascist propaganda of the communist women. Inspired by the heroic role of Soviet women (about sixty thousand of them joined the war),[32] these women activists played a significant role in disseminating antifascist and procommunist ideas among urban and rural women. The Indian People's

Theatre Association (IPTA) became the main instrument of this propaganda. Members of the MARS like Preeti Sarkar, Manikuntla Sen, Kalyanee and Kanak Mukherjee, and Reba Roy, joined the different squads formed by the IPTA. Leading artists of later days, including Tripti Mitra, Shobha Sen, and Suchitra Mitra, played significant roles in the dramas and music composed by the IPTA.

It was an uphill task. As Renu Chakravarti recalled, the organizers, a small group of women,

> worked in a multi-purpose manner. They arranged for the meeting place, did the propaganda for the meeting among women, went round collecting them and often became the main speakers and actors in those grass-root meetings. Organizing street dramas, dancing and singing in the slums and rural areas, a form which deeply appealed to them, this small group of women propagated new ideas. The task was rewarding at the end.[33]

More and more women volunteers joined, started forming local Mahilā Samitis in their areas, and mobilized local women to take initiative in running the groups themselves. By the beginning of 1942, a large number of Mahilā Samitis (women's organizations) had grown up in Mymensingh, Pabna, Calcutta, Hoogly, Baly, Chinsura, Barisal, and Dhaka. New *samitis* were being formed in other areas, too. Thus, a new type of mass organization of women emerged, and for maintaining solidarity among these scattered and distant Mahilā Samitis, a coordination committee was essential. In this background, the Mahilā Ātmarakṣā Samiti (Women's Self-Defense League) was formed by a few leading women activists on April 13, 1942, as a central body of different Mahilā Samitis. Thus, in Renu Chakravarti's view the first seeds were sown, out of which was to sprout a big mass organization of women throughout Bengal districts.

Activities

MARS started its work when the antifascist movement reached its highest watermark, the fear of Japanese aggression was looming large in Bengal, and the food crisis became acute, eventually developing into the Great Bengal Famine of 1943.[34] MARS appealed to women of all classes to shed their political differences and stand together to resist the national calamity. Though formed with a strong leftist orientation, its role was seldom sectarian. Instead it adopted different measures to make it a real mass organization and worked in cooperation with other organizations and political parties. They valued most the support of the existing women's organizations like AIWC and Congress Mahilā Saṅgha for achieving the aims. But real solidarity was not possible because of the political differences between the Congress Mahilā Saṅgha and MARS. Even AIWC, a nonpolitical organization with which MARS had so long been working, differed with it on questions relating to the scale of organization. AIWC wanted to keep it limited, by retaining three rupees as the annual membership fee; MARS wanted to make it a mass organization by lowering the membership fee to four annas (one fourth of a rupee) per year. Because the majority of AIWC members were opposed to this reduction, "the possibility of turning it into a living mass organization could not be realized."[35] When the communist women failed to take up a joint program with AIWC, they concentrated on MARS. Perhaps, for this reason, MARS was branded as a "Mass Front of the CP" (the Communist party). It has also been stated that of 43, 000 MARS members in 1943, about half were party members.[36] Such statements are of doubtful validity. According to the *Party Bulletin*, March 1943, there were only 151 women members in Bengal. The total number of party members in Bengal in July 1943 was 900.[37]

The first group of activists, such as Renu Chakravarti, the late Manikuntala Sen, and Kanak Mukherjee, tell us how, in order to involve the noncommunist women in MARS in the early forties, the organization prepared a common program acceptable to all. The three main planks were (1) defense of the country, (2) release of political prisoners and formation of a national government, and (3) saving the population from starvation and death. The programs were designed to draw various women's communities into the organization. The third one was adopted exclusively for the famine-stricken, who eventually formed the largest section of the women rallied around MARS. MARS was thus also a humanitarian organization that was carrying on relief work among the famine- and epidemic-stricken people in 1943 and 1944. Though the organizers' dream of making MARS a united, nonsectarian mass women's organization that cut across political, communal, and cultural lines was not realized, it was remarkably successful in mobilizing the women masses throughout Bengal through its branches all over the province.

Method of Mobilization

In the beginning, middle-class women from Calcutta and other towns helped lower-class women in identifying, formulating, and executing the MARS-sponsored program, one of the main supporters of which was IPTA. Later on, as the famine devastated the entire rural Bengal, spontaneous response came from the village women now in the grip of a crisis. So, in the first phase of their work in mid-1943, MARS took the initiative in encouraging the masses of women to organize and participate in *baiṭhaks* (closed-door meetings, study circles where a schoolboy was usually drafted to read to them) and adult literacy centers. The attendance was quite encouraging. A large number of women gathered to watch the dramas organized by IPTA and listen to their songs. So the branches of MARS rapidly grew all over Bengal. By mid-1944, the *Samiti* had 390 primary committees in all the twenty-seven districts of undivided Bengal and two-thirds of the committees being formed in the present Bangladesh. MARS held district conferences in twenty-six districts in that year, and the number of its members rose from 22,000 in May 1943 to 43,000 in May 1944.[38]

The rapid growth was partly due to the devastating famine of 1943, and MARS struggled to save its victims through relief centers. It was one of the first organizations to engage in charitable social work. Through their selfless, sustained work, they won the confidence of the rural people, and poor peasant women became members of MARS with the hope that this organization could bring an end to their days of hunger and exploitation.

While organizing the food centers during the tragic Bengal famine, MARS also vehemently criticized the food policy of the government. It was the first women's organization to declare that the famine was not due to a shortage of food but due to hoarding and maldistribution amounting to maladministration.[39] In fact, it reiterated the view of the Communist party in this regard. So the statement "Because of its reluctance to criticize the Allies the CPI did not even expose British complicity in creating the famine"[40] seems to be of doubtful validity. A large-scale protest movement against the government relief policy, hoarders, and black markteers that demanded proper supply at controlled prices was a unique contribution of MARS.[41]

MARS pointed out that the duty of government was to provide food for all. With this specific demand, MARS organized hunger marches of women— a novelty in the history of the women's movement in India—in different districts and Calcutta. The first-ever hunger march was organized by MARS in the remote town of Dinajpur on January 20, 1943.[42] It was unthinkable in those days that such a militant procession could be organized from a backward place like Dinajpur. Next was the memorable hunger march of five thousand starving women to the Assembly House on March 17, 1943 (which reminds us of the hungry women's march from Paris to Versailles on August 5, 1789). Organized by MARS and Muslim Women Defense League (sponsored by MARS), the marching women came from slums in Calcutta and North-South suburban villages. The impact was remarkable. Fazlul Haq, then the chief minister, had to distribute one hundred *maunds* (20 kg) of rice among the women. MARS also demanded fairer price shops and proper distribution of ration cards (only twenty thousand ration cards for two million people in Calcutta at that time). It organized similar hunger marches in different areas of Bankura, Midinapur, Chattagram, Noakhali, Dhaka, Barisal, and other places. A large number of Muslim women joined them, particularly in Bogura and Mymensingh.[43] Even at the height of the Muslim separatist movement in the 1940s, led by the All India Muslim League, the leaders of the women's branch of the league, such as Sahajadi Begum, Safeda Khatun, Daulatunnesa, and Mrs. Momin, continued to cooperate with MARS. Sakina Begum was one of the founding-members of MARS. About five hundred Muslim women laborers, led by Nazimunnesa Ahmed, joined MARS-organized rallies in 1942 in Calcutta. In the Muslim-majority districts of East Bengal, the Muslim women played a significant role in organizing the MARS programe. In the Satkshira subdivision of Khulna district, now in Bangladesh, Tasmina Begum was the organizing secretary of the local branch of MARS.

The other programs of MARS during the famine included a movement against hoarders and black marketeers to force them to distribute food grains in rural Bengal. The form of this collective protest against lack of food was a new feature of the women's movement. Activities such as opening famine relief centers and organizing gruel kitchens, milk distribution, and child-care centers were most intensive in the famine-stricken areas. This kind of work at the grassroots level bore fruit. These areas became the main centers of MARS activities. In their first provincial conference (May 7, 1943), half of the delegates came from peasant and working-class backgrounds."[44]

One of the major contributions of MARS was to assist the rehabilitation of the urban and rural destitute. The famine made a large number of women homeless. Deserted by their husbands and families and devastated by hunger, these women became easy victims of the women traders. The famine, as Manikuntala Sen stated, not only killed 3.5 million people but also killed the ideas of social morality and promoted trading in immoral traffic.[45] Contemporary Bengali literature vividly portrayed this dismal state of womanhood.

Against this background, MARS thought it had a duty to save these women. What destitution meant for women could be realized from the statistics supplied by the Government Medical Report of the Department of Venereal Diseases. From 1943 to 1944, the number of brothel inmates increased from 20, 000 to 45, 000. MARS started an action-oriented program to save the women from further dishonor. To restore and rebuild social life, Ela Reid, secretary of MARS, called on women workers to extend their helping hands to these women, who had suffered the most during the famine.[46]

In April, 1944, MARS joined nineteen other women's and relief organizations to form Nārī Sevā Saṅgha. Self-help and self-employment was the main aim of this *saṅgha.* Such a spirit was seen in mofussil Bengal even before the Nārī Sevā Saṅgha (Institute for Help for Women) opened its center in South Calcutta in late 1944. Narī Jṇāna Bhavan (Institute for Women's Education) at Barisal, with work centers at different villages of Barisal, was formed under the leadership of Manorama Basu in May 1944. Centers were started at Noakhali, Tamluk in Medinipur, Howrah, 24-Paraganas, Falta, Joynagar, and Bashirhat. All these centers had small homes attached to them, and all of them became linked with the Nārī Sevā Saṅgha. The Saṅgha promoted self-employment opportunities through handicrafts and other handiwork. Nārī Sevā Saṅgha's handicraft exhibition still attracts a large Calcutta crowd. The Saṅgha first taught women how to become self-reliant and self-respecting. The extent of their work was quite remarkable. The Hajang tribal women from Mymensingh and poor peasant women from Medinipur, all members of MARS, regularly sent hand-loomed products, leather bags, and woolen garments to the exhibition.[47] The famine relief work of MARS, impressive as it was, was a temporary affair, but this self-help program initiated by MARS had more lasting effects. It was no longer a question of charity to the poor. What became imperative was the initiative of common women in the struggle for achieving their right to a dignified existence.

The Legal Rights Movement

Though MARS insisted that there should be one uniform civil code for the whole of India, it first took up the question of a Hindu code on marriage and inheritance, in hopes that the uniform code would gradually take place. Such an attempt intensified the debate between conservative and progressive opinions over the legal status of women. The conservative section led by the Hindu Mahā Sabhā (a political party founded in 1915), tried its best to thwart this movement of MARS. However, the conservative efforts were frustrated by the militant demonstrations MARS organized in collaboration with other women's organizations. In this struggle, women of all sorts joined together, and AIWC took a significant role in organizing big campaigns in favor of the Rao Committee recommendations, which later formed the basis of the Hindu Code Bill.[48]

MARS mobilized a large number of women through its campaigns in the interior villages of almost every district of Bengal. It also started a signature campaign and took the whole issue down to the women of villages and urban slums. By August 27, 1943, two thousand signatures were collected. Women's meetings were held in different villages to discuss the question of women's rights in marriage and inheritance.

Their struggle bore fruit after independence (1947), when some major changes in the law reflected the impact of radical public opinion organized by MARS. The Hindu Marriage Act (1955) permitted divorce by mutual consent and made polygamy a punishable offense. Under the Hindu Succession Act (1956), women acquired the right to inherit property, and the Hindu Adoption and Maintenance Act (1956) permitted Hindu Women to adopt and enabled women to claim maintenance from their former husbands.

All these acts considerably improved the legal status of women. Even now, however, millions of them are unaware of their legal rights, and the successor organizations of MARS are trying best to create awareness of rights.

The Tebhāgā Struggle

We have thus far excluded the role of women in the famous Tebhāgā struggle of 1946 and 1947. This particular topic has often been discussed.[49] In the autumn of 1946, the Tebhāgā movement erupted like a volcano. Thousands of sharecroppers from hundreds of villages who had experienced hunger and seen death in 1943 and 1944 demanded a two-thirds share of the crop instead of half. Thousands of peasant women, coming mostly from scheduled caste and tribal families joined the movement. On the crest of the movement, illiterate peasant women emerged as local leaders, continued to mobilize women in this land struggle, and sometimes overpowered the police. The movement was intense all over the northern districts of Bengal, Dinajpur, Jalpaiguri, and Rangpur and also in Medinipur and the 24-Paraganas. Tribal peasant women, Oraons, Mundas, Kharias, and Santals were in the forefront of the movement for the first time. The Rajbanshi women of North Bengal formed the majority of the village meetings; some of them were local leaders of MARS. The potential role of peasant women in strengthening agrarian movements was revealed by MARS. The ethnic solidarity that explained the intensity of the movement was created by the day-to-day determined efforts of the activists of MARS and the Kiṣān Sabhā.

We have interviewed many of MARS activists like Rani Dasgupta and Bina Guha; Aloka Majumdar (Chattopadhyay) of Dinajpur; Manikuntala Sen, who toured the districts to organize the branches of MARS; and Geeta Mukherjee, who worked among the Medinipur peasants from 1952 onward and mentally prepared them for such a struggle for existence. We have also interviewed some rural women activists, like Saroj Nandini Sarkar of Dinajpur, Poko Oraon and Jamuna Oraon of Jalpaiguri, Nirupama Chatterjee of Bagnan, Ila Basu of Kakdvip, and Lakshmi Bala Doloi of Medinipur, who participated in the Tebhāgā movement between 1946 and 1950.[50]

From these interviews, we may conclude that, although MARS played a relatively insignificant role in organizing peasant women during the militant Tebhāgā struggle, they tried to remold women's social outlook and link them up with the broader movement for social and economic charge. Hundreds of tribal and poor village women became the members of Kṛṣak Samities during 1946 and 1947. Much of the credit goes to MARS activities from 1943-1946; while conducting the postfamine relief work, MARS activists made them aware of "feudal" injustice and exploitation. A number of protest meetings were held against atrocities on women at the time of the Tebhāgā struggle. A committee of women even went around Dinajpur to investigate charges of rape.[51] Given this background, it is difficult to accept the view the "MARS was a passive spectator" to the sexual atrocities committed by the landlords and their husbands on peasant women.[52]

Epilogue

Two contradictory views have emerged regarding the extent of success of radical women's movements such as MARS.

The women activists, founders, and organizers of the movement emphasize that, though MARS could not appreciably improve the status of underprivileged women it did succeed in creating team spirit among them. Peasant women, long neglected and ignored by society, became aware of their own power of collective bargaining. A large number of them could mobilize themselves for the battle against injustice and local vested interests. Some of them were resourceful enough to lead the movement (particularly during the Tebhāgā struggle).

Such movements sharply contrasted with middle-class women's movements. During the struggle for freedom, urban educated women came out on the streets and articulated their nationalist aspirations, but when it came to the question of leadership they were marginalized. In the upper echelons of the political organization structure, their influence was negligible.

The independent initiative of MARS, particularly during the Tebhāgā struggle, constitutes a striking contrast. In the movement led by Kiṣān Sabhā (1946 to 1950), women's participation surpassed that of men, as the activities intensified and an increasing number of male participants were arrested. In the most active centers of the Tebhāgā struggle (Dinajpur and 24-Paraganas), the women participated at all levels: in the forcible reaping of crops, in meetings, demonstrations, and delegations. Scheduled caste and tribal women were the most active participants. Even Muslim women joined in some cases, and there was an unprecedented solidarity between Hindu and Muslim women during a period of communal strife elsewhere. Tremendous repression in the affected areas necessitated their active participation to protect their homes and families. The early organizers of MARS also point out that the aim of their movement has always been to emphasize women's equal right of participation in nationalist and class struggles. Herein lay the great success of the movement.

Another school of opinion, highlighting the marginalization of the women's role in the national movement, tries to project it on the cases of MARS-led mass movements, too. They think that, in these movements, women's issues have not received adequate attention. The women remained doubly exploited: exploited by the feudal society and by the male-dominated home, even during the period of the movement organized by MARS. They argue that the question of women's liberation

—as opposed to national and workers' liberation—has been merely subsumed under class struggle.[53]

Moreover, this school argues, MARS has never done much to integrate women in development programs at the rural level. They never raised the basic question of the fundamental reorganization of rural society. They never presented the rural women's demands for sharing responsibility for the management of rural produce and the improvement of their status in village society. Such measures could elevate women from their traditional minor role (in theory, Indian women remained minor throughout their lives as they moved from their fathers' to their husbands' and ultimately to their sons' guardianship) and increase their potential as a social force. Because MARS could not link up the struggle for economic gains with a movement for social change, its success remained limited.

But the ultimate success of the MARS movement cannot be measured this way. It might have been unsuccessful as a feminist organization, yet its role in uplifting grassroots level women should be acknowledged.

MARS left a precious legacy for the future generation. The women's organizations in West Bengal carry forward the tradition built by MARS. The split within the Communist party of India (CPI) in November 1964 (following an ideological conflict within the party) did not affect MARS organizationally. It was only in 1970 that MARS split into two groups: The C.P.I. dominated West Bengal Mahilā Samiti and C.P.I. (Marxist) dominated West Bengal Gaṇatāntrik (democratic) Mahilā Samiti.

Moreover, these leftist women's organizations maintain a firm, principled stand on minority rights, secularism, caste, and social reforms. Their roles remain educational in attacking feudal exploitation, capitalist interests, and religious fundamentalism.

It should also be pointed out that, working as an agent for change, MARS set the trend for understanding the revolutionary potential of tribal and other underprivileged women. Through its activities, it also sharply demonstrated the value of the grassroots organization. It is now widely accepted that without such organizations among the rural women, no successful women's movement can be organized.

Notes

1. Omvedt (1979), p. 377.
2. Forbes (1981), pp. 49–82.
3. Sarkar (1973), pp. 287–288, 305, 397, 470–471.
4. Everett (1979), p. 68.
5. Choudhurani (1911), 344–350.
6. For details of this supportive role, see Chaudhuri (1995), chapter 3, pp. 70–126.
7. A form of Gandhian passive resistance, literally meaning "truth force" or search for truth.
8. Basanti Devi was the wife of Bengal's foremost leader of the freedom movement, Deshabandhu ("Friend of the Nation") Chitta Ranjan Das.
9. Forbes (1988), p. 68.

10. In an article in *Young India* (December 15, 1921), he urged his countrywomen to follow the Calcutta "model."

11. Forbes (1988), pp. 65–66, 70. See also Mies (1980), pp. 124–129.

12. Forbes (1988), p. 84.

13. Interview with Sudha Roy (leader of the Labour party and activist in women's movements from 1943), February 12, 1983. See also Sen (1985), pp. 27–28.

14. Forbes (1988), p. 68.

15. *The Report of the AIWC*, Lahore, 1931, pp. 165–176. See also Kaur (1968), pp. 222–223.

16. Matangini Hazra, who was killed by police fire in Medinipur, is still revered as a martyred symbol of women's courage.

17. Omvedt (1979), p. 373.

18. Omvedt (1978). See also Mies (1976), pp. 472–482; Jain (1984); and Sharma, Pandey and Nantiyal (1985), pp. 173–193.

19. Desai (1985), pp. 10–12, 55–56.

20. Forbes (1988), pp. 65–66. See also Everett (1981), pp. 169–178.

21. Everett (1979), p. 198, (1981), p. 178.

22. Basu (1981), p. 219.

23. Jayawardena (1989), p. 359.

24. Omvedt (1979), p. 163.

25. Basu (1989b), pp. 216, 220, 231.

26. Everett (1979), p. 195.

27. The British government persecuted the Communist party of India (CPI) from its inception in 1924. The party was illegal between 1934 and 1942. From 1934 onward, the renewed labor and communist militancy alarmed the government, which led to the formal ban on the CPI on July 23, 1934, under the old 1908 act against seditious associations. Despite the lifting of the ban in July 1942, the CPI could not operate freely even afterward.

28. Chakravarti (1980), p. 147.

29. Interview with Renu Chakravarti, founding-member of MARS, Calcutta, February 25, 1983.

30. The resolution of the CPI characterized the war as the "People's War" after the Nazi attack on the Soviet Union was adopted after a prolonged debate within the party over the question. The resolution was endorsed in December 1941.

31. Interview with Alaka Chattopaddhay (Majumdar), General Secretary, Chhātrī Saṅgha, 1945–46, Calcutta, March 12, 1983.

32. *Always a Woman* (1987), p. 6.

33. Chakravarti (1980), p. 21.

34. For the causes and impact of the Bengal famine of 1943, see the report of the Famine Enquiry Commission (1945); See also Sen (1981) and Bhatia (1963). For the role of the CPI during the famine, see memo of the CPI (in the evidence published by the Famine Enquiry Commission.

35. Sarkar (1973), p. 196.

36. Basu (1981), p. 221.

37. *People's War*, August 1, 1943; and *Report of the DIG IB Bengal*, May 17, 1945, p. 20.

38. *Report on the Second Annual Conference of the* MARS (1944), p. 23.

39. Interview with Manikuntala Sen, founding member of the MARS, Calcutta, January 27, 1983.

40. Basu (1989 a), p. 218.

41. *Report of the DIG IB, Bengal*, May 17, 1945: "The [Communist] party papers—*Peoples' War and Janayuddha*—have been virulent and abusive in arraigning the government for mismanagement, high handedness, corruption and inefficiency" (p. 20).

42. *People's War*, April 4, 1943. *The Calcutta* and other newspapers under instructions from the government did not publish any report on this historical women's food march. See Confidential File No. 103/43, 1943: "Subversive Activities in Dinajpur of Miss Alaka Majumdar"; and Letter from the Commissioner's Office, Rajshahi Division, to J. R. Blair, Chief Secretary to the Government of Bengal, February 1, 1943, Confidential File No. 98e. I have learned from Alaka Majumdar, the leader of the march, that most of the participants were Rajabanshi tribal women.

43. *Report of the Annual Conference of the MARS*, March 27, 1943.

44. *People's War*, May 23, 1943.

45. Interview with Manikuntala Sen, January 27, 1983.

46. *The Statesman*, March 28, September 20, September 29, 1944; See also Sen (1944).

47. *Report of the DIG IB Bengal*, May 18, 1945, p. 20.

48. The government appointed the Rao Committee in 1941, and it toured the whole of Bengal to take evidence. It made its recommendations in 1943 in favor of a change in the legal position of women. The committee visited the United provinces, Andhra Pradesh, and the Punjab in 1945, and the AIWC, the Andhra Mahilā Saṅgham and the Punjab Women's Self-Defense League organized meetings for mass mobilization in its favor.

49. Sen (1985), chapter. 4; see also Cooper (1988), Custers (1987), and Majumdar (1993).

50. I took most of these interviews in 1983 as a member of a research team, led by Professor Sunil Kumar Sen, working on "The Working Women in West Bengal: A Study in Popular Movements and Women's Organizations." The project was sponsored by the International Labour Organization and published from Geneva (Muntensba, ed., *Rural Development and Women*, 1985), pp. 195–222.

51. Majumdar (1993), p. 215.

52. Basu (1989 b), p. 218.

53. Jayawardena (1989), p. 359.

References

Always a Woman. Moscow: Raduga Publishers, 1987.

Basu, Amrita. "Democratic Centralism in the Home and the World: Bengali Women and the Conmmunist Movement" in Kruks, Rapp, and Young, eds. *Prommissory Notes* (1989 a).

———. "Democratic Centralism in West Bengal." In Kruks, Rapp, and Young, eds. *Promissory Notes*, (1989 b).

———. "The faces of Protest: Alternative Forms of Women's Mobilization in West Bengal and Maharashtra." In G. Minault, ed., *The Extended Family*. Delhi: Chanakya Publications, 1981.

Bhatia, B. M. *Famines in India: A Study in Some Aspects of the Economic History of India*. Delhi: Asia Publishing House, 1963.

Chakravarti, Renu. *Communitists in Indian Women's Movements*. New Delhi: People's Publishing House, 1980.

Chaudhari, Barbara Southard. "The Women's Movement and Colonial Politics in Bengal: The Quest for Political Rights." In *Education and Social Reform Legislation, 1921–1936*. New Delhi: Manohar Publishers, 1995.

Choudharani, Sarala Devi. "A Women's Movement." *Modern Review*, October 1911, pp. 344–50.

Cooper, Adrienne. *Sharecropping and Sharecroppers' Struggles in Bengal, 1930–1950*. Calcutta. K. P. Bagchi,1988.

Custers, Peter. *Women in the Tebhāgā Uprising: Rural Poor Women and Revolutionary Leadership, 1946–47*. Calcutta: Naya Prakash, 1987.

Desai, Neera, ed. *Indian Women, Change and Challenges in the International Decade, 1975–85*. Bombay: Popular Prakashan, 1985.

Everett, Jene."'Women Question' in India: From Maternalism to Mobilization." *Women Studies International Quarterly*. Vol. 4, No. 2, 1981.

———. *Women and Social Change in India*. New Delhi: Heritage, 1979.

Famine Enquiry Commission, Bengal, 1945, Evidence, Vol. 1.

Forbes, Geraldine. "The Indian Women's Movement: a Struggle for Women's Rights or National Liberation?" In Gail Minault, ed., *The Extended Family: Women and Political Participation in India and Pakistan*. Delhi: Chanakya Publishers, 1981.

———. "The Politics of Respectability: The Indian National Congress Centenary Hindsights." In D. A. Low, ed., *The Indian National Congress Centeary Hindsights*. Delhi: Oxford University Press, 1988.

Government of Bengal. Confidential File No. 103/43, 1943. "Subversive Activities in Dinajpur of Miss Alaka Majumdar."

Hizer, Gerrit, and Bruce Mannheim, eds. *The Politics of Anthropology: From Colonalism and Sexism towards a View from Below*. The Hauge: Mouton, 1979.

Interview with Alaka Chattopadhay (Majumdar), General Secretary, Chātrī Saṅgha, 1945–46, Calcutta, March 12, 1983.

Interview with Manikuntala Sen, Founder-member of MARS, Calcutta, January 27, 1983.

Interview with Renu Chakravati, Founader-member, MARS, Calcutta, February 25, 1983.

Jain, Savita. "Women and People's (Chipko) Ecological Movement." *Economic and Political Weekly*, October 13, 1984.

Jayawardhena, Kumari. "Some Thoughts on the Left and the 'Woman Question' in South Asia." In Kruks, Rapp, and Young, eds., *Promissory Notes*, 1989.

Kaur, Manmohan. *Role of Women in the Freedom Movement: 1857–1947*. Delhi: Sterling Publishers, 1968.

Kruks, Sonia, Rayna Rapp, and Marilyn B. Young, eds., *Promissory Notes: Women in the Transition to Socialism*. New York: Monthly Review Press, 1989.

Letter from the Commisioner's Office, Rajshahi Division to J. R. Blair. Chief Secretary to the Government of Bengal, Confidential File No. 98e, February 1, 1943.

Majumdar, Ashok. *Peasant Protest in Indian Politics: Tebhāgā Movement in Bengal*. New Delhi: NIB Publishers, 1993.

Mies, Maria. *Indian Women and Patriarchy: Conflicts and Dilemmas of Students and Working Women*. New Delhi: Concept Publishing, 1980.

———. "The Shahada Movement: A Peasant Movement in Maharashtra (India)—Its Development and Its Perspectives." *Journal of Peasant Studies*, Vol. 4, July 1976, pp. 472–482.

Muntensba, Shimwaaji, ed. *Rural Development and Women: Lessons from the field*. Geneva: International Labour Organization, 1985.

Omvedt, Gail. "On the Participant Study of Women's Movements: Methodological, Definitional and Action Considerations." In Hizer and Mannheim, eds., *The Politics of Anthropology* (1979).

———. *We Will Smash the Prison*. London: Zed Books, 1980.

———. "Women and Rural Revolt in India." *Journal of Peasant Studies*, April 1978.

Peoples' War, April 4, May 23, and August 1, 1943.

Report of the AIWC, Lahore, 1931.

Report of the Annual Conference of MARS, March 27, 1943.

Report of the DIG IB Bengal, May 18, 1945.

Report of the Famine Enquiry Commision. Bengal, 1945.

Report on the Second Annual Conference of the MARS, held in Barisal, presided over by Nellie Sen Gupta, May 4–7, 1944.

Sarkar, Sumit. *The Swadeshi Movement in Bengal, 1903–1908*. New Delhi: People's Publishing House, 1973.

Sen, Amartya. *Poverty and Famines: An Essay on Entitlement and Deprivation*. Oxford: Clarendon, 1981.

Sen, Ela. *Darkening Days*. With drawings by Zainal Abedin. Calcutta. Sushil Gupta, 1944.

Sen, Sunil. *The Working Women and Popular Movements in Bengali: From the Gandhi Era to the Present Day*. Calcutta: K. P. Bagchi, 1985.

Sharma, Kumud, Balaji Pandey, and Kusum Nanityal. "The Chipko Movement in the Uttrakhand region, Utter Pradesh, India: Women's Role and Participation." In Muntensba, ed., *Rural Development and Women* (1985).

The Statesman, March 28, September 20, September 29, 1944.

Young India, December 15, 1921.

MAITREYI CHATTERJEE

The Feminist Movement in West Bengal

From the 1980s to the 1990s

Preamble

The term "*feminist*" creates a mental block in West Bengal. The image of a feminist is not one that many women would like to have. Feminism has been variously associated with aggressiveness, sexual permissiveness, immodesty, lack of womanly virtues and antimotherhood and antifamily attitudes. In fact, it is a cocky counter to the "ideal woman," who is selfless, obedient and home loving. The best adjective that can be bestowed on a Bengali woman is *gharoa*, usually translated as "homely," actually meaning a homebody. The matrimonial columns in Bengali and English dailies abound in the standard formula, "Wanted: fair, educated, homely bride."

Why this stress on *gharoa*? Many scholars have traced it to the influence of colonialism, when the colonized created an inner world that was safe and away from the prying eyes of the outside world. It was seen as the last bastion of a community against outside invasion. The home became the repository of the traits, practices, and values of a besieged community, and women were marked out to be the keepers of this identity within the home. Nineteenth-century Bengali writing is full of lessons on the nature of an ideal home life. It is possible that this insistence on the home as the nodal point internalized the concept of the ideal woman as *gharoa*. The highest compliment for a Bengali woman is "she is so educated, so accomplished, yet so homely." Long live *gharoa*!

In a culture where the bottom line for women is "homeliness," it is doubly difficult for feminism to take root. Women's liberation is viewed as a Western import not only by the Bharatiya Janata party (BJP) leader Murli Manohar Joshi but also by liberal-thinking Bengalis, including leftist intellectuals. They also think that the ideological basis of feminism and the women's liberation movement is hatred for men. A feminist is not expected to be a good cook. If she is, then she has betrayed her tribe! A nonsmoking and teetotaler feminist is also somewhat unusual. Is it then very surprising that the majority of even educated urban Bengali women wince if termed feminist? The well-known actress Shaonli Mitra, whose remarkable productions *Nāthavatī Anāthavat* and *Kathā Amṛta Samāna* are really very strong feminist tracts, vehemently denied being a feminist in newspaper interviews. *Nāthavatī Anāthavat* views the *Mahābhārata* from Draupadī's point of view. Draupadī had five husbands, yet she was an unprotected woman. Mitra castigates male values and attitudes that reduced a woman to the status of a pawn to be given away as the prize in a game of dice. *Kathā Amṛta Samāna* tells the story of women characters in the *Mahābhārata*, again from their points of view. These are genuine voices of protest against a male-dominated society, yet their creator disowns feminism.

The feminist movement of the 1990s in West Bengal has to be viewed against this backdrop. This chapter is an attempt to define this feminist movement, which has an autonomous identity because it is non-aligned with political parties, government control, and foreign funding. It is in the absolute sense of the term, a voluntary movement.

The Legacy of the Past

In the nineteenth century, there were reform movements to improve the conditions of women. Votaries of the male-dominated society use these reform movements to beat today's feminists, particularly by invoking the contributions of those activists of the nineteenth century, both men and women, who ushered in reforms to change women's lives in India without being feminists. The reform movement was strongest in Bengal and Maharashtra. Raja Rammohan Roy used *śāstric* sanction to get the British to abolish *satī* in Bengal in 1818. Another man, Ishwar Chandra Vidyasagar, campaigned for the remarriage of widows. He, too, gathered a formidable pile of *śāstric* support and ultimately got the British to pass the Widow Remarriage Act in 1856, which legalized widows' remarriage. Vidyasagar was also a prime mover in the arena of women's education. Recalling the work of these reformers, critics in West Bengal today have chastised feminists for aping the West and creating gender conflict. Even women well-ensconced in the patriarchal hierarchy have parroted the line that "our men have always been with us."

The reform movement and the *Brāhmo* movement did clear the decks for women's education in West Bengal, at least for the middle class. But education for every woman remained a distant dream. With education also came the slow venture outside the four walls of the home for jobs befitting the social status of the family. Teaching in girls' schools was the approved vocation. Beyond that, women found it difficult to pursue a professional life. Nursing was dominated by women from the Anglo-Indian community and later by the Keralan Christians.

If we follow Sheila Rowbotham's definition, then feminism in India for women began with participation of women in the nationalist movement, which believed in armed struggle. The revolutionary movement and, before that, the proposed partition of Bengal in 1905 saw women come out, at first tentatively and later with confidence. Though in the resistance to the partition women's roles were restricted, they expanded in the *svadeśi* movement (1905–1908). The famous decision to boycott British goods and its emotional appeal have been accurately documented in Tagore's novel *Ghare Bāire* (*The Home and the World*). Women's spontaneous responses and gestures did not pass by the shrewd male politicians. A conscious decision was taken to include them even in the revolutionary armed struggle. Legends like Pritilata Wahddedar, Kalpana Joshi, Bina Das, Shanti and Suniti Gupta, and Matangini Hazra were noted. But women in every household became part of the nationalist struggle through the men in the family. They formed important support groups, many of them carried messages for revolutionaries, and some even provided shelter. History has not recorded their names. The trade unions also had important women like Santosh Kumari, Prabhabati, and Maitreyi Bose.

The tradition of women's participation was enlarged under the leadership of Gandhi, who realized their potential for mass action. Women in Bengal were active participants in the Quit India movement. The ground was thus being prepared for women to mobilize themselves. One important landmark was the formation of the All India Women's Conference in the mid-1920s, which looked at inheritance laws for women and demanded changes and uniformity for women of all communities. The other important landmark was the founding of the Mahilā Atmarakṣā Samiti (Women's Self-Protection League) in 1942 by women from the Communist party. At that time, the *samiti* performed a remarkable role not only in mobilizing women but also in relief and rehabilitation work in response to the successive crises brought on by the war, famine, communal riots, and the partition. Two other organizations of this period engaged in relief and rehabilitation were the Nārī Sevā Saṅgha (Association for Women's Services) and the All Bengal Women's Union. Another similar outfit was the Sarojinī Dutta Memorial Association established by Gurusaday Dutta, an eminent member of the Indian Civil Service.

All these women's organizations performed vital tasks during a difficult period and are historically important. This tradition of social welfare continued even after Independence. In independent India, an important development was the formation of the National Federation of Indian Women (NFIW) in 1954. In the 1950s it was a landmark in women's political organization as the women's wing of the Communist party of India. The NFIW was radically different from existing women's organizations because it went beyond the urban middle class to women of the working class.

Bengal in the 1970s

Political turmoil became a standard feature of the political process in West Bengal right after independence. It began with the Tebhāgā movement, which saw active and prolonged participation by women, and then the food movement, again marked by women's activism. In the 1960s, the political instability increased, with frequent clashes between the ruling Congress party and the leftist opposition. In 1967, the Left came to power in West Bengal under the banner of the United Front. The intervening years till 1977 saw the birth of the radical Left movement, named after the remote village Naxalbari in the North Bengal foothills. Naxalbari ideology attracted youth and entrenched itself, ironically, in the elitist Presidency College in Calcutta. Women were also drawn into the folds of the movement and stayed on, even after the movement went underground. During this period, the movement experienced unprecedented state repression through indiscriminate arrests, torture, and fake encounter killings. The declaration of a state of emergency in India in the late 1970s by Prime Minister Indira Gandhi exacerbated matters. A large number of followers of the Naxalbari movement went into hiding, running from shelter to shelter to escape from the police, rival political parties, and factions within the movement itself. Then came 1977, the fall of the Congress government, and the return of the Left in West Bengal. The first issue before the new government was the release of political prisoners. A vigorous movement was launched by mainly leftist intellectuals, cultural activists and many members of the erstwhile Naxalite party. Women, many of them from leftist groups, formed an impressive sector of this initiative.

Toward Equality?

By the end of the 1970s, both on the international scene and the national scene, the feminist movement in the West had asserted its presence and jolted complacent governments. Even the United Nations admitted that all was not right in the condition of women. In India, the report of the Status of Women Committee, "Towards Equality," created a furor with its findings. Twenty-seven years after independence, Indian women's condition had not improved. The mirage of equality created by the Constitution was exposed. Women were angry, disillusioned, and dismayed that the inequality and gender oppression of the preindependence days had not been eradicated by the coming of India's independence. Women who had placed their hope in leftist movements were also disenchanted with the existing male hierarchy within the movements. Their aspirations and frustrations began to demand increasingly greater public attention, especially in view of the UN's declaration of 1975 as International Women's Year and then a Women's Decade.

A Rape Judgment

At this time, the Supreme Court of India announced a judgment in favor of the police that acquitted them of the charge of raping a minor, Mathura, while in custody. The lower court had dismissed Mathura's allegation because the defense pointed out that she had eloped with a boyfriend. Therefore, she did not meet the criterion of credibility. In other words, only virtuous women could be raped. With the not-so-virtuous, it was not rape "but intercourse with mutual consent." The Supreme Court agreed with this argument. Before that, in Hyderabad, Ramiza, a poor woman, had been raped in the police station, and her rickshaw-puller husband was killed for protesting and trying to prevent the rape. The police branded Ramiza as a prostitute and her husband as a pimp. However, the feminist groups, which were being formed all over the country after the emergency, took to the streets with protests. The entire incident ultimately escalated into a grave law-and-order situation, as infuriated masses demonstrated against the police. The government instituted a commission of inquiry, which found the police guilty. However, the lower court still rejected the charge of rape. In Mathura's case, it was the judgment that caused anger. A Delhi group of feminists sent an open letter to the Supreme Court. Mathura's rape judgment triggered off protests in seven cities.

In West Bengal, too, these reactions found ripples. Small units of women's organizations were formed by women from diverse political backgrounds. The Pragatiśīl Mahilā Samiti (Progressive Women's Association, or PMS) were activists who had been part of the many leftist movements and other democratic struggles of these troubled years. India in 1978 was still under almost a reign of state terror, though the dictatorial government at the center had fallen. The young members of PMS took a courageous and principled stand against police torture of women political prisoners and atrocities against women in general. At that time, a South Calcutta housewife, Devyani Banik, had been murdered by her husband and her father-in-law because she had failed to persuade her rich father to invest heavily in a cold storage project owned by her husband and in-laws. After the brutal killing, her body was dumped in the back verandah of their house under discarded old mattresses. Before her in-laws could dispose of the body, an anonymous call brought the police. The husband, his father, and his sisters, were arrested. The brutality of the murder created a sense of horror and revulsion. When the culprits were produced in court, PMS demonstrated against them. They even picketed a famous lawyer's house when they found out that he had taken up the accused's case. No other women's organization came forward.

Again in 1978, when the Archana Guha case came up, PMS demonstrated against police torture in custody. Archana Guha had been arrested and tortured in police custody. While in prison, her health broke down and she became disabled. The government released her on parole, but only when the Congress government lost the elections did the police withdraw the charges against her under the Maintenance of Internal Security and National Security Act. Throughout her ordeal, especially her attempts in 1977 to bring charges against the police, when she had to be carried into the courtroom on a stretcher, PMS gave her case wide publicity.

The group also mobilized slum women and lower-middle class women. But when it decided to forge an alliance with the Indian People's Front, the front organization of the underground Communist party of India (Marxist-Leninist), a number of active professional women left the group because they had strong reservations against radical Left movements and politics by violent means.

An Experiment in Collective Action

In 1983, PMS took up a case of wife burning in an area where it had a strong following. After the initial boycott of the husband's family, it contacted other women's groups for a procession and street-corner meeting. As a gesture of solidarity, several groups responded. The result of the joint effort was an effective show of strength, which set women's groups to thinking. Why not form a platform for collective action on specific issues? The idea floated by PMS was accepted by other groups. Discussion began on the contentious issue of membership criteria. There were long discussions and ultimately the Nārī Niryātana Pratirodha Mañca (Forum against the Oppression of Women, FAOW, also known as Mañcha) was formed. The members came from the Pragatiśīl Mahilā Samiti, Sachetanā (Awareness), Women's Research Centre, Women's Library, Women's Study Circle, Laharī (the Wave), and Prativídhāna (Redress).

The forum decided that members of all groups working for women would be eligible for membership except those who belonged to the following:

1. Women's wings of political parties
2. Religious organizations
3. Foreign funded groups

Women's activism outside the control of political parties had clearly established that the goals and attitudes of party-affiliated women's units were in the interest of the parties rather than in the interest of women. Most members expressed strong reservations regarding the role of religion in keeping women in subservience. The forum agreed that all religions oppressed women and discriminated against them. As for groups with foreign funding, their real purposes came under question, with opinion divided on the issue, but it was generally agreed that foreign funding killed initiative at the local level. The other serious allegation was that the rules and conditions of funding agencies discourraged poilitical activism. It was acknowledged that religion remained an important part of the lives of most women, but the forum excluded religious affiliation because the members believed that religion extended its influence beyond the personal sphere into the public arena, where it became a tool of oppression against women.

The action plan was not easy to develop. The new women's forum needed to function out of an office. A contact address and a contact person were other necessities. The members decided to dispense with the hierarchy of official positions and take decisions collectively. Each constituent organization would contribute a monthly subscription.

The National Situation

The times were then such that finding issues was not difficult for the forum. At the national level, the spontaneous women's movement had crystallized into a definite philosophy of action and had chalked out an agenda for change. The goals of the movement were political, economical, and social equality. The following steps were outlined for the realization of these aims:

1. Continuing the fight to end sexual violence, unemployment, dependency, and medical and religious control over women's bodies and to win their natural and legal rights.
2. Researching to gain insights into the process of politicization.
3. Highlighting the issue of women's unpaid housework for their families.
4. Working for changes in personal law. A new way of looking at the law was a top issue on the agenda, which recognized individual women's need for religion in their personal lives but not in civil matters like

maintenance, inheritance, custody, and or divorce. This demand was a major issue of the autonomous women's movement in India till 1985. At the 1985 Women's Movement Conference in Bombay, women from all communities supported the demand for a secular law for women of all communities. The scenario changed after the Shahbano judgment. Under the country's laws (Indian Penal Code, IPC Sec. 125), the Supreme Court awarded Shahbano maintenance from her divorced husband. It created a controversy when Muslim fundamentalists opposed the judgment. To silence them, a new bill was enacted in Parliament in 1986. The Muslim Women Protection Bill put Muslim women beyond the purview of Section 125, a red flag for Hindu fundamentalists. The Bharatiya Janata party made a uniform civil code for all communities a major campaign plank, but it targeted the Muslim community's practice of polygamy and triple *talaq* (i.e., formalizing a man's divorce of his wife by uttering the word *talaq* three times), so all previous supporters of a common code fell silent because they did not want to appear communal.

5. Re-examining working relationships with leftist groups as an important policy matter.
6. Ensuring that violence against women is recognized and made visible and the reasons behind it highlighted. The two main reasons identified behind violence against women were the economic dependence of women and control of their sexuality. Sexual harassment, pornography, dowry, prostitution, and domestic violence were clearly marked as results of dependency and control.
7. Putting agitation high on the agenda. The objective must be to create an atmosphere of public protests against atrocities perpetrated against women.
8. Listing services and support systems, along with the possible expectations they may arouse among victimized women.
9. Recognizing the ultimate aim of the movement as social reform, political participation, and social change. The autonomous women's movement's crystal gazing had not included the new economic policy, the Gatt treaty and the SAP (structural adjustment policy, which became part of their agenda only in 1994, at the Tirupati Conference)

The West Bengal Experience

After the initial teething trouble, the Calcutta FAOW was able to set out a distinct program. The first issue to be taken up was the gang-rape of three juvenile Ranchi tribals by the police. When the report appeared in newspapers, a protest meeting and procession were organized and a memorandum was served to the representative of Bihar government in West Bengal. Just before that, the forum made its first public appearance at the Calcutta Book Fair, a popular and highly respected annual gathering, where all the member organizations jointly took a stall and sold posters, cards, books by women writers, feminist literature, tracts, and leaflets. It was immensely successful and created awareness about the existence of the forum. Apart from the bookstall, the forum had a procession of members and a cultural program at the Book Fair auditorium. The feminist themes of the songs, poems, and skits were something different and created an impact despite the fact that the artistic standards were not too high.

The forum then took up the unnatural deaths of two young female domestic workers. One girl was prepuberty, and the other only twelve years old. The forum's advocacy of these two cases gave it important lessons for its future function. In both cases, the decision for action was taken after reading newspaper reports. It was found that the domestic workers in both the neighborhoods where the crimes had taken place had organized themselves and protested against the deaths. The employers in each case were upper-class people, and when at one protest meeting in front of one of the houses during the women's demonstration some hoodlums pelted stones and broke a few glass panes, public attention immediately shifted from the death of the girl to the creation of disturbances and property offenses. The police were informed. Instead of registering a complaint against the employers, they arrested some of the agitating domestic workers. At this juncture, the forum took up the case. It organized a meeting with the domestics of the locality (Laketown). A further problem had been created for the arrested women, whose husbands refused to take them back. All the domestics of the locality participated in the protest meeting. They raised money for a microphone and the incidental expenses of a procession through the area. When the forum representatives met with the police, they were given short shrift. The arrested women were unconditionally released, but on their next visit to the locality the forum members found that the domestics' usual daytime meeting place had been put out of bounds for them. Many of the participants had been sacked by their employers for their role in the agitation, and local political groups had become extremely hostile toward them for listening to outsiders—meaning forum members.

In the second case, again the reactions were similar. After the forum members organized a meeting and procession, hoodlums from the nearby slums took over. They threw stones at police vans, and the word went around that the forum had instigated them. Most of the domestic workers who had voluntarily come to the forum office stayed away from a follow-up meeting. On inquiry, it was discovered that the local hoodlums patronized by the women's unit of one of the ruling Left Front partners had threatened the domestics for having gone out of the locality with their problems. They felt scared and vulnerable.

The forum then decided a change in their modus operandi. There was no point in jumping into the fray in Robin Hood style. It was decided to take up cases only when specially approached and to restrict operations within reasonable geographical limits. This case-oriented approach, of course, left state terrorism, violence, and antiwoman policies out of the forum's specific planning, though not out of its consideration and, in fact, an essential part of the forum's campaigning platform. Within two years of its formation, the forum acquired a visibility that became embarrassing because the groups felt that they were not yet ready to meet the rising expectations. The forum observed Woman's Day at public places, drawing the passing crowd. However, many of the organizations thought that the forum was acting more for ad hoc reasons than by long-term planning. There was a grain of truth in the criticism, but at the same time compulsions of the moment often decided forum programs.

Even though it was Calcutta based, the forum did not acquire an elitist image because of this so-called ad hocism. As and when issues were thrown up, the forum reacted. It had to. Otherwise, the trust placed by ordinary women would have been lost. There were individual cases, often impossible to solve, but the forum had to make efforts.

Campaigns in the 1980s

Two very important campaigns were protests against police torture and the fate of several hundred innocent girls lodged in the prisons of West Bengal for so-called safe custody. When the torture victim Archana Guha approached the forum for moral support, there were some voices of dissent. They thought that as a women's organization, the problems of political prisoners were beyond its purview. Another equally vocal section thought that, even though it was a difficult case and members would be liable to all kinds of police harassment, the forum had the moral duty to take up the challenge. The Association for the Protection of Democratic Rights (APDR), a human rights organization, also asked the forum to support them in their campaign for justice for Archana Guha. The powerful police officer who had carried out the torture during Congress rule was equally powerful during Left Front rule. By police service rules, he should have been suspended till proved innocent. However, the state instead gave him promotions, and not surprisingly he misused his position to manipulate the legal proceedings and kept on delaying the trial with frivolous and legally untenable appeals to the courts. The forum joined APDR in its campaign and demanded the suspension of Police Officer Runu Guha Neogy and a speedy trial. This support did not endear the forum to either the police or the government. However, the public acclaimed the two groups. It was one of the forum's most vital campaigns.

The other campaign that really gave visibility to the forum was the effort to help noncriminal women prisoners. A story in a Bengali daily newspaper reported that a minor rape victim had been languishing in jail for four years while the rapists had been acquitted and were free. Maya Barui somehow managed to smuggle out an appeal to a young lawyer, Shivshankar Chakravarty, who took up her case. The judge ordered the government to release her immediately. After being released, she told the lawyer that seventy-eight girls who had not committed any crime were languishing in prison. Shivshankar Chakravarty again took up the cudgel on their behalf. A sordid story of callousness and intrigue came out. Many of the girls had been charged under the vagrancy act and put in prison for safekeeping but were routinely smuggled out with the connivance of the prison staff and pimps and landed in the brothels of Calcutta.

The forum supported Chakravarty in his campaign for the release of these women. Members attended court hearings, wrote articles in newspapers and periodicals and organized a convention to demand their unconditional release in which leading women politicians supported the stand taken by the forum. The forum also participated in a twelve-hour hunger strike to press its demands. Government officials met with forum representatives and assured them that it would organize release and rehabilitation. The newspaper coverage led a reader in South India to file a public interest case in the Supreme Court, which directed the state government to take suitable remedial action.

Cracks in the Edifice

The militancy of the forum over these two issues created differences of opinion within the organization itself. One of its constituent member organizations, which had sympathies for the major partner in the Left Front government, took a stand contrary to that of the forum's. Their representative said that, unless the girls could be properly rehabilitated, there was no point in releasing them and that it was not right to present their case as a civil liberties issue.

The criticism of the state's support to the guilty police officer was also a contentious issue, especially over the forum's association in this matter with the APDR, which was very vocal about custodial deaths and other violations of human rights by the government. Gradually, the attendance at campaigns thinned. As it was very difficult to carry on in this manner, a meeting was called. Four organizations—the Women's Research Centre, Sachetanā, Pragatiśīla Mahilā Samiti, and Pratividhāna—decided to opt out of the forum. The issue that generated the most heat was the question of action by individual members. The logic behind accepting their help was simple. It was generally difficult to get volunteers for the kind of political activism that was the forum's aim, so it was decided not to discourage willing members. But some of the forum's constituent groups found this too disorderly. This difference of opinion became a crisis when, after several meetings, no consensus could be arrived at. The exit of those who disagreed with the forum's policies was a threat to its survival, but it managed to overcome these difficulties; since the end of 1989, it has continued to function as a single organization.

The 1990s

The forum renewed its work in the 1990s with important campaigns. Its area of action was divided into three broad categories: campaigning, counseling, and demonstration. It received cases of individual victims and tried to provide emotional and legal support. These campaigns included custodial rape, the discriminatory population policy, mothers' rights, and the rights of workers in the sex trade. One important area of campaigning was to combat the rising communalism that began in the early 1990s. Since 1990, the forum has also mounted theme-oriented campaigns on International Women's Day. So far, it has published pamphlets on the history of March 8, mothers' rights, a uniform civil code, the population policy, atrocities against women in West Bengal, communalism and its dangers for the women's movement, state terrorism, and other issues. It has compiled a legal handbook in Bengali, helps in bringing out a quarterly newsletter on women and the media, and has published leaflets against custodial rape.

Current campaigns include lobbying for laws for gender justice and bringing out a women's manifesto (on behalf of the International Women's Day Forum 1996) to pressure political parties to form a positive women's program.

Conclusion

The formation of the forum and its functioning are typical of the autonomous women's movement in India, which began in the 1970s. This movement is truly feminist because, for the first time, women themselves have come forward with demands that arise out of a sense of being denied their full potential. This movement is not guided by anyone but women themselves, who have joined together out of their own self-awareness rather than at the behest of others.

All the movements, from the reformist to the nationalist initiatives, and the social welfare movements that succeeded them, as well as steps taken by the political parties, made women targets. The reformist movement had the interest of the family and society at the root of its action. Women needed to be emancipated because the changed social order made men need wives who were educated and articulate. The wife would provide within the home all the ingredients that made family life better for the new Bengali gentleman. The reforms also meant to put Hinduism in a better light. Widow remarriage was advocated to keep women morally pure. In the autonomous movement of women, feminists have not turned away from including the rights of sex workers, traditionally viewed as moral pollutants, in women's battles for justice because they are exploited and oppressed just like the "pure" women of the family idealized in male rhetoric.

The fight for the recognition of domestic violence as a crime has aimed at destroying the insulation of the private from the public. Woman has now demanded rights over her own body and her own sexuality. These demands have made leftists ridicule the movement as urban, elitist, and out of tune with reality. The inherent misogyny of Hinduism is reflected even in left-wing thinking, which has strengthened the deeroticization of women. Even leftist activists do not address women as comrades but as mother and sister. Leftist resistance to discussing any aspect of the oppression of women not directly related to class exploitation has made them mistrust the feminist movement. This is true for even the women on the Left, whose selective protests have resulted in a loss of credibility for the women's movement in general . The ghastly Bāntalā carnage in 1990, in which three women social workers were dragged from their car, brutally assaulted, and lynched (one of them, Anitā Dewan, died, as did the driver of the vehicle) at 7:30 in the evening in a crowded marketplace, was described by a leftist woman member of parliament as an isolated incident by a few hardhearted antisocials, not a sign of mass misogyny.

Communalism has also marginalized the feminist movement in India, and West Bengal is no exception. The feminists' demands in the 1980s for action against these divisive forces, which target women regularly as pawns in the strategy of terror as political leverage, have been now appropriated by the government and political parties. Whether this welcome move is motivated by concern for women and other minorities or by political expediency remains to be seen.

The feminist movement in West Bengal has had a special impact in rural areas, where funded organizations have mobilized women on the lines of the demands of the autonomous groups. There are pockets in the suburbs where women are coming out and organizing themselves. The 33% reservation of seats for women in local self-government saw parties picking up women activists from nongovernment organizations (NGOs) as candidates. Again, though this is no doubt driven by opportunism, it is, in effect, an indirect recognition of the growing power of the feminist movement.

In the late 1990s, with the Left set for years of state power in West Bengal, militant feminist organizations like the forum are reconciled to being left out of government bodies like the state-women's commission and all state-sponsored activities. But the changes that have already taken place will not be rolled back. When the history of the autonomous movement is written, this contribution will have to be acknowledged.

Postscript

After the collapse of the collective platform in 1989, another effort was made in the post-Beijing period to form a women's network in Calcutta. Just before the Beijing Conference, the 1995 International Women's Day was jointly observed by twenty women's groups with a booklet that highlighted state violence against women. This cooperation encouraged for a more concrete joint platform, and Maitree (Friendship) was formed as a network of twenty-two women's organizations and several concerned individuals. As 1996 was an election year, they decided to present the political parties in West Bengal with a women's manifesto that charted women's expectations and demands. The forum actively participated in the network.

The modus operandi of the network is this. One member organization takes charge for four months. It organizes monthly meetings (the first Saturday of every month), sends out minutes, collects subscriptions, and is responsible for the overall networking with other members. Maitree has so far avoided discussing in detail the contentious issues of individual membership, whether women units of political parties would be allowed into the network, and the question of religious organizations. These are complicated issues because several churchbased women's units are now in the network. The question of individual membership remains to be thrashed out, if and when any of the constituent organizations takes a stand on the issue.

Maitree has gained acceptance and visibility with its campaigns against domestic violence, sexual harassment, and interactions with the police. It was thought during meetings with police top brass that better results would be obtained if there was gender sensitization at the local police station level. The Calcutta police administration accepted Maitree's suggestion and requested it to prepare a training module. This has been so far a successful effort.

But the times, they are a-changing. The new economic policies, liberalization, and globalization have affected the outlook of the feminist movement in India. West Bengal, too, has not been able to escape the fallout. Access to foreign funds has meant a growth of NGOs, and these organizations, while appropriating many of the demands of the women's movement, have not accepted its insistence on working through the nonhierarchical organizational structures that feminists consider essential for the promotion of equality. It is hard to ignore the frequently voiced suspicion that women who work for the new NGO's are there not out of a sense of service or commitment to the women's movement but out of career considerations. Corporate culture prevails in the majority of these organizations, whose action plans seem to be modeled on typical corporate reliance on lobbying for the fulfillment of demands rather than on mass struggle and people's movements. Antiestablishment stances, if at all present, are highly diluted. The state machinery is given added recognition and responsibility. For example, recently a Women's Resource Guide brought out by two NGOs was formally released by the Calcutta police chief. Co-option has become difficult to avoid. The political ideology of feminism is systematically watered down or even altogether repudiated by a supposedly liberating relativism, as expressed in declarations such as "feminism means different things to different women."

Will the nonpoliticization of the women's movement isolate it from India's larger mass movements? This question has been worrying women who do believe in the politics of feminism. No sure answer can be offered to this very difficult question, but experience suggests that women's grassroots initiatives in India have a way of rising above the opportunism of organizations that attempt to expropriate them.

Index

Some words in the text may have variant spellings and diacritical notations, reflecting regional usage. They are listed in the index in their most common forms.

Printed in the United States
35136LVS00002B/299

9 780195 122299